AF593687

THE CERTIFICATE LIBRARY

* * *

BRITISH HISTORY

THE CERTIFICATE LIBRARY

THIS SERIES of books has been designed to cover the various syllabuses of the Ordinary Level Examination for the General Certificate of Education. The books are equally suitable for all students who wish to improve their standards of learning in the subjects of the various volumes, and together they form an invaluable reference library.

The Editor of each book is an experienced Examiner for one or more of the various Examination Boards. The writers are all specialist teachers who have taught in the classroom the subject about which they write; many of them have also had experience as Examiners.

Each volume is comprehensive and self-contained and therefore has far more than an ordinary class textbook: each has a full treatment of the subject; numerous illustrations; questions on the chapters with answers at the end of the book; and a Revision Summary for each section of the book.

These summaries give the information in a concise and compact way so that examination candidates may easily revise the whole contents of the book—they can soon see how much they readily know, and how much they have forgotten and need to study again. The facts in these summaries serve, therefore, as a series of major pegs upon which the whole fabric of the book hangs.

Advice is given on answering the examination paper and there are questions of examination standard together with suggested answers.

Series Executive Editor

B. E. COPPING, B.A.HONS.

THE CERTIFICATE LIBRARY

* * *

BRITISH HISTORY

Edited by

C. EMMOTT, B.A., B.Litt.

Headmaster, Hales Owen Grammar School.

Contributors:

R. K. GILKES, M.A.

Senior History Master, Fairfield Grammar School, Bristol.

J. B. DALZIEL, M.A.

Headmaster, Elmhurst Grammar School, Street, Somerset.

and

C. EMMOTT

THE GROLIER SOCIETY LIMITED

LONDON

First published 1965
Reprinted 1971

ISBN 0 7172 7709 7

Made and printed in Great Britain by
Odhams (Watford) Ltd., Watford, Herts

PREFACE

Nearly a dozen Boards conduct G.C.E. examinations. Each has its own history syllabus, and within it several alternative schemes. Each scheme is a statement of what is liable to be examined, not of what must be taught; and every teacher makes his own selection of material within the scheme, taking care to see that his selection is sufficiently wide to make possible a reasonable choice of questions for his pupils.

This book is based on the same principle of *selection*, since one book of this length cannot hope to cover all the prescribed work in the necessary detail. Attention has been concentrated mainly on political history and, within this framework, on the years after 1714 because these are the most popularly chosen for study and examination.

This volume is based on the presentation of topics rather than a continuous chronological narrative. This means that repetition and cross-reference has been unavoidable, but this should be a help to the student, both as a reminder and as revision. From the late eighteenth century onwards major political figures have been studied, rather than aspects of the period. This, it is hoped, is an approach best calculated to supplement existing textbooks. Advantage has, however, been taken of the Specimen Examination Paper and its suggested answers to look at topics which could not adequately be covered in the text of the relevant chapters.

The numerous illustrations and maps, the questions at the end of each chapter and their outline answers, the hints on note-making and the summaries, the suggestions on examination technique, the hypothetical specimen examination paper and the answers thereto are all intended to provide a guide both for the student working alone and for the student seeking additional preparation outside regular classes.

C. EMMOTT

CONTENTS

BY R. K. GILKES

BY C. EMMOTT

BY J. B. DALZIEL

CONTENTS

Coloured Illustrations and Maps

At the State Opening of Parliament the Queen initiates a new session with all the pageantry merited by such an historic occasion.

CHAPTER 1

ENGLAND AND NORMANDY

DEVELOPMENT of English society after the Roman withdrawal was based upon three principles brought to this country by the Saxon peoples: the *comitatus*, or following, which assured the leaders of a band of devoted followers; the *free nation*, implying rights and privileges to individuals within that society; and *kinship*, the cement which held the state together. From these developed a pattern of society, in which the most important element was the king, surrounded by warriors and officials bound to him by close personal ties, in which each man had his place, and in which inequality was accepted as of immemorial custom.

After the Conquest, the phrase "the laws of Edward the Confessor" assumed an almost mystical power and meaning, but it is misleading to conclude from this that there existed a single body of law, codified and universally binding. The laws were varying local customs of the people, applied in the people's assemblies, the moots of the township, the hundred, borough and shire. Here matters of everyday local administration were dealt with, the shire moot deciding more serious and complicated problems. This pattern of administration had been formed in the tenth century, and, in essentials (including geographical limitations of shires), remained unchanged for centuries more. Presiding official in each shire was the reeve (shire-reeve or sheriff), who had taken over from the ealdorman, earlier joint president with the diocesan bishop of the shire court, but who, with development of provincial government in the century before the Conquest and the growing complication of national politics, had withdrawn to take charge of several shires. The reeve, chosen by the king for the administration of justice and finance, was guardian of those customs by which the shire was governed in the king's name.

Local and Central Government

The king's thegns, often holders of large estates, may be regarded as a ruling class. Having wide local influence and judicial privileges within their own estates, and having the right to advise the king in his Great Council (Witan), they stood as an essential element of government. The Witan illustrates the principle of the free nation, for, although it cannot be magnified to parliament, yet it had enormous potential, as it ensured that the king was no autocrat; he was subject to the advice of the most important section, economically and socially, of his people, even if advice could only be given when he requested it.

But the growth of power of these local magnates could be detrimental to the king's authority. Cnut, in 1017, had divided the country into four districts, Northumbria, Mercia, East Anglia and Wessex; and in each of these, authority was in the hands of one man. Although this division was short-lived, it did at least foreshadow the appearance later of powerful provincial governors like those of the house of Godwin, who in Edward the Confessor's reign ruled Wessex, East Anglia and the south Midland shires, rivalling the house of Leofric in the north, and creating problems which Edward tried ably but unsuccessfully to solve. The over-mighty subject was beginning to be a problem of English politics.

The Church

Unifying forces were the monarchy and, above all, the Church. The king was God's representative among his people, sworn to uphold justice and good government, and to protect the Church. As such he had the support of the Church, which he also virtually controlled through an accepted ecclesiastical patronage. Theoretically, the monarchy was elective, for the late king's council had to choose his successor. Five out of eight kings ruling between 899 and 1016 were formally designated ruler by the Witan, as indeed were Harold of Wessex and William of Normandy in 1066.

The Church, moreover, was a European link in a religious and cultural exchange of men and ideas. Religious life, which had blossomed with Biscop and Bede in the seventh century, was renewed in the tenth century, stemming from the drive of Dunstan of Canterbury, Ethelwold of Winchester and Oswald of Worcester and York. The Archbishop stood at the king's right hand, and an educated clergy was indispensable to the government of successive rulers.

The ideal of political unity was universally accepted in 1066, and William of Normandy, like Henry Tudor in 1485, found to his hand adequate machinery to use for its realization.

William of Normandy's Claim to the English Throne

At the end of 1065 Edward the Confessor was known to be dying. He had no son to succeed him, and his heir, another Edward, son of Edmund Ironside, had died in 1057; this Edward's son, Edgar, was not even considered. Three men were ambitious for the crown: Harold Hardrada, King of Norway; Harold, Earl of Wessex; and William, Duke of Normandy. Edward's own choice was William; and William was ready to fight for what he regarded as his incontestable right to the throne of England.

WILLIAM'S CLAIM TO THE ENGLISH THRONE

The English connexion with Normandy had begun in 1002, when Ethelred II married Emma, sister of the Duke of Normandy; after Ethelred's death she married Cnut, whose sister Estrith married Robert I of Normandy. For Ethelred, Normandy had been a temporary refuge in 1013; for his sons, Alfred and Edward, it was a place of almost permanent exile. Alfred was killed in 1036 and Edward was invited to England by Harthacnut in 1041, became a member of the royal household, and was nominated heir to the throne. With the end of Harthacnut's brief career in 1042, Edward became king.

Twenty-five years absent from England, Edward naturally looked to Normandy for his friends. He patronized Norman knights and appointed Norman priests to English benefices, but he did not surround himself with foreign favourites; his concern was to counter the overweening political ambition and territorial preponderance of the house of Godwin. Duke William himself may have visited England in 1051, and about this time, although the circumstances are unknown, Edward clearly promised William that he would succeed to the English throne; in gratitude he could do no less.

Popular support in England was on the side of the house of Godwin; and on the Earl's death in 1053 his son, Harold, became first man in the kingdom and, to all intents and purposes, the king's right hand. However, Harold seems to have been almost persuaded to accept William's succession; in 1064, apparently on a mission from Edward to the Continent, Harold was captured by the Count of Ponthieu, and surrendered to William in Normandy, where he became William's man by swearing an oath to support William's interests in England.

Then, at a Council held at Christmas, 1065, Edward, concerned with the security of his country, chose Harold as his successor. On 6 January, 1066, the day after Edward's death, Harold "succeeded to the kingdom as the king granted it to him and as he was chosen thereto."

The acceptance of Harold by leading members of the king's council was inevitable, for the occasion demanded qualities that Harold undoubtedly possessed. Though Edward, in spite of his piety and his preoccupation with re-founding Westminster Abbey, was no cipher, he lacked the ruthlessness, determination, physical prowess and leadership of a successful king. Moreover, he was virtually a foreigner, and one can appreciate why, with invasion threatening from Norway and Normandy, and from an unholy alliance between Harold's half-brother, Tostig, and Malcolm of Scotland, the majority of Englishmen gave their allegiance to Harold. His skill as a general had already reduced the power of Gruffydd ap Llywelyn in Wales, and was later to shatter Hardrada and Tostig at Stamford Bridge; and, had he not been in such an unreasonable hurry, he might have accounted as thoroughly for Duke William at the battle of Hastings.

One of the fifty-eight scenes of the Bayeux tapestry. Here Harold, touching two shrines, takes an oath of allegiance to William, who looks on from his throne.

The Bayeux Tapestry

Designed and made within twenty years of the Norman Conquest for Odo, Bishop of Bayeux, the Bayeux Tapestry vividly records the main sequence of events affecting England and Normandy from the start of Harold's mission to the Continent to his death at Hastings. These events are recorded in fifty-eight scenes, which are embroidered (strictly speaking it is not a tapestry) on a strip of coarse, buff-coloured linen 231 feet long and 19½ inches wide. Woollen threads in eight colours (red, brown, grey, three shades of blue and two shades of green) are arbitrarily used. A 3-inch border top and bottom contains queer birds and queerer beasties, farming and hunting scenes, Halley's comet, pictures from Aesop's fables, and beneath the battle scenes a liberal assortment of bowmen, equipment and corpses—whole or in parts; beneath the top border runs a Latin commentary. A great work of art, the Bayeux Tapestry is "an inexhaustible storehouse of information about the life of the eleventh century," giving details of costume, arms and armour, ships and castles, besides an accurate account of the Norman Conquest.

QUESTIONS

1. How far is it true to say that the Norman Conquest of England was half completed before the Battle of Hastings?

2. Why did William, Duke of Normandy, decide to invade England in 1066? Give reasons for his success.

CHAPTER 2

THE NORMAN CONQUEST

WHILE celebrating his victory at Stamford Bridge, Harold had news of Duke William's landing at Pevensey on 28 September. He decided upon an immediate march south, but his military resources were exhausted, and he faced William's seven thousand men with only his household troops and the militia of the southern shires. He could, and should, have waited for reinforcements; but his military judgement seems to have been dissipated by his victory in the north, and on Saturday, 14 October, just outside Hastings, Harold and his two brothers fell in battle while the shire levies were still marching to join them.

England was not shocked into submission, and London declared the Confessor's great-nephew, Edgar, as Harold's successor; but William was prepared to wait. From Hastings he marched his force along the south-east coast, through Romney and Dover to Canterbury; and still London hesitated to take action against him. From Canterbury to Wallingford William marched, thence to Berkhamsted, destroying crops and villages on his progress to encircle London. His deliberate manoeuvre had the desired effect; at Berkhamsted he received the Londoners' submission, and on Christmas Day 1066 he was crowned King of England.

Meeting Opposition and Rebellion

William was king but he lacked a kingdom, for not until 1071 was the conquest complete and the last resolute but unco-ordinated English resistance overcome. In 1067 William returned to Normandy, leaving as regents William FitzOsbern and Bishop Odo. FitzOsbern was at Norwich, Odo at Dover expecting a Danish attack, when the men of Kent rose in support of Count Eustace of Boulogne, who had fallen out with William and now intended to oust him from the throne. Dover Castle held out, Eustace returned to his Continental estates, and the rising collapsed.

There remained, however, a mounting spirit of rebellion. The citizens of Exeter defied William in 1067, refused him fealty, closed the town gates to him, and clearly stated that they had no intention of giving him more than the customary payments which they had made to his predecessors. Exeter resisted William and his army for eighteen days, and though forced to surrender they did so on acceptable terms and there were no reprisals.

Much more serious trouble was brewing in the north, and William, to nip it in the bud, put on a show of strength at York. It afforded only a temporary check. The defeat of Robert of Comines and an unsuccessful English attack on York in 1069 was followed by a far more serious rising, when Swein, king of Denmark and Cnut's heir, sailed up the Humber. A combined Danish and English force took York, but then, by wasting time in plunder, gave William time in which to act. Wessex, Devon, Cornwall, Somerset, Dorset and Mercia, which had reacted sympathetically to the rising in the north, were subdued, and William, using the devastation tactics that had won him London, moved on York. The Danes, bought off by William, took to their ships; the rebellion was over. To discourage Yorkshire and Mercia from similar opposition in the future, William ordered the devastation of the north, when a wide belt of territory through Yorkshire, Derbyshire, Staffordshire, Cheshire and Shropshire was made derelict. Much was still a barren waste twenty years later.

The last kick of English opposition came from East Anglia where Hereward, a tenant of Peterborough abbey, gathered around him the most daring English outlaws, including Bishop Ethelwine of Durham, and conducted a guerilla campaign from Ely. Their hope was a forlorn one, even though they were joined by Swein of Denmark; in 1071 Ely surrendered and Hereward, it is believed, fled. Now William could regard himself as king of all England, and the failure of the Rising of the Three Earls in 1075 indicates that a majority of Englishmen was resigned to the fact.

Royal Forests

The royal forests did not arouse militant protest, but they created deep bitterness against the Conqueror. Saxon kings had had their hunting parks, areas of woodland and open waste with a bank and ditch round them to ward off poachers. These areas were not extensive, and in Saxon times Englishmen hunted in open woodlands, and took wood for fuel and building and meat for the pot. This situation was transformed to satisfy the Norman passion for hunting; by royal proclamation William declared wide areas of forest and common land, villages, farms and hamlets included, as royal forests subject to Forest Law. In these areas (and only Kent, Norfolk, Suffolk and the barren north escaped) deer and wild boar were protected beasts for the king's hunting, although the king granted to some of his subjects the right to hunt other wild creatures that might worry the deer.

For those living within a royal forest there was the extra burden of coping with forest courts as well as ordinary local courts, and also the liability to additional penalties. Punishments were severe, and the forest officials—Chief Forester, Wardens, Verderers and Foresters—were unpopular, for they often administered laws of their own making, an objectionable habit practised also by those Norman nobles who set out their own private forests (chases) more often than not, in the later Norman period, without the king's permission. Royal forests were extended during the next hundred years, and were greatest under Henry II when they covered about one-third of all England. Under Richard I and John there was steady deforestation, due not to a change of heart, but to the royal need for money. However, the grievances created by the royal forests and the harshness of Forest Law were not remedied until the Forest Charter of Henry III in 1217.

Transfer of Land Ownership

William provided himself with land by confiscating the estates of Englishmen killed at Hastings, and of those who refused to acknowledge his position. Now he could reward those who had invaded England with him. But his attitude towards the conquered English was one of compromise, not general plunder; and his victory saw neither a greedy scramble for land, nor the wholesale ejection of Englishmen from their estates and offices to let in a swarm of fortune-hunting Normans. William envisaged an Anglo-Norman partnership, and until 1069 he had no plans for Norman domination, for two-thirds of England were still represented by English earls, most sheriffs were English, and there were few changes in the episcopate from the situation as Edward the Confessor had left it.

The revolts of 1069-70 changed all this, and in a short time a great deal of land passed into Norman hands. Confiscation followed suppression of the risings, and for future security Yorkshire and Mercia were subjected to Norman plantation. The transition was not disruptive of society; the Norman lord simply took over his English predecessor's estates, complete with all rights and jurisdictions. Within twenty years of Hastings only two Englishmen south of the river Tees still held great estates directly of the king.

The Norman Castle

An essential factor in the successful establishment of the new Norman ruling class in England was the rapid and extensive building of castles, "the symbol of the feudal age." Most of England's castles were founded in the century after the Conquest; Domesday records forty-nine built between 1066 and 1086. Although William built some of stone (e.g. London and Pevensey) the first Norman castles were of the *motte-and-bailey* type, which had the great merit of being cheap, easy and quick to construct (the motte or mound could be raised in just over a week), and extremely effective.

Not a single county was without its castle, although of particular importance were those built to guard the south-east coast against attack from the Continent, the troublesome northern border against Scotland, and the Marches, at first to preserve, and then to advance, the frontier with Wales.

Trouble from the Midlands and North accelerated the process, and when William went on progress in 1067 he had castles raised at Huntingdon, Cambridge, Warwick, Nottingham, Lincoln and York, and garrisoned them strongly. The Mercian rising saw the building of castles at Shrewsbury, Chester and Stafford; and after his son Robert's punitive expedition to Scotland in 1080, William built a castle on the site of what was later Newcastle to strengthen Northumbrian defences.

The Feudal System

In one respect William was an innovator. His victory at Hastings was gained by a new military technique, based not only on the castle but also on the disciplined and up-to-date knight. Consolidation and preservation of his position as king would depend on these knights, so he had to make radical changes in the social organization of England to provide for their maintenance. This changed pattern of society, present only in embryo in the Confessor's time, is called the *feudal system*, a description first applied by a seventeenth-century French historian. The feudal system, however, was anything but systematic, and although the Conqueror made it less confusing, it still remains, in the words of a modern historian, "the feudal labyrinth."

Feudal society was essentially a military society based upon land, and this is where it differed from the pre-Conquest pattern. The land was the king's, granted him by God. He kept about a quarter of it for himself, the rest he distributed unevenly among some 180 lay or ecclesiastical barons (*tenants-in-chief*), part of whose rent was to supply the king with a certain number of knights, fully equipped and mounted. How many knights each baron was to provide was assessed in proportion to the amount of land (called a *fief*) which he held direct from the king. Somewhat optimistically, William reckoned that the whole country was capable of supplying six thousand such knights. The tenants-in-chief sub-let parts of their estates to *lesser tenants*, in return for the service of a certain number of knights. Each knight was then awarded an estate, or *fee*, the extent of which varied in different areas. Possession of a fee made this professional soldier a wealthy man, and his social status was much improved. In return for it he spent in peacetime forty days each year in military training or on royal castle garrison duty, while in war he served his feudal overlord for a minimum of two months at his own expense.

In addition to providing military service for his fief, the tenant-in-chief, as vassal to the king, knelt before his overlord and became his man (*homage*); at the same time he took on the Gospels an oath of faithfulness (*fealty*) to him. For his part the king as overlord granted his vassal protection in return. Lesser tenants acted in the same way towards their tenants-in-chief, and so on down the social scale. Thus was erected a feudal pyramid, based on the

XXVI

Geoffrey Orlatele
holds BALHAM
without gift of the King and without
warrant. Anschil held
it of Earl Harold. Then it
was assessed for 5 hides; now
for nothing. There is land for 2 ploughs.
In demesne is one (plough); and there are one villein
and one bordar with half a plough.
One serf there and 8 acres of meadow.
In the time of King Edward it was worth 6 pounds; afterwards,
20 shillings; now, 40 shillings.

Domesday Book entry; on the left is a line-by-line translation.

knights, and tapering up through the lesser tenants and tenants-in-chief to the king at the summit, the whole structure cemented by homage and fealty.

A baron's fief was made up of manors, usually scattered widely over the whole country. Although William made no bones about his intention of breaking up the vast, menacing land-holding of the house of Godwin, this scattering was not deliberate policy. Some of the barons held only ten or twenty manors, but others, like the king's brothers, Odo, Earl of Kent, and Robert, Count of Mortain, and the holders of the great frontier earldoms of Northumbria, Hereford and Chester, held between seven hundred and eight hundred; in fact, half the land granted to lay tenants was in the hands of only ten of the king's feudal tenants.

But the feudal system was an imperfect instrument, not least in that it did not satisfy military needs. Mercenaries were always used, as archers, infantry and even cavalry. William's assessment of six thousand knights for his army was too high; there were never so many knights' fees in England, and as, with the development of plate armour in the fourteenth century, a knight's equipment became more expensive, the number demanded of a tenant-in-chief was reduced. As early as 1100, holders of knights' fees were not always able to fulfil their military obligations in person, so instead they paid *scutage* (shield money), a sum sufficient to hire a substitute knight.

Payment of certain other feudal dues was demanded:

(*a*) *Aid.* This was a feudal payment originating in the tenant's obligation to give financial as well as military help to his overlord in an emergency. By

Magna Carta, regular aids were fixed at three, payable when the lord's eldest daughter married, when his eldest son was knighted, and when the lord required a ransom (as did Richard I in 1193-4). The first two aids were demanded by medieval kings, by Henry VII and by James I; but feudal aids and military tenures were abolished in 1660.

(*b*) *Relief*. This was a succession duty, a payment which had to be made by an heir before he could take over his inheritance. As with aids, excessive reliefs could be demanded by the king, as they were by William II and John.

(c) *Wardship*. The heir to an estate, if under age on the death of his predecessor, became a ward of his lord. This lord then enjoyed all profits from the estate during the minority. The right was often much abused, with estates impoverished or ruined.

Domesday Survey, 1086-7

At his Royal Council held in Gloucester at Christmas 1085, William I "had important deliberations and exhaustive discussions . . . about this land, how it was peopled, and with what sort of men." This resulted in a decision to make a vast nation-wide survey to find out the extent of royal possessions, the extent of the land of the great feudal vassals, and generally to confirm the title and responsibility of all who held land. Incidentally, the survey would be of great value in assessing Danegeld.

To collect information, groups of commissioners were sent to every part of England. Questions were put to locally elected juries to discover the name of the manor or village, who held it in the Confessor's time and who now; its area, and how much was cultivated as the lord's demesne, how much by the peasants, and how many peasants there were; number and value of stock; area of woodland, pasture, arable and waste; details of deerhays, eyries, water-mills, sources of fish, quarries and salt works. All this was checked by a second set of commissioners. In this way a mountain of facts was amassed from more than thirty shires; information was gathered together at local centres, and then summarized at Winchester into one massive volume, *Great Domesday* (now in the Public Record Office). The remarkable thing is that the whole survey was made and recorded in less than two years.

The making of Domesday Book was not popular with the English, who regarded it as official snooping; but this first report of a Royal Commission in England is a unique monument to the amazing thoroughness and organizing ability of the Normans, and to the vision of the Conqueror himself.

QUESTIONS

1. What measures did William I take to make his position secure?

2. Describe the main features of feudalism as developed in England by William I.

CHAPTER 3

RELATIONS BETWEEN CHURCH AND STATE

WILLIAM I, succeeding as he believed to his lawful inheritance, had no intention of blatantly disrupting the continuity of the English monarchy, and he maintained the close link between Crown and Church which had existed from Saxon times. Indeed, the effect of Norman influence on the English Church was not to change it, but to create a new Anglo-Norman institution, which brought together the best of both churches.

The corrupt Stigand, archbishop in 1066, was a poor advertisement for the English Church, which was not in need of a religious revival. Contact with religious life and thought of the European mainland, maintained since Saxon times, extended and deepened during the Confessor's reign; and in religious art, painting and sculpture the English Church was far in advance of that of Normandy. Moreover, the impetus of the deep and far-reaching monastic revival of the tenth century had certainly not disappeared; at the time of the Conquest monastic reform was continuing steadily under such men as the saintly scholar Wulfstán, Bishop of Worcester.

Reasonably enough, therefore, William's approach to religious matters in England was quietly cautious. Even Stigand, certainly no friend of William's, continued as archbishop for two years, and was only deposed in 1070 at the Pope's instigation. With Lanfranc's appointment as archbishop, however, William moved with greater confidence and clearer purpose. Norman churchmen were appointed to vacancies in the Church, so that by William's death all bishops (with the single exception of Wulfstan of Worcester) and most of the abbots were men new to England. Spiritually there was nothing to choose between them and their predecessors, but in administrative ability and in the typically Norman passion for building they had more to offer; magnificent cathedrals, like those of Durham, Norwich and Winchester, stand as their most lasting memorial.

William and Papal Claims

In fulfilling his aims for the Church, William had to ward off the wide claims of Pope Gregory VII (1073-1085) who saw himself as leader of a world-wide ecclesiastical empire. "The Christian religion," he wrote to William, "has so disposed that after God the royal power should be governed by the care and authority of the Apostolic See." This did not suit William at all. He kept up payment of Peter's Pence, but had no intention of paying homage to the Pope for the papal blessing on his English enterprise, as Gregory felt he should. He made no bones about this in his reply: "I have not consented to pay fealty, nor will I now, because I never promised it, nor do I find that my predecessors ever paid it to your predecessors."

In their thorough reorganization of the English Church, William and Lanfranc worked hand in glove. Both opposed the principle of direct government from Rome, believing in a national Church controlled by the partnership of king and primate, and one can see why: churchmen had a dual responsibility, as spiritual leaders and as feudal tenants of the Crown. Thus, for the sake of the country it was vital that William should control these ecclesiastical magnates just as he did his other subjects. He demonstrated the point clearly when he replied to the Pope's protest at the imprisonment of Bishop Odo in 1082. Odo had rebelled against the king, so William sent the Pope the mail shirt which his half-brother was wearing when captured, with the pertinent comment, "Is this thy son's shirt?"

Archbishop Lanfranc

Lanfranc's contribution must not be under-estimated; it was greater than that of any other archbishop excepting Theodore of Tarsus (669-690). A scholar and supreme administrator, with a wide understanding of men and affairs and "granite strength" of mind and character, he reformed the calendar of the English Church, and drew up a new up-to-date code of monastic discipline to replace the *Regularis Concordia*, which had regulated monastic life since 970. To Lanfranc monasteries were vitally important, as a means of revitalizing the spiritual life of the country and as a training ground for scholars, church dignitaries and statesmen; and although his customs were only enforced in his own monastery, St. Augustine's at Canterbury, he nevertheless expected that they would be followed elsewhere.

He called frequent church councils, which developed amongst the clergy a sense of community; but this paved the way for future trouble between Church and State. Clerical independence was further encouraged by William's edict, which separated clerical from lay jurisdiction. The episcopate was reformed, and Lanfranc's view that a bishop should establish his seat at the main centre of population in his diocese materialized in 1075, with provision for the bishops of Lichfield, Selsey and Sherborne to move to Chester, Chichester and Salisbury. At the same time, with William's support, he claimed that he was "primate of all Britain," and drew from the Archbishop of York reluctant admission of the primacy of Canterbury.

Lanfranc accepted the Pope's intervention in Church affairs only in technical matters such as conferring the archbishop's scarf of office; beyond that, his duty was to the king. He could not receive a papal legate unless he first had the king's permission, and he accepted William's refusal to allow him to obey a papal summons to Rome. Nevertheless, this does not mean that Lanfranc denied the principle of the Gregorian reform; indeed, he attacked simony and marriage of the clergy, just as Gregory did. With regard to the latter he agreed that married priests could keep their wives, but issued decrees to the effect that in future preferment in the Church would not be offered to married priests. Such decrees were not popular with either English or Norman clergy, and their distaste for celibacy was amply demonstrated when two supporters of the reform were nearly lynched, one by the clergy, the other by their unrepentant wives.

William II and Anselm

The harmony of William I and Lanfranc gave way to the discord of William II and Anselm. This is partly explained by the contrasting character and outlook of the two archbishops. Lanfranc, who became a monk only at the age of thirty-five, knew and understood the world, and this gave him a breadth of vision and prudence quite foreign to his gentle, saintly, cloister-pledged pupil, Anselm. Also, Lanfranc belonged to the period before the Gregorian reform, Anselm to a younger generation which saw nothing unreasonable in the Pope's insistence on the primacy of Rome; this being so, Anselm was bound to view with something more than mere misgiving the close ties between Church and Crown in England; and being as firm as Lanfranc in what he believed to be right, and with such a king as William Rufus, a clash was inevitable. Contemptuous of Church and churchmen, Rufus aroused the anger of the chroniclers. "He feared God but little, and man not at all," wrote William of Malmesbury; while the writer of the *Anglo-Saxon Chronicle* bewailed the fact that "everything that was hateful to God and to righteous men was the daily practice in this land during his reign."

Glad enough of Lanfranc's support during the troubles of his first two years as king, on the archbishop's death in 1089 Rufus made no attempt to choose a successor, but enjoyed the Canterbury revenues while the monks of St. Augustine's barely existed on the pittance he grudgingly allowed them. He diplomatically honoured his father's memory by a few benefactions, but saw no reason to continue such an expensive exercise. What pleased him better was using the Church as a source of wealth. When a bishop or abbot died, Rufus appropriated and milked the estates, delaying years before appointing a successor; even then he exacted a heavy payment before the new holder was allowed to take up his appointment. At Rufus' death in 1100 the estates and revenues of three bishoprics and twelve abbeys were in the king's hands. Canterbury remained vacant until 1093 when Rufus, then seriously ill, gave in and made Anselm archbishop. It was with great difficulty that Anselm had been persuaded to come to England from his monastery of

Bec, and when he learned what was in store he protested that his supporters were proposing to "yoke a weak old sheep to an untamed bull," a particularly apt description of the king.

As soon as he recovered, Rufus declared that he had been tricked, and renewed his attack on the Church and on Anselm. Ignoring a promise made to Anselm, he claimed the right to choose which of the rival popes, Clement III or Urban II, should have the allegiance of England. His claim misfired at the Council of Rockingham in 1095, as Anselm and the Norman Church had already given their allegiance to Urban II, and the Council was unable to say that the archbishop's action was inconsistent with his allegiance to the king. Shortly afterwards the papal legate persuaded Rufus to acknowledge Urban, but Rufus' determination to be rid of Anselm was stronger than ever. He accused the archbishop before the Council of being half-hearted in honouring his feudal obligations in the Welsh war, and Anselm, weary of this relentless harrying, left England in 1097 to take the Pope's advice. Urban, however, had no wish to offend the king of England, and Anselm's visit proved fruitless; he retired to Lyons and remained there until Rufus died, struck down, the chroniclers were convinced, by the avenging hand of God.

Henry I, Stephen, and the Church

Henry I, to make a favourable impression in the face of possible opposition, recalled Anselm in 1100 and made peace with the Church. Three years later the archbishop was in exile again. The trouble arose over the question of lay investiture. In his anxiety to make a fresh start, Henry wanted Anselm to renew his homage and to be again invested with his archbishopric by receiving from the king the ring and pastoral staff, symbols of his office. Henry's demand was not an innovation; it was, in fact, almost common form in the European kingdoms, but the trouble was that lay investiture had been expressly condemned by Gregory VII in 1075, and subsequently by several papal councils. Anselm was on the side of the Pope, fighting, so he believed, for the cause of divine law against utter worldliness, and he refused to consecrate bishops invested by the king. Henry was equally adamant, and here again the double role of the bishops is underlined: the king valued highly their prayers and their counsel, but equally important was their feudal contribution of knight service, and for this reason it was essential that they should be chosen by the king. Faced with this deadlock Anselm wearily returned to exile in 1103 after the Synod of Westminster.

Henry had to give way; under threat of excommunication in 1105, he agreed, in consultation with Anselm, to a working formula: he would give up his investiture claim, but would retain his right to receive the customary homage and oath of fealty from his bishops. The Church had scored a very valuable point, and had moved one step nearer the complete reduction of

Reconstruction of Canterbury cathedral as it was in the time of Henry II and Becket.

royal power over the Church; for although the Pope accepted this settlement, he regarded the homage clause as valid only during Henry's own lifetime.

In 1107 Anselm, glad to be able to fulfil again his duties as archbishop, returned. In the two years of life still left to him he gave canonical consecration to king-appointed bishops, supported Henry in quelling feudal disorder, and tightened clerical discipline. Inferior to Lanfranc as a statesman, he nevertheless overshadowed him as saint and thinker, and "as a human being he reaches a higher level than his first master."

Fortune favoured the Church during the anarchy of Stephen's reign. With the decline of royal power, the Church, under the able leadership of Theobald, was quick to consolidate and further extend its authority at the expense of the otherwise occupied Crown. The important concession, made by Stephen in 1136, that "justice and power over ecclesiastical persons and all the clergy, and their goods, and the distribution of ecclesiastical property, are to be in the hands of the bishops," established an authority that was to provide so dramatic an issue between Henry II and Becket.

The Worldly Chancellor

Thomas Becket, after a period of study at Paris and a spell as a financial clerk in the city of London, entered the household of Archbishop Theobald. Advanced by the patronage of Theobald, Becket's sole desire was pleasure and profit. As archdeacon he pocketed money from any source, including the revenues of vacant abbacies and bishoprics; and his ruthless brilliance and efficiency were decked in flamboyant and unashamedly worldly display. He was an ambitious man, whose appointment as Chancellor in 1154, at the age of thirty-six, had certainly been angled for, perhaps even paid for. Now his extravagance was unbounded, with his lavish household and men-at-arms; and he put himself wholeheartedly at the service of King Henry II. Between the two men grew a deep (and for Becket, unique) attachment. To Theobald, however, who had undoubtedly furthered his archdeacon's career for the benefit of the Church, it seemed that he had sponsored a changeling; and Becket made him drain his cup of bitterness to the dregs, for he ignored his patron's dying wish to see him in 1161. In 1162 Henry made his roistering Chancellor Archbishop of Canterbury.

The separate ecclesiastical courts recognized by William I had by Henry's reign become notorious for both the inadequacy of their punishments and the abuse of their jurisdiction. Although ecclesiastical courts were intended to try only men in holy orders, yet bellringers, gravediggers, and all who could recite a word or two of Latin, or who could read a verse from the fifty-first Psalm, were classed as clerks, and could be tried in a church court.

In these courts even the gravest offences were punished only by degradation, or at most excommunication. Such evasion offended Henry, and his aim was that punishments in church courts should conform to those awarded by civil courts. For such a change the support of the archbishop was vital, so what better insurance for success than to promote his boon companion to the vacant see of Canterbury?

The Saintly Archbishop

Certainly Becket had not angled for the Primacy; and now he resisted the suggestion, partly because he was enjoying himself as Chancellor, but also because he could never be the pliant tool that Henry obviously wanted. His final acceptance brought a new Becket, strict in his religious observances, and an impassioned champion of the Church against the king. In 1162 he was ordained priest, and the next day consecrated archbishop.

Immediately he reclaimed the property of his see, gave up the Chancellorship, and went out of his way to annoy the king by insisting that knights holding church lands should pay homage to him, and not to the king; he even resisted Henry's proposal for a tax reform which as Chancellor he would have supported without question. But Henry was not a king to be crossed by a subject, and his friendship for Becket turned, as suddenly as Becket himself had changed, into cold hatred which, given Becket's churlish attitude, could have only one end.

At the Council of Westminster in 1163 Henry raised the question of "criminous clerks," and voiced his complaints against the church courts. From the bishops he demanded a promise to observe the "customs of his grandfather." Their proviso that they would do so "saving their order," inspired by Becket, infuriated the king.

The following year at the Council of Clarendon, Henry demanded the Church's assent to sixteen constitutions which, he claimed, were merely a restatement of ancient practice. There were two important clauses, one restricting appeals to Rome without the king's consent, the other providing that "criminous clerks" were to be degraded in a church court, then handed over to a civil court for trial. Becket wavered, accepted, then, regretting his weakness, begged the Pope for forgiveness. Becket had recovered himself when the Council met at Northampton; and having denied the competence of a lay tribunal to censure him, he fled to Pontigny. As a reprisal Henry appropriated the Canterbury revenues and banished Becket's kindred.

Both king and archbishop had now no intention of seeking a solution. By 1169 Becket seems to have convinced himself that only his death could win a victory for the Church, and his subsequent actions support this; as John of Salisbury protested to him in his cathedral on the fateful December afternoon in 1170, "Not a soul here except yourself is asking to die." At Fréteval in 1170 a reconciliation was patched up between Henry and Becket, but it could not last; indeed, Becket intended that it should not. During his exile, Henry II insisted that his eldest son, another Henry, be crowned during his own lifetime by the Archbishop of York and the Bishops of London and Salisbury. Becket chose this moment to excommunicate them for usurping his rightful duty, and the necessary papal bulls could not have been issued at a more inopportune time.

Henry heard about the excommunications in France. His violent Angevin temper was provoked, and his ravings prompted four knights to cross to England and murder the archbishop on the steps before the high altar in his own Christ Church at Canterbury, only four weeks after his return from exile.

By his death Becket won, as he knew he would, a famous victory. The Clarendon Constitutions relating to appeals to Rome and to "criminous clerks" were repealed, and Henry's attempt to restore royal authority as a barrier against the unlimited exercise of papal authority in England had failed.

Finally, what are we to make of Becket? Do we write him off as charlatan or hypocrite, or do we see him as an actor of consummate skill, called upon to play two contrasting roles, and deciding in the end on the final touch of artistry that would crown a masterly performance?

QUESTIONS

1. Why were there disputes with the Church in the twelfth century?

2. What was the importance of the career of Becket?

CHAPTER 4

THE NORMAN KINGS AND HENRY II: PROBLEMS AND ACHIEVEMENTS

IT WAS as a reward for his second son's constant loyalty that William the Conqueror chose William Rufus to succeed him as King of England in 1087. Robert Curthose, his rebellious eldest son, he designated Duke of Normandy. Such an arrangement invited trouble, but Rufus, although lacking the powerful dignity of the Conqueror, was as masterful, and militarily as competent as his father, and was equal to the occasion. He enlisted the support of his subjects in 1088 in crushing a baronial revolt, which had been joined by most of his father's followers, with the notable exception of Lanfranc, and as decisively dealt with a second rebellion in 1095, which his own severe government had provoked.

This keeping of the peace, his extension of his dominions in northern England at the expense of the king of Scotland, and his acquisition of Normandy in 1095 when his pious elder brother took the Cross and of necessity gave him his duchy in pawn, earned the respect of his subjects; but his contempt for the Church and his doubtful morals more than cancelled out these achievements in the chroniclers' eyes. To them his violent death while hunting in the New Forest was divinely appropriate; the circumstances were certainly mysterious. Generally accepted as an accident engineered by God or the Devil, it has recently been suggested that Rufus was murdered and that his brother Henry was implicated. Certainly Henry, who was one of the hunting party, acted with suspicious speed in securing the royal treasury at Winchester and getting himself crowned king. all within three days of Rufus' death; but it is scarcely credible that he would have risked the stigma merited by the murder of his brother and liege lord.

Henry I

Henry I suited the chroniclers better. Thorough and ruthlessly efficient, he was a man to inspire fear and respect, but also trust. He continued in the mould of capable Norman administration, working always through traditional instruments of government. He would stand no nonsense from the nobles, and after a rebellion in 1102 they did not trouble him. Indeed, on his death in 1135 the baronage was decidedly weaker than on his accession in 1100.

Not the least achievement of the "Lion of Justice" was his employment

William Rufus' Westminster Hall, later used for Charles I's trial.

of a group of clerical and lay advisers, men already proved in royal service, of knightly training, and certainly not low-born social climbers. No king was better served by his officers than was Henry I by Bishop Roger of Salisbury, whose family held the royal Treasurership (a new office set up at the turn of the eleventh century) until the early thirteenth century; or Aubrey de Vere, appointed Henry's Master Chamberlain in 1133, who, together with the royal Justice, Richard Basset, had already been responsible for a reform of English local jurisdiction.

In 1120 William the Aetheling, Henry's only son, was lost in the wreck of the White Ship, leaving next in succession Henry's daughter Mathilda, a young lady only too anxious to occupy the throne. On the death of her first husband, the Emperor Henry V, in 1125, Mathilda returned to England; and at Henry's wish the English barons, including Stephen of Blois who held two large English fiefs, acknowledged her claim to the English throne. However, in 1128 she married Geoffrey, Count of Anjou. To the barons this created an impossible situation, because by the marriage agreement Geoffrey could become both Duke of Normandy and King of England, an arrangement which Henry himself regretted having made. The barons renewed their oath to Mathilda in 1131 when she was repudiated by Geoffrey, but the separation was only temporary, and the future Henry II was born in 1133. On Henry I's death in 1135 the Council in England, exercising the old English custom of electing the ruler from the royal house, offered the crown to Stephen of Blois, overriding Geoffrey's claim and the right of Mathilda.

King Stephen

Royal authority took an immediate tumble when Stephen, nephew and favourite of the late king, acting in haste to forestall the claim of his elder brother Theobald, nominee of the royal council in Normandy, accepted the crown of England; for he was the barons' puppet, chosen not merely in preference to an unpopular woman, but also as an expression of baronial reaction to the strong, uncompromising government of Henry I.

With Mathilda as a threatened alternative choice, Stephen's kingship depended on the support of the nobles. Immediately therefore he compromised himself still further to gain a wider following. London's support was bought by the grant of extensive privileges, not in the best interests of the Crown; and fickle King David of Scotland was bribed by the cession of land in northern England which had been secured by Rufus. The greatest concession, however, was made for the support of the Church. Stephen promised to restore the liberties of the Church as they were in the days before Rufus' reign, permitting free election and legislation in church courts, and allowing these courts exclusive jurisdiction over all ecclesiastical persons and property.

But Stephen was to have little peace. In 1138 Geoffrey of Anjou invaded Normandy, while in England Mathilda's half-brother, the Earl of Gloucester, rebelled in league with the King of Scotland. The Scots were defeated at the Battle of the Standard and the rebellion crushed, but the landing of Mathilda in England in 1139 plunged the country into civil war and the administration into chaos.

The feudal barons, released like a wound-up spring, threw off their feudal obligations and defied their overlord. This defiance, the *diffidatio*, was an unpleasant aspect of continental feudalism that William I had deliberately kept out of England by his requirement of the Oath of Salisbury from all his Norman followers in 1086. But Stephen was as weak as William had been strong, and by adopting the *diffidatio* the barons were now making themselves free to pay off old scores and to satisfy their ambitions by playing off one side against the other.

Mathilda gave up the contest in 1148 and returned to Normandy, which her husband had taken in 1145 and which passed on his death in 1151 to their son Henry. This same Henry, by the treaty with Stephen at Wallingford in 1153, was to succeed as King of England on Stephen's death. As his eldest son Eustace had died, and as his second son William was content to remain Earl of Surrey, Stephen had no alternative. In 1154 Stephen died after a reign, as a chronicler wistfully expressed it, of "nineteen long winters."

Henry II

To Henry II, Stephen's reign was an unfortunate interlude best forgotten. He was to carry on the work of his grandfather, Henry I. The two Henrys were much alike, thorough, ruthless and deeply concerned to preserve order and justice; but the most striking things about Henry II were his capacity for work and his fantastic energy. He was for ever on the move, leading his household a relentless dance to his French lands (he was in France from 1158 to 1163 and from 1166 to 1170) and to all parts of England.

Henry could ignore Stephen's reign, but he could not overlook the chaos which it had brought. His first practical steps were to dismiss all foreign mercenaries employed in the civil wars, to dismantle four hundred unlicensed castles which had mushroomed since 1135, and to take back the crown lands which had been freely bartered by both sides for the fluctuating loyalty of self-interested supporters. Encroaching Welsh princes were thrown back, and Henry chased the King of Scotland to his own country, forcing him to restore Northumberland, Westmorland and Cumberland, and to acknowledge his English master with homage paid at Chester.

Next, Henry had to counter the disruptive power of military feudalism, to be sure that his reign would not be disturbed by baronial excesses. His Norman predecessors (except Stephen) had kept the barons in check, and he himself had clipped their wings when he razed their castles; if he respected their rights Henry saw no reason for them to combine against him, but he saw no harm in applying a little financial discipline. Sheriffs were to pay the customary revenues of the Crown regularly into the Exchequer under the eagle eye of Henry's Treasurer, Nigel of Ely. By an extension of scutage, Henry avoided military dependence on the barons and provided himself with the means of hiring mercenaries in time of war. In Rufus' time ecclesiastical tenants had paid scutage in lieu of military service, and now lay tenants were allowed to commute personal service for a money payment. Similarly, to be able to hire garrisons for his own castles, Henry collected ward money instead of demanding personal guard duty.

Reform of the Law

To ensure establishment and maintenance of good order as Henry II understood it, there had to be a single code of law, emanating from the king, to which all would be subject. This would end the confusion and irregularities of private courts, manor courts and the public courts of shire and hundred, whose justice was perverted in Stephen's reign by over-ambitious sheriffs.

Henry gained control of the shire and hundred courts and reduced the sheriffs' power by sending out barons on annual progresses through four groups of counties called *circuits*, to keep an eye on the king's affairs up and down the country. Gradually they took over the chief judicial powers of the sheriffs, many of whom were replaced in 1170 following an inquiry into their actions. The strength of these itinerant justices was that not only were they trained judges, but being lesser men than the feudal magnates they could also be relied upon "to do justice habitually." Other such judges sat in Westminster Hall as a permanent judicial court of the Curia Regis to hear the people's complaints. Gradually this tribunal became separated from the royal council and the king, and by the time of Edward I had developed into the Court of King's Bench and the Court of Common Pleas.

To help detection of crime, the Assizes (laws or edicts issued by the King's Court) of Clarendon (1166) and Northampton (1176) required local juries of twelve men from each hundred and four from each township to report to the sheriff or justices the names of any criminals.

Finally, machinery had to be set up to ensure that justice was done in the constant disputes over ownership of land, many arising from the civil war. To settle such matters by trial-by-battle, invoking the judgment of God but depending on the biceps of man, was not Henry's idea of justice. The new procedure was for a plaintiff to purchase a writ (or written order issued by the royal Chancery in the king's name) to ensure equitable settlement of the dispute. For example, a *Writ of Right* restored a freeman's lands if they had been forcibly taken from him; under a *Writ of Praecipe* a sheriff had to order the overlord of any seized land to restore it immediately, or answer for his neglect to the King's Court. In land disputes, a *Writ of Novel Disseisin* provided trial before the king's judges, with judgment to be given by "twelve free and lawful men of the neighbourhood," instead of trial by battle; and a *Writ of Mort d'Ancestor* protected a freeholder's heir to his estates.

Henry's Family

That Henry accomplished so much after almost twenty years of anarchy is remarkable enough; but his achievement would have been greater still had he not been plagued by the concerted rebellion of his embittered wife and turbulent sons. He married Eleanor of Aquitaine in 1152 and, though hardly a model of virtue herself, she was infuriated by Henry's repeated infidelities. In 1173 she incited Princes Henry, Richard and Geoffrey to rebel against their father, with the support of Louis VII of France, the Count of Flanders, and William, King of Scotland. Henry was able to deal with the threat, and Eleanor was imprisoned for sixteen years, but the sons continued to trouble their father. Prince Henry, who had been crowned already at his father's insistence, died in 1183 and Geoffrey in 1186; but when Henry II himself died in 1189, Richard and his favourite son John were plotting with Philip II of France against him.

Empire of Henry II

Normandy, taken from Stephen by Geoffrey of Anjou in the name of Geoffrey's son (Henry II) in 1145, passed to Henry in 1151 on Geoffrey's death. His son, Prince Henry, became Duke of Normandy.

Brittany was gained by the marriage of Henry's son Geoffrey to Constance, heiress and daughter of Duke Conan of Brittany. In 1169 Henry II forced the Bretons to recognize Geoffrey as heir to the dukedom.

Maine, Anjou and Touraine were inherited from his father Geoffrey, hereditary Count of Anjou, in 1151. Henry II's eldest surviving son, Prince Henry, became Duke of Anjou. Maine had passed by marriage to the Count of Anjou in 1110, and Touraine had been subject to the Counts of Anjou since 1040.

Aquitaine was gained by Henry's marriage to Eleanor, heiress of Aquitaine, after her marriage to Louis VII of France had been annulled. Henry II's son, later Richard I, was made Duke of Aquitaine in 1172.

In Ireland, Henry took over the Irish conquests of "Strongbow," Richard de Clare, Earl of Pembroke. From 1171 until 1172 Henry was in Ireland, taking possession of coastal towns, accepting homage from warring Irish rulers and setting up stable government at Dublin under Justiciar Hugh de Lacey. The leading English invaders were settled on large estates, mainly in east and central Ireland. At the Synod of Cashel (1172) the Irish Church submitted to Henry. In 1177 John, youngest son of Henry II, was granted the lordship of Ireland. He went to Ireland in 1185 to take over the government and to complete the conquest, but his expedition was a dismal failure, and he was recalled within a few months.

In 1157 Malcolm IV of Scotland did homage to Henry at Chester, and homage was exacted again in 1163 at Woodstock. William the Lion of Scotland joined a rebellion against Henry, formed by Prince Henry and the Earls of Chester, Leicester and Norfolk in 1173. In 1174 William was defeated at Alnwick by the barons of Yorkshire under Ranulf Glanvill, later Henry II's Justiciar; William was taken prisoner, and by the Treaty of Valognes he did homage to Henry for his kingdom, his barons paid homage for their estates, and his clergy swore obedience to the Archbishop of York.

QUESTIONS

1. Explain why Henry II is regarded as one of the greatest of the kings of England.
2. Account for and describe the unsettled condition of England during the reign of Stephen.

CHAPTER 5

PILGRIMAGES AND CRUSADES

IN THE Middle Ages, prayers to saints, especially if made at their place of burial, were considered of immense benefit as a cure for all spiritual and bodily ills. At the shrine of the saint, or at the altar of the chapel which might contain a relic of the saint it commemorated, a pilgrim would say his prayers, make an offering, and feel that he had laid up for himself in Heaven a credit balance of merit that would sustain him in his lifetime and mitigate his suffering in Purgatory. A pilgrimage was also a holiday, an excuse to travel, and became highly commercialized. Inns flourished on the pilgrim routes, and guardians of less fashionable shrines or relics were not above fabricating stories of miraculous happenings to establish popular appeal.

The most famous objects of pilgrimage in England were the jewelled image of Our Lady of Walsingham and the shrine of St. Thomas Becket at Canterbury, which later attracted no less a pilgrim than Henry VIII. The pilgrim had ample choice: he might see the Holy Blood of Hales, the Rood of Boxley, the tomb of St. Cuthbert at Durham, or the rooted staff of Joseph of Arimathea at Glastonbury; if he had a special need he would go to Repton Priory, to the bell of St. Guthlac, which cured diseases of the head; to be rid of toothache he would go to the tomb of a bishop of Wells; and if his cow had strayed the statue of St. Bride at Arden would surely restore it. If his tastes were more bizarre there were Simon de Montfort's foot at Alnwick Abbey and Thomas of Lancaster's felt hat at Pontefract.

There were many shrines in France and Spain, and at Rome, where St. Peter and St. Paul were buried, and where there was a host of relics: Aaron's rod, fragments of the loaves and fishes, the swaddling clothes of the infant Jesus, and hay from the manger at Bethlehem. Not less impressive were the heads of St. John the Baptist, one at Amiens, the other at Constantinople! But the greatest of all pilgrimages was to the Holy Land.

Causes of the Crusades

In 1071 the Seljuk Turks captured Jerusalem. The Eastern Emperor, ruling at Constantinople, appealed to Pope Gregory VII for help, an appeal strengthened by stories of pilgrims' sufferings at the hands of the Turk. Gregory was unable to arouse sufficient enthusiasm, and the project languished until 1095, when Pope Urban II appealed at the Council of Clermont

ANGLO-SAXON HOMESTEAD IN THE ELEVENTH CENTURY

ANGLO-SAXON SCENES AND PEOPLE

for an international crusade; his aim was to found a Latin state in Palestine to defend Jerusalem. The response was immediate: "The Welshman left his forest-hunting, the Scotsman forsook his friendly lice, the Dane abandoned his endless drinking bouts, the Norwegian deserted his raw fish." Declining to lead the crusade in person, Urban was nevertheless nominal leader of the movement, and (for a while at least) Christendom was united under his command.

East and West experienced an upsurge of energy in the eleventh century which, combined with the differences of race, religion, and political ideals, produced an inevitable conflict.

Further, the Turkish advance across Syria and most of Asia Minor not only put an obstacle in the way of the pilgrim, but also played havoc with the commercial zeal of the merchant; and merchants constituted a growing political force, prepared to wage war to safeguard their trade. Indeed, a movement allegedly religious in origin all too quickly became a mere commercial gambit to secure treasures on earth rather than in Heaven. Fortune seekers flocked to join the crusades, knights intent on carving out a patrimony, poor peasants eager for booty.

The crusade suited Pope Urban's foreign and domestic policy, for not only would the frontiers of Christendom be extended (and possibly further still by reconciliation with the Greek Church), but also reality would be given to the Truce of God by diverting men's quarrelsome energies, besides alleviating discord and indiscipline in the Church.

Medieval pilgrim's badge depicting the mounted figure of St. Thomas of Canterbury which was recovered from the Thames. A modern parallel can be found in the badges which travellers of today wear on rucksacks.

Richard I and the Third Crusade

Three European rulers set out in 1189 to join the Third Crusade: the Emperor Frederick Barbarossa, Philip Augustus of France, and Richard I (Coeur de Lion) of England. Barbarossa was drowned en route in Armenia, and although a part of his force carried on, it was a meagre and demoralized contingent.

Richard I embarked with a force

of eight thousand men in one hundred ships, gathered from the Cinque Ports, Shoreham and Southampton, as well as from private persons and ports of Normandy and Poitou.

Richard embarked from Marseilles, Philip from Genoa, and they met at Messina in Sicily. Here Richard wasted what remained of the sailing season in argument with Tancred, ruler of Sicily, who refused to pay a legacy and dowry to the late ruler's widow Joanna, Richard's sister. Richard stormed Messina, Tancred made peace with gold, and in 1191 Philip sailed on to the Holy Land.

Meanwhile Richard seized control of Cyprus, and there awaited the arrival of Berengaria, daughter of the King of Navarre, whom he married before re-embarking for Acre, where he arrived on 8 June, 1191, almost two months after Philip.

Possession of Acre was essential as a base for operations against Jerusalem, and it was now being besieged, but to little advantage, the Saracen garrison being confident and well-supplied, the Crusaders depressed and near-defeated by disease and discord.

Richard's arrival reinforced the reputation that had preceded him; the Crusaders, temporarily united, renewed the siege, and the garrison capitulated on 12 July. Next month Philip returned to France, sick and unable to work with Richard any longer, but content to intrigue in Angevin affairs whilst Richard was out of the way.

Richard now had the double task of restoring the Kingdom of Jerusalem and recovering the Holy City. Count Henry of Champagne was elected king of the Latin kingdom, over Richard's candidate Guy of Lusignan, whom Richard compensated with the gift of Cyprus. Richard reached Beit-nuba, twelve miles from Jerusalem, but realized that it could not be taken; and, harassed by fever, he was anxious to withdraw. In 1192, after prolonged negotiations, Saladin and Richard concluded a three-year truce, by which the Crusaders surrendered Ascalon but retained Jaffa, Caesarea, Haifa, Tyre, Acre, Lydda and Ramleh.

On the way home Richard avoided France, only to fall into the unfriendly hands of Duke Leopold of Austria who had never forgiven Richard for flinging the Austrian flag into a ditch when Acre fell. To the dismay of Europe he handed the prisoner to the Emperor Henry VI, with whom Richard remained until ransomed for 100,000 marks of silver.

Little had been achieved. From the first this Crusade had been bedevilled by bad blood between Richard and Philip, for which Richard, bad-tempered like all the Angevins, must bear much of the blame. Although vassal to Philip for his fief of Normandy, Richard would not bow to French overlordship. Pledged to marry Philip's sister Alice, Richard had insultingly repudiated her by marrying Berengaria. Above all, Philip, who was intelligent but no soldier, was deeply jealous of Richard's powers of leadership and his courage and skill in battle. From the failure of the Third Crusade there is a change in the character of the whole movement; merchants followed upon the Crusaders' heels and the future of the movement lay with them.

Effects of the Crusade on England

The Third Crusade was a great financial drain upon England, not only for the equipment of fleets and armies, but also for paying Richard's ransom money.

Richard's absence abroad encouraged lawlessness, anti-Jewish outbreaks engineered by crusader knights who had fallen in debt to Jewish money-lenders, and rebellions aroused by Prince John. However, Henry II's administrative measures stood the test; and with the absence of the king and many of his nobles abroad England managed without them.

Results of the Crusades

The Crusades failed to achieve their purpose, and the vast expenditure of human life can be neither justified nor excused. Indirectly, however, the crusades had a marked effect on Europe.

Contact with Syria, established before 1095, was much increased. Eastern products became familiar in the West, at least to those who could afford them: sugar, spices, new fruits (lemons and apricots), new materials (cotton, muslin, damask and silk), precious metals, carpets and tapestries.

With this expansion of trade, towns developed, particularly in northern Italy where Venice and Genoa predominated and lay at the hub of European land-routes with Syria and the East, and with north-western Europe.

Arab mathematics, science and medicine reached the West through Spain, but Western knowledge of the lands and peoples of Syria, Egypt and Asia Minor increased, and growing contact with Constantinople revived interest in the Greek language and Byzantine culture. Henceforth France and her neighbours replaced Constantinople as the cultural centre of Christendom.

The power and influence of the papacy were enhanced, although popes were not above preaching a crusade to raise money. The Crusades created direct taxation, for the Third Crusade was financed by the Saladin Tithe levied in 1188 by Henry II; this proved so profitable that it became a regular tax.

QUESTIONS

1. Explain the origin, purpose and results of the Crusades.

2. Describe the shortcomings and the successes of Richard Coeur de Lion.

CHAPTER 6

THE SONS OF HENRY II, AND THE MONARCHY IN DECLINE

IT WOULD be too much to expect outstanding merit from Henry II's pack of ill-conditioned sons; but of the two who succeeded him, Richard and John, it is the latter who can claim to have earned favourable comparison with his illustrious father.

To Richard, tradition has been unreasonably kind. Of a nine-and-a-half-year reign he spent only five months in England, devoted to high-pressure fund-raising to sustain his restless war-mongering. With the barrels of silver pennies (zealously gathered by his thrifty father) quickly emptied, he resorted to selling castles, lordships, town charters and even, to the King of Scotland, freedom from vassalage. By all manner of means he "relieved all those whose money was a burden to them."

This battle-drunk boor, "lionhearted but soulless," seems ill-cast for the rôle of perfect gentle knight. As Duke of Aquitaine he had spread terror among his vassals by harrying their estates with a marauding band of thugs; and there was more tinsel than gold in a man who, as Gerald of Wales wrote, "cared for no success that was not reached by a path cut by his own sword and stained with the blood of his adversaries."

King John

Richard's foolhardy death in 1199 beneath the walls of Châlus, victim of a crossbowman sniping from behind a frying pan, set a succession problem. As there was no hard and fast rule governing the succession, twelve-year-old Arthur of Brittany (grandson of Henry II) might have challenged, had he been older, the claim of his uncle John. As it was, the barons of Normandy and Aquitaine gave their support to John, whom Richard himself in all likelihood regarded as his rightful successor.

Not that King John was the sort of person one would choose to have about the house. He was cruel, and his cruelty merged into a warped sense of humour. Thoroughly spoilt by his father, he shared with his family the volcanic Angevin temper; and he moved in a world of mistrust and suspicion of his own making. Modern research has not been concerned to whitewash John, but simply to disentangle fact and fiction, and to demonstrate the great abilities of this intelligent king, and the difficulties he had to face.

John was devoted to the business of governing, and expected nothing less from his servants. By constant progresses (reminiscent of his father) from one to another of his seventy castles he was able to maintain a strict watch on the administration of the country as a whole, and ensured its steady and orderly development; and if his coming was dreaded by a laggard official, sight of the royal caravan delighted those many suitors who preferred that their cases should be tried before the king, because only then could they be sure of justice. Cheaper justice and solid judicial reform were outstanding contributions made by John himself, just as it was his own administrative activity that fostered a really efficient bureaucracy

John's early career had held out little hope for his success as king. His stupidity in Ireland in 1185 had led to ignominious recall after only eight months, and he had dabbled in treason, against his father in 1189 and against his brother Richard in 1194, thus meriting sentence of excommunication from Archbishop Hubert and Bishop Hugh of Lincoln. Nevertheless to some extent he turned over a new leaf in 1199, determined to follow in his father's footsteps, to reign and to rule; but his impatience, and lack of discernment and of boldness in action, held him back from success, quite apart from the magnitude of other problems which confronted him.

A major anxiety would be keeping the Angevin Empire intact. Communications were poor, and Philip Augustus, King of France 1180-1223, who controlled only a small part of France, was eagerly awaiting a chance

Engraving of the tomb of King John in Worcester Cathedral.

to stir up latent disaffection against John and deprive him of his French lands. Two deep-rooted obstacles which in the end proved insurmountable, were the rapid rise in prices (which increased the king's expenses but did nothing to raise his revenues) and the murmurings of a baronage induced to protest by long experience of the restrictive policies of the Crown.

There can be no doubt that the barons were a very awkward rabble to deal with, but they were not impossible; and, slow-witted as they were, they could at least understand and respect a king who faced them squarely. Henry II, for example, was harsh but impartial; and even Richard's constant tax-gathering hit everybody alike and was done for a clear purpose. With John it was different; his rule was not especially oppressive, nor did he devise any new and sinister schemes for extending royal power, but he could not be trusted, and this is the key to an understanding of his reign.

John could not inspire trust because he himself trusted no one, and he hedged himself round with a sinister protective screen. He had an armed bodyguard, his household servants acted as spies to report any signs of discontent, and orders to agents were given and acknowledged by a complicated system of secret signs. His nobles and even his favoured mercenary captains were obliged to give hostages to the king, and these he used unhesitatingly as a vicious means of persuasion. His constant tours of his kingdom were not so much progresses as organized prowls, and it is small wonder that some barons felt it well worth while to try and keep on the right side of this suspicious king by goodwill offerings to the Royal Treasury. John's anger was quite unpredictable, and he could hound to destruction any who offended him, as he did William de Briouze, whose only offence was that John had made him too powerful. So deep was the barons' fear of the king that only an outstanding man like William Marshall, Earl of Pembroke, or Ranulf, Earl of Chester, could stand alone against him.

John's Financial Demands

In a period of rising prosperity only the king seemed faced with the impossibility of making both ends meet, and his financial demands were bound to be heavy. However, the crushing weight of Richard's taxation had so soured the country that even moderate demands by John would have been unpopular. As it was, he completely overstepped the mark. Whereas Henry II had raised eight scutages in thirty-four years, and Richard three in ten years, John demanded eleven in his seventeen years, some at more than twice the rate accepted by his predecessors.

In 1201 John summoned his barons to Portsmouth in preparation for an assault on France, relieved them of all the money they had brought with them, then called off the expedition. He consistently abused his right of wardship, exploiting estates in his care and leaving them in a ruinous condition for the new lord, and he demanded heavy reliefs far in excess of what had come to be regarded as reasonable charges.

Loss of Normandy, 1204

In 1199 the barons of Anjou, Maine and Poitou, supported by Philip of France, declared John's nephew Arthur to be their lawful overlord. Although a settlement was patched up, by 1202 Philip and John were at war.

In 1200 John repudiated his wife, Hadwisa of Gloucester, by whom he had no child, and married twelve-year-old Isabella, daughter of the Count of Angoulême, who was already betrothed to Hugh of Lusignan, one of John's Poitevin vassals. This offended feudal law, and John was deprived of his French lands by Philip, to whom Hugh had appealed for redress. Normandy was attacked in 1202, but by a brilliant manoeuvre against Mirebeau, John demonstrated his military ability, and at one stroke captured the rebel leaders together with his nephew Arthur.

Then, as so often, John ruined everything by ill-judged action. He alienated his supporter William des Roches, Seneschal of Anjou, and in 1203 played into Philip's hands by murdering Arthur. Perhaps the murder was prompted by John's awareness of mounting opposition to him in England; its effect was to arouse anger in France, particularly in Brittany. Philip took Château Gaillard after a six-month battering in 1204, forced Rouen to surrender, and the Duchy of Normandy (except for the Channel Islands) was in his hands.

A lavish expedition prepared by John in 1205 to salvage his loss had to be called off because his barons refused to support him. The loss of Normandy deepened John's distrust of his barons, and deprived him of a valuable source of income which he could ill afford to lose.

Canterbury Election, 1205

Tradition had established that the king should play the major part in selecting a successor to Archbishop Hubert Walter in 1205, but the monks of Canterbury, suspicious of the king and anxious to forestall the bishops of the southern province (who claimed a share in such an election), chose one of their number, Reginald, as the new archbishop. They had not even waited for John's permission to hold an election, so the situation was one that John could not and would not allow. He forced monks and bishops together to elect his own nominee, John de Gray, Bishop of Norwich.

However, Pope Innocent II had already been appealed to by the monks to recognize the election they had made, and by the bishops to acknowledge their right to participate in the election, and he hit upon an unfortunate solution. He overruled the bishops' claim and cancelled the monks' and the king's elections. John could not be expected to tolerate this. He refused to accept Stephen Langton, whom the Pope had decided should be chosen as archbishop, expelled the monks and took over their estates as well as the English benefices held by Italians.

The Pope countered this justifiable challenge to papal authority by placing England under an interdict. All churches were closed and public services ceased; and although there is no record of general discontent as a result of the interdict, undoubtedly in a deeply religious age the loss of worship was felt very keenly, and John's reputation with his people can hardly have been improved.

Perhaps the fact that the king was feared more than the Pope softened the blow of the interdict; but the Pope played his trump card in 1209, when he excommunicated John. All but two bishops submitted to the Pope. The estates of the others were confiscated by the king, and swelled the revenue already secured from the Canterbury estates taken over after the interdict. For a time these lands were administered by sheriffs, but soon John allowed the clergy to pay for their recovery, and to continue administering them, although with the lion's share of the revenue still surrendered to the Crown.

Capitulation to the Pope, 1213

The Pope took John's peace offer in 1212 with an outsize pinch of salt, but John knew what he was doing. With unrest in Scotland and Wales, and the Pope and Philip of France arrayed against him, he drove a wedge in their alliance by a complete capitulation. John became the Pope's vassal, surrendering England and Ireland as feudal fiefs and agreeing to pay an annual tribute to Rome. He accepted Stephen Langton as archbishop, and promised to reinstate all exiled ecclesiastics, to restore church lands and to compensate the Church for his exactions.

John received absolution from the sentence of excommunication from Langton in Winchester Cathedral in 1213, and in the following year terms were settled with the Cardinal Bishop of Tusculum, acting for the Pope, for lifting the interdict. By his right-about-turn policy John now had the Pope on his side against Philip of France and against the gathering storm of baronial discontent.

Mounting Opposition

The baronial attitude (for they were not organized and had no policy) was one of "sulk-and-skulk"; and John, as we have seen, had created it. He had excluded the barons from any position of prestige and influence, and preferred the service of low-born prying civil servants and the confidence of mercenary captains like Gerard d'Athée, notorious enough to get himself and his family unfavourable mention in Magna Carta.

In 1206, 1209 and 1212 there were ominous grumblings from the barons. These John effectively but temporarily checked by his usual crippling demands

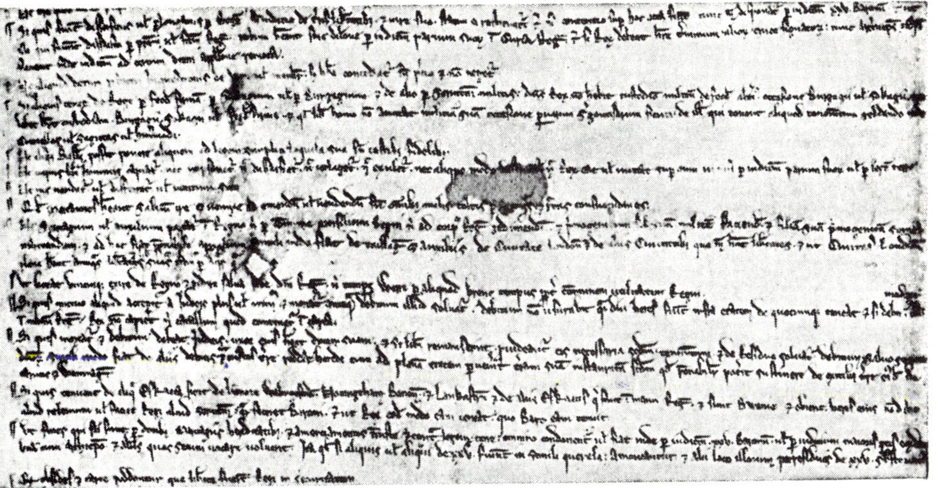

Part of Magna Carta containing the demands of the barons which were granted by King John on 15 June, 1215.

for hostages. After the settlement with the Pope in 1213, the barons found the leaders they needed, when Eustace de Vesci and Robert FitzWalter returned from exile. Fortunately Stephen Langton returned at the same time, and so ennobled by his guidance what would otherwise have been a sordid feudal brawl.

Anxious to settle old scores with Philip, John summoned the feudal host to Portsmouth in 1213. Taking their cue from the barons from northern England, the rest refused the feudal summons, and only Langton's intervention prevented John from marching his mercenary army against them. He embarked for France in 1214 without them, but their defection, and the desertion of the Poitevin barons when Philip could well have been routed at Roche-au-Moine, ruined John's hopes; and with the resounding defeat at Bouvines of the Earl of Salisbury, who had landed his force in Flanders, the king's cause was beyond help.

Magna Carta

John returned to England breathing fire against the barons. Extremists among them refused him hostages and, after a temporary truce, renounced their allegiance. They entered London and appealed for French help. At this point Langton and William Marshall, at the head of moderate opinion, intervened to avoid civil war, negotiating in turn with the barons at Staines and the king at Windsor. A settlement was finally reached at Runnymede, and on 19 June, 1215, the Great Charter was sealed, king and barons agreeing to honour its terms.

The Charter, derived from the coronation charter of Henry I, was drawn up for the best of practical reasons, to check the King's excesses and to define the feudal relationship between him and his barons. It is not a document bursting with lofty ideals and intimations of democracy; this was a mirage created by seventeenth century lawyers who conveniently read far too much significance into Clause 29:

> "No freeman shall be arrested or imprisoned or deprived of his freehold or banished or in any way ruined, nor will we take or order any action against him, except by the lawful judgement of his equals and according to the law of the land."

This was only the barons' insurance against sharing the fate of William de Briouze.

Nor were the king's baronial opponents striking a blow for any cause but their own; indeed it can be argued that they hoped that John would not honour the Charter, and so give them the excuse they wanted to break him. Nevertheless the Charter did promise "present help for present ills to all the articulate classes of the day"; and Clause 61, which provided for the setting up of a baronial committee of twenty-five as watchdogs of the realm to seek redress of wrongs committed by the king or his servants, and in default to deprive him of his castles, estates and possessions, was a novel provision echoed in Henry III's reign in the baronial plan of reform.

Ireland, Scotland and Wales

Effective administration was secured in Ireland under John's Justiciars, Meiler FitzHenry and John de Gray, Bishop of Norwich. In 1210 John himself was in Ireland with an army, reducing the power of the great Irish lords and establishing his own authority firmly.

In 1212 William the Lion of Scotland was forced to pay homage, his oath secured by the surrender to John of his two daughters as hostages, and the promise to pay 15,000 marks within two years.

Wales was similarly contained by John. He married his daughter Joan to Llywelyn ap Iorworth, lord of Anglesey and North Wales; and Llywelyn's attempt to demonstrate his independent power was defeated by John's Welsh campaign of 1211.

> "There was now no one in Ireland, Scotland or Wales, who did not bow to his nod, a situation which, as is well known, none of his predecessors had achieved."
>
> (*The Annals of Barnwell Priory*)

QUESTIONS

1. John has been described as one of the worst kings of England. Explain why this opinion was held and whether you consider it should be modified in any way.

2. Explain why various sections of the people became dissatisfied with the rule of John. Outline the importance of Magna Carta.

CHAPTER 7

THE STRUGGLE FOR THE CHARTER: JOHN AND HENRY III

KING JOHN had been cornered at Runnymede, but the struggle for the Charter was only just beginning. John was a slippery customer, and, basking in the unaccustomed warmth of papal support, he was intent on destroying those truculent barons who had remained in arms against him. They were excommunicated by his bishops on the Pope's instructions, thus setting aside Stephen Langton's argument that the Charter itself invalidated the Pope's position in authorizing such action.

Langton was suspended from office, and began a saddened mission of justification to Rome. In 1215 John received the Pope's letter cancelling the Great Charter, and promptly set off on the warpath.

In the civil war that followed, the rebel barons, drawing support from the eastern counties, the north, Wales and Scotland, established their headquarters at London, and anxiously negotiated for assistance from France.

John wasted no time. He captured Rochester Castle; then, instead of directing a decisive attack on London, chose to move north, harrying his opponents' estates, clearing the Scots from Newcastle and Berwick, and forcing Alexander to defend himself in the Scottish lowlands. This done, in 1216 John turned towards a still defiant London, fortified now by the landing

Seals showing Richard of Cornwall (left) and Simon de Montfort.

of Louis, son of King Philip of France. With two-thirds of his nobles in rebellion against him, John went from Winchester to Cambridge, Lynn, Lincoln and Wisbech, losing "everything he valued most" crossing the Wallstream estuary.

John's Death and the Accession of Henry III

After John's death at Newark in 1216 his nine-year-old son was crowned Henry III by the Bishop of Winchester in the Abbey church at Gloucester. The barons' struggle had been against John, not a blameless child, and now their loyalty was stirred. The tide turned so strongly against Louis that he made peace in 1217; indeed, he had no alternative. The overwhelming defeat at Lincoln, derisively called "the Fair of Lincoln," had seen the capture of half the rebel knights by the regent, William the Marshal, and the rest of Louis' English allies were eager to join the new king. The siege of Dover was raised, and after Philip Daubeny had routed a French fleet off Sandwich, Louis agreed to the Treaty of Kingston. A general amnesty was declared, with full restitution of lands; Louis, who undertook to give no further assistance to English rebels, received 10,000 marks (a quarter of the Crown's revenue), which to the royalists was money well spent to get rid of him.

Henry III, 1216-72

In 1216 the king's followers met in council at Bristol and the regents, William the Marshal and Cardinal Guala, set their seals to a revised Great Charter, so that now it stood as a symbol of equity and security, and seemed to guarantee a working alliance between king and barons.

Much now depended on the king, who, though he modelled himself on Edward the Confessor, nevertheless fell far short of that ideal, and inherited sufficient of his father's suspicious nature and furtive fear of treachery to ensure the forfeiture of his barons' trust. Henry was a misfit; irresolution, petulance and an exalted view of the power of the crown made this child-like ruler totally unfit for the hurly-burly of politics and war. Chroniclers noted a "waxen pliability," and his lack of political insight and his inadequacy in action made civil war inevitable.

The reign of Henry III falls easily into three periods:

(*a*) from his accession to 1227, when (at the suggestion of Stephen Langton and with the permission of the Pope) he declared himself of age;

(*b*) from then until 1258, during which time control was in the hands of the king and his ministers;

(*c*) the final period up to his death in 1272, when both government and king were in the hands of his barons, or of his son, the Lord Edward.

Guala left England in 1218, William the Marshal died in 1219, and until 1232 the major role in government was taken by the Justiciar, high-handed and tactless Hubert de Burgh. He survived only because he had Langton's support, for Hubert, who had clambered from the ranks of the gentry to win the favour of King John and the hand of a Scottish princess, was not popular with the barons. His tenure of authority was bound to be short, and when the king's favour blew in the opposite direction in 1232, Hubert was imprisoned to make way for Peter des Roches, Bishop of Winchester.

Alien Influences

Himself a Poitevin, Peter filled offices at court and in the administration with foreigners, none more influential than his nephew, Peter des Rivaux, sheriff of twenty counties, Treasurer, and Keeper of the Wardrobe and the Privy Seal. In taking only their advice, although Peter des Rivaux was efficient and carried out a much-needed overhaul of the administration, the king was circumventing the Great Council of barons, who had been consulted during the king's minority, and whose position as advisers was traditionally accepted, if not in practice established. Therefore, the conflict between an absolutist king and a baronage out to control both king and government was already present in 1234.

Richard Marshal, Earl of Pembroke, supported by the Marcher lords and Llywelyn ap Iorworth, defied the king on the Poitevin issue in 1233. In 1234 the royal forces were driven from Wales, and Henry agreed to the dismissal of des Roches and des Rivaux. The subsequent murder of Pembroke in the king's name served only to reinforce baronial success.

Beginnings of Baronial Reform

The growth of baronial complaints of misgovernment led to the gradual development of a plan of reform. In the February Parliament of 1244 they renewed their attack on Henry's alien advisers, and demanded that their complaints be satisfied before the king was granted the money he required. Besides demanding a re-issue of Magna Carta, and that the king should have English advisers, they moved a significant step further by claiming the right to share in the appointment of the Justiciar, and of the Chancellor and Treasurer, who now headed separate departments of government, the Chancery and the Treasury having grown away from the royal household.

Not least of the barons' concerns, and of the king's too, at this February Parliament was Henry's need for money. Generally the reign was a period of prosperity, but Henry lived well beyond the Crown means, already restricted by Magna Carta and devalued by rising prices. Various expensive projects, for example the twenty-five-year rebuilding of Westminster Abbey, had already set the king borrowing from Florentine and Siennese money-lenders. But the bitterest cause of financial difficulties was "the yawning gulf of papal need." Henry had cause to be grateful to Rome, but persistent papal demands for subsidies and provisions (comfortable benefices, or rather the comfortable income of benefices, for Roman officials and protégés) had gone beyond all reason; in one year alone the Bishops of Lincoln and Salisbury had to provide for three hundred such papal parasites. As a result Henry felt his gratitude growing threadbare, and even Bishop Grosseteste of Lincoln, champion of Rome, led clerical opposition to this excessive papal demand.

The Sicilian Project

In these circumstances Henry's acceptance of the Pope's offer of Sicily for his younger son Edmund in 1254, and of the crown of Germany in 1257 for his brother Richard of Cornwall, precipitated a conflict with the barons. On the death of the Emperor Frederick II in 1250, Pope Innocent IV, whose hostility to the German family of Hohenstaufen bordered on hysteria, resolved that Germany and Sicily should not again be under one ruler, and that the Hohenstaufens should be excluded from both. Hence the offer to Henry, and Henry's acceptance, were ill-judged because of the impracticability and expense of the scheme. Germany, difficult enough for a German to control, was not likely to respond to a foreigner; and by 1257 Sicily was firmly in the hands of the Hohenstaufen Manfred. Henry's acceptance of these explosive gifts had been secret, but the financial drain involved could not be kept from the barons. Even threats of excommunication from Pope Alexander IV could not squeeze blood from a stone, and served only to unite church and barons against the king.

Baronial Grievances and Remedies, 1258-9

Bad weather and poor harvests in 1257-8, floods in the Severn valley and the threat of famine goaded the barons to positive action at the Hock-tide (Easter) Parliament in 1258. Under the rich and influential earls of Gloucester and Hertford, a group of nobles (including the king's brother-in-law, the Gascon, Simon de Montfort) pledged themselves to constrain the king and reform the government. In May Roger Bigod, spokesman for the determined barons, told the king ". . . all aliens should flee from your presence and ours . . . Swear total observance to our counsels . . . Swear, touching Holy Gospel, you and your son and heir Edward that you will not act without the advice of twenty-four good men of England, namely, the elected bishops, earls, and barons . . ." Henry agreed, for himself and for Edward.

The Mad Parliament at Oxford in June 1258 drew up the Provisions of Oxford, by which this commission of twenty-four (twelve nominated by the king and twelve by the barons) was to provide for reform of the civil administration, the Church, and the king's household.

The central feature of their scheme was a Council of Fifteen chosen from the original twenty-four, seven earls (including Simon de Montfort), five

Frequent summoning of parliaments was a definite policy of Edward I

leading barons, the Archbishop of Canterbury, the Bishop of Worcester and a royal clerk. Its functions were to advise the king and to appoint the Justiciar, Chancellor and Treasurer, who were then responsible, not to the king, but to the Council of Fifteen. The Council was to report on its work to parliaments held three times a year, at Michaelmas and Candlemas and in June, and it soon got down to business. The Sicilian adventure was abandoned, foreigners were expelled, and Henry's enforced renunciation of his claim to Normandy, Anjou and Poitou in the Treaty of Paris with Louis IX of France was the swan song of the Angevin Empire. Provision was made for an overhaul of royal administration by the Council's appointment of four knights from each shire to draw up a list of grievances for presentation to the king's judges.

What is interesting is the maturity of the barons' outlook on government in 1258, by comparison with that of their predecessors in 1215. Still more striking is the extension of constitutional reform to the land-owning class by a set of ordinances, published in the February Parliament of 1259, in which Henry made it known that barons of the Council were prepared to extend to their tenants the same concessions granted by the king to his vassals. Complaints of the lesser nobles, that the barons had looked after themselves but "had done nothing of what they had promised for the good of the realm," were met in the Provisions of Westminster, "the most enduring monument of the baronial revolution."

By 1260, however, the barons who had united in drawing up the Provisions of Oxford were at sixes and sevens, in particular two dominant personalities, the Earl of Gloucester and Simon de Montfort. The steps that had been taken were novel, and many of the nobles, Gloucester included, felt uneasy that all had been accomplished without the king's willing approval.

To de Montfort the Provisions of Oxford were a second Magna Carta, to be defended to the last, and he found a temporary ally in the heir to the throne, Edward. Such an alliance could not last, for sooner or later the fundamental difference between Simon's concept of the Council as a controller of the king and Edward's view that it could only be an advisory committee would range them on opposing sides.

Henry and the Provisions of Oxford, 1260-4

Henry made capital of the division in the baronial ranks to circumvent the restrictions of the council. Through Richard of Cornwall he reached agreement with the leading barons in 1261-2, and completed wriggling out of the Provisions of Oxford in 1262, when the Pope absolved him from his oath to observe them.

Henry was independent again, but his approach to government had not changed. Discontent smouldered on, and in 1263 Simon de Montfort was called to lead the baronial faction. He insisted on a return to the Provisions of Oxford, but the spirit of 1258 had evaporated; by the end of the year the Lord Edward had deserted Simon, taking with him a band of young hotheads, and greater and lesser nobles followed his example. An uneasy truce was made between Simon and the king, and Louis of France was invited to arbitrate in their quarrel.

Louis' judgment, contained in the Mise of Amiens, came down on Henry's side, condemning the Provisions of Oxford. De Montfort could not accept the Mise, and prepared to defend the settlement of 1258. Louis had stated that Henry was bound by all charters, liberties and customs which existed before 1258, and this gave Simon his loophole, for even in these terms

NORMAN VILLAGE AND FORTIFIED MANOR HOUSE

EVERYDAY SCENES FROM NORMAN LIFE

Henry's government stood condemned. At Lewes the king's forces, commanded by the Lord Edward, were defeated, the king and Richard of Cornwall (who had returned from Germany in 1262) were captured, and Edward was surrendered to Simon as hostage to guarantee the king's good behaviour.

Simon de Montfort rules England

From May 1264 to his death in August 1265, Simon ruled England, and pinned his hopes on the principles of the Provisions of Oxford. With the young Earl of Gloucester and the Bishop of Chichester he governed in the king's name. For assistance he looked to a Council of Nine, but more particularly to the Great Council, which already in 1265 was becoming a far more representative body with its lay and ecclesiastical barons, knights and burgesses.

But although the gentry supported Simon, he soon lost the barons' support. The Earl of Gloucester grew increasingly sceptical of Simon's attempt to rule on behalf of the king, and joined with the Lord Edward (who escaped from Hereford with Gloucester's connivance) against him. At Ludlow they agreed, in their new version of the Provisions of Oxford, that the old laws should be observed, that evil customs should be eliminated, and that the country should be ruled by the advice of the faithful native-born.

Simon had to fight for his political faith, and at Evesham he was outmanoeuvred, defeated and killed by the skill of his military pupil Edward.

Baronial Achievement

Deprived of their estates after Evesham, Simon's supporters were hunted down; but the Dictum of Kenilworth of 1266 allowed them to buy back their estates at a fair price. This reveals the influence of the Lord Edward, as does the Statute of Marlborough in 1267, which confirmed the principles of the Provisions of Oxford and Westminster. Edward, the Earl of Gloucester, and the papal legate Cardinal Ottobuono, who shared in the making of this settlement, realized how practical much of the baronial plan of reform was.

Simon de Montfort had not died for a vain cause. Legislative reforms assembled in the Statute of Marlborough derived from the reform movement, and the stipulation that parliament should meet three times a year were notable contributions to the development of that English institution. Above all, the barons had shown themselves capable of intelligent political thinking, and well able to shoulder the task of responsible administration.

QUESTIONS

1. Describe the career of Simon de Montfort and explain his importance.

2. Describe the character and difficulties of Henry III.

OCL/HIST/1—D

CHAPTER 8

EDWARD I

THE capture of Kenilworth in 1266 ended the Barons' War; and the Statute of Marlborough in 1267 indicated that England was again under the control of law, virtually of a new king, for Henry III had conceded his real power to his son, the Lord Edward.

Perhaps Henry's shortcomings as a ruler provided Edward with the determination to succeed where his father had failed; but the most formative influence in his life was undoubtedly his godfather, Simon de Montfort, who had seen in him all the qualities that Henry III lacked.

Edward's youth had been wild, but he began to learn responsibility early, for in 1252-4 his father granted him Gascony, Ireland, lands in Wales, the towns of Bristol, Stamford and Grantham, and the Earldom of Chester; successful management of these estates, besides providing revenue, gave him valuable insight into problems of administration that, on a larger scale, would concern him later as king.

At the age of fifteen he married Eleanor of Castile. In 1270 he went to Acre on a crusade, and distinguished himself by his bravery, although the poisoned dagger of the Emir of Jaffa almost ended his days in 1272, the year in which his father died. After a leisurely progress from Sicily, Edward "Longshanks" landed in England and was jubilantly crowned in 1274.

Principles of Government

Edward knew his people's needs and intended to satisfy them by good laws, emanating from a strong royal authority. For him, good government was that in which all classes played their part; from nobles and clergy he sought advice; from knights of the shires he demanded greater participation in both local and national business; and burgesses from the towns he summoned to the assembly of parliament. In this he was no democrat; his concern was to cultivate the means of checking the magnates' power.

Like Henry II, Edward had to clear away the evils arising from civil war, and the first twenty years of his reign were occupied with the establishment of orderly government.

Immediatcly he instituted an investigation into the extent of crown lands, and into baronial immunities and jurisdictions which stood in the way of his own judicial rights. The inquiry was diligently conducted; forty questions were put to juries in every county by his commissioners, and the replies were embodied in the Hundred Rolls.

Legislation

This inquiry demonstrates Edward's concern for definition, and his willingness to respect valid rights, but to come down heavily on usurpation; it was followed by the Statute of Gloucester of 1278, which ordered justices on progress, armed with information from the Hundred Rolls, to inquire "by what warrant" (i.e. by writs of *Quo Warranto*, which had been in use since Richard I's time) the magnates administered royal justice in their franchises. Edward's insistence on documentary proof set many magnates, whose right rested on custom and not on royal charter, angrily in defence of their jurisdictions; so Edward was forced to compromise. In 1290 uninterrupted possession of a franchise from the beginning of Richard I's reign was considered a sufficient title, and very few franchises were abolished, because Edward was always willing to placate an angry baron (and secure a contribution to his exchequer) by granting a charter of acceptance in return for a substantial fine; but, and this was the important thing, Edward had put a stop to the unlicensed assumption of royal jurisdiction by individuals.

The first Statute of Westminster (1275) dealt with administrative abuses revealed by the 1274 inquiry, and ensured that feudal reforms indicated in the State of Marlborough were carried out. These statutes and the Statute of Winchester (1285) which revived the jurisdiction of local courts, and by its reorganization of the militia (now to be used for maintaining internal order) brought up-to-date Henry II's Assize of Arms (1181), seem to be part of an anti-feudal policy. However, Edward's Statute of Mortmain in 1279 was designed to protect the rights of the feudal barons, and his own as the greatest feudal lord, and was directed particularly against the Church.

This statute forbade transference of fiefs to the "dead hand" (*mortmain*) of religious bodies or other corporations. A practice which had grown up was for a baron to transfer his fief to a religious house, then receive it back again as an ecclesiastical, not a royal, fief, thereby owing no military service to the king and depriving him of the profits of wardship, marriage and relief. This had been forbidden by Magna Carta as reissued in 1217 and 1225, but still land was being freed from the duty of military service by this means; so from 1279 no land was to be transferred in this way without licence from the king.

The Third Statute of Westminster (*Quia Emptores*), 1290, was designed to protect the interests of the feudal class by prohibition of subinfeudation. This was a process of feudal sub-letting, often carried so far that the nominal holder of the fief had insufficient left in his own hands to enable him to perform his required services. In the long run *Quia Emptores* hastened the end of feudalism, because it made land marketable; however, the statute immediately benefited the king, because it increased the number of tenants holding land in-chief (i.e. direct) from him.

As law-giver and administrator, Edward is outstanding among English kings. The three departments of administration, Exchequer, Chancery and the Wardrobe, worked together smoothly, and Edward was well served by men like Robert Burnell, his first Chancellor and chief minister, 1274-92, Walter Langton who was Treasurer, 1295-1307, and John of Benstead, one of many capable civil servants of the Wardrobe.

Edward's reign also saw the development of the three great Courts of Law, Exchequer, King's Bench and Common Pleas, with administration of justice falling more and more into the capable hands of trained lawyers sent on regular circuits from the Curia Regis.

Edward and the Church

Edward was not anti-papal, but with one so tenacious of his rights it was hardly likely that the Church would be exempt from his claim to judicial supremacy. Papal provision of bishops was an inevitable grievance, and twice the Canterbury chapter's choice of an archbishop was set aside in favour of the Pope's mendicant nominees, Kilwardby and Pecham.

An important clause in the Statute of Westminster 1275 echoed Henry II's dispute; it ordered lay juries to bring in a preliminary verdict against any clerical offender, before he was handed on to the church court. The Statute of Mortmain, as we have seen, was part of a policy designed to curb the undue political influence of the Church; and the writ *Circumspecte agatis*, issued to itinerant justices in Norfolk in 1286, distinguished between those questions which came under church courts (breaches of morality, matters concerning tithes, mortuaries, wills, marriages, defamation and assault against the clergy) and the rest, which were the province of temporal courts.

Edward's relations with Church and barons deteriorated towards the end of his reign. Until 1294 Edward had conducted successful war and diplomacy in Wales, France and Scotland, tailoring his policy to fit his resources. After 1294, however, the king over-reached himself, over-taxing his resources; his policy towards France and Scotland went awry, and there was mounting opposition at home beneath the banner of "the Charters."

Edward and Wales

Defence of his borders was essential to Edward, and Wales first demanded his attention. Since the Norman Conquest, Marcher earls had encroached into east and south Wales; but a principality of north and central Wales, under the rule of Llywelyn ap Gruffydd, had been recognized in 1267 by the Treaty of Montgomery. Llywelyn refused to do homage to Edward or to

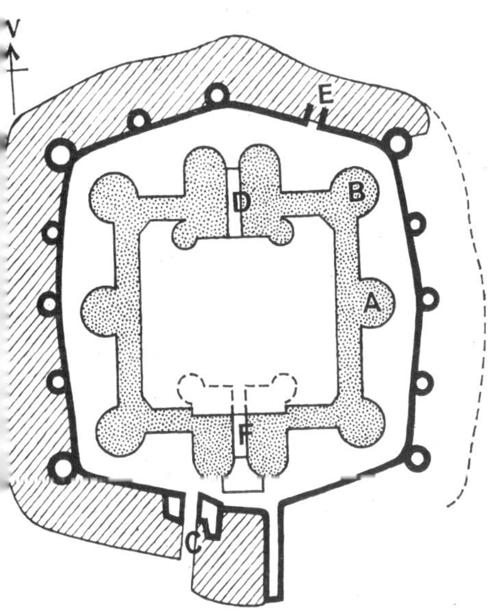

Beaumaris Castle: (A) Chapel. (B) Prison. (C) Drawbridge. (D) Northern gatehouse. (E) North gate. (F) Gate near the sea.

attend his coronation, but this did not directly lead to war; that came in 1277 after one of Edward's ships captured Eleanor de Montfort, Simon's daughter, on her way from France to marry Llywelyn.

In the campaigns that followed, the thoroughness of Edward's military training was clearly demonstrated. When the Marches had been cleared by forays into Cardigan, Brecon and the upper Severn, Edward with his main force ("the best controlled, as it was the best led, that had been gathered in Britain since the Norman Conquest") moved into Gwynedd. This land force was supported by a fleet from the Cinque Ports, which cut Llywelyn off from Anglesey and his food supply. Such an impressive display of force disorganized Llywelyn, and he capitulated in 1277 and agreed to the Treaty of Conway; fines and homage were paid to Edward, and Llywelyn, remaining prince of a small area of north-west Wales, married Lady Eleanor.

This agreement could only be temporary. Llywelyn disputed with the Marcher lords the possession of Arwystli and other districts on the fringe of his principality and the Marcher lands; and in 1282, when his brother David, who had received land in Wales from Edward, rebelled against his overlord and captured Roger Clifford, Justiciar of North Wales, Llywelyn joined him and drew first blood with his defeat of the Earl of Gloucester at Llandeilo.

The pattern of Edward's attack in 1277 was now repeated with equal success. From Rhuddlan his large mercenary force, supported by a blockading fleet, marched into north Wales. Llywelyn was killed in an attack on Builth, and his brother was captured in 1283 and executed at Shrewsbury. The Statute of Wales, drawn up on the advice of a baronial assembly at Rhuddlan in 1283, declared Edward's conquest of Wales complete. North and west

Wales the king held directly, the rest was divided among the Marcher lords.

To guard against a Welsh rising, Edward built strategic castles at Flint, Rhuddlan, Builth, Aberystwyth, Conway, Harlech, Caernarvon and Beaumaris. These great concentric defences incorporated the latest developments in castle design. They succeeded in their purpose and Wales remained largely undisturbed until Glyndwr's rebellion in the fifteenth century.

Edward and Scotland

Scotland proved an impossible nut to crack. Edward's design (accepted by some Scottish nobles in the Treaty of Brigham, 1290) to marry his son Edward to Margaret, heiress to the Scottish throne since the death of her grandfather Alexander III in 1286, had been wrecked by Margaret's death. In 1291 Edward met the Scottish nobles at Norham, at their request, to decide between thirteen candidates for the Scottish throne. The two strongest contenders were John Balliol and Robert Bruce, and in 1292 Edward decided in favour of Balliol.

The Scots at Norham had acknowledged Edward supreme lord of Scotland, Balliol had done homage to him, and Edward had no intention of relinquishing his authority. The Scots, however, did not envisage annexation by England; in 1295 Balliol, defying Edward, joined an alliance with France against England. In a lightning campaign conducted by combined sea and land forces, Edward moved from Newcastle to Berwick and Dunbar, where the Scots were defeated. Balliol abdicated and was confined at Hertford, while the Scots' homage was received at Berwick, and the Earl of Surrey was installed as Edward's viceroy in Scotland.

Scotland was a difficult country to control; communications were poor, the land made campaigning hazardous, and the Scots wanted independence. Nor were they short of leaders. In 1297 William Wallace defeated Surrey at Stirling Bridge and ravaged northern England. Edward led expeditions against him in 1300, 1301 and 1303 (shipping prefabricated bridge sections from Lynn for crossing the Forth), and Wallace was reduced to conducting guerrilla warfare until betrayed to Edward and executed at Tyburn in 1305.

By that time it seemed that Edward had Scotland under control, its government in the hands of the Earl of Richmond, assisted by a Scots council. But in 1306 Scotland was again in ferment; Robert Bruce, grandson of the Bruce candidate for the throne in 1290, was crowned King of Scotland at Scone. In 1307 Edward died at Burgh-on-Sands on his way north yet again.

His son Edward II was no match for Bruce. Between 1312 and 1314 the English strongholds of Perth, Linlithgow, Roxburgh and Edinburgh were taken, and raids were made into Northumberland and Durham. At Bannockburn in 1314 the English were routed, and Bruce was secure. Too many of Edward II's nobles were in league with the Scots for him to unite them in a renewal of English claims. The Truce of Newcastle in 1323 put an end to hostilities in Edward II's reign, and by the Treaty of Northampton in 1328 Bruce was at last recognized as king of an independent Scotland.

Edward I and France

Just as Edward was aiming to annex Scotland, so Philip the Fair of France had his eye on Gascony, which, after the Treaty of Paris in 1259, remained under English control. A dispute between English and Gascon pirates in 1293 gave him the lead he wanted. Edward I, summoned as the King of France's vassal to Paris, refused to appear and was promptly deprived of Gascony.

An expedition against such a formidable opponent as Philip was difficult, but Edward launched small-scale expeditions in 1294 and 1296. The preparation of a large force was made impossible by risings in Wales and Scotland, and mounting discontent in England. In 1297 the English nobles, led by the earls of Norfolk and Hereford, refused to go to Gascony, so Edward was forced to accept a truce with Philip, which through the Pope's mediation led to a treaty in 1303 restoring Gascony to Edward.

The Last Years: the Struggle for the Charters

Edward, in dire need of money for his French expedition of 1297, proceeded to arbitrary taxation and precipitated a constitutional crisis. Heavy duties on wool exports (1294-7) were followed by seizure of the merchants' wool. Archbishop Winchelsey and the clergy, heavily taxed in 1294 and 1295, now obeyed the Pope's Bull *Clericis Laicos* of 1296 and refused the king money from their ecclesiastical revenues. Edward was now at odds with barons (taxed in 1294, 1295 and 1296) and clergy, and these two formidable forces combined, under the earls of Norfolk and Hereford and Archbishop Winchelsey. In 1297 they forced the regent (the king was in Flanders) to agree to a confirmation of the charters (Magna Carta of 1215 and the Charter of the Forest, 1217) and to accept the principle that taxation should not be levied without consent of the "community of the realm."

The charters were confirmed again in 1297 and a third and final time in 1301, and in 1300 Edward accepted the *Articuli Super Cartas*, twenty articles supplementing the charters of 1215 and 1217, the most important of which appointed commissioners (shades of 1258!) to investigate reported infringements of the charters. Nevertheless, in 1303 Edward violated his word by a new scheme of wool taxation, *Carta Mercatoria*, which he agreed, not with his people, but with foreign merchants only.

A stroke of luck at last enabled Edward to get the better of his opponents. In 1305 one of his Gascon subjects became Pope Clement V, and Edward's representative at the papal coronation, to pay off an old score, persuaded the Pope to suspend Winchelsey and summon him to Rome. Edward would not lift a finger to help; he had received all he wanted from the Pope in 1306, release from his oath to the confirmation of the charters.

Development of Parliament

Parliament, meaning *a conference*, was by 1250 specially used for conferences held by the king for purposes of government. In Saxon times the king settled important matters with the counsel and consent of his Thegns and leaders of the Church in the Witan. Despotic Norman kings turned this body into a feudal court, and so it remained until the reign of Henry III, although Henry II's use of a jury to assess the Saladin tithe in 1188 had brought together the ideas of taxation and representation. In 1254 two knights, representing the freemen of each county, were summoned to consider the financial aid they would give the king. They were called again in 1258, 1264 and 1265, when Simon de Montfort summoned burgesses representing the towns; his reason was to have as broad a base of support as possible for his plan of reform. Edward I also sought general support for ambitious projects. In 1283 he summoned two assemblies, one for the north and one for the south; and in 1295, to what has been called the Model Parliament, he called archbishops, bishops, abbots, barons, lesser clergy, two knights from each shire, two citizens from each city and two burgesses from each borough—representatives of the three classes into which medieval society can be divided, those who prayed, those who fought and those who worked. In practice the clergy (except the higher clergy who were feudal lords and landowners as well) preferred to meet in their own assembly, Convocation; and as the knights threw in their lot with the citizens and burgesses, by the end of the fourteenth century parliament had become an assembly of two Houses, Lords and Commons. Also by the end of the fourteenth century, parliament had established two important principles of taxation:

(1) the king could not impose direct taxes without their consent;

(2) parliament could impose all kinds of taxes, direct and indirect.

In the fourteenth and fifteenth centuries parliament's political power grew considerably; parliament resolved on Edward II's deposition in 1327, and on Richard II's in 1399. Finally, the formula of acts of parliament ("Be it enacted by the King's most Excellent Majesty, by and with the advice and consent of the Lords Spiritual and Temporal, and Commons, in this present Parliament assembled, and by the authority of the same, as follows") used since Henry VII's reign had grown to that form in the medieval period.

QUESTIONS

1. Why is Edward I considered to have been a great king?
2. Explain the origins of parliament, and trace its development to the end of the fourteenth century.

CHAPTER 9

THE HUNDRED YEARS' WAR

EDWARD III, eldest son of Edward II and Isabella, became guardian of the kingdom in 1326 three months before the enforced abdication of his father; but in 1330, by overthrowing the usurped authority of his mother, he took the government into his own hands. He had no ambition to establish himself as a great administrator or legislator, but only to shine as a paragon of knightly virtues, the supreme champion of chivalry.

He immediately renewed English intervention in Scotland against David II (1329-71), Robert Bruce's son. In 1333 he routed the Scots at Halidon Hill, and Edward Balliol was foisted on the Scots in place of their nine-year-old king, who fled to France. The arrangement was not reasonable, and further campaigns were necessary in 1335 and 1336. But these Scottish excursions were a mere sideline compared with Edward's main interest, war with France.

Since 1066 and the acquisition of a French empire by England, the feudal relationship between the English and French kings had been a constant source of conflict between the two countries. France, not unnaturally, was intent on securing those French territories held by England; England was just as determined to retain, and if possible extend, her dominion in France. The Hundred Years' War is simply the ultimate stage in this long struggle.

Retention of a French empire became more a matter of prestige to England than a vital national interest. Some headway had been made by 1259 when, by the Treaty of Paris between Henry III and St. Louis of France, Henry abandoned English claims to Normandy, Anjou, Touraine and Poitou, and promised to pay homage for the Duchy of Gascony and a number of additional fiefs on the borders of Aquitaine. In fact these promised fiefs were not under French control, so a major part of the bargain was not fulfilled; and on the English side it was argued that the homage due to the French king need not therefore be paid. French piracy in the Channel, and constant border encroachments, which had increased during Edward II's reign, added to English determination on this point. Obviously, negotiations could never resolve such a fundamental deadlock, and clearly Edward III's attitude was to humour France until his power had grown enough to right these (to him) persistent wrongs by force.

Other facts, such as constant French support for Robert Bruce and his son David II in Scotland, Philip VI's attempt to stop trade between England and

Flanders, French attacks on English shipping and English ports, and even Edward's claim to the throne of France, were merely excuses for a war which both Edward and Philip were determined to fight. In 1336 Parliament granted Edward subsidies in the event of war; Philip replied by announcing that Edward's failure to pay homage must be punished by the confiscation of Gascony. At the same time Edward revived his claim to the French throne (through his mother who was the daughter of Philip the Fair), assuming the title "King of France" and contemptuously referring to the Valois king as "*Philippe qui se dit roi de France.*"

English Success, 1337-60

The Hundred Years' War began in 1337 and continued until 1453, but was rather a series of separate wars with intervals of up to twenty-eight years between them. It began with a period of English success from 1337 to 1364, followed by a French revival up to 1396; it was reopened in 1415 by Henry V, who was brilliantly successful until 1422, and the final stage ended with a complete French victory in 1453.

To take on France was a tough proposition, and Edward began by gathering alliances against Philip. He succeeded in gaining the support of the dukes of Brabant and Gueldres, the Count of Hainault (his father-in-law) and the counts of Berg, Juliers, Cleves, Limburg and Mark, as well as Emperor Lewis V of Germany, who thought that it might be profitable for him financially. Economic pressure (a ban on the export of wool, and the shifting of the Staple from Flanders to Brabant) forced the Count of Flanders to renounce his alliance with France.

The war got off to a desultory start, with Edward simply progressing through Brabant and West Germany in 1338, and in 1339 fighting a small campaign on the border of France near Cambrai. The first real battle of the war, against a Franco-Castilian fleet, was fought at sea off Sluys, at the mouth of the River Scheldt, in 1340, when Edward was crossing to take advantage of the pro-English revolt in the cloth-making towns of Ghent, Bruges and Ypres against their overlord, the King of France. The battle was "right fierce and terrible," and Edward's motley fleet of some two hundred ships achieved an overwhelming victory.

The edge of victory, however, was dulled by a nagging need of money, and the Truce of Esplèchin in 1340 was Edward's only course of action. Edward, whose military enthusiasm had far outrun his financial common sense, believed he had been "stabbed in the back" by corrupt officials and a dithering council. On his return to England he vented his unreasonable spleen on the president of the council, John Stratford, Archbishop of Canterbury. He also dismissed the Chancellor, Robert Stratford, Bishop of Chichester, replacing him with the first lay Chancellor, Sir Robert Bourchier, and appointed a layman as Treasurer in place of Roger Northburgh, Bishop of Coventry. The archbishop was restored to favour, but the financial problem remained.

By 1342 Edward had abandoned his policy of alliances against France. The Flemish rising under James van Artevelde had helped him little, and the Emperor, lukewarm from the start, slid quietly into neutrality, as did the Count of Hainault also. This was the time for direct attacks on France. In 1342 Edward overran Brittany, and in 1345 the Earl of Derby landed at Bordeaux to harass the French on the borders of Gascony.

Landing in Normandy in 1346 Edward, assisted by Derby's diversion in the south, sacked Caen and, moving to the Somme, encountered the French at Crécy. French cavalry crumpled before English infantry and the English longbow. At home the raiding Scots were defeated by the northern earls at Neville's Cross, and David II was taken prisoner. Calais was captured in 1347, then the outbreak of the Black Death ended hostilities until 1355.

When war was renewed, France had a new but ineffective king, John II (1350-64). Edward's campaign was cut short by further trouble from Scotland, but his son, Edward the Black Prince, who had fought at Crécy, landed a force at Bordeaux and ravaged France as far as the Mediterranean coast. He moved northward in 1356, first to Berry, then westward to Tours; and at Poitiers he defeated a huge French army, taking the French king prisoner.

France was eager for peace. Military defeat, capture of their king and the political upset which resulted, the Black Death, the peasant revolt of the Jacquerie in 1358, and ceaseless marauding by the English free companies, forced France to accept the Treaty of Brétigny in 1360. By this treaty Edward demanded a ransom for King John of three million gold crowns, five times Edward's annual revenue. The whole Duchy of Aquitaine was to be added to English Gascony, together with Calais and the surrounding country of Guines and Ponthieu; and provided the French king withdrew his claim over these districts, Edward agreed to withdraw his claim to the French throne, a clause which was not in fact fulfilled. Edward III had become sovereign in his own right of one third of France, and in 1362 the Black Prince arrived at Bordeaux as Duke of Aquitaine.

French Revival: Charles V

The death of King John of France in 1364 "sounded the knell of the Treaty of Brétigny." Although the new king Charles V (1364-80) was a most unwarlike man, he nevertheless worked to satisfy his desire for revenge, and his confiscation of Aquitaine in 1369, on the grounds that some terms of the Treaty of Brétigny had not been honoured by Edward, made war inevitable.

In the period 1369-96 no real battles were fought, but this was deliberate policy on the part of the French. Flamboyant unsupported cavalry charges had been France's downfall at Crécy and Poitiers. Now, on the advice of

Bertrand du Guesclin, the French avoided pitched battles and successfully wore down the English armies by guerrilla warfare. Edward III, with approaching senility, was finding less interest in military exploits. The Black Prince died in 1376, his father in 1377, and the crown passed to the Black Prince's ten-year-old son, Richard II.

English policy, under the influence of John of Gaunt before the new king came of age, was to strike at France through her allies, Flanders, Scotland and Castile; then, when France had been lulled into a false sense of security, a direct attack could be made. Richard's policy, however, when he took over personal control of the kingdom in 1389, was one of agreement with France and an end to hostilities, for he could foresee a time when he might need

English archers at the battle of Agincourt, from the film of "Henry V."

French help at home. Parliament in 1391 authorized peace negotiations, welcomed by both sides because of financial exhaustion. A truce was agreed in 1392, and extended in 1393 and 1394; and the truce with France was sealed in 1396 by Richard's marriage to Isabel, daughter of Charles VI.

War Renewed: Henry V, 1415-22

Throughout the Middle Ages the English attitude towards France fluctuated between affection and enmity, and in the period 1396-1413 the latter sentiment came uppermost. So great was the rising suspicion that by Henry V's accession in 1413 England was in a state of war fever. Henry did nothing to discourage this; as a soldier he was anxious to find glory in the pursuit of arms, just as Edward III had been, and as the son of Henry Bolingbroke he was not unaware of the value of a national war to rally his people.

His negotiations with France were therefore "a hollow sham," and the expedition prepared for 1415 was no hasty compilation. He needed 1,500 vessels to transport his force of some 10,000 men and his ancillary services. The fleet sailed to Harfleur, which was reduced in a five-weeks' siege.

Sickness had been the expedition's major enemy at Harfleur, and having only about 6,000 men left when the sick had been sent home, Henry abandoned his plan to march on Paris. His council of war advised complete withdrawal, but Henry determined to stay in France, to march his troops through Normandy and then to embark at Calais.

From Béthencourt, King Henry moved north towards Calais, but at Agincourt the numerically much superior French army lay across his path. Henry's iron discipline had sustained his small force on a seventeen-days' march with only one day's rest over 260 miles. The French army had not been dawdling either and had covered 180 miles in ten days, but where most of the English were on foot, the majority of the 24,000 French were mounted.

Before battle Henry attempted to bargain, offering the return of Harfleur for a clear run for his army to Calais. The confident French offered impossible terms, and laid wagers on the forthcoming fate of Henry, even making ready a painted cart to drive him prisoner through the streets of Paris.

But where Henry's discipline was perfect, the French array was an undisciplined rabble, drawn from all parts of France and beyond and with no undisputed leader. The battle was a rout. Forgetting the tactics of Du Guesclin, the French cavalry jostled in their packed ranks into a hail of English arrows, which forced them back into the dismounted ranks behind; although the battle lasted four hours, the first half-hour decided the issue. English casualties were some 400 against about 10,000 French killed, including the Constable of France, three dukes, ninety lords and 1,560 knights.

From Agincourt Henry marched to Calais and embarked for England. Subsequently, in a second campaign 1417-19 the conquest of Normandy was completed at Rouen, and in 1420 the Treaty of Troyes was concluded between Henry and Charles VI. On the death of Charles, French and English crowns were to be united in one person, Henry V or his successor. The remaining provision of the treaty was fulfilled in 1420 when Henry married Catherine, daughter of the French king.

Just as the death of John the Good of France wrecked the Treaty of Brétigny, so the death of Henry V in 1422 ruined the Treaty of Troyes. This great leader's successor was a nine-month-old baby. Henry's very able brother, John, Duke of Bedford, determined to maintain the Treaty of Troyes, and proclaimed Henry's infant son Henry VI of England and France. But the tide of war had turned against England.

English Failure After 1422

When Joan of Arc appeared on the scene in 1429, the morale of French troops received a boost that not even her capture and execution in 1430 could diminish. The coronation of Charles VII (1422-61) at Rheims similarly raised French morale. The Duke of Bedford contributed two diplomatic blunders. The first was over the coronation of Henry VI in Paris in 1430; English rites were used, Cardinal Beaufort (not the Bishop of Paris) performed the ceremony, and Bedford failed to get on the right side of the Paris mob who looked for alms and tax remission. The second blunder was his alienation of the Duke of Burgundy by his own second marriage to a daughter of the Count of St. Pol. Nevertheless the death of Bedford in 1435 was an irreparable loss to the English cause, for he alone could offer the prospect of success. Finally, the crippling taxation of Edward III and Henry V to pay for their continental campaigns imposed burdens that England could not bear.

An English revival under a brilliant tactician, John, Lord Talbot, after 1436 could not alter the balance of military power, which had now passed to France. At Formigny in 1450 an English army was practically wiped out, and after the fall of Cherbourg Normandy was lost. In 1453 at Castillon, Talbot and the Earl of Shrewsbury were defeated and killed. Gascony was now lost and the Hundred Years' War was over.

Its passing was not marked by any peace treaty, and the English claim to the French throne was not dropped until 1801.

QUESTIONS

1. State the importance in Anglo-French relations of (*a*) the Treaty of Paris of 1259, (*b*) the Treaty of Brétigny of 1360, and (*c*) the Treaty of Troyes of 1420.
2. Why did Henry V reopen the Hundred Years' War with France? What success did he gain?

CHAPTER 10

THE MEDIEVAL VILLAGE

IN 1066 vast areas of England were still in a natural state, with wide areas of forest; but after the Conquest these woodlands were steadily cleared, and moorland too, while marshland and fenland were drained, bringing hundreds of square miles of new land into cultivation.

Of the total population of England (in 1086 some $1\frac{1}{4}$ million people), perhaps one-tenth lived in the boroughs, the rural remainder in thousands of small, self-contained communities (manors) of fifty, one hundred, or in exceptional cases several hundred, inhabitants. Manor and village were not the same thing. A manor was the estate worked by a lord with the help of tenants; sometimes everybody in the village was a tenant of the same lord but very often (in East Anglia, for instance) one village was divided between two or more manors. Local variations make it impossible to speak of a typical manor or of a typical village, but nevertheless, all country-dwellers shared a common life, bound to the soil and to a lord to whom they owed certain fixed services.

Walk Around the Village

The church was the centre of a village, and radiating from it there were tracks beside which the one- or two-roomed cottages of the villagers were grouped. These cottages were constructed from a wooden framework, covered with wattle and daub; roofs were thatched and a hole was cut to allow smoke from the wood, peat or dung fire to escape. Window openings were covered with canvas or rough wooden shutters, because glass was far too expensive. A small shed at the back of the cottage would serve as a byre for animals, and provide a threshing floor and a place to store farm implements.

Behind each cottage was a small close, where a villager could grow what he pleased: peas and beans, cabbages, onions, leeks, as well as apple, pear and cherry trees. From this little plot he might hope to grow sufficient to supplement his ordinary diet of rye bread, cheese and ale, with perhaps herrings or dried fish supplied by the lord on feast days. For a villager meat was rare, although poaching was common and an occasional rabbit or hare, hunted and snared in the lord's woods, no doubt found its way to the cooking pot to give some variety to the monotony of pottage. Other cooking utensils of earthenware or metal would be arrayed round the iron plate or clay slab on which the fire was set. Bowls, platters and spoons would be home-made from beech or oak, as were stools, trestle-table, and the chest to hold the scanty store of best clothes. At night, bags of straw or flock, thrown on the trodden earth floor around the hearth, served as beds.

Next to the church stood the priest's two-roomed house, and alongside it the tithe barn, a building of ample proportions in which was stored his own produce and his tithe, one-tenth of each man's produce every year. Near at hand was an ale-house, "the Devil's kitchen" as medieval moralists lugubriously called it. Many families brewed their own ale, but the ale-house was a centre of gossip and communal jollification.

Then there were the workshops of village craftsmen; the wheelwright whose ten years' apprenticeship was an indication of the skill of his craft, the carpenter making and mending fences, gates and wagons, shaping cruck frames for village houses, beams and rafters, doors and furniture, platters and bowls, and the blacksmith busy all the year round shoeing horses, mending ploughs and harrows, sharpening scythes and sickles, and (as time went on, becoming very important indeed) cunningly fashioning lances, knives and daggers, swords and armour.

Beside the stream which, if there was no well, provided the village water supply, might be a water mill, or on higher ground a post mill which could be turned round to catch the wind behind its sails. The lord owned the mill, and all villagers had to have their grain ground into flour there, the lord receiving a payment of part of the grain, while the miller often took an unofficial share for himself.

The Open Fields: Meadow, Common and Waste

Surrounding the village were great common fields, the meadow, common grazing land, woodland and waste. The two or three great unfenced arable fields were each of a few hundred acres, and were divided into several large sections called *furlongs*; these were further divided into many strips, separated from one another by a deeper furrow and marked by hazel twigs or stones. These strips were distributed among members of the village community, usually excepting the serfs but including the lord, whose manor house stood, fringed perhaps by his orchard, deer park and private demesne, on the outskirts of the village. Generally speaking, one man's holding of strips would be scattered to ensure fair distribution, so that each had his share of good and poor land, although in Kent and East Anglia the villagers' holdings were compacted together.

Only two of the three fields (or one where there were only two great fields) grew crops in any one year, the fallow field being rested; within temporary fencing animals were put to graze on it, to keep down the weeds and manure

MEDIEVAL CASTLE WITH ITS VARIOUS BUILDINGS

SCENES FROM THE LATER MIDDLE AGES

the land at the same time. Medieval farmers understood the need for constant manuring, and in the absence of sufficient animal manure often went to a great deal of trouble to carry marl or lime with which to treat their land. One of the arable fields would have been sown in September with wheat or rye, the second with barley or oats in the Spring. The decision on which crops were to be grown each year was made in the manor court, and everyone had to abide by it.

The hay meadow was fenced from March until August, after which it was open for grazing. Here again the meadow was divided among the villagers, divisions being marked by sticks or stones, and the hayward would ensure that markers had not been moved. On common land, horses and cattle were grazed, guarded by herds, serfs who numbered this among their many jobs.

Waste land was a continual source of benefit. Here goats were tethered and poultry run, and pigs were grazed to feed on the acorns and beech mast; payment for this privilege (*pannage*) had to be made to the lord. The lord, in return for a money payment, would grant plots of forest or waste for conversion into arable land; the additional growing space, free of customary work, enabled a villager to augment his food production. Wood and peat for fuel, timber for building and repairs, turves for roofing and sedge for thatching were also obtained from the waste.

Classes of Peasants

The largest holders of land in the village were the villeins with some thirty acres (in some areas as many as sixty acres, or as few as ten). Then there were cottars, who held only up to five acres of land; as they had fewer services to perform for the lord and had more time, they often became hired labourers, working for the lord and for the more prosperous villeins at busy times in the farming year. Serfs, who (like the villeins and cottars) were not free men, often held no land at all and so had no alternative but to work entirely on the lord's land. Only a few peasants were free tenants, having bought exemption from the usual manorial services, so that their only obligation was payment of an annual rent. In terms of land-holding being a freeman meant nothing; often they held far less than a villein and, like a cottar, might of necessity spend some time working on a villein's land.

A Villein's Services

The custom of the manor, that is the terms of service which had grown up between a lord and his villagers, demanded that a villein should work two or three days in each week until noon on the lord's land (*week work*). At harvest time *harvest work* of three days a week till noon was required; and in addition at busy times a lord could demand *boon service*. In theory

OCL/HIST/1—E*

boon service was given freely by tenants out of love for their lord; but when it is remembered that a tenant wanted to get his own corn and hay harvest in too, and was hindered from doing so by the lord's prior claim, one can imagine that the term *love boon* was something of a misnomer. All the family, except the housewife and her marriageable daughters, had to attend; and although a *wet boon*, when ale and cider were liberally provided by the lord, was at least tolerable, a *dry boon*, with only water to drink, was most unpopular.

Besides work in the fields, repairs to the manor house and its outbuildings were usually carried out by the peasants as labourers for the carpenters and masons who might be employed; and serfs additionally had their time fully occupied, in carting dung, tending the lord's garden, hedging and ditching, and jobs in and around the manor. When a villager's daughter married, a fine for the lord's consent had to be paid; and often the requirement was extended to include sons as well. And, as if what the peasant had performed during his lifetime were not enough, when he died his best beast or article was taken by the lord as *heriot*, a demand which often caused great hardship to a dead man's family, particularly when the lord was merciless in maintenance of his rights.

The Farming Year

The ceaseless agricultural pattern of the year was as demanding as any lord. In autumn the fallow field would be ploughed and sown with wheat. Plough teams of eight oxen were used, four for the morning and four for the afternoon, and seed was scattered broadcast; harrowing followed. At Martinmas (11 November) pigs were killed and their meat salted down (salt and iron were generally the only essential items that had to be brought into the village); as medieval man had no root crops and insufficient fodder to keep his cattle alive through the winter, all except store beasts were slaughtered. Using flails, grain was threshed and winnowed, and stored in the lord's barns and the peasants' sheds until taken for grinding to the mill.

In March, after the winter months had been occupied with repairing tools and sawing timber, another of the great fields had to be ploughed and sown. Farm livestock were turned out to pasture and sheep were carefully examined for disease. May, June and July were the months of hay harvest and sheep-shearing, a time when manure was carted from the sheep folds and from outside the village cottages to the fallow field, which was ploughed twice, to turn under the stubble and to keep down weeds.

Lammas Day (1 August) marked the beginning of corn harvest. The corn gathered, sheep were folded on the harvest fields, and cattle turned out to graze. Then, after the celebration of Harvest Home, the cycle began again with threshing and autumn ploughing.

Nor must the many other jobs be forgotten—the housewife's care of poultry and bees (honey was used for sweetening), butter- and cheese-making, brewing, care of lambs, calves and foals, repair of houses, and gathering of firewood or digging of peat for fuel.

Administration of the Manor

As the lord often held several manors, much of his time was spent moving from one to another. This meant that administration of each manor had to be in the hands of officials acting on the lord's behalf. Chief of these was the steward, the lord's direct representative, and invariably a man of some social standing. In the lord's absence, his steward presided over the manor court, held in the hall of the manor house two or three times a year or, in some manors, once every three weeks. Tenants would be summoned by an announcement in church, or directly by bailiff or beadle. After the beadle had called the tenants to attention with his thrice repeated "Oyez!" ("Hear ye!"), the proceedings would begin.

Excuses would be made for those prevented from attending the court through illness or accident. Then complaints would be heard: a neighbour's strips were being neglected and weeds were spreading as a result, or he had been moving marker stones between the strips; perhaps a man's pig had died and he was accusing the swineherd's wife of having bewitched it. Minor offences presented by the tithing men (cases of brawling in the churchyard, roistering in the ale-house, assaulting one of the manor officials, or perhaps grinding corn on a hand-mill instead of at the lord's mill) would be investi-

Tithe barn at Bradford-on-Avon.

gated, and punished by fines of two, three, or six pence. Finally requests could be considered, for a man's son to be allowed to go to grammar school, or for the lord to forgo his heriot in the case of a poor widow.

Next in importance to the steward was the bailiff, who lived in the manor house at the lord's expense and who was paid perhaps £6 a year. He saw that manorial services were fulfilled and that the agricultural policy of the manor was carried out, and each year he had to face a financial enquiry by the lord's auditors into the affairs of the manor.

The reeve was a villein, chosen annually at Michaelmas at the manor court, although it often became virtually a permanent appointment. He was the man-on-the-spot, and for his efforts he might receive sixteen shillings a year, as well as being excused rent and services; additional rewards might be a share of the lord's crop, and a free ration of food daily from the manor house. At the practical level a reeve controlled the manor; he arranged the work, supervised the farming calendar, and kept and prepared the annual manorial accounts.

The beadle has already been mentioned; he warned tenants when a boon was required, seized straying cattle and shut them in the pound, and often combined these duties with those of hayward, the official who was really foreman of the field work. He would not be paid, but he would be excused rent, he ate at the lord's table at harvest time, and he sometimes got a share of the harvest for himself.

Merrie England

The medieval peasant would seem to have been held in the vice-like grip of his endless battle with the soil and the demands of his lord. His life was certainly not a sylvan idyll of mincepies and maypoles. Nevertheless, occasional opportunities for enjoyment did come his way, not least at the great church festivals of Easter and Christmas. Some celebrations undoubtedly took place at the manor house between Christmas Eve and Twelfth Night, with yule logs and greenery and plenty to eat and drink. The pagan festivals of May Day and Midsummer were also times of merrymaking. Marriage and death provided an excuse for immoderate ale consumption, a temptation continually deplored but eventually accepted by the Church. The farming year also gave rise to a number of festivals, Plough Monday, Hock Day, Midsummer Eve, Martinmas and the Harvest Home. But the lord cared little how the villagers spent their time after their work was done, and it is well to remember that "these and like pleasures gave but few enough happy moments in lives which otherwise were so bare."

CHAPTER 11

THE DECLINE OF THE MANORIAL SYSTEM

IN the period 1350–1600 the manorial system broke up completely, and the peasant's obligations to his lord were replaced by an entirely new relationship, which allowed the unfree man his freedom not only within the manor, but outside it as well.

Such a change was inevitable, for the temptation had always been strong to make a dash to a neighbouring manor or to the nearest town and, with luck, to remain there for a year and a day and so acquire freedom. But it was never easy to break from the familiar world into which one had been born, to adventure into the great unknown beyond the open fields. Such a course of escape was not uncommon, but to the majority it was a case of accepting circumstances and by constant gnawing to wear away the bonds woven by the manor and its lord.

Break-up of the Manor: Commutation and Alienation of the Demesne

Rendering fixed services and works to the lord, to the detriment of his own husbandry, was hated by the unfree man. As early as the twelfth century, particularly in Kent, East Anglia and the north-west, many tenants were paying money to the lord instead of labour and payments in kind; this process, called *commutation*, continued increasingly to replace first week work, then harvest work, until finally boon work disappeared as well.

The second main reason for the break-up of the manor was the process of *alienation of the demesne*. Sometimes the lord would decide to keep his demesne, despite the fact that his relationship with his tenants had changed; and he would use his income from rents to hire free labour to cultivate his land. More often he preferred to give up management of his estate to a farmer, who would take over lock, stock and barrel on the basis of a rent in kind or money. Thus the lord himself ceased to be a farmer and became a landlord. Organization of the manor had not changed; it still had its lord and manor officials, and its tenants holding their land in accordance with local custom and the will of the landlord; but the status of tenants had changed. By his own exertions the serf had saved enough to buy his charter of *manumission* (freedom) from his lord; the villein was now a *copyholder* (his possession of land was recorded in a copy of the court roll of his manor), and cottagers were joined by hired labour from outside, so that they now stood in relation to the landlord as employee to employer, not bondman to feudal lord.

These factors were noticeably at work in the thirteenth century and were stimulated considerably in the fourteenth century, not least as a result of the Black Death.

The Black Death

In the winter of 1348-9 the plague struck England. From the Far East plague-bearing fleas, carried by black rats, made their way westwards across Asia and Europe, via the trade routes of the world, for the rats were carried by merchant ships, and in bales of merchandise. In less than a year the plague had wiped out some 25 million people, more than were killed in both World Wars.

The first European outbreak occurred at the Black Sea port of Kaffa in 1347. Thence it spread to Constantinople, and through Italy, Spain and Southern France to England. The first outbreaks in the autumn of 1348 were in Dorset and Hampshire, and from there the plague, often spread by those from the affected areas seeking to escape it, moved through the West Country, eastwards to London (November) and East Anglia (January 1349) and through the Midlands to the North. Scottish cattle rustlers, raiding northern England, carried it to Scotland by the end of 1349.

Medieval medicine was helpless, for to Europe this was a new disease. In a few months the population of England was reduced by almost half, from 4 million to about 2,500,000; some villages were completely depopulated, although others were hardly touched.

Inevitably England was profoundly affected. Disintegration of the old manorial order was speeded up; before the Black Death there had been a surplus of labour, now there was a dearth of villeins and free labourers. Freemen who survived could claim a scarcity price for their labour, while surviving villeins schemed for the freedom which provided a passport to comparative prosperity. Commutation was accelerated, and newly-freed men were given a privileged position in wage bargaining; with nearly half the available labourers killed, land produced less and prices of produce went up, so the purchasing power of money went down. This provided labourers with a justification for demanding higher wages, and on many manors they were paid what they asked.

Men now began to move to other manors or to the towns, looking for the highest wages. A competitive spirit was aroused, for a free man or a rich villein could rent the deserted holdings of dead neighbours and, by exploiting this position, become prosperous. Enclosure had been going on in parts of England since the twelfth century, but now it was accelerated. After the Black Death the acquisition of land, and the incentive to put arable land down to pasture for cattle and sheep greatly encouraged enclosure.

In 1351 the government passed the Statute of Labourers, an attempt to fix wages at pre-Black-Death rates, to peg rents and to check the disruptive mobility of labour. The policy failed, for it was necessary to reissue the statute in 1357, 1361, and again in the fifteenth century. The statute was ignored by many landlords whose main concern was to keep their own land under cultivation.

Military landowners, knights and burgesses, however, pressed for stricter enforcement of the Statutes of Labourers, and urged that branding should be the punishment for anyone who demanded more than the wage rates in operation in 1346. Such an attitude only increased labouring resentment of measures designed to check wages.

Finally, a morbid preoccupation with death and decay was an important legacy of the Black Death, which broke out again in 1356, in 1361-2 and in 1368-9, and which remained a regular scourge until the last outbreak in England in 1665.

The second half of the fourteenth century was a period of deep social unrest, but the Black Death did not cause the Peasants' Revolt; it simply gave rise to a feeling of discontent which found its outlet in 1381.

The Peasants' Revolt

This was not just a peasants' revolt, but a revolt of all who had a grievance against authority—the rise in rents and the attempt to restore manorial dues and services, encroachments and hardships caused by sheep-farming lords, taxes to pay for the French wars and a corrupt and incompetent court, and privileges enjoyed by foreigners, in both trade and Church.

The area of England affected by the revolt was south and east of a line drawn from Scarborough through Chester to Plymouth. Travelling chapmen, tinkers, players and the whole wayfaring army of the Middle Ages spread word of local injustices up and down the country, creating a treasury of indignities. In addition, the imagination and enthusiasm of the aggrieved commons were fired by moral tales and ballads of Robin Hood, where right triumphed over wrong, poor over rich. Langland's *Piers Plowman*, with its attack on Idle Rich and Grasping Greedy, provided more ammunition; but, above all, the commons were affected by the propaganda of priests, who were as discontented as their flocks, and who took as their theme:

> "When Adam delf [dug] and Eve span,
> Who was thanne a gentilman?"

In 1381, "England was full of inflammable material and at the mercy of a spark."

The poll tax, invented in 1377 by royal officials, required payment of one groat (4*d.*) by everyone over the age of fourteen to the royal exchequer. This was unjust because the poor were to pay the same as the rich. In 1379 the government was still in need of money; forced loans were raised from landowners, towns and monasteries, and parliament agreed to a second poll tax. This time, remembering the poor yield of the 1377 tax, a sliding scale of payment was arranged, ten marks to be paid by the Duke of Gloucester and the archbishops, down to a groat, which all over sixteen had to pay. Again the yield was disappointing; so in 1380 parliament agreed to a third poll tax. This time the sliding scale disappeared, although it was suggested that the rich should help the poor. The rich, however, had no pretensions to philanthropy, and every adult (defined now as over fifteen) had to pay three groats, the equivalent in some cases of a month's wages. Considering that the authorities were well aware of the discontent in the country, this heavy tax was asking for trouble; and in Essex in 1381 the spark was provided to set off the revolt.

Thomas Brampton, a collector of the poll tax, summoned the inhabitants of the Essex villages of Fobbing, Corringham and Stanford-le-Hope to meet him at Brentwood to hear the amount of tax they would have to pay. Brampton was thrown out, and when Chief Justice Belknap was sent to Essex to restore order he also was driven out, and his jurors and three of Brampton's clerks were seized and beheaded.

This was not mob violence. Artisans and well-to-do landholders, as well as villeins, made up the rebel ranks, and they felt the moment had come to protest, not only against an unjust tax, but also against the corrupt government of a boy king, which did nothing to remedy social grievances; although their immediate complaint was taxation, the aim of their demand was, as a contemporary wrote, "for freedom, to be made equal to their lords, and never again to be held in servitude to any man."

News of the Essex protest spread. By 2 June freemen of Kent, roused by the poll tax and determined to retain their freedom, assembled at Erith. At Gravesend there was open revolt when an escaped villein was reclaimed and thrown into Rochester Castle by the men of Sir Simon Burley, tutor to the fourteen-year-old King Richard II.

Four days after their first protest the Kent rebels seized Rochester Castle, releasing Burley's villein and holding the governor as hostage. On 7 June they were at Maidstone; on the 8th they entered Canterbury and interrupted Mass in the cathedral in an unsuccessful search for the archbishop, Thomas Sudbury, who, as Chancellor, was especially hated by the commons. Leaving some of their number to look after civil affairs in Canterbury, the remainder of the rebels marched to London. At Blackheath the rebels from Essex and Kent joined forces, and London was at their mercy.

The rebel leaders were both thrown up by the Kent uprising. Little is

The Peasants' Revolt: Wat Tyler arrested by the Lord Mayor (left).

known of Wat Tyler of Maidstone, but his qualities as a leader, his discipline, skill and courage as spokesman for the rebels in London, are established beyond any doubt. John Ball was a priest who in more than twenty years of preaching had earned the love of ordinary people and had put their feelings into words when he attacked the Church, particularly the Church hierarchy. What Ball wanted was the confiscation of Church estates, the proceeds to be devoted to the common good; in place of the hierarchy he saw only himself as archbishop. In a sermon to the rebels at Blackheath he stated his simple yet inflammatory theme: ". . . that from the beginning all men were created equal by nature and that servitude had been introduced by the unjust oppressions of evil men, against the will of God. . . ."

An unfruitful meeting between Tyler and Richard II incensed the rebels and they overran London, releasing prisoners from gaol, destroying John of Gaunt's palace at the Savoy and the house of the hated Treasurer Hales, ransacking the Inns of the Temple and massacring any foreigners they could lay hands on.

The king and Court were in the Tower, but his ministers planned to outwit the rebels. The king would meet the rebels at Mile End and, to get rid of them, agree to their demands; then, the danger over, all concessions could be cancelled as having been obtained by force alone. The king's courage was equal to the occasion, and at Mile End he accepted the rebels' demand for the abolition of villeinage, for a fixed rent of 4*d.* per acre to replace feudal services, and for a general pardon for all rebels. The ministers, through the king, had achieved a tactical victory; thousands of rebels dispersed, although many smelled a rat and kept together. One group broke into the Tower and dragged off Archbishop Sudbury and Treasurer Hales to execution on Tower Hill.

A third meeting between the king and Tyler ended in confusion and near massacre. Tyler rudely demanded an end of serfdom and villeinage, and repeated Ball's plan for the confiscation of Church lands. When the king promised to agree to all that he could, one of his company accused Tyler of being a thief; feelings were roused and Tyler was mortally wounded by Walworth, the Lord Mayor of London, while resisting arrest. An ugly situation was prevented by the king's presence of mind and his call to the rebels, "Let me be your leader!" As their argument had never been against the king, the rebels loyally followed him to Clerkenwell Fields, where, after Tyler's severed head had been exhibited, they agreed to go home. By the end of 1381 the revolt had petered out altogether.

For the rebels, success soon turned to defeat. The king toured counties north of the Thames, the Earl of Salisbury those to the south, and any vestiges of rebellion were ruthlessly crushed. The king now revoked the concessions granted at Mile End, because they had been granted "perforce and in haste." When the last kick of revolt came from Kent in September 1381, the demand, understandably but unreasonably, was for the head of the king who had betrayed them.

The break-up of manor and manorial system continued after 1381, but the pace of change was not increased much by the Peasants' Revolt. The landed classes emerged with their knees knocking, but in a short while they were as powerful as ever. What then had the rebels achieved? Immediately, very little, although no poll tax was levied for another hundred years; but they had proved that the old order of society was dying and that a decisive factor for the future was the growing strength of the people.

Richard II

Richard, son of the Black Prince and the "Fair Maid of Kent," succeeded Edward III as king in 1377 at the age of ten. His early promise, shown in 1381, was not fulfilled. Cultured, devout and loyal to his friends, he was also tactless and unable to keep his temper, and he had an almost mystical belief in his royal prerogative. During his minority (1377-81) government was in the hands of Richard's three uncles, John of Gaunt, Edmund, Duke of York, and Thomas, Duke of Gloucester. After a struggle for power (1381-6) when he attempted to rule through men appointed by himself, Richard was forced by his uncle Gloucester to accept the rule of eleven "Appellants." In the

Merciless Parliament of 1388, Richard's friends were attacked, some destroyed, and he himself was humiliated. From this time, his aim was revenge against the Appellants, and establishment of an autocracy.

In 1389 Richard II claimed the right to rule, being then twenty-two. This made the position of the Appellants rather insecure, but Richard took no action against them from 1390 until 1397. By 1397 he had built up a party at court, and had an army and the support of some of the greatest lords; so the three leading Appellants, Gloucester, Arundel and Warwick, were charged with treason. Arundel was executed, Warwick went into exile, and Gloucester was sent to Calais where he died. The work of the Merciless Parliament was rescinded, and Richard's absolute power seemed complete.

In attacking the remaining Appellants, however, he made too many mistakes. Gaunt's son, Henry Bolingbroke, and Thomas Mowbray, Duke of Norfolk, accused one another of treason and were banished, Bolingbroke for six years, Norfolk for life. Richard had promised Bolingbroke that he would succeed to his father's estates, but on Gaunt's death in 1399 he extended Bolingbroke's term of exile to life and confiscated his estates, thus giving him the strongest of all reasons to return to England to claim his lawful inheritance. Richard's second mistake was to undertake a second Irish expedition in 1399, leaving the Duke of York as regent, so that England was wide open for Bolingbroke, who landed at Ravenspur. Richard was deposed by Parliament, being declared "utterly unworthy and useless to rule and govern," and Bolingbroke claimed the throne on fictitious arguments. Few nobles supported Richard, whose military incapacity ruined his chances of succeeding as a medieval king, and whose insistence on the supreme power of the king had alienated popular opinion. An attempt to overthrow Bolingbroke, now Henry IV, ended in the "Slaughter of Cirencester," and shortly afterwards Richard was murdered, probably at Pontefract.

Richard tried to do what Edward IV and Henry VII later succeeded in doing, to crush the nobles, subordinate the Church, keep free of European wars, and rule through parliament and his ministers—a policy likely to succeed after the Wars of the Roses, but not before. The mystery of Richard's disappearance gave rise to a rumour that he was still alive and had fled to Scotland. A strange cult grew up around the murdered king, and gave rise to the doctrine of the Divine Right of Kings, which was to trouble England in the seventeenth century.

QUESTIONS

1. Outline the various causes of the Peasants' Revolt of 1381, and describe its results.

2. Describe the reign of Richard II.

CHAPTER 12

THE TOWN

A MEDIEVAL town was a small community within high walls, but still very close to the countryside. Townsmen were still countrymen, and were to remain so until the industrial revolution of the eighteenth century.

The Saxons, who loved the countryside and at first avoided the towns which the Romans had built to symbolize the superior culture of their Mediterranean world, had seen to it that in every shire there was at least one fortified borough to afford a safe place for markets, a place where money could be minted and, in time of war, a place of refuge. Protection was one of the main motives behind the establishment of early towns, but although the town was primarily a stronghold (as its battlemented walls testify) it was also the natural centre for a district's trade.

Rivers were extremely important in the location of towns. A ford made an admirable site, for here road and river routes met, as at Banbury, Oxford and Hereford. Navigable rivers also offered a town site at the lowest point to which sea-borne ships could come; in this way grew up London, originally the port for Roman Verulamium (St. Albans), Norwich and Bristol. Southampton with its double tides, Plymouth and Dover developed because they had good harbours, as did Chester and Rye until they silted up. At the meeting point of roads, Cirencester, Salisbury, Huntingdon and Winchester (where six roads met) were established. Often a town grew up around a castle to supply its needs and to shelter under its protection, as at Ludlow, Newcastle-on-Tyne and Devizes; and places of particular attraction, like the great monasteries of St. Albans, Bury St. Edmunds or Peterborough, which drew eager pilgrims, and Bath, whose warm springs attracted rheumatic sufferers, frequently developed into thriving towns.

Town Population—Manorial Restrictions

In the middle of the fifteenth century London had a population four times that of any other town in Britain. The second largest, York, had about 15,000, only slightly more than Bristol, with declining Norwich and Coventry next on the list. Winchester, Canterbury, Colchester, Exeter, Shrewsbury, Nottingham, Chester and Lincoln had about 5,000 inhabitants each. But in 1086 only five of the eighty towns listed in the Domesday Survey (London, Norwich, York, Lincoln and Winchester) had a population of over 1,000.

Towns were small because their working population was in early days largely non-resident; country folk only visited the town market, and returned to their homes outside the walls. Gradually, however, particularly in the reigns of Henry I and Henry II, towns grew as country folk came and stayed, setting up shops and workshops and living over them.

But towns were mostly on the king's own land, so feudal dues were still enforced and market tolls had to be paid to him; town-dwellers were obliged to fulfil their feudal work obligations. No less inconvenient for the citizens were the quarterly visits of the king's sheriff to collect his dues, and at the same time to cast an inquisitive eye over the affairs of each of them.

This situation gave rise to bargains between townsfolk and their lord, whereby they bought themselves out of their feudal obligations. Such bargains were called *charters*, and in a written promise the lord granted certain privileges, most important of which was the townsfolks' right to govern themselves by their own elected officials, a council of twelve or twenty-four, presided over by a mayor or (as he was called in some places) reeve, provost or bailiff. These officials calculated the tax payable by each citizen, in the light of the lump sum that the lord of the manor had agreed to receive instead of feudal services.

In addition, a charter might grant a town the right to try those who broke its customs and rules, to hold a market or fair, to have its own mill, or to bake and brew as it pleased.

Gaining a charter was no easy business, and many towns were successful only after a long struggle with their lord. It was not until the fifteenth century that the chief towns, having won their local struggles, secured from the king a charter of liberties which included the right to organize as counties.

Municipal office was both dignified and demanding, and refusal to serve was strictly dealt with in the fifteenth century, and indeed for a long time afterwards. In the Cinque Ports anyone who refused local office might have his house pulled down, while Stephen Fabyn, elected alderman of Bridge ward in the city of London but refusing to serve because he had not "the estate to maintain his dignity," was immediately committed to Newgate gaol until his contention had been examined.

Town Features

The twelfth and thirteenth centuries saw a "fever of borough creation." Some new towns were laid out on a simple grid-iron plan, but the majority were allowed to grow haphazardly within a specified area.

This area, enclosed by walls of stone or earth and timber, was not entirely built up; there were gardens, orchards and fields, and most townsmen owned some livestock which they pastured on common land outside the town. Indeed, fields were as important as houses and shops, and great importance

The Shambles in York: this is the oldest street in Britain.

was attached to the annual walking of the boundaries, for the right to pasture cattle in the town meadows was a valuable right of citizenship.

In the town, geese and ducks waddled in the open channels which ran down the streets, and pigs (although this was technically forbidden) happily snorted through the piles of rubbish accumulating at street ends and in narrow cul-de-sacs. The centre of a town was its market place, in the middle of which was a market cross where proclamations were read; close by were the gildhall and principal church. Even the church was brought into the commercial hurly-burly; goods were bought and sold in the churchyard, rubbish was dumped there, and hay and straw stored until a buyer could be found.

There was a distinctive beauty about a medieval town, but if there was much to please the eye, there was even more to offend the nostrils. Sanitation was primitive and hygienic sewage disposal unknown. To the stench of ordure and garbage tossed habitually into the streets were added smells from the Shambles, where reeking entrails of slaughtered beasts and rotting fish guts were seldom cleared away, from the dyers' and tanners' workshops, and from the latrines, which projected over open streams and ditches running through the town. The first urban sanitary act in our history, the Statute of Barnwell issued in 1388, laid down primitive regulations for the removal of refuse, because the air was becoming "greatly corrupt and infect," but little was accomplished until the nineteenth century.

Then there were the noises: incessant ringing of church bells, as mourning or warning or marking feasts of the Church, clatter of hooves, grinding cartwheels, shouting apprentices tumbling together at football, or in their traditional trade feuds, frenzied yawling of bull-baiting, and the headlong panic of a hue-and-cry.

Merchant and Craft Gilds

To control buying and selling, each large town had a merchant gild whose membership originally embraced all those engaged in trade. All members had the right to buy and sell within the borough without payment of tolls, but foreigners (anyone, that is, from outside the borough) had to pay on all goods they bought or sold. Primarily the gild stood for honesty and plain dealing, and condemned current sharp practices like "regrating," where goods were bought up for resale at a higher price, and "forestalling," where loads of provisions were intercepted and bought before they had reached town.

In the twelfth century the merchant gild was challenged successfully by many craft gilds, which were to become the most important feature of medieval town life. The craft gild, a society of artisans of a particular trade, aimed at providing a sound article at a fair price; it enforced regulations concerning prices, wages and hours, and set necessary standards of quality and craftsmanship. (It is tempting to say that craft gilds were like trade unions, but the striking difference between them must be noted—trade unions raise storms over members' wages, but seldom display much concern over standards of work.) It also demanded that members give absolute obedience to gild officers, the *warden* (himself a master of the trade), *searchers* (who, as their name implies, had to see that gild requirements were carried out) and *masters* (who owned their own workshops and employed journeymen and trained apprentices, how many of each being strictly limited by the gild).

Apprentices served a master for seven, ten or twelve years. Their contract of service, or indentures, bound them to a master who would train them in his craft, lodge, clothe, feed and discipline them. Besides town children, sons of local gentry and yeoman families became apprentices, and a member of a wealthy manufacturing gild might demand a £5 premium before accepting an apprentice, with an annual payment as well.

After he had served his time, the apprentice was brought by his master before the warden of the gild as a candidate for full membership, and the warden presented him to the mayor as being qualified for town citizenship. He would then become a *journeyman* (= a man hired for the day), and if an example of his work (his *masterpiece*) was considered good enough, and if he had enough money to set up for himself, he could become a master.

The mayor exercised a controlling hand over every gild; their regulations had to be approved by him, he gave warden and masters the weight of his authority, and he kept peace between the gilds (no small consideration when even a small town might have between thirty and forty separate gilds).

Gilds also fulfilled a social service for members. In times of sickness a member would receive payment from the gild, in hard times he would get financial help, and if he died in poverty the gild not only met his burial expenses and arranged the appropriate Masses, but also supported his widow and set any children to apprenticeship.

Gild Processions and Plays

Each gild had its patron saint signifying its close link with the Church, a link which complemented its intense pride in its own town. Civic pride was demonstrated in a double muster in arms by the gilds on Midsummer's Eve (23 June) and the Eve of SS. Peter and Paul (28 June), when they staged their "marching watch"; streets were decorated with greenery and against a setting of bonfires and festivity the members of craft gilds, armed with bows and spears, marched in torchlight procession through the streets.

On the Church festival of Corpus Christi, the gilds paraded through the town and presented plays on Biblical themes. These plays, particularly in the Midlands and North, aroused special interest. The Coventry plays were the most famous; here ten plays were performed, each a cluster of small plays, and each small play the responsibility of a different gild; they were staged on ten wagons, and played in each of the ten city wards. York held a one-day festival of some fifty different pageants.

A lot of trouble was taken over these productions, and a gild might spend the equivalent of £150 on its play, the money being raised by the collection of "pageant-pence" from every gild member. Actors were paid, and surviving pageant accounts make fascinating reading with such entries as:

"For mending the white and black souls' coats, 8*d.*";

"Paid to Fawston for hanging Judas, 4*d.*";

Although subjects were religious, the treatment was often worldly with a strong element of farce, the object being to entertain. The Devil would leap from a trap-door to firecracker accompaniment; and Herod ranted and roared, foamed at the mouth, and crowned a sterling display by beating his head on the cobbles. Pageant days were holidays, and a medieval townsman had altogether about forty holidays in a year, including the main Church festivals and saints' days besides these gild and municipal occasions.

Markets and Fairs

Market day and fair time were also of importance in the trade and life of the town. Markets were held weekly (daily in London), often on the regular weekly holy day. Country folk would come into town to sell surplus produce, and would buy in return the townsmen's goods. To hold a market the king's permission was required, and this was granted to the lord of the manor or to the mayor and council; it was a valuable grant, and the king

MEDIEVAL MONASTERY—ITS BUILDINGS AND GROUNDS

archbishop

stained-glass window

monk illuminating a manuscript

monks fishing and hoeing

barefoot friar preaching

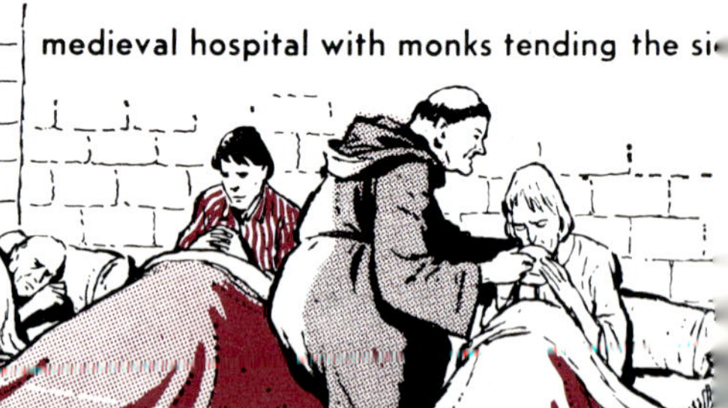
medieval hospital with monks tending the si

ASPECTS OF RELIGIOUS LIFE IN THE MIDDLE AGES

received good payment. Tolls were charged on goods brought into town, and rent was paid for a stall or for a standing space.

Town officials collected tolls; they also had to implement a massive array of market regulations, testing weights and measures, setting standards for bread, ale and wine, inspecting fish and meat and assuring themselves that it was "wholesome for man's body." These restrictions were imposed by the gilds, determined to protect townsfolk against unscrupulous victuallers, to favour their own people over foreigners, and to wage constant war on fraud. A Court of Pie Powder (*pied poudreux* = *dusty foot*) exercised summary jurisdiction, punishing by fine or by a spell in stocks or pillory.

Fairs were simply glorified markets, attracting traders from abroad, from Gascony, Flanders, the Baltic and the East, as well as from all parts of England. Great English fairs which acquired an international reputation were St. Bartholomew's in London, St. Giles' at Winchester, St. Botolph's at Boston and St. Ives' in Huntingdonshire.

Some fairs lasted only one or two days, others over a month; and, as with markets, a royal charter was necessary before a fair could be held. During his reign King John granted 117 such charters, while Henry III had already granted 500 by the time he had been on the throne for eleven years.

The fair ground was fenced off and whole streets of stalls were put up. Watchmen were employed to keep an eye open in case of theft or fire. For the period of the fair, shops were closed; entry of traders to the fair ground was controlled, tolls were collected, weights and measures checked, the Court of Pie Powder kept the peace. Fairs were usually held in spring or autumn, the times when those in charge of large households would lay in stocks of spices, wines and cloth for summer or winter use.

With the rapid growth of trade after the Conquest, fairs had become extremely important, but in the fifteenth century they began to decline as commercial organization developed; it is the entertainment side of the medieval fair, sword-swallower, tumblers, minstrels, dancers and performing animals, that has survived in our own times, although it is interesting to note a revival of the medieval concept in the trade fairs which are playing an increasingly important rôle in the present-day development of international trade.

Medieval English Wool Trade

The Romans found a developed wool industry in the Cotswolds, with its centre at Cirencester, and encouraged it by the establishment (at Winchester and elsewhere) of what might be called factories where the various processes in wool cloth manufacture were carried out. Saxon invasions led to virtual destruction of the industry, but after the Conquest there was a great increase in sheep breeding, and by the twelfth century manufacturing centres had been set up at Bristol and Exeter. Henry I founded the Scottish industry at the mouth of the Tweed in 1111. When ransom money for Richard I was needed, the whole wool clip of the great Cistercian monasteries was commandeered. Up to 1300 England's main concern was trade in raw wool, not cloth, and sheep were on the increase; in 1259 the Bishop of Winchester's estates had 29,000 sheep, and at Swyncombe in Oxfordshire in 1275 even serfs owned fifty sheep apiece; after the Black Death the number of sheep in the country increased to about 8 million. The wool clip from small owners would be collected by large landowners, sent to a local market or sold to the "wool-gathering" agent of an exporter, probably Flemish or Italian, who also bought by advance contract the entire clip of manors and religious houses. In 1313 Edward II ordered that wool for sale abroad should be sent to the Staple, a depot controlled by the Merchant Staplers. The first Staple was sited at Antwerp, but it was often shifted until finally fixed at Calais in 1398. Here foreign merchants came to buy wool, and here the king's officers collected export tax. Exclusion of foreign merchants from England led to the rise of English woolmen who, by buying small clips and selling in bulk to the merchants, made modest fortunes, built fine "wool" churches, houses and schools.

Wool cloth was made in all parts of England. In Henry I's reign there were gilds of weavers in London, Winchester, Lincoln, Oxford and Huntingdon, and a fullers' gild at Winchester. The cloth called *worsted* (from the village of Worstead near Norwich) was an English speciality, with broadcloth made in Somerset, Gloucestershire and Wiltshire. Edward III revitalized the cloth industry; in 1331 he invited Flemish weaver John Kempe to settle at Norwich; other Flemish weavers settled in Yorkshire. In the second half of the fourteenth century production of broadcloth trebled and the amount exported increased ninefold, so by 1400 cloth was replacing raw wool as "the flower and strength and revenue and blood of England."

The wool trade was an integral part of the expanding commerce of the Middle Ages. In return for wool, England received wine from Gascony and Bordeaux, glass-ware from Venice and Genoa and cloth from Flanders. Moreover, the wool trade provided revenue for the Crown, a weapon of diplomacy, and the foundation of many individual fortunes, not only for powerful merchants, but for small tenant farmers and villeins who kept sheep. The Woolsack, seat of the Lord Chancellor in the House of Lords since the fifteenth century, can be regarded as a symbol of the importance of wool in the economy of medieval England.

QUESTIONS

1. Why did towns develop during the Middle Ages, and how was trade regulated in them?
2. Describe the Gild System of medieval times.

CHAPTER 13

THE CHURCH

MEDIEVAL man lived under the shadow of the Church, a shadow which was cast by fear and deepened by ignorance. In the buildings he found instruction, consolation in his fearful struggle against "the Devil and all his works" and temporary relief from fear of death. The mystery of life was deepened for him by the narrowness of his own existence, his ignorance and his superstitious nature, which made his faith a mixture of God and goblins, Mass and magic.

The Church did not help; stark moralities painted on church walls, the fates of the good and the damned depicted on either side of the chancel arch taught of a God more concerned to punish than to forgive; the elaborate Latin service cut off a simple unlettered man from real communion with his God; and the path was further cluttered by the Church's deliberate stifling of inquiry, its encouragement of superstition and its emphasis on the supernatural.

The Church tried to give a Christian meaning to pagan beliefs and customs, rather than arouse prejudice by stamping them out, but the resultant blend was an unhappy one. May Day and Midsummer were pagan festivals celebrated along with Christian Christmas and Easter; and Yule log and greenery put a pagan wreath around the stable at Bethlehem. A wise woman's charm could drive away evil spirits as effectively as the exorcism of a priest; and even the Host, crushed and sprinkled over the cabbages, was expected to keep off caterpillars.

In medieval times, many aspects of secular life were constant reminders of the Church—shrines and crosses, palmers and pilgrims, preaching friars, payments called for by the Church (Mass pennies and Peter's Pence), as well as daily contact with the parish priest.

The Parish Priest

Between 1066 and the end of the fourteenth century, several thousand churches had been built, most of them in the period 1150-1250 when England was divided into ecclesiastical parishes; the parish church, therefore, grew up as the centre of a new community, with the priest as guide and mentor.

He saw to it that people came to church on Sundays and saints' days; he conducted all services and, as these were in Latin, explained their meaning to his illiterate flock. He taught his parishioners the Creed, Ten Commandments and Lord's Prayer; and occasionally he would preach a sermon.

The priest administered baptism, heard the confessions of his parishioners, enjoined penance upon them and absolved them from their sins; he married them and rendered the consolations of the Church to them as they lay dying, and at the last he laid them to rest in God's holy acre. A good priest represented the way of salvation, and stood as a bulwark for his flock against the doubts and fears that troubled them. Nevertheless, many priests were ill-educated and inefficient, sometimes barely able to mumble through the services, content to preach a halting sermon the statutory four times a year but for the rest to leave their "sheep encumbered in the mire."

The priest was also an agriculturalist, and this aspect of his work might take precedence over spiritual duties. He had his share of strips in the great fields and meadow, and shared his parishioners' grazing rights on the common land. This was the priest's glebe for which, as a freeman, he owed no service. Other sources of income were fees for baptisms, marriages, burials, offerings and masses, and the hated *tithe*, a tenth of all produce; a man unwillingly paid to the priest a tenth of his corn and hay, a tenth of his wool clip and of the cheese made from milk given by his cows, goats and ewes, the tenth calf, lamb and piglet born in the year, the tenth chicken hatched, a tenth of his honey, eggs, nuts and even of the vegetables and herbs grown in his cottage garden. In towns the priest took one-tenth of a craftsman's work and of all that he sold in his shop or at market. Furthermore, on the assumption that a man did not faithfully pay tithe on all gains, when he died the priest took his second-best beast, bed or garment as a *mortuary*. Tithe and mortuary did not improve relations between a priest and his flock, for the priest was often of villein stock himself or, as we have seen, a tardy shepherd, while his power to excommunicate those who did not pay tithe made him doubly unpopular.

For church organization, the parish was part of an archdeaconry, the archdeaconry part of a bishop's diocese. The archdeacon visited the priest, admonished and exhorted him, and in his archdeacon's court punished absenteeism, or the not infrequent moral lapses among the clergy.

Three Great Monastic Orders: Benedictine, Carthusian, Cistercian

From the earliest days of Christianity there have been men who have felt a call to live apart from the world and its distractions, and to spend their time in prayer and meditation. In 529 St. Benedict of Nursia built a monastery at Monte Cassino in Italy, where such men could live together as a community, and for this community he drew up the *Rule of St. Benedict* to guide and regulate their everyday life; it was based upon moderation, and, in place of the earlier ascetism, it established a system which contained "nothing

The ruins of Netley Abbey:

(1) Church. (2) Library. (3) Chapter house. (4) Abbot's lodging. (5) Parlour. (6) Dormitory. (7) Store room. (8) Infirmary. (9) Warming house. (10) Refectory. (11) Kitchen. (12) Guest house, or lay brothers' quarters. (13) Cloister. The abbey was suppressed, 1536.

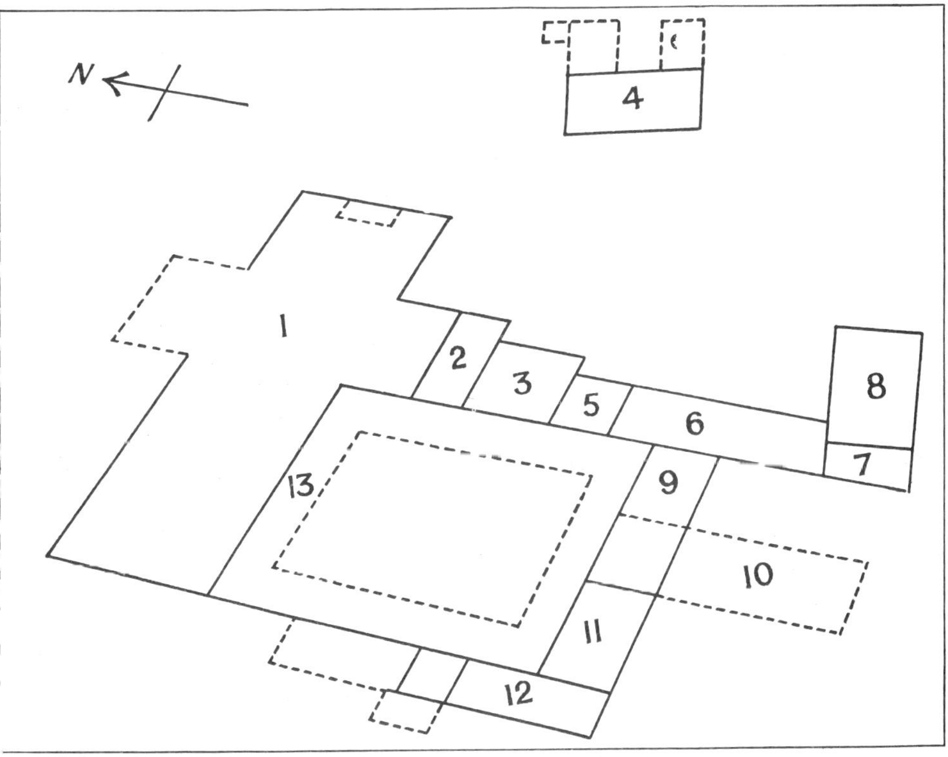

harsh, nothing burdensome." In each day four hours were set apart for worship, four for meditation, and six for domestic and manual labour.

This Benedictine order (Black Monks), the first and greatest, was introduced into England by St. Augustine in 597; the Celtic monasteries of the north turned Benedictine after the Synod of Whitby in 664. Viking invasions destroyed most of the monasteries, and even after the tenth-century monastic revival there were only about sixty religious houses in England (forty-eight for men and twelve for women). Development was rapid after 1066; by 1100 about one hundred new Benedictine monasteries had been founded, many of them given to foreign communities by Norman lords ("alien priories"); by the middle of the thirteenth century there were in England some 345 houses for men and 140 for women, with a total of nearly 6,000 monks and nuns.

Carthusians were the most austere of the religious orders. Founded at Chartreuse in 1086 by St. Bruno of Cologne, Carthusians abandoned the communal life of the parent Benedictine order, and lived in separate cells, mostly in silence, devoted to a life of solitary worship and contemplation. The work in their monasteries, or Charterhouses as they were called, was carried out by lay brothers who had not taken the complete vows of a monk.

Such a strict order had only limited appeal among Englishmen, and the Charterhouse founded by Henry II at Witham in Somerset in 1175-76 was the first of only nine Carthusian houses in England.

Stephen Harding, born at Sherborne in Dorset, was the real founder of the Cistercian order. It had been established at Cîteaux in Burgundy by St. Robert of Molêsme in 1098, and Harding was Prior of this community; but in 1109 he became Abbot, and in his *Charter of Love* (1117) he set out the rules governing the Cistercian order. This order, the White Monks, stressed the importance of manual labour and made great use of lay brothers. The first Cistercian house in England was founded at Waverley, Surrey, in 1128 but the two greatest were Rievaulx (1131) and Fountains (1132). The order was very popular; fifty-one houses were established between 1128 and 1154 (although the final figure for England is seventy-six), and it soon became wealthy as the result of participation in the wool trade. The Cistercians were also horse-breeders, while a couple of their abbeys occupied a prominent place in the English iron industry.

Monastic Vows and Duties

Apprentice monks were called *novices* and, after a period of training in the monastery under their novice-master, they were admitted as monks by taking three vows, poverty, chastity and obedience. Their life henceforth was dedicated to certain tasks. First and most important was prayer, for God's Church and for all mankind. When the monasteries were dissolved later, this was the monastic function most missed, for what better way was there to escape the fires of Hell and find the bliss of Heaven than through the intercession of holy men and women?

Religious observances occupied a fair amount of their time, as did work in the fields and about the monastery itself; study occupied an increasingly small amount of their time as the Middle Ages progressed. Next to prayer, the prime duties of monks were almsgiving and hospitality. Monasteries dispensed food and money to the poor, who attended at an almonry by the monastery gate; the guest house was always ready to receive and shelter a traveller. In northern England, where inns were few and far between, this service was especially valuable, and the fact that its bread was whiter, its ale better and its beds less bug-ridden, gave the monastery a distinct advantage over any medieval inn. St. Benedict laid great stress on hospitality, and according to his Rule every guest had to be received "as if he were Christ."

Benedictine Monk's Day

Daily routine varied according to the time of year, because a monk's day ran from sunrise to sunset (with a regular commitment in the small hours of the morning). Services were distributed evenly over the day: Mattins (or Nocturns) and Lauds from midnight until 1.30 a.m., Prime at dawn, and Terce and Sext in the forenoon, together with Mass in the early part of the day; then between noon and sunset were None, Vespers and Compline. This was the framework of a monk's day.

At midnight he got up from his pallet in the dormitory and made his way into church for Mattins and Lauds. In winter he was allowed a pair of lined boots, as the church would be very cold; and because standing for a long time in his choir stall would be too tiring, he could rest his weight on a small ledge on the underside of the tip-up seat. These *misericords* were often quaintly carved, with biblical or social scenes or strange animals.

Back to bed after Lauds, our monk would be up again at sunrise. He had no breakfast, although sick monks were allowed bread dipped in wine. After Mass a meeting was held each day in the Chapter House, where the abbot would read a chapter from the Benedictine Rule (hence *Chapter* House), and where monks and novices would be given their tasks for the day. When the novices had been dismissed, the monks engaged in brotherly censure, a helpful criticism of each other.

At noon, having washed his hands in a stone trough, the monk would enter the refectory for dinner. Silence was the rule here, as it was in the church, dormitory and cloister; but throughout the meal one of the brethren would read aloud from the Bible or from a religious book. The meal consisted of pottage, fish, water-fowl, eggs, cheese, milk or vegetables and, from the twelfth century onwards, meat, which had been forbidden by the Rule, but which English monks insisted on having. In summer a short rest was allowed after dinner, but then it was back to work. Supper was eaten after Vespers, and before Compline was Collation, a reading from a holy book. After Compline, to bed. This was the routine, year in, year out, the only variations coming with the seasons or with sickness.

The Friars

The twelfth and thirteenth centuries were times of religious unrest in Western Europe. With the development of trade during the Crusades, wealth provided a temptation which weakened the hold of the Church; and poor people, across a widening gulf from the rich merchants and bankers, saw little hope in the Christian message as it was given to them. The Crusades had broadened men's minds; the cramping hold of the Church was no longer bearable, and there was even some questioning of the authority of the Pope and the Church of Rome. The Church was ill-equipped to counter this growing dissatisfaction. Priests, many of whom were ignorant, commanded little respect; bishops were too busy with state affairs; and monks, holy men though they were, were not permitted to work and move outside the monastery. It was to remedy this situation that the friars came into being.

Of the four major orders of friars in medieval England, Franciscans, Dominicans, Augustinians and Carmelites, the Franciscans, founded by St. Francis of Assisi in 1210, were first. St. Francis preached repentance and a return to simple holiness; he and his followers accepted the absolute poverty of Christ, and for food and shelter they relied upon charity. Their aim was to preach and minister to the poor and sick.

A Franciscan friar was free to move about. Soon friars reached all parts of Italy, Germany, France, Spain, Hungary and the Holy Land; and in 1224 a group of nine, led by Agnellus of Pisa and including three Englishmen, landed at Dover. From there they went straight to Canterbury where they were expected, and within a few weeks they had set up houses at London, Oxford, Cambridge and Northampton. Within twenty years over thirty Franciscan houses had been founded, and by 1340 there were fifty. All sorts and conditions of men made up their diocese, lepers, the sick and the wretched; in slum areas of vice and misery these happy men ("God's jesters," as they were called) put up little wattle-and-daub huts, and shared their love of God with their fellow men.

St. Dominic, a Spanish nobleman, founded the Dominican order (or Order of Preachers) in 1215 to combat the heresy which he had encountered as a member of Cardinal Aquaviva's embassy to south-west France. His aim was to explain and defend the true faith of the Church and to defeat heretics by argument; to do this, serious study was essential. A school in every Dominican house was his ideal, and schools in university cities where his followers could work for a degree. In 1221, the order having already spread to Germany and

Poland, the first group of Black Friars reached England from France. Houses were rapidly established at Oxford (1221), Holborn (1223), Norwich (1226), York (1227), Bristol (1230) and Northampton (1232), with a final total of fifty-three. The first university school was established at Paris in 1228, and a similar school was founded at Oxford in 1263.

Friars provided the Church with crack reinforcements of mobile religious commandos. With their preaching they went to the people, and their sermons, carefully prepared and liberally sprinkled with racy anecdotes, had instant appeal. Works of charity received a fillip, and money was diverted from monasteries to institutions for relieving want and suffering. If they upset the monks by this, friars also fell foul of the parish clergy by their encouragement of confession among the laity, because this enticed offerings and legacies away from the Church; when the friars agreed to share such money with the parish priests, they were allowed to preach freely.

Above all, the friars were teachers. Franciscans were particularly active at Oxford and Cambridge; some of the scholars who went to Oxford from Paris in 1229 were friars, and the greatest of them, Alexander of Hales, joined the Franciscans. Robert Grosseteste, master of the schools at Oxford, befriended the friars and promoted the connexion between Oxford and the Franciscans; and their school there became a model for the university's earliest halls and colleges. Dominicans were less active at Oxford and Cambridge, but their educational contribution was through their own schools. They made their name as royal confessors; all the English kings from Henry III to Richard II had Dominican confessors, while most of their Queens had Franciscans.

Decline of the Religious Life

By 1348 there were about one thousand religious houses in England, including about two hundred houses of friars: a total of nearly 17,000 religious men and women. But the early enthusiasm of both monks and friars was becoming diverted from prayer and good works towards the pursuit of land and wealth; the mendicant ideal of poverty was abandoned. Not all monasteries were wealthy; some were on the brink of bankruptcy. But the irreverent speculation that if the Abbot of Glastonbury had married the Abbess of Shaftesbury they would have been richer than the king of England, is an indication that somehow the monastic ideal had lost its way; and men such as John Wyclif were not lacking to attack these representatives of the Church, and through them the Church itself.

QUESTIONS

1. Describe the life of a typical parish priest during the Middle Ages.
2. What were the aims of (*a*) the Franciscans, (*b*) the Dominicans. Describe briefly their work in England.

CHAPTER 14

THE WARS OF THE ROSES

TO REFER to the civil wars fought in the fifteenth century as the Wars of the Roses is convenient but inaccurate. The description is a sixteenth-century invention; and although the white rose was a Yorkist emblem, the red rose, attributed to the house of Lancaster, was in fact a Tudor one, while a white swan was the most usual Lancastrian device. But the roses themselves are not important; what is important is why these wars should have been fought at all, between representatives of two branches of the family of Edward III, York and Lancaster.

Claims to the Throne

Henry IV, when he had overthrown Plantagenet Richard II in 1399, based his Lancastrian right to the throne on descent from Edmund Crouchback, the elder son, he claimed, of Henry III. His argument was ridiculous, suggesting that Edward I (truly the elder son of Henry III, and elder brother of Edmund Crouchback) and all Plantagenet kings since (Edward II, Edward III and Richard II) were mere intruders. Richard II himself declared representatives of the Mortimer family his heirs, but Henry IV buttressed his claim by parliamentary acceptance; and, most important, he actually wore the crown.

To the country as a whole, Henry Bolingbroke was preferable to Richard of Bordeaux, and the house of Lancaster to any other dynasty, but only so long as they were successful; failure would remind people of the watertight legal claim of the Mortimers, represented, after the marriage of Anne Mortimer to the Earl of Cambridge, by Richard, Duke of York. Henry IV hardly survived to 1413, but Henry V, by his French campaigns, revived the flagging fortunes of Lancaster. His premature death, and the succession of feeble Henry VI in 1422, brought about the end of the dynasty.

Henry VI, 1422-71

Henry VI was weak and ineffectual; his court was gloomy and austere. In the 1440s and 1450s his government fell to pieces, and the nobles battened on the royal estates and revenues, growing rich as the king grew poor. His marriage to haughty Margaret of Anjou in 1445 was extremely unpopular at a time when England's fortunes in the Hundred Years' War were at a low ebb. Her influence contributed greatly to the creation of factions at court; and

SUCCESSION TO THE THRONE 1327-1509

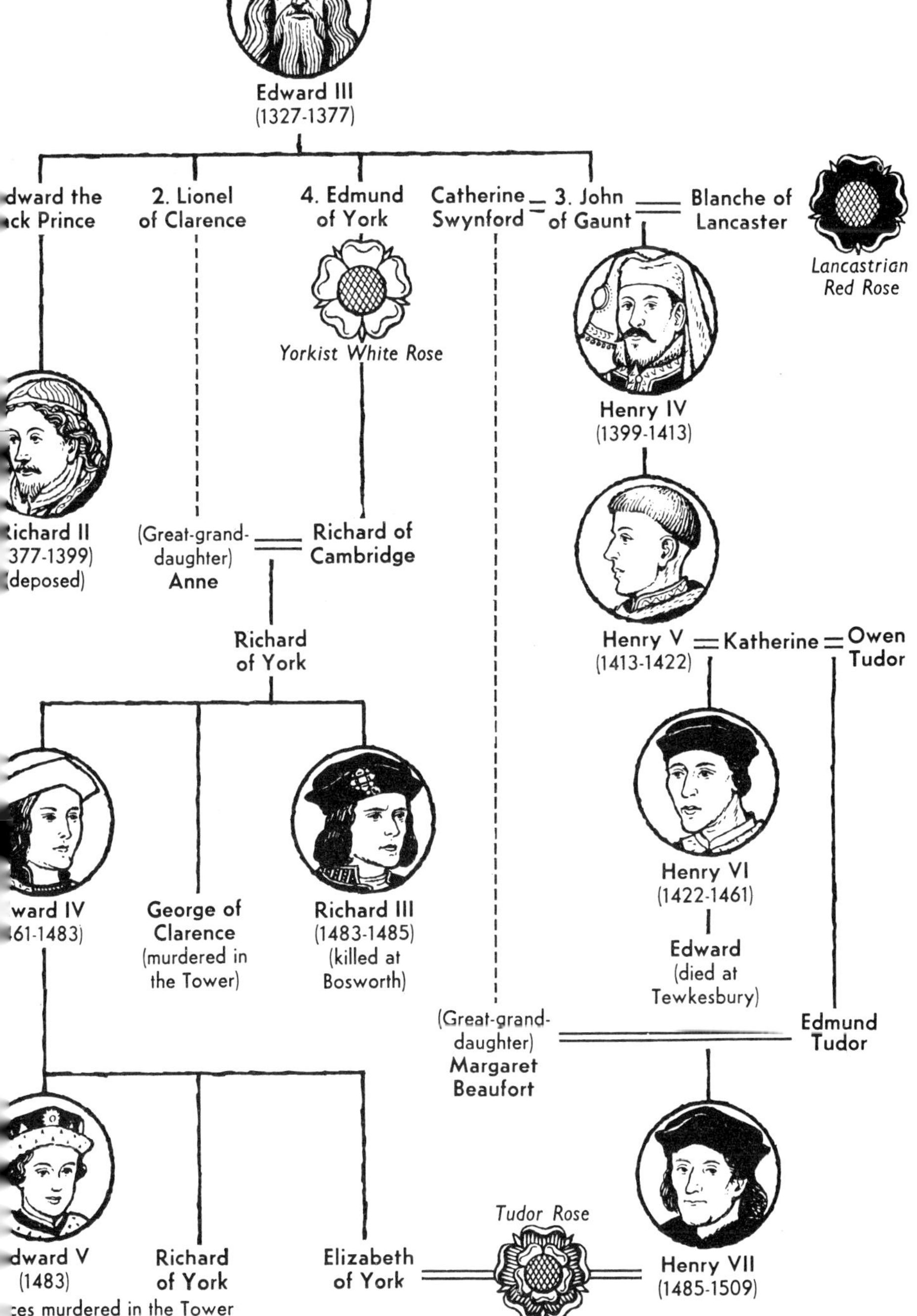

she, with the unpopular Dukes of Somerset and Suffolk, headed the Lancastrian party against the growing opposition party of discontented lords, led by capable Richard, Duke of York. There was plenty for this opposition to complain about, not least the government's conduct of the war in France.

Cade's Rebellion

In 1449 French armies overran Normandy and discontented troops, landing from the Continent, spread begging and robbing through Kent. In 1450 troops waiting to embark at Portsmouth to reinforce Somerset's force in France murdered Bishop Moleyns, one of the court party who had been sent to pay their long-overdue wages. Kent continued to be a trouble spot, with strange agitators finding ready support. Suffolk, attacked by parliament and banished in 1450, was murdered at Dover; and hearing that the Sheriff of Kent and Lord Say (the Treasurer of England) had threatened reprisals against the county, the men of Kent, sick of misrule at home and failure abroad, rallied behind Jack Cade and, with men of Surrey and Sussex, marched to Blackfriars.

The composition of the rebel force, fishermen, sailors, tradesmen, priests and local gentry, reveals the universality of the country's displeasure. They denounced the king's evil councillors for having poisoned the king's mind against his people and his true adviser, the Duke of York; and they demanded an overhaul of the government, as well as legal and financial reform.

London was abandoned to the rebels by the king and his ministers; Lord Say and William Crowmer, Sheriff of Kent, were summarily executed; but then the discipline of the rebels collapsed. They looted indiscriminately, arousing a London counter-rebellion which brought the movement to an end. But Cade's rebellion had focused national dissatisfaction, and the Duke of York, returning from Ireland where he had been sent as Governor to get him out of the way, forced on the king the arrest of Somerset and a complete reform of government. In 1453 London made ready for conflict, and the army of three thousand men that York had at his back when he entered the city illustrates another important factor in the causes of civil war.

Livery and Maintenance

By the reign of Henry VI, the old feudal relationship based on land had disappeared to be replaced by a system based on a money-and-influence connexion called *livery and maintenance*. It was a system of patronage, lesser men joining with greater for protection and profit. In return for service, usually armed service, a retainer received from his lord some form of payment, wore the lord's badge (*livery*), and could depend on the lord to protect him if he fell foul of the law or even if he had private scores to settle (*maintenance*). Such a system enabled great families, like the Nevilles on the

Yorkist side and their rivals the Percies who supported Lancaster, to build up private armies which in times of "lack of governance" could be exercised in gang warfare. Now that the French wars were over, the nobles were only too ready to work off the stiffness of their sword arms in civil war.

Taking Sides

In 1453 Henry VI went mad; and with Richard of York as heir to the throne, the end of misgovernment and the house of Lancaster seemed in sight. A few weeks later, however, the queen gave birth to a son, Prince Edward, and she was prepared to fight to maintain his right to the throne, and to retain power in her own hands. Authority passed to the council, Somerset was sent to the Tower, and York became Protector of England; but only until 1454, when Henry regained his wits, and York's appointment was annulled. The queen and Somerset now planned revenge against York. He was forced to retire to the north, where his adherents joined him, and with a small army he marched on London, simply to survive. Civil war had now begun.

It is a mistake to think of the Wars of the Roses as just a nobles' affair, but it would be equally wrong to imagine that a clarion call, "For York or Lancaster!" went out to all England. Few people considered the pros and cons of either party. The lower classes had been restless for a hundred years and more, but the lawlessness of the times hit them hardest, and so they supported York, just to have a change from Lancaster.

Landowners and nobles were simply out for what they could get, supporting that side most likely to bring about an increase in their fortunes. The main struggle was York versus Lancaster, but many private wars went on under that canopy, as the experiences of the Paston family in Norfolk amply testify. There were few men of principle, Henry VI was totally out of his depth in the blood and thunder of civil war; and Richard, Duke of York, whose sole interest was in the establishment of good government, claimed the throne in 1460 only to save England from anarchy.

The Wars, 1455-64

The years 1455-71 were a vicious playtime of what Sir John Fortescue called "the overmighty subjects." Law and order went by the board, justice was misused, juries were notoriously corrupt and the times were "out of joint for all." After the first battle at St. Albans in 1455 (when the Duke of York and the Earl of Warwick defeated the royal forces, killing Somerset and taking Henry VI prisoner), there was an interval until 1459-61 when six battles were fought. In 1464 two battles were fought, and the wars ended after four more battles between 1469 and 1471.

The queen regained control of the king in 1456, and left London to rally support in Cheshire and Lancashire, where feudalism was still strong, trade was undeveloped, and reforming ideas had hardly penetrated; the Yorkist lords withdrew to their strongholds. Trade languished as English merchants, lacking government support, wilted in the face of foreign competition; and the port of Sandwich was disdainfully plundered by a French fleet.

The queen moved against York at Ludlow (1459) and by treachery forced the Yorkist leaders into flight, Richard to Ireland, Salisbury, the Earl of March (Richard's second son, later Edward IV) and the Earl of Warwick to Calais. This reverse aroused popular sympathy for the Yorkist leaders among townsmen and gentry of the southern counties, who flocked to join Warwick and the Earl of March when they landed at Sandwich from Calais in 1460.

At Northampton the "Calais earls" routed the king's army; the queen escaped to Wales, but Henry was again taken. This was the point when York, to the earls' surprise, demanded the crown. A compromise was reached, York agreeing to be named heir to the throne; but Margaret could not accept this injustice to her son. She feverishly rallied supporters in the north, defeated and killed the Duke of York at Wakefield, and moved south to defeat Warwick at the second battle of St. Albans, recapturing the king.

While this was happening, another Lancastrian army was defeated at Mortimer's Cross, and the victor, York's heir Edward, joined Warwick in London and on 4 March, 1460, was acclaimed King Edward IV. Margaret retired north, losing support to the Yorkists by the pillaging she allowed. Edward and Warwick, joined by men from East Anglia, the southern counties, Bristol and other towns as they advanced through the Midlands, faced the Lancastrians at Towton (1461). This was the greatest battle of the wars, with about 75,000 men taking part, and with total casualties in the region of 25,000. The Yorkists were victorious, Margaret retired to France (1463), and with two more defeats at Hedgeley Moor and Hexham (1464) and the recapture of King Henry VI, the Lancastrian cause seemed irretrievably lost. And so it would have been, had not the Yorkists fallen out.

Edward IV and Warwick

Edward IV had no intention of being a puppet of Warwick and the Neville faction, who were strongly entrenched in power—Warwick as "Conductor of the Kingdom," his brother the Bishop of Exeter (later Archbishop of Canterbury) as Chancellor, and the Earl of Northumberland as virtual ruler of the north. It would be a long and tricky task, but Edward set out to outmanoeuvre Warwick.

Edward's secret marriage to Elizabeth Woodville, widow of the Lancastrian Sir John Grey, in 1464 ruined Warwick's plans for a French match for him, and gave him a bevy of in-laws to counteract the Neville interest. He dismissed the Chancellor in 1467, and again wrecked Warwick's plans for a French alliance by concluding one with Burgundy instead.

Warwick was infuriated, and under threat of arms Edward agreed to do as he was told, and was lodged in Warwick Castle. In this, Warwick and George, Duke of Clarence (Edward's brother), who had joined with the "Kingmaker," miscalculated, for Edward's popularity grew while Warwick's influence declined. When a Lancastrian rising broke out on the Scottish border, Warwick actually had to appeal to Edward for help in putting it down.

The rising crushed, Edward seized his chance. Independent of the Nevilles he summoned his supporters to Pontefract and informed Warwick that he was returning to London. Warwick and Clarence, clearly outdone, joined with Lancastrian sympathizers in Lincolnshire, but, defeated at "Lose-coat Field" (1470), they fled to France. Within a few months they returned triumphantly with the unaccustomed blessing of Queen Margaret.

Caught on the wrong foot, Edward crossed to the Low Countries, while Henry VI was brought from the Tower to resume the crown, but only for a little longer. Events moved quickly. In 1471 Edward was back again with money and a fleet supplied by his ally Burgundy, landing at Ravenspur in Yorkshire where Henry Bolingbroke had landed in 1399. Without a blow being struck he marched from York to London; thence to Barnet, where the Lancastrian army was routed, and Warwick the Kingmaker was slain. In the west Queen Margaret, after landing at Weymouth, was defeated at Tewkesbury (1471), her son killed, and she herself taken prisoner. That night Henry VI was murdered in the Tower. His queen was more fortunate; ransomed by Louis XI of France (1475), she died in France in 1482. War between the white rose and the white swan was at an end.

Edward IV, 1461-83

A recent writer on this period (P. M. Kendall) has claimed that Edward's achievement has been under-estimated. Edward lacked the shrewdness of Henry VII, but he compares very favourably in other respects. Anxious to restore order and justice after the civil wars, he won the allegiance of former enemies, then set about clearing his debts, increasing his revenue, and reforming his household administration. Trade was encouraged by a new charter to the Merchant Adventurers, allowing them wide scope in regulating trade with the Low Countries and Burgundy, and French markets were opened up to English trade after the Treaty of Picquigny in 1475. He encouraged native shipbuilding, insisting that English ships be used whenever possible, and himself purchased a number of ships to participate in the wool and cloth trade, and later in the export of tin and lead. The customs were overhauled, as was the administration of royal estates; and titles to land were investigated to check illegal seizure of property which had occurred during the wars. In the *Black Book of the Household of Edward IV* a comprehensive code was drawn up by which his household was to be administered. A man of wide tastes, he was a great builder and patron of the arts and scholarship, and by his death in 1483 he had established a strong monarchy and had earned the affection and esteem of his people.

Richard III, 1483-5

Edward intended that his brother Richard, Duke of Gloucester, the loyal and efficient ruler of northern England, should be regent for his twelve-year-old son, Edward V; but the queen, supported by her relations, by Lord Stanley and Lord Hastings, usurped this rôle. Hating the Woodvilles, who had so damaged his brother's government by their avarice and ambition, Richard joined with the Duke of Buckingham, seized the king, and became Protector. Within weeks he had set his eyes on the crown. Hastings was executed, and Richard staked the amazing claim in parliament that Edward IV's marriage had been invalid, and that his child, Edward V, was therefore illegitimate. Edward V and his younger brother Richard were put in the Tower and murdered, probably by, or on the instructions of, Richard III himself. A rebellion by Buckingham in 1483, supported by the Woodvilles and in favour of Henry Tudor, failed; but in 1485 this same Henry, Earl of Richmond, defeated and killed Richard at Bosworth.

The country was at a standstill, and the prevailing numbness of a punch-drunk nation was shown by the fact that, to contemporaries at least, the battle of Bosworth might never have taken place.

Richard himself remains a mystery. Tudor propagandists painted him jet black to make the natural grey of Henry VII appear pure white. Certainly Shakespeare's "bottled spider, that poisonous bunchback'd toad" is an assessment extremely wide of the mark, as are the claims of those who have tried to whitewash him. Richard was efficient and respected, a wise and trusted counsellor, a vigorous administrator in the Scottish Marches, and a good soldier who fought at Barnet and Tewkesbury. Devoted to his brother, why should he have snatched the crown, by deceit and probable murder, from his brother's child? The answer perhaps lies in his ambition, aroused by the prospect of a wasting minority exploited by the despised Woodvilles, and encouraged by the general acceptance by the country of his seizure of the crown. At the end, after the death of his only son and his wife, he may well have believed that God's hand was upon him, and that his furious and fearless death at Bosworth was the only way of atonement.

QUESTIONS

1. Explain the causes of the fifteenth-century struggle between Lancastrians and Yorkists?

2. Richard III is usually regarded as a wicked king. What is your opinion of his character and career?

REVISION SUMMARY OF CHAPTERS 1-14

For final revision, notes in some form are essential. Dictated or ready-made notes are not as good as those the student makes for himself, provided he brings thought and care to the task, because making good notes involves understanding what is being read, grasping the main theme of each paragraph, and finding out what facts build up the theme. This does much to fix the matter in the mind. Understanding of this kind precedes learning, and halves the difficulties. It cultivates an eye for the relevant point, and in an examination relevance is vital to success. In history papers more students fail through irrelevance than through ignorance. It is therefore important that the student should learn to distinguish clearly between causes and events, and between events and results. Careful note-making should help considerably.

The layout of the notes is important. A summary or précis in continuous prose is of little use. What is needed is an arrangement which has pattern and shape. In this way visual memory reinforces verbal recollection.

The following pages contain for each chapter an outline scheme only, round which the student can build his own notes. For CHAPTER 2 a fully expanded note has been provided in order to suggest how the student may best use the outlines. In this expanded note the material in italics is what the student should add for himself. Before attempting to use the other outlines, the student would be well advised to study the example carefully in relation to the text of the chapter on which it is based.

THE NORMAN CONQUEST

(expanded notes on CHAPTER 2)

A. WILLIAM'S MILITARY SUCCESS

1. Fall of Harold (p. 13)

(*a*) Harold's handicaps and mistakes

(*i*) *His military resources were weak after Stamford Bridge.*

(*ii*) *He should therefore have awaited reinforcements before marching to meet William.*

(*iii*) *His failure to do so was a lapse of military judgment.*

(*b*) William's successful approach to London

(*i*) *Death of Harold and his brothers at Hastings.*

(*ii*) *London declared against William, but took no measures to defend itself or to oppose William's progress.*

(*iii*) *Hence William was able to encircle London, which then had no alternative but to admit him and submit.*

(*iv*) *Coronation of William, 25th December* 1066.

2. Consolidation of William's power in the south (p. 13)

(*a*) Suppression of opposition in Kent

(*i*) *Temporary return of William to Normandy in* 1067; *William FitzOsbern and Bishop Odo were regents.*

(*ii*) *Defection of Eustace of Boulogne from William.*

(*iii*) *Kentish rising in support of Eustace.*

(*iv*) *FitzOsbern successfully held Dover Castle.*

(*v*) *Eustace returned to the continent.*

(*vi*) *Collapse of Kentish rising.*

(*b*) Failure of opposition in Exeter

(*i*) *Exeter refused fealty, and closed its gates to William.*

(*ii*) *Surrender on acceptable terms; no reprisals.*

3. Suppression of the north (p. 14)

(*a*) Anglo-Danish resistance

(*i*) *Landing of Swein and the Danes from the Humber.*

(*ii*) *Anglo-Danish capture of York.*

(*iii*) *Failure of rebels to exploit their success.*

(*iv*) *Sympathetic reaction in Wessex, Devon, Cornwall, Somerset, Dorset and Mercia.*

(*b*) William's counter measures

(*i*) *Sympathetic reactions repressed.*

(*ii*) *Norman advance to York and devastation on the way.*

(*iii*) *Danes bought off; collapse of English rebels.*

(*iv*) *Punitive devastation of North Midlands and Yorkshire.*

4. Final suppression of opposition (p. 14)

(*a*) Resistance in East Anglia

(*i*) *English stand under Hereward and the Bishop of Durham.*

(*ii*) *Guerrilla warfare conducted from base at Ely.*

(*iii*) *Support afforded to the rebels by Swein of Denmark.*

(*b*) Failure

(*i*) 1071, *surrender of Ethelwine and flight of Hereward.*

(*ii*) *Failure of rising of the Three Earls in* 1075.

B. NORMAN RE-ORGANIZATION

1. Forests and forest law (p. 14)

(*a*) Position in Saxon England

(*i*) *Royal hunting parks existed, but were not extensive.*

(*ii*) *People had rights of hunting in them and for gathering wood for fuel and building.*

(*b*) Norman changes

(*i*) *Extensive areas of forest, common, villages and hamlets declared subject to forest law.*

(*ii*) *In these areas deer and boar were protected for royal hunting only.*

(*iii*) *Popular rights confined to hunting of creatures which were enemies of deer.*

(*iv*) *Forest courts and officers appointed to enforce forest law by severe penalties.*

(*v*) *Establishment of private forests by Norman nobility.*

(*vi*) *Consequent hardship and resentment of the people.*

(*c*) Development to 1217

(*i*) *Forest extensions*, 1066-1166.

(*ii*) *Diminished by royal need for money under Richard I and John.*

(*iii*) *But a serious grievance until Henry III's Forest Charter of* 1217.

2. Land redistribution (p. 15)

(*a*) Initial phase

(*i*) *Confiscation only of lands of Englishmen killed at Hastings or of those who refused to acknowledge William.*

(*ii*) *English earls, sheriffs and bishops left largely unchanged until* 1069.

(*b*) Later phase

(*i*) *Revolts of* 1069-70 *led to a change of policy and deliberate large-scale confiscation of land.*

(*ii*) *Norman plantation of Yorkshire and Mercia for security reasons.*

3. Castles (p. 15)

(*a*) Early phase

(*i*) *Immediate castle construction in each county for security.*

(*ii*) *Motte-and-bailey type for quickness and cheapness.*

(*iii*) *A few only of stone.*

(*b*) Purpose

(*i*) *General security.*

(*ii*) *To guard against special danger in particular areas, e.g. south-east coast against invasion; Scottish border; Welsh Marches.*

(*c*) Later extensions

(*i*) *In Midlands and the north after rebellion.*

(*ii*) *At Shrewsbury, Chester and Stafford after the Mercian rebellion.*

(*iii*) 1080, *on site of later Newcastle against reprisals after Norman raid into Scotland.*

C. THE FEUDAL SYSTEM

1. Social innovation (p. 16)

(*a*) The necessity from the Norman standpoint

(*i*) *Norman military success depended on the professional soldier, the knight.*

(*ii*) *The knight had to be rewarded and maintained.*

(*iii*) *The means adopted to do this was to make him a landowner.*

(*b*) Nature of the social innovation

(*i*) *All land was assumed to belong to the king.*

(*ii*) *Grants of land were made by the king to his barons, by the barons to lesser tenants, and to knights either directly by the barons or by lesser tenants.*

(*iii*) *Barons and their sub-tenants were responsible for provision of knights for the king's service.*

(*iv*) *Such provision was part of the "rent" paid for land granted.*

(*v*) *The number of knights to be provided was conditional on the amount of land held.*

(*vi*) *Knights "rented" their land by military service.*

2. Feudal services, fiefs and dues (p. 17)

(*a*) Services

(*i*) *A knight in peacetime spent forty days annually in military training or garrison duty.*

(*ii*) *In war he served for two months at his own expense, having been endowed as a wealthy landowner.*

(*iii*) *The Oath of Homage bound a subordinate (vassal) to the service of his overlord.*

(*iv*) *The Oath of Fealty was a pledge of loyalty by vassal to overlord.*

(*v*) *The overlord in return promised protection to his vassal.*

(*b*) Baronial fiefs

(*i*) *Made up of scattered manors.*

(*ii*) *Usual holding, twenty to thirty manors.*

(*iii*) *King's brothers and frontier earls might hold* 700-800.

(*c*) Feudal dues

(*i*) *Aids: financial payments to his overlord by a vassal, at the marriage of the overlord's eldest daughter, at the knighting of his eldest son, or as ransom.*

(*ii*) *Relief: payment by an heir to his overlord on assuming an inheritance.*

(*iii*) *Wardship: an heir was the ward of his overlord during his minority, and the overlord enjoyed the profits of the estate during this time.*

3. Domesday Survey (p. 18)

(*a*) Purpose

(*i*) *To discover the extent of William's possessions.*

(*ii*) *To give a clear picture of land ownership and land values.*

(*b*) Method

(*i*) *Commissioners to conduct on-the-spot inquiries.*

(*ii*) *Details required: name of locality, pre-Conquest ownership, present ownership, value, population, stock, acreage, use.*

(*c*) Importance

(*i*) *Added to Norman unpopularity with the English.*

(*ii*) *First report of a Royal Commission.*

(*iii*) *Evidence of Norman organization and thoroughness.*

ENGLAND AND NORMANDY

THE NORMAN CONQUEST

(See example of the fully expanded notes, page 105)

CHURCH AND STATE

EDWARD I

CHAPTER 15

HENRY VII, THE FIRST TUDOR

ON THE field of Bosworth, Henry Tudor collected a Crown and with it many problems. In the long struggle of the Wars of the Roses many had picked up that same Crown only to have it struck swiftly from their heads. How was Henry to succeed in retaining what so many had lost? Weak kings in the fifteenth century had opened the way to power for ruthless, ambitious noblemen. How was Henry to re-assert the power of the king? Civil war had meant a diminishing respect for law and order. How was Henry to restore that respect? No government could function without money. How was Henry, who had staged his bid for the throne on borrowed supplies, to make himself financially secure without putting himself under obligation to wealthy subjects by asking them for loans, or alienating the people by raising taxes through Parliamentary grants? These were Henry's formidable problems.

Measures to Secure Throne and Dynasty

Knowing that there were claimants with better legal title to the throne than his own, Henry was content to declare himself king without stating the basis on which his claim rested. Next he caused a dangerous rival, Edward, Earl of Warwick, son of Richard III's murdered brother the Duke of Clarence, to be lodged a virtual prisoner in the Tower. Then Henry married Elizabeth of York, daughter of Edward IV, but delayed doing so until 1486 lest his enemies allege that he sat on the throne by virtue of his wife's right rather than his own. Nevertheless, this marriage went far to conciliate the Yorkists.

As far as possible Henry treated false pretenders like Lambert Simnel and Perkin Warbeck, sons respectively of an English baker and a Flemish boatman, with ridicule. For the former he found menial employment in the royal kitchen; the latter, more dangerous because he had European and Scottish support, was first imprisoned in the Tower, and executed only in 1499 on a charge of conspiracy with the Earl of Warwick against the king's life. Finally the birth of two sons, Prince Arthur in 1486 and Prince Henry in 1491, gave hope of an undisputed succession when Henry VII died.

Henry had to make himself king in reality as well as in title. Great medieval kings like Edward I had exercised considerable personal power on and in their Councils; but weaker monarchs of the fifteenth century had allowed government to fall into the hands of powerful councillors, and the crown itself to become a prize for the most ambitious or unscrupulous. Henry VII reverted to the example of the stronger medieval rulers, and his first step was to subdue the feudal barons from whose ranks the Council was drawn.

The barons were already weakened by their long wars with each other and the Crown. Many noblemen had died in the wars without leaving an heir; Henry, exercising his feudal rights in such cases, resumed possession of estates thus rendered ownerless. He gained more estates by confiscation of the lands of those who had fought for Richard III. In 1487 earlier acts limiting the number of liveried retainers a nobleman might keep in his service were revived, consolidated and enforced, making it difficult to maintain private armies.

As Henry reformed his Council, few of the aristocracy found places in it. Instead, Henry enlisted men from the growing middle class who, owing their careers to him, were more likely to be loyal.

Thus the feudal baronage began to lose its grip on the machinery of government. Similarly in local government the king's representatives became Justices of the Peace drawn from the ranks of country gentlemen and town merchants, rather than sheriffs drawn from the nobility.

Measures to Enforce Law and Order and Secure Revenue

The measures described above to re-assert the king's power went far towards making a new respect for law and order possible.

Something else was needed, however. A Justice of the Peace might still be unable to enforce his decisions on a powerful local baron. To meet situations of this kind, Henry developed the judicial work of his newly-staffed Council.

Though some Councillors always accompanied the king as he moved about the country, others were always on duty in London, hearing the pleas of poorer people or, in a room known as the Star Chamber, dealing with major offences against the King's Peace which other judicial bodies such as the Justices' courts were not powerful enough to handle. In this way the powers of what came to be known as the Court of Requests and the Court of Star Chamber began to expand. In 1487 the latter Court was empowered by statute to deal with cases of bribery of jurors, rioting and illegal assemblies. Away from London, where there might be special danger, Henry established special bodies such as the Council of the Marches which in 1502 was charged with the task of keeping peace in the western shires.

Henry devoted himself to ensuring that monies legally due to him as king were paid. Whereas some of his immediate predecessors had made grants of land to win supporters, Henry made a point of collecting into his own hands as much land as possible, for this was a basic source of Crown income. Tunnage (duty on wine) and poundage (duty on goods) his first Parliament granted to him for life, as was customary. He sought to promote trade, to increase the yield from duties on exports, mainly wool, which were

Prince Arthur's Chantry in Worcester Cathedral.

legally his due. He revoked freedom from customs duties granted to foreign merchants by his impecunious predecessors.

Further, he re-asserted the Crown's feudal rights of relief, wardship and escheat. He preferred to exact fines as legal penalties rather than impose physical punishment, since such monies accrued to the Crown.

Thus Henry restored the Crown revenue, enabling the king to "live of his own" without recourse to Parliament for grants nor to wealthy subjects for loans except, as was usual, in circumstances involving abnormal expense, for example the probability or occurrence of war. So successful was he that only on four occasions did he find it necessary to summon Parliament, and at his death he left a well-filled treasury for his successor.

He set the seal on his financial security by reviving an efficient system of monetary administration. The Court of the Exchequer was cumbersome, and the first three Edwards and Richard III had used the machinery of the Royal Household for collecting and auditing most of their revenue. Henry VII followed their example and by 1487 the Treasurer of the Household was, in fact if not in name, chief financial officer in the kingdom.

There were, as Henry was shrewd enough to know, always those who would attempt to avoid their financial obligations. To check their activities he employed special agents, of whom Empson and Dudley were the most famous, to enquire into debts and evasions. Such agents were loyal, keen and ruthless in executing their duties; but they were efficient administrators, not malicious extortioners.

Henry VII's Foreign Policy

In 1492 Henry made the Treaty of Etaples, securing peace with France. The heir to the English throne, Prince Arthur, was married to Catherine of Aragon in 1501, and when Arthur died a few months later, Catherine was betrothed to the new heir, Prince Henry. Thus Henry VII had secured recognition of his kingship from both France and Spain. To reduce the threat from Scotland and France, Henry's daughter Margaret was married to James IV of Scotland and an alliance with France made in 1502.

Henry also sought to promote trade; the Intercursus Magnus, signed in 1496 between England and Flanders, helped the English wool trade with Flanders, as well as withdrawing Flemish support for Perkin Warbeck. The privileges of English wool merchants in Flanders were extended in 1506.

The foreign policy which Henry followed had many far-reaching results. England's position as an important international power was restored, and Europe recognized the Tudor dynasty. Increased trade gained the support of merchants and traders, and added considerably to the royal revenue. Henry avoided serious wars, to save money and to prevent opportunities for rebellion in England. He also prepared the way for the union of the crowns of Scotland and England, and (unwittingly) laid the foundations for Henry VIII's break with the papacy. He was, however, only partly successful in weakening the Franco-Scottish alliance against England.

During the civil wars, central government had broken down, and the Irish parliament had become independent. The Irish had strong Yorkist sympathies, and supported Simnel and Warbeck. Henry hoped to re-establish central government, subordinate the Irish parliament and secure Ireland.

Sir Edward Poynings became Deputy Governor (1494-96), and persuaded the Irish parliament to pass Poynings' Act (1494) by which it was agreed that the Irish parliament would not meet except on the king's summons, and would discuss no laws not previously approved by the king; all English legislation would henceforth be automatically binding on Ireland. Annual accounts of Irish revenue were to be submitted to the English Exchequer.

QUESTIONS

1. What was the effect of the reign of Henry VII on English prestige abroad?
2. Describe Henry VII's aims and methods, and show to what extent they were new or old.

CHAPTER 16

HENRY VIII IN THE YEARS OF WOLSEY'S SUPREMACY

At his father's death, Henry VIII was a youth of eighteen, vigorous, lively and a far more attractive personality than the cautious older man whom he succeeded. He was devoted to sport, music and study, but already selfish and potentially ruthless, as was shown by his approval of the execution of his father's faithful servants Empson and Dudley in order to win easy popularity.

At his side from 1513 to 1530 stood Thomas Wolsey, Archbishop, Cardinal, Legate and Lord Chancellor, avaricious, unscrupulous, vain, self-centred, insatiable in his appetite for power and inordinately ambitious. His shortcomings were partially redeemed by his genuine ability, capacity for hard work, faithfulness to his master and courage in making even the most noble and powerful subjects bow before the king's will. These were the men of a new reign.

Rise of Wolsey

Wolsey was born in 1472, of a prosperous middle-class family in East Anglia. Educated at Oxford, he became a priest in 1498, and entered the service of Bishop Fox of Winchester. By 1502 he had become chaplain to the Archbishop of Canterbury, and in 1507 was appointed chaplain to Henry VII. Two years later he became the king's almoner, and in 1511 was made a privy councillor. In 1514 he became Bishop of Lincoln and Archbishop of York; at various times he became Bishop of Bath and Wells, of Durham and of Winchester. In 1515 he was made a Cardinal, and in the same year he also became Lord Chancellor.

Wolsey and the State: Administration of Justice

Once appointed as Lord Chancellor, Wolsey used his position to make himself (on behalf of the king) the supreme and final authority on all aspects of government administration. Wolsey devised policy, the king approved it and Wolsey saw it put into execution. The king's Council continued to exist, but did less and less, Wolsey transacting most state business through the Court of Star Chamber (a prerogative court rather than one of the courts of common law) in which Wolsey presided in the king's name.

In some ways the nation benefited from his exercise of power. Wolsey improved the Court of Chancery, the body which handled matters relating to property, trusts and wills. He increased its business, speeded up its processes and saw that decisions were enforced. The Court of Star Chamber, as well as taking over much administrative work hitherto performed in Council, also relieved the Church Courts of jurisdiction in matters of perjury, libel and forgery. It became, until its abolition in the next century, an almost regular feature of the judicial and administrative system of the country. By summoning some half-dozen of the greatest noblemen in the land before Star Chamber when their offences had gone unpunished in the Courts of Common Law, and compelling them to accept its jurisdiction, Wolsey made it clear that the king's writ applied to all subjects without regard to rank, position or wealth. The king's justice could be neither bought nor defied.

A price had to be paid for these benefits; it was the ever-growing power of one man, Wolsey. This proved too high a price, for the more Wolsey concentrated business in his own hands the less he was able to give it the attention it needed. His justice became rough; urgent affairs accumulated, awaiting his attention; much-needed reforms were never undertaken. Centralization of authority destroyed the efficiency it was intended to promote.

Wolsey and the State: Financial Administration

Wolsey's record in financial administration had even less to recommend it than his administration of justice. True, scrutiny of the king's finances was put on a systematic basis by annual appointment through parliament of two surveyors of Crown lands, to administer income from this source and to audit other revenue.

At the same time, Wolsey soon exhausted the well-filled treasury Henry VII had left, largely because foreign policy was adventurous and therefore expensive. In 1514 a tax of one shilling in the pound was imposed on all income derived from land and wages. In 1522 a forced loan was levied, although this means of raising money had been declared illegal in the time of Richard III. The nation still expected the king to "live of his own" and constant demands for special revenue were resented. In 1523, when Wolsey demanded from parliament a tax of four shillings in the pound, parliament was politely but firmly critical, and he had to be content with two shillings in the pound. When Wolsey tried to collect another forced loan in 1525 he had to face not merely parliamentary criticism but widespread discontent in the country. The king intervened and withdrew the demand; unlike his Chancellor, he was not prepared to ride for a fall.

Wolsey and the Church

Wolsey used the Church even more obviously for his own ends than he used the state. As Chancellor, his power and position were subject to his ability to convince the king of the rightness of his policy; but the final

Hampton Court Palace, built by Cardinal Wolsey.

authority in ecclesiastical matters was the Pope, who was far away in Italy.

Wolsey's own career in the Church shows how badly the Church needed reform, for he broke or ignored its regulations wholesale. It was an offence against Church law for a man to hold more than one ecclesiastical benefice at one time, yet Wolsey always held at least one Bishopric as well as his Archbishopric of York. Clergymen took a vow of celibacy, yet Wolsey had several children. Never in monastic orders, he was for a time Abbot of St. Albans. In several cases he appointed absentee foreigners to English benefices and drew the revenues himself. A large part of his personal wealth was drawn improperly from the Church.

It is thus not surprising that Wolsey failed to undertake any effective Church reform beyond closing a few small and unimportant monastic houses. Yet he constantly professed his intention and desire to carry through reform, and it was on the plea that he was about to do so that he won from the Pope the extraordinary concession which made him permanently *legate a latere*, resident ruler of the Church in England and the first Churchman to have legal authority in spiritual matters over Canterbury and York alike.

Wolsey's use of this unique position did little good to the Church in England. His appointment of absentee foreigners to bishoprics weakened the authority of the episcopal bench. Not merely did he curtail the jurisdiction of Church courts. but he also reduced the legal status of these judicial bodies by withdrawing particular cases from an episcopal court to his own legatine court. Intent on imposing his will on the Church, he so arranged matters that provincial convocations ceased to meet except when parliament met; and if Wolsey's demands for money for state business were heavy on parliament, those he made upon convocation were even heavier. Wolsey made himself unpopular among the clergy; and he made the Pope, from whom his authority was derived, unpopular with the nation. For one whose ambition it was to become Pope himself, Wolsey's Church policy was singularly ill-devised.

Wolsey and Europe

This ambition, rather than any patriotic desire to see his country dominant in European affairs, or any far-sighted plan to establish the balance of power as the basis of international relations, was the motive which governed the policy towards other European powers which Wolsey urged upon a partly willing king and a wholly unwilling nation.

Henry VIII had celebrated his accession to power by plunging recklessly into war with France, with the dream of reviving English claims to the French crown. The first of two short wars was wholly inglorious; the second produced two spectacular successes, one over the French at the Battle of the Spurs and the other over their Scots allies at the Battle of Flodden in the same year, 1513. These successes had been largely due to the administrative ability shown by Wolsey as victualler to the forces. Wolsey was also responsible for diplomatic negotiations which led to peace in 1514.

This brief experience of active kingship was enough for the time being for King Henry. For the next twenty years he was content to leave detailed direction of domestic and foreign policy to his loyal servant, whom he made successively Archbishop of York and Lord Chancellor.

Wolsey and the Papacy

The peace which Wolsey arranged in 1514 did not last long. By 1516 there were three young men ruling respectively in France (Francis I), in Spain (Charles I, later Emperor Charles V) and in England, all of them ambitious and each to some extent jealous of the others.

The fiercest rivalry was between Charles and Francis, and their battlefield was Italy. This involved the papacy in their contest, for the Popes were secular Italian rulers. As such they had no desire to see either France or Spain too powerful in Italy.

Papal support swung to and fro between the rivals as the fortunes of war varied. Wolsey's policy shifted with that of the papacy, in the hope that by championing papal power in Italy his services might one day be rewarded by election to supreme office in the Church. If that day came, Wolsey was anxious that papal sovereignty should be a reality rather than a shadow. Henry VIII's support was given to Wolsey partly out of jealousy of Francis I, partly (up to 1527) to support Queen Catherine's nephew, Charles, and partly (after 1527) in the hope that the Pope would grant that dissolution of marriage which Henry was by then seeking. When this hope finally had to be abandoned, Wolsey and the king no longer saw eye to eye and Wolsey's supremacy came to an end.

Nevertheless, so long as he had the king's favour Wolsey persisted. When Francis I had overwhelmed Spain in 1515 at the Battle of Marignano in Italy, Wolsey sought to organize an anti-French coalition of the papacy, Venice, Spain and the Empire, an effort rendered useless when Francis I and Charles signed the Treaty of Noyon in 1516.

Still with his eye on the papacy, Wolsey tried to turn this new situation to his advantage. He negotiated an alliance between England, France and Spain in 1518, officially for the purpose of checking the growth of Turkish power in western Europe. Wolsey hoped that by uniting these Christian kings against the Mohammedan Turks he would stand out in the eyes of all churchmen, and in those of the College of Cardinals in particular, as champion of the Faith. At the same time, an anti-Turkish venture would divert the energies of France and Spain from Italy, thereby removing a potential threat to the temporal power of the papacy. On both counts he hoped to enhance his chances of election as pope when the office fell vacant.

Almost at once his hopes were destroyed. Charles I of Spain was elected Holy Roman Emperor as Charles V. Francis I, the defeated candidate in the election, now found Hapsburg power threatening to encircle his country. Conflict was bound to be renewed, and both parties courted English support.

Failure of Wolsey's Foreign Policy

Henry and Wolsey parleyed with both Charles and Francis. Henry met the latter at the Field of the Cloth of Gold in 1520, avoided committing himself to an alliance, and moved elsewhere to explore the possibilities of joint action with Spain. Wolsey, hoping that Charles would ensure his succession to the papacy, persuaded Henry to form an alliance with Charles; Henry agreed, and war with France followed.

Militarily and diplomatically it was a failure. There were no English victories to celebrate; the papacy fell vacant and Wolsey was not elected; the English parliament and people resented the taxation involved; the Scots invaded the north of England; and imperial troops sacked Rome. Promptly Wolsey switched from alliance with Charles to one with Francis.

No sooner had he done so, largely because the Pope was virtually a prisoner in Charles' hands, than again circumstances worked against him. The Pope came to terms with Charles, and Charles came to terms with Francis in the Peace of Cambrai, 1529. Henry VIII realized that the Pope neither could nor would annul the marriage of his ally's aunt. England was isolated in Europe; Wolsey was dismissed from office and died a few months later.

Panelling from the Court of Star Chamber, now in Windsor Castle.

The Importance of Wolsey

Wolsey, the last great ecclesiastical statesman in the medieval tradition, continued the work of Henry VII in strengthening the rule of law and order and in enforcing the king's peace. He laid the foundations of royal absolutism by subordinating Church law to state law, by subordinating common law to special royal courts, and by the aggrandizement of the Court of Star Chamber as a means of by-passing normal legal channels, thus enforcing the king's will and carrying out the king's policy.

Wolsey unintentionally prepared the way for the Reformation: he alienated the king from the papacy by his failure to persuade the Pope to agree to the king's wishes concerning the annulment of Henry's marriage to Catherine; he alienated the English clergy from the papacy by using his delegated papal authority to encroach on the privileges of the Church in England. His failure to carry out much-needed reforms in the Church, and his own bad example as a churchman, turned many people from the Church.

QUESTIONS

1. Explain what services Wolsey rendered to his king and account for his fall from power.

2. What did Wolsey accomplish in the administration of justice?

CHAPTER 17

HENRY VIII AND THE REFORMATION IN ENGLAND

WE HAVE seen in the previous chapter that Henry VIII's matrimonial problems had a decisive influence on Wolsey's policy and career. These problems we must now examine for out of them grew important changes in the religious life of the country.

The Succession Problem

Soon after his accession, Henry VIII married, for state reasons and influenced by his late father's wishes, Catherine of Aragon, widow of his elder brother Arthur. By 1525 it was obvious that the queen would bear no more children, and the only one who had survived was a girl, Mary. The king was afraid that, if the heir to the throne was a girl, the succession might be disputed and the troubles of the previous century repeated. He must, he felt, find a way of freeing himself from Catherine so that he could re-marry and produce a male heir.

At the time of his marriage there had been doubt whether a man might according to the rules of the Church, marry his brother's widow. Those doubts were thought to have been resolved by a papal dispensation. In 1525 however Henry's doubts revived. Was it not a sign of God's displeasure that no son had been born of the marriage? Had there not always been some churchmen who had questioned the Pope's power to grant that dispensation on which he had relied? Could it be that Catherine and Henry were not truly married? The question gradually became a conviction in Henry's mind, especially after his eye fell on Anne Boleyn.

Efforts for a Papal Solution

There was a simple solution to the problem in Henry's mind. One Pope had pronounced the marriage valid; another must now be persuaded to say that his predecessor was mistaken. Wolsey was told to arrange matters.

Thus in 1527, with his prior consent, Henry was summoned to appear before Wolsey's Legatine Court to explain why he was living in sin with his brother's widow. Henry, it was arranged, would plead guilty, the court would find that the marriage had never been valid, and the Pope would confirm the court's decision. However, while Catherine offered strenuous opposition, the Pope fell a virtual prisoner into the hands of her nephew Charles V with the result that the first attempt to solve the problem legally came to nothing.

By the next year the Pope was his own master again and had to yield to Wolsey's pressure to appoint a commission to consider Henry's predicament. Wolsey and Cardinal Campeggio were the commissioners, but the latter had secret instructions to delay a decision, and did so. The hearing was adjourned in 1529 and never resumed, Pope and Emperor having resumed their friendship at the Peace of Cambrai. All hope of securing a decree of nullity with papal consent had to be abandoned, and Wolsey, chief author of this solution, lost the king's confidence and was deprived of power.

Threats to Force the Pope's Hand

From 1529 to 1532 the policy was to frighten the Pope into compliance by attacking his power over the Church in England. Wolsey's years of supremacy had fed the fires of anti-clericalism, and the king decided to encourage them to burn. In 1529 he summoned the parliament which has become known as the Reformation Parliament, and gave it every encouragement to attack Church abuses and papal power in England. At the same time he canvassed university opinion on the validity of his marriage; majority opinion was on the king's side. When these steps were not enough to induce the Pope to conform to his wishes, Henry attacked him through the English clergy by declaring them guilty of breaking the Statute of Praemunire when they accepted Wolsey's Legatine authority. Since this could mean confiscation of clerical wealth and possessions, the clergy purchased pardon by paying the king £100,000 as a fine and by recognizing him as Head of the Church in England "as far as the law of Christ will allow."

Yet in spite of these threats the Pope remained adamant. In 1532 he formally forbad Henry to contract a second marriage, his only concession being to refrain from declaring the first marriage lawful; the king was thwarted, but he remained determined.

Break with Rome

It was at this point that the king found another loyal servant, Thomas Cromwell, to replace Wolsey. Cromwell was prepared to lead the king towards a more radical solution of his difficulties than had yet been tried, the destruction of papal authority over the Church in England. Parliament was only too ready to support such a policy.

The Reformation Parliament resumed work. In 1532 it enacted that Convocation should not legislate for Church affairs without the king's permission. Payment of annates to the papacy was suspended until the Pope submitted to the king's wishes. In 1533, though with the Pope's approval, a new Archbishop of Canterbury was appointed, known to be sympathetic to the Continental reform movement; this was Thomas Cranmer. In the same year Parliament declared appeals to Rome illegal, and this enabled Henry to seek the opinion of Convocation on the validity of his marriage. Convocation pronounced against the marriage of Henry and Catherine. Henry, already secretly married to Anne Boleyn, had her crowned as queen, and a baby was born to them—unfortunately (from Henry's point of view) another girl, Elizabeth.

The Pope reacted to this destruction of his authority in England by declaring Henry excommunicate; the king counteracted by confirming non-payment not only of annates but also of Peter's Pence and all other revenues. The political break with Rome was complete.

Subordination of Church to State

In this same year, 1534, Parliament declared that all archbishops and bishops in England were to be elected on the king's nomination alone. Convocation was not to meet save when summoned by the king and succession to the throne was vested in the children of Henry and Anne Boleyn; Mary, since her mother's marriage was invalid, was regarded as illegitimate. Finally, in this fateful year 1534, the king was declared Supreme Head of the Church of England without any saving qualification, and shortly thereafter all clerics and Crown servants were required to take an oath recognizing him as such.

A revolution had been peacefully accomplished; the Church in England had become the Church of England. It was not however as yet "reformation" so much as assertion of the control of Church by state—subordination of the former to the latter.

Dissolution of the Monasteries

The work of the Reformation Parliament did not end with subordination of Church to state. One pocket of papal influence remained, namely the monasteries. Their heads had always owed direct allegiance in spiritual matters to the papacy. This exception to the king's supremacy could no longer be tolerated, and the monasteries were in no position to defend themselves.

Diocesan bishops had no great love for them, since the monasteries were outside their jurisdiction. Government and lay magnates envied their wealth. Monastic ideals were seldom exemplified in the lives of those pledged to them; spiritually monasticism was dead. As landlords, abbots were no more tender towards tenants than were laymen. Apart from some contribution to education and the wool trade, monasteries no longer performed the social services that they had once offered. Deprived of papal protection, they were an easy target for government attack.

Cromwell, architect of the king's victory over Rome, was appointed Vicar-General, an office which made him directly responsible for Church affairs, although he was a layman. He immediately issued orders for a visitation of the monasteries. His commissioners knew what he wanted, and by reporting only deficiencies and abuses they produced a formidable indictment of the institutions they visited. On the strength of these reports Parliament had no hesitation in suppressing the smaller monasteries in 1536, and abbots of the larger houses acquiesced in the vain hope that their institutions would be left alone.

Ineffective Opposition to the Reformation Parliament

Dissolution of the smaller monasteries was followed by dissolution of the Reformation Parliament itself. It had been a ready tool in the hands of the king since his schemes suited the mood of the country.

For this reason changes effected between 1532 and 1536 aroused little opposition. It is true that an emotionally unbalanced girl, the Maid of Kent, had been encouraged to confront the king in person and denounce his second marriage on moral grounds; she forfeited her head. So, in 1535, did Bishop Fisher and Sir Thomas More, when on conscientious grounds they refused the oath recognizing the king's supremacy.

More general opposition, fundamentally economic in origin, was brought to a head by dissolution of the smaller monasteries. There were risings in Lincolnshire and Yorkshire; that led by Robert Aske, in Yorkshire, was known as the Pilgrimage of Grace. Both risings were pro-monastic and anti-Cromwell rather than anti-king, but Henry was not the man to recognize distinctions of this kind. After temporizing until he felt sure of his position, he firmly repressed these rebellions; their leaders were executed, and the Council of the North was charged with preventing similar demonstrations.

Suppression of the Larger Monasteries and Results of the Dissolution

Some monks from larger monasteries having been involved in the futile risings of 1536, the government was provided with an excuse for the final suppression of monasticism. Parliament was summoned again, and in 1539 the remaining monasteries were dissolved.

With them went the last vestiges of papal authority in the religious life of the country. The Crown was enriched, monastic land and wealth passing to the king, and only a negligible fraction of it being devoted to pensions for the dispossessed or to the foundation of schools and colleges. Some land was sold, so many now had a vested interest in the revolution. Ecclesiastical influence in parliament was diminished by the disappearance of the mitred abbots from the House of Lords. Finally, a more rational church administration was established by the creation of six new episcopal dioceses. Such were the immediate results of the dissolution of the monasteries; the long-term economic consequences belong to a later chapter of history.

May Day celebrations in the early sixteenth century.

Controversy on Church Doctrine

Papal power having been destroyed, the vexed problem of his marriage settled, and Church subordinated to State, Henry VIII had no further quarrel with Roman Catholicism. In 1521 he had refuted the teachings of the German Protestant reformer, Martin Luther, and had been rewarded with the title Defender of the Faith; his beliefs, apart from papal supremacy, remained the same in 1539. He had sought to make his position clear in 1536 when, at his request, parliament approved the Ten Articles. These re-affirmed the Catholic view on Holy Communion and Salvation, and only leaned towards Protestantism in their emphasis on the Bible as the source of doctrine.

Cromwell and Cranmer were more sympathetic towards new teachings than was the king. Cromwell issued injunctions against "Popish Practices," as a result of which centres of pilgrimage were attacked and images destroyed. The Great Bible produced under Cranmer, a translation of the Scriptures into

English, had Protestant leanings, and this version was ordered to be read in churches in 1538. The "reformation" party of Cromwell and Cranmer had strong opponents whose influence led in 1539 to the enactment of the Statutes of the Six Articles, the famous "whip with six strings," which re-asserted the essentials of Catholic doctrine and made denial of them punishable by death.

Although the Reformation had thus begun in the reign of Henry VIII, it had by no means finished, even though the six articles were enforced for little more than a year. The completion of the doctrinal reformation proved in fact to require another twenty years.

Causes of the Reformation

Though the consequences of Henry VIII's succession and marriage problems were closely connected with the Reformation it would be wrong to think that these were the sole, or even the main, causes of religious changes. There was, for example, strong anti-papist, anti-clerical feeling in the country, caused partly by the obvious wealth of the Church and by the heavy financial demands which the Church made, for payment of Annates (the first year's revenue of an ecclesiastical benefice, paid to the papacy), Peter's Pence (an ecclesiastical tax in England, also paid to the papacy), Tithes (a tax of one-tenth of everyone's income, which had to be paid to the parish priest), and Probate (a fee payable on the proving of a will). The common people disliked the extent of ecclesiastical jurisdiction, because the procedure in Church courts was slow, expensive and corrupt; but many legal matters came under Church control, for example marriage settlements and disputed wills. In addition to the obviously wealthy men of the Church, commoners resented the many ignorant and worldly parish priests who were unequal to their tasks. The clergy had certain special privileges; they were in some cases exempted from trial by a secular court, and as we have seen, ecclesiastical courts were corrupt. Certain ecclesiastical property was outside the royal jurisdiction, and criminals could gain sanctuary there.

All these causes for discontent were the original basis for the Reformation in England, and the continental reformation movement and new Renaissance outlook came later, to influence the already-existing movement.

Religious Change and Foreign Policy

England's greatest danger during this period was that the Catholic powers, France and Spain, would attack England in order to restore papal authority.

Henry had a choice of policy: he could either maintain England's isolation and avoid any foreign alliance, which was what he personally would have preferred to do; or he could make an alliance with an anti-papal power, for example the German Lutheran states, which was Cromwell's policy.

Henry maintained an alliance with France against Charles V until 1533, when France began to show disapproval of the break with Rome. For the next two years, overtures were made to the German Lutherans, but without result. In 1536, an approach was made to the Catholic Emperor Charles V, who was at that time on bad terms with France, but a year later Charles was reconciled with France, and England renewed her approaches to the German Lutherans.

In 1540 Cromwell negotiated an alliance with the Duke of Cleves, and Henry VIII married Anne of Cleves only to divorce her almost immediately, and Cromwell was beheaded later in the same year. In 1543 England made war on France, but failed to prevent negotiations for the marriage of Mary Queen of Scots to the French heir. Henry died in 1547, while preparations were being made for a fresh attack on France.

Wales, Ireland and Scotland

While so largely occupied with matrimonial adventure and religious change, Henry VIII did not neglect the challenge presented by Welsh, Irish and Scottish affairs.

In 1536 Wales was incorporated with England. Welshmen were henceforth to have the same rights as Englishmen, and English land laws were to apply equally to Wales. In 1543 Wales was divided into twelve counties, and arrangements were made for Welsh counties and boroughs to be represented in parliament.

Henry assumed the title King of Ireland, and imposed the English land laws, judicial system and language on the Irish. He forced Irish recognition of his supremacy in the Church, dissolved the monasteries, and used their wealth to create a vested interest of laymen in the new order, as he had done in England. This Anglicanization of Ireland led to serious problems later.

Henry began war with Scotland, anticipating a Scottish invasion to restore papal authority. He defeated the Scots in 1542 at Solway Moss. Then James V of Scotland died, and his heir was the six-day-old infant Mary, so Henry demanded the crown of Scotland; he also negotiated the preliminaries of a marriage treaty between Mary and his own son, Edward. The Scottish regent repudiated this treaty, however, and Henry angrily attacked Scotland ("the English Wooing"), capturing Edinburgh in 1544. The regent of Scotland arranged a marriage treaty with France, whither Mary was sent for several years, with a view to her eventual marriage to the French heir. This arrangement strengthened the ties between France and Scotland. Henry made peace with the Scots in 1546, as part of a peace with France.

QUESTIONS

1. Describe how Henry VIII dealt with the problems facing him after 1529.
2. Why and how did Henry VIII break away from the Church of Rome? Was Henry a Protestant?

CHAPTER 18

EDWARD VI AND MARY: FACTION AND REACTION

THE system of strong central government dependent on the monarchy, built up by the first two Tudors, faced a severe test on the death of Henry VIII. His successor was a sickly boy, and there were ambitious men in the Privy Council. Might not the civil conflict of the fifteenth century begin again?

Henry VIII had always been sensitive to this possibility. As far as he could, he had sought to provide against it, first by his matrimonial adventures, and at the end of his life by securing parliamentary approval to his determination of the succession.

His will left the succession to his three surviving children, beginning with his son Edward. Until Edward was of age to assume personal power, administration was to be in the hands of a Privy Council, all its members equal in power and authority.

This last proviso was an unworkable one which immediately broke down when the Council recognized the young king's uncle, the Duke of Somerset, as Protector. He was a man of unusual character for his times: ambitious but not ruthless, aloof towards equals but sympathetic to the poor, a well-intentioned idealist but an inefficient administrator, a competent army commander but an inept politician.

Inevitably he proved no match for his rival, the Duke of Northumberland, whose ambition knew no bounds. Northumberland was unscrupulous, prepared to exploit all causes for personal advantage, oppressive towards the poor, but in intrigue and administration he far surpassed Somerset. For the moment he had to watch, while Somerset assumed responsibility for the government of the country.

Somerset's Problems and Attempted Solutions

That responsibility was heavy. England was at war with Scotland; the nation was divided on the question of religion; the government was Protestant in its subordination of Church to State, but Catholic in doctrine; the falling value of money, rising prices, the enclosure of common and church land and the change from arable to pastoral farming created unemployment, and that in turn created discontent.

Somerset's approach to these problems lacked thoroughness. He decisively

Derest Uncle by your lettres and reporte of the messenger, we have at good length understanded to our great comfort, the good succese, it hathe pleased god to graunt us against the Scottes by your good courage and wise forsight, for the wich and other the benefites of god heaped upon us, like as we ar most bounden to yeld him most humble thankes, and to seke bi al waies we mai his true honour, So do we give unto you, good Uncle our most hartie thankes, praying you to thanke also most hartelie in our name, our good Cosin therle of Warwike, and all the othere of the noble men, gentlemen, and others that have served in this iournei, of whose service they shall all be well assured, we will not (god graunte us lief) shew our selfes unmindful, but be redy ever to consider the same as anie occasion shall serue. yeuen at our house of Otlandes, the eightenth of Septem ber.

your good neuew
Edward

Letter from Edward VI to Somerset after the Battle of Pinkie.

defeated the Scots at the Battle of Pinkie in 1547, but abandoned Henry VIII's policy of seeking to unite the crowns of the two countries and to destroy the Franco-Scottish alliance. Mary Queen of Scots married the Dauphin of France, later Francis II.

In religious matters Somerset carried the country further towards Protestantism, but by no means all the way. Parliament in 1547 repealed the Statute of Six Articles, and sanctioned the marriage of clergy. In the same year the chantries (small foundations for educational or religious purposes) were dissolved and their endowments taken into the Treasury and sold to wealthy laymen, though a very small portion was used for the foundation of a few grammar schools. Gardiner, Bishop of Winchester, the chief defender of Catholicism, was removed from the Council and sent to the Tower. In 1549 the First Prayer Book was issued. This was ambiguous in its definition of doctrine, but it simplified ritual; its use in all churches was made compulsory by the Act of Uniformity of 1549. All this displeased Catholics without satisfying Protestants. His approach to social problems was Somerset's final undoing. He sympathized with the grievances of the poor, and when landowners in parliament refused to pass laws against enclosure and condemned vagrants to slavery, Somerset in 1548 forced the Council to condemn enclosure and to send out commissioners to investigate the situation. When active rebellion broke out in the west, he left its suppression to others.

His sympathy with social hardship earned Somerset much popular support, but lost him the trust of his fellow councillors. He was arrested and imprisoned. Northumberland, who replaced him and indeed secured his release, was for almost two years unable to take further action against him. Not until 1552 did Northumberland feel strong enough to have him executed on an insubstantial charge of treason.

Northumberland's Administration

There are signs that, given time, Northumberland might have effectively restored the weakening financial administration of the country, in spite of his ruthless defence of the interests of the land-owning nobility. His tenure of office was brief, however, and his efforts were devoted to building up a solid group of supporters. To this end, and not from conviction, he identified himself with the Protestant cause and pushed ahead with religious changes.

Catholic bishops such as Gardiner and Bonner were deprived of their sees and replaced by such Protestant zealots as Hooper and Ridley. In 1550 minor clerical orders were abolished, and next year the Catholic doctrine of transubstantiation was formally rejected. Communion tables replaced altars; images and stained glass windows were destroyed. In 1552 a Second Prayer Book, more uncompromisingly Protestant in doctrine, was issued and made compulsory by the second Act of Uniformity. Finally, church doctrine was defined in forty-two articles which rejected Catholic teaching and accepted the Protestant standpoint. The Reformation had triumphed in England.

This triumph was no sooner achieved than it was threatened, for the young king's health was increasingly precarious. To save himself, Northumberland must save Protestantism; and since the Catholic Princess Mary was next in line to the throne, the succession must be diverted elsewhere.

Northumberland persuaded Edward VI to bastardize his half-sisters, and to will the succession to Lady Jane Grey, Northumberland's daughter-in-law. The king died; Lady Jane was proclaimed in London; and Mary fled to Catholic Norfolk and was proclaimed there.

Northumberland hurried off to suppress the Marian faction in Norfolk; but free of his power and influence in London, the Privy Council drew back from the prospect of civil war, and proclaimed its allegiance to Mary. When this news reached Norfolk, Northumberland tried to save himself by supporting Mary, but it was too late. He and his son and daughter-in-law were imprisoned and finally executed.

Marian Reaction

Catholic though she was, Mary was Henry VIII's daughter. The first two Tudors had done their work so well that loyalty to the dynasty outweighed loyalty to the Reformation. London and the landowners apart, national sympathies were still anti-clerical rather than pro-Protestant.

Mary began with almost everything in her favour. Majority opinion would have been content with a state-controlled church teaching Catholic doctrine and practising the old forms of worship. The silent dignity with which Mary and her mother had accepted the humiliations heaped upon them in the reign of Henry VIII had won admiration and sympathy from the people. The recent attempt to make England fully Protestant had brought the country to the verge of civil war, and this had not made the cause of the Reformers popular; Mary clearly was.

Her first measures chimed well with the mood of the nation. Catholic Bishop Gardiner was released from the Tower; Protestant Cranmer became a prisoner there. Gardiner became Lord Chancellor and Edward's Protestant bishops were deposed. Edward's prayer books were suppressed, his Acts of Uniformity repealed. Married clergy were expelled from their livings and Mass was once more celebrated in England. The religious situation was what it had been in the last years of Henry VIII, and the nation was satisfied.

Marian Persecution

Mary, however, was not. All that had been done she had accomplished by virtue of her position as Head of the Church, with parliamentary legislation. She achieved this by using a power which she did not believe rightfully hers; she wanted to bring the English church back to papal allegiance, to restore church lands filched by greedy laymen and to unite herself in marriage to the great Catholic state of the day, Spain. When her acts revealed these hopes, Mary's popularity waned.

In some of these ambitions Mary was more papal than the Pope. Both he and the Emperor Charles V realized better than Mary that there were limits in undoing the Reformation beyond which even a Tudor could not go. The Pope sent Cardinal Pole as Legate to England with power to grant the nation absolution, in the hope that Mary would be satisfied. She was not, but she met defeat; parliament refused to restore Church lands, and only grudgingly restored the payment of annates to Rome. Mary persisted with the Spanish marriage in spite of parliamentary opposition, the anger of the people, and a rebellion led by Sir Thomas Wyatt in 1554. It was not a happy match. Her husband soon became Philip II of Spain and left his wife for his native country, making thereafter only one short return visit. The marriage failed to produce what the queen dearly wanted, an heir to perpetuate the Catholic faith in England.

Frustration, disappointment and disease made Mary bitter and stubborn. With the encouragement of Gardiner and Bonner she embarked on a policy of persecution. Henry IV's statute for burning heretics was re-enacted in 1555, and Bishops Hooper, Ridley and Latimer were among its first victims. Cranmer was taken from the Tower to martyrdom, and altogether three hundred people died for their faith. It was a highly unpopular policy which had the opposite effect to that which Mary had intended. Far from frightening the nation into fervent Catholicism, it turned the nation to genuine Protestantism. Catholicism was for the next two centuries a hated cause. How long Mary could have maintained the persecution and held her throne, we shall never know. In 1558 Mary was to die, and her half-sister Elizabeth, product of their father's breach with Rome, to reign in her stead. The Marian reaction was destined to fail and the Reformation was to be secure.

Parliamentary Opposition to the Crown

If the Reformation later emerged strengthened from the Marian Persecution the Crown did not. Henry VIII had taught parliament to share in government when he unleashed it against the Pope. Somerset and Northumberland had had to rely upon it for support. It began to practise the lessons thus learned at the Crown's expense under Mary. Her first parliament in 1553 made plain its opposition to the restitution of Church lands, and protested against the Spanish marriage. Her second parliament in 1554 opposed the revival of heresy laws and offended Mary by limiting the powers in England of her Spanish husband. The third parliament in 1554 was more co-operative, the government having exercised some influence on the elections. The last parliament showed its resentment of this fact by discussing, though it did not enact, a bill to exclude from membership all office-holders under the Crown, for these could always be relied upon to support Crown policy. The effectiveness of this opposition was seen in the last days of the reign when Mary had recourse to a forced loan to raise supplies for the French war of 1558. Clouds of a later conflict between Crown and parliament were as yet no bigger than a man's hand, but they were there.

Foreign Affairs, 1547-58

The truce with France, established by Henry VIII in 1546, was broken when Somerset declared war on France as a consequence of the marriage of Mary Queen of Scots to the Dauphin; but Somerset failed to secure an alliance with the Emperor, and Northumberland made peace, surrendering Boulogne to the French.

The projected marriage between Mary Tudor and Philip of Spain would have secured an English alliance with Spain, thus balancing the alliance between France and Scotland. As Spain controlled Flanders, such an alliance would also have benefited the English wool trade. The marriage was nevertheless unpopular: Spain refused to allow English merchants to trade with Spanish possessions in South America; many people felt that England might be reduced to a mere appendage of Spain, and become involved in continental wars which served only the interests of Spain.

So unpopular was the proposed marriage alliance with Spain that in 1554 Sir Thomas Wyatt led a rebellion against it. He aimed to make Elizabeth

Court of Wards and Liveries in the sixteenth century.

queen in Mary's place, and to marry her to Edward Courtenay, great-grandson of Edward IV. Courtenay betrayed the plot, however, and the rebellion was suppressed. Elizabeth was sent to the Tower for a time, and the rebellion was made the excuse for executing Lady Jane Grey and her husband, although neither of them was involved.

When the marriage treaty was drawn up, certain safeguards were included. Philip, although he was to have the title of King, was not to be crowned, and would have no powers in England. Any child of the marriage was barred from ruling Spain and England at the same time. But the queen's hopes of an heir to continue the Catholic faith in England were not fulfilled, and Philip was soon kept abroad by his duties as King of Spain. As a consequence of the marriage, England became involved in renewed war with France.

Philip had quarrelled with Pope Paul IV about certain Italian issues, and the Pope invoked French help in a war against Spain. Philip asked Mary for English help against France, and this led to the French capturing England's last remaining French possession, Calais, in 1558.

QUESTIONS

1. Trace the course of religious change in England, from the fall of Thomas Cromwell to the death of Edward VI.

2. How do you account for the popularity of Mary Tudor at the beginning of her reign, and her unpopularity at the end of it?

CHAPTER 19

ECONOMIC AND SOCIAL CHANGE IN THE TUDOR AGE

INNOVATION in religion was not the only break with the past in the Tudor period; changes in economic and social life were almost equally important and these two "revolutions" were not unconnected.

Much land passed into the Crown's possession at the dissolution of the monasteries; more was seized from the dioceses in the reign of Edward VI when Catholic bishops were replaced by Protestant bishops. Some of this land was wisely used for educational endowments, some for resettlement of displaced clergy and some was retained by the Crown; but most of it was sold to wealthy merchants or given to the lay nobility.

Rising Prices and Rents

All buyers were not members of the aristocracy. The flow of precious metal from the new world led to a rise in prices, more marked on the continent than in England. English merchants engaged in the profitable Flanders wool trade accumulated capital. Since social position depended largely on land ownership, many merchants were prepared to invest surplus profit in land, to raise their social status. Wanting a profit on this investment, they began to raise the rents of tenants on the land they bought.

Rising prices compelled established landowners to follow the example of these new men. The old rents no longer enabled the landed gentry to maintain their accustomed standards of living. They welcomed the opportunity which availability of Church property gave them of increasing their estates, and they also raised rents.

The Crown was adversely affected by this rise in prices, for it derived its income from fixed revenues on land sublet to tenants. As nominal protector of its subjects, the Crown could not resort to rent-raising to the same extent as other landowners. Instead Henry VIII reduced the amount of precious metal in the coinage, and with the silver saved he minted additional money. While this expedient temporarily increased his income by increasing the amount of money in circulation, it only served to add to the difficulty created by the influx of silver from abroad, and thus led to a further rise in prices. Debasement of the coinage was not a remedy for financial problems; it merely aggravated them.

Increasing lack of adequate revenue threw Tudor monarchs after Henry

VIII back either upon illegal devices such as forced loans, excessive fines and the like, or upon parliament for money raised by taxation. By the reign of Elizabeth, parliament, dominated by the gentry who had found other ways of surmounting the financial difficulties of the time, was beginning to realize the strength of its position. Never very willing to sanction taxes, it was more unwilling to do so when these taxes were to be used in furtherance of policies it disliked. This increasing financial dependence of Crown on parliament made it possible for the latter in Mary's reign to refuse to return Church lands at her bidding, and in Elizabeth's reign to dare to advise her to marry and even to suggest possible husbands. The resulting angry exchanges between the last of the Tudors and her parliaments were omens of the bitter conflict to come between the first Stuarts and their parliaments.

New Farming

Not merely did land find new owners; owners found new uses for land. Raising rents was only one way of making land more profitable; another was to grow less crops but keep more sheep. By this change from crops to animals, the same acreage could be tended by fewer men; and less labour meant less expense. Further, up to the mid-sixteenth century trade in wool was booming; profits from sheep-rearing were thus far higher than those from arable farming. When, in the latter half of the century, the wool trade was less prosperous, sheep still yielded a good profit when sold as meat.

Arable farming, where it continued, did not however stand still. Tentative use was made of marl as a means of improving the quality of lighter soils, though this did not become widespread until the eighteenth century. Cultivation of hops was developed in Kent, and horses gradually replaced oxen as farm draught animals.

Enclosures

The new farming could hardly have been carried out had the old medieval strip system of land allocation remained unchanged. It had already been modified in the previous century, and the process was carried further in the Tudor period. Large landowners concentrated their holding around their houses, sometimes for the purpose of pastoral farming, sometimes to create private park-lands for their enjoyment. Others went further and enclosed the "commons" of the village, to the distress and anger of the poor. It is however easy to exaggerate the distress thus caused. The enclosure movement of the sixteenth century was by no means universal throughout the country; it was mainly concentrated in the Midlands. The distress experienced by poorer people was in the main due to rising prices, but because this was not understood at the time, the enclosure movement received much unmerited blame.

The government understood the causes of social evils as little as did the victims. The state made strenuous efforts to check enclosures, believing that these were the root of all the trouble. In 1489 an act was passed restricting sheep-farming, and was enforced as far as possible by the Court of Star Chamber. Wolsey in 1517 instituted a review of all enclosures which had taken place since 1488; but, though many offenders were identified and fined, this review and similar later measures achieved very little. Many parliamentarians and magistrates were landowners, and were unco-operative to Crown and Council. Somerset's sympathy with the victims of enclosure was, as we have seen, a major factor in his fall from power.

Social Effects of Economic Changes

By the end of the Tudor period two effects arising from these economic changes were apparent. There had been a marked increase in the number of land-owning gentry. From the sixteenth to the mid-nineteenth century this social group dominated the country through its monopoly of parliamentary representation. In the second place there was an undoubted increase in the number of paupers, some unable to work, others unwilling to work, others genuinely unemployed, and some rogues and vagabonds.

Lavenham Guildhall has always had close connexions with the wool trade.

The Church, with varying effectiveness, had hitherto done something to mitigate the hardships of poverty. With the monasteries dissolved and the Church shorn of wealth, she was no longer able to serve in this way. Belatedly and reluctantly the State had to assume this responsibility.

Of the two outstanding pieces of legislation on this issue, the first was the Act of 1536 which distinguished between "sturdy beggar" and "impotent poor". The former was to be whipped, the latter to be provided for by collections made by the churchwardens on Sundays. The second piece of legislation was the Poor Law Code of 1601, by which each parish was responsible for its own poor. Overseers were to levy a poor rate to be used to relieve the needs of those unable to work, and to promote employment for those unemployed but able-bodied. Pauper children were to be apprenticed; the idle were to be compulsorily trained to work in Houses of Correction, parish institutions which were half prison, half workhouse. Rogues, vagabonds and sturdy beggars were to be whipped or branded and, if found outside their parish, to be returned there. The Poor Law was a harsh forerunner of the Welfare State of Elizabeth II, but it was an ancestor nonetheless.

Industrial Development During the Tudor Period

The opening of new markets overseas, in Africa and in America especially, led to increased industry at home. The end of the Venetian monopoly of trade with the Near East also encouraged English trade.

Protestant refugees from Europe brought new skills to England, and new industries developed; for example, glass manufacture brought over by the Huguenots. New machines, such as the stocking-frame, were invented and used. Some of the new industries needed coal, which now became increasingly important in manufacture.

The Gilds declined, but Livery Companies increased in power. Wool was still the main commodity around which trade centred, but the wool trade was increasingly dominated by middlemen. And in spite of the growth of industry, the majority of English men remained engaged in rural pursuits.

The Statute of Apprentices of 1563 was an attempt to organize labour, and laid down certain regulations. All able-bodied men not already employed were to work on the land, and hours of work were fixed, from 5 a.m. to 7.30 p.m. in summer, and from dawn to dusk in winter. Magistrates were empowered to fix local wage-rates with due regard to price levels. Seven-year apprenticeships for industrial training were enforced.

QUESTIONS

1. Describe the causes and effects of enclosure in Tudor times.
2. What effect did the Reformation have on the social and economic life of Tudor England?

CHAPTER 20

ELIZABETH I, ANGLICANS, CATHOLICS AND PURITANS

AT ELIZABETH'S accession in 1558, the most pressing problem was religion. The nation neither wished, nor after the Marian persecution expected, Anne Boleyn's daughter to perpetuate the return to Catholicism and its implied subordination to Spain. Country gentry enjoying possession of former church property made easy converts for the ardent reformers who came flooding back from continental exile when Mary died. To return to Henry VIII's compromise, a state Church which was Catholic in doctrine, was impossible in these circumstances; a new solution had to be found and this was to prove a major problem to Elizabeth.

Attitude of Queen and Parliament

Religion was an issue on which the queen, unlike her late half-sister, had no strong convictions, only prejudices. She was not prepared to tolerate Mass, but she liked candles and vestments. By appearing uncommitted, she hoped to lull the Catholic powers of Europe into the belief that England might yet be re-united with Rome by peaceful means. A conservative, ambiguous settlement would have suited her best, and her chief adviser, William Cecil, later Lord Burghley, was of the same mind.

Not so parliament. In the Commons there was an influential group of Protestant gentry; in the Lords vacant episcopal sees left the Catholic bishops of Mary's reign less effective in advocacy of the Roman cause. If it was to avoid a radically Protestant solution to the religious problem, the government had to act quickly. Even so, the laws passed committed Elizabeth further than she wished.

The Elizabethan Settlement

Parliament began by repealing the Catholic legislation of Mary's reign, and went on to pass two acts hastily drafted by the government. The first, the Act of Supremacy (1559), declared the sovereign Supreme Governor of the Church, required all clergy and officers of the Crown to acknowledge the queen as such by oath, and authorized her to delegate the exercise of her governorship to ecclesiastical commissioners.

The second measure, the Act of Uniformity (1559), re-introduced compulsory use of the Prayer Book of 1552, modified only by removal of the more insulting references to Catholicism. Church ritual could no longer be changed except by consent of Crown-in-Parliament.

By authorizing the queen to delegate her ecclesiastical powers and by legislating for Church ritual, parliament now shared with the Crown the power to determine Church affairs, a situation which Elizabeth resented, and which the Stuarts sought to reverse, with important constitutional results.

The Anglican Church

To the Anglican Church thus established, its own legislative body (Convocation) gave a defined body of doctrine in 1563 by reducing the forty-two articles of religion of Edward VI's reign to thirty-nine. Since these articles condemned such major Catholic doctrines as transubstantiation, justification by works and purgatory, and reduced the sacraments from seven to two, while permitting the marriage of the clergy and communion in both kinds, it was clear that the now-established Church was a Reformed Church. At the same time, since it continued to recognize the office of bishops and to use the ring in the marriage service and the sign of the cross in baptism as well as the cassock and surplice as clerical vestments, it was hoped that the new dispensation would look not too unlike the old. The government reinforced its hopes by the practical measure, incorporated in the Act of Uniformity, of making attendance at church compulsory on Sundays and Holy days under penalty of a fine of twelve pence for failure to do so.

Philip II of Spain was the husband of Mary Tudor, but in 1588 he launched the Armada against Elizabeth I and England.

The majority accepted this moderate degree of Protestantism, but extremists on both sides were dissatisfied. Devout Catholics could neither accept the queen's supremacy nor renounce the Mass; ardent Protestants, soon known as Puritans, found in church ritual and organization too many resemblances to the old Catholic form; and neither party was as yet reconciled to the notion of final defeat.

The Government and the Catholics

The government for some years showed considerable forbearance to both groups of extremists, but more particularly perhaps to the Roman Catholics. Such an attitude avoided giving excuse for foreign intervention on behalf of the old faith. There was the hope also that it would discourage plots against the queen's life, a hope by no means fulfilled. Nevertheless the government persisted; in 1563, when parliament made it a treasonable offence to refuse the Oath of Supremacy a second time, the queen ordered Archbishop Parker to refrain from administering the oath a second time to those who had already refused to take it. In such ways, a policy of leniency towards Roman Catholics was pursued up to 1571, but then the situation changed.

In 1570 Pope Pius V issued a Bull of Excommunication releasing English Roman Catholics from allegiance to their queen. Moreover priests trained abroad arrived secretly in the country, charged with encouraging Catholics in loyalty to their faith, and re-converting as many as possible who had accepted the Elizabethan settlement. The worst fears of the government were confirmed when a plot to assassinate the queen organized by a Florentine named Ridolfi was discovered by Cecil in 1571. Parliament reacted vigorously. An act was passed making it a treasonable offence to introduce a Papal Bull into England. In 1580 any attempt to convert the queen's subjects to Catholicism was declared treasonable. In 1581 the fine for non-attendance at church was increased to twenty pounds per month, while the fine for attending Mass was fixed at one hundred marks. Finally in 1585 Catholic priests, especially Jesuits, were expelled from the country. To be a Catholic priest was now in itself a capital offence.

For the rest of Elizabeth's reign, Catholics were subjected to persecution. Legally their crime was treason; but in fact they suffered torture, fines, imprisonment and death for their religion, few of them having designs on either the queen's life or the security of the state. The most that can be said in explanation of government policy is that the administration feared revolution and invasion, and that victims who paid the extreme penalty were not as numerous as those who had died for Protestantism in the previous reign.

The Government and the Puritans

Her advisers feared Catholics, but Elizabeth disliked Puritans. They were numerous among the lower clergy and more importantly among country gentry, from whom members of the House of Commons were mainly drawn. By constantly pressing for further reforms in the ritual and organization of the Church, the Puritans incurred the queen's anger; by so doing, they were, in her opinion, encroaching upon her prerogatives. Matters of religion, she maintained, were her exclusive concern. This the Puritan gentry in the Commons would not accept. Their pleas for discontinuance of

I

A Myrror for Martiniſts.

When I call to minde the graue ſentence of our ſauiour Chriſt, Wiſedome is iuſtified of her children, and doe beholde the miſerable contentions with which the Church of England at this day is ſo vexed and turmoiled by the children of follie, I cannot but on the one ſide condemne the late Martine libellers, and their fauorites, who hauing a bad cauſe, do as leudly handle the ſame: and on the other ſide miſlike ſome repliers, who notwithſtanding Math.11.19.

Part of one of the Martin Marprelate Tracts. These pamphlets widened the rift between Puritans and the Church of England.

the use of surplices, the ring in the marriage service and the sign of the cross in baptism, and for the institution of an elected ministry instead of episcopacy, seemed to the queen intolerable presumption. A proposal for the abolition of the episcopacy, and another in 1571 for reform of the prayer book, provoked Elizabeth into open avowal of opposition, and were in consequence defeated.

Since Puritans were likely neither to plot against her life nor to receive foreign aid, the queen was swifter to adopt repressive measures than she was to take such action against Catholicism. In 1565 Archbishop Parker, with the queen's ultimate approval, issued instructions enforcing use of the surplice. The result was suspension from their benefices of some London clergy who were not prepared to conform. In 1576 Grindal, who had succeeded Parker as Archbishop of Canterbury, was himself suspended from his duties because of his refusal to suppress meetings of the clergy for study of the Scriptures, largely attended by those of Puritan views.

Whitgift, who succeeded Grindal in 1583, was a more determined opponent of Puritanism. His Six Articles of that year required the clergy to acknowledge the supremacy of the Crown and to admit that the Prayer Book and Thirty-nine Articles contained nothing contrary to Scriptures; as a consequence, two hundred clergymen were suspended from duty. Henceforth anti-Puritan measures were vigorously enforced through the Court of High Commission, a body entrusted with the task because too many local magistrates were in sympathy with Puritanism and could not be relied upon to enforce the law.

So far Puritanism had been a reform movement within the Church. Having failed to win official support, it now became to some extent a separatist movement. Led by Henry Barrow and Robert Browne, some Puritans in Norwich set up independent congregations and became known as Congregationalists. They set forward their views in a series of pamphlets (1588-99) called *Martin Marprelate Tracts.* This challenge provoked the government into ruthless reprisals; there were some executions, and in 1593 the Conventicles Act made non-attendance at church or attendance at unauthorized "conventicles" punishable by exile or death. Temporarily the Puritans were muzzled.

The Crown and the Puritan Parliamentary Opposition

Apart from her dislike of their religious views, Elizabeth was angered by the way in which the Puritans tried to use parliament as a means of opposing her wishes and policy. When in 1566 Elizabeth ordered the Commons not to discuss her marriage or her successor, the Puritan Peter Wentworth asked whether such an order was not a breach of the privileges of the House. It was Wentworth again who in 1572 and 1575 asserted the right of free speech in parliament and protested against the queen's habit of seeking to influence parliamentary opinion by conveying messages through the Speaker. When in 1588 the queen intervened while parliament was discussing alteration of the Prayer Book, Wentworth questioned the right of anyone save parliament to alter the laws of the land, and even asked whether the queen was independent of parliament.

Wentworth paid the price of his temerity by imprisonment in the Tower; but Elizabeth did not dare to order Wentworth's execution as her father would have done. Elizabeth raged at these challenges to royal authority but had on occasions to admit defeat, as when in 1566 she withdrew her order forbidding discussion of her marriage. Further, the most stringent anti-Catholic laws were a reflection of the will of Parliament and Council rather than of the queen; just as the settlement of 1559 was more Protestant in tone as the result of Puritan opinion in the Commons than the queen would have wished.

Rebellion and Conspiracy

Parliament's sense of urgency about the queen's marriage is better understood if we examine in more detail the rebellions to which passing reference has already been made.

The Northern Rebellion of 1569 was caused by the survival of old feudal loyalties in the north of England, and by the strong Catholic feeling of the

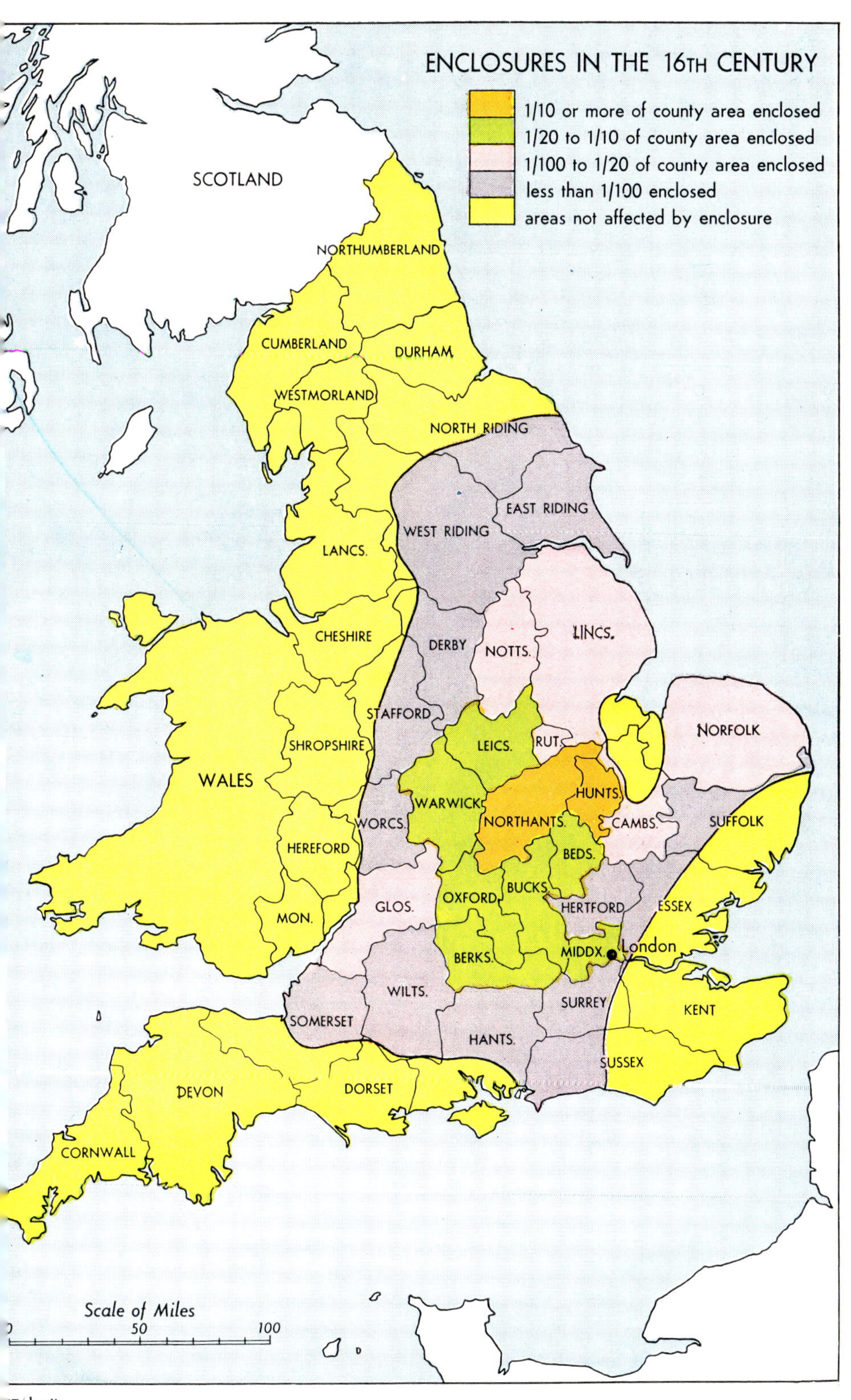

ENCLOSURES IN THE 16TH CENTURY
1/10 or more of county area enclosed
1/20 to 1/10 of county area enclosed
1/100 to 1/20 of county area enclosed
less than 1/100 enclosed
areas not affected by enclosure
SCOTLAND
NORTHUMBERLAND
CUMBERLAND
DURHAM
WESTMORLAND
NORTH RIDING
EAST RIDING
WEST RIDING
LANCS.
CHESHIRE
DERBY
NOTTS.
LINCS.
STAFFORD
SHROPSHIRE
LEICS.
RUT.
NORFOLK
WALES
WARWICK
NORTHANTS.
HUNTS.
CAMBS.
SUFFOLK
WORCS.
HEREFORD
BEDS.
BUCKS
OXFORD
HERTFORD
ESSEX
GLOS.
MON.
MIDDX.
London
BERKS.
WILTS.
SURREY
KENT
SOMERSET
HANTS.
SUSSEX
DEVON
DORSET
CORNWALL
Scale of Miles
50
100

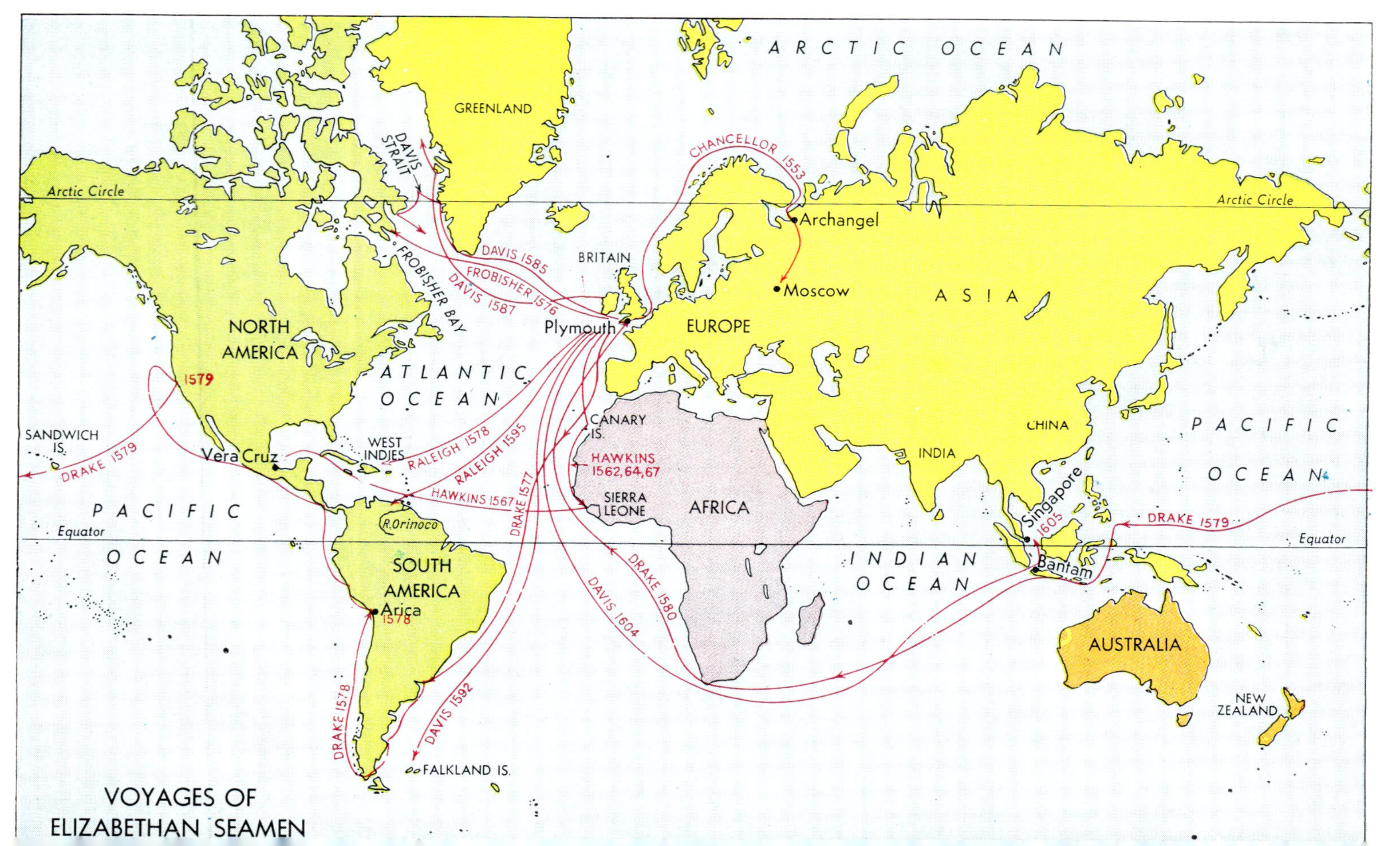

VOYAGES OF ELIZABETHAN SEAMEN

area. It was aggravated by the Duke of Norfolk's dislike of the growing influence of Lord Burghley.

With encouragement from the Duke of Norfolk, the earls of Westmorland and Northumberland agreed to raise troops in support of Mary Queen of Scots, against Elizabeth. Norfolk submitted on being summoned to London, but the earls captured Durham, heard Mass in the cathedral there, and burned copies of the English Prayer Book and Bible. They advanced as far as Tadcaster, but were then forced to retreat. The leaders fled to Scotland, but eight hundred rebels were caught and executed. The Northern Rebellion failed because Elizabeth gained the support of Murray, regent of Scotland, while Spain failed to give more than financial support to the rebels; moreover the rebellion did not gain support from other areas of England.

The Ridolfi Plot

The papal Bull of Excommunication against Elizabeth led to the Ridolfi Plot of 1571. Mary Queen of Scots and the Spanish intrigued to arrange the assassination of Elizabeth, to be followed by a Spanish invasion of England from the Netherlands, under the command of the Duke of Alva. While Philip of Spain and the Duke of Alva were still hesitating, Lord Burghley discovered the plot. The Spanish ambassador was expelled from England and the Duke of Norfolk was executed for treason. It was now that the introduction of a papal Bull was made illegal. Parliament demanded Mary Stuart's execution. England sought an alliance with France.

Strong Catholic feeling in Ireland, and the activities of an anti-English Jesuit mission, led to Desmond's Irish Rebellion in 1579. The rebellion was led by the Earl of Desmond, and a body of Italian troops supported him, but he was defeated and killed.

The Throckmorton Plot of 1583 was prompted by a new Spanish ambassador name Mendoza, who schemed with Philip of Spain, Francis Throckmorton and Mary Queen of Scots to put Mary on the English throne. The plot, discovered by Walsingham, led to the expulsion of Mendoza and the Jesuits from England.

The Babington Plot of 1586 also sought to replace Elizabeth by Mary Queen of Scots, and the conspirators included Anthony Babington, Father Ballard and Mary. This plot was discovered, and led to the trial and execution of Mary Queen of Scots.

QUESTIONS

1. Describe, and estimate the success of, Elizabeth's policy in dealing with
   (*a*) Puritans, and
   (*b*) Catholics.

2. Give an account of the attempts made to dethrone Elizabeth.

OCL/HIST/1—K*

CHAPTER 21

THE DANGER FROM FRANCE AND SCOTLAND

RELIGION was not the only problem which confronted Elizabeth on her accession in 1558; her relations with the two major powers of Europe, both Catholic, presented even greater difficulties.

Of these two powers, France and Spain, the former in 1558 seemed to offer the greater threat to English security. The strongly Catholic family of Guise had risen to power at the French court; they had married one of their number, Mary of Guise, to James V of Scotland, and she, now widow of James V, ruled Scotland as Regent for her daughter Mary Queen of Scots. In 1559 the Guise influence in France was further enhanced when Mary Queen of Scots became Queen of France on the accession of her husband Francis II. Further, this queen of Scotland and France was (as grand-daughter of Margaret Tudor) heir presumptive to the throne of England so long as Elizabeth remained unmarried and childless. In Catholic eyes her claim to the English throne was stronger than that of Elizabeth, tainted as the latter was with heresy and illegitimacy. English statesmen sincerely thought that they must reckon with the possibility that France might, under influence of the Guises and in the interests of a Catholic revival in England, seek to enforce Mary's claims either by force of arms or through the assassination of Elizabeth. Small wonder that they urged their queen to marry or to name her successor. It seemed to them that only her life stood between the country and war, international, civil or both. Should the French embark on an adventure of this kind, their path into England was clearly indicated, so long as Mary of Guise was Regent of Scotland or her daughter Queen.

The danger from Spain, though it could not be overlooked, was not quite so pressing; for though it was true that Philip II was the widower of Mary Tudor of England and had lately brought the long struggle in Italy between France and Spain to an end by the Peace of Cateau-Cambrésis, he had not yet adopted the role of political champion of Catholicism in Europe nor had he an ally within the British Isles, as had France.

Aims of Elizabeth's Foreign Policy

Parliament saw a solution to this dangerous situation in the queen's early marriage and the hope of an heir, but Elizabeth thought otherwise. Her marriage with either a French or a Spanish suitor would put England in pawn to one of these powers. Elizabeth's aim was at all costs to preserve England's independence. So long as the Catholic powers thought they saw a hope of reconverting England through marriage, they were not likely to resort to other methods. The prospect of a marriage alliance seemed to Elizabeth a better bargaining counter than fulfilment of a marriage contract. This consideration ruled out marriage to an Englishman as surely as it did to a foreigner. The aspirations of the Earls of Arundel or Leicester were as vain as those of the French Dukes of Anjou and Alençon.

Maintenance of peace was as dear to Elizabeth as preservation of independence. Peace would enable her religious settlement to win its way among the majority of her subjects. Peace would enable her to nurse the country's finances, avoid widening the gap between revenue and expenditure, and so reduce the frequency with which parliament must be humoured or bullied into granting special taxes. Elizabeth's frugality was not entirely the niggardliness of a mean woman; it was largely a political necessity.

Elizabeth's prospects of success in 1558 were brighter than Parliament thought. Though France and Spain had composed their differences, it was not likely that Spain would countenance a French attempt to extend her sphere of influence from Scotland to England. Such a development would tilt the balance of power too heavily to Spain's disadvantage. Moreover, France was on the brink of civil war over religion, and the nobility were not slow to exploit this situation when the crown passed to a succession of weak, childless kings whose interests had to be protected by the Queen Mother, Catherine de Medici.

Elizabeth I, from a silver medal commemorating the Armada.

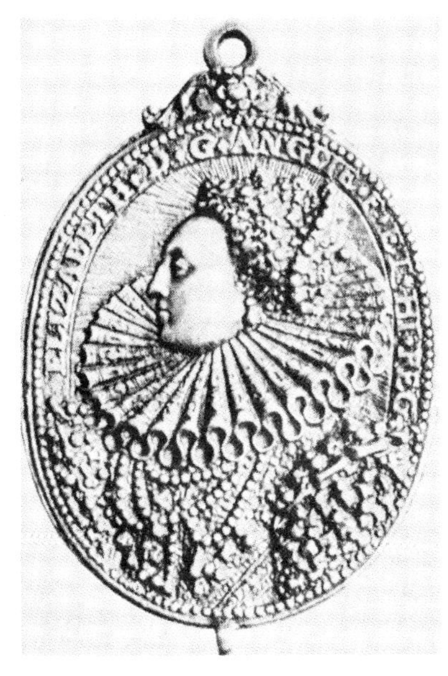

Spain, too was almost immediately faced with an acute problem when the Low Countries revolted and sought to achieve independence. With Philip II thus occupied, Elizabeth had few qualms about rejecting his proposal of marriage in 1559.

Situation in Scotland

In Scotland, too, Elizabeth was not without friends, for the country was divided by religion, the Reformation having made rapid progress under the leadership of John Knox and the Lords of the Congregation.

John Knox, Scottish Calvinist.

Until he was thirty years old, Knox was in Catholic orders. In 1544 he came into contact with a reformer, George Wishart, who was burned at the stake in 1546. In reply, Wishart's friends murdered Cardinal Beaton; and as one of them, Knox became a French galley slave for the next eighteen months. On his release, he returned to England and became chaplain to Edward VI. While Mary Tudor reigned, Knox travelled in France and Switzerland, where he became friendly with Calvin, leader of the reformation in Geneva and founder of Calvinism.

Knox returned to Scotland in 1559, and henceforth Scottish Protestantism became Calvinist in nature. A sermon by Knox in 1559 provoked mob violence against the Church in Scotland, and St. Andrew's cathedral was sacked in 1560.

The First Blast of the Trumpet against the Monstrous Regiment of Women, a famous tract by Knox, although directed against the Scottish regent, Mary of Guise, appeared just as Elizabeth succeeded to the throne of England; and since the tract argued that government by a woman was contrary to natural and divine law, it earned Knox the disapproval of the English queen. This personal feud was the more unfortunate since the Scottish Protestant party was, like Elizabeth, opposed to French influence in Scotland and was making good progress. Parliament rejected papal authority, declared Mass illegal, and dissolved monasteries. A Confession of Faith was adopted, defining Protestant doctrine for Scotland on the lines of Calvinism and replacing bishops and priests by elders or presbyters in Church administration. Moreover, the Lords of the Congregation had their eyes set on the expulsion of the Regent, Mary of Guise.

Initial Success and Failure

Elimination of French influence from Scotland was so clearly to Elizabeth's advantage that when the Lords of the Congregation led a revolt against the Regent, Elizabeth lent them aid by raising a loan on their behalf on the continent, sending troops to their assistance (though the latter made a poor showing at Leith), and despatching a fleet to the Forth. This latter contributed vitally to the rebels' success. The Regent's party surrendered, and by the Treaty of Edinburgh (1560) the French withdrew from Scotland and government was entrusted to a committee of twelve, the Earl of Murray subsequently becoming Regent.

The death of Francis II of France in the same year further weakened the links binding Scotland and France. One threat to Elizabeth's security had been appreciably diminished by the skill with which she had exploited the difficulties of potential enemies.

Elizabeth met with defeat, however, when she tried by the same methods to recover Calais from France. By 1562 France was in the first phase of her long wars of religion, and Elizabeth formed an alliance with the Huguenots (French Protestants). Catherine de Medici met this foreign intervention by temporarily persuading Huguenots and Catholics to make peace and join together to expel the invader. Elizabeth had strengthened rather than weakened the power she feared, and was no nearer recovering Calais.

Challenge of Mary Queen of Scots

In 1561, Mary Queen of Scots returned to Scotland. At first she made no attempt to challenge her Protestant subjects, but quickly showed her desire to be recognized as heir to the crown of England. She began by asking Elizabeth to name her as next in succession. When Elizabeth refused, Mary tried to exert pressure by marrying the Earl of Darnley, like herself a grandchild of Margaret Tudor. As a Catholic, Darnley might expect the support of co-religionists in England. In 1566 the claims of Mary and Darnley were united in their son, the future James VI of Scotland and James I of England. Alarmed, the English parliament once more urged Elizabeth to marry, but Elizabeth rejected their request, refused to name even the infant James as her heir, and continued to hope that time would provide a solution to her problems.

Time and Mary played for Elizabeth. Mary embarked upon a pro-Catholic policy in Scotland, and found herself at odds with her Protestant people and government. She tired of Darnley (not surprisingly, for he was by no means an estimable character), sought comfort from her secretary David Rizzio, and when her husband countenanced the murder of Rizzio, became party to the murder of her husband. Within months she married her lover, the Earl of Bothwell, generally believed to be the murderer of Darnley. Such conduct was more than her Calvinist subjects could tolerate. A revolt headed by the Earl of Murray led to the defeat of the Marian faction at Carberry Hill and Lochleven. Mary fled for her life to England and threw herself upon the mercy of her cousin Elizabeth.

Mary Queen of Scots in later life. For nearly nineteen years she was held captive by Elizabeth until her execution in February, 1587.

Mary Stuart in England

To Elizabeth, Mary was now an embarrassment as well as a danger. Unwilling to approve the deposition of a fellow sovereign, Elizabeth could not, on the other hand, risk war with Scotland by restoring Mary to the Scottish throne by force. She could not hand Mary over to the new government in Scotland, for that would lead to Mary's death. She could not send Mary abroad, for that would tempt foreign powers to enforce a Catholic restoration in Scotland and possibly in England. The English parliament saw only one solution; while Mary lived, neither Elizabeth nor English Protestantism was safe, so Mary must die. Mary and her friends seemed to justify such an opinion; the plots of 1571-86 all centred round Mary Queen of Scots, and she was certainly a party to some of them even if she was ignorant of others.

For nineteen years Elizabeth temporized. She received her unwelcome guest with cold friendship, and heard Mary's accusers and Mary's defence. She found no cause to condemn the action taken by Mary's rebellious subjects, and no case proved against Mary herself. She put Mary under supervision, and ordered her close confinement.

She allowed her to be brought to trial after discovery of the Babington Plot in 1586, and to be condemned to death, but tried hard to avoid signing the death warrant. When finally she brought herself to do so, she charged her secretary with the warrant's safe custody. When he allowed it to become operative and Mary was executed at Fotheringay Castle on 8 February, 1587, Elizabeth protested that he had exceeded his duty, and imprisoned him in the Tower, only to release and reinstate him when the indignant protests from Europe had died away. For years Elizabeth deliberately, and Mary despairingly, gambled with their lives; Elizabeth won, but at a price she never wished to pay.

QUESTIONS

1. Explain and illustrate Elizabeth's foreign policy with regard to France and Scotland.

2. Justify or criticize Elizabeth's treatment of Mary Queen of Scots.

CHAPTER 22

THE CONFLICT WITH SPAIN

IN THE duel between Elizabeth and Mary Queen of Scots, Philip II of Spain played a curious part. After Mary became Elizabeth's prisoner, Philip, through his ambassadors in London, was a party to plots against the English queen in favour of her rival, one of which plots was instrumental in determining Mary's death. Mary, if placed on the English throne by Spanish support, would have been no danger to Philip; but before 1568, Mary, as an ally of France and Queen of Scotland, would not have been welcomed by Spain as Queen of England.

Anglo-Spanish Relations

Thus, up to 1568 Anglo-Spanish relations were not actively hostile, though not cordial. Spain had no desire to see Mary of Scotland carry French influence into England. England for her part was ready to follow her traditional policy of friendship with whatever power controlled Flanders, whose ports were entrances through which English wool passed to the continent. English merchants had no desire to see these entrances closed, nor could the government, in an age of rising administrative costs and an income derived from fixed sources, afford to see such a closure. Since Flanders was part of the Spanish empire in Europe, England was anxious to avoid any step which might lead to open war. Philip II, in the years before the deposition of Mary of Scotland, was equally unwilling to respond to papal promptings that he should, by force if necessary, destroy England's heretical queen. Yet the effort to keep the peace became an increasing strain to both parties.

One cause of friction was the activity of Elizabethan sea-captains. Ever since Christopher Columbus found land on the other side of the Atlantic, European countries had taken an increasing interest in the New World. Spain and Portugal had been leaders in this exploratory work; England, recovering from the Wars of the Roses and acclimatizing herself to a new dynasty and a new religious faith, had been slower to share this new interest. When in the second half of the sixteenth century she was ready to do so, she found her way barred by the division of the New World into two spheres of influence, allotted respectively to Spain and Portugal by Pope Alexander VI.

When in 1562 John Hawkins began to raid the coasts of Africa, round up natives from the coastal villages, cram them into the holds of his ships, carry them across to the Spanish American colonies and sell them into slavery, his actions were illegal as well as immoral. The right to trade with her colonies was in Spanish opinion exclusively Spain's. Hawkins was an interloper.

Yet when he sailed on his second voyage, Elizabeth was among those who lent money to equip the expedition in hope of sharing the profits—hardly a friendly act towards a neighbour with whom she was supposed to be on good terms. Philip showed himself capable of answering double-dealing with double-dealing when, on Hawkins' third voyage, the Spanish fleet allowed the Englishman into the harbour of San Juan d'Ulloa and then attacked him.

The activities of Sir Francis Drake were even more provocative than those of Sir John Hawkins, amounting to undisguised piracy. During his voyage to the Indies in 1572 Drake met the Spanish treasure fleet homeward bound from the mines of Peru. He seized a large part of its cargo, to the embarrassment of the Spanish treasury and the enrichment of England. Between 1577 and 1580 he made his famous voyage round the world, and took the opportunity to sack and plunder the Spanish ports of Valparaiso and Santiago, and to sink much Spanish shipping.

Spanish protests about such activities were received by Elizabeth with little more than "diplomatic" sympathy; she officially rebuked the offenders, but secretly encouraged them in their enterprises. Even secrecy was abandoned when Drake was knighted in 1580.

Revolt of the Netherlands

By 1580 tension between England and Spain had mounted dangerously, for England had added to Spanish difficulties in the Netherlands.

Philip II of Spain wished to impose royal absolutism on all seventeen provinces of the Netherlands, but the Netherlanders were determined to maintain their local provincial rights of limited self-government. Also, Philip wished to restore Catholicism in the northern provinces, but these provinces were anxious to remain Protestant.

The Duke of Alva marched from Italy to take control of the Netherlands in 1567. The Council of Troubles (nicknamed the Council of Blood) was established to sentence all who had revolted against Spain. Refugees from the vengeance of Spain formed a naval unit, known as the Sea-Beggars, and William the Silent of Orange assumed leadership of the opposition in 1568. The Sea-Beggars captured Brill and Flushing from the Spanish in 1572, and Alva was defeated in 1573. He was recalled to Spain in the same year, and de Requesnes was sent to replace him.

De Requesnes wished to follow a policy of reconciliation between Spain and the Netherlands, but due to his own inefficiency, and to the stubbornness of both Philip and William, he failed in his attempts.

Don John of Austria replaced de Requesnes in 1576, and the northern

The Armada (from the film "Fire over England").

and southern provinces of the Netherlands temporarily united against him, under William the Silent. Don John died two years later, without having executed his plans for the subjugation of the Netherlands.

The Duke of Parma became Governor-General in 1578. The unity of the northern and southern provinces was destroyed, and the Protestant north formed the Union of Utrecht for joint action against Spain, and for a measure of central government. In 1584 William the Silent was assassinated, and was succeeded by his son Maurice. The struggle continued, with frequent attacks on Spanish commerce, until in 1609 a twelve-year truce was established. Thereafter the struggle between Spain and the Netherlands became merged in the Thirty Years' War, and when the Peace of Westphalia ended the war in 1648, Dutch independence was recognized by Spain.

England and the Netherlands

After Alva's entry into the Netherlands, England showed herself sympathetic to the rebels, though Elizabeth hesitated before committing herself to active intervention. Meanwhile she welcomed refugees from Alva's terror, who enriched England with their skills and industries. Further, when an Italian ship carrying money borrowed by Philip to finance operations in the Netherlands was compelled by bad weather to put in at an English port, Elizabeth "borrowed" the money herself. In retaliation Alva seized goods belonging to English merchants in Flanders. England replied by seizing Flemish merchants' goods in England, and the Spanish ambassador in London became a party to the Northern Rebellion. War seemed imminent.

Elizabeth now became more cautious in her policy towards the Netherlands, and sought additional safety in an alliance with the French in 1572. She even toyed with the notion of marriage to a French prince, the Duke of Anjou. Though Elizabeth's intentions were never serious, her performance was sufficiently convincing to induce Spain to seek an accommodation with England. By a series of agreements (1573) trade with the Netherlands was resumed and England undertook to deny her ports to Flemish rebels.

Friendlier relations did not last long. In 1576 when Don John made it clear that he was determined to crush this long-standing revolt and, having done so, was prepared to turn against England, Elizabeth tried to frustrate his intentions by renewing her unofficial support of the Netherlands. William the Silent protested that this was not enough and, failing to get more from Elizabeth, turned to France. France responded by despatching troops under the Duke of Alençon. Elizabeth had no desire to see French influence replace that of Spain in the Netherlands. Again she made a most realistic pretence of prospective marriage, with Alençon. The latter wasted precious time in England, and his troops in the Netherlands got out of hand and turned on those they had been sent to help. French influence had not been established in the Netherlands, but the rebels had not been finally suppressed.

Religious and Economic Rivalry

Underlying all these twists and turns of diplomacy were fundamental differences between England and Spain unlikely ever to be peaceably resolved. Both countries believed that national prosperity depended upon accumulating a reserve of precious metal; each country sought to sell abroad more than it bought abroad, so that the difference would have to be made up in bullion. To further this policy each country imposed duties on goods imported from the other. Thus two tariff walls were constructed, the effect of which was to hamper the free flow of trade and create tension between the two countries.

As the years passed it became more and more plain that England represented the Reformation and Spain the interests of the old Catholic faith, now endeavouring, in a movement known as the Counter Reformation, to recover the ground it had lost. These two forms of Christianity had not yet realized that it was possible to live side by side in mutual toleration. Increasingly after 1568 Philip II came to regard it as his divinely appointed duty to destroy the Protestant heresy.

Events Leading to War, 1584-85

Developments in France finally forced Elizabeth to abandon her policy of strenuous resistance to Spain short of total war. The death of the Duke of Alençon, last surviving brother of the childless Henry III of France, in 1584 left Protestant Henry of Navarre as heir to the French throne. The

Sir Walter Raleigh in the New World.

powerful Catholic Guise family resolved to put Cardinal Bourbon, Henry of Navarre's uncle, on the throne, and Spain, in the interests of the Counter Reformation, was ready to help. If this scheme had succeeded, the combined might of France and Spain would have been turned on England and the Netherlands. Elizabeth realized that she could compromise no longer, when the designs of Spain were clearly indicated by help given to a papal attack on Ireland, connivance at the installation of a Guise adviser to young James VI of Scotland, and participation with Mary Queen of Scots in the Throckmorton plot. Elizabeth showed her hand by expelling all Jesuit priests from England, embarking upon active persecution of her Catholic subjects and ordering the Spanish ambassador to leave the country. Finally the Earl of Leicester was sent, officially this time, with an English force to help the Netherlanders, now handicapped by the murder of William the Silent in 1584. England and Spain in 1585 were openly at war.

The war was fought not merely in Europe but also in the New World. Spain relied on imports of precious metal from the colonies to finance her efforts in Europe. If her treasure fleets could be captured or her communications with colonies interrupted, Spain's capacity to make war in Europe would be markedly hampered. In 1586 Sir Francis Drake, though he failed to capture that year's treasure fleet, seriously injured Spain's communications with her colonies by his destruction of the chief towns in the Cape Verde Islands, by his capture of San Domingo and Cartagena and by the ransom he demanded before his departure from these Spanish territories. News of Drake's exploits damaged Philip's credit in Europe. He was unable to borrow money from bankers, and was in consequence unable to provision his armies.

War in Europe: The Armada

Back in home waters Drake inflicted further humiliation on Philip by destroying Spanish shipping in the harbour of Cadiz and maintaining a patrol off the Spanish coast, thus demonstrating English control of the seas.

Had Drake's patrol been sustained the Armada might have been longer delayed, but Elizabeth had become alarmed by the success of another new commander in the Netherlands, the Duke of Parma. In 1588 she ordered Drake to remain in port while she attempted to negotiate with Parma. This gave Philip an opportunity to instruct the Armada to sail. The intention was to embark Parma's troops from the Netherlands and land them in England.

Before the Armada could reach the Netherlands, however, it was intercepted by English ships. For over a week the battle raged, strong winds and heavy seas giving the advantage to the English ships. Half Philip's fleet was destroyed; the rest made a disordered way home. The invasion, dreaded for nearly twenty years, had failed; and it had removed another danger from Elizabeth's path by provoking her, as we have seen in an earlier chapter, to sign the death warrant of Mary Queen of Scots in 1587.

Later Events of the War with Spain

Revolt in the Netherlands and civil war in France outlived both Elizabeth and Philip II. While she lived, Elizabeth intervened from time to time in both countries, never decisively but always sufficiently to keep Spanish attention directed elsewhere than towards England. She even made sporadic attacks on Spain itself, and Spain as sporadically replied in kind. There was a feeble Spanish landing in Cornwall in 1595. The Earl of Essex replied with a raid on Cadiz in 1596. During the following two years other Armadas were prepared, but storms and English control of the channel kept them in port. In 1601 there was a Spanish landing in Ireland. Spain and England were still at war when Philip died in 1598 and Elizabeth in 1603. It was left to their successors, Philip III and James I, to make peace in 1604.

QUESTIONS

1. Describe the motives of both Elizabeth and Philip II for delaying the outbreak of war for the better part of thirty years.

2. How did the foreign policy of Elizabeth differ from that of Henry VIII?

CHAPTER 23

TUDOR EXPANSION

WE HAVE seen in the last chapter that the skill of English seamen played an important part in the struggle with Spain and that the war was fought out in the New World as well as in Europe. We must now retrace our steps and examine in more detail the story of English expansion overseas during the Tudor period.

The reasons which led Englishmen to take an interest in realms beyond their own shores were many. In part it was because they shared the spirit of enquiry characteristic of the age in which they lived, a desire to know more about the past and to explore the unknown. This was one aspect of the Renaissance. Adventure overseas provided an outlet for the courage, ambition, initiative and enterprise so disastrously mis-employed in the civil wars (now happily concluded) of the previous century. The government had realized that if the new dynasty and new religion were to survive, the country must be able to frustrate attempted invasion, and that demanded a strong navy and experienced sailors. The government was therefore prepared to support any development to promote these ends. Economic conditions and theories directed attention to the desirability of expansion. New markets overseas would stimulate internal trade and so create more work, in a century which knew a good deal of unemployment. The New World was thought to be a boundless source of precious metal; and to an age which believed that a country's wealth was measured by its surplus bullion, this theory (known as Mercantilism) was a strong incentive to gain control of these valuable regions. Finally, to those who believed that England was over-populated, the idea of settling some people elsewhere, whether in America or nearer home in Ireland, seemed very desirable.

Exploration and Discovery

These differing motives led to differing forms of activity, and exploration was one of the earliest. Ever since the Turkish advance into Europe in the fifteenth century rendered the overland route to the Far East hazardous, men had been searching for an alternative sea route. By now the idea that the earth was a sphere was generally accepted, and men argued that it should be possible to reach the east by sailing west. Henry VII was too slow in his response to Columbus' request for support to permit England to share the glory of America's discovery, but in 1497 he encouraged John Cabot's attempt to find a western sea-way to Asia. Just as Columbus mistook America for the Indies, so Cabot mistook Newfoundland for Asia. Had the season allowed him to explore further, he was sure he would have found China and Japan, known from Marco Polo's account of his overland travels to those parts. Backed by Bristol merchants, Cabot set off again in 1498, equipped to trade with the countries he thought he had found. From this voyage he did not return to tell the story of his failure.

His efforts served, however, to reveal that a hitherto unknown continent barred the western sea-route to Asia. Attention was now concentrated on attempts to circumvent this obstacle by a north-west or north-east passage.

In 1508 John Cabot's son Sebastian took up his father's work, sailed south of Greenland and north-west across the Davis Strait into a wide expanse of ocean which we now know as Hudson Bay, but which Cabot took to be the Pacific. Compelled at this point to put back by his crew's unwillingness to face the danger of floating ice, he returned convinced that he had found the long-desired north-west passage. John Rut renewed the search in 1527, but failing, made for the West Indies and was repelled by the Spaniards when he tried to trade with San Domingo. In the reign of Elizabeth the quest was taken up by Martin Frobisher, who in the years 1567, 1568 and 1569 made three unsuccessful attempts to find this desirable north-west passage. On his first voyage an opening in Baffin Island convinced him of success, but two subsequent trading expeditions revealed his error and led to bankruptcy of the Cathay Company, formed to finance the hoped-for trade. Later attempts by John Davis in 1585, 1586 and 1587 were similarly unsuccessful.

While these men sought the north-west passage, others (notably Willoughby and Chancellor in the reign of Mary I) looked for a north-east passage. Willoughby's expedition of 1554 rounded the North Cape, but perished while wintering in Lapland. Chancellor, who set off with Willoughby but became separated from him, reached the White Sea and Archangel, whence he visited Ivan IV in Moscow with advantageous results for English trade, as we shall see later. Neither explorer found the north-east passage to Asia for which he had been searching.

Development of Trade

Oceanic enterprise produced traders as well as explorers. In 1530 William Hawkins broke the Portuguese monopoly of trade with Brazil and Guinea. In Brazil he exchanged English knives and hatchets for dye-wood, useful to the English cloth trade; in Guinea he exchanged the same English commodities for ivory and pepper.

It was from the early sixteenth century also that Bristol seamen began a regular trade in fish between Newfoundland and Europe. It was in the reign

John White, governor of Roanoke in 1589, spent much of his time recording the life of the Indians in detailed drawings.

of Edward VI, however, on the initiative of the Earl of Northumberland, that the government made a determined effort to expand English trade overseas. If new markets could be found, much of the economic distress and consequent political unrest might be remedied. Northumberland sought the advice of Sebastian Cabot, now an old man with immense practical knowledge of the New World, and of John Dee, a young man with immense knowledge of all that medieval travellers had written about Asia and the East. Under their stimulus trade was begun with Morocco in 1551. English goods were bartered for Moroccan dates, sugar and gum-arabic, the latter useful to the cloth-finishing trade.

It was with Northumberland's encouragement that Thomas Wyndham undertook his first voyage to the Gold Coast in 1553, followed in subsequent years by other traders. Here English goods were paid for by gold or gold-dust, a most profitable exchange and an import warmly welcomed by an impoverished government, in spite of Portuguese protests. At this point we may notice the important trade which resulted from Chancellor's unsuccessful search for a north-east passage. He was warmly welcomed in Moscow where Ivan IV was anxious to break the monopoly which Hanse merchants held of European trade with Russia. Chancellor's visit led to the formation in 1555 of the Muscovy Company and the beginning of direct trade between England and Russia. In 1560 this led to the development by Anthony Jenkinson of trade with the East through Persia and Russia. When Turkey conquered Persia the Turkey Company was formed, and this trade with the East carried on by a more direct route through the Mediterranean.

The most significant development in Tudor overseas trade, however, was the establishment in 1600 of the East India Company. This was a joint stock company in which named merchants were given the monopoly, so far as England was concerned, of trade with India. The first expedition sailed in 1601 and a connection between England and India was formed which was to endure for three centuries.

Colonization of the New World

Tudor trading expansion was infinitely more successful than Tudor efforts to establish colonies. All attempts made to establish English settlements on the American continent failed.

The first attempt was made in Newfoundland. In 1583 Sir Humphrey Gilbert took formal possession of the island in the queen's name. When he sailed for home he left a few settlers, ill-equipped to maintain themselves in a virgin land since their store ship had foundered. Gilbert intended to return with reinforcements the following year, but his ship was also wrecked on the homeward voyage. Gilbert's settlers were left to fend for themselves, but failed to do so.

In 1584, under the patronage of Sir Walter Raleigh, a scheme was drawn up for the establishment of a settlement at Roanoke (now North Carolina). The territory was formally annexed by Barlow, who reported favourably on the prospects of settlement there. Raleigh, courtier as well as sailor, decided that the settlement should be named Virginia as a compliment to the Virgin Queen. Sir Richard Grenville was entrusted with the expedition which landed the first settlers. These founding fathers were more intent upon exploitation of the territory than on its development. They provoked the hostility of the Indians, and when Drake put in there in 1585 they decided to return with him to England. Raleigh renewed his efforts to establish a settlement at Roanoke in 1587, a bad time to choose for such a venture. The Armada crisis prevented the sailing of reinforcements until 1589. They

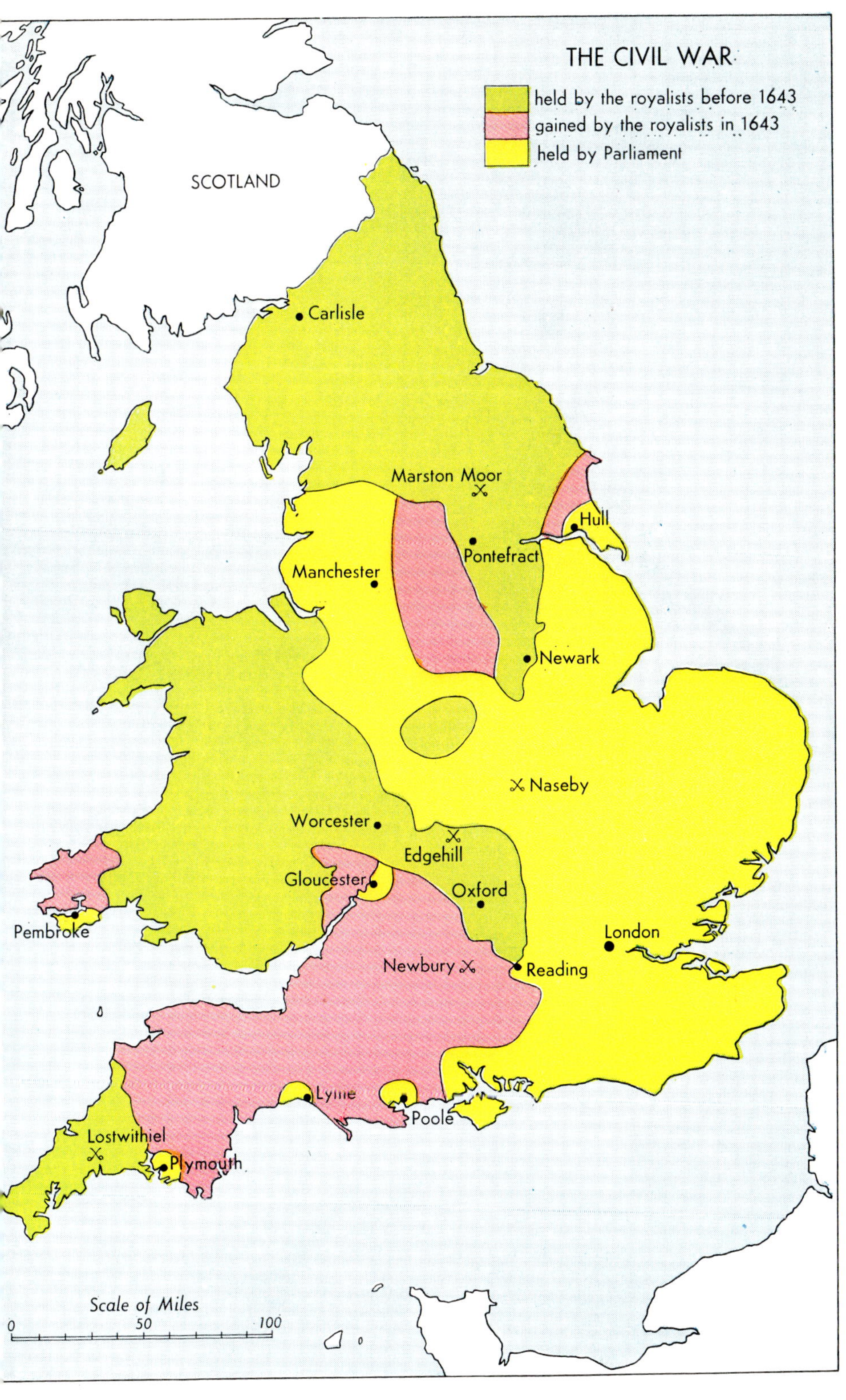
THE CIVIL WAR
held by the royalists before 1643
gained by the royalists in 1643
held by Parliament
SCOTLAND
Carlisle
Marston Moor
Hull
Pontefract
Manchester
Newark
Naseby
Worcester
Edgehill
Gloucester
Oxford
Pembroke
London
Newbury
Reading
Lyme
Poole
Lostwithiel
Plymouth
Scale of Miles
0
50
100

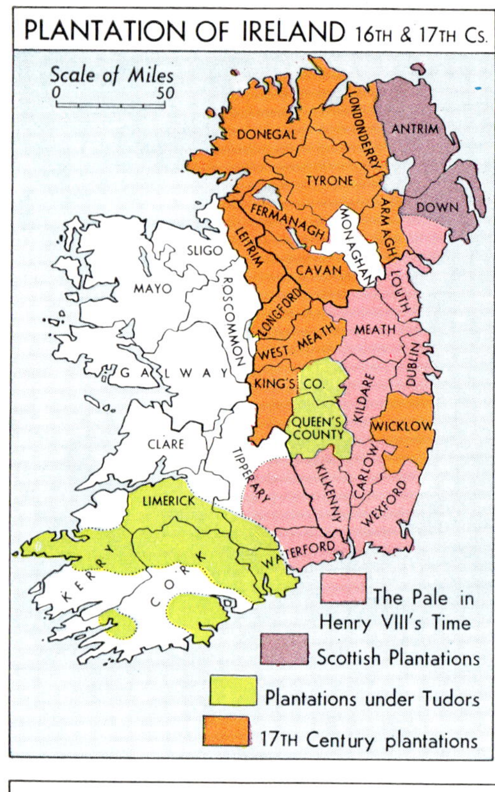

PLANTATION OF IRELAND 16TH & 17TH Cs.
Scale of Miles
0 50
DONEGAL
LONDONDERRY
ANTRIM
TYRONE
DOWN
FERMANAGH
ARMAGH
MONAGHAN
LEITRIM
SLIGO
CAVAN
LOUTH
MAYO
ROSCOMMON
LONGFORD
MEATH
WEST MEATH
DUBLIN
GALWAY
KING'S CO.
KILDARE
QUEEN'S COUNTY
WICKLOW
CLARE
TIPPERARY
KILKENNY
CARLOW
LIMERICK
WEXFORD
WATERFORD
KERRY
CORK
The Pale in Henry VIII's Time
Scottish Plantations
Plantations under Tudors
17TH Century plantations

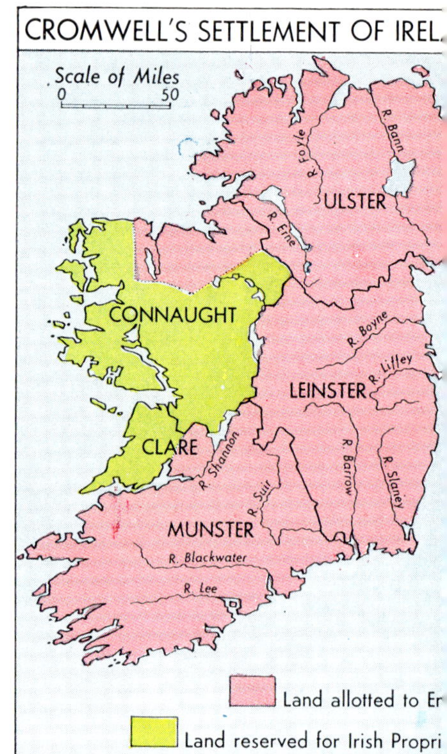

CROMWELL'S SETTLEMENT OF IREL
Scale of Miles
0 50
R. Foyle
R. Bann
ULSTER
R. Erne
CONNAUGHT
R. Boyne
R. Liffey
LEINSTER
CLARE
R. Shannon
R. Barrow
R. Slaney
R. Suir
MUNSTER
R. Blackwater
R. Lee
Land allotted to Er
Land reserved for Irish Propri

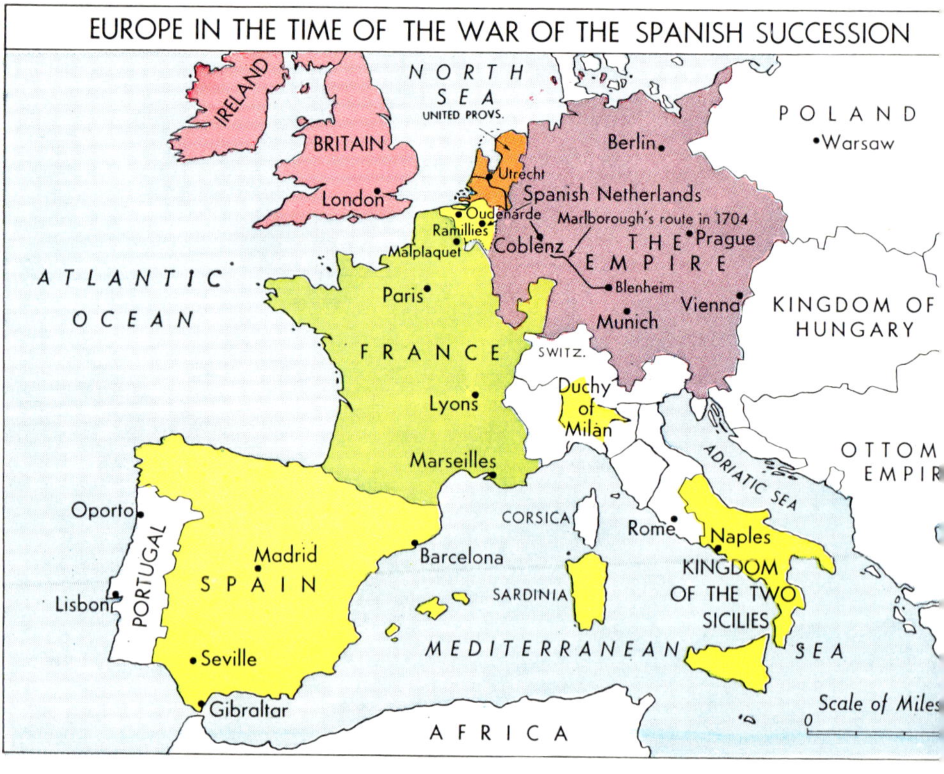

EUROPE IN THE TIME OF THE WAR OF THE SPANISH SUCCESSION
IRELAND
NORTH SEA
UNITED PROVS.
POLAND
Warsaw
BRITAIN
Berlin
Utrecht
London
Spanish Netherlands
Oudenarde
Marlborough's route in 1704
Ramillies
THE EMPIRE
Prague
Malplaquet
Coblenz
ATLANTIC OCEAN
Blenheim
Paris
Vienna
KINGDOM OF HUNGARY
Munich
FRANCE
SWITZ.
Duchy of Milan
Lyons
ADRIATIC SEA
OTTOM EMPIR
Marseilles
CORSICA
Oporto
Rome
Naples
Madrid
Barcelona
KINGDOM OF THE TWO SICILIES
PORTUGAL
SPAIN
Lisbon
SARDINIA
MEDITERRANEAN SEA
Seville
Gibraltar
Scale of Miles
0
AFRICA

arrived too late and could find no trace of their predecessors, only the deserted ruins of the colony.

A third equally unsuccessful effort at colonization was made in Guiana, South America; Raleigh was again its sponsor, this time in person. Though he explored the region between the Orinoco and the Amazon and reported favourably on its suitability for colonial settlement, the scheme was not pursued and England was still without an American colony when the Tudor period ended with the death of Queen Elizabeth.

Plantation in Ireland

Those who believed that England had a surplus population for which new living-room should be found had some success in Ireland. Efforts made by the first two Tudors to establish the authority of the English Crown in Ireland were followed by the attempts of Edward VI to establish the Reformation there and of Mary to re-introduce Roman Catholicism. One method adopted was to encourage Englishmen to emigrate to Ireland, and in this way the anglicized area known as the Pale was extended by addition of the King's Country and the Queen's Country.

Even so, when Elizabeth became queen Ireland was still dominated by its native chiefs, with tribal jealousies and violent objection to centralized administration. The Elizabethan government did not succeed in extending the English settlement of Ireland, but prepared the way for such an extension by the inroads it made on the power of the clans and chiefs.

Ulster remained reasonably loyal after Sir Henry Sidney successfully united many of the clans opposed to the hitherto dominant O'Neills. Munster was so severely devastated after the rebellion with Spanish help under the Earl of Desmond between 1579 and 1583 that it gave no help to the Armada. More serious was the revolt of Hugh O'Neill, Earl of Tyrone, in 1598. Elizabeth's favourite, the Earl of Essex, was sent to suppress the rising, but in 1599 he made a treaty with Tyrone which virtually made the rebel an independent sovereign in that part of Ireland. The Queen's affection for Essex did not save him from the consequences of his folly; he was recalled from Ireland and executed for treason in 1601. Lord Mountjoy replaced him in Ireland, and in three years pacified the rebellious province, defeating Tyrone and building forts to prevent a further rising. The full fruits of this work were not reaped until some seven years after the death of Elizabeth, for the settlement of English people in Ulster did not take place until 1610.

QUESTIONS

1. Write an account of three of the chief English voyages of discovery during the Tudor period.
2. Describe the treatment of Ireland by the English in the reign of Elizabeth.

OCL/HIST 1—!

CHAPTER 24

CROWN *v.* PARLIAMENTARY GENTRY: THE RIVAL THEORIES

WHEN the Tudor dynasty gave way to the Stuarts in 1603, old issues began to take new forms. The result was a bitter controversy between court and Crown on one side, and the parliamentary gentry on the other, as to the way in which the country was to be governed. The first faint rumblings of this storm had been heard in the last ten years of the reign of Elizabeth Tudor, but the clouds thickened in the reign of James I, and burst upon the unfortunate Charles I. Before we examine the story of these two reigns in detail, it will help if we try to understand what this conflict was about.

The Nature of Tudor Government

The way in which Tudor sovereigns, more especially the two Henrys and Elizabeth, governed the nation is sometimes described as Tudor Despotism. In as much as this phrase means that the sovereign personally decided the policies his ministers should execute, the description serves well enough; but if used to imply that these policies were arbitrarily imposed on a wholly unwilling nation, it needs modification.

For the greater part of the Tudor age there was close agreement between Crown and country. Henry VII had been welcomed as a shield against the selfish ambitions of over-mighty subjects and civil war. Parliament eagerly supported Henry VIII's reformation of the Church as the sole means by which the nation could free itself from the foreign influence of the papacy in English affairs. The careers of Somerset and Northumberland in the reign of Edward VI had been an unwelcome but timely reminder of how essential strong personal government was to the nation's peace. Mary died before the disadvantages of such government became wholly intolerable. Under Elizabeth, country supported Crown as the best safeguard against the threatened foreign invasion. In any case, the idea that sovereigns should rule as well as reign was a commonly accepted notion throughout western Europe in the sixteenth century and continued to be so until almost the end of the eighteenth century.

Declining Need for Personal Government after 1588

In England in the last ten years of the reign of Elizabeth I, however, there were signs that this form of government was no longer so essential. Reasons are not difficult to find. Danger from over-mighty subjects had greatly diminished, and nobility and gentry alike had been happily accorded a legal place in the administration of the country, by being entrusted with the execution of Crown policy in their own localities. There was no danger of successful restoration of papal influence, and the threat of foreign conquest faded with the defeat of the Armada. In short, pressures making for unity of interest between Crown and country had weakened; the two could now afford to re-examine their relationship.

Accordingly, as we have already seen in an earlier chapter, in the later years of her reign Elizabeth I had found it increasingly difficult to bend parliament to the royal will, and the Commons had begun to claim privileges which it was beyond the power of the Crown to deny. The queen's angry reaction was to avoid summoning parliament, a quite proper course of action, since it was still established practice for that body to meet only at the sovereign's pleasure.

Stuart Theory of the Divine Right of Kings

Elizabeth believed, as did her father, that the king's will should be law; but she realized that the temper of parliament had changed in the intervening years, and she was realist enough to evade the challenge rather than provoke head-on conflict.

The first two Stuart kings lacked Elizabeth's practical wisdom. James I had already, as King of Scotland, formulated his theory of kingship in a book *The True Law of Free Monarchies*. A keen student of theology, James proved to his own satisfaction by appeal to scripture that kings were appointed by God, that they were responsible to God alone for exercise of their power, that their subjects' only duty was obedience, that bad kings were a divine infliction for national sins, and that rebellion was a sin against God. He had been a successful king in Scotland, and looked forward with confidence to sharing his learning on these matters with his new subjects. In England he expected, to be "the great schoolmaster of the whole land."

James I's daughter Elizabeth married the Elector Palatine, thus involving England in central European politics.

Thus, at a time when, as a result of the Tudor habit of using parliament as the agent of their will, that body had become conscious of its strength and experience, there came to the throne a king sincerely convinced that all political wisdom and authority was vested in himself. Moreover he thought that he only needed to expound this theory for its truth to be instantly recognized and accepted. His son and successor Charles I fully shared these views, and learned nothing from his father's failure to induce parliament to accept them.

The country gentlemen who in the House of Commons formed the backbone of opposition to the Stuarts had no carefully-worked-out theory with which to reply to the king, and were reduced to improvised answers. Antiquarians among them sought for historical precedents to show that parliament had a right to share with the king in government of the country. Lawyers among them tried to prove that both king and subject were amenable to Common Law. Philosophers argued that there was such a thing as Natural Law, binding on ruler and ruled alike.

This difference of theory between the Stuarts and their English subjects might have been a purely academic matter, had it not been for two practical considerations.

Reasons for Conflict

The first of these was that on almost all day-to-day issues of policy, king and parliament held opposite opinions. The second was that crown revenue, as we have seen in an earlier chapter, was no longer sufficient to meet the expenses of government; the king repeatedly had to summon parliament to ask for additional supplies. This financial dependence of Crown on parliament was parliament's strong suit. The Commons were unwilling to supply taxes for the king to carry out policies which they thought misguided. When parliament insisted on discussing the king's policies in religion or foreign affairs instead of obediently voting him the money he needed, theories about government became important. The king denied his subjects' right to criticize his policies; his subjects asserted their right to do so, and also to withhold money until the king reshaped his action in conformity with their wishes. In these circumstances the king claimed the right to levy taxes at his own pleasure. Parliament declared this beyond his power. To kings who believed in Divine Right, this was treason. When nearly forty years of argument resulted in deadlock, the final resort was civil war.

QUESTIONS

1. Why was the Tudor Despotism challenged under the Stuarts?
2. Describe the theory of the Divine Right of kings, and show how it affected relations between Crown and parliament under the first two Stuarts.

CHAPTER 25

CROWN *v.* PARLIAMENTARY GENTRY: THE GATHERING STORM

THE Puritans, who had been a parliamentary irritation to Elizabeth, entertained high hopes of James I. If he had identified himself with the cause of episcopacy in Scotland, it was also true that he was a considerable theologian and had been brought up under Calvinist influence. Hence with lively expectations the English Puritans met James while he was in progress from Scotland to London and presented to him their Millenary Petition, in which they asked that clergymen of the Church of England should be allowed to exercise discretion about wearing a surplice, and that providing they used the Prayer Book in public worship the clergy should not be required to declare belief in its absolute truth; the petition also listed minor modifications in church ceremonies which they would like to see permitted.

The Hampton Court Conference, 1604

James promised to give the petition consideration, and once in London he summoned leading Puritan sympathizers among the Anglican clergy to meet some of the bishops under his chairmanship at Hampton Court to consider these requests. As chairman, James soon showed himself far from impartial; the bishops, feeling they could count on the king's sympathy, were far from accommodating. One Puritan clergyman was incautious enough to mention the word "presbytery," the kind of ecclesiastical organization James had been at pains to combat in Scotland. The word frightened the king into supposing that he was about to be asked to dispense with episcopacy. He declared that a presbytery agreed as well with monarchy as God with the Devil, and if that was what Puritanism meant he would make the party conform or harry them out of the land. "No bishop," he said, "no king."

Only one good thing came out of the conference and that was the appointment of a committee to prepare an official translation of the Bible. Seven years' labour at this task led to the publication of our Authorized Version in 1611.

The Puritan Ejection

James followed his rejection of the Millenary Petition by a proclamation ordering all clergymen to conform strictly to all existing rules of church

Gunpowder Plot conspirators: Guy Fawkes is third from right.

ritual on pain of losing their livings. Three hundred clergy were ejected, and went to swell the ranks of free-lance preachers and those opposed to royal absolutism.

In 1618 James gave further offence to Puritan opinion by issuing the Book of Sports, authorizing (but not commanding) continuance of old English games on Sundays, a custom strongly disapproved of by Puritans, who held that the Sabbath should be strictly observed as a day for rest and worship. Though a minor matter, this was one more example of James' tactlessness in dealing with those whose opinions differed from his own.

James I and the Catholics

Like the Puritans, the Catholics also had high hopes of James I on his accession. Theirs had been his mother's faith, and her adherence to that faith had been a factor contributing to her execution. To James in 1603, however, this was an unhappy story of the past. When the Catholics saw that their expectations were not likely to be fulfilled, they resorted to the old policy of plots against the throne. Of these the Gunpowder Plot was the most serious, and its discovery brought severe penalties on Catholic heads. By the Recusancy Laws of 1605, Catholics were excluded from all professions, from court and from London. Fines for non-attendance at Church of England services were greatly increased.

This was a policy Parliament eagerly, and James reluctantly, accepted; for the king was prepared to deal leniently with Catholics in the interests of the foreign policy he was pursuing. Later, in 1618, in furtherance of diplomatic negotiations with Spain, James relaxed the Recusancy Laws and (in 1623) went so far as to promise freedom of worship for Catholics in England to facilitate a marriage between his son Charles and a Catholic princess of France.

Parliamentary Reaction to James' Religious Policy

In James' first parliament of 1604 the House of Commons supported the Millenary Petition, and was displeased with its rejection. Puritanism began to gather support from the wealthier country gentry, and it was from this social group that parliamentary representatives of town and county were drawn. Puritanism and parliamentary opposition to the Crown now tended to march side by side. When the Crown sought parliamentary supplies, religious reform became a grievance which must be discussed before supplies were considered. In the parliament of 1614, James' refusal to concede religious changes was one of the reasons why the king was unable to secure the taxation he genuinely needed.

James' tenderness towards Catholics angered parliament as much as did his hostility towards Puritans. The Earl of Salisbury, an adviser whom the king inherited from Elizabeth, shared the fear which his father Lord Burghley had had of Catholicism, and welcomed the Gunpowder Plot as an excuse for frightening James into accepting the Recusancy Laws. Thereafter parliament was keen to see these laws strictly enforced, and their repeated demands to this end antagonized the king.

James the Peace-Maker

James' opinion of himself as a diplomatist was as unbounded as his confidence in himself as a theologian, and his success as meagre. He hated war, and immediately on accession resolved to make peace with Spain. This he achieved in 1604, and thereafter sought to establish himself as general peace-maker of Europe. His method was to ally himself through his children's marriages with Catholic Europe on the one hand and Protestant Europe on the other. In pursuance of this aim he successfully negotiated the marriage of his daughter Elizabeth to the Protestant Frederick Elector Palatine. His attempt to marry his son Charles to a Spanish princess failed, however, in spite of his sacrifice of Raleigh to the executioner's block in an attempt to please Spain, and of the visit of Charles (and James' latest adviser, the Duke of Buckingham) to Madrid in 1623.

The Thirty Years' War

James' ambitious scheme failed long before 1623, though he refused to face the fact. Religious war which was to last for thirty years broke out in Germany in 1618, and its first victim was James' son-in-law Frederick, whose territory was overrun by Spaniards supporting the Catholic cause in Germany. James persisted in pursuing diplomatic negotiations with Spain, hoping thereby to secure his son-in-law's restoration without recourse to war. Not until Charles and Buckingham urged a change of policy after their fruitless visit to Madrid did James abandon his hopes. In 1624 negotiations with Spain were broken off, military help was sent to the Elector and (France being at odds with Spain) proposals were made for the marriage of Charles and Henrietta Maria of France.

Parliamentary Reaction to James' Foreign Policy

Parliament disliked the peace with Spain of 1604; they found it difficult to believe that Spain was no longer the dangerous enemy she had been for so long. They bitterly opposed the projected Spanish match, were angered by the execution of Raleigh, and rejoiced when the Madrid visit failed.

From the outbreak of the Thirty Years' War parliament advocated active aid for Frederick of the Palatinate, and despised James' efforts to find a diplomatic solution. They welcomed the failure of those efforts and the change of policy in 1624, but their joy was tempered by the decision to seek a French and therefore Catholic bride for the heir to the throne, particularly when it transpired that concessions to Catholics in England were part of the bargain. Parliament in 1621 demanded a Protestant marriage; James replied that since this issue was a matter of foreign policy it was beyond the power of parliament even to discuss it. The Commons retorted with a resolution to the effect that any matter of state was a fit subject for discussion. James in anger not only dissolved parliament, but himself tore this record from the House journals. Thus foreign policy, like religious policy, led back to the question of where the king's power ended and that of parliament began.

Financial Difficulty

In his dealings with parliament, the king's weak spot was money. James had inherited an empty Treasury, a fixed source of income in an age of rising prices and falling monetary values, a public opinion which still expected the Crown to "live of its own," no machinery for assessing the private wealth of his subjects, and subjects unwilling to share their growing prosperity with the government.

The normal remedy for inadequate revenue was special votes of additional taxes by parliament. When parliament refused to grant such aid, James declared his right to raise what he needed at his own pleasure. He had good precedent; Elizabeth had avoided meeting critical parliamentary opinion in the latter years of her reign, and raised the revenue she required by selling offices and honours to those wealthy enough to buy them. She had also sold the exclusive right to trade in specific commodities to wealthy bidders, and these monopolies had ultimately met with strong parliamentary criticism, but no one had gone so far as to tell Elizabeth that all monies raised without parliamentary consent or approval were illegal.

The Earl of Salisbury tried to come to the king's rescue in 1610 by putting forward a scheme known as the Great Contract. Had parliament agreed, the king would have surrendered his right to what remained of the old feudal dues in return for an annual income of £200,000; but parliament would have none of it. If the king was financially independent, he could dispense with parliament; necessity would not oblige him to summon it.

Between 1614 and 1621 James did attempt to govern the country without recourse to parliamentary advice or help, and during these years he resorted to various devices to raise the revenue he needed to be independent. He had already issued a new Book of Rates in 1610, increasing duties on imported goods. Now he began to sell offices, both lay and ecclesiastical. He created a new order of baronets at £1,000 a time, and many subjects were more or less compelled to buy these titles. He exacted forced loans, and extracted benevolences or "free" gifts from his subjects. Finally he revived Elizabeth's practice of monopolies.

Parliamentary Reaction to Royal Finance

Parliament's reaction, when it finally had to be summoned, was to declare that taxes imposed without its consent were illegal. Refusing to recognize facts, the Commons insisted that the king's ordinary sources of revenue would be quite adequate if the king were less extravagant and his ministers less incompetent. The increased customs duties were not taxes, but impositions. Finally the Parliament of 1621-22 not only condemned monopolies, but impeached Sir Giles Mompesson, one of the greatest monopolists.

Thus finance joined religion and foreign policy in raising the crucial issue of the nature of royal prerogative and the extent of parliamentary liberties. This became the overriding problem in relations between James' successor Charles I and his parliaments, about which they argued up to 1642 and fought thereafter.

Plots Against James I

The tension in the nation created by James I led to plots against his life. The Bye Plot of 1603 was formed by William Watson, a Catholic priest. It was caused by the enforcement of fines on Catholics for non-attendance at Church of England services, in contravention of the king's promise that such fines should not be enforced. The plotters intended to seize the king, and obtain pledges that Catholics should enjoy complete equality of rights with Protestants. The plot was impractical, and was therefore betrayed by Jesuits. To show his gratitude James ceased to enforce the fines for a time.

After an unsuccessful journey in search of a Spanish bride, Charles I contracted an unpopular marriage to Henrietta Maria of France.

The Main Plot of 1603 was hatched by Catholics and Protestants, who aimed to replace James by his cousin Arabella Stuart, and to secure toleration for Catholics and Puritans. The leaders Cobham and Grey were imprisoned; Raleigh was executed in 1618. This plot led to the reimposition of fines on Catholics, and to the expulsion of Catholic priests from London.

The Gunpowder Plot of 1605, led by Catesby and Guy Fawkes, planned to blow up king and Commons at the assembly of parliament on 5 November, 1605. They planned to secure Catholic freedom by making James' daughter Elizabeth queen, and educating her as a Catholic. The conspirators warned their friends in parliament, and the plot was discovered. It resulted in increased fear of Catholicism among parliament and the general public, and in the passing of the Recusancy Laws.

Ministers and Favourites of James I

With one exception, the men whom James took into his confidence were as unpopular, and rightly so, as the king himself. The one exception was Robert Cecil, the son of Queen Elizabeth's Lord Burghley. Made a member of Council during the last years of Elizabeth's reign, he was influential in securing the peaceful accession of James I, who for this reason created him Earl of Salisbury and confirmed him in office. He was a competent statesman who opposed leniency to Catholics, exposed the Gunpowder Plot and supported the Recusancy Laws. He opposed the Spanish marriage proposed for Prince Charles, and might have saved James from his worst mistakes if he had not died in 1612.

Robert Carr, Lord Rochester and Earl of Somerset, was a handsome young page who became the king's favourite. He gained wealth when given the estates confiscated from Raleigh, and grew powerful by his marriage to Lady Francis Howard, after contriving her divorce. After the revelation that Lady Francis had been party to murder to obtain her divorce, Carr fell from power and was imprisoned for six years.

Francis Bacon, Viscount St. Albans, was a man of many parts: historian, essayist, philosopher, Attorney-General and Lord Chancellor. He was a strong supporter of monarchy, but saw the necessity of harmony between king and parliament. He upheld the theory that judges should support the Crown, and was therefore unpopular with parliament. Impeached on a charge of accepting bribes, he was sacrificed by James to save Buckingham.

George Villiers, Duke of Buckingham, was another handsome young courtier who attracted James' affection; he was a fine administrator, though a poor statesman. He supported the Spanish marriage for Charles, and was responsible for the unsuccessful visit to Madrid. Angry at Spanish indifference, Buckingham urged James to abandon negotiations with Spain. When Charles I came to the throne, he confirmed Buckingham in office. Buckingham was responsible for the failure of Charles' foreign policy, and was impeached by parliament. Charles' defence of Buckingham added to the difficulties between king and parliament.

Charles I and Parliament, 1624-1629

Parliament took the initiative immediately on the new king's accession. It was customary at the beginning of a new reign to confirm, as a normal source of revenue, the king's right to collect duty on wine and wool for life. This was known as tunnage and poundage. In 1625, Parliament took the unusual step of granting tunnage and poundage for one year only, and further showed its distrust of Charles I by voting only seven subsidies instead of the twelve the king had asked for to pursue his policy of war with Spain.

In 1626 the Commons demanded an enquiry into the conduct of the Spanish war and, when Charles refused to agree, impeached his adviser the Duke of Buckingham, thus asserting their right to influence the king's policy and to hold his ministers accountable to parliament for their actions. To save Buckingham and his own royal prerogative, Charles dissolved parliament.

Two years later a third parliament met. In the interval the king's foreign policy had met with further disaster, and the king had raised money on his own authority. He levied a forced loan, and imprisoned five knights who refused to pay it on the ground that the king's action in demanding it was not legal. The parliament of 1628 took up the challenge, and refused to vote any supplies until the king gave his assent to their Petition of Right. This asked the king to agree that all loans and taxes raised without consent of parliament were illegal, that no subject should be imprisoned without trial, and that the country should not be ruled by martial law in times of peace.

Reluctantly the king accepted the petition, but in 1629 parliament protested that he was not observing its provisions. Charles ordered parliament to dissolve but it refused to do so until Eliot's three resolutions had been passed, condemning as an enemy to the kingdom anyone who proposed innovations in religion, levied taxes without consent of parliament or paid taxes so levied. The first clause was an attack on the king's religious advisers who had tried to make Church of England services more elaborate; the second was a direct condemnation of the king himself and an attempt to curb his prerogative; and the third was an encouragement to the king's subjects to resist his authority.

This was more than the king could tolerate. By the king's orders Eliot was arrested, imprisoned and left to die in the Tower. Charles determined to establish his personal rule and dispense entirely with parliament. Thus in 1629 began the so-called "eleven years' tyranny."

Charles I's Foreign Policy

With so many problems at home Charles I was unable to follow a vigorous foreign policy. In 1625 he promised to pay Denmark £360,000 yearly to support the Protestant cause in the Thirty Years' War, but he paid only one instalment of £46,000; Denmark was defeated, and compelled to withdraw from the war.

Charles decided to attack Spain, in the hope of inducing Spain to press the Emperor to restore the English king's brother-in-law Frederick. An attack on Cadiz in 1625 failed, and parliament demanded an inquiry, which Charles resisted.

Charles was involved in difficulties with France because he was unable to fulfil promises, made at the time of his marriage to Henrietta Maria, to aid the French government against French Protestants and to grant toleration to English Catholics. This led to war with France in 1627. Buckingham led an expedition to the Isle of Rhé, to help French Protestants against their government, but it was a failure; a second expedition was abandoned after the death of Buckingham.

Charles was prevented from pursuing any further active foreign policy by his attempt to dispense with parliament after 1629. He lacked the financial means to do so.

QUESTIONS

1. Why was James I increasingly unpopular during the period 1603-25?

2. On what subjects did Charles I quarrel with his first three parliaments?

CHAPTER 26

THE FAILURE OF CROWN GOVERNMENT, 1629-42

THE "eleven years' tyranny" as a description of the personal rule of Charles I from 1629 to 1640 represents the point of view of the king's opponents. The magnates and country gentry who ultimately defeated the king fought against him because they found his rule worked to their personal disadvantage. Precisely for this reason, however, the wage-earner, the poor and the small farmer in many parts of the country enjoyed during these years a greater measure of protection against their social superiors than they were to experience again for many generations. Moreover, in seeking to govern the country without advice from parliament, the king's action was not nearly so unconstitutional as it appears to us today. The king was defending an established system, and it was his opponents who were innovators, seeking to secure as a right a degree of participation in government which had hitherto come their way by royal grace, royal convenience or royal weakness. In the appeal to ancient custom which both sides made, the king's case was better founded than that of his opponents.

Royal Finance

The king could refrain from calling parliament only so long as he could raise money without recourse to special taxation. His first problem therefore was a financial one.

Many of the king's expedients for solution of this problem were perfectly legal. His rigid insistence of full discharge of feudal obligations was a proper course of action; fines on local magnates for encroachment on forest land were strictly within the king's powers, and served to protect some interests of his humbler subjects; the same comment can be made of fines for enclosure of common land.

Other expedients were at worst matters of questionable legality. Such were the fines imposed on gentry who refused to obey the king's proclamation ordering them to leave London and live on their estates. So were fines imposed by the royal Courts of Star Chamber and High Commission, though these again affected magnates and gentry rather than wage-earners. Indeed the jurisdiction of these courts often served to secure justice for humble people which magistrates' courts, dominated by the gentry, failed to provide. As for the king's increase of customs duties, and the fines he exacted for their evasion, he could properly plead the judges' decision when his father tested the matter in the courts. In defence of his continued collection of tunnage and poundage he could argue that parliament had broken with tradition when it sought to restrict his right to one year only, and in so doing had itself been guilty of exceeding its powers. Even sale of monopolies could be defended on the ground that the act of 1624 which condemned the practice referred only to those sold to individuals, whereas Charles was careful to sell only to companies. His demands for loans and benevolences were clearly illegal, but here again the king could argue that the financial condition of the country was precarious, and that as king he had the duty to recognize this fact and the right to take measures necessary for the nation's security. On the other hand it was open to parliament to reply that this exercise of royal power could be employed only in exceptional circumstances, and that mere shortage of revenue did not constitute such a crisis, especially since parliament had not been asked to supply the deficiency.

A test case arose when, between 1634 and 1636, the king sought to maintain a fleet for the protection of the nation without recourse to parliamentary supplies, by demanding "ship-money," first in 1634 from seaport towns and then in the next two years from the whole country. The king's case was that he had the right to levy such a tax in times of danger and that he was sole judge of the existence of such danger. When John Hampden was brought to trial in 1637 for refusal to pay, judgement was given for the king by seven judges to two.

"Thorough" Government

So long as the country remained at peace, the king's financial expedients were adequate to meet the expenses of normal administration; and while magnates and gentry might chafe at the king's successful attack on their pockets and privileges, there were other social classes who had reason to be pleased with these years of personal rule.

Charles found loyal and competent ministers. Bishop Juxon as Lord Treasurer was scrupulous in seeing that poor relief was fairly and adequately administered, a state of affairs that would not have obtained had the matter been left in the hands of justices of the peace. Again (though this was not necessarily the work of Juxon) highways and bridges were maintained in a fashion never again equalled until the nineteenth century. As far as he could, Juxon ensured strict regulation of prices and wages which prevented the rich from exploiting the poor. It was the ranks of magnates and country gentry, rather than the people at large, who saw the king's personal rule as tyranny, and then only because it put limits to their power over their social inferiors and protected the poor.

In the north Charles had an able lieutenant in Thomas Wentworth, Earl of Strafford, who gave the king invaluable service as President of the Council of the North. Far from believing in, or being an agent of, tyranny, Strafford aimed at efficient and thorough government, administered with justice and impartiality, in the interests not of particular social groups but of the nation generally. He was convinced that this kind of government could be most readily established through king and Council rather than through the less speedy parliamentary system. A capable administrator, Strafford ensured through the Council of the North a degree of justice for the small farmer which was often denied by local magistrates; he strictly enforced apprenticeship laws and so protected apprentices from exploitation by unscrupulous masters; he safeguarded the interests of villagers by vigorous execution of laws against enclosure, and like Juxon did his best to see that wages and prices were regulated according to law. The end of the "eleven years' tyranny" was a social disaster for the poor, wage-earners and small farmers, from which they did not recover until the nineteenth century.

Strafford was equally successful when sent to take charge of Irish affairs. The limited group of families who had hitherto ruled Ireland for their own benefit were sent about their business. Almost for the first time, Ireland enjoyed an impartial judicial system and fair taxation. Roads were constructed and new industries set up, and an efficient army was raised. Henceforth the king's opponents in Ireland were not so much the common people as former wealthy corrupt administrators whom Strafford ruthlessly exposed.

Thomas Wentworth, Earl of Strafford.

Religious Uniformity

It was the application of the policy of "thorough" government in the sphere of religion, under the leadership of William Laud, Archbishop of Canterbury, that proved to be the king's undoing.

Laud had no sympathy with Puritans. He stood for the idea of religious uniformity throughout the nation, and the religious system he favoured was that of the Prayer Book, the legal religion of the state. If there were to be innovations, he favoured those which leaned towards beauty in ritual and order in worship. Above all, Laud was a convinced champion of royal supremacy in church government.

He followed a strong anti-Puritan policy. In 1633 he re-issued James I's Book of Sports, and expelled from their livings those clergy who took exception to his action. Through the Court of High Commission he enforced order and uniformity in clerical dress and conduct of worship, bringing before the court clergy whom on his arch-episcopal visitations in the province of Canterbury he had found to be non-conformist in these matters. Ejected clergy were forbidden to preach, to lecture or to publish their writings. Punishments were severe; in 1633 Prynne, a London barrister who had published a book expressing the usual Puritan disapproval of actors and acting, was sentenced to lose his ears and to pay a fine of five thousand pounds as well as to suffer imprisonment for life. When in 1637, Prynne from his prison joined with two other Puritans, Bastwick and Burton, in an attack on episcopacy, his two collaborators incurred the same penalties.

Charles and Laud made their greatest mistake when they decided to apply Laud's rigorous religious policy in Scotland. They began by increasing the number and powers of bishops in Scotland, a country in which most people were firmly wedded to the Presbyterian, non-episcopal form of church organization. They carried their policy a stage further by ordering compulsory use of the surplice by clergymen, finally drawing up a special Prayer Book for use in Scotland and making its use obligatory.

The Scottish reply was given in 1638 by the General Assembly of the Church, held at Glasgow. The assembly declared the Prayer Book and the office of bishop abolished, appointed a committee to control national religious affairs and pledged themselves by their signatures to the National Covenant to maintain the presbyterian form of church administration. The king ordered the assembly to disperse, the assembly declined, and both sides prepared for armed conflict.

The Bishops' Wars

Two short wars followed. The first, in 1639, was indecisive. To win, Charles needed money for better troops. His financial expedients were quite insufficient to stand the strain of war. Strafford from Ireland offered, and advised the use of, the army he had raised there; but Charles, conscious of his rightness and, uncomprehending of the eagerness with which his opponents in England and Scotland were looking for an opportunity to bring his personal rule to an end, decided to seek the money he needed from parliament. The Short Parliament of 1640 refused to grant money until Charles changed both his English and his Scottish policies; the king refused and parliament was dissolved.

The second Bishop's War followed in 1640. Charles was decisively defeated at Newburn, and the Scots refused to withdraw from English territory until the king had paid the expenses they had incurred in the campaign. For this

Charles had no resources. A meeting of the Great Council of Peers at York advised him to recall parliament, and the king had no alternative.

Three factors combined to bring the king to this humiliation.

(*a*) His finances were adequate for normal government expenses only; he had involved himself in a war he could not afford, by his attempt to enforce Laudian religious conformity in Scotland.

(*b*) He had no regular trained army and was not wise enough to accept Strafford's offer of Irish help.

(*c*) Above all, influential wealthy social groups in England were more than ready to exploit to their own advantage the difficulty in which the king had placed himself and his advisers.

Work of the Long Parliament up to 1642

The parliament which Charles was compelled to summon in 1640 has inevitably earned the name of the Long Parliament, because it did not finally dissolve until 1653. Its most important work was done in its first two years, when it dismantled beyond hope of reconstruction the whole machinery of Crown government. In 1640 Strafford was impeached and condemned, and in 1641 the king, against his conscience and with a deep sense of shame, was compelled to sign his adviser's death warrant. Laud was also impeached and condemned in 1641, and languished in prison until his execution in 1645. Having disposed of the king's advisers, parliament turned to the king's powers.

In 1641 tunnage and poundage, ship money and other royal financial expedients were all declared illegal unless imposed with consent of parliament. In the same year the royal courts of Star Chamber and High Commission were abolished, and a Triennial Act passed requiring the king to ensure that parliament met at least every three years. Charles had no alternative but to consent to this legislation, and by so doing deprived himself of all possibility of ruling without parliament on any legal basis.

Moderate parliamentary opinion might well have been content to stop at this point, but Puritan and republican extremists were becoming increasingly well-organized in their management of the House of Commons. In 1641 they came near success with their Root and Branch Bill, which would have abolished episcopal government of the Church of England. Later in the year they were completely successful in inducing parliament to pass the Grand Remonstrance. This was in effect a summary of all Charles' acts of "misgovernment," with no mention of the fact that he had consented to reforms made by parliament between 1640 and 1641; hence it was unfair to the king, and won to his cause a large section of national opinion which had so far been neutral in the struggle between Crown and parliamentary gentry. By dividing both parliament and nation into king's men, soon known as

OCL/HIST/1—M

Cavaliers, and parliament's men, destined to be remembered as Roundheads, the Grand Remonstrance made civil war almost inevitable.

Leaders of the Parliamentary Opposition

Parliament was now being led by capable men. John Hampden, a member of a county family in Buckinghamshire, was a cousin of Oliver Cromwell. Educated under Puritan influences at Oxford, he subsequently had legal training at the Inner Temple. In 1621 he became an M.P., and was in the first three parliaments of Charles I, the Short Parliament and the Long Parliament. He helped to prepare charges against the Duke of Buckingham. In 1627 he refused payment of a forced loan, and ten years later he also refused to pay ship money. He was one of the managers of Strafford's prosecution. He opposed episcopacy, and supported the Grand Remonstrance. He raised a troop to support the parliamentary cause in Buckinghamshire, and died in 1643, after the battle of Chalgrove Field.

Sir John Eliot, educated at Oxford and trained in law, became an M.P. in 1614. He was a friend of Buckingham, was knighted in 1618, and appointed Vice-Admiral of Devon. In 1625 he urged enforcement of laws against Catholics, and broke his friendship with Buckingham. By 1626 he was virtually leader of the Commons opposition to the Crown. He attacked Buckingham, and criticized the Cadiz expedition. He supported the impeachment of Buckingham, and was dismissed from his position as Vice-Admiral of Devon. In 1627 he was imprisoned for a short time, for refusing to pay a forced loan. In 1628 he opposed royal taxation, and was the author of the Three Resolutions of that year. He also attacked ritualism in religion. Although confined in the Tower, he refused to compromise. He wrote political works defending parliamentary participation in government and justifying his own attitude. In 1632, still in prison, he died.

John Pym, educated at Oxford and trained in law, urged suppression of Catholics in 1621. He asserted parliamentary rights in a Commons protest, and was for a short time under house arrest. He led opposition to the Crown in the Short Parliament. In the Long Parliament, Pym pressed for the impeachment of Strafford and Laud. He voted for the Root and Branch Bill, he organized parliamentary finance for the civil war, and was the architect of the parliamentary alliance with the Scots. He was always an opponent of royal autocracy, rather than a convinced Puritan. He died in 1643.

QUESTIONS

1. Describe and account for the action taken by the Long Parliament with regard to (*a*) Strafford and (*b*) Archbishop Laud.
2. Describe the methods by which Charles I sought to raise money during his period of personal government 1629-40.

CHAPTER 27

THE CIVIL WAR, 1642-49

THE fanaticism of parliamentary extremists responsible for passing the Grand Remonstrance was matched only by the belated stubbornness of the king, and events moved grimly and inevitably to war.

Certainly it was the Grand Remonstrance which provoked the king into one of his most disastrous and illegal acts. He took a troop of soldiers to the House of Commons, intending to arrest five members who had recently been his severest critics (one of whom was John Pym). Warned of what was afoot, they were absent when the king arrived. The illegality of his action was made worse from his point of view by its utter ineffectiveness. There followed the Bishops Act (the Rabbling of the Bishops) depriving bishops of their seats in the House of Lords and thereby removing from parliament the king's strongest supporters. Two more extreme actions on the part of parliament still further divided that assembly as well as widening the gulf between the king and his opponents. Parliament demanded control of the militia, and the king's consent to nineteen propositions which, had he accepted them, would have deprived him of all power. The king rejected these requests and both sides reached for their weapons.

Resources of King and Parliament at the Outbreak of War

When Charles raised his standard at Nottingham in the late summer of 1642, after parliament had seized Hull and denied the king admission, the nation was sadly divided. Of the contending religious parties, Anglicans were for the king; so were the Catholics, since their bitterest antagonists, the Puritans, were for parliament. Moderate political opinion sided with the king, fearing that parliament, increasingly dominated by the intolerant Presbyterian faction among the Puritans, might if successful set up a tyranny far more oppressive than the personal rule of the Crown.

The king had the support of three-fifths of the peers, and his military strength lay in the cavalry, led by his nephew Prince Rupert. Parliament, with only a minority of peers on its side, was weak in cavalry but (with the support of yeomen and merchants) stronger in infantry.

Financially parliament was stronger than the king. Being now the effective government, it controlled national revenue, and had strong support from the commercial classes. The king was dependent on the wealth of his followers.

six 20

1 You ar to accuse those joyntlie & seueralie

2 you ar to reserue the power of making additionalls

3 When the Comittie for examination is a naming (wch you must press to be close & under tey of secresie) if either Essex, Warwick, Holland, Say, Wharton, or Brooke be named, you must desyre that they may be spared because you ar to examine them as witnesses for me

Charles R

Charles I's orders for the arrest of the five members.

Geographically the king was supported by the north of England (except south Lancashire and the north Midlands) together with Wales, Devon and Cornwall, and by 1643 he had captured the south as far as a line from Gloucester to Newbury. These were on the whole poor areas; a quick victory was essential to the success of the royalist cause. Parliament, on the other hand, was strongest in the east, the south (up to 1643), Manchester, the cloth towns of the West Riding of Yorkshire, and London. Hence parliament possessed the chief ports, and controlled customs, and could thus afford a long war. Finally, although the king had the universities, a valuable source of initial wealth, behind him, parliament had control of the navy and could prevent foreign aid reaching Charles. Scottish intervention told heavily against the king up to 1646, and did him no service when in 1648 it switched to his side.

Nature of the Civil War up to 1646

To almost all the broad generalizations above, exceptions may be found. If towns were strongly parliamentarian, in all of them existed a royalist minority. If country areas were predominantly royalist, yeomen farmers of the south and east were the parliamentary exception. One of the chief features of the Civil War is the fact that there was no clear-cut geographical or social division between sides. Families were divided in their loyalties. Oliver Cromwell might be the architect of parliament's military victory, but his old uncle, Sir Oliver Cromwell of Hinchingbrooke, was to his death in 1653 an enthusiastic royalist. To be for or against the king was the dividing issue, a matter of allegiance to principle, at least up to 1646; the Civil War is therefore perhaps better called the Great Rebellion.

Again it resembled a rebellion rather than a war in its military character. It was a series of local engagements rather than a nationally co-ordinated campaign, conducted on both sides (prior to the emergence of Cromwell and the New Model Army) by commanders of no great military ability (save perhaps Prince Rupert) leading "train bands" pressed into parliamentary service from the towns; or troops of horse similarly assembled by local royalist gentry. The soldiers were not trained professionals, and only some of their leaders had battle experience.

Main Events of the Civil Wars to 1646

The indecisive battle of Edgehill in 1642 diverted the king from his march on London. In 1643 the king captured Reading after failing to prevent the retreat to London of the Roundheads under the leadership of Essex. By the end of 1643 the king had control of three-quarters of the kingdom.

In 1644 both sides sought help from outside. Parliament made the Solemn League and Covenant with the Scots, whereby the Scots promised to help parliament, and parliament agreed to establish the Presbyterian form of Puritanism as the national religion of England. In the same year Charles agreed to recognize Catholicism in Ireland, and the Irish promised ten thousand troops to assist the king.

Charles now began to find difficulty in raising funds for the war. Cromwell won a victory at the battle of Marston Moor in 1644, with the help of Scottish troops, and the king lost control of the north of England. Essex was defeated at Lostwithiel.

The parliamentary group reorganized their command by the Self-Denying Ordinance of 1644, which excluded M.P.s from command of the parliamentary armies. Command was given to Sir Thomas Fairfax; an exception to the Ordinance was made for Cromwell, who was appointed second-in-command. The New Model Army was formed, and carefully trained.

At the battle of Naseby in 1645 the king lost control of the Midlands. Montrose was defeated at Philiphaugh in the same year, and the Royalist cause was ruined in Scotland. Charles surrendered to the Scots, who handed him over to parliament.

New Model Army

Cromwell's creation of the New Model Army was one of the decisive developments of the Civil War. By 1644 leadership of the parliamentary forces was growing dangerously weak. Pym and Hampden were both dead;

Oliver Cromwell (left) developed the New Model Army from the Eastern Association. Prince Rupert (right), nephew of Charles I, led the Royalist cavalry, but his forces proved no match for the disciplined parliamentary troops.

confidence in the leadership of Essex had been destroyed by his defeat and narrow escape after an engagement at Lostwithiel in Cornwall. To clear the field, parliament passed the Self-Denying Ordinance requiring all members of both Houses to resign military commands. This left the way open for appointment of new commanders. The Self-Denying Ordinance was respected by giving the supreme command to Sir Thomas Fairfax, but broken in spirit by appointing Cromwell, a member of the Commons, as his immediate subordinate.

These two men had for some time been training a force known as the Eastern Association. They now applied their programme throughout the parliamentary forces. Eventually they had an army of 80,000 which, though it contained some pressed men, contained far more men of conviction dedicated to Puritanism, freedom and toleration. It was systematically drilled, well organized and (up to 1646) regularly paid; but its overwhelming virtue was its high morale and intense belief in the cause for which it fought. This New Model Army gave parliament complete victory within twelve months.

Nature of the Civil War after 1646

After 1646 the nature of the conflict underwent subtle changes. From 1646 to 1648 the professional army was opposed to irregulars. Moreover the struggle became a three-party affair of parliament, army and king, rather than a straight fight between crown and rebel subjects. Parliament misused victory to adopt intolerant measures against Anglicans and Royalists. Prayer Book services were prohibited, two thousand clergy were expelled from their livings and Presbyterian preachers intruded in their place. When next you visit an ancient parish church in which is displayed a list of incumbents, examine it carefully between 1640 and 1665 and you will probably see numerous changes and short tenures. It will be unusual if it does not reflect the ebb and flow between Anglican and Puritan during this period.

After dealing thus intolerantly with Anglican clergy, parliament turned on royalist landowners. Those who had fought for the king were required to pay fines varying from 15 to 50 per cent of their estates. This common suffering of parson and squire was the beginning of a close alliance between the two which dominated English social life well into the nineteenth century.

It was the Presbyterian intolerance of parliament which damaged its relations with the army. Puritan sects known as Baptists and Independents, which dominated the army, were as loth to submit to Presbyterian uniformity as to Anglican uniformity. When in addition parliament tried to disband the New Model Army without final payment, the army took matters in its own hands, dispossessed parliament of the king and in 1647 sought to negotiate its own peace terms, known as the Heads of the Proposals.

At this point the king committed his crowning act of folly. He tried to play off the army against parliament and both against the Scots to such an extent that all parties lost faith in his word. His stupidity at this point led to renewal of war, and to his ultimate execution.

The short campaign of 1648 was much more a civil war than the first had been. It was fought between the army (Cromwell's Ironsides, as they were known) on the one side and Presbyterians (parliamentary and Scottish) and Royalists on the other. This was less a quarrel about the constitution than a struggle for power. Cromwell's victory at the battle of Preston in 1648 and Pride's Purge of parliament immediately afterwards settled the issue and doomed the king.

Reasons for the King's Failure

Apart from his final mishandling of the situation in 1648, the king had virtually lost his cause in 1646. Fundamentally the king's weakness was lack of money. Parliament's resources were continuous; the king's were limited by the resources of those loyal to him. Had he been able to obtain foreign aid, in men or money, this disadvantage might have been offset; but defection of the navy, always strongly Protestant and fearful that Laud's religious policy might be a step back towards Catholicism, removed any hope of foreign support. The king's difficulties in these respects were emphasized by parliamentary possession of London and the ports.

After 1643 and 1645 the scales were further weighted against the king by the superior discipline, organization and training of the parliamentary forces compared with his own. The well-drilled enthusiasts of the New Model

Army were more than a match for the king's pressed levies and his enthusiastic but amateur cavalry.

Finally it must be admitted that Charles contributed to his own undoing by errors of tactics, judgement and character. His negotiations for a French invasion in 1645 and his promise to establish Catholicism in Ireland in return for Irish help alienated many of his supporters. Equally his transparent attempts to play off parliament against the army and both against the Scots destroyed any prospect the royalist cause might have had of profiting from the disunity of its opponents.

Comments on the King's Execution

The king's apparent duplicity and untrustworthiness revealed during the last two years of his life went far to make his execution inevitable; but it did not make it legal or even advisable. A special court had to be set up to bring him to justice, and its jurisdiction was open to question. A new interpretation had to be given to the law of treason; hitherto treason had been an offence against the king, but Charles could hardly be tried for self-betrayal. By 1649 the Long Parliament, by reason of natural death and death in battle as well as party purges, could only doubtfully claim to be representative of the nation; and the Peers did not agree to the trial. In challenging the legality of the court which sat in judgement on him, Charles was on strong ground.

The advisability of the king's execution was also open to question. Dead, he came to be regarded as a martyr. With his execution, royalists rallied round his son Prince Charles, too young to be identified with his father's follies, and therefore presented to the nation as blameless. Republican sentiment was a minority opinion; the king's death did not automatically restore national unity. Indeed England, Scotland and Ireland all had to be compelled by further force of arms to accept the Commonwealth, and ultimately no republican constitution proved workable.

Yet it is hard to see what practical alternative to execution could have been adopted. That Charles would have loyally observed the terms of any compromise settlement which limited the powers and prerogatives of the Crown is extremely doubtful; he was too sincerely convinced of the divine nature of kingship. To have deposed him and kept him prisoner would have meant constant threat of war, foreign invasion on the king's behalf or plots to restore him to power. Cromwell's verdict on the king's execution remains valid; it was, he said, "a cruel necessity."

QUESTIONS

1. Why did parliament win the Civil War?

2. What part did Scotland play in English affairs just before and during the Civil War?

CHAPTER 28

THE FAILURE OF CONSTITUTIONAL EXPERIMENT

CHARLES I was executed, not because the majority of his subjects objected to monarchy, but because they found Charles himself an impossible monarch. His death therefore left unsolved the problem as to how government of the country was to be carried on.

For the moment, what was left by 1649 of the Long Parliament of 1640 was legally in charge of the country's affairs; but it had triumphed over Charles I by virtue of the army's defeat of the king's forces. The Rump, as this remnant of the Long Parliament came to be called, was thus dependant on the continued support of the army. This was clearly demonstrated when Ireland and Scotland refused to recognize the new regime in England and pledged their loyalty to Prince Charles. It was the army (under Cromwell, his son-in-law Ireton, and General Monk) which had to enforce by military conquest the recognition in these countries of the new Commonwealth.

Establishment of the Commonwealth in Ireland and Scotland

On the execution of Charles I, all political parties in Ireland combined to support Prince Charles against the Rump. Cromwell took an army to Ireland in 1649, successfully stormed the chief Irish forts of Drogheda and Wexford, and established control of the whole east coast except Waterford. His son-in-law Ireton completed the conquest by 1652. The needless violence and cruelty with which the conquest was effected permanently soured relations between Ireland and England.

Cromwell's troops and other Protestant settlers were given extensive lands in Ireland, thus intensifying the division of Ireland between native Catholic and planted Protestant. The Catholic religion was made illegal.

In Scotland there were two Royalist parties: the one, led by the Duke of Argyll, wanted Prince Charles to accept the Covenant, and promise to impose Presbyterianism in England; the other, led by the Duke of Montrose, supported Prince Charles unconditionally. In 1650 Montrose headed an unsuccessful Highland rising in favour of Prince Charles, and was defeated, captured and hanged. The Prince was forced to come to terms with Argyll.

In the subsequent war between England and Scotland, the Scots were defeated at the battles of Dunbar (1650) and Worcester (1651). Scotland lost her independence, and was governed during the Interregnum by General

Monk and an English army, with the temporary union of the two kingdoms.

Once civil war had ended, it became obvious that there was a marked difference of outlook between the Rump and the army on which it depended. In religious matters the Rump represented the Presbyterian aspect of Puritanism, and wished to enforce that system of church organization throughout England. The army, on the other hand, represented independent sects, and was anxious to establish a large measure of religious toleration. The Rump, moreover, was as eager to establish its own monopoly of political power as Charles I had been, whilst the army was ready to promote measures of political reform, and pinned its faith for realization of its hopes on elections and a new parliament. True, it quickly suppressed an extremist group (the Levellers, led by John Lilbourne) with dreams of annual parliaments, manhood suffrage and common ownership of land; but it took alarm when the Rump proposed that its ninety remaining members should automatically retain their seats in any new parliament and have the right to exclude any new members they thought undesirable. To prevent these proposals being enacted, Cromwell took troops into the Commons and forceably dissolved the Rump. Thus one of Charles I's judges was compelled to take a course dangerously similar to that which, when taken by Charles in 1642, had been denounced as tyranny.

First Experiment: Barebones' Parliament, 1653

All that the Rump had done towards solving the problem of Britain's future government was to declare Britain a Commonwealth and to entrust administration to a Council of State. Partly for this reason the domestic history of the years between 1649 and 1660 is largely the story of a series of constitutional experiments.

With the dissolution of the Rump, the Council of State, dominated by the Independent Puritan influence of the army, tried the experiment of having a new parliament chosen by members of independent Puritan congregations throughout the country. This resulted in 1653 in the assembly of 140 worthy and well-intentioned but, as events proved, not very effective Puritan legislators, among whom was Praise-God Barebones, by whose name this parliament has become known.

Measures proposed or enacted by this legislature were impractical and unsuccessful. They angered lawyers and disrupted the country's legal system by abolishing the Court of Chancery after only one day's debate, and setting up no alternative. In similar fashion it offended the army by a series of complicated proposals for raising money for army maintenance. Its eagerness to establish religious toleration earned the hostility of Presbyterian opinion, while its condemnation of financing the church through payment of tithes, without alternative suggestions, would have ruined church finances.

"The Great Seal of England 1651" *has on its reverse the House of Commons during the Interregnum. This shows the House in session, the Speaker sitting in the Chair and a Member is addressing the House from the floor. Two clerks can be seen at the table, upon which the mace rests. This is the Second Seal used by the Commonwealth, and is attached to a document dated* 8 *September*, 1656.

The result of all this impossible legislation was the realization by a few practical members that most of their colleagues were unequal to the task to which they had been called. These few therefore carried a surprise vote for voluntary dissolution, and the handing over of power to Cromwell.

The Second Experiment: The Instrument of Government, 1653

With greatness suddenly thrust upon him, Cromwell turned to the army for advice. As a result the army council drew up the Instrument of Government. Under the terms of this document, England, Ireland and Scotland were to be a Protectorate with Cromwell as Lord Protector, assisted by a Council of Fifteen. Parliament was to be elected on a new franchise, from re-organized constituencies; the life of parliament was to be limited to three years, and no parliament was to be dissolved before it had sat for five months. Parliament was to make laws and determine taxes, while the Protector was to administer revenue thus raised, to make ordinances in conformity with parliamentary legislation, but to have no power of veto over such enactments. Finally there was to be religious toleration for all save papists, episcopalians, the blasphemous and the licentious.

First Protectorate Parliament

This scheme, Britain's first written constitution, had much to commend it. It involved re-organization of electoral constituencies and re-distribution of seats in parliament; it provided for the parliamentary union of the British Isles. Less happily, it balanced too nicely the powers of parliament and Protector, and provided no means of removing the latter if unsatisfactory.

The First Protectorate Parliament got off to a bad beginning. It had been elected on too narrow a franchise; instead of being elected by all free-holders of property worth forty shillings a year, voting was restricted to owners of property worth £200 a year. Efforts of the Council to "manage" the election were not wholly successful, and an active minority of Presbyterian members indulged in criticism of the Instrument of Government; in consequence thirty members were expelled from the House. The remainder, anxious to safeguard themselves from a similar fate if their proposals displeased the army, tried to reduce military expenditure and to limit still further Cromwell's powers as Protector. Finding the legislature not merely unco-operative but even hostile, Cromwell exercised his power to dissolve the assembly at the end of five lunar months, though the Instrument of Government had merely said "five months," and probably meant calendar months.

Third Experiment: Rule of the Major-Generals

Thereafter for almost two years Cromwell, like Charles I between 1629 and 1640, administered the country without parliament. For purposes of local government the country was divided into eleven districts, each under the rule of a Major-General. These officers were empowered to supervise the militia, prevent royalist plots and enforce laws regulating conduct and morality of a narrow Puritan kind. From this period dates what is known as the English Sunday, with closure of shops and inns and prohibition of games and sport. Juries were elected and newspapers suppressed; never were gaols so full, nor so many ships heavily loaded with deportees to the colonies. So earnest were the efforts made to produce a godly nation that ungodliness itself became a crime. It is not surprising that this third experiment was resented as a military and religious despotism; yet the depth of the impression it made on the nation is indicated by the survival to our own day of features of the Puritan Sunday.

Second Protectorate Parliament, 1656: The Humble Petition and Advice

Financial necessity, rather than unpopularity, brought the rule of the Major-Generals to its end. Like the first two Stuart kings, Cromwell found it impossible to run the country and fight a war without special taxation; and by now Cromwell, as we shall see in the next chapter, was involved in war with Spain. By now too the principle that taxes could be imposed only by parliament was no longer a matter of legal dispute; it had been written into the constitution by the Instrument of Government.

Hence in 1656 Cromwell again tried to establish constitutional parliamentary government. The Second Protectorate Parliament in its first session suggested fresh proposals for government of the country. In the Humble Petition and Advice it suggested abolition of the Council of State, re-establishment of a second House of Parliament, enlargement of the Protector's powers and restoration of the monarchy with Oliver Cromwell as the new king.

These changes, save one, Cromwell accepted. The exception was restoration of the monarchy in his person. The army was firmly opposed to the notion of King Cromwell, and since Cromwell's power depended on army support, he could not risk accepting the title.

In the second session of 1658, parliament was less co-operative. Many members who had initiated and supported the Humble Petition and Advice had been moved to the new second chamber; their replacements in the lower House represented a different outlook, and launched a strong attack on both the upper House and the extension of the Protector's powers. Cromwell and the army regarded the constitutional issue as settled; they wanted parliament to address itself to the purpose for which it had been summoned, provision of funds for war against Spain. When it showed no inclination to do so, but every determination to check the power of the administration, Cromwell, disillusioned by its unco-operativeness, had no alternative but to dissolve it. If at times Cromwell's relations with parliament seem strangely similar to those of Charles I, it must be remembered that while Charles would not co-operate with parliament, it was now parliament who would not co-operate with Cromwell. After the dissolution of the second Protectorate Parliament, Cromwell had no opportunity to try again. Seven months after the dissolution, he was dead.

The End of Constitutional Experiment

Though Cromwell had refused the title of King, he was succeeded as Protector by his son Richard as if the office was hereditary. Richard however lacked the qualities of leadership which his father had possessed. His ineffectiveness aroused discontent in the army, and within a year Richard resigned, realizing his inadequacy for the role in which birth had placed him. The depleted ranks of the Rump reassembled to take charge of the situation, but were expelled by the army, whose leaders began to quarrel.

In this confused situation Cromwell's lieutenant in Scotland, General Monk, took the initiative, and in 1660 marched on London. There he re-assembled the Rump, to compel it to bring itself to a legal end by voting its own dissolution. Monk then made arrangements for the election of a new parliament which, when it met, proved to have a royalist majority.

At this point Prince Charles helped matters along by issuing from his exile in Holland the Declaration of Breda. He promised an amnesty for all political offences against himself and his father, save such as should be exempted by parliament. He likewise declared himself in favour of toleration for all religious parties except those which disturbed the peace. He further undertook to leave parliament to decide the validity of the change of ownership of land which had taken place during the years of his exile.

In the light of these fair promises the Convention Parliament had no hesitation in declaring that government of the country should be by "King, Lords and Commons," and in inviting Prince Charles to ascend the throne as Charles II. He landed at Dover to an enthusiastic welcome on 25 May, 1660, and the period of constitutional experiment was over.

Merits and Demerits of the Interregnum

Clearly public opinion had not found the attempt to dispense with the Crown any more to its liking than it had found the efforts of the Crown to dispense with parliament, and the people had good cause for dissatisfaction. The freedom enjoyed by the individual was probably no greater under Cromwell than it had been under Charles I. People were still imprisoned without trial and had been subjected to military tyranny. Their amusements had been curtailed by closure of theatres and by enforcement of a narrow Puritan morality, while Roman Catholics had suffered severe penalties. Taxation had increased threefold between 1649 and 1660, yet there remained a formidable national debt.

On the other hand, sound reforms had been attempted. Jews, officially excluded from England since the days of their persecution under Edward I, were re-admitted and allowed the normal rights of a citizen. Together with Quakers and Anglicans, they enjoyed a fair measure of religious toleration. Good order was maintained; and, if there was some restriction of innocent pleasures, many undesirable amusements were rightly suppressed. Some sound changes, such as reduction of the cost of legal processes, temporary parliamentary union of England and Scotland and the remodelling of parliamentary constituencies, were attempted. Finally, Cromwell's regime paid greater attention to colonial affairs than any previous seventeenth-century government had done, while its foreign policy re-established the international standing of England as a major power of Europe. It is to this latter aspect of the period 1649-60 that we must turn in the next chapter.

Cromwell's rule was personal, and its collapse after his death was almost inevitable. Experiments in government without a monarch never commanded the support of the majority, and had always rested on military strength. Hence there had always been strong sympathy in the country for the monarchy and Anglicanism. The rule of the Major-Generals had been highly unpopular, and public opinion had been offended by interference in private life. The nation was tired of experiments, and wanted settled government.

QUESTIONS

1. How did Cromwell deal with Scotland and Ireland?
2. What attempts at constitutional rule did Cromwell make, and why did they fail?

CHAPTER 29

THE INTERREGNUM, THE EMPIRE AND EUROPE

THOUGH neither Commonwealth nor Protectorate succeeded in solving domestic problems, both contributed to the revival of England's prestige as one of the major powers of Europe, as well as to the growth of the Empire.

England's pre-occupation with domestic quarrels between 1629 and 1649 left little time for development of a successful foreign policy. After 1629 England virtually withdrew from any position of influence in Continental affairs, and proved powerless to prevent Dutch privateers from raiding English coasts or Dutch ships from taking over the English carrying trade.

Indirectly, however, quarrels at home contributed to growth of the Empire overseas. Failure of attempts to plant colonies during the reign of Elizabeth was redeemed by success under James I. By 1619 Virginia had established a sound economy on the cultivation of tobacco on estates owned by emigrants from England and cultivated by native labour. Adjoining Virginia was Maryland, established in 1632 by Lord Baltimore under a charter granted by

"Mayflower II," a replica of the Pilgrim Fathers' ship, at New York.

Charles I; here refugees from religious intolerance in the mother country had established the principle of religious toleration, and Puritan and Catholic lived happily side by side.

This aspect of life in Maryland serves to show that motives other than commercial enterprise had begun to prompt colonial expansion. As early as 1620 a group of Puritans, in despair of practising their religion undisturbed at home, had sailed for the New World, landed in America and given their new home the name of the town whence they had sailed, Plymouth. These Pilgrim Fathers had been followed by another group of oppressed Puritans, who formed the colony of Massachusetts in 1630, and thereafter received a steady flow of new emigrants as Laud's religious policy grew more intolerable. Ultimately there were four Puritan (New England) settlements on the American coast, Rhode Island, Connecticut, New Hampshire and Massachusetts.

While Puritans found refuge in New England, Royalist gentlemen reinforced a settlement first made in Barbados in 1625; and Royalist churchmen predominated in the Bermudas. Thus tensions at home were reflected in the Empire overseas; and though unhappy divisions served to weaken England in Europe, they thus served to extend the Empire, although the link with the mother country only narrowly survived conflicts in England. The Puritan New England colonies came together in a confederation in 1643 to resist possible interference in their internal affairs by Laud, while Cromwell had to threaten an attack on Royalist Virginia, Barbados and Bermuda before they would recognize the Commonwealth.

Colonial Policy, 1649-58

The Commonwealth made its contribution to colonial development by challenging the most powerful naval power of the day, Holland. Much profit which might have accrued to England from overseas possessions was lost because by the mid-seventeenth century the Dutch had become the great ship-owning and naval trading power of the day. English trade with her overseas possessions was carried on in Dutch ships, which diminished the profitability of colonial trade.

For this reason the Rump passed an Act requiring that all goods brought to England from America, Africa or Asia should be carried in ships owned and manned by English or Colonial subjects. Had this Navigation Act been enforced immediately, prosperity of the colonies would have been seriously curtailed; for due to neglect during the civil wars, English shipping was inadequate to cope with the trade entailed. Nevertheless, the act was a severe blow to the Dutch, and a powerful stimulus to the growth of English trade.

The Protectorate, as well as the Commonwealth, promoted colonial development. In the course of a war with Spain which we shall examine presently, Cromwell despatched an expedition to the Spanish West Indies, and Jamaica

ELIZABETHAN THEATRE, SUCH AS SHAKESPEARE USED

LIFE IN THE DAYS OF ELIZABETH I

was captured in 1657. Although leaders of the enterprise were given little credit for their exploit Jamaica was to prove a most valuable possession.

The Commonwealth's War with the Dutch

The Navigation Act of 1651 was one cause of the war which the Commonwealth waged with the Dutch, but not the only one. Taking advantage of England's feebleness during the years 1629-49, the Dutch virtually excluded English traders from the East Indies. They challenged English control over the Channel by refusing to salute English men-of-war in these narrow seas, as well as disputing England's right in time of war to search suspected ships sailing in this area.

The war, when it came in 1651, began badly for England; Admiral Blake was defeated in an engagement with Dutch Von Tromp off Dungeness. But Blake turned the tables and re-asserted English control of the Channel by defeating Von Tromp off Portland. Monk carried war home to the Dutch by defeating them off Texel, and the English navy was able to establish a blockade of Holland.

The Protectorate and Foreign Powers

It was left to Cromwell to reap the fruits of the Commonwealth's conflict with the Dutch. By the Peace of Westminster which Cromwell negotiated in 1654, the Dutch agreed to expel refugee Stuarts from the Netherlands, to salute the English flag in English seas and to accept the Navigation Act of 1651. The hey-day of Dutch naval and commercial supremacy in Europe was brought to the beginning of its end, and England ultimately inherited what the Dutch surrendered.

Cromwell had been pleased to make peace with the Dutch, for it seemed to him ungodly that two Protestant powers should be at war with each other. He wanted to be free to defend Protestantism wherever it was threatened, and would have liked to make a league of northern Protestant powers of Europe against the champions of Catholicism, Austria or Spain and France, but this was out of the question. Not merely were the northern powers unsympathetic to Cromwell's religious zeal, but two major Catholic powers, France and Spain, were at odds with each other and in competition for England's support. At one time it seemed likely that Cromwell might join Spain against France, but Spain was not prepared to pay Cromwell's price for an alliance. She felt she could not grant religious toleration to English merchants resident in Spain, allow English ships to share trade with Spanish American colonies or surrender Dunkirk.

These were the concessions Cromwell wanted; and when he could not get them by negotiation, they became adequate reasons for war. Without waiting for a formal declaration of hostilities, Cromwell launched a raid on the

Spanish Main, and entered into an anti-Spanish alliance with France. An English expedition to the West Indies failed to take San Domingo but, as we have already seen, had no difficulty in capturing Jamaica. A severe blow at Spain's capacity for continuing the war was struck by capture of the Spanish treasure fleet in the harbour of Santa Cruz; and final victory for Cromwell came with the defeat of Spain at the Battle of the Dunes, and the capture of Dunkirk in 1658.

Cromwell's desire to serve the Protestant cause in Europe, frustrated on a large scale, had one small success. He used his influence with France to induce the French government to compel the Duke of Savoy to cease persecuting the Vaudois, a small Protestant sect in the Italian Alps.

For the most part, however, Cromwell's foreign policy served the national advancement of England rather than Protestantism in Europe. With Sweden he made a commercial treaty facilitating supply of naval stores from the Baltic to England and opening up the Sound to English shipping. Cromwell, though ready to plunge England into civil war in 1642, did much to prove himself a sound patriot.

Comments on Cromwell's Foreign Policy

One result of Cromwell's keen defence of British interests in Europe was the restoration of British prestige abroad. A contemporary admirer said of him that he "carried the keys of the Continent at his girdle and made all the neighbour princes fear him." Certainly he re-established English naval power and secured its recognition by European rivals. His commercial treaties secured important concessions for English trade, though his war with Spain, by affording hostile pirates an excuse for attacks on the carrying trade, prevented England from reaping benefits which might otherwise have accrued. The fact that England acquired a new colony as a result of the war was no adequate compensation for losses in other directions.

Losses there certainly were. In attacking Spain, Cromwell was merely delivering the final fatal blows at an already dying power, at the same time contributing to the strength of a thriving potential enemy, France. Above all, his expensive foreign policy prevented him from achieving the constitutional pacification he would have liked to establish in domestic affairs. Cromwell bequeathed to those who followed him only a renewal of issues for which parliament had fought and Charles I had died, and for this lamentable legacy his foreign policy was largely to blame.

QUESTIONS

1. Give an account of Cromwell's foreign policy during the Protectorate.
2. Why was Cromwell so anxious to make peace with the Dutch, but so ready to make war upon Spain?

CHAPTER 30

THE RESTORATION, 1660-67

THE Restoration of 1660 did not mean solely the return of a king to the throne of England; it was equally the restoration of parliament and of the Church of England. It was not so much an event as a process, gradually carried out during the first seven years of the reign of Charles II.

It was impossible to undo all the work of the Commonwealth and Oliver Cromwell. Edward Hyde, Earl of Clarendon, the king's adviser during these first seven years, aimed largely at re-establishing the state of affairs which had existed by the middle of 1641, accepting much of the work of the Long Parliament. The Convention Parliament (1660-61) sincerely tried to honour the pledges Charles had given in the Declaration of Breda. It was the Cavalier Parliament (1661-79) which proved more royalist than the king.

Thus Charles II was as free as any sovereign since the time of Elizabeth I to choose his advisers and decide on policy; but, like Elizabeth in her later years, he would have to persuade parliament to accept both policy and ministers. Crown lands were restored to the king, even those sold during the Commonwealth; and income derived from them, together with tunnage and poundage, was to be the normal revenue of the kingdom. No other financial demands were to be levied except by parliamentary consent. Neither feudal dues nor special royal courts were revived, so the king was deprived of these sources of non-parliamentary revenue. Judges were to be appointed for life, and not at the king's pleasure, so the king could not use judges to define the law in such a way as to make his will prevail over that of parliament.

The effect of these arrangements was to make the king very dependent on parliament, particularly since money produced from Crown lands was hardly sufficient for the expenses of government even in times of peace, much less during war. Charles II had repeatedly to seek parliamentary approval for taxation, not necessarily because he was extravagant but because he was poor. Not until the last few years of his reign, when owing to an increase in trade there was a greater yield from tunnage and poundage and excise duties, was he able to dispense with parliament.

Thus the restoration was as much a restoration of parliament as of the king, especially since the House of Lords was revived, together with the old constituencies and franchise qualifications of pre-Commonwealth days.

It was when the Convention Parliament sought to deal with land which

Charles II dancing with Mary of Orange at a ball at the Hague on the eve of his departure for England, 1660.

had changed hands during the Commonwealth that restoration proved most difficult. As we have seen, Crown lands were recovered by the king. Much land, however, had been sold by royalists during the civil wars to raise money for the king's cause. Other royalists, when the fighting was over, had been heavily fined for their support of the king. The fine had sometimes taken the form of confiscation of their estates; at other times, when the fine had been a monetary one, they had been compelled to put estates on the market to raise money to meet the penalty. With the king restored, these cavaliers hoped for a reversal of their fortunes, but many were disappointed. Lands were restored only to royalists whose estates had been confiscated by the Commonwealth without payment of compensation; those which had been sold were retained by their new owners. Thus among the wealthy landed gentry of post-restoration England there were many new families, but within a generation or two they had become absorbed into the ranks of the aristocracy. A major social revolution had been confirmed.

Restoration of the Church of England

Re-organization of the religious life of the country proved the most controversial problem of all. Charles II, in the Declaration of Breda, had promised religious toleration; and the Convention Parliament made proposals on this matter which would have gone far to redeem the king's pledge. The proposals were, however, defeated by hostility between the parties concerned; and at the Savoy Conference of 1661, which was called to try to reach a compromise on points which divided Anglican and non-Anglican, Bishop Sheldon ensured failure when he refused to make any concessions to his opponents.

In the Cavalier Parliament of 1661 non-Anglicans of all kinds were but thinly represented, and this parliament showed itself as strongly anti-Nonconformist as it was anti-Roman Catholic, and sought to restore the Church of England to the exclusive position it had occupied before the civil war.

This it did by a series of laws, passed between 1661 and 1665, known as the Clarendon Code (in spite of the fact that the policy they presented was neither Clarendon's nor the king's). The Corporation Act of 1661 required all members of county and borough corporations to be communicant members of the Church of England. The Act of Uniformity of 1662 declined to recognize a clergyman not ordained by a bishop of the Anglican Church, and demanded that all clergy and schoolmasters should declare acceptance of the Prayer Book. The result of this act was the expulsion from, or resignation of, their livings of one-fifth of the most learned and respected clergy.

The Conventicle Act of 1664 forbade any meeting of more than five persons for worship, unless conducted according to ceremonies set out in the Prayer Book. This was designed to curtail the popularity of dispossessed clergy who continued to teach and to minister acceptably to people who sympathized with them and shared their views. Finally the Five Mile Act of 1665 forbade all expelled clergy to teach in schools, or to come within five miles of any corporate town or borough. This deprived Nonconformist clergy of the most obvious way of earning a living, and was intended to remove their influence. The total result of the Clarendon Code was to intensify conflict between Anglican church and Nonconformist chapel.

Continuity of Foreign Policy, 1660-67: Alliance with France

In their relations with foreign powers, king and parliament in 1660 did not so much reverse the state of affairs they found as continue where Cromwell had left off. In the duel between France and Spain, Cromwell had adopted an anti-Spanish and to that extent pro-French line. Charles II went further and sought to build up an Anglo-French alliance, not moved purely by his admiration for all things French nor by consideration of the best interests of England. He disliked being dependent on parliament for finance, and was willing to become a pensioner of France if thereby he could deliver himself from this dependence. Louis XIV hoped to see Catholicism tolerated, if not established, in England, and knew that Charles would never be able to carry such a policy so long as parliament controlled his purse. Moreover Louis had designs on Holland, and saw in England his most likely ally.

These considerations drew the two sovereigns together. Charles married Catherine of Braganza, a princess of France's ally Portugal. He made no bones about selling Dunkirk to France, and agreed to aid France in an attack on Holland or at least to remain neutral. In return Charles was promised financial support.

The results of these developments were the acquisition of Bombay as part of the dowry of Queen Catherine, the increasing unpopularity of Clarendon who was unjustly blamed for the sale of Dunkirk, and finally for war between Holland and England.

Second Dutch War, 1665-67

For war with Holland there were causes other than the alliance with France. Across the Atlantic, Dutch colonists of New Amsterdam were at odds with English colonists of Virginia; and Charles II was angered when, Holland having become a republic, his nephew William of Orange was excluded from the Presidency.

The opening stages of war were successful for England; in 1664 New Amsterdam was captured from the Dutch, and only partly offset by the Dutch capture of part of Guiana. In the next year the Duke of York had a spectacular victory over the Dutch fleet off Lowestoft. Thereafter the story was one of disaster. Louis XIV, alarmed by possible growth of English naval power, deserted England for the Dutch. Charles II and parliament alike had their attention distracted from the war by the Great Plague of 1665 and the Fire of London of the following year. Parliament, never in sympathy with the war, had voted supplies grudgingly and now refused to vote any more. In 1666 the English navy met defeat off North Foreland. In the following year the fleet had to be laid up in Chatham docks through lack of money, and the crowning disgrace occurred when the Dutch sailed up the Medway and fired the ships as they stood useless in dock.

When the Peace of Breda was negotiated in 1667 all that England had to show for her efforts was recognition of her conquest of New Amsterdam; but this was an important gain since it linked up the New England states with the older colony of Virginia.

Parliament urged the dismissal of Clarendon, and demanded a break with France and an alliance with Holland. Charles, rather than consent, immediately prorogued parliament. The honeymoon of the restoration was over; Crown and parliament were at odds again.

QUESTIONS

1. In what ways did the Restoration settlement honour the undertakings given in the Declaration of Breda?
2. "The foreign policy of Charles II during the first seven years of his reign was no more than a continuation of that of Oliver Cromwell." Do you agree?

CHAPTER 31

CONSTITUTIONAL CONFLICT RENEWED, 1667-85

CROWN and parliament were at odds again by 1667 because the so-called Restoration Settlement of 1660 had in practice settled very little. By leaving the choice of ministers and determination of policy to the Crown while leaving the Crown dependent on parliament for money, it had placed both in an unworkable position. Was it likely that parliament would pay for a policy of which it disapproved? And what became of the king's right to determine policy, if parliament could bring policy to naught by refusing necessary supplies?

Only so long as king and parliament saw eye to eye on policy could such a system function; and the dismissal of Clarendon was virtually the last issue on which Charles II and parliament agreed. Even so they willed a common purpose for very different reasons. Many members of the House of Lords were angered that Clarendon had not produced a settlement of the land

Painted tiles in the Victoria and Albert Museum. These tell the story of the Popish Plot in pictures.

question more favourable to pre-Commonwealth owners, and they further resented the marriage of Clarendon's daughter Anne Hyde to James, Duke of York, heir presumptive to the throne, though in fairness to Clarendon we have to remember that he himself deplored the match. The House of Commons regarded Clarendon as the king's man, unresponsive to their wishes. The nation at large, since he was the man in power, held him responsible for everything disastrous during his years of office, from the sale of Dunkirk and the Second Dutch War to the Great Plague and Great Fire of London.

The king, on the other hand, had grown tired of playing pupil to Master Clarendon. Clarendon's high moral code was a constant reproach to the libertine king, and the minister's frequent rebukes to Charles on this score widened the gulf between them. Deprived of the support of both king and parliament, Clarendon had to go.

Having rid himself of Clarendon, Charles had no intention of submitting to another mentor. He called to his service not one man but five, Clifford, Arlington, Buckingham, Ashley and Lauderdale. Since their surname initials formed the word Cabal, they were soon known by this label. Charles hoped through them to exercise a more personal influence over policy than hitherto, and he was careful to choose men who were more sympathetic to his point of view than Clarendon had been.

The Triple Alliance, 1668

Both parliament and king were concerned to foster national power and prosperity, but divided as to how this would be best accomplished. Parliament saw the growth of French influence as the greatest threat to English security; the king saw the Dutch as a more pressing menace, especially to expansion of English trade and commerce. His hope was to use French power to destroy Holland; parliament would have preferred to help Holland to curb French aggression in Europe.

For the moment Charles sought to pursue both lines of policy. Officially an alliance was made (1668) with Holland and Sweden against France. It had the effect of halting a French attack on the Netherlands, and of inducing Louis XIV to find some means of securing English goodwill. Thus, the Triple Alliance notwithstanding, Louis and Charles entered into negotiations to this end.

Secret Treaty of Dover, 1670

Overtures were carried on in great secrecy for two years. Not even all the members of the Cabal were party to them, and the main agent was Henrietta, sister of Charles and sister-in-law of Louis XIV. The result was the secret Treaty of Dover, which provided for a joint Anglo-French attack on Holland and a return payment of £300,000 a year by Louis to Charles. Charles undertook, when he judged the time suitable, to declare himself a Catholic and to reintroduce Catholicism to England. When he had done so, he was to receive an additional £200,000 a year and a French army to suppress any rebellion his action might provoke.

The first overt sign of this secret change of policy was the outbreak of the Third Dutch War in 1672. In spite of some indecisive engagements, the Dutch were sufficiently alarmed to agree in the Treaty of Westminster (1674) to salute the English flag in the English Channel and to cede the island of St. Helena.

Declaration of Indulgence, 1673

While the Dutch war was in progress Charles moved towards fulfilment of the religious aspect of the secret Treaty of Dover by issuing, without consulting parliament, a Declaration of Indulgence suspending all laws which penalized Roman Catholics. Charles extended the same relief to Nonconformists; not only did this extension disguise his intentions, but it also enabled him to defend his action on the ground that he was anxious, not so much to promote the Catholic cause, as to establish a wider measure of religious toleration. He was hopeful that with Nonconformist support he might be able to withstand the Anglican opposition which parliament was sure to offer.

In this he was disappointed. Dislike of Catholicism was too strong for Nonconformists to buy their liberty by countenancing an increase in the liberty of those who adhered to the old faith. Disappointed, and faced with strong parliamentary opposition on the grounds that the king had no legal power to override laws made jointly by himself and parliament, Charles accepted defeat and withdrew the declaration.

Test Act, 1673

Parliament followed up its victory by compelling Charles to approve the Test Act. This required all persons holding office under the Crown to take Communion according to the rites of the Church of England, and expressly to renounce Roman Catholic teaching about the doctrine of transubstantiation.

This conflict between Charles and parliament led to the break-up of the Cabal. Ashley, prominent later in the reign as Earl of Shaftesbury, found himself out of sympathy with the king's Catholic leanings and shocked by the king's attempt to override parliament. Clifford, Lord Treasurer, as a Catholic felt unable to conform with the terms of the Test Act, and therefore resigned office. With this break-up of the Cabal came the king's third defeat. He took as his minister the Earl of Danby, not a king's man, but one after parliament's own heart, a staunch Anglican and a firm opponent of France. He promptly switched back to the policy of good relations with Holland by arranging a marriage between Princess Mary of York, daughter of the English heir presumptive, and William of Orange.

Popish Plot, 1678

Foreign affairs were for the time being overshadowed by domestic events. The country had been gravely disquieted when, as a result of the Test Act, James, Duke of York, publicly declared allegiance to Catholicism by resigning his office of High Admiral. If Charles II had no legitimate son, it now appeared that renewal of religious conflict was a strong possibility.

In this nervous state, public opinion readily accepted allegations, made before a magistrate by Titus Oates, of a Catholic plot to murder the king, enthrone the Duke of York and organize a massacre of Protestants. Subsequent murder of the magistrate who had taken Oates' deposition gave credibility to the story. No one was prepared to stop and reflect that this murder might well have been the normal work of a highwayman or the deliberate crime of one of Oates' party to bolster up their story. Magistrates now began to enforce strictly the laws against Catholics; many were imprisoned and even executed on no more than suspicion of illegal conduct. In 1678 Catholics were formally excluded from parliament.

Fall of Danby, 1679

Faced with this wave of hysteria, Charles could do little save wait for it to exhaust itself. He advised his brother James to retire to Scotland. For the rest he astutely prepared to rid himself of Danby, who was technically the king's secretary. As such, Charles required him to sign a letter suggesting a renewal of Anglo-French friendship. In the hope of destroying Danby, Louis revealed the letter to ardent parliamentarians. They immediately suspected Danby of double-dealing and impeached him. Charles, content with this and fearing that the impeachment might reveal too much of his pro-French leanings, dissolved parliament but left Danby languishing in imprisonment.

Before dissolution, however, parliament had had time to pass the Habeas Corpus Act (1679), designed to make it more difficult for the government to keep anyone in prison indefinitely before bringing him to trial. While this act did not extend the liberty of the king's subjects, it did much to protect their exercise of the liberty that they were supposed to enjoy.

Exclusion Bill, 1679-81, and the King's Victory

Meanwhile the anti-Catholic fever continued. Shaftesbury and his followers introduced into parliament a Bill to exclude James, Duke of York, from the throne because of his Catholicism. The dissolution of parliament in 1679 not only put an end to the impeachment of Danby but also prevented the Exclusion Bill from getting beyond a second reading. Shaftesbury, however,

Harvington Hall, Worcestershire, a Roman Catholic family stronghold, has several well-hidden "priests' holes."

kept the issue alive during and after the elections by organizing demonstrations among the London mob. When parliament met again in 1680 the Exclusion Bill got through the Commons but was rejected by the Lords. The answer of the Commons was a resolution to vote no more monetary supplies until the Bill was passed. The king dissolved parliament yet again.

Shaftesbury's organization of public opinion now provoked a counter organization. Shaftesbury's followers, presenting petitions for the recall of parliament, became known as Petitioners; their opponents, expressing abhorrence at such a means of bringing pressure to bear on the king, earned the name of Abhorrers. Here we have the beginnings of political groups known in the next century as Whigs and Tories.

Charles sought to counter Shaftesbury's influence in London by summoning the next parliament to meet in Oxford. This he did confidently because he had reached a financial agreement with France. The Popish Plot had been proved an invention, and opinion in consequence was turning against those who had exploited the plot for their own ends. Finally, not only had Charles come to terms with France, but, more important, an increase in trade had considerably increased the king's income from tunnage, poundage and excise duties. With these resources and peace abroad, Charles was at last financially independent of parliament. When at Oxford his opponents proved as intractable as ever, Charles surprised them by dissolving parliament. For the four remaining years of his reign, Charles had no need to recall parliament.

Charles took steady advantage of his victory. A feeble though genuine conspiracy against the king's life, the Rye House Plot of 1683, was made the excuse to arrest and put on trial leading members of the opposition. Two were executed, Titus Oates at last met with deserved imprisonment and Shaftesbury fled the country. Thus the opposition was divided, discomforted and defeated.

With an eye to the day when parliament would have to be recalled, for example on the king's death, the government sought to ensure that Crown supporters would predominate among elected candidates. To this end, city and borough charters were, wherever possible, remodelled to give control of these bodies to government influences. Finally, as he lay dying, Charles II asked for a priest and declared himself Roman Catholic.

Economic Growth, 1660-85

An important factor in the Crown's victory was the post-Restoration economic growth.

As a result of the Navigation Act of 1660, England secured an increased share of Baltic trade at the expense of the Dutch. This led to the growth of English shipping and ship-building, and to the expansion of many English ports, such as Bristol, London and Liverpool.

The growth of the colonies also increased prosperity in England. The volume of trade transacted by overseas trading companies such as the East India Company, the African Company and the Hudson's Bay Company brought more wealth to England, as did development of the re-export trade consequent upon the expansion of tobacco, sugar and cotton crops in the colonies. English industries engaged in finishing processes of imported colonial produce such as cotton and sugar grew rapidly.

Such developments meant that English prosperity was no longer dependent on wool and woollen goods only. Imports led to a much increased revenue from customs and excise, so the Crown became more independent of parliamentary taxation for finance. In this way parliament temporarily lost its chief weapon of control over Crown policy, and this led to the ultimate necessity of a revolution (1688) to re-establish parliamentary participation with the Crown in government administration and policy.

QUESTIONS

1. How did Charles II come into conflict with Shaftesbury and his supporters, and what were the results of the struggle?
2. Charles II said that he had no intention of going on his travels again. How did he achieve his aim?

CHAPTER 32

JAMES II, THE REVOLUTION, AND THE REVOLUTION SETTLEMENT

AFTER the accession of James II in 1685, it soon became clear that the fears entertained in 1680 of possible dire consequences of Charles II's death had been justified. James II lacked the wily patience of his brother, and was a more bigoted man. Shaftesbury and his partisans in exile at once determined to achieve by force of arms the purpose they had failed to accomplish by parliamentary means.

Encouraged by these ambitious politicians, the Duke of Monmouth, an illegitimate son of Charles II, landed in the south west and raised the standard of armed rebellion. His hopes of an immediate national response to his landing were disappointed, and his locally-recruited ill-armed sympathizers were no match for the disciplined troops sent against them by the king. Monmouth was defeated at the Battle of Sedgemoor in 1685, was taken prisoner and executed; and Judge Jeffreys was dispatched to hold special trials of those of Monmouth's followers who had been taken prisoner. Jeffreys only too faithfully discharged his instructions to strike terror into disaffected districts, ordering execution or transportation of over a thousand captives in about three weeks. He wasted no time carefully balancing the evidence of the guilt or innocence of those who came before him, did not even pretend to be impartial, and seemed to relish the savagery of sentences he imposed. His reward by a grateful king was appointment as Lord Chancellor, and by posterity the perpetuation of his name with these Bloody Assizes.

Support for Monmouth had been lukewarm because the nation had no desire to embark on a long civil war; not all Petitioners of the time of Charles II were prepared to go as far as Shaftesbury and his faction. James II had no heir and seemed unlikely to produce one; the heir presumptive was the anti-French Protestant William of Orange, by virtue of the title of his wife Mary, daughter of James II and Anne Hyde. Even among former Petitioners there were those who thought that there was no point in resorting to force when a better result might be obtained by time and patience.

The Attempt of James II to Re-establish Catholicism

The actions of James II soon made clear that much would meanwhile have to be endured. The ease with which Monmouth's rebellion had been crushed deceived James into thinking that he had little to fear by way of opposition. He had an effective army, and the money he needed; extremist leaders of any opposition were in exile. His brother, with assets such as these, had been able to dispense with parliament; power was his by Divine Right, and the way, he thought, was clear. He would restore Catholicism by exercise of the royal will.

One of James's earliest steps in this disastrous policy was the appointment of Sir Edward Hales, a Roman Catholic, as governor of Dover, with commissioned rank in the army. With the king's secret approval this action was challenged in the courts, and eleven out of twelve judges who heard the case ruled that the king had power to dispense with parliamentary laws and that he had rightly exercised such power in this case. Armed with this decision, James went ahead with his policy. Roman Catholics were quickly appointed to the command of the army in Ireland, the Lord-Lieutenancy of Ireland, and command of the English fleet. Two Catholics shared with two Protestants the office of Lord Treasurer, and Catholic Robert Spencer Earl of Sutherland became Lord President of the Council.

As a Catholic himself, James did not care to exercise his powers as head of the Church of England. In 1686 he established a court of commissioners to whom he could hand over his powers in this respect. Unhappily this seemed to the nation a revival of that Court of High Commission which had been declared illegal in 1641. Moreover, James used this court to establish Catholics in the universities of Cambridge and Oxford. The Vice-Chancellor of Cambridge, when he refused to confer a degree on a Catholic monk, was dismissed. Similarly the Fellows of Magdalen College, Oxford, who refused to elect the king's Catholic nominee as President of the College, were deprived of their fellowships.

Crisis of 1687

To re-establish Catholicism by means of exercising his dispensing power in particular cases was too slow a process for impatient James II. In 1687 he transformed his dispensing power into a suspending power by issuing a Declaration of Indulgence making inoperative the limitations imposed upon Catholics and Nonconformists alike under the Test Act of 1673. He tried, but failed, to ensure that when parliament next met it would contain a majority of members likely to support his policy. He postponed the recall of parliament and meanwhile, finding that magistrates were ignoring his Declaration of Indulgence, issued a second one, coupled with an instruction to all bishops to see that it was read by the clergy from their pulpits on a specified date.

Seven bishops, including the Archbishop of Canterbury, refused to accept this instruction, and three hundred clergy followed their example. Moreover the bishops dared to present to His Majesty in person a petition in defence of their point of view.

By James's orders the bishops were arrested, lodged in the Tower and brought to trial. For James it was a fatal mistake. The bishops were acquitted, and the nation went wild with joy. Celebration bonfires burned even among the army encamped on Hounslow Heath, an ominous sign which James would have been wise to heed.

National rejoicing soon turned to dismay when it was learned that at last the queen had given birth to a son. There was now a Prince of Wales who would be brought up as a Catholic and imbued with belief in the Divine

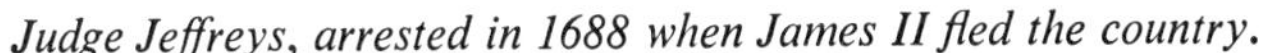

Judge Jeffreys, arrested in 1688 when James II fled the country.

Right of Kings. In him the struggle between king and parliament, Catholic and Protestant, might well be perpetuated for another generation at least. Time was no longer on the side of the nation, and the nation could no longer afford to be patient.

Revolution of 1688-9

In the face of prospects of this kind, a group of politicians of all shades of opinion put faction aside and took collective action by sending an invitation to William of Orange to come and assume the crown of England. William landed at Torbay, and the Hounslow army under John Churchill, later Duke of Marlborough, deserted James. Yorkshire rose to arms in support of William, and James's offer of concessions failed to avert the disaster his foolish haste had provoked.

James, compelled to acknowledge defeat, sent his queen and infant son to France, and tried to follow them. He was caught and brought back to London, but ultimately allowed to escape. Meanwhile William confidently marched on London. Parliament declared that James had vacated his throne, and invited William and Mary to be joint sovereigns.

Opposition to the Revolution

Their accession did not go unchallenged. A section of opinion in parliament tried hard to secure Mary's recognition as queen with William as her consort. This proposal was defeated by William's refusal to agree to such a scheme and by Mary's support of her husband's objections.

Similarly, when an oath of allegiance to William and Mary as sovereigns was demanded, a number of clergy in the Church of England found it contrary to their conscience to take such an oath. The Archbishop of Canterbury, six bishops and four hundred clergymen were for this refusal deprived of their titles or livings; expelled from Anglicanism, they formed a separate sect, known henceforward as Non-jurors.

The opposition from abroad was more serious. Under William of Orange, Holland had long been a thorn in the side of Louis XIV of France, and Louis was not prepared to stand by and watch his enemy strengthened at the expense of Catholicism and a Divine Right king. France therefore, refusing to recognize William as king of England, gave aid to James II and his supporters, henceforward known as Jacobites. In the War of the English Succession (or Grand Alliance) which ensued from 1689 to 1697, France found Austria, Spain, Holland and England arrayed against her. A Jacobite stand in Scotland was defeated; and a similar movement in Ireland, though encouraged by the return of James II in person, met with final disaster at the Battle of the Boyne. In 1697 France was ready to make peace, and the Treaty of Ryswick was signed. By then, a far more important throne than

GREAT FIRE OF LONDON IN CHARLES II's REIGN

SCENES FROM LATE STUART TIMES

that of England, from the French point of view, was at stake. Spain and the important Spanish overseas empire lacked a direct heir. Within three years of the signing of the Treaty of Ryswick, Europe was convulsed by the War of the Spanish Succession. Not until 1715 were the exiled Stuarts able to secure active foreign aid for an attempt to recover the throne they had lost. This gave England time to consolidate the revolution of 1688.

Legislation Arising from the Revolution of 1688

Between 1689 and 1701 a series of parliamentary Acts tried to settle permanently some of the issues which had so long divided the country. The Declaration and the Bill of Rights (1688), the Mutiny Act and the Toleration Act (all of 1689) were followed by the Triennial Act (1694) and the Act of Settlement (1701).

This legislation defined again the limits of the king's power. The Court of High Commission, suspending and dispensing powers, and maintenance of a standing army in time of peace were declared illegal. Henceforth the king could not himself be, nor could he marry, a Roman Catholic. Judges, once appointed, were, as before, to hold office so long as they were of good conduct, and not at the king's pleasure. Finally the king was not to leave the country except with consent of parliament.

Every effort was made to exclude exiled James II or his heirs from succession to the throne. William and Mary were declared king and queen, each in his or her own right; the survivor of the pair was to continue to rule until death. They were to be followed by their children, or those of Mary if William died first and Mary made a second marriage. If both these possibilities failed, succession was to pass to Mary's sister Anne, and thence to her children. If in turn Anne died childless, assuming that William had outlived Mary, remarried and produced children, such children should inherit the throne.

By 1701 it was apparent that all these provisions were not enough; William, Mary and Anne were all childless. This situation led to the Act of Settlement, which named the Electress Sophia of Hanover (granddaughter of James I) and her Protestant descendants as heirs. It was this act which in 1714 brought George, the Elector of Hanover, to the throne as George I of England.

The King's Position After 1689

Not only did this legislation subordinate the king to the laws of the land; it also made him financially subordinate to parliament. The money which the king needed to carry on government of the nation was now separated from the money he needed for his own private purse. Henceforth the former was voted annually by parliament; the latter was voted to the king for life on his accession. The Lord Treasurer was made responsible for seeing that the distinction between private and public expenditure was observed, while parliament appointed auditors to see that public funds were spent only on the purposes for which they had been granted.

While the king's powers were thus limited, they were not destroyed. Ministers were still the king's ministers, and in theory he was free to choose whom he wished to serve him. He himself remained an active member of the ministerial team, presiding over meetings and helping to shape, and at times to determine, policy.

In practice however, as William III ultimately found, it was necessary to shape policy in a way which parliament was likely to digest, and to present it through ministers who enjoyed the confidence of the Commons as well as that of the Crown. Otherwise no money was forthcoming to execute policy, and the king could no longer impose taxes on his own authority.

Nor could he refrain from summoning parliament. Supplies for army upkeep were voted for only one year at a time. So long as he wished to maintain an army the king had to call parliament at least once each year; and with an exiled royal family still hoping to recover the throne it had lost, neither William, Anne nor the early Hanoverians could do otherwise. On the other hand, to prevent the king from keeping a docile parliament indefinitely, the Triennial Act limited the life of any parliament to a maximum of three years.

Religious Aspects of the Revolution Settlement

Religious problems which had complicated the relations of king, parliament and people in the seventeenth century did not demand so complex a solution as did political problems. In general, a solution was found in partial acceptance of the principle of toleration, which meant freedom of worship and of opinion without loss of rights as a citizen. The state began to abandon its claim to dictate the religious beliefs of its members. Though the Act of Uniformity of 1662 and the Conventicle Act of 1664 were not repealed, they were modified inasmuch as the Toleration Act of 1689 relieved Nonconformists of penalties they could incur under the two earlier laws. This did not give the Nonconformists all that they would have liked; it still left the Test and Corporation Acts in full operation, thus continuing exclusion of Nonconformists from the full rights of citizenship; but it made their life more tolerable. On the other hand, Catholicism remained outside the law; no concessions were made to members of the old faith, and this weighed particularly heavily on the people of Ireland.

Importance of the Revolution Settlement

The revolution of 1688 was an important turning-point. In domestic affairs it meant that England was to differ increasingly from her neighbours on the

The seven bishops (of Chichester, Bath and Wells, St. Asaph, Peterborough, Bristol, Ely, and the Archbishop of Canterbury—(centre), who refused to read the Declaration of Indulgence.

continent. While they continued to be ruled by absolute monarchs, sometimes benevolent but always despotic, England evolved a form of limited monarchy which proved both practical and enduring; by so doing England avoided any upheaval so violent as that which engulfed France a hundred years later. Future rulers of England could hardly claim to rule by Divine Right when William and Mary had become sovereigns by invitation. Since the Hanoverians came to the throne by an Act of Parliament, parliament was henceforth an essential and permanent part of the machinery of government. In religion, partial toleration had been granted; it was only a matter of time before it was extended. The attempt to achieve uniformity had been abandoned and England became the refuge of persecuted minorities from less tolerant countries.

In Scotland and Ireland the revolution was an equally important landmark. Scotland followed the English settlement, and a way was thus prepared for the eventual peaceful union of the two nations. Ireland, on the other hand, tried to reject the revolution but had it forced on her by military conquest; this bitter memory was one of the roots of a conflict with England which was not resolved until the early years of the twentieth century.

Abroad, the period of Anglo-French friendship came to an end, to be replaced by a relationship of strenuous rivalry, the first phase of which was the War of the Grand Alliance or the English Succession. Jacobites, Nonjurors and the exiled House of Stuart found encouragement in France. Louis XIV refused to recognize William of Orange as King of England.

War of the English Succession

In the ensuing war, England did not lack allies. As king of Holland, William had long been ambitious to check the growing power of France in Europe. Thus Holland fought side by side with England. Austria came to their support in the hope of securing English and Dutch sympathy later, in her claim to the Spanish Succession. Spain joined them, too, to defend the Spanish Netherlands from the aggressive designs of France which were a growing threat to the whole of Europe.

John Graham of Claverhouse, Viscount Dundee, raised the Highlanders in support of James II, and defeated William's forces at the Battle of Killiecrankie. Dundee's death led to the collapse of Scottish resistance, which was in any case a minority movement.

James II, supported by French troops, invaded Ireland. Irish Protestants were besieged by Irish Catholics in Londonderry and Enniskillen; Londonderry was relieved, and the beseiged in Enniskillen made a successful sortie. The invaders were defeated by William III at the Battle of the Boyne (1690), and James II fled to France. John Churchill captured Cork and Kinsale; and war ended by the surrender of Limerick to English forces.

In 1690 the French Admiral Tourville defeated the English and Dutch fleets off Beachy Head, but two years later the allies regained command of the sea by defeating the French off Cape La Hogue, a victory which saved England from invasion.

On the continent the French captured Namur and Mons, and William III was defeated at Steinkirk and Neerwinden. Later the English recaptured Namur.

War came to an end by the Treaty of Ryswick, 1697. By the terms of this treaty, Louis XIV of France recognized William III as king of England, and promised to withdraw his support from James II. The Dutch were to garrison barrier fortresses between the Spanish Netherlands and Holland. Louis XIV agreed to restore all French conquests in Europe since 1678, with the exception of Strasburg. This proved, however, to be but an interlude in a long Anglo-French struggle.

QUESTIONS

1. Show how Charles II and James II supported Roman Catholics in England, and describe briefly the opposition they met.
2. State the main terms of the Revolution Settlement of 1689, and explain why both William and Mary were placed on the throne.

CHAPTER 33

THE WAR OF THE SPANISH SUCCESSION, 1701-14

THE war of the Spanish Succession, which so quickly followed the war of the English Succession, was only one stage in the Anglo-French rivalry for dominance in Europe and overseas which lasted, with interruptions, until 1783.

Apart from particular issues leading to particular wars there were deep, long-continuing reasons for this conflict. France under Louis XIV aimed at considerable extension of her territory in Europe. She felt that the Rhine was the boundary which geography intended to be hers. To achieve this meant conquering both the United Provinces (Holland) and the Spanish Netherlands (Belgium). Not merely William of Orange (as ruler of Holland and England) was opposed to this project; England under any king with the country's interests at heart could hardly approve it. Possession of these territories would give France access to the North Sea. England could not tolerate a more extended hostile coast-line opposite her shores, especially with expelled Stuarts threatening from the continent. Such a state of affairs would be a menace to both English naval supremacy and national security.

French ambition did not stop at the Rhine. In the childlessness of Charles II of Spain, Louis XIV saw an opportunity to add the Spanish crown to his own. Such a union would confer on him unchallengeable mastery of Europe· no other power would be able to withstand the will of a sovereign who ruled from the Mediterranean to the North Sea, especially as his resources of money would have been swollen by the wealth of Spanish colonies in America and revenue from trade with these possessions. William III was not the only European ruler who felt that realization of such a dream could not be permitted.

Colonial rivalry was already a factor impairing relations between France and England. England had helped Spain, during the war of the Grand Alliance, to repel French attacks on the Spanish West Indies. In North America the French had never reconciled themselves to the incorporation of the Hudson's Bay Company in 1670, or to English participation in trade with Canada. None of the colonial issues had been settled by the Treaty of Ryswick, and neither nation was content with the situation as it had been left by that treaty.

Finally, in spite of the undertaking she had given at Ryswick, France was as unwilling to recognize a Protestant succession in England as William III was determined to thwart the ambitions of Louis XIV.

Origins of the War of the Spanish Succession

The Treaty of Ryswick was in fact merely a truce arranged to give the powers of Europe time to take up positions for conflict over the Spanish succession. In absence of any direct heir to Charles II of Spain, there were three or four claimants to his crown. Louis XIV could argue that his wife's claim must be considered, since though she had made a conditional renunciation at the time of their marriage, the conditions had never been fulfilled. Realizing however that Europe was not likely to tolerate his own claim, he prepared to support that of his young grandson Philip. French claimants apart, there were others in the field. Elector Joseph of Bavaria was the grandson of Charles II's sister Margaret, and great-great-grandson of Philip III of Spain. Moreover, his grandmother Margaret had been named by her father's will as heiress, should her brother Charles II die childless. This was precisely the situation which had now arisen. Finally there was Archduke Charles of Austria, later Emperor Charles VI, great-grandson of Philip III.

Between 1698 and 1701 attempts were made to settle the issue by diplomatic negotiation based on the principle of dividing the prize between contestants. The first of these attempts (or Partition Treaties) was undone by the death of Joseph of Bavaria (1699), principal beneficiary under the treaty. The second Partition Treaty (1700) failed to achieve a peaceful solution to the problem through the joint action of Charles II of Spain and Louis XIV of France. When Charles died almost immediately after the treaty had been made, it was found that in his will he had named Philip of France as his heir, providing that Louis XIV supported his grandson. This temptation was too much for Louis who, in spite of being a signatory to the second Partition Treaty, now renounced it and accepted the will of Charles II. Europe was prepared to accept neither the will nor Louis's renunciation of the treaty; and diplomacy having failed, recourse was had to war.

Political Factions at the Outbreak of War

The detailed story of the war is as much a matter of European as of English history. Only the main outlines can be noted here. England, Holland and Austria were joined by many German princes; France and Spain stood alone. Louis XIV had by this time lost most of the great military leaders who brought success to his armies in earlier wars; the allies, on the other hand, had at their disposal the military genius of John Churchill. Behind him, for the first year of the war, stood William III, determined to fight until France was defeated. After William's death in 1702, his resolve was preserved by a group of English politicians dominating the House of Commons from 1702 until 1710 whom, as we shall see later, we can now fairly begin to call the Whigs. These were keen supporters of the Protestant succession, the strongest opponents of the Stuarts and among all factions there were some shrewd business men profoundly irritated by Louis XIV's decrees excluding the Dutch and English from trade with Spanish America.

Thus the death of William III and the accession of Queen Anne made little difference to English determination to continue the war. In any case, William III was for the most part an unpopular figure. He was too exclusively interested in foreign politics, suspected of using English resources in furtherance of his ambition to humiliate Louis XIV. He was distrusted by the more conservative Anglicans because he himself held Calvinist views. He tried to ignore the power groupings in parliament and to rule with administrations drawn impartially from the main factions. Not until the Whigs determined to resist France did William find it easy to carry parliament with him.

Main Events of the War on Land

With a group of politicians solidly behind the war effort and John Churchill, later Duke of Marlborough, in command, the opening stages of the war quickly brought success. Removal of the French threat to Holland was achieved when Marlborough (1703), having secured the Meuse, drove the French from the lower Rhine and captured Bonn.

In the following year Louis XIV planned to eliminate Austria, so as to be able to turn all his forces westward. Marlborough frustrated this plan by halting the French advance on Vienna at the Battle of Blenheim (1704).

The French forces were driven from Belgium in 1706 as a result of the battle of Ramilles, and the initiative was seized (but not held) by the allies in the advance of Archduke Charles on Madrid, which he captured but failed to hold. The Austrian forces had more success in an attack on French possessions in Italy, capturing Milan and Naples.

The Library, Blenheim Palace. The palace was a gift to John Churchill, first Duke of Marlborough, from a grateful nation.

The recovery of the French by a successful re-entry into Belgium in 1707 was short lived, since Marlborough at the battle of Oudenarde (1708) again freed Belgium from her invaders. Finally the battle of Malplaquet in 1709 opened the way for invasion of France itself.

Meanwhile, the English navy had contributed to Marlborough's success. Not merely had it retained control of the English Channel and so kept open his lines of communication, but it had won victories of its own. In 1704 the capture of Gibraltar marked the beginning of English naval supremacy in the Mediterranean; four years later that supremacy was confirmed by the capture of Minorca. English command of the sea had spread the conflict to North America, and English influence had grown at the expense of France in the Hudson's Bay territory, Newfoundland and Nova Scotia.

Faced with undeniable defeat on land and at sea, and exposed to invasion, France was by 1710 ready to open negotiations for peace. Fortunately for her, enthusiasm had begun to wane in England; but Churchill and the Whigs were as war-minded as ever, and hence as general enthusiasm declined the Whigs lost favour and power. Elections for a new parliament in 1710 found the Tories the largest single group in the new House of Commons.

In the early eighteenth century this was not enough to bring about a change of policy; the queen's sympathies must be enlisted in the cause of peace if the Tories were to bring war to an end. Queen Anne had long relied exclusively on the Duchess of Marlborough among her personal attendants, so the Tories enlisted another of the queen's servants in their cause. Mrs. Masham, a cousin of the Duchess of Marlborough by whom she had been introduced into the queen's service, was also a relative of Robert Harley, later Earl of Oxford, head of the new Tory administration. Mrs. Masham transferred her loyalty to the party in power, and gradually replaced the duchess in the queen's confidence. Whigs also played into Tory hands by prosecuting a popular London clergyman, Dr. Sacheverell, for expressing what they considered to be Tory opinions in his sermons. There was, too, a general fear of the ambitions of the successful Duke of Marlborough.

The Peace of Utrecht, 1713

Thus the new government began negotiations for peace, concentrating on purely English interests and neglecting those of their allies. Indeed, when the conference began at Utrecht England had virtually made her own arrangements with France, and at best acted as arbitrator between her enemy and her allies, much to the anger and disgust of the latter.

By the terms ultimately agreed, Philip of France was allowed to succeed to the Spanish throne; Archduke Charles, who was in possession of Spain by right of conquest in the late war, had no alternative but to withdraw. It was, in consequence, some time before Austria was willing to ally herself again with England, in spite of the fact that she received Belgium, Milan, Naples and Sardinia. Philip promised that the crowns of France and Spain should never be united, and France undertook to expel the Old Pretender (son of James II of England) and to recognize the Protestant succession in England.

England made the biggest gains. She kept Gibraltar, Minorca, Hudson's Bay territory and Nova Scotia. She was accorded the right to send one ship each year to trade with Spanish American possessions and, by the Asiento Treaty, the sole right of exporting negro slaves from Africa to America, a disgraceful but profitable trade.

From the English point of view the Peace of Utrecht contributed markedly to the growth of the country's trade and to her standing as a colonial power. Rivalry with European neighbours was not finished, but her acquisitions immensely strengthened her position in the struggle for imperial supremacy.

It marked too her status as leading naval power of Europe; the days of Dutch naval supremacy were over, and in the struggle with France the advantage now lay with England. Even in the Mediterranean, French naval power had been eclipsed; that sea could never become a French lake while England held Gibraltar and Minorca.

Finally, the foreign threat to the Protestant succession in England was removed. The Jacobite risings of 1715 and 1745 were no more than exhausted stirrings of a dying tornado.

On the other hand, the Peace of Utrecht was not without disadvantages for England. England had feathered her own nest with scant regard to the interests of her allies, and had obtained much; they had obtained far less than they had hoped for. The bulk of the Spanish prize had gone to the French candidate, and it was to prevent this that the war had been fought. For this unsatisfactory result her allies held England blameworthy. In consequence England was left for some years in a position of dangerous isolation, friendless in Europe while possessing much that European powers coveted. Early Hanoverian statesmen, particularly Stanhope, had to work hard to restore Europe's faith in the value of alliance with England.

Moreover, her gains had been almost too much. Neither Spain nor France was reconciled to the profits England had made at their expense. Their desire to recoup their losses led to further wars and in this way the peace of 1713 planted the seeds of future conflict.

QUESTIONS

1. Describe the causes of the War of the Spanish Succession, and give the main terms of the Peace of Utrecht.

2. Show how William III and Marlborough tried to check the ambitions of Louis XIV.

CHAPTER 34

DOMESTIC AFFAIRS, 1689-1714

THE wars between 1689 and 1714 had been costly not only in men but also in money. The government of William and Mary was by 1697 in debt to the extent of £21,000,000; only £5,000,000 of this had been repaid when Anne came to the throne in 1702. The War of the Spanish Succession pushed the total debt up to £54,000,000. It was the need to pay for this war policy which led to new developments in the national financial system.

The Bank of England and the National Debt

We have seen how in 1689 parliament tried to settle the vexed question of national finance by separating the king's personal income (Civil List) from his public income (Supply Services), voting the former to him for life on his accession while making the latter dependent on an annual parliamentary vote. This public income was invariably fixed to meet the ordinary needs of government in time of peace, but was quite inadequate to cover the cost of a major war. Since England was almost continually at war between 1689 and 1714, some means had to be found to meet the cost.

In 1692 parliament levied a new direct tax on landowners, at four shillings in the pound. This was destined to remain long after the war was over, and to become the main source of government revenue in the eighteenth century. By itself, however, it was not sufficient to discharge the cost of Marlborough's wars, and the government had to borrow money from the goldsmiths of London who had long acted as bankers. The goldsmiths were not eager to lend money to the Crown, ever since Charles II in 1672 refused to repay loans secured from them. William's borrowings, however, differed from those of Charles II inasmuch as they were sanctioned by parliament, who guaranteed to pay the interest.

In 1693 a loan of £12,000,000 was obtained from a group of goldsmiths on new conditions. In return for the loan, lenders were given a Royal Charter allowing them to form a bank to be known as the Bank of England, and conferring on them the sole right of issuing bank notes in London. In return for these privileges the bankers agreed to accept an interest rate of 8 per cent, a more moderate charge than usual, and not to expect repayment of capital so long as interest was regularly forthcoming.

Thus in 1693 a new way of looking at the national debt was introduced.

Glencoe, where the Campbells were entertained by the Macdonalds and massacred their hosts on 13 February, 1692.

It was no longer a temporary advance to be paid off in a limited time. Instead it became a permanent fund, and investors could buy and sell their share in it as in any other financial venture. Surplus money could now be profitably placed not only in private businesses but also with the government.

This funding of the national debt, as the process of making it a permanent feature of the financial system came to be called, together with establishment of the Bank of England, had important political as well as economic results. The two developments meant that the moneyed classes were now more than ever bound to the cause of the Protestant succession of 1689, since there was always the fear that a restored Stuart might refuse to honour the debts of his "usurping" predecessors. Moreover, since wealthy Tories as well as Whigs had shares in the national debt, it helped to weaken Tory support for the Jacobite cause.

Another step to put national finance in order was the decision in 1694 to reform silver coinage. Coins were supposed to contain precious metal roughly corresponding in quantity to their face value. In fact they did not; many old coins were in circulation, worn thin with constant usage. Many others had been clipped, or deliberately reduced in circumference, by dishonest people and bits shorn or clipped off had then been melted down and forged into new additional coinage. This illegal increase in the amount of money in circulation had contributed to a rise in prices and a corresponding fall in the purchasing power of money.

The government of William III undertook to put this right. Debased, old and defective coins were taken out of circulation, and new coinage of standard value was issued, with milled edges to make clipping impossible. Expensive though this reform was, it had good results; sound coinage provided a stimulus to trade and in the long run was a help to meeting the financial stress of war expenditure.

England and Scotland

These financial developments of the late seventeenth century were not the only ways in which England began to assume more modern shape.

When in 1603 James VI of Scotland had become James I of England, only the crowns of the two kingdoms had been united. The kingdoms themselves remained separate and, as we have seen in earlier chapters, both the Commonwealth in 1649 and the Revolution of 1689 had to be imposed by English armies on an unwilling Scotland.

Obstacles to Union

Even in the early eighteenth century there were serious obstacles to be overcome before the two kingdoms could be united. Scotland was jealously determined to defend her Presbyterian faith and historic legal system, and loth to surrender her independence. In England there was still distrust of the enemy across the border who had so often allied with England's foes. Expulsion of the Stuarts in 1688 (the royal family Scotland had given to England) still rankled in the highlands, which remained strongly Jacobite in sympathies.

The massacre of Glencoe in 1692 had done nothing to endear the English Protestant succession and the new ruler to the north of Scotland. Highland chiefs who had opposed the accession of William and Mary were promised pardon if they took an oath of allegiance before 31 December, 1691. Macdonald of Glencoe, through no fault of his own, was unable to take the oath before 6 January, 1692. A warrant was issued for the extirpation of the Macdonald clan, and execution entrusted to their enemies, the Campbells.

The Macdonalds entertained the Campbells at Glencoe for twelve days. Then, in a sudden night attack, the Campbells murdered thirty-eight of their Macdonald hosts, on 13 February, 1692.

The English government failed to punish the offenders; as a result of this, Scots resentment increased the difficulty of uniting Scotland and England. The massacre strengthened the Jacobite cause in the Highlands.

The massacre was mainly a Highland grievance, but the whole country resented the fact that for purposes of trade England treated Scotland as a foreign country. The failure of the Darien Scheme between 1695 and 1699 seemed to the Scots a clear case in point. A scheme was put forward to establish a Scottish settlement on the Isthmus of Darien, in order to attract

Asiatic trade from the Cape route to a route across Panama. A Scottish trading company, similar to the English East India Company, was formed, approved and financed by the Scottish parliament.

The Spanish, supported by William III in the interests of the anti-French League of Augsburg which he had recently organized, opposed the scheme. Also, unsuitable goods were sent out to be exchanged for Asiatic products. The scheme failed; money invested in it was lost, and the project abandoned.

Further cause for offence was given when in 1701 the English parliament settled the succession on the Hanoverians without reference to Scotland. Outraged, the Scottish parliament in 1704 declared that Scotland would choose her own ruler on the death of Queen Anne.

Factors Favouring Union

There were however some factors tending to draw the two countries together. Scotland was anxious to share the benefits which had steadily accrued to English trade and shipping from operation of the Navigation Acts, but only union with England would remove her foreign status under those Acts.

Moreover, Scotland was divided against herself. The Highlands were a disorderly, ungovernable area, and the more law-abiding and industrious Lowlands suffered from frequent raids made by men from the north. The gulf between these two areas had been further widened by recognition (1689) of Presbyterianism as the established religion of Scotland. This served to reconcile the Lowlands to the English revolution settlement, while leaving the Highlands to defend the lost causes of Catholicism and Jacobitism.

Finally, existence of separate parliaments made government of the two kingdoms not merely difficult, but dangerous, as the Scottish Act of Security of 1704 clearly revealed.

Act of Union, 1707

Negotiations for union of the two kingdoms were long and difficult, but were brought to a successful conclusion in 1707. By the Act of Union Scotland retained her own legal system, and the Presbyterian Church was the established state Church. She was to contribute $2\frac{1}{2}$ per cent to the joint national revenue, and to have sixteen representative peers in the English House of Lords and forty-five members in the House of Commons; no longer was there to be a separate parliament for Scotland. In return for these concessions there was to be free trade between England and Scotland, and the Scots would now benefit from the Navigation Acts.

The Union of 1707, though not wholly satisfying to Scottish national pride, has on the whole been of immense benefit to Scotland. From the eighteenth century onwards there has been steady industrial and commercial progress

Founded in 1693, by 1790 the Bank of England was well established.

especially of shipbuilding in such areas as the Clyde valley. Equally England benefited from the export by Scotland of many of her sons; their industry and talent enriched many aspects of British life, and development of the resources of the former British Empire owed a great deal to the contribution made by Scottish enterprise, thrift and skill.

These were the long-term benefits; others were more immediate. The Union was a severe blow to Jacobite hopes of recovering the throne of England, and equally served to strengthen the Protestant succession. The Union also helped to preserve Britain from internal disruption during the long struggle against Revolutionary and Napoleonic France.

Whigs and Tories after 1689

Union with Scotland was all the more welcome since by 1707 political divisions in the country were becoming a permanent feature of British life. Broadly speaking the division was between one group of land-owners known as Whigs and another known as Tories.

Differences between the two groups in the late seventeenth and early eighteenth centuries are not easily definable. Perhaps the clearest distinction was a religious one. Tories remained staunch Anglicans and opponents of Noncomformity. Whigs stood for some degree of religious toleration.

In politics Tories were not so much for the old king or for parliament as opposed to the war policy of William III and Marlborough, which the Whigs supported. These latter were of course strong supporters of the Act of Settlement, and the Hanoverian succession. The Tories were anti-Hanoverian without being ardently Jacobite.

What each party really wanted was control of the machinery of government. Had the Tories been able to install themselves so strongly in the chief offices of Church and state that it would have been impossible for the Hanoverians to carry on administration of the country without them, accession of a new dynasty would have been a matter of indifference to them. Command of political power was what both parties coveted.

The Party System

The Crown was slow and unwilling to recognize the increasing importance of political groups; this development cut too deeply into the legal right of the Crown to choose its servants with unrestricted freedom. Certainly in the eighteenth century a parliamentary election did not mean a change of government; voters made a new parliament only, and the king chose or dismissed ministers as he pleased.

William III, experienced in statecraft in Holland before suceeeding to the English throne, continued to act, as his predecessors had done, as head of his government. His ministers were merely heads of departments of state, executing the king's policy as much as, if not more than, deciding what that policy should be. Until 1694 William's ministers were drawn impartially from Whigs and Tories alike, but in view of the attitude of Tories towards war with France, he ultimately felt compelled to dismiss his Tory ministers for others drawn from the Whigs; Godolphin alone of the Tories remained in office after 1694. With Whig ministers and a Whig parliament, William found his war policy easier to pursue until 1698, when elections of that year returned a Tory parliament. Thereafter with Whig ministers and a Tory parliament William found pursuit of his war policy far more difficult.

Queen Anne and Party Politics

Queen Anne was less experienced and therefore more dependent on advice than William III had been. Her personal loyalty to the Church of England drew her towards the Tories, and from 1702 to 1710 her chief adviser was Lord Godolphin. Whigs and Tories served with him up to 1708, and the war policy continued to hold the field through the influence exercised on the queen by Sarah Duchess of Marlborough. As Tory opposition to the war became stronger by 1708, the queen dispensed with the services of Tory advisers and the ministry became wholly Whig.

Between 1708 and 1710, continuance of war became increasingly unpopular with the nation at large. When Tory Mrs. Masham replaced the Whig Duchess of Marlborough in the queen's personal service, the fate of the Whig administration was sealed. No government could survive long if it lost the confidence of the Crown. The ill-advised persecution of Dr. Sacheverell was the ministry's crowning folly.

In 1710 the queen turned for new ministers to the Tories St. John, later

Viscount Bolingbroke, and Harley, later Earl of Oxford. It was their ministry which won the queen's approval for the dismissal of Marlborough from all his appointments and which brought war with France to an end by the Peace of Utrecht.

The ministry demonstrated its Tory loyalty to the Church of England by passing two acts to diminish the growth and influence of Nonconformity. The Occasional Conformity Act of 1711 put an end to the practice whereby non-Anglicans had qualified for political office by occasionally instead of regularly receiving Communion in an Anglican church. Three years later the Schism Act of 1714 prohibited anyone from teaching unless he was licensed by a bishop. This would have destroyed the educational system Nonconformists had established, had it not remained inoperative by reason of the queen's death before it came into force.

Succession Crisis

The Schism Act brought to a head a quarrel between the two Tory leaders which had been developing since the queen had been taken seriously ill in 1713. Oxford would neither commit himself definitely to the Jacobite cause nor take effective steps to re-insure himself and his party with the Elector of Hanover. Bolingbroke wanted some definite line of policy. Moreover there was jealousy between the two men since the earldom conferred on Oxford was a greater honour than the viscountcy of Bolingbroke. The latter tried in vain to get the queen to dismiss Oxford. He forced the Schism Act through parliament in spite of Oxford's disapproval and this time successfully persuaded the queen to dismiss his rival.

This was almost, but not quite, Anne's last important action; there remained one more. Bolingbroke had not completed reconstruction of his ministry when it became clear that the queen had only a day or two to live. The Council was summoned to the bedside of the dying queen, and she appointed to the vacant office of Treasurer the Whig Duke of Shrewsbury. This meant that Bolingbroke was no longer chief minister; and with a Whig in the most important office, the Hanoverian succession was safe. Bolingbroke, who knew he was not acceptable to the new sovereign, fled abroad; Oxford was impeached and lodged for a time in the Tower. With the Tories divided and dispersed, George Elector of Hanover became George I of Great Britain peacefully and unchallenged.

QUESTIONS

1. What were the main changes in organization of the national finances during the reign of William III, and how do you account for them?
2. Why was there unrest in Scotland between 1689 and the Act of Union in 1707? What did Scotland gain and lose by the terms of the Union?

REVISION SUMMARY OF CHAPTERS 15-34

HENRY VII, THE FIRST TUDOR

HENRY VIII IN THE YEARS OF WOLSEY'S SUPREMACY

OCL/HIST/1—P*

Page

THE CIVIL WAR, 1642-49

THE FAILURE OF CONSTITUTIONAL EXPERIMENT

CHAPTER 35

THE JACOBITE MOVEMENT

THE Jacobite movement began in 1688 when James II fled from England. For the next sixty years attempts were made to regain the English throne for him or his son "James III," the Old Pretender. The battle of Killiecrankie in Scotland in 1689, the Boyne campaign in Ireland in 1690, and the French attempt to invadc Scotland in 1708 were all part of the Jacobite movement; but it was not until 1715 that the first major effort of the English Jacobites took place and by that time the movement had inevitably lost some of its momentum. William III (1688-1702) and Anne (1702-14) were no tyrants and had not stirred up any widespread discontent.

The 1715 Rebellion

The accession of George I in 1714 stimulated Jacobite activity, for he was a coarse, unattractive foreigner. In Scotland widespread resentment existed against the Act of Union of 1707, and there was a natural loyalty towards the Scottish Stuarts. English Jacobites in 1715 included many Tory squires, Anglican churchmen of high rank, M.P.s of both Houses, army officers and 28,000 papists. There were pro-Jacobite riots in London, Oxford and Staffordshire. In their alarm, Hanoverian ministers secured the passing of the Riot Act to increase magistrates' powers to deal with unlawful assemblies. In spite of Louis XIV's promise by the Treaty of Utrecht (1713), French sympathies lay with the exiled Stuarts.

"James III and VIII" was proclaimed at Braemar, and in November, 1715, the Earl of Mar marched towards Edinburgh. He was intercepted by government troops led by the Duke of Argyll at Sheriffmuir, and after an indecisive battle Mar and the Pretender fled to France.

The Duke of Ormonde landed from Ireland in the south-west of England, but failed to gain support in Devon and Cornwall. Forster, who was M.P. for Northumberland, and Lord Derwentwater united with the survivors of Mar's Scottish force, and marched through Carlisle; but they were forced to surrender to government forces at Preston.

In spite of its promising prospects, the rebellion of 1715 therefore failed. Its leadership was uninspiring; its main military leader, Ormonde, lacked energy; Viscount Bolingbroke in France betrayed Jacobite secrets by careless talk; "Bobbing Joan" Mar mishandled his army, and the Old Pretender himself, though no coward, was well out of touch in far-off Lorraine.

By contrast, the Whig leaders Stanhope and Townshend acted swiftly, blockading French ports, suspending the Habeas Corpus Act for six months, threatening Scottish lairds with seizure of their lands, arresting prominent Jacobites like Sir William Wyndham, seizing Jacobite arsenals, and ferreting out Jacobite plans through their astute ambassador in Paris, Lord Stair.

The death in 1715 of Louis XIV, protector of the Stuart house, was a blow to Jacobites, but it is doubtful whether he would have risked another war on their behalf. The Duke of Orleans, regent for Louis XIV's infant successor, was soon to find reasons for friendship with the Hanoverian house, for he too was insecure. Little help therefore came from abroad in 1715.

English Jacobites were ready to drink toasts of loyalty to the "king across the water" but unwilling to lose their lives in his service. There was no bitter sense of injustice in England in 1715. English dislike for the Scots impeded the movement, as did inter-clan jealousies in Scotland, where the most powerful clan, the Campbells under their leader Argyll, fought for the Hanoverians. As always Highlanders were inclined to drift away rapidly after battle.

Perhaps the greatest single factor in losing the support of Englishmen for the Stuart cause was the Roman Catholicism of the Old Pretender. Englishmen had shown in 1688 that they did not want another Roman Catholic king. No help came from the Roman Catholic Irish who had been numbed by the effect of the fierce penal laws of William III's reign; the Protestant Dutch, on the other hand, sent six thousand good troops to assist the Whig government. Finally, Jacobite financial resources were always lean, whereas Whigs had the wealth of the Bank of England behind them.

The rebellion defeated, the Whig government acted with wise foresight. Lords Derwentwater and Kenmure were executed, together with twenty-two less distinguished prisoners in Lancashire and four in London. Hundreds more were transported to the colonies; estates belonging to rebel leaders were confiscated. Marshal Wade drove new roads through the Highlands to facilitate future control.

The 1745 Rebellion

Britain became prosperous under the tolerant rule of Walpole (1721-42) which makes it surprising that there was another Jacobite rebellion thirty years after the first, but it was to come nearer to success. There were some favourable factors. George II's best troops were abroad in the Netherlands, participating in the War of the Austrian Succession, and had just received a sharp defeat at the hands of the French commander Marshal Saxe at Fontenoy. Scotland was held by a scattered garrison of only three thousand Hanoverian troops under incompetent Sir John Cope. Charles Edward, the Young Pretender, was dashing, high-spirited, competent and attractive.

GENEALOGICAL TABLE SHOWING THE DESCENT OF GEORGE I

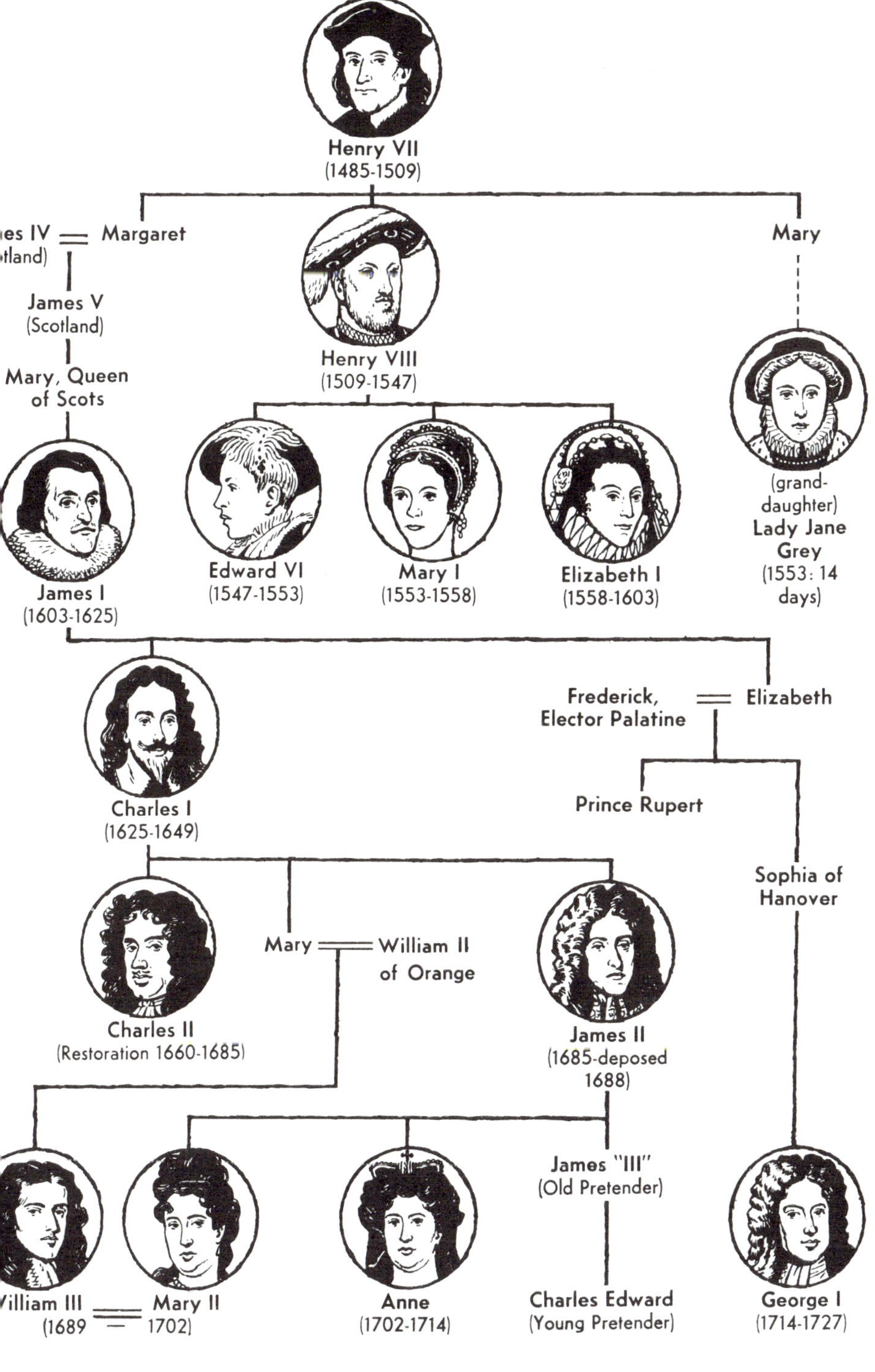

Prince Charles Edward landed at Moidart with seven followers. He succeeded in gathering an army, though one not so numerous as Mar's force in 1715. The absence of government troops in Europe helped the Jacobites, who were able to occupy Edinburgh. A government force was defeated by the Jacobites at Prestonpans, and the young Pretender led his army southwards towards London, by way of Carlisle, Wigan and Manchester as far as Derby. But as the Highlanders left their homeland farther behind, they became less and less enthusiastic. By this time too, the government troops had gathered, and they forced the Jacobites to begin the long retreat northwards, towards Scotland. The Jacobites won a victory at Falkirk in 1746, but at Culloden they were decisively defeated.

The almost complete lack of response from the English was a bitter blow. Hanoverian prosperity had sapped their interest in Jacobitism. Jacobite resources were very scanty in comparison with those of the Hanoverian government. At Culloden, Cumberland had an army twice the size of Charles' force, and eighteen guns while Charles had none. The Roman Catholicism of the Pretender was still a barrier. The Highlanders quarrelled among themselves and became dispirited. As in 1715, little help came from abroad, whereas George II could count on the assistance of twelve thousand Dutch and Hessian troops.

"Butcher" Cumberland wreaked a brutal vengeance on captured Jacobites. In order to break down clan loyalties the Hanoverian government took away from clan chiefs their rights of hereditary jurisdiction and military service. Wearing tartans, playing bagpipes, and bearing arms were all forbidden for the same reason. A genuine attempt to stimulate prosperity in the Highlands followed. Pitt was soon to enlist the fighting qualities of clansmen into regiments of the British army. The failure of the '45 marked the end of Jacobitism as a serious factor in the political life of Great Britain.

Brief Comparison of the Two Rebellions

Though the '45 took place at a less favourable time than the '15 it came nearer to success. The prospects of the '15 were considerably stronger, for Hanoverians were not firmly settled on the English throne. In 1715 the nobility rallied in strength to the Stuart cause, but in 1745 few men of rank joined the rebellion, other than clan chiefs. There was more response in England in 1715 than in 1745. Both rebellions collapsed for largely similar reasons.

QUESTIONS

1. State reasons for the failure of the rebellions of 1715 and 1745.
2. Show that the Jacobite Rebellion of 1745 was more dangerous than that of 1715.

CHAPTER 36

SIR ROBERT WALPOLE

BORN in 1676, Walpole came from a landed Norfolk family and was a typical heavy-drinking, coarse, open-air-loving, eighteenth-century squire. He was a practical man full of common sense. Educated at Eton and King's College, Cambridge, he entered Parliament for the borough of Castle Rising in 1701. Unlike many squires, he was always a Whig. From 1708 to 1710 he was Secretary at War, and from 1710 to 1711 Treasurer of the Navy. He had a spell in the Tower in 1712 on a charge of corruption.

The Whig triumph of 1714 brought Walpole the office of Paymaster of the Forces, and in 1715 that of Chancellor of the Exchequer. He liked to live in style, so he needed the rewards of office; but in 1717 he resigned his post out of loyalty to his brother-in-law Townshend, who quarrelled with George I and Stanhope over foreign policy. He returned as Paymaster in April, 1720, before the South Sea Bubble burst.

South Sea Bubble, 1720

The South Sea Company was founded in 1711, and given a monopoly of trade in the Pacific, arising out of the Asiento Treaty. The company offered to take over £31 million of the national debt, and to pay £7 million for the privilege. The government, who regarded the national debt as something which the country was not able to carry, accepted this offer; but members of the company had bribed M.P.s to support the proposal in Parliament.

As a result of government acceptance, public confidence in the company rose. This led to a speculation mania. Many new companies were formed, some sound, others unsound. Shares in the South Sea Company originally worth £100 rose to £1,060 by 1720.

The South Sea Company prosecuted some bogus companies successfully, but this shook public confidence in investment. The consequent fall in share values affected all companies, including the South Sea Company, and many small investors were ruined. Public anger at this affair caused the fall of Stanhope's ministry, and a temporary collapse of the national finance.

Though the South Sea Bubble gave Walpole his chance he was not so astute over the scheme as is sometimes thought: he would have lost money himself had not his steward taken timely action. Nevertheless, he had a reputation for financial wisdom, and was not one of the promoters of the scheme, which

The speculative merry-go-round: the South Sea Bubble.

disgraced his rivals Sunderland and Aislabie. Fortunately for Walpole too, Stanhope died in 1721, leaving the field clear for Walpole and Townshend. In April, 1721, Walpole became First Lord of the Treasury and then virtually Prime Minister, a position he maintained for the next twenty-one years. He saved the South Sea Company by transferring £18 million of its stock in equal amounts to the East India Company and the Bank of England, thus restoring financial confidence. This was typical of his financial wisdom.

Walpole's General Aims

Walpole wished to increase prosperity in order to stimulate satisfaction with his government, to maintain the Protestant succession of 1714, and to maintain the Whigs and himself in office. He loved both power and the business of administration. He wanted peace at home and abroad so that he could build up Britain's financial strength.

Reasons for Walpole's Long Tenure of Office

Walpole would brook no rival. He deliberately overlooked Pulteney in 1721, sent Carteret to Ireland as Lord Lieutenant in 1724, edged Townshend out of office in 1730 and engineered the dismissal of Chesterfield in 1733 for opposing the Excise Scheme.

Walpole made himself indispensable to the first two Georges as their protector against Jacobitism and as their head of government. Apart from his brief dismissal by George II in 1727, Walpole enjoyed royal support during the whole of his long spell of office. He managed the House of Commons wonderfully well, using patronage to win votes there and at elections. He placated Tory squires by reducing land tax. It took Bolingbroke a considerable time to organize an effective opposition to Walpole. Meanwhile Walpole skilfully damped down any likely opposition by his policy of letting sleeping dogs lie.

Examples of Walpole's Policy

There are a number of good examples of Walpole's determination to let sleeping dogs lie. When William Wood tried to cheat the Irish in 1722 by supplying them with base copper coins, Walpole quietened things down by withdrawing Wood's concession, but gave him a pension. Walpole frequently raided the Sinking Fund rather than raise taxation. He dropped a desirable extension of the Excise Scheme in 1733 to assuage opposition. When Captain Porteous killed some smuggler-protecting hooligans in Edinburgh in 1737 and was hanged by the mob, Walpole dissuaded irate Queen Caroline from punishing the city and stirring up Scottish resentment, but at the same time he granted Porteous' widow a pension.

Walpole's Finance

Walpole's special interest lay in the field of finance. In 1717 he had established his Sinking Fund when the National Debt stood at £54 million with rates of interest up to 9 per cent. When he returned to office he renewed the scheme by which money was set aside each year to reduce the debt, and by 1727 he had reduced it by nearly £9 million. Interest was lowered to a uniform 4 per cent. Though Walpole abused the Sinking Fund, it did create confidence among investors.

He reorganized and simplified collection of duties, and maintained two main taxes, house duty and land tax, at a low level, the latter at only 1*s.* in the pound in 1732 and 1733.

His Excise Scheme of 1723, which applied to coffee, coconuts and chocolate, dealt a blow to smuggling and increased the revenue by £120,000, in spite of which a similar scheme for wines and tobacco was defeated by the opposition in 1733.

Trade was greatly stimulated by reduction of high tariffs on imports, amounting almost to abolition in the case of raw materials, and by removal of duties on export of agricultural produce and over one hundred manufactured articles. Bounties were granted on exports of grain, spirits, silk, sailcloth and refined sugar. At the same time, Walpole carefully protected industries at home from foreign competition.

His policy was one of modified mercantilism. Improvement in British exports between 1720 and 1738 reflected the success of his policies.

Walpole's Colonial Policy and Foreign Affairs

Walpole was inclined to shelve problems which arose in the Colonies, but his tactful interpretation of the Old Colonial System was wiser than the unbending legal attitude of George Grenville later in the century. Walpole encouraged colonists to produce goods needed in Britain by offering them bounties on sugar, tobacco and naval stores. He skilfully placated West Indian sugar-planters by having the Molasses Act passed in 1733, forbidding American colonists to purchase sugar from the French islands; but he avoided strict enforcement of the Act, which would have caused discontent in North America. He left his successors to grasp the colonial nettle more firmly.

At first Walpole left foreign affairs to Townshend, who maintained the policy of friendship with France initiated by Stanhope; but when hostile Chauvelin became Cardinal Fleury's foreign minister in 1727, relations between Britain and France cooled. Walpole refused to be drawn into the War of the Polish Succession in 1733, and allowed British influence on the Continent to decline. France turned to Spain and away from Britain. Peace was Walpole's essential aim.

Religious and Constitutional Affairs

Religious toleration grew during Walpole's tenure of office, and this is greatly to his credit. He realized that repeal of the Test and Corporation Acts (which forbade Nonconformists to hold public offices) would cause a storm, so he had annual Indemnity Acts passed from 1727 onwards to save his Nonconformist supporters from punishment under the earlier Acts.

Peaceful constitutional development resulted from Walpole's long spell in power. We can now see that Walpole approached the position of Prime Minister, though he disclaimed the title, and that the Cabinet system took a firmer root under his strong hand. The House of Commons grew in stature (Walpole remained in it throughout his long ministry), and party government operated more noticeably, but without any strict organization such as exists today.

Growth of Opposition and Loss of Office

Until 1725 Walpole did not meet any serious opposition. His old rival Bolingbroke did not return to England until 1723; and though he was never allowed to re-enter Parliament, it was he who organized those elements hostile to Walpole into a firm opposition. It included discontented Whigs like Pulteney and Carteret, Tories like Sir William Wyndham and George Shippen, "boy patriots" like William Pitt and Henry Fox, and Frederick

Walpole (left) talks to the Speaker.

Prince of Wales, whose residence (Leicester House) became a centre of opposition.

In 1739 the long-standing quarrel with Spain came to a head. The Spaniards resented abuse by Britain's seamen of trading rights in Spanish American colonies granted by the Asiento Treaty of 1713. Spanish coast-guards used over-vigorous methods against British sailors, as the loss of Captain Jenkins' ear proved.

Walpole tried hard to avert war but the opposition drove him into it. His heart was not in it and inevitably the war was not well waged. Walpole's majority declined in the election of 1741 and soon afterwards he was out-voted in the House of Commons. He resigned and moved up to the House of Lords with his new title, the Earl of Orford.

Assessment of Walpole

Walpole had given Britain twenty years of peaceful government, during which the country prospered. Political violence decreased and religious toleration increased. He established the Hanoverians firmly on the throne and Britain's financial strength grew.

He did little to deal with social problems of his day, and his methods did nothing to raise the low moral climate which prevailed. His cautious foreign policy caused some decline in Britain's influence abroad, and his policy of retrenchment led him to neglect the army and navy, so that Britain's performance in the Austrian Succession War (1740-1748) was uninspiring. His determination to oust his rivals from power caused him to surround himself with mediocre men.

Nevertheless Britain gained much from the long spell of peace which Walpole gave her between 1721 and 1739.

QUESTIONS

1. Explain in what ways Walpole followed a policy of "letting sleeping dogs lie."

2. Write an account of Walpole's domestic policy.

CHAPTER 37

PITT THE ELDER

WILLIAM PITT the Elder, born in London in 1708 and educated at Eton and Trinity College, Oxford, entered Parliament for the family borough of Old Sarum in 1735. A brilliant orator, he at once attacked Walpole, who retaliated by taking away Pitt's army commission. Pitt gained revenge by driving Walpole into the Spanish war of 1739, which led to Walpole's downfall. Next he accused Walpole's successor, Carteret, of sacrificing the true interests of Britain in the War of the Austrian Succession to those of Hanover, which he called a "despicable electorate." This earned him the hatred of George II, but Pelham and Newcastle forced the king to accept Pitt's entry into office by themselves resigning in 1745. George II could not replace them, so Pitt became Paymaster of the Forces.

Pitt was Paymaster from 1745 to 1755. Normally men made private fortunes in this office, but Pitt refused to make a personal profit; this unusual purity won him respect and popularity. During these years he was quiet, so his enemies assumed that he had been bought over, but all the while Pitt was busily poring over maps, getting to know the art of military administration, and making the acquaintance of great London merchants like William Beckford. The knowledge gained stood him in good stead during the Seven Years' War. By 1751 he was growing restive in his minor office, but George II's loathing for Pitt made his prospects of promotion slight. Pitt could see that France was preparing to attack in both India and North America, and that Newcastle was failing to make preparations; this caused him to criticize the Duke openly in 1754. The ambush of Braddock's force in North America in 1755 proved to Pitt that his fears were justified, but in the same year he was dismissed.

Outbreak of the Seven Years' War

The War of the Austrian Succession (1740-48) had not left the overseas struggle between Britain and France resolved: nor had it settled Maria Theresa's dispute with Frederick II of Prussia over Silesia. The Austrians had been dissatisfied with the help received from Britain during the war, so they turned to France. George II's fears for Hanover drove him to Frederick, whom he thoroughly disliked. This change of alliances, complete by 1756, became known as the Diplomatic Revolution. War broke out in the same year, and

Death of General Wolfe on the battlefield of the Plains of Abraham.

brought nothing but disaster for Britain, who lost Minorca in the Mediterranean and Fort Oswego in North America, and suffered the disaster known as the Black Hole of Calcutta in India. In spite of his vast control of placemen in the Commons and votes in the boroughs, Newcastle had to go.

Newcastle was replaced by the Devonshire-Pitt ministry. Pitt rapidly put new energy into the conduct of the war by sending German troops out of England to defend Hanover, raising 40,000 soldiers and 50,000 sailors, and despatching reinforcements to North America; but a combination of George II (still prejudiced against Pitt), Cumberland (who refused to take up his command), and Newcastle (smarting at his loss of office and longing to return), overthrew Devonshire and Pitt. For eleven weeks George II tried to form a ministry without Pitt, but had to give way to public clamour and accept him in coalition with Newcastle, and a very successful coalition it proved to be, with Pitt concentrating on winning the war, and Newcastle finding the money and managing Parliament. Pitt said, "I know that I can save the country and that I alone can," and he proved to be right.

Pitt's Conduct of the Seven Years' War, 1757-61

In North America the French had built a chain of forts from Louisbourg to New Orleans, threatening to restrict the more numerous English-speaking colonists from expansion to the Great Plains. In Montcalm they possessed a fine commander who had swept the British from the Hudson-Mohawk valley connecting Canada with New York. Pitt sent able generals to North

America, and backed them to the full. His masterpiece was the three-pronged campaign of 1758, in which Amherst, Wolfe and Boscawen took Louisbourg and Forbes took Duquesne, though Abercromby failed at Ticonderoga. The next year Wolfe took Quebec, and Amherst cleared the French from Ticonderoga and Crown Point. Oswego was recaptured and Fort Niagara was also taken from the French. With the fall of Montreal in 1760, Canada lay in the hands of the British, a triumph indeed for Pitt.

Pitt organized an "army of observation" to defend Hanover and to protect the flank of Frederick the Great. When Ferdinand of Brunswick took over its command from Cumberland in 1757, this army fought brilliantly, defeating the French at Crefeld in 1758 and at Minden in 1759.

Naval operations were equally successful under Pitt's direction. In 1756 the navy was short of ships; Pitt made sure that Admiral Anson, First Lord of the Admiralty, produced more ships rapidly, and ordered a blockade of the main French ports, Brest and Toulon. French fleets were thus prevented from intervening overseas, and when they tried to escape in 1759, as part of a plan to invade England, the Toulon fleet was destroyed by Boscawen at Cape Lagos and the Brest fleet by Hawke at Quiberon Bay. Co-operation between navy and army was most effective. Admiral Saunders helped Wolfe to take Quebec, Clive was ferried from Madras to Bengal by Admiral Watson, and many other overseas expeditions were supported by the navy.

Pitt forecast that he would conquer Canada on the plains of Europe. This he did by faithfully sending Frederick of Prussia an annual subsidy of £700,000 which enabled him to maintain armies in the field against the French, whose soldiers were pinned down in Europe, thus weakening the French effort overseas.

Pitt supported his main campaigns by coastal attacks on Cherbourg, St. Malo and elsewhere. Though these attacks were not successful and brought Pitt criticism, Frederick II pleaded for them to be continued, because they took pressure off him by keeping 30,000 French troops in France.

Pitt had a flair for finding energetic and aggressive commanders like Wolfe, Boscawen, Hawke and Amherst, and he gave them his full support.

Determined to expand the British Empire, Pitt sent expeditions to the West Indies where Grenada, Dominica, Tobago, Guadeloupe and Martinique were taken from the French. In West Africa, Senegal and Goree were captured. He saw the war as a whole, working ceaselessly, sometimes for eighteen hours a day, and by 1759 he had turned dismal defeat into glorious victory.

Pitt's Resignation and the Peace of Paris

By 1760 public adulation of Pitt bordered on idolatry, and it went to his head. He saw that Spain was planning to enter the war on the side of France, and wanted to attack her first. When his colleagues under Lord Granville's influence would not support him, he at once resigned. Pitt's forecast was correct, and when his plans were put into effect they led to the capture of Cuba, Florida and the Philippines from the Spaniards.

War ended with the Treaty of Paris (1763). Britain gained Canada, Cape Breton Island, Grenada, Dominica, Tobago and Senegal from France (who restored Minorca), and Florida from Spain (who recovered Cuba and the Philippines). Pitt considered that the treatment of Britain's enemies was far too lenient. He had won supremacy at sea, in North America and in India.

Pitt was one of Britain's greatest war ministers. He created the first British Empire, and in a corrupt age his political incorruptibility shone out. His championship of liberal causes was fearless and sincere. Had his powers not waned, he might have averted loss of the American colonies. As a politician he made errors of judgement which laid him open to charges of inconsistency, as when he defended Hanover, having earlier attacked Carteret for doing so; but Britain was fortunate to find such a leader in the Seven Years' War.

In 1763 Pitt refused to join the ministry of Grenville, his brother-in-law. He defended freedom of speech in Wilkes' case, and condemned general warrants. In 1766 he opposed the Stamp Act introduced to tax the American colonists. Also in 1766, Pitt became Earl of Chatham, and moved up to the House of Lords. He formed a ministry (1766-68), but ill-health distracted him, and the ministry was a failure. Recovering somewhat, he later spoke in the Lords, about Wilkes and the Middlesex election. He also criticized the East India Company. After 1770, he strove in vain for eight years to avert an American war and the loss of the colonies, and he also advocated moderate parliamentary reform. He died in 1778.

Extent of the British Empire in 1756 and 1763

1756	Added in 1763
Thirteen American colonies.	The rest of Canada.
Nova Scotia. Newfoundland.	North America east of the Mississippi and west of the Appalachians.
Hudson's Bay Territory.	Florida.
Gibraltar. Minorca.	Grenada. St. Vincent.
Bermudas. Barbados. Jamaica.	Tobago. Dominica.
Montserrat. St. Christopher.	Senegal.
St. Eustatius. St. Kitts.	Bengal.
Antigua. Ivory Coast. Gambia.	
Bombay. Calcutta. Carnatic.	

QUESTIONS

1. Outline the career of the Elder Pitt, describing his achievements briefly.
2. Describe the Elder Pitt's leadership during the Seven Years' War, and explain what Britain gained by the Treaty of Paris, 1763.

CHAPTER 38

GEORGE III

GEORGE III was twenty-two years old in 1760 when he came to the throne, and like most young men he wished to distinguish himself. Grandson of George II, he was brought up by his unintelligent German mother, Augusta of Saxe-Coburg, to hate his grandfather and his grandfather's ministers. Jacobitism was dead, so George had no need to tie himself to the Whig factions. He was not endowed with strong intellect, but his sense of duty was high. He was to raise the moral tone of the court to a respectable level after the sordidness of the first two Georges; he was less concerned with Hanover than they had been, and gloried in the name of Britain.

George III did not come to the throne with a definite political programme and certainly entertained no intention of establishing absolute rule. He saw as his special mission that of purifying politics, but was to find that the influence which won support for an eighteenth-century government was not easily dispensed with. There was no sudden break in constitutional development in 1760. George wished to see party ministries replaced by national, patriotic ministries. He exercised strong personal influence on political life and though this influence declined because of the loss of the American colonies (for which he was partly responsible), it did not disappear until 1811, when he became permanently insane.

Unstable Administrations, 1760-70

There were rapid changes of ministry in the first ten years of George III's reign, and this has been interpreted to mean that the king was searching for a man who would endorse without question the king's policies, but George III did not arbitrarily dismiss men who disagreed with him; he merely refrained from giving them his support. Thus he did nothing to dissuade Pitt from resignation in 1761: thereafter it was Pitt's aloofness from other politicians, rather than George's interference, which weakened ministries. George identified Newcastle with the hated Whig factions, but he was quite within his rights when he resumed personal control of royal patronage. The fact that this undermined the basis on which Newcastle's following in the Commons rested was a secondary consideration. Yet with this basis lost to him, Newcastle had little alternative but to resign. Sensitive Bute (1762-63) was hurt not by the king (who liked him), but by parliamentary criticism of his Treaty of Paris. It was this that drove him from office. George Grenville

1784 election scene at Covent Garden, by R. Dighton.

(1763-65), by tactless handling of almost every problem, lost the confidence of king and parliament alike. Rockingham (1765-66) failed to placate the American colonists or to unite his ministerial colleagues in a common policy.

Party leaders having failed him, George III turned to Chatham (1766-68), a man who like himself sought to stand above the party, in the hope that this elder statesman would be able to command the respect of the Commons through support of that group of independent members unfairly labelled by opponents "the king's friends". Chatham's health proving unequal to the task given him, George turned back to a party man, the Duke of Grafton (1768-70), but the American problem was the Duke's undoing as it had been that of some of his predecessors. It looked as if the party system was the only way by which government of the country could be carried on, and that further decline of royal initiative was inevitable. It was at this stage that George called Lord North to his aid.

Lord North has been much maligned. He was thirty-seven in 1770 and was to provide twelve years of settled administration. He had been Chancellor of the Exchequer since 1767. He did not lead a clan of supporters, nor did he owe his position entirely to royal support, for he steadily won the approval of county members by a policy of economy. He was easy-going and met problems as they arose, and suited George III far better than his predecessors. North was a quiet administrator whose tact and attitude of compromise won him fresh support in the election of 1774. His popularity began to wane as bad news came from across the Atlantic, and it is true that George III sustained North in power during the later years of his ministry against the will of the country; but he exercised less royal authority in doing so than George II had done in keeping Walpole from 1739 to 1742. North fostered the idea of the supremacy of royal influence by lamenting that he was forced to stay in office.

Attacks on George III

John Wilkes, the scoundrelly editor of the controversial weekly *North Britain*, accidentally strengthened constitutional liberty. In 1763 he was arrested on a General Warrant. These warrants were often misused because they did not name any particular person. After his release Wilkes campaigned successfully to have General Warrants made illegal, and won damages for wrongful search and arrest. After five years abroad, Wilkes was elected M.P. for Middlesex, but was charged with libel and expelled from Parliament. The electors returned him three times, but the Commons refused to admit him. Riots in Wilkes' support followed, and Parliament had to allow him to take his seat in 1774. The motion which had expelled him was erased from the Statute Book in 1782. George III and his ministers had lost their battle.

As a magistrate, Wilkes contributed to the freedom of the Press by dismissing government prosecutions brought against a reporter and a printer who had published accounts of parliamentary debates.

Anonymous letters by Junius appeared in 1769 in the *Morning Advertiser*, criticizing Grafton mercilessly, and George indirectly. Edmund Burke's *Thoughts on Present Discontents*, published in 1770, argued the case for party government and lamented the turn politics had taken since 1760.

Emboldened by government failures in the American war, the opposition in England began to talk of corrupt majorities and the excessive influence of the Crown. Jebb and Wyvill, both clergymen, began to organize attacks on the executive power, and were joined by Sir George Saville, member for Yorkshire. A great petitioning movement sprang up, demanding more county M.P.s independent of party control, more economy, and annual parliaments, all with reduction of royal influence in mind. The Rockingham and Shelburne groups joined the petitioning bandwagon. In 1780 Dunning secured the passing of his famous motion "that the influence of the Crown has increased, is increasing, and ought to be diminished". It was fair that George III should share with North the blame for loss of the American colonies, since he had consistently regarded the colonists as insubordinate rebels and had interfered constantly in the conduct of the war against them.

Ministries, 1782-83

The resignation of North in 1782 marks a decline in George III's personal ascendancy in the government. George wished to continue war against the colonists, but North's successor, Rockingham, wanted peace, and George had to give way. The passing of Crewe's Act (disfranchising revenue officers) and Clerk's Act (disqualifying government contractors from sitting in parliament) weakened the influence the Crown could exercise through Treasury patronage.

When Rockingham died in 1782, George III used his prerogative to appoint Shelburne as his successor, in spite of the fact that Fox and North between them mustered 210 votes to Shelburne's 140 in the Commons; but his new ministry was short-lived.

The Fox-North coalition (1783) was a defeat for George, who despaired of finding an alternative arrangement; but he was able to defeat the coalition by his personal influence over the House of Lords, when he engineered its rejection of Fox's India Bill. The power of the Crown was by no means spent!

Pitt's Emergence, 1783

Pitt the Younger became the next leader of the king's government. In the ensuing months he was repeatedly out-voted in the Commons, though by decreasing majorities. George's ability to maintain him in office proves that the royal prerogative was still very strong. The election of 1784 brought Pitt (and therefore George III) a great victory.

As Pitt's stature grew and as George III aged, the king's personal intervention in day-to-day administration of the country became less frequent; but he certainly did not become a functionless appendage of the constitution. Throughout the long ministry of Pitt, George III continued in countless ways to rule as well as to reign. In 1801 his opposition to Catholic Emancipation brought the end of the ministry. In 1804 he kept Fox out of office against Pitt's wishes. In 1806 George successfully resisted relief for dissenters when Grenville was Prime Minister. Pitt's re-establishment of the position of Prime Minister inevitably loosened the grip that George III had had over the administration during North's ministry, and it was a grip never fully regained.

QUESTIONS

1. Describe George III's attempts to revive the power of the Crown. Why did he give up this policy?
2. What do you know of the political aims of George III? How did they affect his reign between 1760 and 1783?

CHAPTER 39

ROBERT CLIVE AND WARREN HASTINGS

THE East India Company was founded in 1600, and by 1700 it had stations at Surat, Masulipatnam, Madras, Calcutta and Bombay. The break-up of the Mogul Empire in 1707 on the death of the Emperor offered a great opportunity to European traders, who gained concessions from the rulers of Hyderabad, the Carnatic, Bengal and Mysore in return for military help. Joseph Dupleix, French governor-general in 1741, made brilliant use of the situation. His aim was supremacy in India and expulsion of the British. The French were established at Pondicherry, Mahé and Chandernagore. During the War of the Austrian Succession, the French captured Madras, but it was restored to the British in 1748 by the Treaty of Aix-la-Chapelle. Had Clive not arrived on the scene and devoted himself to the British interest Dupleix might have achieved his ambition.

Clive's First Visit to India, 1743-53

Robert Clive, born in 1725, was sent to India as a company clerk. In 1746 when the French attacked he escaped from Madras, and took a commission in the army. Dupleix placed a French puppet on the throne of Hyderabad in 1748, and when the Nawab of the Carnatic died in 1749 Dupleix proposed to do the same there, his candidate being Chunda Sahib; the British candidate was Mohammed Ali. By 1751 Mohammed Ali was besieged in Trichinopoli, and the position was desperate for the British Company, whose position in southern India was endangered.

Clive persuaded the Madras governor to let him take two hundred British soldiers and six hundred sepoys to Arcot, capital of the Carnatic. This caused Chunda Sahib to raise the siege of Trichinopoli and march to Arcot, where Clive held out for two months of the monsoon season against superior forces. In 1752 Clive and Major Lawrence relieved Trichinopoli, thus saving Mohammed Ali, and British prestige soared. Mohammed Ali became ruler of the Carnatic, Dupleix was recalled to France in disgrace, and Madras was saved. Clive was back in England in 1753, his reputation already established, and with the British secure in southern India.

Clive's Second Visit to India, 1756-60

Clive returned to India in 1756 with a small naval force under Admiral Watson. Count de Lally had reached Indian waters with a large French fleet,

Robert Clive (1725-74) won an empire for the East India Company.

and the Frenchman de Bussy still dominated Hyderabad. With his men, Sirajud-dowlah, the new ruler of Bengal, had perpetrated the Black Hole of Calcutta. Clive and Watson at once made for Bengal, where Clive took Chandernagore. Meer Jafeer, the Nawab's treasurer, played traitor to Sirajud-dowlah, leading troops over to Clive's side at Plassey in 1757. As a result, Clive gained a remarkable victory over vastly superior numbers, and secured Bengal, the richest province in India, for the East India Company. Meer Jafeer, firmly under British influence, became its ruler. Finally, when Sir Eyre Coote defeated de Lally and de Bussy at Wandewash, Britain became the supreme European power in India.

Clive's Third Visit to India, 1765-67

Clive tried in vain to persuade Pitt to assume control of Bengal; the East India Company had won an Empire without wanting it, for armies swallowed up its profits. When Clive returned to England in 1760 Company servants corruptly amassed huge fortunes by cheating the Bengalese. Consequently British prestige sagged. In 1764 the Nawab of Oudh and the Mogul Emperor attacked Bengal and were defeated by a small force under Major Munro, Oudh and the Emperor coming into the Company's contol.

In 1765 Clive was back in India as Governor of Bengal. In the next two years, until his health failed, he tried to restore order by making a treaty with Oudh, arranging for the Company to collect the revenues of Bengal while retaining the Nawab as ruler (the dual system), restricting private trading and raising the salaries of Company servants; but he failed. Private trading continued; a famine in 1770 killed one-third of the population, yet Company servants callously withheld corn to sell at high prices; Madras became involved in a dangerous quarrel with Hyder Ali of Mysore; the Mahrattas threatened Oudh, and the Company was forced to borrow £1 million to remain solvent. Like most other servants of the Company, Clive had become wealthy by accepting gifts from Indians. In 1772 he was accused of corruption and found guilty, but also praised for his work. To Clive, this condemnation outweighed the commendation and he committed suicide in 1774.

Warren Hastings

Hastings, born in 1732, sailed for India as a junior servant of the Company. After a spell in Bengal he returned to England in 1764, but was back at Madras in 1769. To his surprise the directors asked him to become Governor of Bengal in 1772. Here he inherited the problems left by Clive. Hastings swept aside Clive's dual system, made Calcutta the centre of administration, established a new system of justice incorporating Moslem and Hindu law, appointed a collector for each district to ensure fair taxation and just application of laws, and minimized corrupt trading.

North's Regulating Act and the Council

North's Regulating Act of 1773 gave the government at home much more control over political matters in India. It set up a Supreme Court at Bengal, made the Governor of Bengal also Governor-General of India (a wise step), but imposed a Council of four upon him. The new councillors arrived in 1774. One of them, Philip Francis, soon became Hastings' deadly enemy; and, winning over two colleagues to his side, he was able to block Hastings' every move. Only when one of the two died in 1776 was Hastings able to use a casting vote. Francis, after fighting a duel with Hastings in 1780, returned home to spread prejudice against him.

During the War of American Independence (1775-83), when the French tried to regain their lost supremacy in India, Hastings saved British power in India almost single-handed, receiving little help from the hard-pressed government at home.

Britain faced a hostile confederacy of the Mahrattas, Hyderabad and Mysore. Madras was involved in a foolhardy quarrel with both Mysore and the Mahrattas, who also threatened Bombay. A powerful French fleet was allowed to escape from Europe to India.

The Campaigns of Warren Hastings

Hastings seized French ports (so that their fleet had no bases); sent an army to help Bombay; despatched Eyre Coote to Madras, which was saved by victory over Hyder Ali at Porto Novo in 1781; and broke up the hostile confederacy by skilled diplomacy. Admiral Hughes successfully fought off the French with inferior forces. Hastings' desperate need for money to support these campaigns led to the forceful actions which later brought about his impeachment. Pitt's India Act of 1784 was passed without any reference to Hastings who returned in disgust to England in 1785. He was greatly respected in India and was probably the greatest statesman the British ever had there.

Impeachment of Warren Hastings

Hastings became a target for all who were prejudiced against Indian "nabobs". The Whigs prepared an elaborate attack directed by three powerful orators, Charles Fox, Richard Sheridan and Edmund Burke. Hastings was accused of corruption and the intimidation of Indians; his trial, beginning in 1788 and lasting until 1795, cost him a private fortune. In 1774 he had helped Oudh to obtain tribute from an Afghan hill tribe which Oudh had protected, but much blood was shed in carrying out the task and it led to one of the charges against Hastings. He was also accused of engineering in 1776 the condemnation and execution for forgery of Nuncomar, a disreputable Hindu banker, with whom he had quarrelled. In 1780 he had deposed the wealthy Rajah of Benares for refusing to pay tribute to the Company; and in 1781, in desperate need for money, had allowed some vigour to be used to extract tribute from the mother and grandmother (the Begums) of the ruler of Oudh. These actions led to the charges against him.

Results of the Impeachment

On all these counts he was eventually cleared. To be so treated after giving such services was unjust; but it had the good effect of inspiring future Empire builders to treat native peoples with greater humanity. The Company gave Hastings a pension and he lived until 1818, almost forgotten in his last years.

QUESTIONS

1. What were Clive's main achievements in India?
2. Describe the work of Warren Hastings in India and explain why he was impeached.

CHAPTER 40

JOHN WESLEY AND METHODISM

AFTER successfully defending itself in the seventeenth century from Puritan and Catholic alike, the Church of England gradually became complacent, so that by the reigns of the first Georges it had lost its vigour and enthusiasm. Its leaders, such as Joseph Butler, Bishop of Durham, were men of intellect, but they concerned themselves with theological disputes rather than evangelism. There were many abuses within the Church. Bishoprics and livings became rewards for political service, few new churches were built, enthusiasm was frowned upon, pluralism and non-residence abounded. Bishop Hoadly of Bangor never once visited his diocese in six years! The vicar of Cheddar lived in London. Bishop Keppel of Exeter was also Dean of Windsor. In 1809, 7,358 clergy out of 11,194 were non-resident. With their spiritual needs neglected, the moral standards of rich and poor in early eighteenth-century England were low. Bull-baiting, cock-fighting and drinking gin were the main interests of the poor, gambling and port-drinking those of the rich. Religion everywhere was marking time, though in fairness it must be said that many a poorly-paid parish priest was loved by his flock and performed his duties conscientiously, and most bishops were upright men. Rapid growth of new industrial areas in the second half of the century raised new problems with which the Anglican Church was slow to deal.

The life of John Wesley changed this situation by leading to a revival of religious enthusiasm. He was born in 1703 at Epworth, Lincolnshire, where his father, Samuel, was rector. He was educated at Charterhouse School and Christ Church, Oxford, and ordained in the Anglican Church; he also became a fellow of Lincoln College, Oxford. John frequently preached at Oxford where in 1729 his brother Charles became the centre of a religious group known derisively as Methodists. This group of young men read the Greek Testament, attended Communion regularly every week, visited prisons and the sick, and distributed their money among the poor. It was the strictness and regularity of their lives which earned them their description as Methodists.

In 1735 Charles Wesley was ordained, and he and his brother set sail for Georgia as chaplains for the Society for the Propagation of the Gospel, hoping to lead a mission to the Indians. Their visit was not a success and they returned to England. On their voyage they had come into contact with some Moravians, a German Protestant sect. At Aldersgate Street in London

John Wesley (left), and his brother Charles, who wrote over 6,500 hymns.

in 1738, at a Moravian meeting, John Wesley experienced a sudden conviction of personal salvation that changed his whole life. The Wesleyan Society was founded at Moorfields in London in 1739. John and Charles began to travel all over England to preach, John to Newcastle and the West Riding, Charles (ordained in 1735) to Wednesbury, Leeds and Cornwall. In 1747 John paid his first visit to Ireland, and in 1751 to Scotland. They were joined in their work by a more powerful preacher than either—George Whitefield, who was eleven years younger than John Wesley. Whitefield was born at Gloucester, and educated at Pembroke College, Oxford, where he joined the Methodist group. He preached to tough miners at Kingswood, Bristol, resorting to the open fields when churches were closed to him.

Spread of Methodism

Wesley's good health enabled him to travel 5,000 miles each year, preaching as many as fifteen sermons a week. Charles wrote 6,500 hymns. Wherever the three preachers went, conversions followed; men and women fainted or became hysterical; rough colliers were moved to tears. Sometimes the preachers suffered from violence but faced it bravely. John possessed great aptitude for organization, otherwise the Methodist movement might not have lasted. He began to organize Methodist societies all over the British Isles, placed under men whom he could trust. Lists of rules were drawn up to ensure uniformity of practice. Members made weekly contributions, and lay assistants were appointed. From 1744 onwards an annual conference was held, a practice which has continued to this day.

Division and Separation

Wesley always regarded himself as a loyal Anglican, and never ceased to exhort against separation; but his actions tended towards it. In 1784 he consecrated Dr. Coke and Francis Ashbury as superintendents for America. In 1785 three lay preachers were appointed for Scotland, and others later for Ireland and the West Indies. By 1797, organization of the Methodist movement was completely separated from the Church of England, six years after John Wesley's death, when Methodists numbered 100,000. He left a movement with 294 preachers in Great Britain and 43,000 members in the United States of America. There were members in Ceylon and the West Indies. Methodism, however, did not remain united; Welsh Calvinistic Methodists came into existence in 1770, the Methodist New Connection in 1797, Independent Methodists in 1806 and soon afterwards the Primitive Methodists.

Influence of the Methodist Movement

John Wesley was responsible for a great religious revival in the second half of the eighteenth century. Methodism renewed personal religion, and resulted in an improvement in general morality. It broke through barriers of class, and had a civilizing effect on the new industrial masses of the North, the Midlands and South Wales, who were neglected by the Anglican Church; relief for the poor was organized in these areas, and educational facilities were provided by the Methodists, with cheap but good literature. Social discontent was canalized into spiritual channels, and Methodism possibly staved off a revolution in England comparable with that which convulsed France in 1789; the Methodists opposed violence, and Wesley advocated observance of law and order. Industry and sobriety increased among the lower classes. In addition to their work for the poor, the Methodists also demanded the abolition of slavery, and supported the movement for prison reform. The rise of Methodism considerably increased the number of Dissenters in Britain.

Methodism was an emotional (some would say too emotional), rather than an intellectual, movement, but it was unfortunate that Methodism failed to win the general support of the established Anglican Church.

QUESTIONS

1. Describe the rise of Methodism, and estimate its effect.
2. Why were the Wesleys dissatisfied with the condition of England, and how did they seek to change matters?

CHAPTER 41

REVOLT OF THE AMERICAN COLONIES

ALMOST from the first establishment of colonies along the North American seaboard there were certain fundamental causes of friction and misunderstanding between them and the mother country. As the population of the colonies grew and trade expanded, sources of friction became magnified. Tempers on both sides became so frayed that war ensued in 1775.

Old Colonial System

Of the long-standing causes of this quarrel, perhaps the most vital was what has become known as the Old Colonial System. This system assumed that colonies existed for the benefit of the mother country. American colonists were forced to supply Britain with raw materials and a market for finished goods. Certain enumerated goods such as tobacco, sugar, cotton and wool, could be sent only to Britain, Ireland or a British colony. Even non-enumerated goods had to be shipped to Britain before being sent to a foreign country, though Walpole relaxed restrictions on sugar and rice.

The imports of colonies were equally restricted. No goods, other than British, might be imported unless they had first been shipped to Britain. The purpose behind this regulation was to increase British revenue from customs, since duty had to be paid on colonial imports as they passed through British ports.

Colonial manufacturers were similarly subordinated to British interests. Colonists could only manufacture goods which were not manufactured in Britain. This applied to copper, iron and even fur hats!

Increasingly irksome though this restrictive system proved, it was not without advantages from the colonial point of view. Avoidance of restrictions by wholesale smuggling was common practice, usually ignored by the home government. Agriculture was the colonists' main livelihood and therefore restriction on manufacture was not the serious issue it might seem to be. Colonial tobacco enjoyed a monopoly in the British market and bounties were paid on colonial naval stores, iron and other products.

Other Causes of Discontent

In most colonies the governor was appointed by the Crown and found himself with no police, no civil service and little control of military forces.

The Boston Tea Party, one of the events which sparked off war.

He was therefore at a disadvantage in the frequent quarrels which arose between him and his elected assembly. Often the latter was responsible for his salary and so could exert pressure by threatening to withhold payment.

The Puritan colonies of New England lived in constant fear of having Anglican bishops thrust upon them. When Lord North's Quebec Act of 1774 gave concessions to French Catholics in Canada, a wave of anger arose in New England.

In 1754, at the Albany conference, to which many colonies sent representatives, no agreement was reached on matters of defence against French and Indians, so the burden continued to fall upon the British army and navy and therefore upon the British taxpayer. During the Seven Years' War colonists refused to pay their share of the cost of their defence and even traded illegally with the enemy. Britain emerged from the war with a national debt of £130,000,000. By 1764 it cost Britain £350,000 per year to administer the American colonies. A great Indian raid upon Virginia and neighbouring colonies in that year, the Conspiracy of the Pontiac, proved that colonists still could not defend themselves, yet they felt less need of the support of the British when Pitt removed the French threat by his successful campaigns.

Massachusetts led the demand for independence which was strongest in the New England colonies. This was not surprising because they were inhabited by descendants of the Puritans who were driven from England by religious persecution in the seventeenth century. Travel across the Atlantic was slow and took months, so that colonies and home country developed in different ways, and misunderstandings inevitably arose.

Events which led to War

In 1765 Grenville imposed a stamp duty on legal and commercial documents, newspapers and pamphlets, in order to raise more revenue from colonists to pay for the cost of their defence. He had given them a year in which to make counter-suggestions, but none came. New duties were imposed upon coffee, white sugar and indigo and an effort was made to curtail smuggling. All this produced a storm in the colonies. The cry was raised "no taxation without representation." It was the first direct taxation imposed by Britain in America. British merchants persuaded the Rockingham government to repeal the measure in 1766 because they lost so much money from a colonial boycott of their goods. Instead of letting the outcry simmer down, Rockingham proceeded to secure the passing of a Declaratory Act in the same year to assert that the right to impose taxation still rested with the mother parliament. Fuel was added to the fire when Charles Townshend, Chatham's Chancellor of the Exchequer, imposed duties in 1767 on glass, red and white lead, painters' colours, paper and tea. All these duties except that on tea had to be rescinded in 1773. The colonists rescued a smuggling sloop from the customs authorities in 1770, a breach of discipline in the eyes of George III's government. A scuffle between troops and civilians in Boston in 1770 led to the death by gunfire of five or six civilians, the Boston Massacre. Tempers mounted. When *H.M.S. Gaspee* pursued smugglers in 1772 she was burned by the colonists.

There were faults on both sides. The East India Company was having a difficult time, so the home government allowed it to send its tea direct to North America with complete exemption from tax in Britain. Not only did this cut American merchants out of a share of the profits but, by reducing the price of tea, it looked like a subtle attempt to undermine the colonists' stand upon their principles. As a result a group of Boston extremists dressed as Red Indians threw £15,000 worth of tea into the harbour. This Boston Tea Party revealed absence of respect for Britain, and revolution became inevitable. In 1774 George III's government closed the port of Boston, and withdrew the charter of Massachusetts. At a Continental Congress in the same year, to which all colonists except Georgia sent representatives, resistance against Britain was prepared. Lord North offered to impose only taxes which regulated trade, but the concession came too late.

Main Events of the War, 1775-83

In 1775 General Gage tried to seize colonial arms in a skirmish at Lexington, Massachusetts, and attempted to drive colonists from their position at

Bunker's Hill, near Boston. In 1776 the colonists issued their Declaration of Independence.

Owing to a misunderstanding between Generals Burgoyne and Howe, an attempt to seal off the New England colonies in 1777 ended in the ambush and surrender of Burgoyne at Saratoga to a colonial army under General Gates. In the same year, Howe defeated George Washington at Brandywine, and captured Philadelphia.

France entered the war on the American side in 1778, and Spain joined France a year later. In 1780 Holland also entered the war against the British. Russia, Denmark, Sweden, Prussia and the Emperor formed the League of Armed Neutrality, to protest against Britain's searching of neutral ships for contraband.

General Clinton captured Charleston for the British in 1780, and at Camden (South Carolina) Cornwallis crushed an American army. But the following year Cornwallis faced the Americans under Washington on land and the French fleet under de Grasse at sea; he was forced to capitulate at Yorktown, and the American colonies were lost.

In 1782 Admiral Rodney retrieved the reputation of the British navy by defeating de Grasse at Les Saintes, in the West Indies. Minorca was captured by the French, but Gibraltar held out against the Spanish.

By the Peace of Versailles of 1783, Britain recognized the independence of the United States of America, and lost Tobago to the French and Florida and Minorca to the Spanish.

Reasons for Britain's Defeat

In neither origins nor conduct was the War of American Independence a struggle which reflected any credit on Britain, and her defeat was neither undeserved nor surprising. Her armies were called upon to fight in a badly-charted country three thousand miles from home against an enemy who knew the terrain much better. There was no single centre of resistance whose capture would have led to the collapse of the colonial effort. The capture of neither New York nor Philadelphia was sufficient to induce the colonists to sue for peace. The fact that they were fighting passionately for their own independence gave them a motive which George III's mercenaries lacked. Of the British Generals, Howe, Clinton and Cornwallis, only the latter had the degree of ability the situation demanded; whereas on the colonial side George Washington was not only a sound soldier but a man with outstanding gifts of leadership, courage and pertinacity. In his hands colonial strategy and its execution were largely combined; on the British side strategy was too often planned in London by Lord Sandwich for the navy, and by Lord George Germaine for the army. Neither of these two noblemen was distinguished for his competence or effectiveness. Finally, Britain's European

The American Declaration of Independence was signed in 1776.

enemies rejoiced in her discomfiture to the extent of aiding the colonists. With France, Spain and Holland against her, Britain lost command of the seas, and this was her undoing; she had to reconcile herself to American independence, and loss of her first colonial empire.

Results of Loss of the Colonies

The immediate result of the defeat of Britain was the birth of a new nation, the United States of America. In Britain the first reaction was a bitter one. The discovery that colonies could not indefinitely be subordinated to the interests of the mother country led to doubts about the value or usefulness of colonial enterprise. Gradually wiser reflections were prompted and a more enlightened colonial policy adopted. George III's personal direction of political affairs suffered a humiliation from which it never recovered.

Abroad, France derived little profit from the defeat she had helped to inflict upon her old rival. The expense she had incurred in helping the Americans drove her further towards bankruptcy; while ideas of liberty and freedom brought back by returning armies drove her further towards revolution.

QUESTIONS

1. Describe the events which led to the outbreak of the War of American Independence.

2. Describe briefly the War of American Independence, and explain why Britain lost.

CHAPTER 42

PITT THE YOUNGER

WILLIAM PITT the Younger, son of the Earl of Chatham, was born in 1759 and educated at Pembroke College, Cambridge, being subsequently called to the Bar in 1780. In the same year he entered the Commons for the borough of Appleby. In 1782 he served as Chancellor of the Exchequer under Shelburne and was called upon to form a ministry to replace the Fox-North coalition in 1783. The election of 1784 entrenched him firmly in power for the next seventeen years.

Never a popular man, Pitt had few personal friends and his political colleagues did not always find him congenial since he was too stiff and dictatorial in manner. Even the blamelessness of his personal life and the probity of his public conduct failed to compensate for the coldness of his approach to his fellows.

In the early years of his ministry Pitt revealed liberal tendencies. In 1785 he tried to persuade parliament to transfer the seats of thirty-six rotten and pocket boroughs to more populous areas. He sympathized with demands for abolition of the slave trade, greater religious freedom and a more generous policy towards Ireland and her trade. Vested interests, however, proved too strong for him and none of the measures was acceptable to parliament.

Pitt's Financial Work

England needed an able financier after the strain imposed by the American War, which added £114,500,000 to the National Debt. It stood at £250,000,000 on which £9,500,000 interest had to be paid annually. Pitt planned to wipe out the Debt by the establishment of a Sinking Fund, to which £1,000,000 was allotted annually out of revenue. This money was to be used to buy Government stock, while interest on the holdings was to be used to buy further stock. An independent board of commissioners ran the scheme, which seemed to be merely paying out of one hand into another, but it stimulated public confidence, and reduced the debt.

Pitt would not allow his government to undertake expenditure greater than its revenue, and always attempted to balance his budgets. Unfortunately the war which came in 1793 caused expenditure to leap ahead of revenue so that the public debt rose rapidly, for Pitt was slow to introduce new taxes.

When government loans were raised, Pitt refused to offer them as bribes to friends, but opened them to competition and accepted the best terms available.

To reduce losses caused by smuggling, Pitt lowered duties on tea and spirits, that on tea being reduced from 119 per cent to 12½ per cent. Where several duties had been levied on one article Pitt replaced them by one duty, which simplified collection. He endeavoured to tax luxuries like racehorses, gauzes and ribbons so that he could lighten taxes upon necessities.

Pitt was considerably influenced by the teaching of Adam Smith in his *Wealth of Nations* which advocated free trade. In 1786 Pitt concluded a commercial treaty with France, known as the Eden Treaty, by which each country opened its ports to, and reduced tariffs on, the other's goods.

Pitt's Imperial Policy

Pitt did much to restore confidence in the Empire after the disastrous loss of the American colonies. His India Act of 1784 took responsibility for political matters in India from the inadequate shoulders of the East India Company by establishing a Government Board of Control in London; the company retained control of commercial matters. Pitt's Canada Act of 1791 helped to settle fifty thousand United Empire Loyalists who had migrated from the American colonies. It created two new governments in Upper and Lower Canada (Ontario and Quebec) each having representative assemblies which controlled revenue. Finally it was under the direction of Pitt's Home Secretary, Lord Sydney, that the first white settlement of Australia took place when Captain Phillip took seven hundred convicts to Botany Bay.

Pitt's Foreign Policy in time of Peace

Britain emerged from the American war with no allies and with her prestige at a low ebb. Pitt steadily restored her position between 1783 and 1793. He gained allies by the Triple Alliance of 1788 whose members (Britain, Holland and Prussia) came together to check French interference in Dutch affairs. He successfully demanded compensation when Spain seized British ships at Nootka Sound off Vancouver Island, thus safeguarding the future of western Canada, though he suffered a setback when parliament would not support him in his attempt to prevent Catherine II of Russia from seizing the Black Sea fortress of Oczakoff from the Turks.

Effects of the French Revolution on Pitt

At first Pitt welcomed the French Revolution of 1789, but when its violence increased, and political agitation took place in Manchester, Leeds and Norwich, and when a new spirit of resistance arose in Ireland and Burke's *Reflections on the French Revolution* turned public opinion against the revolution, Pitt abandoned his projects for liberal reform and embarked upon a policy which made serious invasions upon the liberty of the subject. In 1793 a Bill was passed subjecting immigrants to police supervision, and the Corresponding Societies Act suppressed all societies which imposed oaths or which concealed the names of their members. In 1794 the Habeas Corpus Act was suspended, and in 1795 new Treasons and Seditious Meetings Bills were passed to punish plots against king or constitution, and to forbid meetings of over fifty people if a magistrate's permission was lacking. In 1799 and 1800 Combination Acts were passed forbidding workmen to combine in order to secure better wages and conditions of labour. Trials followed these acts which resulted in fierce sentences of transportation for some members of the Corresponding Societies, though two prominent leaders of such societies which maintained contact with the revolutionary movement in France were acquitted by London juries.

Pitt as a War Minister

Pitt, essentially a constructive peace minister, was forced into war with revolutionary France in 1793 for several reasons. The revolutionary armies invaded Belgium, and Britain regarded this as a threat to her security. Pitt also feared French interference in Holland. When the French opened the mouth of the river Scheldt to navigation, Britain regarded it as a high-handed breach of the Treaty of Utrecht of 1713. The French government, by the November Decrees of 1792, offered help to peoples who wished to rise against their governments, thus asserting their right to interfere in the internal affairs of other states. British opinion was also shocked by the execution of Louis XVI in January 1793, but it was France who declared war on Britain in February, 1793. Pitt laboured hard to combat both the ardent fervour of revolutionary leaders and the genius of Napoleon but he died before victory had been achieved.

Pitt's Failure

For his failure to achieve final victory there are many reasons. Because the French government was bankrupt, Pitt based his wartime finance on the assumption that the war would be a short one; in fact it lasted twenty-one years. He under-estimated the ardour of revolutionary France, and found no great military leaders to match his opponent Napoleon. Without his father's genius for directing a war, he largely adopted his father's policy of attacking France's overseas possessions, blind to the fact that in the circumstances of his time it was no longer an effective course of action. It is true that his colonial expeditions led to the capture of valuable territories such as Tobago, Martinique, St. Lucia, Ceylon, the Cape of Good Hope, Trinidad and Demerara, but they cost the lives of nearly 100,000 men who might well have been better employed on the continent of Europe. Moreover, Britain's allies

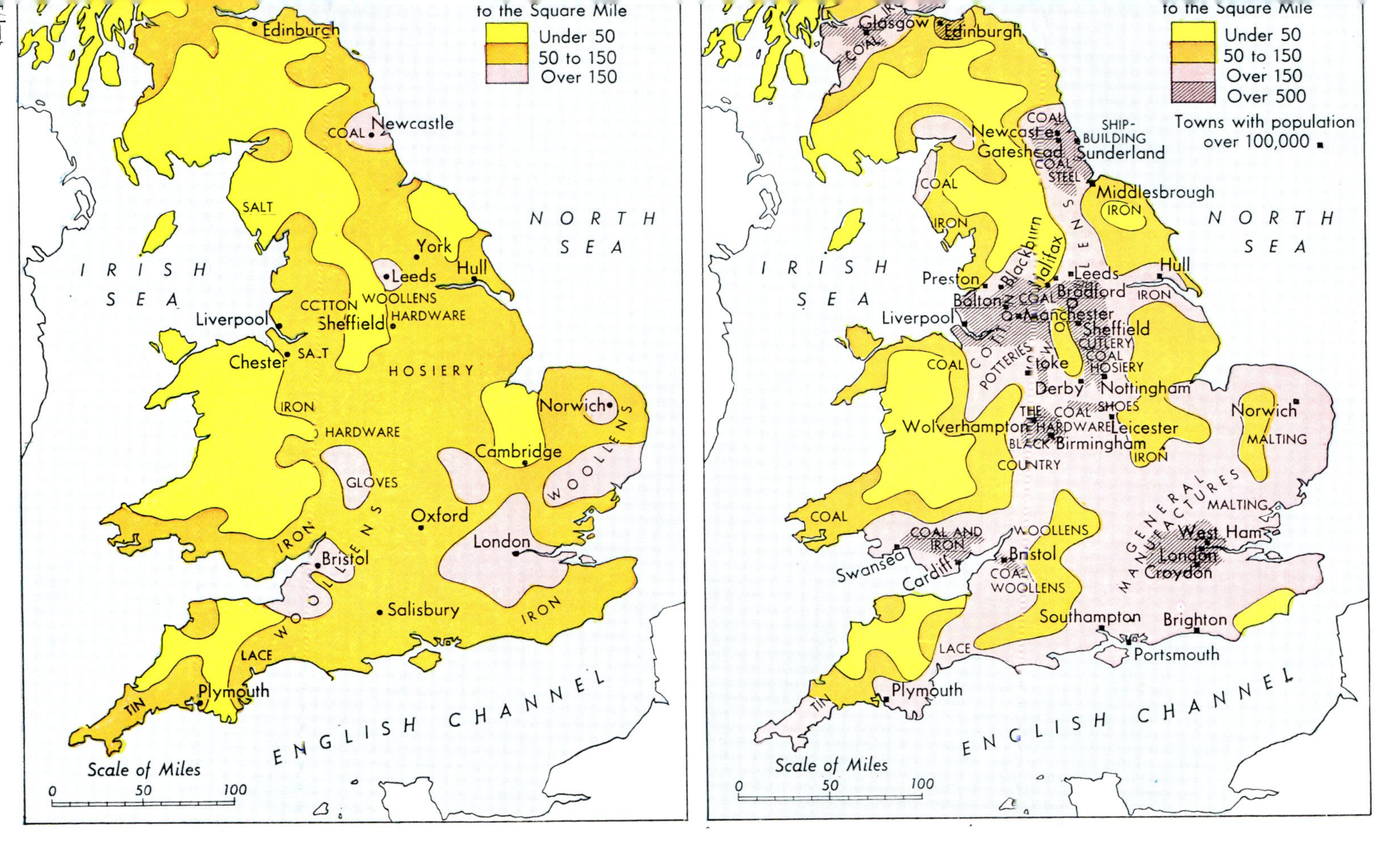
to the Square Mile
Under 50
50 to 150
Over 150
Edinburgh
Newcastle
COAL
SALT
NORTH SEA
IRISH SEA
York
Leeds
Hull
COTTON
WOOLLENS
HARDWARE
Liverpool
Sheffield
Chester
SALT
HOSIERY
IRON
HARDWARE
Norwich
WOOLLENS
Cambridge
GLOVES
Oxford
London
IRON
Bristol
WOOLLENS
Salisbury
IRON
LACE
Plymouth
TIN
ENGLISH CHANNEL
Scale of Miles
0
50
100
to the Square Mile
Under 50
50 to 150
Over 150
Over 500
Towns with population over 100,000
Glasgow
COAL
Edinburgh
COAL
Newcastle
SHIP-BUILDING
Gateshead
Sunderland
COAL
STEEL
COAL
Middlesbrough
IRON
IRON
NORTH SEA
WOOLLENS
IRISH SEA
Blackburn
Halifax
Preston
Leeds
Hull
Bolton
COAL
Bradford
IRON
Liverpool
Manchester
Sheffield
COTTON
CUTLERY
COAL
POTTERIES
Stoke
COAL
HOSIERY
Derby
Nottingham
THE
COAL
SHOES
Norwich
HARDWARE
Leicester
Wolverhampton
BLACK
Birmingham
MALTING
COUNTRY
IRON
GENERAL MANUFACTURES
MALTING
COAL
COAL AND IRON
WOOLLENS
West Ham
Bristol
London
Swansea
Cardiff
COAL
WOOLLENS
Croydon
Southampton
Brighton
LACE
Portsmouth
Plymouth
TIN
ENGLISH CHANNEL
Scale of Miles
0
50
100

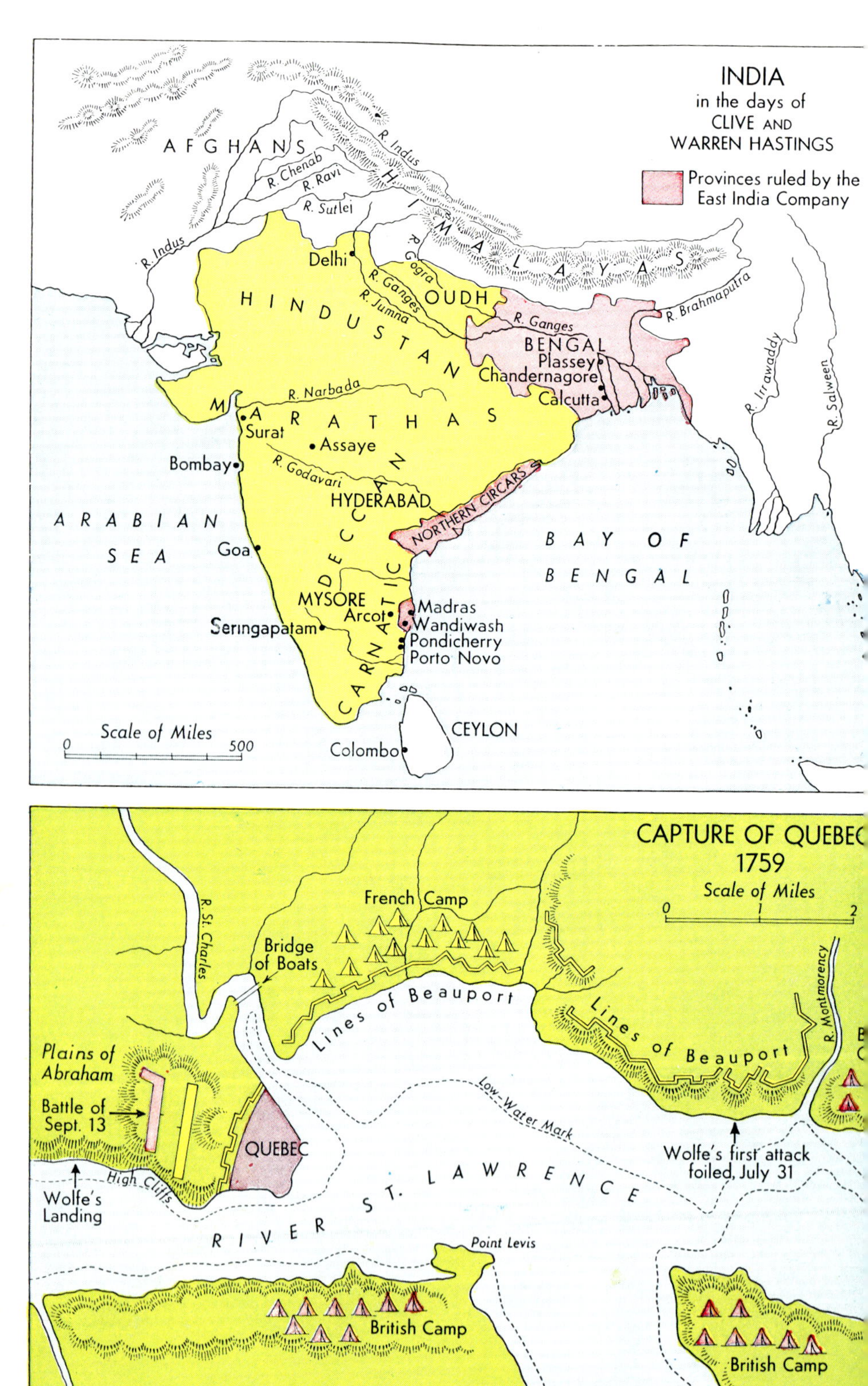
INDIA
in the days of
CLIVE AND
WARREN HASTINGS
Provinces ruled by the East India Company
AFGHANS
HIMALAYAS
R. Indus
R. Chenab
R. Ravi
R. Sutlej
R. Gogra
R. Ganges
R. Jumna
R. Brahmaputra
R. Irrawaddy
R. Salween
R. Narbada
R. Godavari
Delhi
HINDUSTAN
OUDH
BENGAL
Plassey
Chandernagore
Calcutta
MARATHAS
Surat
Assaye
Bombay
HYDERABAD
NORTHERN CIRCARS
DECCAN
ARABIAN SEA
BAY OF BENGAL
Goa
MYSORE
Arcot
Madras
Wandiwash
Pondicherry
Porto Novo
Seringapatam
CARNATIC
CEYLON
Colombo
Scale of Miles
0
500
CAPTURE OF QUEBEC
1759
Scale of Miles
0
1
2
R. St. Charles
French Camp
Bridge of Boats
Lines of Beauport
Lines of Beauport
R. Montmorency
Plains of Abraham
Battle of Sept. 13
QUEBEC
Low-Water Mark
High Cliffs
Wolfe's Landing
Wolfe's first attack foiled, July 31
RIVER ST. LAWRENCE
Point Levis
British Camp
British Camp
ISLE OF ORLEANS

in the coalitions Pitt so tirelessly formed and re-formed saw these colonial adventures as proof that Britain was more interested in extending her empire than in defeating France or Napoleon.

With his forces so divided between New World and Old, it is not surprising that Pitt's operations in Europe were unsuccessful. In 1793 an attack on Dunkirk failed, and Toulon was lost because insufficient troops were sent there. In 1794 the Duke of York was chased out of the Austrian Netherlands, and in 1795 a landing at Quiberon Bay was a fiasco. Again, in 1799 the Duke of York failed at Alkmaar in Holland. Pitt placed too little reliance upon effective British action on the continent and too much faith in the European coalitions he built. The First Coalition (1793-97) fell to pieces because Austria and Prussia quarrelled about partitioning Poland. Austria and Russia quarrelled bitterly in the Second Coalition (1799-1801), the latter accusing the former of lack of co-operation; while the Third Coalition (1805-06) could not survive Napoleon's shattering victories.

Pitt and the Navy

Only in his naval direction was Pitt really successful. He had built up the navy before war began in 1793, so on the outbreak of hostilities ninety ships were ready for action. The result was a series of resounding naval victories; the Glorious First of June 1794, Cape St. Vincent 1797, Camperdown 1797, the Nile 1798, Copenhagen 1801, and Trafalgar 1805. These victories gave Britain complete command of the seas. Pitt discovered Nelson, Jervis, Duncan and Collingwood, all great commanders. He was truly "the pilot who weathered the storm," riding it out magnificently at sea and battling against it with courage, determination and persistence, if not with complete success, on land. He was unfortunate in having to face such a brilliant foe as Napoleon.

Truce of 1802-03 and Renewal of War in 1803

Between 1793 and 1815 there was only one brief period of peace. In 1802 a truce was arranged because war had reached a stalemate: France was unbeatable on land, Britain unconquered at sea, and both sides were exhausted. Addington, who had replaced Pitt as head of the administration in England, wanted peace.

By the Treaty of Amiens, Britain was to restore most of the colonial conquests made during the war, including Malta. France agreed to withdraw from the Papal States and from Naples. Both countries were to withdraw their forces from Egypt.

The truce was, however, short-lived. Britain failed to withdraw from Malta, as promised. The continued presence of French troops in Dutch territory angered Britain. Napoleon was unwilling to revive the Anglo-French

Pitt the Younger addresses the House of Commons from the floor.

commercial agreement. Also he resented insulting personal references to him in the British Press, and refused to believe that the British government could not prevent them. Britain feared that he was planning fresh assaults on Italy and Egypt.

Pitt's Second Ministry, 1804-06

In 1801 Pitt had resigned when George III refused to countenance Catholic Emancipation for Ireland in fulfilment of his minister's pledge at the Act of Union (1800).

The king recalled him to office in 1804, when Napoleon was known to be making serious plans for the invasion of England. Pitt was encouraged by the defeat of these plans as a result of effective naval action by Nelson and Calder and Napoleon's discovery that Austria was again mobilizing her forces for a new military campaign. But news of the French victory over Austria and Russia at Austerlitz in 1805 was too much for Pitt. He died, a disappointed and almost despairing man, in 1806.

QUESTIONS

1. How did the French Revolution affect the Younger' Pitt's domestic policy?
2. Write an account of the Younger Pitt's political career up to 1793.

CHAPTER 43

THE AGRICULTURAL REVOLUTION

THE eighteenth century saw the development of a business spirit in agriculture, cultivators increasingly considering their land as capital from which better income could be drawn by improved methods. Greatly improved transportation made it possible to send produce farther afield than hitherto. The joint working of these two factors led to the final disappearance of the old open field system.

Open Field System

In 1700 about half the arable land of England was still farmed under the medieval open field system, in which village lands were divided usually into three large fields and these sub-divided into strips. The system was widespread across a broad belt from Hampshire and Dorset through the midlands to Yorkshire. It was not found much in the south-west, Wales, Welsh border counties, or the north-west. Where it existed, villagers were able to use common lands for grazing their beasts and gathering fuel. Squatters, with no lands of their own to farm, were entirely dependent upon the commons. Of these squatters, some lived in squalor and others were lazy, even criminal.

Advantages and Disadvantages of the System

A system which had prevailed for centuries was obviously not without advantages. The open-field system ensured that cultivation did not fall below certain standards. It was more flexible than is sometimes thought, and in places individual small farmers grew on their strips crops different from those of their neighbours. In normal years a peasant cultivator could supply most of his own needs: yet changes were necessary.

One of the three huge fields was by custom left fallow each year to allow the soil to recover; this was wasteful of land. Further, when a farmer owning two hundred acres had his strips of land scattered in ten or twenty places, perhaps two miles apart, time was wasted. Since cattle could not be segregated in unhedged holdings, breeding could not be controlled, and disease spread quickly among them. The quality of livestock reared under this system was by modern standards poor. Winter fodder was nearly always short, so there had to be wholesale slaughtering of beasts in the autumn. The system tended to kill initiative. Implements were clumsy. Where strips were divided by balks it was very difficult for a man to drain his land effectively. Moreover there were endless disputes over boundaries. Strips were too narrow for cross-ploughing or cross-harrowing, and common land was overcrowded.

Enclosure

If progress was to be made, clearly one man's land had to be consolidated and separated from that of his neighbour. For this reason a widespread enclosure movement took place in the second half of the eighteenth century. Such enclosures were not new, but whereas in the sixteenth century, as we have seen on page 142, they had been opposed by the government, in the eighteenth century they were encouraged by parliament.

Enclosures could be effected either by local agreement or by act of parliament. Between 1700 and 1815, over three thousand enclosure acts were passed, affecting seventeen per cent of the total area of the country. Consent of the owners of four-fifths of the land in question was needed to set in motion an enclosure bill. Often, three or four men might hold this proportion of the land under consideration, and when this was the case the interests of many smaller holders were frequently overlooked. Villagers rarely dared to voice their opposition. Squatters were in the worst position; enclosures often embraced common land and, having no legal entitlement to this, squatters had no means of legal redress when dispossessed.

Effects of Enclosure

The Board of Agriculture admitted that out of sixty-eight enclosure acts they examined, fifty-three injured the poor; but harsh effects of the movement have been grossly exaggerated. There is no evidence of large-scale rural unemployment. New agricultural practices, such as growing root-crops and grasses, maintenance of large dairy herds, and winter hedging and ditching, created new demands for labour. There was no mass eviction. The population of agricultural villages increased at a rate not much less than that of industrial areas. It has been stated that the small farmer was swamped by enclosure: in fact, the number of small farmers actually increased during the period. If agricultural workers left the land, it was not because they were driven from it, but because they were attracted by the higher wages to be earned in towns. Freeholders, copy-holders and tenants-for-life often received compensation in land for loss of their rights in common fields. Even common-right cottagers who previously had no land of their own were able to buy small plots from large proprietors who disposed of fragments to help defray the heavy cost which an enclosure bill entailed. The rise in price of foodstuffs enabled small cultivators to survive. If there had been no enclosure movement to increase the yield from the soil, there might have been a national catastrophe, for the

Aerial photograph showing the enclosure of strip fields in Buckinghamshire.

total population grew rapidly during this period. A number of improving landlords introduced better farming methods during the eighteenth century.

Pioneers of Scientific Farming

Jethro Tull (1674-1741) invented a drill to sow seed neatly in rows, which was more economical than the old hand-scattering method. Tull advocated deep ploughing and regular hoeing. His invention of a horse-drawn plough in 1714 heralded mechanical farming. In 1731 he published *The New Horse-Hoeing Husbandry.*

"Turnip" Townshend (1674-1738) retired from politics in 1730, and thereafter concentrated all his energies on farming. He drained his Norfolk estate, adding marl to the lighter soils; his land was ploughed deeply and well manured. He popularized the turnip as a field crop, and as winter food for cattle. Townshend established the Norfolk Rotation of crops (barley-roots-clover-wheat), thus dispensing with the very wasteful fallow year.

Robert Bakewell (1725-95) experimented in stock improvement, by careful attention to feeding and by selecting the best animals for breeding. He produced a strain of horses particularly suitable for farm work, and established the famous New Leicestershire breed of sheep, produced for meat rather than for wool. Bakewell also established the New Leicestershire longhorn cattle, his work complementing that of Charles Colling (1751-1836), who improved the shorthorn breed of cattle.

George III, the "farmer" king.

Coke of Norfolk, Earl of Leicester (1752-1842), gave his tenants long leases on their holdings, to make it worthwhile for them to improve the land. He also improved the implements used, and bred Southdown sheep and Devon cattle.

Arthur Young (1741-1820) was the propagandist of new farming methods, although he failed as a practical farmer. He toured the country collecting information about the new farming, and in 1784 published *The Annals of Agriculture.* In 1793 Young became first secretary to the newly-formed Board of Agriculture, and organized publication of books about farming, establishment of farmers' clubs, ploughing matches, agricultural shows and societies.

King George III (1760-1820) set a fashion by his interest in agriculture. He wrote pamphlets, and reared merino sheep on his model farm at Windsor.

General Results of Agricultural Revolution

The enclosure movement and improved methods of farming together constitute the gradual agricultural revolution of the eighteenth century. Its results were vastly important. England began to grow far more food than ever before and the area of land under cultivation was considerably increased. Moreover all the land worked was put to more profitable use. It became possible to provide winter fodder, avoid seasonal slaughtering of livestock and so improve the quality of sheep and cattle as well as their numbers. Compact estates and hedged fields appeared, so that the countryside took on its modern pattern. If some poorer men suffered in all this, their number has been grossly exaggerated.

QUESTIONS

1. Describe the main changes in agriculture in England during the eighteenth century.
2. What were the main causes and results of the enclosure of open fields in the eighteenth century?

CHAPTER 44

THE INDUSTRIAL REVOLUTION

THE term *Industrial Revolution* is applied to a long process involving many changes in the economic life of Britain. It denotes the passing of the time when British people earned their living by agricultural pursuits, and the coming of the time when most were engaged in industry. It also includes the reorganization of industry whereby people ceased to work in their own homes but became increasingly employed in factories. This in turn entailed the decline of work by hand and expansion of machine work. All these changes gathered momentum in the eighteenth century and have continued ever since.

Factors favouring Industrial Revolution in Great Britain

Conditions of social and political life in Great Britain were peculiarly favourable to such changes in the eighteenth century. Constitutional struggles had been settled in the previous century, and internal stability followed. The country also possessed a reserve of capital accumulated from overseas trade. There were no internal customs barriers between one part of the country and another, such as existed in France. Trade and craft gilds, which might have restricted enterprise, had already decayed. Britain possessed iron ore and coal in abundance, and these were two essentials for industrialization. The banking system was well established, and credit sound, so that monetary facilities for industrial expansion were readily available. Finally there were men of technical and scientific skill eager to experiment. Six hundred and ninety-seven patents were registered between 1617 and 1760.

Revolution in Textiles

The silk industry had been organized on a factory basis from its beginning, when John Lombe opened a silk factory in 1721 near Derby; this supplied the model for cotton mills.

The cotton industry expanded during the eighteenth century to such an extent that the supply of yarn fell short of what was required. When John Kay invented his flying shuttle in 1733, as a result of which one man could weave the quantity of broadcloth which previously two men had produced, the shortage became greater. A series of spinning inventions rectified the position. In 1770 James Hargreaves patented his Spinning Jenny by which eight spindles worked from one wheel. His first machines were destroyed by hostile mobs, fearful of finding themselves thrown out of employment, but by 1788 there were twenty thousand "Jennies" in use in the country.

The thread that Hargreaves' machine produced was too weak to be used as warp. That made on Arkwright's water-frame (1769) avoided this fault but was too coarse to be used in making fine fabrics. It was however the water-frame which fully established the factory system in the cotton industry, and Samuel Crompton's Spinning Mule of 1779 (combining principles of Jenny and water-frame) made continuance of this form of industrial organization inevitable.

Weaving now lagged behind spinning and this stimulated Edmund Cartwright to produce a power loom in 1785 and, when it proved successful, to set up a factory at Doncaster in 1787. His loom was more widely adopted after it had been improved by Radcliffe and Horrocks and constructed of iron instead of wood. From this point steam power was rapidly applied to spinning and weaving machinery alike, and factories grew apace. By 1813 Manchester possessed 43 cotton mills and the value of cotton goods exported rose from £23,000 in 1701 to over £7,000,000 in 1801.

Many inventors whose work made this expansion possible were from Lancashire, where there was an extensive coalfield and a climate suitable to the industry. Moreover Lancashire's ports were as near as any to the United States of America, whence raw cotton was imported. It was for reasons such as these that England became the main centre of the cotton industry.

The older woollen industry was slow to change. It was widely scattered, and for technical reasons machinery was less easily applied than to cotton. Being long-established, the industry was tied by traditions and restrictions. There was no rapidly-expanding supply of raw material, for only a trickle of raw wool had reached Britain from Australia by 1815, whereas cotton imports from the United States increased by leaps and bounds. It was not until 1840 that power looms were widely used in the woollen industry.

Revolution in the Coal Industry and the Development of Steam Power

Coal had been used domestically for many centuries, but its mining raised many problems which remained unsolved before the eighteenth century, though Thomas Savery had invented a heavy steam engine for pumping water from mines in 1698. Progress began to be made when in 1705 Thomas Newcomen produced a steam engine for the same purpose; it had, however, one serious defect—it used vast quantities of fuel. So it fell to James Watt to patent a more efficient steam engine in 1769 after he had experimented with Newcomen's machine. He carried his work a stage further in 1781 by harnessing the new motive-power to a rotary motion so that the steam engine could now drive machinery in factories, and in fact be applied for innumer-

Hargreaves's Spinning Jenny was a major advance in textile manufacture.

able other purposes. Matthew Boulton and William Murdoch helped Watt to establish a factory in Birmingham from which poured a steady supply of steam engines.

Increased use of steam and expansion of the iron industry stimulated the demand for coal, while the steam engine had already solved one mining problem. Mines were now dug deeper, but poisonous gases were encountered. John Buddle's fan of 1809, which sucked foul air out of the up-shaft so that fresh air would rush down the other shaft, improved the situation. Sir Humphry Davy's invention of the safety-lamp in 1815, by enabling foul gas to be detected more easily, added to the miners' safety. Metal rails used first by Richard Reynolds in 1768 increased the ease with which coal could be moved from coal-face and pit-head, and winding machinery patented by Oxley in 1763 was an additional aid. Timber props replaced coal pillars as supports for roofs of galleries in mines, and were an additional safety factor. The net result was that coal output rose from 6,000,000 tons in 1770 to 10,000,000 tons in 1800.

Revolution in the Iron and Steel Industry

At the beginning of the eighteenth century Britain's great natural deposits of iron ore were almost entirely unworked. Her iron industry had declined because of shortage of fuel, for it depended upon charcoal, and forests had been seriously depleted. In these circumstances the industry was scattered throughout the country, continuing only where there were forests still able to yield charcoal. Frequently a foundry and the source of its iron ore were many miles apart. In 1709 Abraham Darby I discovered that by reducing coal to coke he could use this latter fuel to smelt iron ore. Darby concealed his discovery and his new method was in consequence slow to spread, but once the secret leaked out the use of charcoal gradually ceased. Output of iron was increased by using blast for furnaces, a Newcomen engine being employed for this purpose. In 1768 John Smeaton introduced a greatly-improved blast apparatus at Carron ironworks in Scotland.

Unfortunately pig-iron produced by coke-smelting was unsuitable for refining into wrought iron, and charcoal still had to be used for this process. It was expensive; the weight of charcoal used almost equalled the weight of wrought iron produced. Henry Cort solved the problem in 1784; his "puddling process" produced an iron less brittle and containing less carbon. Reduced from great lumps to bars by rolling, this new iron could be worked into all kinds of shapes, and began to replace wood in the manufacture of machinery.

There were other great iron-masters like "Iron-mad Wilkinson" who built the first iron bridge with Abraham Darby II. He was also responsible for an iron ship in 1787, iron pipes for water systems and accurate metal cylinders so essential for machines of all kinds. The Carron ironworks which Smeaton improved had been founded in 1760 by John Roebuck, and were famous for the huge guns produced there.

Steel had been used in small quantities for many years to make shears, knives and swords. In 1742 Benjamin Huntsman discovered the crucible process which speeded up production of steel, though use of this metal remained limited by the fact that it was still, in spite of Huntsman, four times as costly as iron.

The number of blast furnaces in Britain grew from 59 in 1720 to 221 in 1806. Output of pig-iron rose from 17,000 tons in 1720 to 205,000 tons in 1806, and the industry became firmly established in the coalfields of the Midlands, Yorkshire, Derbyshire and South Wales.

Improvement of Transport and Communications

One result of great industrial changes was a rapid development of better communications. At the beginning of the eighteenth century roads were few, and those that existed were quagmires in winter and deeply rutted in summer. Parishes had largely neglected their responsibilities for upkeep of roads. In 1763 the first turnpike trust appeared; a board of men obtained permission from parliament to build a road and to levy tolls for its use. This brought some improvement, though some turnpike roads were bad. Radical improvements in road-making were effected by Blind John Metcalf of Knaresborough, who constructed roads in Yorkshire, Lancashire and Cheshire. Thomas

Telford, son of a Scottish shepherd, as public surveyor for the roads of Shropshire, built 42 bridges and many roads. He used a hard foundation, camber, and good drainage. The elegant suspension bridge over the Menai Straits was his work. Another Scot, John McAdam, surveyor for roads in the Bristol area, built many miles of fine roads, whose surface was of several layers of small stones compounded together. Improved roads speeded up travel and despatch of mail, but heavy goods could not be sent by road.

To provide cheap transport by water, rivers were widened and their channels deepened from the seventeenth century onwards. A rapid development of canal building followed construction of the Worsley to Manchester canal by James Brindley in 1761. This canal connected the Duke of Bridgewater's collieries to Manchester, where the price of coal fell by a half as a result. The Grand Trunk canal, completed in 1777, connected the Mersey with the Trent, assisting the growth of the Lancashire textile industry, Midland hardware manufacture, and the pottery industry of north Staffordshire. The Grand Junction canal linked the Thames with the Trent. In Scotland, under Telford's direction, the Caledonian canal linked two sides of the country. Between 1758 and 1801, no less than 165 acts of parliament were passed for the construction of canals. Too many were constructed, and some soon fell into disuse.

General Results of the Industrial Revolution

The Industrial Revolution led to an increased demand for labour. The employment of children encouraged people to have large families. The increased population was concentrated in large towns of the industrial Midlands, the North, the West Riding of Yorkshire and South Wales; cities such as Birmingham, Manchester and Leeds grew rapidly.

Increased production in older industries, and development of new industries such as engineering, led to a greater volume of trade, more exports and greater national wealth, and put Britain well ahead of her European competitors.

Nevertheless the great wealth of Britain was unevenly distributed, employers growing very rich, but workers remaining in poverty. In large towns the houses were inadequate, and overcrowding led to the growth of slums. Grasping factory owners paid very low wages, and did little to improve conditions in their factories. Such abuses led to a demand for parliamentary reform, and contributed to the growth of trade unionism.

QUESTIONS

1. Show how the textile industries were affected by the industrial revolution and by inventions in the eighteenth century.
2. Describe the development of road and canal transport during the eighteenth century.

CHAPTER 45

THE BRITISH NAVY AND THE FRENCH WARS

THE period 1793-1815 was dominated by the long war against France Until 1802, Britain strove in vain to secure victory. Revolutionary enthusiasm, the appeal of the revolutionary ideals in many parts of Europe, the apathy of Britain's allies and their lack of unity, combined to ensure failure. After 1803, the character of the war changed. It became a struggle to check the imperial ambitions of Napoleon. By 1815, Britain's complete mastery of the seas, the rise of European nationalism in protest against the tyranny and aggression of Napoleon, the recovery of the British army, and the new-found unity of purpose among the allies led to the complete overthrow of the French Emperor.

The detailed story of the continental campaign is a matter for European, rather than for British, history; but the part played throughout by the British navy, and the part played in the overthrow of Napoleon by the British army may rightly concern us.

The Task of the Navy

The British navy, which had not been handled well during the War of American Independence, was now to experience great success. It was on this occasion much better prepared, because Pitt and Admiral Howe had seen to it that ninety ships of the line were ready for sea in 1793.

Its contribution was by no means restricted to the battles it fought. It had to seal the French fleet in its home ports. It had to carry detachments of the British army to the Netherlands, Spain, Egypt, India, Canada and Buenos Aires. It had to obliterate the sea-borne traffic of France. It eventually had to watch almost every port on the continent of Europe. It had to see that Britain was not starved, and that her foreign trade was not destroyed, merchant ships having to be protected in convoy against French and later against American privateers. These duties kept ships tirelessly patrolling the seas, in fair weather or foul, year after year.

Toulon, 1793

The navy at first suffered a reverse. Royalists at Toulon, holding out against much larger Jacobin forces, invited the British and Spanish fleets into harbour to support them. British sailors fought well in the land battle which ensued, but numbers were inadequate and Admiral Hood, under severe artillery fire from the guns of young Bonaparte, had to withdraw.

The Glorious First of June, 1794

The next action in which the navy was involved was likewise not a complete success. A powerful French squadron was convoying from the United States of America ships containing grain, sorely needed in France. Another large French fleet was in Brest. Admiral Howe had the difficult tasks of blockading the Brest fleet and intercepting the great convoy. He could not do both, so he intercepted the convoy, and broke up the French fleet which was maimed and dispersed, leaving six great ships in British hands; but since the grain ships reached Brest unscathed the operation was, in one important respect, unsuccessful.

Wax effigy of Horatio, Viscount Nelson. He was buried in St. Paul's Cathedral, and this portrait was made to be placed in Westminster Abbey.

Cape St. Vincent and the Spithead Mutiny, 1797

By 1797 Pitt's First Coalition against the French had largely collapsed. If France could, by invasion, force Britain to give up the struggle, she would become mistress of Europe. Her plan was to unite the fleets of subjugated Spain and Holland with her own, thus outnumbering the British fleet. Early in 1797 the Spanish fleet left Cartagena to effect a junction with the French fleet from Brest. Admiral John Jervis with fifteen excellent ships faced twenty-seven badly equipped and badly manned Spanish ships. As the two fleets bore down upon each other, the Spaniards having the wind advantage, Commodore Nelson in the *Captain*, thirteenth in the line, realized that the enemy might escape. He therefore wheeled his ship out of line to head off the Spaniards. Though his ship was badly shattered, Nelson captured the *San Nicolas* and the *San Josef*. He had risked his career but saved the day. Four Spanish ships were captured and the rest dispersed. Jervis became Earl St. Vincent and Nelson an admiral. Stern though he was, Jervis generously acknowledged his debt to Nelson. A severe blow had been dealt to French plans for the invasion of Britain.

No one could defend conditions of service in the British navy at this time. Pay was very poor, shore leave almost non-existent, and food thoroughly bad. Sailors of the Channel fleet based on Spithead mutinied in protest, but were persuaded by the popular Howe to return to service after a firm promise had been made to redress their grievances. At the Nore station in the Thames estuary, a second mutiny was led by Richard Parker which was political in flavour and less justifiable; the Admiralty hanged the ringleaders. Britain's peril was great when her first line of defence was impaired in this way.

Camperdown, 1797

During 1797 Admiral Duncan, not so strong a disciplinarian as Jervis, had the task of watching the Dutch fleet off Texel. Most of his ships deserted him to join the Nore mutiny. He cleverly deluded the Dutch by false signals into thinking that he was in touch with a larger fleet farther off. In October he was obliged to put back to Yarmouth to refit, whereupon de Winter, the Dutch admiral, swept across to the English coast with fifteen battleships and twelve frigates, but soon turned towards home. Duncan pursued and caught him, and in the ensuing mêlee disabled eleven Dutch ships. As a result, Dutch naval power was almost destroyed, and French invasion schemes were completely thwarted. The navy had once more proved itself a trusty shield.

Battle of the Nile, 1798

Between 1797 and the late spring of 1798, Britain deserted the Mediterranean. Then at forty, Nelson was promoted to rear-admiral and given the task of restoring British naval power there. Napoleon eluded him and set sail with a large invasion force from Toulon, with the intention of conquering Egypt and attacking the British in India by marching overland. Having captured Malta, Napoleon landed at Alexandria, his fleet under de Brueys anchoring close to shore in apparent security at Aboukir Bay nearby. Nelson found the French stationed in a curve, and de Brueys felt so certain of safety in this curved formation along the bay that his ships were almost undefended on the side nearest to land. Realizing this, Nelson sent some of his vessels to sail in close between the French and the shore, attacking their weakest side. His remaining ships attacked from such an angle that the other French ships, unable to sail against the wind, could not help the one under attack, and Nelson was able to deal with the French fleet piece-meal.

The battle did not begin until evening, and Nelson's policy of discussing his plans fully with his officers beforehand ensured that the English knew what was happening in the darkness around them, whereas the French were baffled by it. The British fleet was smaller than that of the French, and one of the British ships was prevented from taking part because it ran aground on a sandbank; but in spite of this, the British won a sweeping victory, and only two French battleships out of thirteen escaped, together with two frigates, all under the command of Villeneuve, later Nelson's adversary at Trafalgar.

The British navy had ruined Napoleon's prospects by cutting him off from contact with France. British India was saved. Britain had also successfully reasserted her naval supremacy in the Mediterranean. The victory gave some encouragement to Britain's allies, Austria and Russia. It enhanced Nelson's reputation still further, and his grateful nation made him Baron Nelson of the Nile. One of his younger officers, Commodore Sir Sidney Smith, held up Napoleon at Acre, in 1799, where his sailors fought valiantly on land, assisting the Turks. Once again the British navy had thwarted Napoleon's ambitions, for his aim had been to reach Constantinople.

First Battle of Copenhagen, 1801

In all her modern wars, Britain has used her naval strength to stifle her enemies' commerce. It has necessitated searching neutral ships at sea, a constant source of irritation to neutral powers. In 1801 this caused Russia, Sweden and Denmark to form the Armed Neutrality of the North as a protest, and Britain was threatened with complete loss of valuable naval stores from the Baltic. Sir Hyde Parker was sent with a fleet to demonstrate Britain's power in the Baltic with Nelson as second-in-command. It was decided to attack and seize the Danish fleet which lay under the protection of shore batteries at Copenhagen. The battle was so fierce that Parker hoisted the signal "leave off action"; Nelson ignored it by placing a telescope to his blind eye, and then pressed so close that the Danes could not employ their shore batteries. Copenhagen thus came under the fire of British guns. The action caused the Armed Neutrality to collapse.

The Final Engagements, 1805-07

From 1803 to 1805, Nelson was engaged in the Mediterranean. When the Peace of Amiens broke down in 1803, Napoleon began to plan the overthrow of Britain, his most persistent enemy, by a great invasion. He hoped that the French fleets of Toulon, Rochefort and Brest, and the Spanish fleets of Cartagena, Cadiz and Corunna, would escape British blockading fleets and rendezvous at a secret destination, Martinique in the West Indies. Having drawn British fleets away from Europe the combined French and Spanish naval forces could then descend upon the Channel to cover an invasion. Fleets did escape from Toulon, Rochefort and Cadiz. Nelson located them in the West Indies, but not before they had begun to return to Europe. He despatched a fast frigate, the *Curieux*, to outsail them and to warn Lord Barham at the Admiralty. Barham reinforced Sir Robert Calder off Corunna, where he met Villeneuve returning from the West Indies, and captured two of his ships. Nelson handed over his fleet to Cornwallis who was still blockading Brest, and returned for a hard-earned rest in England. Napoleon's plans for invasion had been foiled.

Taunted by Napoleon, Villeneuve left Cadiz with his thirty-three Franco-Spanish ships to meet a refreshed Nelson, now in command of twenty-seven ships, off Cape Trafalgar. Nelson decided to attack the enemy line with two columns, one of twelve ships led by his own *Victory*, another under Collingwood. The manoeuvre was brilliantly successful: it led to the destruction and capture of twenty enemy ships in one of the most decisive naval battles ever fought. Nelson was mortally wounded early in the battle, but lived long enough to know that the British fleet had won.

Britain lost Nelson, but gained complete supremacy of the seas for the rest of the war. Her security from invasion was confirmed. Most important of all, Trafalgar drove Napoleon into the fatal Continental System.

At Tilsit Napoleon and Alexander I of Russia planned to lay their hands on all battleships owned by the continental powers, 180 in all. Denmark possessed the most useful fleet, and Napoleon meant to have it. The British Government decided to forestall the plan. Admiral Gambier therefore sailed to demand surrender of the Danish fleet, though Denmark was not at war with Britain. The Danes naturally refused, so Gambier bombarded Copenhagen and seized seventy Danish warships. This action was unscrupulous, but deprived the French of valuable war material and naval reinforcements.

Conclusion

The navy had now fought its major battles. It next concentrated on defeating Napoleon's Continental System by organizing wholesale smuggling of British goods into Europe through Lisbon, Sicily, the Ionian Islands, Heligoland and elsewhere. It imposed a crippling counter-blockade, depriving Europe of tropical and equatorial goods like coffee, sugar and tobacco, and making French rule highly unpopular. When the Peninsular War broke out in 1808, the navy played a great part in the victory of Wellington's army, by supplying it through Lisbon, and later through Santander, and by assisting the Spanish guerrilla forces. After Trafalgar the navy seized almost all Dutch and French possessions overseas, such as the Cape of Good Hope (1806), Martinique (1809), Guadeloupe, the Ile de Bourbon and Mauritius (all in 1810), the Dutch East Indies (1811) and St. Lucia (1813), founding a new Empire.

QUESTIONS

1. Explain the importance of the British Navy during the Revolutionary and Napoleonic wars.
2. Describe Nelson's great victories, and show what dangers they averted.

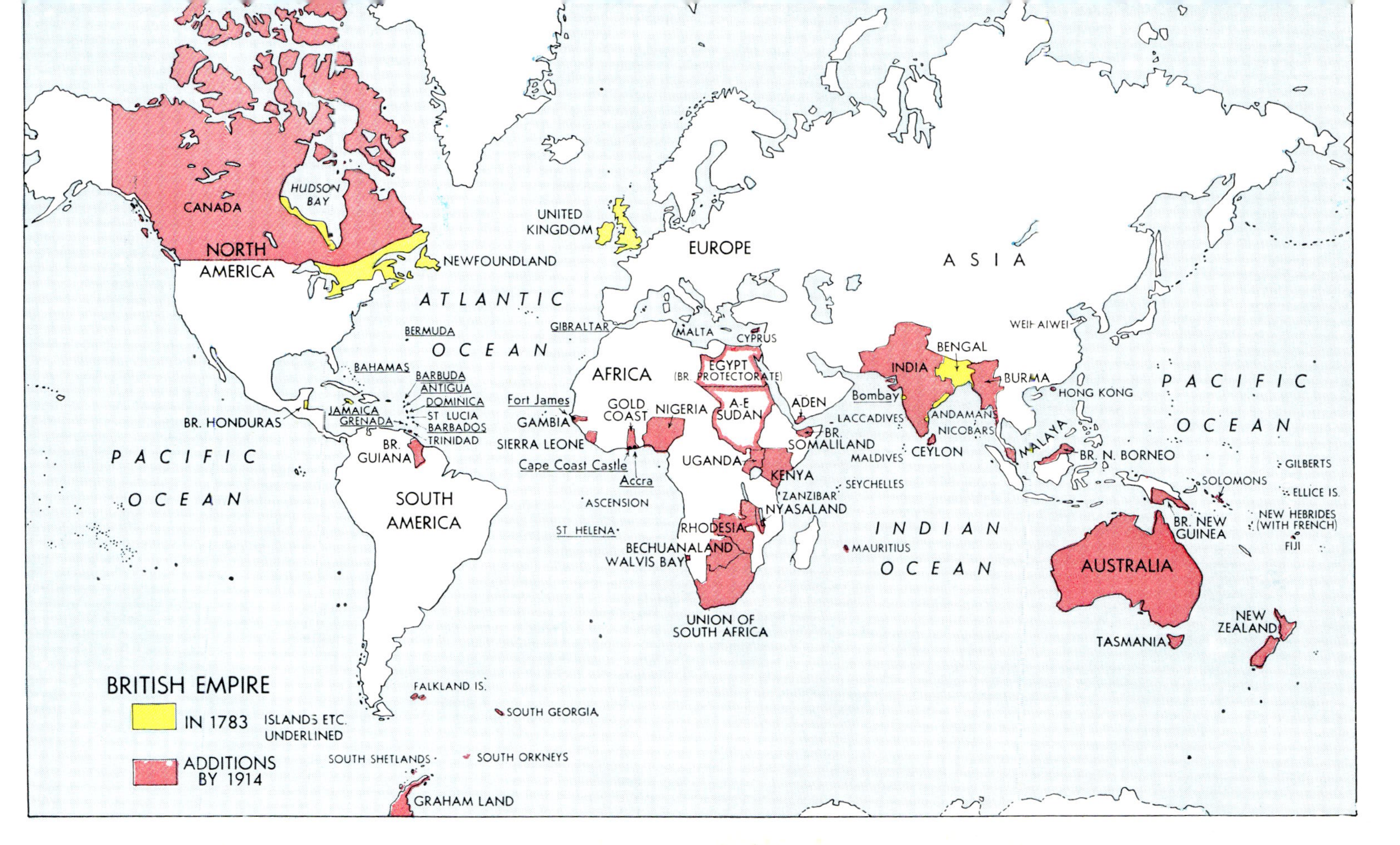
BRITISH EMPIRE
IN 1783
ISLANDS ETC. UNDERLINED
ADDITIONS BY 1914
CANADA
HUDSON BAY
NORTH AMERICA
NEWFOUNDLAND
UNITED KINGDOM
EUROPE
ASIA
ATLANTIC OCEAN
PACIFIC OCEAN
PACIFIC OCEAN
INDIAN OCEAN
BERMUDA
BAHAMAS
BARBUDA
ANTIGUA
DOMINICA
ST LUCIA
BARBADOS
TRINIDAD
JAMAICA
GRENADA
BR. HONDURAS
BR. GUIANA
SOUTH AMERICA
FALKLAND IS.
SOUTH GEORGIA
SOUTH SHETLANDS
SOUTH ORKNEYS
GRAHAM LAND
GIBRALTAR
MALTA
CYPRUS
AFRICA
EGYPT (BR. PROTECTORATE)
A-E SUDAN
Fort James
GAMBIA
SIERRA LEONE
GOLD COAST
NIGERIA
Cape Coast Castle
Accra
ASCENSION
ST HELENA
ADEN
BR. SOMALILAND
UGANDA
KENYA
ZANZIBAR
NYASALAND
RHODESIA
BECHUANALAND
WALVIS BAY
UNION OF SOUTH AFRICA
SEYCHELLES
MAURITIUS
LACCADIVES
MALDIVES
Bombay
INDIA
BENGAL
CEYLON
ANDAMANS
NICOBARS
BURMA
WEI-HAI-WEI
HONG KONG
MALAYA
BR. N. BORNEO
GILBERTS
SOLOMONS
ELLICE IS.
BR. NEW GUINEA
NEW HEBRIDES (WITH FRENCH)
FIJI
AUSTRALIA
TASMANIA
NEW ZEALAND

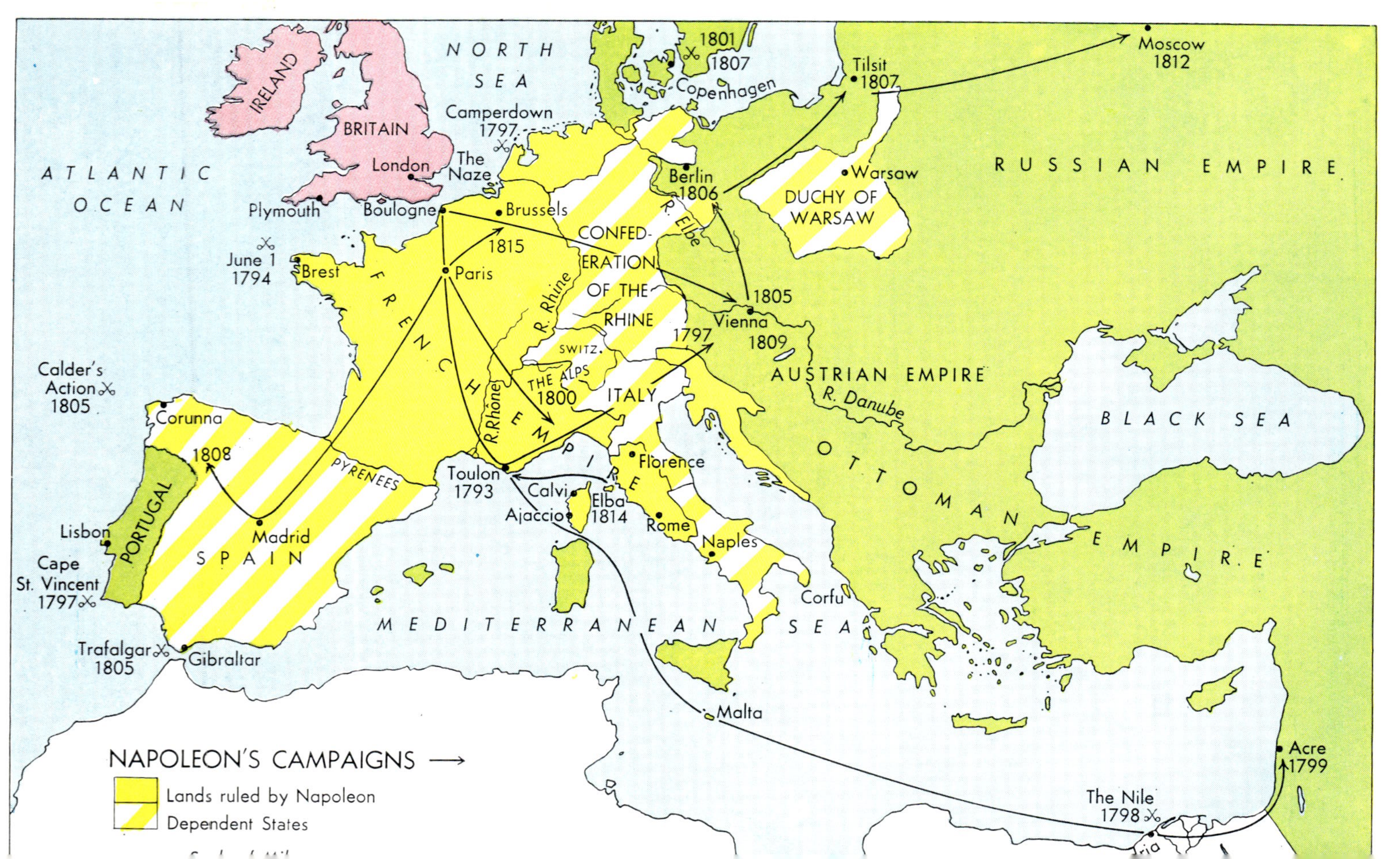

NAPOLEON'S CAMPAIGNS ⟶
Lands ruled by Napoleon
Dependent States
ATLANTIC OCEAN
NORTH SEA
IRELAND
BRITAIN
London
Plymouth
Camperdown 1797
The Naze
Boulogne
Brussels
1815
Paris
Brest
June 1 1794
FRENCH EMPIRE
CONFEDERATION OF THE RHINE
R. Rhine
R. Elbe
R. Rhône
SWITZ.
THE ALPS
1800
ITALY
1797
Toulon 1793
Calvi
Ajaccio
Elba 1814
Florence
Rome
Naples
Corfu
Copenhagen
1801 1807
Berlin 1806
Tilsit 1807
Moscow 1812
Warsaw
DUCHY OF WARSAW
RUSSIAN EMPIRE
1805
Vienna 1809
AUSTRIAN EMPIRE
R. Danube
BLACK SEA
OTTOMAN EMPIRE
MEDITERRANEAN SEA
Malta
The Nile 1798
Acre 1799
Calder's Action 1805
Corunna
1808
PYRENEES
PORTUGAL
Lisbon
Madrid
SPAIN
Cape St. Vincent 1797
Trafalgar 1805
Gibraltar

CHAPTER 46

THE BRITISH ARMY AND THE FRENCH WARS

THE record of the British army for much of the long war against Revolutionary and Napoleonic France was rather dismal, but it recovered its prestige by 1815 largely because of success in Spain and at Waterloo. In 1793, after ten years of economy following the American war, it had been reduced to a skeleton. Recruiting was inefficient, but even the French did not employ conscription for service overseas until 1788. At the outset of war there was no commander-in-chief, and the Secretary of State for War, Dundas, did not bother to shed his other ministerial jobs. At the same time, with ruthless generals and plenty of expendable amateur soldiers, the French drove back their enemies everywhere.

In 1793 the Duke of York was repulsed by the French at Hondschoote in Flanders, and driven back to Ostend; a retreat through the Low Countries followed, all discipline being lost, and by 1795 only six thousand troops were left to embark at Bremen. At Toulon in 1793 a small British force arrived only in time to take part in withdrawal from the port. Better success was gained in the West Indies, where Guadeloupe, St. Lucia, Marie Galante and Les Saintes were taken, but by 1796 the British had lost eighty thousand troops who could more effectively have been used in Europe.

In 1795, when Holland changed sides, Britain took the Cape of Good Hope, Ceylon, Malacca, Amboyna and Banda; but while she lorded it in the east, she was powerless to affect the balance of force in Europe. Charles Stuart took Minorca in 1798, but this was offset by another failure by the Duke of York in 1799 at Alkmaar, where he agreed to withdraw from Holland. In India Arthur Wellesley, later Duke of Wellington, defeated Tippoo Sahib of Mysore in 1799, revealing talents which were to serve his country well in Spain; but on the whole Britain appeared militarily second-rate. The necessity of suppressing the Irish rebellion of 1798 further taxed her feeble resources.

Turn of the Tide

Early in the nineteenth century the British army began to show that it could give the French a taste of defeat. Abercromby defeated the army which Bonaparte had deserted in Egypt (1801). British forces led by Sir John Stuart

The Duke of Wellington (just left of centre) at the battle of Waterloo. The lines of battle stretch almost to the horizon.

in Sicily, 4,800 in number, attacked 7,000 French at Maida in southern Italy (1806), and the British bayonet won the day. To assist the navy to capture the Danish fleet in 1807, the army landed on Zeeland and captured the Danish capital. In 1806 the Cape of Good Hope was recaptured, though the army failed at Buenos Aires. The greatest triumph, however, was to be won by Wellesley in Spain.

Napoleon, intent on mastering all of western Europe, declared war on Portugal; this inevitably involved him in the squalid politics of Spain, In 1808 at Bayonne he forced the imbecile Charles IV and his son Ferdinand to sign away their rights to the Spanish throne, placing his elder brother Joseph in their stead. The Spanish people rose spontaneously to resist the tyrant. The British government saw that an opportunity had arisen to obtain use of ports on the European coastline; Portugal, who was now being threatened, was an old ally whose plea must be answered.

Wellesley's Early Career

Arthur Wellesley was born in Dublin in 1769, the son of Earl Mornington. Entering the army in 1787, he passed through various regiments until he held the rank of colonel in 1793; his promotion had been purchased, and he had not yet seen a shot fired in anger! He served with the Duke of York in the Low Countries, learning the necessity of discipline and efficient staff work. Next he was sent to India where, after his triumph at Seringapatam in 1799 against Tippoo Sahib, he scored two brilliant victories over the Mahrattas at Assaye and Argaum in 1803, returning to Britain as Major-General Sir Arthur Wellesley. He entered parliament for Rye, and by 1807 was Chief

Secretary for Ireland, but in this same year he took part in the attack on Copenhagen. By 1808 he was a Lieutenant-General, and was appointed to take ten thousand troops to drive Marshal Junot from Portugal.

The Peninsular War, 1808-14

Wellesley deliberately involved the French in a lengthy campaign, because he realized that their practice of living off the land, which enabled them to strike down enemies with staggering speed in northern Europe, would fail in Spain, which had never been a rich country. The French advance in Spain was also made difficult because river valleys and chains of mountains ran across the direction of advance.

In 1808 Wellesley defeated Junot at Vimeiro, but was superseded by Sir Hew Dalrymple, a superior officer. Dalrymple concluded the Convention of Cintra with the French, by which they were to be evacuated from Portugal back to France in British ships. Wellesley returned to England, but was sent to Portugal again in the following year.

In 1809 Napoleon advanced into Spain to restore Joseph Bonaparte to Madrid. Sir John Moore led 30,000 British troops to attack the rear of 250,000 French; and although Moore himself was killed, he had managed to prevent the subjugation of Southern Spain by the French.

Wellesley drove Soult out of Portugal, and defeated Joseph Bonaparte at Talavera in 1809, but realized that he would have to base his army on Portugal for some time; and indeed Lisbon was an excellent base. In 1809 he ordered engineers to construct triple defence lines to the north of Lisbon. Having stripped the north of anything which might be useful to the French, Wellesley withdrew his army (and many Portuguese peasants) within the lines. Masséna, the French commander, was taken completely by surprise. He could not make a frontal attack against hills bristling with guns, and he could not outflank Wellesley, who had the sea on his left and the broad river Tagus on his right, from which all boats had been prudently removed. The French had come up against a British commander of genius!

Until 1811, Wellesley, now Viscount Wellington, followed the policy of striking out at the French and then retiring to Lisbon again. In 1810 he defeated Masséna at Busaço, and then withdrew behind the triple lines of Torres Vedras; the French lost 25,000 men.

Between 1811 and 1812 Wellington cleared the French from the frontier between Spain and Portugal; he strove to secure control over three key fortresses, Almeida, Ciudad Rodrigo and Badajoz. He held Masséna off at Fuentes d'Onoro, and captured Almeida in 1811 and Ciudad Rodrigo and Badajoz in 1812. Wellington then defeated Marmont at Salamanca, and drove Joseph Bonaparte from Madrid; but once more he retired into Portugal.

During 1813 he left Portugal and struck at the Burgos road, the only good

Cartoon of 1805. "The Plumb-pudding in danger; or State Epicures taking un petit souper." Napoleon carves out Europe for himself; Pitt takes Oceania.

route from Madrid to France, with the aim of drawing French armies from the south to safeguard their only line of retreat. His strategy had the desired effect, and by the end of the year the French were pouring across the Pyrenees. Wellington's army was the first allied force to enter France, where he defeated Soult at Toulouse in 1814.

Reasons for the Success in Spain

There are many reasons for the British success in Spain. Though unreliable in set-pieces, the Spaniards wore down the French by constant attacks on supply lines, cutting down stragglers and intercepting despatches. As a result the French could never afford to concentrate their armies against Wellington; they had to be scattered throughout Spain to hold down the Spaniards. The British navy was able to intervene effectively along the extended coastline of the peninsula, and supplied Wellington through Lisbon and later through northern ports. French marshals quarrelled bitterly with each other. Napoleon himself appeared only once in Spain and was inclined to under-estimate the difficulties of the campaign there. The Moscow campaign of 1812 led him to remove many of his best soldiers from the peninsula. The part played by

Wellington personally can hardly be over-estimated. By fierce discipline he moulded his army into one of the best fighting units in Europe. He ordered his staff to compile special maps of areas over which he fought: this gave him a distinct advantage over the French.

There is no doubt about the importance of the Peninsular War. It proved to Europe that Napoleon's armies could be beaten, and set an example of national resistance to French imperialism. At the height of the war 200,000 French troops were pinned down in Spain. It served to restore the morale and prestige of the British army, and ensured a continuous leakage in Napoleon's Continental System.

Waterloo, 1815

Wellington and Napoleon met only once on the field of battle, and Wellington won. His victory at Waterloo was a tremendous achievement, since many of his veterans had been sent to North America and he had a new staff to direct. Foreigners outnumbered British by two to one in his army: among them, the Dutch and Belgians were unreliable. Driven by Ney from Quatre Bras, Wellington selected his site at Waterloo on the crest of a hill. Once again his calmness and the steadiness of the "thin red line" of British infantrymen proved superior to French dash and the French column. The timely arrival of Blücher's Prussians enabled Wellington to put the French to flight, and so to end Napoleon's career.

Wellington's Subsequent Career

In 1814 Wellington was made a duke. Four years later he became Master-General of Ordnance, and sat in Lord Liverpool's cabinet. He acted as British representative at the Congress of Verona in 1822, succeeded the Duke of York as Commander-in-Chief, and in 1828 became Tory Prime Minister. He shepherded through the repeal of the Test and Corporation Acts (1828) and Catholic Emancipation (1829). He opposed the Reform Bill in 1831, but eventually used his influence to persuade the House of Lords to accept it.

In 1834 Wellington again served as Prime Minister, for three weeks only, while Peel formed his first ministry. He served in Peel's 1841-46 ministry without holding specific office, supporting Peel over repeal of the Corn Laws. At the time of the Chartist riots of 1848 Wellington was entrusted with the defence of London. He died in 1852.

QUESTIONS

1. Outline the main events of the Peninsular war, and show how it contributed to Napoleon's overthrow.
2. Write a brief account of Wellington's military achievements between 1808 and 1815.

CHAPTER 47

THE YEARS OF DISTRESS, 1815-22

EVERY great war is inevitably followed by a painful period of recovery, but the years following Waterloo were unusually bleak and difficult.

Misery brought by the Industrial and Agrarian Revolutions has been exaggerated, but any vast process of economic change must cause suffering. Workers resented discipline imposed upon them in the new factories. Domestic workers had to find other employment. Those who had dwelt on common land found themselves dislodged. The economic warfare waged with Napoleon, and the post-war boom and slump, accentuated all these factors.

Swift demobilization of 200,000 soldiers and sailors increased unemployment, the strength of the navy being reduced from 100,000 in 1815 to 35,000 in 1816. Withdrawal of government contracts for uniforms, guns and naval stores, and the slow change-over to peace-time production, caused others to lose their jobs. One particularly hard-hit group were the hand-loom weavers who had been so prosperous before the French wars. The Anglo-American war (1812-14) had cut off supplies of raw cotton, and the power-loom had come into widespread use; as a result, wages for hand-loom weavers fell from 21*s*. per week in 1800 to 8*s*. in 1820, at a time when prices were rising steadily. Wages generally failed to keep pace with prices; while prices doubled, the wages of agricultural workers rose from 9*s*. per week to 13*s*. only.

War led to increased taxation and although income-tax was introduced in 1797, additional revenue was gathered mostly by indirect taxation on commonly-used articles like tea, sugar and soap, the burden falling chiefly on the poor. In 1816 income-tax was abolished, so indirect taxation increased still more.

Lord Liverpool's government, anxious to avoid dependence on foreign foodstuffs, introduced the Corn Law of 1815 by which foreign wheat could not be imported until the price of home-grown wheat reached 80*s*. per quarter. This could be interpreted as a class measure since it was passed by a parliament in which landowners predominated, but in fact, the Corn Law probably did little good to landowners and much less harm to consumers than is usually assumed. If anyone gained, it was the corn-dealer. The low purchasing power of the greater part of the population made it impossible for them to buy bread. Certainly the Corn Law was widely hated.

It was expected that foreign trade would recover rapidly when the war ended, but this did not happen. European countries were too impoverished to buy large quantities of British goods, and Britain lost that war-time monopoly of trade which command of the seas gave her. During the war France developed a sugar-beet industry, with encouragement from Napoleon: similarly a West Prussian textile industry was developed. When war ended, governments employed tariffs to protect these new industries, and British sugar and textiles were excluded from some continental markets.

Yet another cause of economic difficulty was instability of currency. Use of paper money during the war had led to price inflation. When a parliamentary committee recommended return to the gold standard in 1819, commodity prices fell; but the fall caused unemployment, so the poor were no better off. The working classes might have improved their lot by direct action, but the Combination Laws of 1799 and 1800 forbade combination of workers for the purpose of bargaining with employers.

The Speenhamland System

In 1795 the well-meaning magistrates of Speenhamland introduced a form of poor-relief by which assistance was given in proportion to the size of a family and to the prevailing price of bread; the system spread to other counties. Unfortunately it caused employers to pay low wages in the knowledge that these would be subsidized, but employers soon found that the poor rate mounted to crippling proportions. By 1815 the Speenhamland system had failed, but there was no attempt to replace it by a better scheme.

Agricultural labourers whose families faced starvation naturally took to poaching the well-stocked estates of nearby landowners, but they faced fierce penalties under the game laws passed by a parliament which readily preserved the interests of the landed class. In 1816 a law was passed punishing with seven years' transportation anyone found in possession of a rabbit net!

Lord Eldon, a learned lawyer and Lord Chancellor, saw to it that a formidable list of capital offences was preserved to check crime. Over two hundred such offences existed. A man could be hanged for impersonating a Chelsea Pensioner, or for damaging Westminster Bridge! In 1815, 101 persons were hanged for forgery. This can hardly be called enlightened government. The law fell into disrepute.

Apart from accepting full responsibility for maintaining order, the government of 1815 pursued a policy of laissez-faire, which caused them to make little effort to direct the economy in order to alleviate suffering.

Expressions of Unrest

There were frequent outbreaks of violence during the years after 1815, usually when bread was expensive. In 1817 the price of wheat rose to 111*s*. per quarter after a bad harvest: outbreaks of disorder followed.

Henry "Orator" Hunt, a leading Radical, and his associates, organized a great meeting at Spa Fields on the outskirts of London in 1816. Some more violent elements broke into a gunsmith's shop, and this development of the situation led the lord mayor to collect a force to disperse the mob.

In 1817 the unemployed of Manchester planned a march to London to petition the Regent. Because they carried blankets, they were called Blanketeers, but their march never really got under way. Leaders were arrested in Manchester, others held up at Stockport, while most of the rest went no farther than Macclesfield.

In Derbyshire in the same year, unemployed textile workers led by Jeremiah Brandreth marched on Nottingham. Government agents acted and Brandreth and three of his associates were hanged, fourteen others being transported.

The Peterloo Massacre

By 1819, unemployment was rife again. Reformers in Manchester invited Hunt to speak in the open at St. Peter's Fields to fifty thousand people. There was no disorder, but the magistrates, who had brought in special constables and detachments of yeomanry, lost their nerve. Soldiers tried to arrest Hunt, sabres were drawn and in the general stampede eleven people were killed (including two women) and about four hundred wounded. There was great indignation in the country against this Peterloo Massacre, but the Regent congratulated the magistrates.

A plot to seize London and murder the Cabinet was hatched in 1820 by Arthur Thistlewood, an agitator who had just completed a prison sentence. It was rather absurd and became known to the government, who arrested the conspirators in Cato Street. Thistlewood was beheaded.

Policy of Lord Liverpool's Government

Most important members of Liverpool's government had lived through the violent period of the French Revolution, and could never forget their fear of a similar outbreak in Britain. Their policy was largely one of repression: they never attempted to seek out causes of unrest with the aim of removing them. Eldon, Lord Sidmouth (Home Secretary) and Castlereagh (Leader of the House of Commons) were the dominant figures.

In their defence it should be stated that they possessed inadequate security forces in the absence of a strong police system, and that they sincerely felt that they must keep order and defend property. Sidmouth employed spies and informers, and even *agents provocateurs*.

The Habeas Corpus Act was suspended soon after the Spa Fields disturbance and measures against both seditious meetings and attempts to weaken the loyalty of the troops were pushed through.

The Peterloo disturbance led to the passing of the Six Acts, three of which

Contemporary illustration of the Peterloo Massacre. The banners read "No Corn Laws," "Universal Suffrage," and "Order."

were not unreasonable. They dealt with procedure for bringing cases to trial, prohibiting of military exercises, and issue of search warrants. The other three laws were more open to question. One limited meetings for drawing up petitions to residents of the parish in which the meeting was held. Another allowed magistrates to seize blasphemous and seditious literature. The final act extended the Stamp Act to all papers and periodical pamphlets of a certain size: this was directed against Radical literature like William Cobbett's *Weekly Political Register*.

Only when Peel replaced Sidmouth as Home Secretary in 1822 and Castlereagh died in the same year did a more enlightened attitude appear.

QUESTIONS

1. Describe the main causes of political discontent in Britain between 1815 and 1822, and attempts made to deal with them.

2. State briefly the political and economic difficulties which faced Britain in 1815.

CHAPTER 48

THE FOREIGN POLICY OF CASTLEREAGH AND CANNING

ROBERT STEWART, Viscount Castlereagh and second Marquis of Londonderry, was born at Mountstewart, County Down, and educated at St. John's College, Cambridge. He entered parliament in 1790, and was Chief Secretary for Ireland in 1799, steering the Act of Union through the Irish parliament. A believer in Catholic Emancipation, he resigned on this issue in 1801. In 1802 he became president of the Indian Board of Control and was War and Colonial Secretary in 1805 and again from 1807 to 1809. Canning held him responsible for the Walcheren disaster of 1809, and the two men fought a duel which led to their resignation. From 1812 to 1822 Castlereagh served as Foreign Secretary under Liverpool.

Castlereagh was an impressive man of fine appearance, good manners, self-control, courage and industry, though he neither gained popularity nor courted it. He saw no reason why he should explain or defend his policy to gain popular support, and he was, in any case, a hesitant speaker. Only recently has he been given full credit for his achievements in foreign affairs.

Castlereagh and the Fourth Coalition, 1813

When Castlereagh became Foreign Secretary in 1812, Europe was still struggling against Napoleonic imperialism. He played a strong role in bringing about the alliance (Russia, Prussia, Austria, Great Britain and Sweden) which was to cause the ultimate downfall of that imperialism. He implored the allies to remain united and to frame a common basis for peace. In 1814 he persuaded his allies into the Treaty of Chaumont, by which all four great powers agreed to place 150,000 men in the field. In the same year he brought the Anglo-American War to an end by the Treaty of Ghent. He joined the Tsar in checking the revengeful spirit of the Prussians, insisting that the only lasting peace would be one which the French could regard as just: this was statesmanship of a high order. Castlereagh was to play a part in settling European affairs rarely equalled by that of any other British statesman. Wellington's military successes strengthened his hand.

Castlereagh and the Treaty of Vienna, 1815

It was Castlereagh who insisted on a general settlement for Europe, and much of the settlement was directly his work. He favoured creation of barriers against future French aggression, such as the Kingdom of the United Netherlands, Rhenish Prussia, and a strengthened Piedmont. He intervened strongly to prevent Prussia from gaining the whole of Saxony. It was his policy to restore the Bourbons. He persuaded Louis XVIII that it was essential to accept the role of a constitutional monarch in order to win acceptance by Frenchmen. After Waterloo, Castlereagh saved France from harsh retribution. He secured promises from European powers to put an end to the slave trade. He was prominent in launching the congress system, by which the great powers were to meet to preserve the settlement. Castlereagh saw also that Britain did not emerge from the conference empty-handed and she acquired the Cape of Good Hope, Mauritius, Ceylon, Heligoland, Malta, the Ionian Islands, Trinidad, St. Lucia and Tobago.

Castlereagh and the Holy Alliance, 1815

Castlereagh knew most sovereigns and leading ministers of Europe, and continued to exercise considerable influence during the years after 1815. The burden of work upon him was tremendous, for the Foreign Office had only twenty-eight persons working for it in 1821! He had no sympathy with Alexander I's Holy Alliance of Christian rulers of 1815, regarding it as "a piece of sublime mysticism and nonsense." It was difficult for a parliamentary state like Great Britain to oppose all constitutional movements in Europe, as the three eastern autocracies (Russia, Prussia and Austria) tended to do.

Castlereagh and the Concert of Europe

The congress system possessed no rules of procedure, and was largely an improvisation. The first congress met at Aix-la-Chapelle in 1818, to consider the whole question of France. The country had rapidly paid off its war indemnity, and showed internal stability. Castlereagh and Wellington were mainly responsible for securing French admission to the ranks of the great powers once more. Theirs was a wise and moderate policy, but already Britain was pulling away from her wartime allies.

Castlereagh and the Congresses of Troppau and Laibach, 1820-21

When Spanish liberals rebelled against Ferdinand VII in 1820, Castlereagh maintained that the affair did not threaten the great powers, and he opposed intervention. British public opinion was hostile to Ferdinand. Castlereagh had little sympathy with rebellions, but when the Sicilians revolted in 1820 against Ferdinand I of Naples, he recognized that Austrian interests were threatened, yet maintained that Austria alone should deal with the rising. He strongly opposed the claim of general intervention as asserted in the Troppau Protocol. As a protest he sent only an observer, Lord Stewart, to the Congresses of Troppau (1820) and Laibach (1821).

Viscount Castlereagh (left), and his successor, George Canning.

Castlereagh and the Greek Revolt, 1821

Outbreak of a Greek revolt against the Turks in 1821 changed Britain's position. Castlereagh was now afraid that Russia might intervene on the rebels' side to gain her own advantage and to weaken Turkey. Before the Congress of Verona met to deal with the new situation, Castlereagh, under severe strain imposed by the burden of work which he had undertaken, took his own life (1822).

Castlereagh's Achievements

Castlereagh was one of Britain's greatest foreign secretaries. He helped to overthrow Napoleon, to reconstruct Europe in 1815, to launch a praiseworthy attempt to preserve European peace at the conference table, to maintain the balance of power in Europe and to prevent another war which might have arisen if France had been too harshly treated in 1815. At the same time he carefully upheld British interests. (He established the 49th Parallel as the boundary between Britain and the U.S.A. west of the Great Lakes.)

Early Career and Character of Canning, 1770-1822

George Canning was born in London, the son of a barrister, and was educated at Eton and Christ Church, Oxford. In 1794 he became an M.P. and soon held office as Under-Secretary for Foreign Affairs (1796-99). He was successively Paymaster-General, Treasurer of the Navy and Foreign Secretary from 1807 to 1809. He became President of the Board of Control for India in 1816, and held this post until his resignation in 1820. In 1822 he thought so little of his political prospects at home that he accepted the post of

Governor-General of India, but had not left the country when Castlereagh died. Liverpool promptly made him Foreign Secretary.

Canning and European Affairs

Canning was not new to the work, and could make quick decisions, as shown when he ordered seizure of the Danish and Portuguese fleets in 1807 and 1809. He had been responsible for the expedition to Portugal in 1808, and for selecting Wellington as commander. He mistrusted diplomacy by conference, and wished to keep clear of European intervention. He had not shared Castlereagh's experience of the benefits of co-operation in the overthrow of Napoleon. His mind was more brilliant than Castlereagh's. He was ready always to take parliament and people into his confidence. Collaboration between Great Britain and the Holy Alliance had broken down and Canning wished to emphasize the breakdown.

He despatched Wellington as British representative to the Congress of Verona. On Canning's instructions he protested against French intervention in Spain on behalf of Ferdinand VII. In spite of the protest, French troops in 1823 restored Ferdinand, who dealt cruelly with liberal opponents. Wellington left before the end of the congress, and Canning's antipathy towards the congress system increased.

Canning and the South American Colonies of Spain

Since the breakdown of the Spanish commercial monopoly in South America, British trade there had increased fourteen-fold. Canning had no love for the republics which had been set up by Spanish subjects, but he made it quite clear to eastern European powers and to France that intervention from Europe would mean war with Great Britain. The American Monroe Doctrine of 1823 coincided with his warning, for it opposed European interference (including British). London and Liverpool merchants exercised pressure on Canning (member for Liverpool until 1822) to preserve their South American trade; and though Canning was thwarted in Spain, he succeeded in South America. He recognized the republics of Buenos Aires, Colombia and Mexico as independent states, proclaiming: "I called the New World into existence to redress the balance of the Old," striking a blow for liberty and British commercial interests at the same time.

Canning's Support of Liberalism and Independence

In Portugal a struggle was being waged between the constitutional party who wished to retain young Queen Maria on the throne and the reactionary party who supported the claims of her uncle Dom Miguel. Spain threatened to intervene on behalf of Miguel, so Canning sent a fleet and four thousand troops. Ultimately the forces of Miguel were defeated. Canning had again helped the cause of liberalism, and had preserved Britain's traditional influence in Portugal.

The Greek revolt against the Turks began in 1821, and was very successful. British opinion was highly sympathetic towards the Greeks, and money and volunteers poured in. For Canning, the situation was not so simple. He could hardly display any favour towards the Turks, who had massacred Christians; but he feared that Russia might use the situation to further her own designs in the Balkans. He felt that the only thing to do was to co-operate with Russia, so he sent Wellington to St. Petersburg.

France, Britain and Russia agreed by the Treaty of London of 1827 that Greece should have self-government in practice while still remaining under Turkish rule in theory. When Liverpool died, Canning became for a few months Prime Minister, and then followed Liverpool to the grave. An Anglo-French fleet under Admiral Codrington, ordered into the Mediterranean to enforce an armistice upon Greeks and Turks, sank a Turco-Egyptian fleet at Navarino Bay off the Morea and virtually guaranteed Greek independence but Canning died before this naval battle took place.

Wellington, who succeeded Canning as Prime Minister, pursued a more cautious policy and actually apologized to the Turks. Britain, France and Russia recognized the complete independence of Greece in 1830. Canning had safely averted Russian domination in the Balkan area and helped to bring into being another European state without launching a fresh European war. Austria and Prussia opposed his actions and another blow had been administered to the dying congress system.

Comparison of Castlereagh and Canning

There are interesting similarities and differences between Castlereagh and Canning. Both men were very capable Foreign Secretaries, but Castlereagh disliked intervention by the congress powers in the internal affairs of smaller states, while Canning sometimes intervened on behalf of nationalists and liberals.

Castlereagh was cautious, but Canning was bold. Castlereagh belonged to the High Tories, but Canning had to make his way with few social advantages.

Canning had no love for the congress system, and had not experienced the value of co-operation against Napoleon; his approach was more insular than that of Castlereagh.

Differences in the policies of the two men should not be exaggerated, however. Both men sought to preserve British interests by all possible means.

QUESTIONS

1. Give an account of Castlereagh's foreign policy.

2. Describe Canning's political career.

CHAPTER 49

THE LIBERAL TORIES, 1822-30

THE death of Castlereagh in 1822 marked the end of the old Toryism, for leadership of the House of Commons passed to Canning who soon gave a new tone to the administration, though there were limits to his liberalism. He maintained essential Tory principles and did not favour parliamentary reform: but he supported Catholic Emancipation and realized that the Tory party, in order to survive, must show itself ready to remove abuses.

Huskisson and Robinson

William Huskisson (1770-1830) was as important as Canning in bringing new ideas into the government's commercial and fiscal policies. He was well supported by Frederick "Prosperity" Robinson (1782-1859), Chancellor of the Exchequer, who, having preceded Huskisson at the Board of Trade, had already persuaded parliament to relax the Navigation Laws to attract the commerce of former Spanish colonies and to give British colonists in North America and the West Indies direct access to Europe.

In this partnership, Huskisson was dominant, for he was the abler man. He laid the foundations of Britain's Free Trade policy, but had no intention of abolishing all duties. His aim was to discourage smuggling and to encourage competition. He also wanted to stimulate British industry by admitting raw materials freely. In 1824 duties on rum, silk and wool were reduced. This was followed in 1825 by a reduction of duties on cotton, linen and woollen goods, coffee, glass, books, paper, porcelain, china, copper, zinc, lead and iron.

Huskisson found a general duty of 50 per cent on manufactured goods, and lowered it to 20 per cent. Owing to the refusal of parliament to accept income tax, some duties had to be retained.

He had more vision of the future of the empire than most of his contemporaries. He established a working system of preferential tariffs for colonial goods. For example, Canadian timber was allowed into the country at more favourable rates than timber from other areas, though in a sense this policy was contrary to true Free Trade.

Navigation Laws were modified in the interest of British re-export trade. European goods put into bond were excluded from their application. Reciprocity treaties were introduced whereby foreign ships were allowed free use of British ports if British ships were accorded similar facilities by the countries concerned. In these several ways Huskisson and Robinson stimulated trade and industry. Since economic distress is so often the cause of political agitation, theirs was a wise policy.

Robert Peel (1788-1850), twice became Prime Minister.

Work of Peel

Peel served as Home Secretary under Liverpool (1822-27) and under Wellington (1828-30). During this time he effected three measures for which alone he deserves to be remembered. They were the reform of larger prisons, the humanization of the fierce penal code, and the introduction of the Metropolitan Police Force.

During the eighteenth century, prisons were centres of demoralization, disease and crime. John Howard (1726-90) devoted his life to revealing their state, but the French wars held up reform. M.P.s like Sir Samuel Romilly and Sir Francis Burdett, led agitation for reform, and Elizabeth Fry (a Quaker) took up Howard's work. As on so many occasions, Peel, by nature a liberal, became convinced by the evidence placed before him.

He compelled justices to organize prisons on a prescribed plan, to inspect them regularly, to send quarterly reports upon their condition to the Home Secretary, to place women prisoners under female gaolers and to see that all prisoners were visited by chaplains and surgeons. The pernicious system of rewarding gaolers by fees payable by prisoners was ended and replaced by regular wages. Some attempt was made to rehabilitate prisoners, not merely to punish them. Unfortunately Peel's reforms applied only to prisons of the county justices and to those of London, Westminster and seventeen provincial towns. There was still much to be done in debtors' and the smaller prisons.

Parliament had been singularly unenlightened concerning the penal code. In 1808 Romilly failed to persuade it to remove the death penalty for picking pockets. Later it refused to abolish a similar penalty for stealing 5*s*. from a shop. When Romilly died in 1818, Sir James Mackintosh took up the cause of penal reform. Peel turned his attention to it in 1823 and carried five statutes removing the death penalty from about one hundred felonies. The ferocity of the penal code had been bringing the law into disrepute: juries frequently refused to find a verdict of guilty, even in the face of conclusive evidence, because of the severity of the penalty which would follow.

Having already successfully established a constabulary in Ireland when he served as Chief Secretary, Peel introduced the Metropolitan Police Force in 1829. He saw that crime could hardly be curbed by elderly night watchmen, and that spies and *agents provocateurs* were undesirable. They were replaced by a force armed only with staves, but criminals soon left London to escape them. During the following thirty years similar forces were set up in many large cities. A Commissioner of Police supervised the Metropolitan force from Scotland Yard, and Britain is justly proud of the fine force which has grown from Peel's original three thousand constables.

Repeal of the Combination Laws, 1824-25

Many nineteenth-century reforms resulted from pressure outside parliament. Francis Place (1771-1854) was largely responsible for securing repeal of the Combination Laws in 1824. He was a prosperous London tailor of moderate radical views, whose aim was not revolution but social betterment. J. R. McCulloch (an economist) and Joseph Hume (a radical M.P.) helped him. On Place's suggestion, Hume (1777-1855) packed a parliamentary committee appointed to enquire into the working of the Combination Laws, with the result that it recommended repeal. Hume and Place sincerely believed that the desire to strike would disappear if the right to do so were granted. Here, they were wrong; a wave of strikes followed and Lord Liverpool became seriously alarmed. A second committee was appointed which Hume could not pack, but Place produced evidence which prevented a reactionary panic. In 1825 an Amending Act was passed which permitted peaceful bargaining with employers over wages and hours. Strike action was hardly possible, since any obstruction was disallowed, but trade unions at least had a legal right to exist.

The Sliding Scale, 1828

Huskisson had earlier proposed a sliding scale to replace the Corn Law of 1815, but his measure was not implemented until the Wellington ministry of 1828, when it was enacted that import duty on grain would not be levied unless the price of British wheat fell to 74*s*. per quarter. Duty rose proportionately higher if the price fell lower still. The measure was not a success, however, for fluctuation in prices continued and corn speculators artificially tampered with the market.

Repeal of the Test and Corporation Acts, 1828

Annual Indemnity Acts had long exempted Dissenters from the penalties of the Test and Corporation Acts, so their repeal in 1828 did not remove any deep grievance, but it was an expression of the prevailing liberal attitude. Lord John Russell, a Whig, actually proposed the measure. Its real importance was that it raised the whole question of Catholic Emancipation which was a much more delicate and complex issue.

Catholic Emancipation, 1829

Wellington, in 1828, had weeded out from his ministry several men who had espoused the cause of Catholic Emancipation, yet in 1829 he and Peel introduced a bill to relieve Catholics of their disabilities. This inconsistency was due to a situation which had arisen in Ireland. The Irish leader Daniel O'Connell had just won the County Clare election, in opposition to a popular Protestant landlord, Vesey Fitzgerald. As a Roman Catholic O'Connell could not take his seat. This situation could be repeated all over Ireland and could lead to civil war. Wellington saw it as his duty to avert bloodshed. A rather reluctant Peel introduced the Catholic Relief Bill, which opened to Catholics almost all the great offices of state, but it was only passed with the help of Whig votes. It split the Tory party into three groups: ultra-Tories who opposed repeal, Canningites who refused to serve under Wellington, and Wellington's supporters.

Unfortunately Wellington's government followed repeal with some vindictive measures. Irish freeholders were deprived of the vote and Daniel O'Connell was made to seek re-election on the grounds that the Relief Act had not been passed when he was elected. This caused unnecessary bitterness and Irish gratitude was lost.

Reasons for the Tory Defeat of 1830

Reforms passed by liberal Tories, though frequently a result of influences outside the party or of unforeseen circumstances, possibly averted a political revolution, but they did not serve to keep the Tories in power.

The Tories were defeated in the 1830 election for several reasons. The issue of Catholic Emancipation had hopelessly divided the party. Also, there was a strong public demand for parliamentary reform, which the Tory party (with some significant exceptions, such as Palmerston) opposed; the Whig party, on the other hand, was ready to introduce moderate parliamentary reform.

A fall in trade, and the return of hard times, were naturally blamed on the government. So it was inevitable that the Whigs returned to power as a result of the election.

QUESTIONS

1. Write an account of Tory reforms from 1822 to 1830.
2. Why was the Tory policy from 1822 to 1830 called a policy of liberal reform?

CHAPTER 50

THE PARLIAMENTARY REFORM MOVEMENT

THE parliamentary system which existed before 1832 had many defenders but by modern standards its defects were numerous. The landowning class completely dominated parliament; it has been calculated that 162 landlords nominated as many as 306 M.P.s in the House of Commons. Ireland's hundred seats were controlled by fifty or sixty landowners; Scotland's by 150 patrons. Scotland was represented by forty-five M.P.s, one less than Cornwall, which had only one-eighth Scotland's population. The Industrial Revolution had caused a great shifting of the population, but no adjustment had been made in distribution of seats, so great new towns like Manchester and Birmingham had no separate representation, whereas tiny boroughs were represented on the strength of bygone importance. Old Sarum, a mere mound in Wiltshire, sent two members, as did Gatton with its seven voters, and Dunwich, once in Suffolk, but now tumbled into the sea! Each county sent its two members who were elected by forty-shilling freeholders, but there was no such uniformity in the boroughs. In *rotten* boroughs the few voters sold their votes to the highest bidder: in *pocket* boroughs, the powerful local landowner nominated one or both members. There was no uniform qualification to vote in the boroughs. In some, only members of the corporation voted; in others those who possessed certain dwellings (burgages); in others again, those who paid rates. Fifty-six towns had less than forty voters apiece. Only two hundred M.P.s, a third of the total number, were returned on a free vote. This system had produced able administrators, but no one could say that it was equitable.

There are several reasons why parliamentary reform was held up until 1832. Borough-owners regarded their boroughs as property to be bought and sold, and were prepared to fight hard to retain control. The demand for reform had grown strong after 1780, but the anti-Jacobin spirit which excesses of the French revolution had provoked among the ruling class had held up reform for over forty years. The Tory party, with certain exceptions, was opposed to reform and dominated the political scene during this period.

Crisis of 1830

Matters came to a head by 1830. Radicals like Cobbett and Place stimulated demand for parliamentary reform. Associations like the London Radical

Association and the Birmingham Political Union excited popular demands. Pressure was exerted by the new rich manufacturing class for a share of political influence. George IV, an implacable enemy of reform, died in 1830, and was succeeded by William IV, who was less reactionary. The Whigs won the election of 1830 and were ready to undertake moderate reform. The almost bloodless revolution of 1830 in France, which brought Louis Philippe to power, strengthened the desire in Britain for constitutional change.

Struggle to Pass the Reform Bill of 1832

The first version of a reform bill was introduced into the Commons on 1 March, 1831, having been drawn up by a Cabinet committee. Whigs and Tories alike were surprised by what they considered the far-reaching character of the bill, though, as Peel foresaw, Grey was wrong in thinking that the working class would regard it as a final settlement. After the bill had passed through two readings, the Tories defeated it in committee stage, and William IV was persuaded to dissolve parliament. The ensuing election gave the Whigs an increased majority, which proved that they had the country behind them; they therefore introduced a second bill in June, substantially the same as the first. It passed through the Commons by September, but the Lords threw it out. There had been occasional rioting during and after the election of 1831, but nothing dangerous: now serious disorders occurred in Derby and Nottingham, and at Bristol, where a mob burned the Mansion House and the bishop's palace and opened up the prisons. Mass meetings took place in London. A third bill was introduced in December, 1831, with further minor changes, and by April, 1832, the bill had passed its second reading in the upper house but was held up in the committee stage. Grey asked William IV to create fifty new Whig peers to swamp the Tory majority in the Lords, but the king refused to go beyond twenty. Grey and his colleagues promptly resigned, tired of the long strain. At the king's request, Wellington, always ready to perform his duty, tried to form a ministry; but Peel refused to join him. The king was obliged to accept the Whigs back on their own terms and to promise to create the number of peers which they requested; but there was no need to do so for the Tories in the upper house at last saw that they must give way or lose their supremacy there. The Reform Bill became law in May, 1832.

Terms of the Reform Act of 1832

After the fuss had died down, neither side found the result as dramatic as expected. The act gave the vote in the boroughs to £10 householders, and in the counties to long-lease holders of £10 and short-lease holders of £50, while the old forty-shilling freeholders were allowed to retain the vote. Fifty-five boroughs lost both members, 30 lost one out of two, Higham

Ferrers its one, and Melcombe Regis and Weymouth two of their four, releasing 143 seats in all, of which 65 were given to English and Welsh counties, 22 to large towns (two each), 21 to smaller towns (one each), eight to Scotland, and five to Ireland. Reform Bills were passed in 1832 for Scotland, whose number of seats was increased from 45 to 53, and for Ireland, whose number of seats was increased from 100 to 105.

Results of the 1832 Reform Act

The Act of 1832 was a turning point in modern British history, but it was a modest measure. The electorate of England and Wales was increased by only 217,000 voters; Whigs and Tories had expected a higher figure. The rise in the population and wealth of the country brought a further increase of about 400,000 before 1867. Dishonest practices continued. Landowners multiplied leases and created small freeholdings, to add to the voting strength of their party. One thousand pounds' worth of land could produce five hundred votes. Dead men's names were used and fictitious rent receipts compiled. Efforts were made to disfranchise hostile voters. Some voters who did not qualify under the new provisions actually lost their votes! In the counties, the influence of landlords was still unbroken, and it was also strong in smaller boroughs. The borough representation of England and Wales was still twice as strong as representation of the counties, and the southern half

Spirit flasks of the nineteenth century: Brougham Cordial, William IV the Reform Cordial, and the Free Spirit of Reform.

of England still had a predominance which was not justified by the distribution of population. New towns, however, tended to return Whigs, Liberals or Radicals.

The Act of 1832 did not have much immediate effect on the composition of parliament, for the new one of 1833 contained 217 sons of either peers or baronets. In 1865 the number was still 180, and the landed interest as a whole still mustered some 400 representatives. Radicals nevertheless won seats after 1832. Broadly speaking, the aristocracy had been obliged to admit the middle classes to a share of political power. The act opened the door for a further extension of the franchise.

Reform Act of 1867

When Lord John Russell succeeded Palmerston as Prime Minister in 1865, opinion was widespread that extension of the franchise and considerable redistribution of seats were both necessary. The number of adult males was five million, but the number of voters under one million. Thus five out of every six males were voteless. Russell, who wanted the credit for extending the vote, introduced a bill in 1866 to extend the franchise to £7 householders in the towns and to £14 occupiers in the counties. The Tories led by Lord Cranborne (later Salisbury) and a rebel group of Whigs under Robert Lowe attacked the bill, and it was defeated. Derby formed his third ministry with Disraeli as its spearhead. Disraeli was determined to win for his party the credit for extending parliamentary reform. His attitude drove Cranborne, the Earl of Carnarvon, and General Peel from the government. Prolonged manoeuvres followed, the Liberals forcing Disraeli into a more extreme measure than he had intended. He gave the vote to all householders and to £10 lodgers in the towns, and to £12 occupiers in the counties. One of two members was taken from boroughs of less than 10,000 inhabitants, releasing forty-five seats, twenty-five of which were allotted to the counties, fifteen to new boroughs, a third seat being given to Liverpool, Manchester, Birmingham and Leeds, and one to the University of London.

The act added 938,000 voters to the electorate. In the towns, working-class voters were now in a majority, though they did not return working-class M.P.s. The passing of the act decreased resistance to the popular demand for other reforms. Many feared the results of the act, Carlyle likening it to shooting Niagara and Derby speaking of a "leap in the dark." Contrary to Disraeli's hopes, the fickle electorate returned the Liberals at the next election with a handsome majority.

County Franchise Act of 1884

In his second ministry, Gladstone gave the vote to all householders, in boroughs or in rural areas, who paid £10 or more in rent. The act enfranchised

Suffragette disturbances led to votes for women over thirty in 1918, and for all women over twenty-one in 1928.

the agricultural worker, and many working men in those towns which were not large enough to be separate parliamentary boroughs. It added two million voters, more than the earlier acts combined.

Other Measures of Parliamentary Reform

Jews were admitted to parliament in 1858, and the property qualification for M.P.s was removed in the same year. Gladstone's first ministry (1872) introduced the secret ballot.

A Corrupt Practices Act of 1854 had required an audit of accounts from parliamentary candidates; another, passed in 1883 during Gladstone's second ministry, imposed penalties for indirect bribery, forbade the use of carriages, and limited the amount of money a candidate might spend in attempting to secure election to parliament.

The Redistribution Act of 1885 disfranchised all boroughs of less than 15,000 inhabitants, and merged them into county constituencies. Towns with a population of less than 50,000 were limited to one M.P., and the seats thus released were given to larger towns.

In 1911 the Parliament Act, passed during the Asquith ministry, deprived the House of Lords of power over money bills, and limited its right to hold up other measures to two years. General elections were to take place every five, instead of every seven, years (see Chapter 67). Payment of M.P.s was introduced; they were to receive £400 a year.

Liberal ministries between 1906 and 1916 refused to meet the demands of the Suffragette movement, but in 1918 the vote was given to all men over twenty-one and to all women over thirty, adding twelve million new voters to the electorate. In 1928 a Reform Act gave the vote to all women over twenty-one, thus adding a further five million voters.

QUESTIONS

1. Explain how, and why, parliament was reformed in 1832.

2. Describe changes in parliamentary representation between 1830 and 1872.

CHAPTER 51

WHIG REFORMS, 1833-41

THE Whigs, having had a prolonged struggle to pass the Parliamentary Reform Act of 1832, were by no means filled with the enthusiasm to embark on a further series of sweeping reforms, yet a number of important reforming measures followed. Radicals saved the Whigs from resting upon their laurels, bringing them to the limit of their Whiggish principles. Among the Radicals were men like Sir William Molesworth, Edward Gibbon Wakefield and Lord Durham.

The political philosophy of Jeremy Bentham (1748-1832) also bore fruition in some Whig reforms. Bentham was one of the few great reformers to be appreciated in his own time. He taught that new institutions should be introduced when the old had ceased to be effective (Utilitarianism), though he did not look for too much activity on the part of the government. The government should seek to pursue "the greatest happiness of the greatest number."

Other reformers also had a considerable influence upon Whig government; Wilberforce, Ashley and Rowland Hill may be mentioned. The lack of enthusiasm of the Whig leadership is proved by Melbourne's view that Benthamites were "all fools." He told Queen Victoria in 1839 that Radicals had "neither ability, honesty, nor numbers."

Abolition of Slavery, 1833

Although the slave-trade had been prohibited to British subjects (and to ships flying the British flag) in 1807, it was not brought to an end, for the ban made clandestine voyages very profitable. Slave-carrying ships were crammed with negroes whose sufferings were worse than before. William Wilberforce (1759-1833) and his friends formed an Anti-Slavery Society in 1823 to fight for the end of slavery within the British Empire. In 1833, E. G. Stanley (later Earl of Derby), carried through a scheme for emancipation. All slaves were to receive freedom within twelve months, those employed on agricultural work being apprenticed to their former masters until 1840, and domestic slaves being similarly apprenticed until 1838. Planters, whose representatives at Westminster had held up reform for a long time, were granted £20 million in compensation at the rate of £37 10*s*. per slave. The apprenticeship system, intended to maintain a supply of labour, did not work well.

The measure, entirely justifiable morally, caused dislocation in the West Indian sugar industry and bitterness among Boer farmers in South Africa.

The Factory Act, 1833

In 1802 an act was passed safeguarding the interests of poor-law apprentices in factories: it limited the day's work of these children to twelve hours. The elder Sir Robert Peel, himself a wealthy factory-owner, endeavoured after 1815 to extend the act to all children; his work was rewarded in 1819 when a twelve-hour limit was imposed (exclusive of meal-times) for all children between nine and sixteen. Employment of children under nine was forbidden. This act was largely evaded, for it did not provide for supervision by inspectors. It applied only to cotton mills, and therefore offered no protection to children in other types of mills; and it did nothing for adults.

Michael Sadler (1780-1835), a reformer, obtained a committee of enquiry in 1832 whose findings shocked public opinion and brought Anthony Ashley Cooper (1801-85), later the Earl of Shaftesbury, fully into the movement to improve factory conditions by parliamentary legislation. The Whig Lord Althorp shepherded an act through parliament which applied to all textile factories except those of the silk industry. This act maintained the exclusion of children under nine, and limited the work of children under thirteen to forty-eight hours a week, or nine hours in any one day. No person under eighteen could be employed for more than twelve hours a day or sixty-nine hours a week, daily hours being fixed between 5.30 a.m. and 8.30 p.m. Children under thirteen were to attend school for not less than two hours per day. The most important provision, however, was the appointment of paid inspectors who saw that the act was enforced, and whose reports did much to educate public opinion. Ashley was disappointed because the act did not secure a ten-hour day for all workers under eighteen.

State Aid to Education, 1833

In providing elementary education England lagged well behind Scotland and Prussia. Manufacturers feared labour troubles from an educated working class; others maintained that compulsory education would be an attack on the liberty of the individual. Two religious societies were largely responsible for providing schools for the poor, the Anglican National Society (founded in 1811) and the Nonconformist British and Foreign Schools Society (founded in 1814). Using the monitorial methods of Andrew Bell (1753-1832) and Joseph Lancaster (1778-1838), they provided the rudiments of an education to thousands of poor children who would otherwise have remained illiterate. In 1833, £20,000 was voted to enable the two societies to build more schools. The grant was continued in ensuing years and by 1846 had reached £100,000. It was the first state grant to education (see also Chapter 63).

During a sale of slaves a prospective buyer examines a Negro. Scene from the film "Uncle Tom's Cabin."

Poor Law Amendment Act, 1834

By 1818 the poor law administration of England and Wales cost £8 million —13*s*. 3*d*. per head of population. The Speenhamland system (see page 307) had failed; it weakened the independence and self-respect of labourers, and prevented any rise in agricultural wages. It was unfair to wage-earners in regions where the scheme did not operate, and unfair to employers who tried to pay a living wage. Agrarian disturbances in 1830 brought matters to a head, causing the Whigs to appoint a commission under the chairmanship of Dr. Blomfield, Bishop of London. Its report was issued in March, 1834, most of its recommendations becoming law later in the year.

Able-bodied men and women were no longer to receive outdoor relief but were to be housed in workhouses where they could contribute to their upkeep. Legislators feared that the new workhouses would attract too many paupers, so they intended to make the lot of the able-bodied pauper harder than that of the worst-paid labourer whose condition was often lamentable. The risks were small, for few workhouses were comfortable! At first discipline was fierce, married couples being separated, meals taken in absolute silence, and all smoking within doors forbidden. The commissioners did not intend the work provided to be repellent, but stone-breaking, grinding corn by hand and oakum-picking were nevertheless imposed.

The influence of Bentham was to be seen in the establishment of three commissioners in London to administer the scheme. Their secretary was Edwin Chadwick (1800-90), a tactless, impetuous and cocksure administrator but a man of drive and efficiency. The commissioners found that they had still to offer a greater amount of outdoor relief than they had intended.

This measure was the most hated Whig reform. To the poor, the new workhouses were "the poor man's bastilles." The ruling class was too ready to equate poverty with sin at that time, and there was a constant worry about expense yet at least the problem of widespread poverty was not ignored.

Municipal Reform, 1835

The local administration of England and Wales had long been carried on by unpaid amateur justices of the peace, many of whom were tolerant and careful, but the nineteenth-century industrialization brought administrative problems of great complexity with which they could not adequately cope. New towns had sprung up outside the old municipal boundaries. The old system of parish meetings had broken down under the strain of new burdens.

The municipal corporations of England and Wales, nearly 250 in number, varied in type. Some were oligarchic, some democratic. On the whole the close corporations were less irresponsible than the open ones. Reform of parliament in 1832 made the reform of municipalities logically necessary. The complaint of Nonconformists that corporations were still dominated by Anglicans was largely justified. Any improvement in matters like drainage and water-supplies had been effected by Improvement Commissions established by authority of parliament.

A commission was set up in 1833 by the Whigs to enquire into local government, and the Municipal Corporations Reform Act of 1835 resulted. It abolished close corporations in the boroughs, and substituted a uniform body of councils to be elected by all male ratepayers for a term of three years. Provision was made for towns like Manchester and Birmingham to become boroughs, and the new councils took over the work of the Improvement Committees. Improvement of conditions in large towns took place only very slowly after the act, and in 1842 only one in every five houses in Birmingham had water provided and in Newcastle only one in twelve.

Other Reforms

The Whigs were responsible for a number of other minor reforms. Among the most useful was the introduction of compulsory registration of births, deaths and marriages in 1836, which made it easier to apply the factory acts and to compile the accurate statistics which every efficient government needs. Between 1836 and 1840 the Whigs carried through a number of ecclesiastical reforms; based on the findings of a commission appointed in 1834, they ensured a better distribution of clerical incomes, set up a permanent board of ecclesiastical commissioners to administer church property, checked plurality, and changed payment of tithes from kind to money based on the market price of various grains over a seven-year period.

The ideas of Rowland Hill triumphed in 1840 when Penny Postage was

Ragged and Industrial School, Brook Street, London, 1853.

introduced. Previously poor people could not afford to send letters, because the cost was based on the distance which a letter travelled; a postman waited for payment upon delivery, a cumbersome process. Hill suggested prepayment with a uniform set of charges for all distances, starting with a penny; he also suggested the postage stamp. In spite of resistance from the postal authorities, his scheme was carried through, and proved a great boon to the poor and to commerce. Within twenty-five years the number of letters and packages carried in a year rose from 76 million to 642 million. It was a victory for reason over prejudice.

Reasons for the Whig Defeat of 1841

The Whigs had twice been replaced by the Tories for brief periods between 1830 and 1841, by Peel's first ministry of 1834-35, and in 1839 by Peel's second ministry. In 1841 Peel replaced them more permanently.

Almost every reform which the Whigs had passed aroused hostility. The new Poor Law was hated by the working classes; the clergy disliked the Whig attitude towards the Church; manufacturers resented the 1833 Factory Act; and businessmen disliked the Whig taxation policy. Their ferocity towards the Tolpuddle Martyrs in 1834 (see page 380) earned the Whigs a bad name; and many Englishmen resented their dealings with the Irish leader O'Connell (see pages 389-90). The Whigs never found an adequate Chancellor of the Exchequer, and for this reason they mismanaged financial matters.

QUESTIONS

1. Describe in detail any two reforms passed by the Whigs during the period 1833-41, and explain why they were important.
2. Describe the reforms of the Whig governments of Grey and Melbourne, *after* the 1832 Reform Act.

CHAPTER 52

THE CHARTIST MOVEMENT

THE Chartist movement was almost entirely a working class movement, and political in its aims. Its leaders desired to win for their class a greater influence in the nation's political life so that the economic and social status of the labouring classes could be raised.

The working class had played no small part in securing the Reform Act of 1832, but found that it left most working men without a vote. This inevitably created bitterness. The failure of Robert Owen's massive Grand National Consolidated Trades Union in 1834 (see pages 379-80) destroyed the workers' faith in direct action by trade unionism. They therefore turned to indirect action through their own representatives, whom they hoped to place in parliament. Labourers were full of resentment against the Poor Law of 1834, and the economic depression which began in 1836 not only increased their discontent, but also emphasized the full significance of the prohibition of outdoor relief. Working men felt no gratitude towards the Whigs for reforms which seemed to bring no benefits, whilst the Young England movement launched by Disraeli to win over the lower orders had very little appeal. Great hopes were raised among them by the charter which listed the aims of the Chartist movement.

The origins of the Chartist movement lay in the London Working Men's Association founded in 1836 by William Lovett (1800-77) and his friends, and the Birmingham Political Union founded in 1830 and now revived by Thomas Attwood (1783-1856), a Birmingham banker. The movement soon spread beyond the confines of London and Birmingham.

Leaders of the Movement

Lovett was born in Cornwall, the son of a sea-captain. Though an embittered man, he was not violent. He showed himself to be no great leader of men, and allowed the movement which he launched to fall into the hands of demagogues. Francis Place was an honorary member of the London Working Men's Association; so was James O'Brien (1805-64), an easy and convincing speaker but a man of little originality of thought or critical judgement. Joseph Sturge (1793-1859) became associated with Lovett during the second phase of the Chartist movement (1842). He was a Birmingham Quaker and corn-miller, who urged co-operation with the middle classes. Most famous of all Chartist leaders was Feargus O'Connor (1794-1855) who was to be the ruin of the movement. Entering English politics in 1832 as member for Cork, he became an honorary member of the London Working Men's Association, and then left it to form a rival body, the London Democratic Association, in which he could use his power of invective to greater advantage. In 1837 he took over a Radical newspaper in Leeds called the *Northern Star*; it established O'Connor's position as a political figure and also brought him a great deal of money.

In May, 1838, Francis Place helped Lovett to draw up a list of the political demands of the working class. Thus the People's Charter came into being. It contained six points: annual parliaments, equal electoral districts, removal of the property qualification for M.P.s, universal male suffrage, a secret ballot, and payment of M.P.s. Lovett was alarmed at the great enthusiasm which the charter provoked.

First Petition, 1839

The idea of a national petition to support the charter came from the Birmingham Political Union. A Chartist Convention met in London in February, 1839, to discuss the plan. O'Connor at once used his influence against moderation, and did his best to get rid of cautious Lovett and his friends. A general strike or "Sacred Month" was planned if parliament rejected petition and charter. On 6 May the petition was ready for presentation to the House: it contained 1,200,000 signatures. The London delegates decided to move from London to Birmingham where riots took place in July. The Whig government tried to be moderate, but could hardly ignore the drilling of men and talk of violence, so Sir Charles Napier, an accomplished soldier not unsympathetic to the Radicals, was appointed to keep order. He occupied strong points in Nottingham, Leeds, York, Newcastle and Manchester, and made it clear that violence would be firmly dealt with.

On 12 July the Commons rejected consideration of the national petition. The Chartist Convention therefore declared the Sacred Month, but workers over the country as a whole did not respond, and it was an ignominious failure. In November there was an attempt at armed rebellion in Monmouthshire where John Frost, a Newport draper and magistrate, led an attack on the city. In the fighting which followed, fourteen Chartists were killed outright and another ten died of wounds. Frost and two other leaders were sentenced to death, but the sentence was commuted to transportation.

Second Petition, 1842, and O'Connor's Land Scheme

After 1839, Lovett and other moderates began to consider whether it had been advisable to refuse middle-class help. O'Connor organized a second great national petition which was brought to the House of Commons on

2 May, 1842. Thousands of wretched and half-starved working men caught his impetuous enthusiasm. The petition was signed by 3,317,752 persons, but it was rejected by the House of Commons. In August there were strikes in Lancashire, Scotland and the Midlands which were doomed to failure because they coincided with a period of industrial depression when many firms were only just surviving. O'Connor tried in vain to prevent rioting. He was arrested but not imprisoned. Public opinion was unsympathetic. In Staffordshire fifty-four men were sentenced to long periods of transportation. Lovett's own contribution, the New Move (an attempt to win over the middle classes), also failed, for the middle class was frightened by the disorder.

O'Connor was left in possession of the field after 1842. He thoroughly disliked factories and industrialization and wanted to create a large body of small landowners in Britain. Many a working man hungered for a small plot of land. O'Connor therefore began to collect subscriptions from workers, and with these funds he hoped to provide smallholdings to lucky ones on a lottery basis, charging them a rental. Unfortunately O'Connor was reckless in money matters and his land scheme was financially unsound. Other Chartist leaders warned men against it.

After 1842 there was less agitation and discontent because the price of bread fell, and Peel's reduction of tariffs favoured business enterprise. Emigration provided a means of escape for distressed working men, and the administration of the Poor Law became more humane.

In July, 1847, O'Connor, at the height of his popularity, became M.P. for Nottingham, and won European fame.

Third Petition, 1848

In 1848 O'Connor tried for a third time to arouse and control a great political agitation. News of Louis Philippe's fall in France excited the Chartists greatly, and another national convention was summoned. A new petition was drawn up embodying all the points of the People's Charter with the exception of the secret ballot.

The police would not allow a large procession to take the petition to parliament, and after a crowd had met on Kennington Common, the petition was quietly taken to the Commons in three cabs. The aged Wellington, still Commander-in-Chief, had brought troops into London and concentrated them at important points, but there was little disorder, and the last phase of the Chartist movement soon collapsed.

The last petition was found to contain a large number of bogus signatures like those of Victoria Rex, Sir Robert Peel, the Duke of Wellington and Mr. Punch. O'Connor blustered; there was no one else to blame for failure this time. His Land Company was in distress, for the smallholders could not pay their way. A parliamentary committee found the company bankrupt and

Chartist rally: these processions gave expression to public opinion.

without proper accounts. O'Connor had not been dishonest; the company actually owed him money; but he had been guilty of gross mismanagement and this revelation finally discredited him. He died in an asylum in 1855.

Reasons for the Failure of the Chartist Movement

The Chartist movement failed because there were far too many conflicting schemes, and because leadership of the movement was hopelessly divided between cautious men like Lovett, those of violent speech like O'Connor, and others like Frost who were unwillingly involved in physical violence.

Governments who had to deal with the various outbreaks, on the other hand, usually acted firmly and sensibly. The middle class was never won over to the Chartist cause, preferring the Anti-Corn-Law League. After repeal of the Corn Laws in 1846, economic conditions gradually improved.

Although apparently unsuccessful, the Chartist movement did not fail utterly, for most of its demands were ultimately granted: abolition of property qualifications for M.P.s was won in 1858, the secret ballot in 1872, equal electoral districts in 1867, 1884 and 1918, payment of M.P.s in 1911, and adult male suffrage by 1919. Annual parliaments would not be desirable.

Agitation created by Chartism led to an enquiry into working-class conditions, which was followed by a long series of social reforms.

QUESTIONS

1. Outline the aims and methods of the Chartist movement, and explain the reasons for its collapse in 1848.
2. Describe and account for the rise and fall of Chartism.

CHAPTER 53

SIR ROBERT PEEL

ROBERT PEEL was born in 1788 near Bury in Lancashire. His father sent him to Harrow and Christ Church, Oxford, where he revealed his academic brilliance by gaining firsts in both Classics and Mathematics in 1808. His father's wealth and influence soon procured for the gifted young man a seat in the House of Commons for the borough of Cashel in Tipperary, Ireland (1809). Only one year elapsed before Peel held office as Under-Secretary for War and Colonies in the Perceval Ministry. From 1812 to 1818 he was Chief Secretary for Ireland, where he established a constabulary to maintain order. His special interest in financial affairs was recognized in 1819, when he was asked to serve on the parliamentary committee on currency with Huskisson and David Ricardo, the economist. It recommended a return to the gold standard, which caused an unfortunate fall in prices but countered inflation.

Gladstone thought Peel the greatest man he had ever known. Outside his very happy family life he was frigid and shy; Ashley likened him to an iceberg, and in 1839 Queen Victoria described him as a "cold, odd man," while O'Connell said his smile was "like the silver plate on a coffin." He was tall, dignified and very conscious of his great abilities, though he could never quite forget that he was the son of a rich cotton-spinner, and never felt entirely at ease with the aristocratic elements of his party. He had a natural tendency towards liberalism, and some said that he had joined the wrong party, though throughout his career he remained a Tory. He was always sensitive to injustice and to human suffering.

Peel as Home Secretary, and his Two Short Ministries

In 1822 Peel succeeded Sidmouth at the Home Office. Between 1822 and 1827 he reformed the larger prisons and humanized the penal code (see pages 316-17). Since he was opposed to Catholic Emancipation he would not serve under Canning in 1827 or under Goderich, but returned to the Home Office in 1828 under Wellington. In 1829 he founded the Metropolitan Police Force (see page 317). At this stage he was converted to Catholic Emancipation, but this volte-face cost him his seat for Oxford University in the election of 1830. He found another seat at Tamworth, which he represented for the rest of his life, and proceeded to lead Tory opposition to the Great Reform Bill of 1832.

When Melbourne resigned in 1834 Peel agreed to form a ministry, though he had no majority in the Commons, and the election which followed in 1835 brought the Whigs back. At Tamworth, Peel issued a famous election manifesto in which on behalf of his party he accepted the Reform Act of 1832 and the need for moderate reform; he intended his party to be a progressive one. In 1839 Melbourne again resigned, and Peel was asked to form a ministry. On this occasion, young Queen Victoria petulantly refused to change her Whig Ladies-in-Waiting for ladies of Tory leanings (the "Bedchamber Incident"), so Peel resigned and Melbourne returned.

Peel's Ministry, 1841-46, and his Budgets

In 1841 the Whigs were defeated, and Peel formed a particularly strong ministry. Six of his colleagues had held or were to hold the office of Prime Minister. Among them were Gladstone (President of the Board of Trade), Wellington (without specific office), Lord Aberdeen (foreign affairs) and Viscount Stanley (Secretary for War and Colonies and later Lord Derby).

In the years before 1841, the Whigs had failed to balance their budgets, and Peel therefore gave special attention to finance. Although he had a capable Chancellor of the Exchequer in H. Goulburn, he introduced his own budgets in 1842 and 1845.

He wished to stimulate commerce and industry by encouraging consumption through the lowering of duties. Four-fifths of the revenue came from customs and excise, 1,046 articles being subject to duty. Peel reduced duties on 769 articles, mostly raw materials, in 1842. The deficit in revenue had to be made up, so Peel courageously re-introduced income tax at 7*d.* in the £1 on incomes over £150 per annum. Within three years the increase in consumption had almost caught up with the loss in revenue. By 1846 Peel had abolished duties on 605 articles. He had decreased taxation by £2,500,000 per year and yet balanced his budgets. He had repaid £14 million of the National Debt and reduced the annual interest on the Debt by £1,500,000 per year. This was sound finance. It took Britain nearer to full free trade, created prosperity, and reduced the cost of living.

The Bank Charter Act, 1844

A sound banking system is essential for healthy economic life, but in the early nineteenth century there were too many small banks in Britain which lacked adequate reserves and which tended to over-issue paper money. Seventy such banks failed in 1825 alone. By his Bank Charter Act of 1844, Peel restricted issue of notes by banks other than the Bank of England, and limited the note issue of the Bank of England to £14 million. All issues above this sum were to be covered by coin or bullion. Although Peel's act was a little too restrictive and had to be suspended three times between 1844 and 1866, it created stability in the currency and stimulated confidence.

The Mines Act, 1842

Peel's government was responsible for passing several valuable social reforms. One of them was the Mines Act of 1842, based on the findings of a commission appointed in 1840. The Commission's revelations shocked public opinion, for children under six were employed underground for long hours in semi-darkness and cramped conditions, and women were used as beasts of burden. The Mines Act prohibited employment of women or girls underground, and set an age-limit of ten for employment of boys. Inspectors were appointed to enforce the law.

The Factory Act, 1844

Another report led to the Factory Act of 1844, which secured a day of six-and-a-half hours for children between eight and thirteen and a twelve-hour day for all women and girls. Regulations for the fencing of machinery were inserted mainly in the interests of women and girls, since their clothing was liable to be caught up in shafts or gearing.

Repeal of the Corn Laws, 1846

The demand for repeal of the Corn Laws was revived during a succession of bad harvests after 1836. The Anti-Corn-Law League was founded in London in 1839, but enthusiasm for the campaign declined with the good harvests of 1842, 1843 and 1844. The arguments of Richard Cobden (1804-65), who was elected M.P. for Stockport in 1841, and of John Bright (1811-89), who became M.P. for Durham in 1843, gradually convinced Peel that the Corn Laws must be modified, though he was fully aware that the land-owning section of his party was violently opposed to tampering with them. Peel made his decision before the potato crop in Ireland failed in 1845. This disaster strengthened his conviction. When rain ruined the English harvest in the same year, Peel considered that the question could no longer be postponed. Within his Cabinet, Stanley and others opposed him, so he resigned. Russell could not form a ministry and "handed back the poisoned chalice" to Peel. Lord George Bentinck and Disraeli, leaders of the protectionist Tories, made a strong attack on Peel, but in 1846, with the aid of Whig votes, he secured acceptance of a bill to reduce all duties on wheat, oats and barley to the nominal sum of one shilling a quarter. He could argue that if the Whigs had put the measure through, the Tory Party would have been split in any case. The fact that protectionists soon dropped protection seems to justify Peel's attitude. Soon after Peel's act was accepted, he was defeated over a Coercion

Bill for Ireland. The controversy over repeal was out of proportion to the results which followed, for in good years Britain could supply its own needs of grain, and importation of foreign corn was almost unnecessary.

Peel and Ireland

Peel was firm but constructive in dealing with the problem of Ireland. He faced a powerful campaign directed by O'Connell in favour of repeal of the Act of Union. The Irish leader since 1842 had organized mass meetings: in 1843 he planned a huge meeting at Clontarf to overawe the British government, but Peel was not easily stampeded and forbade the meeting. To his credit O'Connell did not want violence and gave way, but lost influence over his countrymen to more extremist elements. To prove that his attitude was not solely one of repression, Peel increased the grant paid to Maynooth College, an institution for training Roman Catholic priests.

Foreign Policy of Peel and Aberdeen

Peel and Aberdeen were ready to uphold British interests, but they did not employ Palmerston's aggressiveness and were much more conciliatory towards other powers. They concluded Palmerston's war with China (see pages 339-40) by the Treaty of Nanking (1842), which brought Britain financial compensation for the opium which the Chinese had seized. Britain also gained Hong Kong and the right to use five other ports including Shanghai and Canton. Frontier disputes with the United States of America might easily have led to war had they been tactlessly handled. Aberdeen commissioned Lord Ashburton to treat with the American Secretary of State Webster in 1842 over the boundary between Maine and New Brunswick. The two negotiators, both bankers, calmly settled the issue. Since 1818 the 49th parallel of latitude had been recognized by the British and American governments as the frontier between the Lake of the Woods and the Rockies. The section from the Rockies to the Pacific coast was still unsettled. Some belligerent Americans wanted to extend it as far north as Alaska which would have left Canada with no western coastline. Aberdeen stood firm and in 1846, by the Oregon Treaty, President Polk accepted a line which included Vancouver Island within Canada. Friendly relations with France were established when Queen Victoria and Prince Albert visited Paris in 1843. When the French Admiral Dupetit-Thouars high-handedly annexed the island of Tahiti in 1843 and a year later arrested a British missionary named Pritchard, hostility might have grown had not Aberdeen exercised firmness and tact in the matter.

Achievements of Peel

After his defeat in 1846, Peel continued to attend debates in the Commons, but died after a fall from his horse in 1850.

Children, often under the age of six, were still employed in the mines until the Mines Act of 1842. This shows the conditions under which they worked.

Peel achieved many valuable social reforms during his career, including prison reform, humanizing the penal code, and the Mines Act and the Factory Act of 1844. He brought a new progressive spirit into the old reactionary Tory Party and maintained peace abroad while upholding essential British interests. He was the founder of the modern police force. His financial ability had given businessmen confidence, reduced the cost of living and increased prosperity; and he had brought complete free trade nearer, at a time when it suited Great Britain's needs.

Peel's "Betrayals" of the Tories

Peel was accused of betraying his party on three occasions. He accepted Catholic Emancipation in 1829 against the wishes of many of his party, having previously opposed it: he led Tory opposition to the Great Reform Bill (1832), but then accepted the Act by his Tamworth Manifesto three years later: and he removed most import duty on corn in 1846, using Whig votes to do so, when a large group in his own party opposed it.

In Peel's defence it can be said that he prevented his party from becoming reactionary and blind to public opinion; that he was a statesman; and that he rose above narrow party politics.

QUESTIONS

1. Outline briefly the reforms introduced by Sir Robert Peel.

2. Describe the political career of Sir Robert Peel, and explain the importance of his 1841-46 ministry.

CHAPTER 54

LORD PALMERSTON

HENRY JOHN TEMPLE, third Viscount Palmerston, was born at Westminster in 1784. Educated at Harrow and St. John's College, Cambridge, he entered parliament as member for Newport (Isle of Wight) in 1807. His peerage was an Irish one, so he was able to sit throughout his career in the House of Commons. He soon held office, for he became a Lord of the Admiralty in 1808 and served as Secretary at War from 1809 to 1828. He then moved from the Tory Party over to the Whigs, because he favoured moderate parliamentary reform.

For the greater part of his career Palmerston's interest lay in foreign affairs. He was full of prejudices; he distrusted France and Russia and spoke of Austria as "an old woman." He did not work to any system but preferred to improvise. He favoured states which possessed constitutions, but had no fixed friends or enemies. His ill-mannered treatment of foreign countries and foreign statesmen can hardly be justified; diplomatic tact was unknown to him, and his despatches were often deliberately insulting. For much of his time Palmerston directed the foreign policy of a powerful Britain which, by use of her supremacy on the seas, could lord it everywhere. In the years before he died this strong position had waned, and Palmerston found that Bismarck was not to be flustered by words or paper threats, and that military strength was needed to influence European affairs.

Whig Foreign Secretary, 1830-41

In 1830 Palmerston became Whig Foreign Secretary under Grey. At once he had to deal with the problem of Belgian independence. The Belgians had rebelled against union with the Dutch, established in 1815. Austria, Russia and Prussia wished the union to be preserved. Palmerston was willing to accept Belgian independence but feared that France would secure undue influence over Belgium. When the Belgians offered their crown to the Duc de Nemours, a son of Louis Philippe of France, his fears seemed justified; and he was willing to go to war to prevent their possible realization. He persuaded the Great Powers at the London Conference to accept his candidate, Leopold of Saxe-Coburg. The Dutch invaded Belgium but a French army drove them back. Palmerston exerted pressure to force the French to leave Belgium. Then French and British combined to make the Dutch evacuate Antwerp. Eventually the Dutch agreed to recognize the independence of Belgium with frontiers as the Great Powers had designed them. All the Great Powers in 1839 signed the Treaty of London guaranteeing Belgian independence and neutrality and Palmerston had scored a great triumph. He had averted a European war, placed a friendly ruler on the new throne, and safeguarded British security.

From 1828 onwards civil war had raged in Portugal. It was caused by the attempt of Dom Miguel to wrest the throne from his niece Donna Maria. A similar situation existed in Spain, where Don Carlos sought to secure the throne occupied by his two-year-old niece Isabella. Palmerston disliked both Pretenders as reactionaries. He established the Quadruple Alliance of Great Britain, France, Spain and Portugal (1834) to expel the Pretenders, and eventually the liberal cause triumphed in both countries, much to Palmerston's satisfaction.

Mehemet Ali, vassal of the Turkish Sultan, was bitter because the Sultan had not given him adequate reward for his intervention against the Greeks in 1825. He sent his son Ibrahim Pasha to invade Palestine and Syria in 1831. The Egyptian army made such startling progress that it was able to threaten Constantinople itself, and the hard-pressed Sultan appealed to Russia for help. The Treaty of Unkiar-Skelessi of 1833 reduced Turkey almost to a protectorate of the Tsar, and opened the Bosphorus and Dardanelles to Russian warships. This was one of the gravest diplomatic defeats that Palmerston ever suffered, but the revocation of Unkiar-Skelessi eight years later was one of his greatest triumphs.

In 1839 Sultan Mahmoud launched an attack on his powerful vassal, only to suffer a humiliating defeat at Nessib in Syria. This was Palmerston's opportunity; he decided to intervene on behalf of Sultan Abdul Medjid, the boy who had succeeded Mahmoud. At the same time he called a conference of the Great Powers. The presence of British naval units at Acre and Alexandria warned Mehemet Ali that the Great Powers intended to protect the Sultan's interests. By the Straits Convention of 1841, Mehemet Ali became hereditary ruler of Egypt and governor of Nubia and the Sudan for life. The Dardanelles were closed to all foreign warships while Turkey was at peace. Though Palmerston's strong methods of dealing with Egypt almost provoked a war with France, the Treaty of Unkiar-Skelessi was torn into shreds and Britain, rather than Russia, now acted as protector to Turkey, which straddled Britain's vital trade route to India.

The Chinese government, quite justifiably, wished to prevent British merchants from demoralizing many Chinese by importing opium from India into China. In 1839 it seized British-owned opium at Canton; Palmerston retaliated by bombarding Canton. His action was not morally defensible, and reveals Palmerston at his worst. He was too ready to use the might of the British navy to overawe weaker powers. From 1841 to 1846 Palmerston was out of office.

Whig Foreign Secretary, 1846-51

He returned with the Whigs to serve as Foreign Secretary under Lord John Russell from 1846 to 1851. He was soon in conflict with Louis Philippe's France again over the Spanish Marriages Affair (1846). Queen Isabella of Spain and her sister Louisa had attained marriageable age, and the question of providing them with suitable husbands occupied the attention of both France and Great Britain. Palmerston wished to see Leopold of Saxe-Coburg gain the hand of Isabella, and was shocked to hear that she had married her aged cousin, the Duke of Cadiz, and that Louisa had married the Duc de Montpensier, a son of Louis Philippe. He felt that the provision in the Treaty of Utrecht (1713), that the thrones of France and Spain should never be united, was threatened, and he considered that he had been tricked. His attitude towards Louis Philippe became openly hostile and he did nothing to help him during the revolution of 1848 in France two years later.

The 1848 Revolutions in Europe

Palmerston frequently failed to inform Queen Victoria and his Cabinet colleagues of the content of his despatches, and the Queen, who had an able adviser in Prince Albert, became increasingly incensed at his neglect.

Europe was convulsed in 1848 by liberal and national revolts, many within the Austrian Empire. While opposing Austria in Italy, much to the annoyance of pro-Austrian Queen Victoria, Palmerston wished to see the Austrian Empire preserved, for he regarded it as necessary to the balance of power in Europe. Nevertheless he deplored the brutality of Austria's suppression of the Hungarians in 1849, and sent the British navy into the Dardanelles to support the Sultan's refusal to hand over Hungarian and Polish refugees to Austria and Russia. He allowed guns to be sent from Woolwich Arsenal to rebels in Sicily who were in revolt against the King of Naples, and he tried to persuade the Portuguese and Spanish governments to pursue a more liberal policy, though his interference created resentment. His sympathy lay with the rebels, but he did not try actively to intervene on their behalf.

Don Pacifico and General Haynau, 1850

Palmerston's vigour and lack of tact are well illustrated by two incidents which occurred in 1850.

Don Pacifico was a Portuguese Jew who claimed British citizenship because he was born at Gibraltar. He demanded £30,000 in compensation from the Greek government when his house was burned down in riots at Athens. Palmerston knew that Pacifico was a rogue, but considered the

Greeks to be bigger rogues. He therefore instructed the British fleet to blockade the Piraeus until the Greek government gave way on the matter. Peel, Gladstone, Bright, Cobden and Disraeli all attacked Palmerston in the Commons for his high-handed bullying of a smaller power, but he defended himself brilliantly in his greatest speech when he asserted that "a British subject, in whatever land he may be, shall feel confident that the watchful eye and strong arm of England will protect him from injustice and wrong."

General Haynau was an Austrian who had suppressed the Hungarians in 1849 with great brutality. He represented the Austrian court on an official visit to England in 1850 and, when visiting the London brewery of Barclay and Perkins, was manhandled by brewer's draymen. Palmerston sent a very half-hearted apology to the Austrian government and despatched it without referring it to the Queen, who was infuriated by the insult to Vienna. Palmerston's attitude delighted the ordinary people, and revealed his antipathy to foreign reactionaries.

In 1851 Palmerston went too far. Louis Napoleon, President of the Second French Republic since 1848, carried out a coup d'état in order to

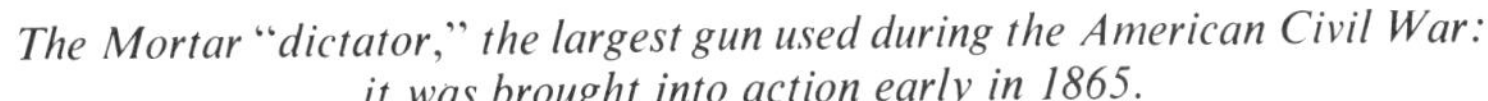

The Mortar "dictator," the largest gun used during the American Civil War: it was brought into action early in 1865.

extend his tenure of office. The British Cabinet decided on a non-committal attitude, only to discover that two days previously Palmerston had independently expressed to the French ambassador his entire approval of Louis Napoleon's action. Russell dismissed him, but three weeks later Palmerston brought about Russell's defeat over a Militia Bill, referring to it as his "tit-for-tat for Johnny Russell"!

Palmerston at the Home Office

The Aberdeen coalition government (1852-55) followed Russell's, and Palmerston accepted the Home Office in it. He found it much less exacting than the Foreign Office, but did not make it an excuse for being idle. He put an end to burials within church buildings in the cause of hygiene; he displayed an interest in factory reform which earned him Shaftesbury's praise; and he supervised schemes for improving the drainage of London so as not to pollute the Thames.

Foreign Policy as Prime Minister, 1855-58

The Aberdeen government drifted into the Crimean War, and then mismanaged it. If Palmerston had been in control of foreign policy in 1854, he would probably have convinced Nicholas I of Russia that Britain would fight, and thus would have prevented a war, for Nicholas did not want a war. Opinion grew in Britain that only Palmerston, who was known to be strongly opposed to Russian aggression in eastern Europe, could direct the war with energy. When Aberdeen resigned in 1855, Palmerston, then seventy, became Prime Minister for the first time.

At once he brought new vigour to the conduct of the war, sending out a commission of enquiry to the Crimea which resulted in an improvement in the provision of supplies for the army. Another commission improved sanitary arrangements. Before war ended, Palmerston had provided a well-clothed and well-equipped army of eighty thousand. The Treaty of Paris (1856) administered a sharp, though temporary, check to Russian ambition.

When news arrived in Britain of a terrible mutiny of Indian sepoys in 1857, Palmerston's calm cheerfulness did much to steady the government. He sent off Sir Colin Campbell on the day after the news arrived, and despatched thirty thousand men to India within the next three months. He sponsored the India Bill, to transfer the powers of the East India Company to the Crown, though it was Derby's government which saw it enacted.

Palmerston was determined to force the Chinese to allow the entry of British commerce into China. When the Chinese boarded the *Arrow*, a lorcha which flew the British flag (though its licence to do so had expired), to retrieve a notorious pirate, Palmerston ordered the bombardment of Canton, thus provoking a war which dragged on until the year 1860, when the Treaty of Tientsin granted foreigners the right to trade in the interior. Cobden made a fierce attack on this policy in 1858, causing Palmerston's defeat in Parliament, but Palmerston won the ensuing election.

In January 1858, an Italian named Orsini made an attempt to assassinate Napoleon III in Paris, and it was discovered that the plot had been hatched in England. Palmerston brought in the Conspiracy to Murder Bill, which made it a crime and not merely a misdemeanour to plan a murder. Remarkably enough, foreigner-hating Palmerston was accused of kow-towing to the French, and his defeat followed.

Palmerston's Second Ministry: Foreign Policy, 1859-65

In July 1859, Palmerston returned to office as Prime Minister upon Derby's resignation. Lord John Russell served as Foreign Secretary and Gladstone, though he disliked Palmerston's blustering foreign policy, became Chancellor of the Exchequer. The ministry was known as the Triumvirate.

Palmerston, Russell and Gladstone all favoured the cause of Italian unity. Their view was shared by most British people, though the court was pro-Austrian. Britain did not intervene when France fought to drive the Austrians from the plain of Lombardy by the battles of Magenta and Solferino in 1859, but Russell did use his influence in favour of plebiscites which brought Tuscany, Modena and Romagna under Sardinian control. When Cavour sent Piedmontese troops into the Papal States in 1860 in the face of opposition from Austria, France, Russia and Prussia, Russell sent a note of approval to him. The presence of the British navy at Marsala helped Garibaldi to land safely in Sicily in 1860, and Britain refused to stop him crossing to the mainland. Thus in many ways Palmerston's government helped to establish Italian unity under the Sardinian king.

Relations between the Federalists and Britain became very strained during the American Civil War (1861-65). When a Northern warship stopped the *Trent*, a British ship, to take off two Southern envoys, Mason and Slidell, Russell prepared a strong note of protest which might have led to hostilities had not the Prince Consort toned it down, an intervention which Palmerston willingly accepted (1861).

Russell failed to prevent the *Alabama* from sailing from the Mersey in 1862 under Southern control. She inflicted untold damage upon Northern shipping before she was sunk, but Russell refused to pay compensation to the Federalists.

In 1863 the Poles rose against their Russian masters. They received encouragement from Palmerston, but he did not intend to help them. His attitude broke up the Anglo-French entente, which was already flimsy, and did no good to Britain's reputation.

When Bismarck and the Austrians launched a joint attack on Denmark in order to take Schleswig and Holstein from Danish control, Palmerston asserted in parliament that "those who made the attempt would find that it was not Denmark alone with which they would have to contend." These were fine words, but they did not check Bismarck, who knew that Britain's military weakness would not permit her to interfere. Palmerston had more than met his match, and British prestige received a bitter set-back. Palmerston's career had ended on a note of failure, for he died in office in 1865 at the age of eighty-one.

Palmerston and Domestic Affairs

It has been said that Palmerston was a Conservative at home and a Liberal abroad. Certainly he delayed parliamentary reform and had a strong prejudice against trade unions; but valuable reforms were carried through during his second ministry. Gladstone, Palmerston's Chancellor, sent Cobden to Paris in 1860 and the Free Trade Treaty with France resulted, after which British trade with France doubled. Gladstone swept away other duties until only sixteen of importance remained. Against the wishes of Palmerston, Gladstone secured repeal of the paper tax, which he called "a tax on knowledge." He reduced income tax to sixpence in the pound. Palmerston's own sympathy with improvement of factory conditions produced a series of legislative measures which protected women and children employed in the bleaching and dyeing industries (1860), the lacemaking industry (1861), and the pottery and match-making industries (1864). An attempt was made in 1864 to prevent chimney sweeps from employing boys, but the measure was not effective.

Conclusion

Palmerston's methods in foreign affairs can hardly be justified, but his shrewdness and vigour are to be admired. He had genuine compassion for the underdog whether factory worker, negro slave, or an oppressed nationality.

Palmerston always had sympathy with liberal, constitutional and nationalist movements abroad, providing these did not conflict with British interests. He opposed the Russian threat to British influence in Eastern Europe, and was against either French or German predominance in Western Europe. Palmerston was determined that British influence would predominate in Europe, and equally determined to protect the rights of British subjects abroad.

QUESTIONS

1. What were Palmerston's achievements in home and foreign affairs from 1855 to 1865?
2. Describe Palmerston's work as Foreign Secretary between 1830 and 1851.

CHAPTER 55

BRITAIN AND THE CRIMEAN WAR

IN THE mid-nineteenth century there was widespread hostility to Russia in Great Britain. It was feared that she intended to expand towards the Mediterranean, where vital British interests existed; she seemed also to be exerting influence upon Afghanistan, through which she could threaten the security of British India. Tsar Nicholas I increased British apprehension when at Windsor in 1844, he asserted that Turkey was "a dying man" and hinted at possible partition of its territories by Great Britain and Russia. Again in 1853 he hinted that Britain should take Egypt and Crete while Russia assumed control over Moldavia, Wallachia, Serbia and Bulgaria, and occupied Constantinople, which would later become a free city. Nicholas was hated in Britain as persecutor of the Poles and Hungarians (whose rising against the Austrians he had suppressed in 1849), and as the upholder of serfdom in Russia. Yet Nicholas did not want a war. He assumed that vacillating Lord Aberdeen, the British Prime Minister (1852-55), would not fight, especially as he was strongly harassed by pacifists like Cobden and Bright. If Palmerston had been at the helm, war might have been avoided, by convincing the Tsar of Britain's will to fight Russia if she seized Turkish territory.

British and French supply ships and warships during the Crimean War.

The British ambassador at Constantinople, Lord Stratford de Redcliffe, a cousin of George Canning, possessed an unrivalled knowledge of the Turks and a powerful influence over the Sultan. Though he regarded a war over Turkey as inevitable, he worked desperately hard to avoid war. At the same time, he was determined to prevent the overbearing Russian ambassador Prince Menschikoff from bullying the Sultan into making concessions, and Stratford's presence at Constantinople probably bolstered up the Turks' will to resist. Britain had not fought in a large war since 1815, almost forty years previously, and the British people in 1854 were very jingoistic having forgotten the suffering and bestiality of war.

Britain's allies were Turkey and France. The former was anxious to avoid further Russian expansion at her expense, and Napoleon III resented Russian non-recognition of his imperial style and title. He had therefore eagerly adopted the cause of the Roman Catholic Church in France in its quarrel with the Russian Orthodox Church over guardianship of the Holy Places in Palestine. A successful war on this issue would strengthen Napoleon III's position at home. Britain also found an unexpected ally in Sardinia who joined the opposition to Russia in order to win French and British recognition of her efforts to lead the movement for Italian Unification.

Events Leading to War

Early in 1853, Nicholas I revived claims to a general protectorate over Christians within the Turkish Empire. As a precaution, Aberdeen sent a British fleet to Besika Bay, outside the Dardanelles, and the French agreed to send a squadron in support. A conference of Great Powers met at Vienna in July 1853, where the Sultan was asked to promise to protect Christians within his domains, but he rejected the request, and declared war on Russia in October 1853. The Russians moved their troops into Moldavia and Wallachia, and destroyed a Turkish naval force at Sinope in the Black Sea. Excitement mounted in France and Britain, where this naval action was regarded as an unwarranted massacre. Nicholas I was asked to withdraw his warships to Sebastopol, but ignored the request; he also refused to withdraw from Moldavia and Wallachia. After Britain and France had declared war, he gave way, partly because the Turks resisted his troops well, and partly because the Austrian government delivered a strong note. Thus the case for war had been removed, but by this time Britain and France were determined to strike a blow against Russia.

Crimean War, 1854-56

The problem was where to strike. A large-scale invasion of Russia was out of the question, for the allies had not the resources, and were not foolish enough to repeat Napoleon I's mistake. It was therefore decided to attack and dismantle Sebastopol, the formidable Russian arsenal and naval base.

The Crimean War was fought by a British army which had seen little service outside India for forty years. There were no commanders of outstanding ability, staff-work was poor, and the war brought little credit to Britain's military reputation. Conditions of life for soldiers on the campaign were unnecessarily hard. Wellington's conservatism was to blame for lack of modernization in the army; few large exercises had been held in peace-time, and soldiers who went to the Crimea did not even know how to cook in the open air. At home there was ridiculous overlapping of authority between the Secretary-at-War, the Secretary-of-War, and the Commander-in-Chief.

A British army landed at Varna in Bulgaria, a move which helped to drive the Russians northwards from Wallachia; but conditions there were unhealthy, and malaria and cholera rapidly decimated the troops. If a swift move had been made on Sebastopol, it might have fallen quickly, but there were endless delays before the French and British landed north of Sebastopol on the Crimean Peninsula at Eupatoria. The Russians could muster 80,000 men in the Crimea, and the allies 60,000, including 26,000 British. The British commander, Lord Raglan, aged sixty-six, who had fought in the Peninsular War, was a brave, conscientious man, of only average ability.

The British drove back the Russians under Menschikoff when his forces tried to prevent them from crossing the river Alma on their way south towards Sebastopol. If the allies had followed up the victory, they might have destroyed the Russian field army, taken the north side of Sebastopol, disabled the Russian fleet by bombardment, and cut Sebastopol from contact with the north and east; but the Russians were allowed to sink seven ships across the harbour, which made attack from the sea impossible.

The Russians knew that they must take the initiative to save Sebastopol, so they made a surprise attack on the British base at Balaclava in October 1854. It was in this battle that the British cavalry distinguished itself in two charges, one by the Heavy Brigade under General Scarlett and the second, the famous charge of the Light Brigade under Lord Cardigan, in which 247 out of 673 horsemen were killed. This last action was magnificent, but achieved little. After suffering heavy losses, the British held their base.

In November 1854, the Russians, reinforced by twenty thousand men from Odessa, tried again to dislodge the allies by the battle of Inkerman but failed, losing twelve thousand men.

The Russian winter then descended. A blizzard destroyed hospital marquees and wrecked twenty-one ships in Balaclava harbour, all carrying vital supplies. The allies spent winter on open ground, and cholera, dysentery and malarial fever killed thousands of soldiers who paid with their lives for the inefficiency of their commanding officers and for their government's economies at home. One in ten soldiers died on the voyage to hospitals at Scutari and Constantinople and those who survived the journey found the hospitals badly managed; in one, half the patients died.

W. H. Russell, war correspondent of the *Times*, revealed these sufferings at home and brought down Aberdeen's government, which was replaced by that of Palmerston. Florence Nightingale, who reached Scutari in November 1854, began to improve hospital conditions and save lives. Palmerston brought more drive to the conduct of the war. Raglan died, and was replaced by the abler General Simpson. In September 1855, largely owing to a great French attack, Sebastopol at last fell.

Treaty of Paris, 1856

Palmerston wanted to continue the war to administer further rebuffs to Russia, but Napoleon III forced him to make peace by threatening to extend the war to one of liberating the Italians, Poles and Hungarians. After Austria had sent an ultimatum, Russia agreed to negotiate, and the Treaty of Paris was signed on 30 March, 1856.

Russia agreed to surrender Southern Bessarabia, thus losing control of the mouth of the Danube, and relinquished her claims to a protectorate over Turkish subjects or Turkish territory. The Dardanelles were to be closed in peacetime to foreign warships, and the Black Sea was to be demilitarized. Turkey was admitted to the ranks of the Great Powers, and her independence guaranteed. Moldavia and Wallachia were to enjoy independence and constitutional government under the nominal sovereignty of the Sultan.

The Treaty of Paris was not, and could not be, a permanent settlement of the eastern question; but the British and French had temporarily succeeded in checking the ambitions of Russia, and had preserved Turkey.

The Sultan's promise to treat Christian subjects more humanely was never kept. The Treaty of Paris was also ignored during the Franco-Prussian War (1870), when Russia, encouraged by Bismarck, sent warships to the Black Sea.

The results of the war hardly justified its cost to Britain. Nevertheless various reforms were carried out in the British army as a result of its failures in the war.

The loss of military prestige suffered by the British is said to have been one cause of the Indian Mutiny of 1857.

QUESTIONS

1. State briefly the causes, important events and results of the Crimean War
2. Explain why Britain took part in the Crimean War, and comment on the terms of the Treaty of Paris.

REVISION SUMMARY OF CHAPTERS 35-55

THE JACOBITE MOVEMENT

SIR ROBERT WALPOLE

PITT THE ELDER

GEORGE III

OCL/HIST/1—Y*

THE AGRICULTURAL REVOLUTION

THE INDUSTRIAL REVOLUTION

LORD PALMERSTON

CHAPTER 56

BENJAMIN DISRAELI

BENJAMIN DISRAELI was the son of Isaac D'Israeli, a Spanish Jew whose family had migrated from Venice to England. Born in London, Benjamin was sent to a private school, and at seventeen was articled to a firm of solicitors. But literature rather than law claimed his attention, and in 1826 he produced his first novel, *Vivien Grey*. Between 1828 and 1831 he went on a long tour of Spain, Italy and Palestine. After several unsuccessful attempts, he entered parliament as member for Maidstone in 1837. Dispensing with his early Radicalism, he became a Tory and in 1839 he married Mrs. Wyndham Lewis, who brought him wealth and social standing. His maiden speech in the House was howled down, for it was full of overcoloured, flamboyant phrases, but the time was to come when he would command the attention of the House. His second novel, *Coningsby*, appeared in 1844, and a third, *Sybil*, in 1845.

Young England Movement

Disraeli was very bitter when Peel overlooked him in forming his ministry of 1841-46, his bright clothes, oiled ringlets and flashing rings hardly appealing to Peel's sober English taste. He became a member of a small group of young aristocrats, led by George Smythe and Lord John Manners, who were rebelling against Peel's cautious party leadership, and who advocated a Romantic Toryism which envisaged a union of the working class with the old aristocracy to oppose the arrogance of the new industrial class. This Young England group gave Disraeli a platform from which he could attack Peel but the group split up over the Maynooth Grant in 1843.

Disraeli and Repeal of the Corn Laws, 1846

Peel's decision to repeal the Corn Laws in 1846 gave Disraeli an opportunity for revenge. Although Lord George Bentinck was head of the protectionist wing of the Tory party, it was Disraeli whose fiery speeches gave weight to its attack. When Bentinck died in 1848, Disraeli was his inevitable successor, though there was still much prejudice against him among the Tories. His willingness later to drop protection has been used to stress his insincerity, though it may also be regarded as political realism, for it was obvious that the country as a whole favoured free trade.

Three Derby-Disraeli Ministries: 1852, 1858-59 and 1866-68

When the Russell ministry fell in 1852, Derby was called upon to form a new ministry and he asked Disraeli to become Chancellor of the Exchequer. Disraeli replied that he knew nothing of financial questions, to which Derby answered, "They give you the figures." The defeat of Disraeli's budget, however, brought down the short-lived ministry. In 1858 the second Derby-Disraeli ministry followed that of Palmerston, and Disraeli again served as Chancellor of the Exchequer. He wanted the party to adopt the cause of electoral reform but the Tories were out of office again by 1859. The third Derby-Disraeli ministry had a longer life (1866-68). Disraeli was its leader in the House of Commons, and the Reform Act of 1867 was largely his work, but was regarded by many prominent members of his party with suspicion (see page 322). After the passing of the bill Derby resigned (February 1868), and Disraeli briefly took his place as Prime Minister: he had "climbed to the top of the greasy pole". From 1868 to 1874 Disraeli was leader of the opposition. Personal hostility to him within his party became weaker, though it never completely disappeared. His youthful eccentricities forgotten, he enjoyed the favour of Queen Victoria, and even found time to write another novel, *Lothair*.

Disraeli's Ministry, 1874-80

In 1874, on the defeat of Gladstone's first ministry, Disraeli at last found himself at the head of an assured majority. His position had been won in the face of immense obstacles by courage and shrewdness; he was now seventy.

Disraeli still cared sincerely for social reform, but he was never a great administrator. He was very fortunate to discover Richard Cross (Home Secretary), who sponsored a whole series of social measures, many of which were passed in 1875.

The Artisan's Dwelling Act aimed to provide better housing for the poor by giving local authorities power to clear slums. The measure enabled Joseph Chamberlain to effect great improvements in Birmingham. A New Public Health Act codified many past acts. The Conspiracy and Protection of Property Act permitted peaceful picketing by trade unionists, and the Employers and Workmen Act made a breach of contract by an employee a civil, not a criminal, offence.

In the first year of the ministry a Factory Act (1874) had cut the working week to fifty-six hours. At last the ten-hour day had been achieved.

An Education Act of 1876 penalized parents who kept their children away from school without official sanction and another act of 1876 limited agricultural enclosure, and saved Epping Forest for Londoners.

Other useful social measures were an Agricultural Holdings Act which provided for compensation for displaced tenants if they had carried out

Contemporary comment on Disraeli's foreign policy. These cartoons deal with the Suez Canal, and the Eastern Question (see page 366).

improvements; a Rivers Pollution Act which checked pollution of rivers by sewage or manufacturing waste; and a Sale of Food and Drugs Act which prohibited use of harmful substances in food preparation. The Universities of Oxford and Cambridge were reformed and obliged to use college revenues to promote learning. Samuel Plimsoll's powerful agitation forced the government to sponsor the Merchant Shipping Act of 1876, which enjoined shipping companies to mark a line on the sides of ships to prevent the overloading which imperilled sailors' lives. The act enabled the Board of Trade to prevent an overloaded ship from leaving port; the measure, unfortunately, was not entirely successful.

Disraeli achieved many improvements by his policy of social reform, but industrial unrest and agricultural depression disturbed the country more and more after 1875, as the full weight of foreign competition began to be felt in Britain.

Imperialism

Disraeli did everything he could to strengthen the British Empire for whose existence he found every justification. By a famous coup he gave Britain powerful influence over management of the Suez Canal, which had been built by a French company and opened in 1869. In 1875 Disraeli heard that Khedive Ismail, spendthrift ruler of Egypt, was proposing to sell his shares in the canal, about 7/16ths of the whole. Hurriedly raising £4,000,000 from the Rothschilds in the face of fierce opposition from his Cabinet, Disraeli secured the shares. It was recognized at home and abroad as an act of national leadership. In subsequent years dividends paid by the company easily repaid the initial cost of shares. The principal result was to obtain more reasonable tolls for British merchant shipping which used the canal (then 4/5ths of the whole). It also gave Britain a special interest in Egypt, where she took control in 1882.

Empress of India, 1876

Not only did Disraeli have great enthusiasm for the empire, but he also revered the monarchy. In 1876 he brought his two interests together when he persuaded Parliament to pass the Royal Titles Bill which gave Queen Victoria the title Empress of India. Disraeli wished to use the special glamour of monarchy to appeal to the oriental imagination. His opponents suggested that he was merely flattering the queen and that the title Empress was un-English.

Annexation of the Transvaal, 1877, and the Zulu War, 1879

By 1876 the problem of black against white in South Africa had reached a crisis. Zululand was a Bantu military monarchy whose king Keshwayo (Cetawayo) maintained a highly drilled army of nearly forty thousand warriors. This force menaced both Natal and the Transvaal. The weak and inefficient government of the Transvaal deliberately provoked the Zulus. In 1877 Disraeli authorized annexation of the Transvaal. Sir Bartle Frere, a new High Commissioner in South Africa, against the will of the home government, committed Britain to a war against the Zulus which led to disaster when a poorly defended camp of British soldiers with native auxiliaries was overrun at Isandlwana, and 1,600 men massacred. At the same time a small force of just over 100 men held out against a large Zulu force at Rorke's Drift. News of Isandlwana was received badly by the public in Britain though the Zulus were crushed at Ulundi in 1879. Disraeli was fiercely attacked for wanton aggression in South Africa, but the Zulus would have continued to disturb the peace of South Africa if their military system had not been crushed.

Afghanistan, 1876-80

Disraeli feared the influence which Russia sought to exercise over Afghanistan, and took steps to check it by exerting a strong British counter-influence there for the sake of the security of British India. He authorized Lord Lytton, Viceroy of India (1876-80), to use military force to place a British Resident in Kabul, the Afghan capital. The Resident was murdered,

Queen Victoria in 1854.

and General Roberts had to be sent to retrieve the situation. Again the news brought a revulsion against Disraeli's "forward" policy, and strengthened the anti-Imperialist campaign of Gladstone.

Disraeli and the Eastern Question

In the sphere of foreign affairs Disraeli (who had become Earl of Beaconsfield in 1876) and his Foreign Secretary, Lord Derby, were mainly concerned with the perennial Eastern Question. After the Crimean War there had been little improvement in the efficiency of Turkish government, and Christian races of the Balkans were still cruelly treated. In 1875 the Serbs of Herzegovina rose against the Turks. Austria, Russia and Germany issued from Berlin a memorandum which suggested Turkish reforms. Disraeli feared, not without some justification, that they were secretly plotting the dismembering of Turkey.

In 1876 the Turks unleashed the Bashi-Bazooks, a band of barbaric irregular soldiers, upon the Bulgarians, who were massacred in great numbers. Beaconsfield was inclined to assume that reports reaching Britain were exaggerated, but they were all too true, and produced Gladstone's tremendous pamphlet *The Bulgarian Horrors and the Question of the East*, which sold forty thousand copies. Beaconsfield sent Lord Salisbury to Constantinople, where a conference took place to try to persuade the Turkish government to accept reform, but the conference failed in its object, and war between Russia and Turkey began in 1877. The resistance of the Turks caused a change of feeling in Britain in their favour. Queen Victoria shared the desire of her people for war with Russia. Beaconsfield sent part of the British fleet through the Dardanelles, but though he wished to check Russian expansion, he did not wish to go to war.

He was shocked by the terms of the Treaty of San Stefano which the Russians imposed on the Turks in 1878, and supported Andrássy, the Austrian minister, in demanding their revision at a European conference. To persuade Russia to agree, Beaconsfield called up reserves at home, summoned seven thousand Indian troops to Malta and replaced pacifist

Lord Derby by the more determined Lord Salisbury at the Foreign Office.

Beaconsfield and Salisbury represented Britain at the Congress of Berlin which followed. Beaconsfield revealed a suave yet formidable bargaining power, once ordering a special train to leave Berlin in order to win his point.

Terms of the Congress of Berlin

By the Treaty of San Stefano, the Sultan had recognized the independence of Serbia, Montenegro, Roumania and a greatly enlarged Bulgaria. Beaconsfield feared that these new states, particularly Bulgaria, would be dominated by Russia. The Congress of Berlin arranged that Bulgaria should be reduced, that Macedonia should remain part of the Turkish Empire, and that a new division called Eastern Rumelia should lie to the south of Bulgaria and be governed by a Christian governor. It was also agreed that Austria should administer Bosnia and Herzegovina, and that Britain should receive Cyprus.

Beaconsfield returned from Berlin to receive wild acclaim in Britain; the Queen rewarded him with the Garter. He said that he had brought back "peace with honour". War had been averted, and Russian designs in the Balkans had been frustrated, but there was much to be criticized in the arrangements. Eastern Rumelia and Bulgaria joined within eight years. Serbian nationalism was affronted by Austrian occupation of Bosnia and Herzegovina. The return of Macedonia to Turkish control ensured continuation of the massacre of Christians, while the damming-up of Russian aspirations in the Balkans was one of the causes of the 1914-18 War. After Britain's occupation of Egypt in 1882, Cyprus proved of little value to her.

The Defeat of Beaconsfield's Ministry, 1880

In 1880 Beaconsfield's government fell for a number of reasons. People feared the possible consequences of his foreign policy, and his ambitious imperialism seemed to lead to costly reverses. The agricultural depression, with its attendant miseries, was blamed on the Conservatives. Gladstone's tremendous Midlothian election campaign made a great impact on electors, and the swing of the political pendulum operated against the government.

Beaconsfield's policies made Britain a respected power in Europe, created pride in the Empire, and gained control of the Suez Canal for Britain. He was responsible for many valuable social reforms, he extended parliamentary reform, and created the modern Conservative party.

QUESTIONS

1. Give an account of Disraeli's foreign and imperial policies.
2. How did Disraeli improve social conditions?

CHAPTER 57

WILLIAM EWART GLADSTONE

WILLIAM EWART GLADSTONE was born at Liverpool in 1809, son of a wealthy merchant of Scottish descent. Educated at Eton and Christ Church, Oxford, he took a double first in Mathematics and Classics as Peel had done. In 1832 he entered the House of Commons as a Tory; Peel made him Under-Secretary for War and Colonies in 1835, and Vice-President of the Board of Trade in 1841. Always a staunch Anglican, Gladstone resigned over the increased grant to Maynooth College in Ireland in 1843, though he returned to office in 1845 as Secretary for War and Colonies. He later supported Peel over the repeal of the Corn Laws.

It has been said that Gladstone's life was spent in unlearning the prejudices of his youth. In a curious way he combined deep conservatism with a fundamental desire for reform. To him every question was a moral question and his sincerity cannot be questioned. His energy was tremendous, and despite his lack of a sense of humour he was the most powerful debater in the Commons for a great part of the nineteenth century. His four outstanding interests were the Anglican Church, economy in public expenditure, peace abroad and peace in Ireland, his best work being accomplished in the realm of finance.

Chancellor of the Exchequer

Twice Gladstone served as Chancellor of the Exchequer, firstly in the Aberdeen Coalition (1852-55) and later under Palmerston and Russell (1859-66). Under Aberdeen he tried to decrease taxation by reducing expenditure. In his great budget of 1853 he abolished duties on foodstuffs and semi-manufactured goods and halved nearly all duties on wholly manufactured goods. He also planned to reduce income-tax until it disappeared in 1859, but the Crimean War raised it from sevenpence to 1*s.* 2*d.* in 1854.

As Palmerston's Chancellor, Gladstone continued a similar policy. His budget of 1860 reduced import duties to such an extent that only sixteen articles continued to make an important contribution to revenue. His proposal to abolish the excise duty on paper, a "tax on knowledge", was strongly opposed by the House of Lords and by Palmerston himself, but Gladstone outmanoeuvred the peers by tacking the measure to the budget of 1861 which the Lords could not reject. He now concluded that it was impossible to abolish income-tax, but in 1863 he reduced it from ninepence to sevenpence, and raised the limit of abatement to £200. By 1865 it stood at sixpence. Duties on tea were lowered in 1863, on sugar in 1864, and on tea again in 1865. This reduction of taxation in three successive years brought Gladstone much popularity. He had brought the policy of Free Trade, inherited from Huskisson and Peel, to its conclusion.

Between 1852 and 1859 Gladstone was politically in the wilderness, until he decided to join Palmerston, for he had little sympathy with the Crimean War. The most able and important of the Peelites, he emerged in 1859 as leader of the Liberal element in the new ministry. His pacifism and zeal for economy brought him into conflict with Palmerston's ebullient foreign policy.

Gladstone's First Ministry, 1868-74

In the autumn of 1868 the Liberals, with Gladstone and Bright in the van, waged a great election campaign which earned them a majority of 112. Gladstone then formed a ministry, and announced that it was his intention to pacify Ireland.

The problem of Ireland was brought before the public in 1868 because of the Fenian outrages at Manchester and Clerkenwell in the previous year (see page 391), but Gladstone had made up his mind to tackle the problem before they took place.

Gladstone's first measure was Disestablishment of the Anglican Church in Ireland (1869), and his second the First Irish Land Act (1870) which failed to solve the agrarian problem (see page 392).

Domestic Reforms

At home Gladstone attempted a great programme of reform. W. E. Forster's Education Act of 1870 laid the foundation of a national system of elementary education by establishing school boards which were to build and run schools where they were needed (see page 405). By the University Tests Act of 1871, Nonconformists were admitted to Oxford and Cambridge on the same terms as Anglicans.

In 1870 entry to the Civil Service was based on competitive examinations (with the exception of the Foreign Office), thus enabling it to tap a greater supply of talent.

Two measures were passed concerning trade unions. An act of 1871 gave trade unions legal status as corporations so that they could hold property and sue dishonest treasurers who absconded with union funds, but a second act, the Criminal Law Amendment Act (also 1871) lost Gladstone the gratitude of the movement, because it made picketing illegal.

The Poor Law Board, the local government section of the Home Office, and the Medical Department of the Privy Council were combined in 1871 to form the Local Government Board, precursor of the Ministry of Health.

Mr. Punch finds Gladstone and Disraeli engaged in a mud-slinging match (left). On the right we see Gladstone's attitude to the Eastern Question which helped to win re-election for the Liberals in 1880.

The Secret Ballot Act of 1872 discouraged any bribery which persisted at elections. There was no great demand for the measure, and some said that secret voting was un-English! It paved the way for election of Irish Nationalists in Ireland, as young Charles Stewart Parnell readily saw, for Irish voters could no longer be intimidated.

Reforms in the Army

Perhaps the most valuable of all reforms of this ministry were the army reforms of brilliant Edward Cardwell. British opinion had been shaken by the superb strength and efficiency of the Prussian army, displayed in the Franco-Prussian War of 1870. In Cardwell efficiency and economy met.

In 1868 he abolished flogging in the army in peace-time, though it was not abolished on active service until 1880. In the face of fierce military opposition, he put an end to the purchase of commissions, thus opening promotion by merit. The War Office was reformed and the Secretary for War given authority over the Commander-in-Chief. By his Army Enlistment (Short Service) Act of 1870, Cardwell replaced the twelve-year period of service by six years' service with the colours and six years on reserve. As a result, recruiting improved and service in the army became more popular, in spite of dismal forecasts by the military hierarchy. Between 1872 and 1874 the infantry was re-armed with the Martini-Henry rifle, a breech-loading weapon, and placed on a regional basis. Cardwell divided Britain and Ireland into sixty-nine military districts, each with a depot for a particular regiment such as the Dorsetshire, Gloucestershire, and Worcestershire regiments. This was the basis of his famous linked-regiment system, whereby one battalion of a regiment was in training at home while another served abroad. In this way replacements were readily available. British soldiers abroad became seasoned warriors, and this accounts for the splendid record of the army between 1871 and 1899. Local patriotism was skilfully used.

There was too much resistance in the cavalry and artillery for Cardwell to effect much change in them. He was worn out by 1874. He had miraculously increased army strength at home by 25 battalions, 156 field guns and abundant stores, and yet reduced military spending.

Bruce's Licensing Act of 1872 was the most unpopular of Gladstone's reforms. Public houses were closed down where too many existed, hours of drinking regulated, and adulteration of drinks attacked. The measure turned every public house into a committee room for the Conservative party! In 1874 Gladstone said, "We have been borne down in a torrent of gin and beer."

One final measure deserves mention. Lord Selborne's Judicature Act of 1873 tidied up the British judicial system on a grand scale.

Foreign Affairs

While Britain could field an army of only 100,000 which had many commitments abroad, Prussia could muster one of 500,000. It was impossible, therefore, for Gladstone and his Foreign Secretary, Lord Granville, to exercise a powerful influence on a European scene dominated by Bismarck. They saw that the neutrality of Belgium was observed during the Franco-Prussian war, but were unable to prevent Russia from breaking the Black Sea clauses of the Treaty of Paris in 1870. British people felt Gladstone let them down. Their opinion was confirmed when he agreed to pay the Americans £3,250,000 in 1872 as compensation for damage inflicted by the *Alabama* during the American Civil War (see page 343).

Reasons for the Defeat of Gladstone's First Ministry, 1874

By 1874 there was a feeling that the Liberals had come to the end of their programme. The upper classes were offended by Gladstone's reforms of the Civil Service and the Army, which removed their privileges. They also disapproved of recognition of trade unions. Anglicans were offended by Irish Disestablishment, and by full admission of Nonconformists to Oxford and Cambridge. Forster's Education Act of 1870 alienated Anglicans and Nonconformists alike. Trade unionists resented the refusal to permit picketing. Property-owners disliked the Irish Land Act; and the lower orders and the wealthy brewing interest jointly attacked the Licensing Act.

Between 1874 and 1879 Gladstone went into semi-retirement, but emerged to attack Disraeli's policy in the Near East. He saw no justification for supporting the Turks and thundered against them in his pamphlet *The Bulgarian Horrors and the Question of the East*. He embarked on a tremendous campaign to win the Conservative seat at Midlothian (1879-80), and largely due to him the Liberals were returned with a majority of 137 in the election of 1880.

Gladstone's Second Ministry, 1880-85

Gladstone was now past seventy, and this ministry was to be by no means as successful as his first. It faced opposition not only from the main body of Conservatives, but also from a small Conservative "Fourth Party" led by the brilliant Randolph Churchill, and from the Irish Nationalists led by Parnell. It was divided within itself, for old Whigs like Hartington had little in common with the new Radicals like Joseph Chamberlain. Ireland was the major problem, and for the rest of his career, Gladstone grappled with it (see also Chapter 61). W. E. Forster's attempts as Chief Secretary to establish order by coercion failed. It was not Gladstone's way to rely upon oppression alone. He steered through his great second Irish Land Act (the Three F's) in 1881. When Parnell stubbornly refused to give the act a trial, Gladstone lost patience and lodged him and other Irish leaders in Kilmainham Gaol. Six months later he released Parnell to conclude the Kilmainham Treaty with him, by which Parnell was to use his influence to put an end to the campaign of violence in Ireland and Gladstone promised to introduce a measure to assist tenants to pay off arrears of rent. Any chance of peace was destroyed by the murder in Phoenix Park of the new Chief Secretary Lord Frederick Cavendish and Under-Secretary Burke in 1882. Gladstone's Land Act and his Arrears Act did something to relieve distress in Ireland, but did not abate the demand for home rule.

A number of useful reforms were carried through by this ministry, with Chamberlain as the driving force behind them. He took up Plimsoll's work in his Seaman's Wages and Grain Cargoes Act. The Married Women's Property Act of 1882 granted to married women the right of separate ownership over every kind of property. A Settled Land Act of 1882 broke down the bars to land transfer. Chamberlain's Bankruptcy Act and his Patent Act, both of 1883, were sound commercial measures. The Corrupt Practices Act of the same year prevented abuses at elections, and parliamentary reform was continued by the Third Reform Act of 1884 and the Redistribution Act of 1885 (see page 323).

The Empire

Gladstone was no imperialist, but problems raised by the Empire had to be faced. The Boers of the recently-annexed Transvaal rebelled and defeated Sir George Colley at Majuba Hill (1881). Gladstone decided by the Pretoria Convention to grant the Boers their independence once more, though they were to remain subject to British sovereignty but the Boers remained arrogant. Gladstone also found it necessary to continue Disraeli's interference in Afghanistan in order to counter the influence of Russia there.

Egypt and the Sudan

After the purchase of the Suez Canal shares in 1875, Britain's interest in Egypt grew, and Gladstone reluctantly had to sanction the occupation of Egypt in 1882. Egypt exercised some sway over the Sudan to the south which was rapidly falling under the control of a religious fanatic, the Mahdi. It was decided to withdraw Egyptian garrisons from the area, but Gladstone's government made the error of sending General Gordon to effect the task. This lion-hearted officer, contrary to the wishes of the Cabinet, stayed at Khartoum where he was surrounded and killed, Gladstone being slow to send a relieving force under Wolseley. When news of Gordon's death at the hands of the Mahdi's hordes reached Britain, it brought a fierce outcry against the Prime Minister.

Reasons for the Fall of Gladstone's Second Ministry, 1885

By 1885 Gladstone's cabinet was hopelessly divided over Chamberlain's project for local self-government in Ireland. Parnell and his followers decided to vote with the Conservative opposition to defeat the Liberal budget. Gladstone's soft policy towards the Boers had lost him support, and the Gordon disaster had made him highly unpopular.

Gladstone's Third Ministry, 1886

After his second ministry had collapsed, Gladstone became converted to home rule as the only solution to the Irish problem. The election of 1886 gave the Liberals a majority of 86 over Conservatives; but since Parnell's Nationalists held 86 seats, Gladstone was dependent on him to form a ministry. When news of Gladstone's conversion to the cause of home rule leaked out through the carelessness of his son Herbert, it appeared as if Gladstone had allowed himself to be bought over by Parnell in order to regain office. Nothing could have been worse for the cause of home rule, or further from the truth.

Gladstone could not woo his leading colleagues to his new point of view. Of Hartington, Chamberlain, Bright, Harcourt and Selborne, only Harcourt came over. By Gladstone's first Home Rule Bill, an Irish parliament was to be set up at Dublin, but control over the army, navy, customs and foreign affairs was to remain at Westminster. The problem of Ulster was largely ignored. The bill never reached the Lords, for it was defeated by 343 votes to 313 on its second reading in the Commons, 93 Liberals voting against it. The ensuing election gave Gladstone's opponents a majority of 118.

Gladstone's Fourth Ministry, 1892-94

Gladstone's prospects of solving the Irish problem suffered a severe blow in 1890, when a divorce suit lost for Parnell the leadership of the Irish Nationalists, who became hopelessly divided. When Gladstone took office for the fourth and last time in 1892, his position was not a strong one. Almost the whole of the Whig peerage in the House of Lords had left him over home rule; many middle- and upper-class supporters did likewise, and his majority was only forty. His second Home Rule Bill passed through the Commons after a prolonged struggle, its deadliest critic being the Liberal Unionist Chamberlain. The bill differed from that of 1886 in that it provided for Irish members at Westminster. As in 1886 the problem of Ulster was ignored. The House of Lords rejected the bill at its second reading by 419 votes to 41.

In 1894 the prudent and assiduous H. H. Fowler achieved the passage of his Local Government Act which established the system of rural and urban district councils. Gladstone resigned in 1894, sixty-one years after making his maiden speech in the House. He died in 1898 at the age of eighty-nine.

Gladstone's Achievements

Gladstone completed Peel's work by establishing complete free trade. He introduced many valuable social reforms, and improved the standard of public finance. He strove valiantly to solve the Irish problem, and had he commanded stronger support might have succeeded. He also extended parliamentary reform, and created the Liberal party.

Reasons why Gladstone failed to Solve the Irish Problem

Gladstone failed to solve the Irish problem for a number of reasons which are discussed at greater length in Chapter 61. There was a deep-rooted prejudice against the Irish in Britain; and this was not lessened by violence in Ireland, especially the Phoenix Park murders. Parnell's disgrace (see pages 395-6) and the problem of Ulster also made a solution of the problem more difficult. Finally, Gladstone was handicapped by his failure to win over his own party, and in particular Joseph Chamberlain, and by Conservative domination of the House of Lords.

QUESTIONS

1. Give an account of Gladstone's attempts to find a solution to the Irish question.
2. Outline Gladstone's 1880-85 ministry, and explain the reasons for his defeat in 1885.

CHAPTER 58

FACTORY REFORM

THE Industrial Revolution brought rapid expansion of the factory system. Few now would defend conditions of labour which prevailed in the first factories, though there was nothing idyllic about the earlier domestic system. In their own homes men, women and children had worked long hours in cramped quarters under bad light, for little reward. At first the factory reform movement directed its attention more to hours and conditions than to wages. Reform began with the cotton mills, and it took nearly fifty years to achieve a ten-hour day. Prominent among leaders of the movement were Robert Owen, John Fielden (a manufacturer), John Doherty (a trade union organizer), Richard Oastler, J. R. Stephens (a Wesleyan minister), Michael Sadler (M.P. for Leeds), and Anthony Ashley, later Earl of Shaftesbury.

Conditions against which these men fought were grim indeed. Children of both sexes were admitted to factories at six or seven years of age, their parents being compelled by economic pressure to send them. They worked from twelve to nineteen hours a day, and overseers imposed a fierce discipline with frequent beatings. Some manufacturers were humane; others callous.

Factory Acts were passed in 1802 and 1819 but were not effective. The first effective one was passed in 1833 by the Whigs (for details see Chapter 51). Years of depression followed the 1833 Act. After 1840 Short-time Committees sprang up to work for the regulation of women's labour; it was felt that if women and young persons worked for shorter hours men's hours would inevitably be shortened also. The next step forward was the Act of 1844, passed by Peel's ministry of 1841-46 (see page 335).

The Ten Hours Act, 1847 and the Print Works Act, 1845

In January 1846 Ashley introduced a Ten Hours Bill, but it was defeated. Fielden introduced another Ten Hours Bill in 1847, and anger against Peel's repeal of the Corn Laws won support for the measure, which was passed. It restricted the labour of women and young persons to ten hours, but not men's labour. It was still possible to work women and young persons in shifts in order to keep the men at work for fifteen hours a day. In 1850 Ashley agreed to a compromise by which the government raised the working day for women and young persons to ten-and-a-half hours but imposed outside limits of 6 a.m. to 6 p.m. Operatives were angered by what

Until the Act of 1864 small boys were often kidnapped by unscrupulous chimney-sweeps to be used as climbing boys.

they regarded as Ashley's treachery, for it remained possible for an employer to use children as assistants to men after women and young persons had left work, but in 1853 the government imposed the normal day on children. Reduction of hours nowhere proved as fatal to production and profits as manufacturers had forecast; ten hours' labour proved as productive as twelve, and profits continued to multiply.

After publication of the report of the Children's Employment Commission of 1843, Ashley obtained the passing of the Print Works Act which prohibited night work in the calico-printing industry by women and young persons under thirteen and employment of children under eight, and required children under thirteen to attend school for thirty days in each half-year. Other trades were left unregulated until well into the second half of the nineteenth century. Between 1860 and 1864 bleaching, dyeing, calendering and finishing were brought under the scope of the Factory Acts, and in 1861 the Lace Works Act placed lace factories, with certain exceptions, also within their scope.

The Factory Extension Acts of 1864 and 1867

In 1863 the Children's Employment Commission began to issue reports on working conditions of children and young persons outside the scope of the

Factory Acts. Their work was found to be frequently unhealthy, dirty and dangerous, with long hours and small rewards. Among industries inspected were paper-staining, fustian cutting, bootmaking, tailoring, pottery manufacture, match-making, glass and metal manufacture and lace making. Eleven thousand children were employed in the potteries. They sometimes worked from 6 a.m. to 9 p.m. Their work gave them rheumatism, tuberculosis and asthma; they were poisoned by lead and arsenic used in the manufacturing process. One in eight employed in lace-making contracted tuberculosis, and many also had impaired eyesight at an early age. By the Factory Acts Extension Act of 1864 pottery manufacture, match-making, percussion-cap-making, cartridge-making, paper-staining and fustian-cutting were brought under Factory Law, so that inspections, rules concerning ventilation and cleanliness, and control of hours were introduced. In 1867 another Factory Acts Extension Act and a Workshops Regulation Act were passed which brought metal, hosiery, printing and other trades under factory law, but many exceptions were allowed and the Workshops Act was permissive and vague.

The Factory Act of 1874 (Disraeli)

By the Factory Act of 1874 changes were made in the law applying to the textile industries. The maximum hours of work for women and young people, which since 1850 had been a ten-and-a-half hour day, were reduced to ten, and the week was limited to fifty-six-and-a-half. In practice, this involved a similar shortening of the hours of men. Children under nine years of age (and after a lapse of a year, under ten) were not to be employed in factories, and the half-time age was raised to fourteen, except in the case of children who had reached a certain standard of education. Working overtime was forbidden, and conditions in the silk mills were brought into line with other establishments.

The Factory and Workshop Acts

In 1878 the Factory and Workshop Act abolished the distinction between factories and workshops as places where more or less than fifty persons were employed. Instead a place using mechanical power was a factory, and one not using it was a workshop. The act brought conditions in factories and workshops into line, but women's workshops and domestic workshops were still inadequately regulated.

In the 1880s attention was drawn to the tailoring trade in which repetitive work was performed for low rates of pay in dark, overcrowded rooms; the Public Health Act and the Factory and Workshop Acts were utterly disregarded. Similar "sweating" existed in boot-making, cabinet-making and nail-making, and in the cutlery and hardware industries. The existing system of inspection was entirely inadequate.

The Factory and Workshop Consolidation Act of 1901 brought together all that was best in existing legislation, adding a "Particulars Clause" which, though it could not prevent "sweating," gave certain workers limited protection by providing that they be given written details of pay and work to be done. The Act applied to all workers except those in men's workshops.

The Mines

The Industrial Revolution made little difference to the mining industry. Hewing and carting coal below ground remained as they had been for centuries. The iniquitous truck system was widely found in the industry: in order to retain their jobs miners had to spend part of their wages in "tommy-shops" although prices were often 25 per cent higher than elsewhere. Payment was irregular, though miners earned more than most workers.

The report of a Commission on mines revealed that female and child labour was widely used beneath the ground, children being sometimes only four years old. They acted as trappers and stayed twelve or fourteen hours underground, opening traps as coal-carts passed. Some children in the winter never saw daylight for months on end. Accidents were frequent. The report of 1841 led to the swift passing of the Mines Act (see page 335).

Safety Measures in Factories

Introduction of safety measures was at first painfully slow. The Employers' Liability Act of 1880 recognized the employer's responsibility for insuring his workpeople against risks. Fencing of machinery was extended from textile to non-textile factories and workshops, and an Act of 1891 required adequate fire-escapes. In 1906 the Workmen's Compensation Act made clearer the workman's right to compensation for an accident at work. The twentieth century saw an increasing list of regulations dealing with dangerous trades; by 1932 over forty codes of regulations dealt with health and safety.

Arbitration

Neither the hours of men nor the wages of any persons were regulated by the Factory Act of 1901; nor had they been by any earlier factory acts. After 1850, however, wages and trade boards (like the Nottingham Hosiery Board and the Building Trades Joint Committee) had developed to arbitrate over wages and conditions. In 1909 the first Trade Boards Act was passed dealing with wages in tailoring, box-making and other "sweated" industries. The Coal Mines Regulating Act of 1908 limited miners' hours to eight per day. By 1922 there were sixty-three trade boards in the United Kingdom covering thirty-nine trades. In 1919 the Industrial Courts Act established the first permanent Arbitration Court, but the better-organized trade unions held aloof from it. Nevertheless, the trade boards effected an improvement.

Climbing Boys

One of the worst forms of employment was that of small boys to climb and sweep the meandering chimneys of big houses. The boys, purchased for £5 each or even kidnapped, were sent up chimneys when only six. An Act of 1834 prohibited apprenticeship of a child under ten to a chimney-sweep, and forbade employment by a chimney-sweep of any child under fourteen who was not an apprentice. In 1840 an act prohibited the climbing of chimneys by all under twenty-one, or the apprenticing of children under sixteen to sweeps, but both acts failed to name an authority to enforce the law, and the number of climbing boys increased. In 1863 the Children's Employment Commission reported that conditions were as bad as ever. Since 1840, twenty-three cases were reported of climbing boys dying, but it was not easy to gain the evidence to prosecute. Lord Shaftesbury championed the cause of the sweeping boys, and a boy's death in 1872 lent weight to his campaign. The Act of 1875 forbade a sweep to carry on his trade without an annual licence. For offences against the earlier Acts of 1840 and 1864 sweeps could lose their licence. The police were made responsible for enforcement of the law, and at last chimney-sweeping abuses were checked.

Factory Act of 1937

The 1901 Factory Act remained the governing Act until the Factory Act of 1937, which abolished the distinction between factory and workshop, and between textile and non-textile factory, and included men's workshops, hitherto excluded. Women and young persons were given a forty-eight hour week in place of sixty hours (fifty-five-and-a-half in textiles). On no day were they to work more than nine hours, or after one o'clock on Saturdays. The earliest hour for starting work was 7 a.m. Young persons under sixteen were not to work beyond 6 p.m. A certain amount of overtime was allowed to women and young persons over sixteen, but none to those under sixteen. Other regulations required medical inspection, more space per worker, and better lighting, heating, ventilation and cleaning. The inspectorate (250 for 200,000 factories and workshops) was increased to enforce the Act, which, like preceding legislation, provided for women and young persons but not for adult men. Before the 1937 Act could be fully operated the Second World War broke out and long hours had to be worked for national survival.

QUESTIONS

1. Describe briefly how conditions in mines and factories were improved between 1833 and 1878.
2. Explain the ways in which working conditions in factories and mines were regulated by Parliament after 1832.

CHAPTER 59

TRADE UNIONISM

THE factory system lent itself much more readily to the organization of workers into trade unions than the domestic system had done, for instead of being isolated in their own homes, workers were now in daily contact with each other. The principle of state intervention to regulate conditions and wages in industry, which had been observed in the famous Statute of Artificers of 1563, was no longer upheld, though as late as 1765 and 1773 Justices of the Peace were directed to formulate wage-schedules for silk weavers. It was natural, therefore, that industrial workers should combine to assert their interests and in the eighteenth century a number of unions developed, particularly those of wool-combers, weavers and tailors. They were almost entirely local at that time.

Combination Laws of 1799 and 1800

In 1799 and 1800 Combination Laws were passed by which associations in restraint of trade were made illegal. These laws applied to associations of masters as well as to those of men, but in practice they were not enforced against masters. Fear among the ruling class of political revolution inspired the passing of the acts. From 1799 to 1824 trade unionism remained illegal, yet trade unions did not entirely cease to exist. They were disguised as friendly societies, given legal status by an act of 1793; these societies received contributions from members, and paid those who were sick or out of work.

Repeal of the Combination Laws in 1824 was achieved largely by two Radicals, Joseph Hume and Francis Place (for details see page 317). As a result, many new unions were formed; and others, previously secret, came out into the open. Funds and organization were both inadequate, and their strikes soon collapsed.

Grand National Consolidated Trades Union, 1834

For several years after 1829, efforts were made to combine small local trade unions into larger organizations. The Grand General Union of the United Kingdom and the National Association for the Protection of Labour enjoyed a brief existence. Most famous of all was Robert Owen's Grand National Consolidated Trades Union of 1834. Robert Owen (1771-1858) was born in Montgomeryshire and apprenticed to a draper in Stamford in 1781.

Tolpuddle, Dorset, home of the six martyrs of 1834.

When he was only nineteen, he became manager of one of the largest factories in Manchester, and by 1800 he was a partner in one of the largest mills in Scotland. He made his own mills at New Lanark a model for the world. He did not preach class warfare, but wished to see society organized into small self-directing communities. Owen intended his great union of 1834 to include all the working class. A general strike against the capitalist system would take place, all competition would cease and manufacture would be carried on by national companies. The disappointment of workers with the Reform Bill of 1832 won Owen much support, but the Grand National Consolidated Trades Union soon collapsed. It was too large and unwieldy; its organization was poor, and the lack of both communication and cheap postage hampered co-ordination. Its failure was a great setback to trade unionism, and thousands of poorly-paid labourers were disappointed. Afterwards unions abandoned revolutionary aims and usually restricted themselves to improving conditions in their particular trades.

The Whig government of Lord Grey (1830-34) became very alarmed at the spread of trade unionism, and chose to make an example of six labourers of Tolpuddle in Dorsetshire who illegally took oaths in forming a branch of the Grand National. They were sentenced to seven years' transportation, but as a result of great petitions they were pardoned and brought home in 1836.

Amalgamated Society of Engineers, 1851

In the 1850s a new type of trade union came into being, well administered by permanent salaried officials. Their funds were substantial, and they used the strike only as a last resort. The 1825 act gave them very inadequate legal protection, for mere announcement of a strike was interpreted by judges as an attempt to intimidate employers.

The model for these new model trade unions was the Amalgamated Society of Engineers, formed in 1851 by William Allen and William Newton. It soon had a membership of 11,000 and an income of £500 a week. Payments in time of sickness and at death were considered equal in importance to allowances during strikes and periods of unemployment. A union similar to the A.S.E. was the Amalgamated Society of Carpenters and Joiners, founded in 1860.

London Trades Council, 1860

The London Trades Council, formed in 1860, was another sign of the improved organization of the trade union movement. It was brought into being by the secretaries of some of the larger societies whose headquarters were in London. Controlled by a junta of five officers, it gave legal assistance all over the country. Similar trades councils sprang up in the large towns.

Royal Commission on Trade Unions, 1867

The growing power of trade unions was viewed with disfavour by employers. Some isolated acts of violence, which were condemned by the better unions, led to a demand for the suppression of these bodies. Since 1825 unions had had no legal status as corporations and therefore could not take action to prosecute officers who absconded with union funds. A royal commission met in 1867 to report on the situation. Some unions had tried to protect their funds by registering as friendly societies under the Friendly Societies Act of 1855, but were not upheld by law-courts.

The majority report of the commission of 1867 was not favourable towards unions, though it recommended relaxation of the Combination Laws, registration of trade unions, protection of their funds, and separation of funds intended for friendly benefits from those designed for trade purposes. A minority report maintained that the larger unions contributed to the stability of trade, while acts of violence had occurred chiefly where there was no union or where the union was weak. Protection for union funds was afforded by the Trade Unions (Protection of Funds) Act of 1869, but this was only a temporary measure.

Trade Union Act, 1871 (Gladstone)

The Trade Union Act of 1871, largely based on the minority report of the royal commission, strengthened the position of the unions. It provided that the purposes of a trade union should not be illegal merely because they were in restraint of trade. A trade union was empowered, but not compelled, to register with the Registrar of Friendly Societies, to whom it was to furnish the address of its office and an annual statement of its expenditure and the extent of its funds. Any registered union was enabled to hold land or buildings, and to bring or defend itself against actions at law. Treasurers of a trade union were compelled to render to the union exact accounts of all monies received by them, and became liable to prosecution for misappropriation of any funds entrusted to them.

A setback to union activity followed, for this right to combine was largely destroyed by the Criminal Law Amendment Act of the same year, which imposed heavy penalties on men found guilty of picketing and intimidation. It became impossible to strike legally and effectively.

Conspiracy and Protection of Property Act, 1875 (Disraeli)

The Conservatives undertook by the Conspiracy and Protection of Property Act of 1875 to legalize picketing and to re-establish the right of workmen to bargain with their employers (and to make that right effective by withholding their labour, if necessary). The act provided that any action or proposed action of two or more persons in connection with a labour dispute should not be regarded as a conspiracy punishable at law if such an action committed by one person only would not be treated as a crime. The Criminal Law Amendment Act was repealed. The Employers and Workmen Act of 1875 also benefited trade unionists by giving them legal parity in the matter of contracts with their employers. (See page 362.)

Growth of Unions among Unskilled Workers

During the 1870s a large number of new unions were formed, but the great trade depression which began at this time had a prejudicial effect on the fortunes of the movement. Unemployment caused union membership and funds to fall. In 1872 Joseph Arch formed the Union of Agricultural Workers, but it ceased to exist in 1894, having met with much resistance from employers (The National Union of Agricultural Workers started only after the First World War.)

Unskilled workers tended to be sceptical of the advantages of trade unionism. Their wages were lower, so it was out of the question for them to make substantial contributions to union funds. In the event of a strike, unskilled workers could be replaced much more easily than skilled workers. Nevertheless, unions of the unskilled came into being. Gas workers, under the leadership of John Burns, Tom Mann, Ben Tillett and Will Thorne, pressed for a substantial reduction in hours of work in 1889, and secured their demands without a strike. A match-girls' strike organized by Annie Besant took place in 1888, and though the girls had neither organization nor funds they won their case, the public raising subscriptions for them. In the summer of 1889, dock workers of the Port of London embarked upon a strike for a minimum wage of sixpence an hour; again, there was much public sympathy, and the strike was successful. These successes caused other unions of the unskilled to be formed.

Miners and Railwaymen

In 1893, mine-owners demanded a 10 per cent cut in wages, which provoked a fifteen-week stoppage in the coal-mines and violence in South Wales. An acute shortage of house-coal arose. In 1898 a six-month strike of coal miners took place backed by the Amalgamated Society of Engineers, but it ended in defeat.

Railway workers were slow to form unions, their earliest union being formed in 1871. The Amalgamated Society of Railway Servants was not formed until 1890 and then was not recognized by the companies.

Towards the end of the nineteenth century, trade unionists began to give more support to the growing Labour movement.

Taff Vale Case, 1901

Early in the twentieth century the trade union movement suffered two severe blows. In 1900 a strike occurred among men employed by the Taff Vale Railway Company which brought an action for damages against the

Robert Owen's model cotton mill at New Lanark.

Amalgamated Society of Railway Servants. The union, which had considered itself covered by the Trade Union Act of 1871 and the Conspiracy and Protection of Property Act of 1875, was ordered to pay the company the sum of £23,000. If similar actions took place, the unions would soon lose all their funds.

Trade Disputes Act, 1906

The presence of twenty-nine members of the Labour Representation Committee in the Parliament of 1906 helped to forward the trade union cause. By the Trade Disputes Act (1906) the Liberals made peaceful picketing permissible. No trade union or any member or official of it was to be actionable at law in respect of any civil wrong committed by or on behalf of the union. When contemplating or committing an act in furtherance of a trade dispute, a man could not be charged in combination for a misdemeanour which would not be chargeable were he acting alone. This act became the charter of trade unionism.

Osborne Judgment, 1909

A second blow came with the Osborne judgment of 1909. It was customary for many trade unions to exact contributions from members for support of the Labour party. Their right to do so was contested by Mr. W. Osborne, a member of the Amalgamated Society of Railway Servants, and his view was ultimately upheld by the courts and by the House of Lords. The Osborne judgment took the Labour party and the trade union movement by surprise. It was a shattering blow to the finances of the Labour party, though payment of M.P.s in 1911 offered some relief.

Trade Union Activity, 1910-13

An atmosphere of violence prevalent in the years before the outbreak of the First World War affected trade union activity. French Syndicalism had an influence which caused some trade unionists to aim at paralysing the State by direct action. Lightning strikes and sympathetic strikes became frequent. In 1910 a strike in north-east England affected the shipbuilding industry: it lasted fourteen weeks, and cost the Boilermakers' Society £100,000 in strike pay. In 1911 there were great strikes of firemen, transport workers and railwaymen. In 1911 the London dockers successfully raised their rate from sixpence to eightpence an hour. In 1912 miners came out all over the country in a strike involving one million men. The government, after employing troops to keep order, ended the miners' strike by securing the passage of a Minimum Wage Act.

Absorbed by their struggle with the Conservative House of Lords over the budget of 1909, the Liberals waited until 1913 before they partially reversed the Osborne judgment. Trade unions were then permitted to engage in political activity and to raise funds for that purpose, though such activity had first to be approved by a majority ballot of members. Political funds were to be kept separate from other funds; and, after giving notice, an individual member could contract out, though in fact few did.

Post-War Period, 1918-39

The post-war slump of 1921 brought trouble among miners. They objected to the return of their industry to private control, and to a reduction in wages. A lock-out took place, lasting several months, but the triple alliance of miners, railwaymen and transport workers broke down, and the miners had to admit defeat. The stoppage cost the country £250,000,000. To meet a decline in profits in 1926, mine-owners asked for a further reduction in wages and a longer working day; their request caused a strike which became national. Though the famous General Strike of 1926 lasted only a week, the miners fought on for seven months and then gave in, their strike funds being completely exhausted.

Trades Disputes Act, 1927

The Conservative government (1924-29) took the opportunity to avert further general strikes by introducing the Trades Disputes Act of 1927 which prohibited strikes intended to coerce the government or inflict hardship on the community. Trade unionists were also to announce their intention of contributing towards political funds. Many did not take the trouble. Widespread unemployment weakened the trade union movement as a whole, and it did not fully recover until after the Second World War. (The Labour Government of 1945-50 repealed the Trades Disputes Act in 1946.)

Trades Union Congress

The Trades Union Congress was set up in 1868, and most unions became affiliated to it. The functions of its General Council, established in 1920, are to adjust disputes among trade unions, to watch over conduct of individual unions in the interests of the movement as a whole, and to take a special interest in labour legislation. It is now a powerful organ in the nation's economic structure.

QUESTIONS

1. Trace the development of the Trade Union Movement from 1867 to 1939.
2. Show the importance in the development of the British Trade Union Movement of the following: The London Dockers' Strike, 1889; the Taff Vale Judgment, 1901; the Osborne Judgment, 1909; the General Strike, 1926.

CHAPTER 60

IRELAND, 1780-1848

THE history of Anglo-Irish relations is a record of inter-racial hatred, bloodshed and broken promises. Bitterness created by the Irish rebellion of 1641, in which thousands of Protestants were slain, and by Cromwell's barbarous retaliation in 1649, lived on into the eighteenth century. Only very wise statesmanship could have established permanent peace in Ireland.

Irish Grievances

For the greater part of the eighteenth century Ireland was quiescent, largely because of the numbing effect of the penal laws of William III's reign, which left Roman Catholics with almost no civil rights, although they made up about 90 per cent of the population. Spirited Irishmen left the country.

Religious discontent was strong, for Irish Catholics were expected to contribute tithes to the Anglican Church in Ireland, which served only about one-seventh of the people and whose bishops were often absent in England. To the Irish it was an alien church. Their own priests were not officially recognized.

The agrarian situation in Ireland also bred discontent. Absentee Protestant landlords, who owned the bulk of the land, employed bailiffs to manage it for them. Peasants received no encouragement to improve standards of farming, and therefore endeavoured to support large families from the growth of potatoes. The land deteriorated, and in times of diseased crops hundreds of people starved.

The Irish had their own parliament at Dublin, but it represented Protestants only and was even more narrowly-based and corrupt than its British counterpart. Moreover by Poyning's Law of 1494, it was subject to the Privy Council in England; and by the Declaratory Act of 1719, acts passed in the British parliament were to be applied to Ireland over the head of the Irish parliament, which was therefore not really an independent assembly at all. Thus the Irish had no political freedom.

The commercial development of Ireland was selfishly stifled by laws passed in Britain, the aim of which was to prevent any competition for British traders and farmers. Cattle and pigs were not to be imported into Britain from Ireland, and yet they were essential products of Irish agriculture.

Early in the reign of George III a party arose within the Protestant Irish

Funeral during the Irish famine of 1846. As a result of the famine about two million emigrants left Ireland between 1846-61.

parliament which began to agitate for greater freedom. Its leaders were Henry Flood (who entered parliament in 1759 and who, by his fiery eloquence, induced the English government to recognize the exclusive right of the Irish parliament to introduce its own money bills) and Henry Grattan, an even more eloquent and forceful figure. Grattan entered the Irish parliament in 1775, the year fighting began in North America. George III's government, hard-pressed across the Atlantic, withdrew forces from Ireland, though American privateers like Paul Jones were operating in Irish waters. Lord Charlemont and Grattan raised a force of eighty thousand patriotic volunteers to defend the country. Grattan skilfully used the presence of this force to demand free trade for Ireland. In 1780 bills were passed in the Westminster parliament which established almost complete commercial equality between Great Britain and Ireland.

Two years later, in 1782, Rockingham's government repealed both Poyning's Law and the Declaratory Act of 1719, and the Irish parliament became independent. It enjoyed its new independence for eighteen years.

Ireland and the French Revolution

Inevitably the French revolution caused excitement in Ireland, and in 1791 the Society of United Irishmen was formed, whose aim was to unite Protestant and Catholic to win complete independence from Britain by force, using French help if need be. Pitt's grant of the vote to Catholics in 1793 won little gratitude, for still only Protestants could be elected to the Irish parliament. The leaders of the United Irishmen were Theobald Wolfe Tone, a young and able barrister, and Lord Edward Fitzgerald.

Pitt made a disastrous mistake in 1794, when he sent Lord Fitzwilliam to Ireland as Lord Lieutenant. Fitzwilliam was known to be friendly to the Catholic cause, but he went beyond the wishes of his government colleagues by promising Catholic Emancipation, and was promptly recalled. This convinced many Irishmen that they could expect no further concessions from the British government unless violence were used.

Irish Rebellion, 1798

In 1796 a French force under General Hoche reached Bantry Bay, only to be dispersed by a storm. Martial law was proclaimed and leaders of the United Irishmen rounded up, Fitzgerald being shot in Dublin when resisting arrest. In 1798 a terrible rebellion of Irish peasants flared up. Under their priests, they fought ferociously against regular British troops and Protestant yeomanry, both sides being guilty of atrocities. Lord Lake defeated the rebels at Vinegar Hill, but shortly afterwards another small French force reached Ireland; it landed at Killala Bay, only to be easily captured. Among the party was Wolfe Tone, who committed suicide while in custody.

Act of Union, 1800

With Britain engaged in a fierce struggle against revolutionary France, Pitt decided that it was necessary to tie Ireland and Britain more closely together in order to avoid such terrible distractions as the 1798 rebellion. In the General Election of 1799 in Ireland, Lord Lieutenant Cornwallis and Chief Secretary Castlereagh were called upon to use every bit of influence they could to secure a majority favourable to union. Honours, places and pensions were liberally scattered. To secure Catholic support for an Act of Union, promises were made which included exemption from payment of tithes to the Anglican Church, payment of salaries to the Roman Catholic priesthood, and above all Catholic Emancipation: but these promises were not kept, and the Act of Union was therefore doomed to fail. Accepted by the Irish parliament in 1800 and ratified by the British parliament, the act provided that:

(*a*) Britain and Ireland should have a common king, parliament, army and flag;
(*b*) Ireland should be represented in the British parliament by one hundred elected members in the Commons and twenty-eight elected peers in the Lords, who were to be joined by four bishops;
(*c*) Free trade should be established between the two countries;
(*d*) The Irish should contribute two-seventeenths of the revenue of the United Kingdom.

The Act of Union brought about the resignation of Pitt, for George III refused to sanction Catholic Emancipation, maintaining that to do so would cause him to break his coronation oath. It would have been wiser of Pitt to have been sure of the king's feelings before allowing Catholic Emancipation to be promised to the Irish. Inevitably the Irish felt that they had been cheated. Instead of bringing economic benefit, complete free trade caused Irish industries to wilt under the impact of British competition. To find their share of the revenue of the combined countries the Irish had to borrow heavily and to raise more in indirect taxation, which increased the burdens of the poor. Religious and agrarian grievances were left untouched. It is not surprising, therefore, that Irishmen remained discontented, and that they worked throughout the nineteenth century to secure repeal of the Act of Union.

Daniel O'Connell, 1775-1847

In Daniel O'Connell the Irish found a leader of genius. A lawyer by profession and a powerful orator, he saw how to use force of numbers without pursuing a policy of bloodshed and violence. He had disapproved of the rebellion of 1798. His aims were chiefly political and religious, his programme included a completely independent Irish parliament, emancipation of Catholics, and disendowment of the Anglican Church in Ireland; but he also demanded fixity of tenure for the peasant, compulsory leasing of land, and taxation of absentee landlords. He was known to the Irish as "the Liberator." It took courage to oppose agrarian crime, but O'Connell consistently did so. He never wished to sever all connection with Great Britain.

In 1823 O'Connell formed the Catholic Association, to which Irish peasants contributed one penny per month. By 1825 the association had an income of £1,000 per week and a reserve of £10,000. O'Connell and his friends began to fight elections in Ireland, though it was still legally impossible for a Catholic to take his seat in the British parliament. They took steps to protect tenant supporters from intimidation by landlords. O'Connell himself contested and won the County Clare election of 1828 against a popular and generous Protestant landlord, Vesey Fitzgerald. This success convinced Wellington that civil war in Ireland would be averted only by Catholic Emancipation. In 1829 all important offices were opened to Roman Catholics except the monarchy, the woolsack and the viceroyalty. As usual, any gratitude which the Irish might have felt was destroyed, for the Irish forty-shilling freeholders were promptly deprived of their vote to prevent O'Connell from gaining too much control, the voting qualification being fixed at £10 per year.

It was now O'Connell's aim to secure what he could from the Whigs. In the face of fierce opposition the Whigs relieved the poorest Irishmen from payment of tithes in 1832. In 1833 they abolished ten Anglican sees in Ireland and taxed the remaining bishoprics and richer benefices; but these measures brought little benefit to the majority of Irishmen. O'Connell, who disliked

Peel, used his influence to bring about Peel's defeat in 1835, making the Lichfield House Compact with the Whigs who introduced the poor law to Ireland, reformed Irish corporations, and agreed to settle the tithe problem. In 1838 tithes were replaced by a rent charge of about three-quarters of the value of the tithes. Nevertheless, O'Connell was disappointed by the results of co-operation with the Whigs. Serious problems were untouched.

When Peel and the Tories came into office in 1841, O'Connell felt that he had little to hope for from them, especially when Peel drafted more troops to Ireland and spoke against repeal of the Act of Union. O'Connell had begun to agitate by means of mass meetings; one such meeting was organized at Clontarf in 1843, but Peel firmly banned it, and O'Connell gave way. This cost him his influence among the Irish, who regarded it as a tame submission. He suffered a year's imprisonment, subsequently left the country, and died at Genoa in 1847. Peel increased the grant to Maynooth College from £9,000 to £26,000 as a conciliatory measure.

Depression and Disunity

Failure of the Irish potato crop in 1845 and 1846 led to the repeal of the Corn Laws (see pages 335-6) because of the starvation of many thousands of Irish men, women and children. Between 1845 and 1850 more than one million people are said to have died of famine. Measures for relief were inadequate, for there was a complete lack of trained officials to direct them. In 1846, 100,000 emigrants left Ireland, and 200,000 in 1847. Similar numbers left in each year from 1849 to 1851, and another million between 1851 and 1861. Emigrants spread their hatred of Britain wherever they went, but particularly in North America, and Ireland's population was reduced by a half.

Young Ireland

O'Connell's influence gave way to the Young Ireland movement, inspired by the Young Italy movement of Mazzini, an Italian nationalist. Its leaders were Thomas Meagher, John Martin, Charles Duffy, Smith O'Brien and John Dillon. Aiming at independence from Britain, they achieved little, for they quarrelled among themselves and lacked powers of organization. They tried to provoke a revolt in 1848 when most of Europe was disturbed by revolutions, but their movement, which served to bridge the gulf between the fall of O'Connell and the rise of the Fenian movement, soon collapsed.

QUESTIONS

1. What circumstances and events led to the Act of Union with Ireland? Summarize the terms of the Act.
2. What did Daniel O'Connell achieve for Ireland?

CHAPTER 61

IRELAND, 1848-1939

AFTER O'Connell's death and the passing of the Young Ireland movement, the Fenian society took up the task of fighting for the liberties of Ireland. The society was American in origin and was founded in 1858 but made little progress in Ireland until 1865. Arms and money were smuggled in from the United States, and violent action was taken in England in 1867 when, in attempts to rescue captured Fenians, a policeman in Manchester and twelve people at Clerkenwell in London were killed; but the vigorous life of the society was short-lived. By 1867 it had ceased to be dangerous. Yet it had served to bring the affairs of Ireland firmly before the British public.

Gladstone's Early Measures

In 1868, Gladstone, now Prime Minister, made it his first task to reduce discontent in Ireland. He decided to deal with religious and agrarian

Parnell, the Irish nationalist, is depicted in this cartoon as Dr. Jekyll and Mr. Hyde. He is shown peacefully negotiating with Gladstone (left), then as "Captain Moonlight" he is shown ready to attack him.

grievances. The Irish Church Disestablishment Act of 1869 disestablished and disendowed the Anglican Church in Ireland, relieving Roman Catholic Irishmen of the burden of paying tithes to an alien church.

The agrarian problem was more intricate. Too many peasants competed for too little land, and they had no security of tenure or compensation for improvement. Methods were crude and led to impoverishment of the soil. Their answer to problems was a violence which alienated British sympathies.

After studying the problem for three months Gladstone secured the passage of his first Irish Land Act in 1870. It limited a landlord's powers of arbitrary eviction and it enforced compensation, establishing a scale of damages for eviction, the scale varying according to the size of holding. But it was not a success. Unscrupulous landlords could evade its provisions by raising rents beyond the amount that tenants could afford. Gladstone failed to satisfy the demand for fair rents and fixity of tenure, and the agricultural depression of 1875 increased the difficulties of tenants. Two years earlier, however, the Home Government Association of Ireland had been founded in Dublin and Home rule was henceforth to be in the centre of Irishmen's attention for the next fifty years.

Rise of Charles Stewart Parnell

The Secret Ballot Act of 1872 had consequences in Ireland which were not foreseen by its authors. It enabled Irish voters to return Irish Nationalists without fear of intimidation. Charles Stewart Parnell, a young landowner of Wicklow County, was very quick to see this possibility. Though a Protestant, he was imbued with a passionate hatred of Britain only matched by his intense love for Ireland. Humourless and ungenerous, he gained rapid control over the Irish Nationalist party by sheer force of character. In 1874, sixty home rulers were returned to the British parliament and were led by the moderate Isaac Butt. Parnell entered parliament at a by-election in 1875, and established a reputation as an obstructionist in 1877, twice keeping the House sitting all through the night. By 1878 he had ousted Butt from the leadership of the Irish party.

Davitt and the Irish Land League

In 1879, Michael Davitt, an ex-Fenian who had served almost eight years in prison, founded the Irish Land League. By 1880, therefore, the British government was faced with a revolutionary party at Westminster and another in the Irish countryside.

Gladstone's Second Irish Land Act, 1881

The problems of Ireland now dominated British politics. A tremendous burst of outrages took place in which ricks were burned, cattle maimed,

GEORGIAN MANSION AND GROUNDS

SCENES FROM LATE GEORGIAN TIMES

houses fired, and graves dug before the front doors of unpopular landlords by the followers of "Captain Moonlight." Gladstone's second Irish Land Act gave Irish tenants fixity of tenure, fair rents and free sale (the "three F's"). It ensured that a tenant could not be evicted if he paid his rent, that the rent should not be excessive, and that he could sell his lease without his landlord's permission to anyone who would give him a fair price for it. In this way he could secure compensation for improvements. The completeness of the measure astonished both English and Irish members, but Gladstone's praiseworthy efforts were marred by the intransigence of Parnell and by the Phoenix Park murders of 1882 (see page 371).

First Home Rule Bill, 1886

The agrarian problem was eased further when the Conservatives under Salisbury introduced the first state-aided scheme of Irish land purchase by Lord Ashbourne's act of 1885. Parnell cared not from whom he obtained home rule, but in 1886 he lent his support to Gladstone's Liberals. Converted to home rule, Gladstone introduced his first Home Rule Bill in the same year, but it was defeated in the Commons (see pages 372-3), and brought the downfall of his ministry.

Balfour and Ireland

During the second Salisbury ministry (1886-92) Salisbury's nephew, A. J. Balfour, was Chief Secretary for Ireland and revealed unexpected firmness. He had to face a plan of campaign by which tenants on each Irish estate were to unite to deal with the landlord. If their offers of rent were not accepted by him, they were to pay the money to a campaign fund. The scheme was promoted by William O'Brien and John Dillon, though Parnell privately disapproved of it. Wholesale evictions followed. Balfour skilfully piloted through a new and drastic Crimes Act to enable the government to suppress disorder. It coincided with publication in *The Times* of a letter dated 1882, purporting to be signed by Parnell, in which he appeared to condone the Phoenix Park murders. Though Parnell denounced the letter as a forgery, it stimulated resentment in Britain against Irish violence. The Crimes Act embodied some concessions to Irish tenants, but three years of warfare between Irish peasants and the British government followed. Three Irishmen were shot at Mitchelstown, and for long afterwards Irish Nationalists used the phrase "remember Mitchelstown" as a rallying cry.

Fall of Parnell

The Times letter proved to be the forgery of a disreputable journalist called Pigott who, when on trial, fled from the witness box and sought asylum in Spain where, after admitting his guilt, he committed suicide. His confession brought Parnell a wave of sympathy and cost *The Times* £250,000. The newspaper had already paid £30,000 for the material it had published! The sympathy that Parnell had gained and the improved prospects for the Irish cause were swept away, however, when Parnell was cited as correspondent in a divorce suit. The Liberals insisted on a change of leadership in the Irish party, which was divided on the issue, forty-four members seceding to Justin McCarthy and twenty-six remaining with Parnell. It took the Irish party some time to regain its unity after Parnell's death in 1891. In that year Balfour steered a valuable Land Purchase Act through Parliament to enable tenants to become proprietors.

Wyndham's Irish Land Purchase Act, 1903

After the defeat of Gladstone's Second Home Rule Bill in 1893, another attack was made on the Irish agrarian problem.

George Wyndham, Chief Secretary for Ireland under Balfour, was responsible for the Land Purchase Act of 1903, one of the most statesmanlike and successful measures ever achieved by any British government in dealing with Ireland. A large cash contribution was made to bridge the gap between what landlords could afford to accept and what tenants could pay. The aim of the act was to provide a means by which the Irish peasant could become the proprietor of his land. He was able to borrow money and to repay it at 3 per cent interest over sixty-nine years. He proved to be very conscientious in making repayments, and the scheme worked well until the Free State Government of Southern Ireland intercepted and appropriated the payments in 1932.

Third Irish Home Rule Bill, 1912, and Rebellion

During the first decade of the twentieth century the agrarian problem was steadily eased by the operation of new land purchase schemes. The leader of the Irish Nationalist party, John Redmond, a great orator, did not hate the British as Parnell had done; but more rebellious and violent organizations had arisen, such as the Gaelic League, the Irish Republican Army and Sinn Fein ("Ourselves alone"), to question the value of moderation.

The Liberal government of 1906-15 was sympathetic towards the cause of home rule, but was too heavily involved in its struggle with the Conservative House of Lords to deal with the matter before 1912. It then introduced a bill which reduced Irish representation in the Imperial parliament to forty-two members and arranged for an Irish parliament at Dublin similar to that which exists in Belfast today.

Since 1886 the Protestant community of Ulster had acquired a much stronger self-consciousness. Belfast was now bigger than Dublin. Yet Redmond knew that he would be expected to obtain home rule with control

1867. *In Manchester an attack on a prison van to release arrested Fenians caused the death of a policeman. The three Fenians executed for his murder became known as the "Manchester Martyrs."*

over Ulster, to which he was prepared to give all safeguards short of exclusion from the new Ireland. Unionist opponents of the Liberals in Britain deliberately stimulated opposition in Ulster to the Home Rule Bill and by 1910 a powerful lawyer, Sir Edward Carson, became leader of the Ulstermen. By 1912 a force of eighty thousand Ulster volunteers existed. Asquith, the Liberal Prime Minister, knew that he could not coerce Ulster, and was himself unenthusiastic about home rule. The third Home Rule Bill passed through the Commons but was twice rejected by the Lords, who held up its operation for two years by the powers left them in the Parliament Act of 1911 (see page 426) and had to be abandoned when the First World War began in 1914.

Irish trade unionists began to organize violent strikes. In Dublin a force of Irish Volunteers sprang up to rival the Ulster Volunteers. By 1914 civil war in Ireland seemed imminent and British army officers mutinied at Curragh, near Dublin, rather than enforce home rule upon Ulster. From Larne thirty thousand rifles and three million rounds of ammunition were run in to the Ulster Volunteers who were outnumbered by Nationalist Volunteers. A conference between Bonar Law (the Conservative leader), Asquith, Carson and Redmond, was called by George V, but produced no agreement. Then the First World War drew attention from Irish affairs.

The 1916 Rebellion

In 1916 the Sinn Fein group organized a rebellion, and precious British troops had to be used to suppress it. It was partly German-inspired: Sir Roger Casement landed from a German submarine to direct it, but he was captured and shot as a traitor. His Irish patriotism has subsequently been tacitly recognized by Britain.

Irish Free State

The election of 1918 in Ireland swept away the old Irish Nationalist party and eighty Sinn Fein republicans were returned. They attempted to set up an independent government at Dublin. Two years of bloodshed followed in which the Irish Republican Army fought against British troops and the special auxiliary police, the Black and Tans. Both sides were guilty of atrocities. In 1920 the British coalition government passed the fourth Home Rule Bill, which amounted to repeal of the Union; but the Sinn Feiners still demanded complete independence for the whole island. Agreement was finally reached in 1921 and in 1922 the Irish Free State Act was passed.

All except north-east Ireland was to become a free state with the status of a Dominion. Extremists who remained dissatisfied had to be suppressed violently in a famous battle in Dublin directed by the new Irish government. At last the Irish problem was settled; but the I.R.A. has continued to work for possession of Ulster.

Relations between the new Irish Free State and Britain were not happy, especially when extreme Republicans came into power under de Valera in 1932. They wanted to sever all connexion with the British Crown, and they stopped payments of money owed to the British and waged a tariff war. Eire's refusal to allow Britain to use her ports during the Second World War was a severe handicap. In 1949 she severed her connexion with the Commonwealth and became, in effect, a foreign country. Bitter memories of strife between the two countries, the unfortunate legacy of centuries of misunderstanding, have not yet wholly faded away.

QUESTIONS

1. Describe Parnell's part in the Irish home rule movement.
2. Explain the importance of the Irish land problem, and describe attempts to solve it during the period 1870-1914.

CHAPTER 62

INDUSTRY AND AGRICULTURE AFTER 1870

THE success of free trade between 1850 and 1870 and a long industrial lead over other powers gave Britain a spell of unprecedented prosperity during the third quarter of the nineteenth century, but after 1870 she experienced increasing competition, and agriculture went into a severe decline. Her strength in 1851 was testified by the success of the Great Exhibition. In 1870 British trade exceeded that of France, Germany and Italy put together.

Iron, Steel and Coal

The supremacy of iron in industry was threatened when Henry Bessemer patented his process for manufacturing steel cheaply in 1856, but it was only in the 1870's that steel began to oust iron. The other process for making steel on a large scale was the Siemens-Martin open-hearth process of 1867. The fact that the Bessemer and Siemens-Martin processes could make use of non-phosphoric ores only was a distinct advantage to Britain, because the main sources of these ores were Spain and Sweden and ore could be imported cheaply to Middlesbrough, South Wales and Barrow-in-Furness; French and German coalfields, well inland, could not advantageously import the raw material, whilst the abundant native supplies of ores were phosphoric.

Paradoxically it was an Englishman, Sidney Gilchrist-Thomas, who discovered how to make steel from phosphoric ores. Experiments in South Wales proved the success of his discovery in 1876. When his discovery reached Germany, Britain lost her advantage in the steel industry although most of her own ores were phosphoric. The development of the gigantic German steel industry in the later stages of the nineteenth century was dependent on the Gilchrist-Thomas method, and would have been impossible without it.

By 1895 Germany's output surpassed Britain, and competition led to curtailment of Britain's trade in steel in the middle eighties. Competition also came from the United States; in 1900 production figures were: America 10,188,000 tons, Germany 6,260,000 tons, the United Kingdom 4,901,000 tons and France 1,540,000 tons. By 1903 Germany also surpassed Britain in pig-iron production. America and Germany made steel in larger and more efficient plants than Britain. In 1908 German steel output doubled the British, yet Germans sold much of their steel to Britain more cheaply than it could be bought in Germany. This was to Britain's advantage because the steel was turned into more remunerative ships, machinery and tinplate. Though Britain lost her lead, she remained a major industrial power.

Before 1871 Britain consistently produced more than half the world's coal supply, but after that year her share decreased. American and German production was greatly expanded during the last phase of the century, and their mining methods were superior to those of Britain.

Reasons for Britain's Decline as the "Workshop of the World"

A number of reasons for the decline of Britain's industrial lead have already been mentioned, such as the discovery of the Gilchrist-Thomas method of producing steel (which helped Germany and France to use their native ores) and the vast increase of American and German competition; but there were other factors at work. German higher education was superior, and enabled her to establish long leads in the chemical and electrical industries. American industrialists were more open to new ideas than conservative British firms. The large corporations of America and state-supported concerns of Germany found more capital for research. British industrial leadership during the nineteenth century bred lethargy and self-complacency. British trade unions, growing stronger throughout the period, exercised a drag on production by their reluctance to see too great an increase in output per man in case it reduced the demand for labour.

Britain found it more and more difficult to sell her main products because of the erection of hostile tariff barriers by states who wished to protect growing native industries. Germany turned to protection in 1879, Russia in 1881 and 1882, and France in 1882; America adopted the same policy. Even within the British Empire high tariffs were imposed by Canada and by Victoria (Australia) in 1879. Britain's answer was to increase exports of machinery, coal and ships, but these increased the ability of foreign powers to compete with British manufactured goods and to dispense with the services of the British mercantile marine. Exported coal could have been more profitably used in British blast furnaces and factories.

Agricultural Decline

Between 1850 and 1870 British agriculture flourished, but thereafter it declined rapidly, largely because of the sudden invasion of American prairie wheat in the 1870's. The rise of prairie wheat in America can be attributed to three factors: the building of railways across the prairies, a sudden abundance of steamer transport, and the introduction of agricultural machinery. Land was cheap in the prairie region, railway freight charges were low, and the soil was fertile. European agriculture was not inefficient, but could not meet prairie prices. The plains of America were ideal for farm machines. By 1879 most European states had to impose a tariff or lose their wheatfields; but two

Iron and steel works at Hindpool near Barrow-in-Furness in 1867.

states failed to do so, Belgium and Britain! The blow inflicted on the British farmer could not have come at a worse time, because from 1875 to 1879 a series of wet summers ruined harvests. A world monetary depression at the same time depressed meat and dairy prices. As if that were not enough, rinderpest visited Britain in 1877, and liver-rot spread among sheep in 1879 and caused the loss of millions of animals. Finally a terrible outbreak of foot-and-mouth disease occurred in 1883.

By 1885 the area under wheat had shrunk by 30 per cent, and between 1871 and 1881 the number of farm labourers at work decreased by 92,250. The decline had disastrous social effects, since as late as the 1890s agriculture employed more people than any other industry. Import of frozen meat from abroad did not, as some have asserted, contribute to the decline of British agriculture, because while it grew rapidly so also did home production of meat, to feed the rapidly-growing population of the cities.

Between 1890 and 1900 British wheatfields shrank to only half the 1870 acreage, although in the early twentieth century there was a slight revival.

Inter-War Years, 1918-39

After the First World War there was a short period of brisk trade, followed by a slump in 1922. Goods piled up in warehouses and unemployment grew. Britain, heavily in debt to the United States, had lost half her overseas investments in paying for the war. Pre-war customers were too impoverished to buy British goods, and much industrial equipment was obsolete. Britain could not compete with America in salesmanship. Lancashire cotton, one of Britain's main exporting industries, met with increasing competition from the cotton exports of India and Japan, which were cheap because of the abundance in those countries of cheap labour. After a brief boom, the coal industry suffered from competition offered by oil, from out-dated methods, and from quarrels between labour and management. Britain also lost her shipping lead, her share of the world's tonnage declining from 39 per cent in 1914 to 26 per cent in 1937.

During the First World War British farms recovered their long-lost prosperity because of the desperate need for food; but between 1921 and 1931 there was an annual fall of 21,000 in the numbers employed in agriculture.

Recovery was gradual, but it did come. Large concerns, for example, Richard Thomas and Baldwin, Imperial Chemical Industries, Lever Brothers and Tate and Lyle, had resources of capital to undertake research, and gained control over the raw materials which they needed and all the processes required to make their products. New industries grew, such as the motor, electrical and radio industries.

Safeguarding of Industries Act, 1921

Britain concluded that she must protect her industries. By the Safeguarding of Industries Act of 1921 the government was empowered to impose a tax of 33⅓ per cent on dyestuffs, drugs and scientific instruments; the list was soon extended. The economic crisis of 1931 led to further protection by the Import Duties Act of 1932.

After 1931 the government adopted a policy of state aid for agriculture which has been pursued ever since. Marketing Boards were set up for milk, bacon, pigs, potatoes and hops to control sale, grading, advertising and transport. In 1934 cattle-breeders received a state subsidy. British agriculture has since become economically much stronger.

In 1933 the number of unemployed in Britain reached the disastrous figure of three million, but by 1937 it had been reduced to half this figure. By 1936 overseas investments had reached £4,000,000,000, the 1913 figure. It is sad to record that preparation for the oncoming war with Hitler's Germany was an important factor contributing to Britain's economic recovery.

QUESTIONS

1. Explain Britain's failure to maintain her position as "Workshop of the World."

2. Describe the difficulties experienced by British agriculture in the period 1875-1914.

CHAPTER 63

DEVELOPMENT OF EDUCATION

THE Industrial Revolution raised more sharply than before the question of education. At the beginning of the nineteenth century there was no state education; governments were reluctant to accept responsibility for education, partly because it was linked with the thorny question of religious teaching, interference with which was liable to cause fierce controversy, and partly because they were slow to accept new responsibility. Yet by the end of the century an imperfect system of State education existed and the population was almost entirely literate.

At the end of the eighteenth century three kinds of schools provided elementary education for the working classes. Schools run for profit charged fees between 4*d.* and 9*d.* per week; anyone could set up such a school, and standards could be very low; Dame schools, where children were often merely "minded", were of this type. Schools supported by private subscription were run by the Nonconformist British and Foreign School Society, founded in 1814, and by the Anglican National Society, founded in 1811. These schools employed a monitorial system for reasons of economy, and used the Bible as a textbook. Their aim was to give an introduction to the three R's, "reading, 'riting and 'rithmetic." In the third group of schools available were the Charity and Sunday schools. A Charity school was usually run by a church or chapel, and Sunday schools existed to instruct young factory workers to read. Robert Raikes of Gloucester founded his first Sunday school in 1780, to keep his pupils from hooliganism on the Sabbath; Hannah More ran such schools for the children of Mendip miners.

The Beginnings of State Primary Education

The upper classes feared that to educate the poor would make them dissatisfied but soon it was realized that ignorance might be more dangerous to public tranquillity than knowledge; Shaftesbury took this view. Others pointed out that workers could hardly acquire the technical skill to keep Britain's industrial lead without being able to read and write. Whigs of the 1830s would have been content to leave the provision of education to private persons or to the Church, but Radicals and Utilitarians regarded it as a national responsibility. As a result the Whig government made a first state grant towards education in 1833 by providing £20,000, for building purposes only; half the cost had to be raised by a school's sponsors before application for government money could be made. The result was that more schools were built in better-to-do areas where the 50 per cent contribution could be more easily raised than in poorer areas. The government fund was administered by the British and Foreign School Society and the National Society, the latter receiving the greater part of the money.

Those who opposed state education for the poor said that if taxpayers bore the financial burden of education it would become unpopular, that the British would resent being forced to educate their children, and that it would place an undesirable power for propaganda in the hands of the government.

In 1837 only one-tenth of the child population of the country went to school. By 1839 the government had appointed a small Committee of the Privy Council to organize the distribution of public money, and for sixty years it was the only body with direct official interest in education. It recommended an increase in the government grant to £30,000 and the appointment of inspectors; its proposals were accepted by parliament in 1839 only after strong opposition. At this time there was little provision for adequate training of teachers, and the government refused to take responsibility for such training until 1846 when it accepted a scheme for training pupil-teachers. The state grant rose by 1848 to £125,000. In 1850 there were twenty-one government inspectors, Anglican, Roman Catholic and non-sectarian.

Payment by Results

In 1857 the Prince Consort presided over a Conference on Elementary Education which found that only two million children were at any kind of elementary school, and half of these stayed for one year only. A Commission met under the Duke of Newcastle in 1858 to consider "the extension of sound and cheap elementary instruction to all classes of people." Only one child in eight was found to be at school (one in seventeen in 1818), one-quarter of these being at private schools. Four-fifths of those at elementary schools left before they were twelve; more than half attended for only 100 days in the year, and two-thirds left school not having mastered the three R's. The Newcastle Commission recommended payment by results, and this was accepted by the Committee of the Privy Council and by parliament; teachers were paid according to the attendance of pupils and their success in passing a test conducted by visiting inspectors. Robert Lowe, Vice-President of the Council, administered the scheme. It was certainly economical, the education grant falling from £813,000 in 1861 to £637,000 in 1865, but in other respects it was thoroughly bad. Bright children were penalized as teachers laboured to bring slower ones to grant-earning standard. It led to cramming, and demoralized the teachers. Schools informed each other of the examination questions, and even sent dull children to a neighbouring school on the day of examination to avoid bringing down the percentage of passes. Attendance registers were sometimes falsified. Grants ceased for children over eleven, so the incentive to keep them at school was decreased. Yet this system lasted for thirty years, in spite of condemnation by inspectors; the Cross Commission of 1888 also condemned it. In 1890 it was curtailed and by 1900 it ended.

Forster Education Act, 1870

The Education Act introduced in 1870 by W. E. Forster, a Liberal Vice-President of the Council, was another landmark in the development of primary education. Forster tried to make the best of both national and voluntary agencies. He divided the country into school districts, the units being boroughs and groups of parishes, in which rate-payers were to elect special boards to provide new schools where needed. Boards could compel attendance if they thought fit. In their schools religious teaching was to be undenominational. These "Board Schools" were to receive financial assistance not only from the state but also from the local rates, which gave them an advantage over voluntary schools which received state aid only. One reason for passing the act was an increasing need for technical competence, and another the need to have an informed electorate after the extension of the franchise by the act of 1867. As Robert Lowe had said, the state must now educate its "masters." Weaknesses of the act were that it failed to establish a national system of education, it left untouched the system of payment by

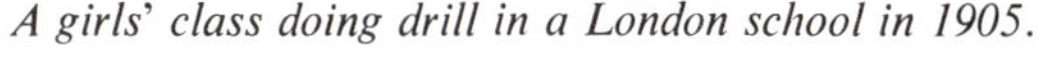

A girls' class doing drill in a London school in 1905.

results, and it applied no direct compulsion to attend, though in fact there were hardly enough schools to permit compulsion. A total of 3,500,000 children needed schooling in 1870 and there were places for only 1,878,000. Only by 1886 was comprehensive provision made.

Compulsory Attendance

Sandon's Act of 1876 declared it the duty of every parent of a child between five and thirteen, subject to a penalty, "to cause such child to receive efficient elementary instruction in reading, writing and arithmetic." Employers were forbidden to employ a child under ten, or a child between ten and thirteen who was not proficient in the three R's. The act was not entirely effective nor universal. Direct compulsion came only with the Mundella Act of 1880, by which school boards were to enforce attendance. It took six years to ensure that all children who should have been enrolled were actually on school registers. Schools were unevenly distributed and parents attempted to dodge the "school-board man" in order to send their offspring to work.

There was a great need to widen the curriculum of primary schools, and more enlightened boards began to introduce art and practical subjects; but they received a setback in 1900, when an auditor of the Local Government Board, T. B. Cockerton, brought a lawsuit against school boards for teaching certain branches of art and science and won his case. It was also ruled that school boards had no authority to provide secondary education.

Balfour Education Act, 1902

The Cockerton Judgment was nullified by the Balfour Act of 1902, largely the work of a very able civil servant, R. L. Morant. It abolished school boards; county councils and county boroughs became the education authorities. In districts of a certain size the borough or district council was permitted to administer elementary education; the actual work was done by education committees which were to include persons co-opted because of special qualifications. Rate aid was extended to voluntary schools in which local authorities were to control the secular teaching. Provision was made for training teachers under the auspices of local authorities, and not before time, for in 1902 36 per cent of existing teachers had never passed the examination for a teacher's certificate and 55 per cent had never been to a college of any kind.

Developments in Primary Education, 1902-39

The administrative structure of the Balfour Act has not been substantially altered. The Hadow reports of 1926 and 1930 recommended the introduction of the Eleven Plus test. An Education Act of 1918 raised the school-leaving age to fourteen, and another of 1936 proposed to raise it to fifteen, but its operation was held up by the outbreak of war in 1939. Since 1902 more and more children have gone on to universities.

Secondary Education

Grammar schools were endowed between the fourteenth and seventeenth centuries for the instruction of poor boys, but as time passed they were monopolized by children of the wealthier classes. Their curriculum at the beginning of the nineteenth century was narrowly classical. Some grew into public schools like Merchant Taylors, St. Paul's and Shrewsbury. A few enlightened headmasters set new standards, particularly Arnold of Rugby (1828-42), Butler of Shrewsbury (1798-1836) and Thring of Uppingham (1853-87). They improved scholarship and introduced modern history, geography and foreign languages; other schools gradually followed suit. Proprietary schools were started by persons who wished to give their sons an education similar to that in public schools, and in this way Cheltenham College (1841), Marlborough (1842) and Rossall (1844) came into being.

In 1861 the Clarendon Commission investigated the position at schools like Eton, Harrow, Westminster and Winchester, and found that classics dominated the curriculum and that teaching was not efficient. At some schools endowments were being misused.

State secondary education came into its own with the Balfour Act of 1902, which enabled local authorities to provide further education and to pay fees for scholars at secondary schools. New secondary schools were built and others aided. In 1904 there were 86,000 secondary-school pupils in England and Wales alone, but by 1943 this had increased to 514,000, more than half in local authority schools.

Education for Girls

There was little provision for higher education of girls until the mid-nineteenth century except where wealthy families engaged governesses. In 1850, however, Miss Buss started the North London Collegiate School and in 1853 Miss Beale established Cheltenham Ladies' College. University education for women began with the building of Bedford College in London (1860), Girton College (1869) and Newnham College (1871) at Cambridge, and Lady Margaret Hall and Somerville Hall at Oxford (1879). Cambridge local examinations were opened to women in 1865, and women were able to take degrees at London in 1878. This concession was granted by Oxford in 1920 and by Cambridge in 1948.

Universities

For centuries the only universities in England were Oxford and Cambridge. The Royal Commission which reported on Oxford in 1852 did not paint a rosy picture. In 1828 the Benthamites established University College, London, where a broader choice of subjects was offered than at the older universities; it was followed by Anglican King's College in 1829, the two being incorporated into London University in 1836. The University of Durham came into existence in 1837. These newer universities were cheaper than Oxford and Cambridge, and open to a much wider class, as were the Scottish Universities of Edinburgh, Aberdeen, Glasgow and St. Andrews. In 1871 the Universities Tests Act abolished religious tests at Oxford and Cambridge. An Act of 1877 required Oxford and Cambridge colleges to contribute more of their revenues to university funds, and gave the Senate at Cambridge and Convocation at Oxford more influence over heads of colleges. Late in the nineteenth and early in the twentieth centuries, universities were founded at Aberystwyth, Cardiff and Bangor (1893), Birmingham (1900), Manchester and Liverpool (1903), Leeds (1904), Sheffield (1905), and Bristol (1909). By 1914 there were university colleges at Nottingham, Newcastle, Reading, Exeter, and Southampton, all of which have subsequently become universities in their own right.

Self-Education and Adult Education

No account of educational development would be complete without mention of praiseworthy attempts to provide illiterate men and women with an elementary education carried on by churches and chapels and by Mechanics' Institutes such as that at Glasgow established in 1799. Mechanics' Institutes spread over the country in the first half of the nineteenth century to provide first technical instruction and later cultural education. Birkbeck College grew from the London Mechanics' Institute, and is now part of London University. These institutes later tended to be taken over by the middle classes.

Adult education was attempted by the Sheffield People's College (1842) and the London Working Men's College (1854). Quakers set up an Adult School at Birmingham in 1852 which still survives. The University of Cambridge instituted external lectures in 1873, Oxford following in 1878. Trade Unions and Co-operative Societies were active in providing classes. Under the inspiration of Albert Mansbridge, the Workers' Educational Association was founded in 1903. At Oxford Ruskin College came into being in 1899 as a residential college for working men.

QUESTIONS

1. Describe the work of the voluntary schools for primary education and show how this was extended by the system of state education developed after 1870.
2. What developments took place in education between 1871 and 1939?

CHAPTER 64

LORD SALISBURY

ROBERT ARTHUR CECIL was born at Hatfield, Hertfordshire, and educated at Eton and Christ Church College, Oxford, where he proved a gifted scholar.

He became M.P. for Stamford in 1853, and early in his career showed himself suspicious of democracy and resistant to change.

In 1865 he became Viscount Cranborne, and in 1866 was appointed Secretary for India in the third Derby administration, but he resigned in 1867 in opposition to Disraeli's household suffrage bill. In 1868 he succeeded his father as Marquess of Salisbury. Disraeli gave him the India Office in the 1874 ministry, and he held the post until 1878 when he replaced Lord Derby as Foreign Secretary. Opposing Russian designs in Asia, he gave his support to Lord Lytton's "forward" policy in Afghanistan.

Lord Salisbury, three times Prime Minister, and chiefly remembered for his achievements in imperial and foreign affairs.

Disraeli sent him to Constantinople in 1876, to attend a conference of Great Powers on the Balkan question. Here he established a reputation as an able diplomatist, though he failed to persuade Turkey to adopt a policy of reform. Salisbury's influence led Bismarck to summon the Congress of Berlin to secure revision of the Treaty of San Stefano, which Russian military success had forced upon the Turks. Salisbury had mastered the facts of the Eastern question more fully than any other British statesman, and Beaconsfield found him a very able lieutenant (see page 366). On Beaconsfield's death in 1881, Salisbury became Conservative leader in the House of Lords, where his party was all-powerful.

A great foreign minister, in home affairs Salisbury represented the merely anti-progressive section of his party; at a period when changing conditions called for legislative action, he nearly always stood for doing nothing.

Prime Minister, 1885

When Gladstone resigned in 1885, Salisbury agreed to form a caretaker ministry, which lasted only seven months. He protested that he disliked the office of Prime Minister, but he was to be Premier for over thirteen and a half of the next seventeen years. Two brilliant newcomers to office were Randolph Churchill (Secretary for India) and A. J. Balfour, Salisbury's nephew (President of the Local Government Board). Two episodes of note occurred during this ministry: Lower Burma was annexed in 1886, and, in order to bring Parnell's support over to the Conservatives, Lord Ashbourne's Irish Land Purchase Act was passed (see page 395). The election held in 1886, however, gave the Liberals a majority of eighty-six over the Conservatives.

Salisbury's Second Ministry, 1886-92

After the defeat of Gladstone's first Home Rule Bill in 1886, a second election was held which resulted in a Conservative victory.

The ministry was hardly established when a storm arose concerning talented Randolph Churchill, now Chancellor of the Exchequer. He planned a budget which demanded economies by the armed forces, and he could not persuade his fellow ministers to agree. He promptly resigned, thinking that he was indispensable. In fact, the Liberal Unionist Goschen proved a very capable successor.

The bright star of the administration was A. J. Balfour, now Secretary for Ireland. A new and drastic Crimes Act of 1887 strengthened the hand of those whose task it was to keep order in Ireland. Balfour had the strength to see that it was rigidly applied; even the Lord Mayor of Dublin was imprisoned at one time! It took over three years to restore order in Ireland, and meanwhile Parnell had been disgraced and had died (see pages 395-6). Then in 1891 a valuable Land Purchase Act was passed.

During the second Salisbury Ministry the "scramble for Africa" took place, and it was largely due to the restraining hands of Bismarck and Salisbury that the powers concerned did not come to blows. Salisbury co-operated in the Berlin Conference of 1884 where some provision was made for peaceful settlement of disputes over African territory. In 1890 he signed agreements with Germany, France and Portugal, and in order to obtain a balance of African advantages, made over Heligoland to Germany. France agreed to recognize British control over Zanzibar in return for British recognition of her control of Madagascar.

In Europe Salisbury recognized the union of Bulgaria and Eastern Rumelia of 1885, though it reversed the Berlin settlement of 1878 which he had helped

VICTORIAN COTTON TOWN

locomotive and carriages

first postage stamps

Albert Hall, London

iron steamship

penny-farthing bicycle

shop and street-lighting

department store

LIFE IN VICTORIAN TIMES

to negotiate. He had concluded that Turkey was not worth propping up, and that more hope lay in the rise of Balkan nationalities. He regarded France and Russia as aggressive powers, and his fears were confirmed when in 1885 Russia threatened Bulgaria and took Penjdeh at the expense of Afghanistan. Salisbury committed himself to a pact with Italy in 1887 in which Austria-Hungary joined. In that same year Bismarck wrote to the British Prime Minister, suggesting an alliance; but nothing resulted because Bismarck would not adopt an attitude of hostility towards Russia. Salisbury never took the lead in European affairs as Bismarck did; his situation and temperament were against it. He can scarcely be placed in the top flight of international statesmen, but ranks high in the second. Abroad there was high regard for his wisdom and calm temper. Backed by the strength of his country's fleet and the first-class performance of her small army, he enabled her to hold her own in world affairs.

The chief domestic achievements of Salisbury's second ministry lay in the spheres of finance, local government and education. Few Chancellors of the Exchequer have brought Goschen's financial experience to bear upon their task. He reduced income tax and duties on tea and tobacco, yet found money for local government development and free education. To meet extra naval expenditure he introduced an estate duty on real and personal estates over £10,000. By converting the national debt in 1888, he saved £1,400,000 immediately, and eventually another £3 million. The County Councils Act was passed in 1888 and elementary school fees abolished in 1891.

The election of 1892 resulted in victory for the home rulers over the Conservatives and Liberal Unionists. As a result, Salisbury became leader of the Opposition from 1892 to 1895.

Salisbury's Third Ministry, 1895-1902

When Lord Rosebery was defeated in 1895, Salisbury became Prime Minister for a third time. His ministry was a strong one, and included the Liberal Unionists Chamberlain at the Colonial Office and Lansdowne at the War Office. Sir Michael Hicks Beach was Chancellor of the Exchequer, and Salisbury acted as his own Foreign Secretary.

Britain was shocked in 1895 when President Cleveland of the U.S.A. intervened in a threatening way in a dispute of long standing between Great Britain and Venezuela over the boundary of British Guiana. Salisbury's calm approach averted any possibility of war; he agreed to submit the matter to arbitration, and in 1899 the principal British claims were recognized.

African problems occupied the attention of this ministry. In 1896 it was embarrassed by the Jameson Raid, over which Salisbury loyally defended Joseph Chamberlain when he was accused of complicity. It was during this ministry that Kitchener reconquered the Sudan by his victory over the

Dervishes at Omdurman in 1898. Salisbury's calmness again averted war, yet preserved British interests, when France and Britain clashed over the Fashoda (Sudan) incident in 1898. By agreement with Delcassé of France, the watershed between the rivers Nile and Congo was fixed as dividing the spheres of influence of the two countries. As Prime Minister, Salisbury was also responsible for the conduct of the Boer War, 1899-1902.

Salisbury became increasingly conscious of Britain's isolation in his last years of office. The Venezuelan dispute and the Boer War both emphasized the need to end it. He authorized Chamberlain's approaches to Germany in 1898 and 1899, but they bore no fruit, and he himself showed no real drive.

Salisbury was concerned at this time by the massacre of Christian Armenians by the Turks, but could do little to help them. He supported control of Crete by the Greeks, at the expense of the Turks.

Salisbury's last ministry was rather barren in social reform, possibly because the driving force in these matters was Chamberlain, and his attention was given to imperial matters. The Workmen's Compensation Act of 1897 was the sole big measure. Accidents which occurred to workmen in industry were now to be paid for by industry.

In 1900 the Khaki Election was timed to take advantage of emotions stirred by military victory. Although Unionists retained office as a result of it, their star was on the wane, and Salisbury at seventy-one was clearly ageing. He gave up the Foreign Office to Lord Lansdowne, a change which produced happy results.

Hicks Beach's careful financial husbandry as Chancellor of the Exchequer saved Britain from bearing too great a burden of debt after the Boer war. Between 1900 and 1902 he raised income tax from 8*d.* to 1*s.* 3*d.* He also increased duties on beer, spirits, tea and tobacco to help to pay for the war.

Resignation of Salisbury, 1902

Salisbury's health was failing fast by 1902 and he resigned, dying thirteen months later. Before he left office he successfully concluded the Boer war by the Treaty of Vereeniging in 1902. He had not been a man to dominate his cabinets. At home he lacked a constructive aim, although he was keen to improve the housing of the poor and to improve sanitary conditions. Under his influence the Conservatives became less forward-looking. His talents and achievements lay in the realm of foreign affairs.

QUESTIONS

1. Describe the foreign policies of Lord Salisbury.
2. Outline the important colonial issues which arose during Salisbury's ministries, and show how they were dealt with.

CHAPTER 65

BALFOUR'S MINISTRY, 1902-05

ARTHUR JAMES BALFOUR, born in 1848 in East Lothian, Scotland, was a Scottish aristocrat. Educated at Eton and Trinity College, Cambridge, he entered the House of Commons for Hatfield, Hertfordshire, in the General Election of 1874. In 1878 he accompanied his uncle, Lord Salisbury, to the Congress of Berlin. He was one of a brilliant group of young Tory politicians known as the Fourth Party which, under Lord Randolph Churchill's leadership, plagued Gladstone during his ministry of 1880-85. In 1885 he entered Salisbury's first Cabinet as President of the Local Government Board.

In 1887 Balfour succeeded Hicks Beach as Chief Secretary for Ireland in the second Salisbury ministry of 1886-92, and proved unexpectedly successful in this office (for details see Chapters 61 and 64). In 1891 he succeeded W. H. Smith as Conservative leader of the House of Commons, and became First Lord of the Treasury, a post which he continued to hold in the third Salisbury ministry of 1895-1902. During the later stages of this ministry, when Salisbury's strength was fading, it was Balfour who came forward to direct its policies.

Prime Minister, 1902-05

Balfour became Prime Minister in 1902, and in a three-year term of office accomplished much for the nation, though his ministry was followed by an overwhelming defeat for his party, for which he has always been blamed. Six memorable measures distinguish his ministry: the Education Act of 1902, the Irish Land Purchase Act of 1903, the Licensing Act of 1904, creation of the Committee of Imperial Defence in 1904, the naval reorganization of 1905, and establishment of the Anglo-French Entente.

Irish and Social Issues

Balfour's Education Act of 1902 can be regarded as one of the most constructive measures of the twentieth century. It was really the work of Robert Morant, but Balfour deserves great credit for forwarding the measure when he knew that he was sacrificing many future votes (see page 406).

Balfour's measure has worked admirably, but it kindled fierce controversy. Though Anglicans and Roman Catholics welcomed it because it saved their schools, Nonconformists were furious. They asserted that the act would place the cost of sectarian teaching on the rates. In some areas, particularly in Wales, Nonconformist children had no choice but to go to Anglican schools, and here there was resistance to payment of rates for educational purposes. Balfour and Morant remained firm and sensible in the face of opposition, with the result that education in Britain took great strides forward.

The Irish Land Purchase Act, 1903

The Irish Land Purchase Act of 1903, the work of George Wyndham, did much to create outright ownership of land by Irish peasants (for details see page 396), and was a very successful and constructive measure.

The Licensing Act, 1904

In passing the Licensing Act of 1904, Balfour's Conservatives were grasping another nettle. It provided for closing redundant public houses whose owners were to be paid compensation from a fund levied on the brewing trade. Nonconformists attacked Balfour for leaning towards the brewing interest, but there is no doubt that there were far too many "ale-houses."

Committee of Imperial Defence

During 1903 and 1904, Balfour turned the Committee of Imperial Defence into a regular organ of government with a permanent secretariat. The Prime Minister acted as its chairman. The sagacity of this step was proved during the First World War of 1914-18, when the committee was in working order and ready to direct the Imperial war effort.

The Cawdor-Fisher Naval Reforms, 1905

In 1904 Sir John Fisher became First Sea Lord. He was a restless man, forward-looking, brilliant and very determined. Prompted by the growing German naval challenge, he and Earl Cawdor, First Lord of the Admiralty, organized a redistribution of the fleet, and laid down the *Dreadnought* and the *Invincible*, prototypes of the First World War battleship and battle-cruiser.

Concluding that Germany's new fleet was directed against Great Britain, Fisher put an end to the traditional policy of scattering the fleet all over the globe, and began to concentrate it in home waters. Semi-obsolete ships, sailing death-traps, were ruthlessly scrapped, saving upkeep and crews. Three fleets were organized, one each for the Mediterranean, the Atlantic, and the Channel (based on Malta, Gibraltar and home ports respectively). The *Dreadnought* made all other battle-ships out-of-date and hit Germany very hard, for she had to widen the Kiel Canal to take ships of this calibre. Cawdor and Fisher planned to build four such ships in 1906 and another four

Mr. Balfour, representing Great Britain, speaks at the League of Nations Conference in February, 1920.

in 1907, but the Campbell-Bannerman Liberal ministry shelved this programme and Britain's advantage was lost.

In the realm of foreign affairs Balfour's ministry was also fruitful, for in 1904 Lord Lansdowne negotiated the Entente Cordiale with France after settling many differences with her (for further detail see pages 434-5). Britain's isolation was well and truly ended.

Economic Policy

Balfour's ministry was undermined by a struggle between free traders and those who wanted tariff reform. When Joseph Chamberlain came out openly in favour of tariff reform, he carried a large part of the Unionist rank and file with him. Balfour and Lansdowne sought a compromise. They were not ready to impose any general tariff or to tax food; they were only prepared to use retaliatory duties to force down foreign tariffs. This did not satisfy Chamberlain, for it did nothing for the Empire. When he and others resigned, Balfour reconstructed his Cabinet with skill and courage, bringing in Chamberlain's son Austen as Chancellor of the Exchequer and Lyttelton as Colonial Secretary.

To the Liberal opposition the tariff issue was a godsend, for it patched up the split in their ranks caused by the Boer war. They united to fight for free trade. In January, 1905, Balfour announced that he was ready to use duties to stop foreigners from dumping surplus goods on the British market, and to establish imperial preference; but it was too late to restore unity to the Conservatives.

In sanctioning the use of indentured Chinese labour in the Rand goldfield in South Africa, Balfour made his one indefensible mistake. Politically it was disastrous. Tens of thousands of young Chinese coolies were shipped thousands of miles and committed to work for years underground, cooped up in compounds when not working and shut off from contact with the outside world. The British working classes condemned Chinese "slavery"; Canada, New Zealand and Australia were offended. Balfour did not understand the attitude of the lower classes, Disraeli's alliance with the working class had disappeared, and the Conservatives had become much more of a one-class party. No other Conservative measure rivalled the use of Chinese labour as a cause of the electoral catastrophe of 1906.

The last important measure of the Balfour government was the Unemployed Workmen Act of 1905 which made provision for local unemployment committees to effect relief by voluntarily contributed funds, and to seek to provide employment for the out-of-work.

Balfour after his Premiership

The election of January, 1906, was a personal disaster for Balfour. Not only did his party suffer eclipse, but he himself failed to retain his Manchester seat. The Liberals won 377 seats, against the Unionists' 157.

Balfour found his way back into the Commons for the City of London. During the Liberal ministries of Campbell-Bannerman and Asquith, he and Lansdowne used the Conservative majority in the Lords to impede Liberal measures, a policy which can hardly be justified on any grounds.

He served as First Lord of the Admiralty, 1915-16, under Asquith, and from 1916-19 as Foreign Secretary under Lloyd George, playing an important part in the Versailles peace settlement. In 1922 he became Earl Balfour, having continued to serve in the Lloyd George coalition after 1918. He had much to do with the re-settlement of Jews in Palestine. He was never again Premier and lived on as an elder statesman until his death in 1930.

QUESTIONS

1. Discuss the achievements of the Balfour ministry, 1902-05.

2. Outline the career, and assess the importance, of A. J. Balfour.

CHAPTER 66

JOSEPH CHAMBERLAIN

JOSEPH CHAMBERLAIN was born in 1836 into a Unitarian family linked by marriage with the Nettlefold family of Birmingham, who owned a large screw-making business. Educated at University College School in London, young Joseph entered the Nettlefold business, and proved so successful that he was able to sell his interest in the firm for £120,000 in 1874 at the age of thirty-eight. Chamberlain became nationally known through the National Education League, whose aims were to expand provision of education for poor children. Then he plunged into local politics in Birmingham, forming a Liberal party caucus or party organization to defeat the reigning oligarchy there. He very soon became mayor. From his drive and administrative ability the city gained cheaper gas and water supplies, slum clearance, an art gallery, libraries and parks; Joseph Chamberlain made many enemies but never made any effort to conciliate opponents, and seemed to take delight in infuriating them.

He entered the House of Commons in 1876 for a Birmingham constituency after winning a by-election. He soon revealed his power in debate and became acknowledged leader of the radical section of the Liberal party.

President of the Board of Trade

In 1880, Gladstone was obliged to recognize Chamberlain's ability and influence by making him President of the Board of Trade, with a seat in the Cabinet. Gladstone's second ministry was an unhappy one, and Chamberlain was unhappy in it. It was a mixture of Whigs, Liberals and Radicals, at variance on almost every question. Chamberlain soon raised the importance of the Board of Trade, and proved his administrative capacity, though his colleagues thought that he was always trying to go too fast. He steered through a Bankruptcy Bill to restrain fraudulent debtors, and a Patents Bill to protect the poor inventor. The Parliamentary Reform Bill of 1884 received his full support. It was at this stage in his career that he formulated his own unauthorized programme, which included free primary education, full local government in the counties, local parliaments for Scotland and Wales under the final authority of the Westminster parliament, financial reform to pay for increased social welfare, land reform to give labourers a share of land, disestablishment of the Church in England, Scotland and Wales, manhood suffrage, and payment of M.P.s. This was a very large-scale and advanced programme for the 1880s.

Chamberlain and Ireland

When the Liberal government was defeated in 1885, Chamberlain and Jesse Collings campaigned for "three acres and a cow" for the farm labourer. He returned to office in Gladstone's third ministry in 1886 as President of the Local Government Board, but was not to hold office for long. He objected wholeheartedly to Gladstone's first Home Rule Bill, considering it tantamount to a proposal of separation. No one contributed more to its defeat than Chamberlain. His motives were quite honest, but many accused him of having unscrupulous ends. In the 1886 election he campaigned all over the country, with the result that seventy-eight Liberal Unionists (opponents of home rule) were returned. Chamberlain moved more closely from this time towards the Conservatives. Though he possessed only a small personal following he exercised enormous influence over the House of Commons, where he advocated old age pensions and other forms of social security.

Chamberlain, a shrewd businessman and a sharp politician, was at heart an idealist. For this reason he now developed visions of imperial unity. He played a major role in defeating Gladstone's second Home Rule Bill in 1893, accusing Gladstone of being the "slave of the Irish Party." He was, in fact, the real leader of the opposition at the time.

Colonial Secretary: the Boer War

In the election of 1895, the Liberals suffered a crushing defeat when Salisbury gained a majority of 152. Chamberlain, now sixty, was offered the post of Colonial Secretary. Still possessing dynamic energy, he was to increase the stature of the Colonial Office tremendously, and to occupy a very prominent position in national life.

He soon showed his vigour by ordering the annexation of Ashanti in West Africa, when the King of Ashanti refused to stop slave-trading and human sacrifice and would not pay an indemnity to the British government. He took up the cause of the Uitlanders of Johannesburg, taking a strong line with Kruger. The Jameson Raid of 1896 was highly embarrassing to Chamberlain, for he was accused of being in league with Jameson. In 1897 Chamberlain declared that Britain must remain the paramount power in South Africa, and affirmed British sovereignty over the Transvaal in no uncertain terms. He sent Sir Alfred Milner as High Commissioner, knowing that he had appointed a man strong enough to negotiate with Kruger. Chamberlain did not want war with the Boers, but was not willing to sacrifice the Uitlanders.

As a prominent member of the Conservative government, Chamberlain played an important part in the conduct of the Boer War, and the Khaki

Joseph Chamberlain, photographed in the 1880s.

Election held in 1900 was a personal triumph for him; he spoke at meetings all over the country. After the war he travelled widely in South Africa, and won great respect by his attempts to reconcile Briton and Boer.

Queen Victoria's Diamond Jubilee, 1897

Chamberlain not only reflected the interest in the Empire displayed in the late nineteenth century by the people of Britain, but he also stimulated it. In 1897 he was determined to display to the world the spectacle of the Empire united under its venerable sovereign. The Diamond Jubilee of 1897 was an astonishingly popular celebration. Chamberlain took advantage of the presence of colonial premiers to hold a Colonial Conference to discuss defence and trade. In 1901 he played some part in the establishment of the Commonwealth of Australia, and in 1902 he organized another Colonial Conference, though colonial premiers were unwilling to tie their hands too closely.

Chamberlain and Foreign Affairs

Since Chamberlain was one of the three most powerful ministers in the Salisbury government of 1895-1902, he was allowed to exercise considerable influence over foreign policy. He believed that Britain needed to end her isolation, and favoured France as an ally; but the openly hostile attitude of France over the Fashoda incident (1898) and the Boer war led him to approach the Germans. German arrogance killed Chamberlain's hopes of success, and after 1902 he made no further effort to gain a German alliance.

Chamberlain countered French ambitions to create a vast area of control between the Atlantic, the Red Sea, the Mediterranean and the Congo. His West African Frontier Force held its own with the French Senegalese force in West Africa, and his firmness led to a peaceful and advantageous settlement by 1899. In 1897 Chamberlain had travelled across the Atlantic to Washington to arrange for the calling of an arbitration tribunal to settle a border dispute between British Guiana and Venezuela. In 1899 it unanimously upheld

British claims almost completely: its decision was a triumph for Chamberlain. When Salisbury resigned in 1902, Chamberlain served on as Colonial Secretary under Balfour, his successor.

Balfour Ministry and Tariff Reform

His position was a strong one. Thousands of working men supported the Conservative administration solely because Chamberlain was in it. Chamberlain felt increasingly that the bonds of the Empire could be more tightly drawn by colonial preference. When Ritchie, Chancellor of the Exchequer, opposed the scheme, Chamberlain unfurled the banner of tariff reform. The issue split the Conservative Party when fifty-four Conservative M.P.s formed a Free Food League to oppose Chamberlain. No one quite knew what the government policy was. Chamberlain resigned to organize a tariff reform campaign.

The country was prosperous, however, and national complacency was hard to shake. Liberals raised the cry that Chamberlain wanted to tax the people's food. A Tariff Reform League was organized with all Chamberlain's customary drive and efficiency, but made little impact. The great Liberal victory in the election of 1906 was a blow to him, but his campaign was less the cause of it than the storm over Chinese labour in South Africa.

In 1906 Chamberlain's health failed, and his political career came to an end, but he continued to live in retirement until 1914.

Importance of Joseph Chamberlain's Career

Chamberlain at his best was described as "the best speaker in the House with one exception, and the best debater without exception." He was both a destroyer and a builder; he broke the Liberal Party, but it returned to power in 1906 with a larger majority than it had ever known. With Salisbury, Chamberlain rescued the Conservative Party from the slough of reaction into which it had fallen on the death of Disraeli; it has always since been ready to undertake social and political reforms. Chamberlain twice defeated home rule, and was probably mistaken in his attitude to it; but subsequent history has justified his advocacy of tariff reform. His imperialism made a great impact at the time.

Though apparently inconsistent, Chamberlain was always sincere, and was the last man to claim that he never changed his mind. His administrative achievements in both local and national affairs were considerable.

QUESTIONS

1. Trace Joseph Chamberlain's career and achievements.
2. Write an account of Joseph Chamberlain's services as Colonial Secretary, from 1895 to 1902.

CHAPTER 67

CAMPBELL-BANNERMAN AND ASQUITH, 1906-14

THE advent of the Liberal ministries of 1906-14 gave rise to a period of extensive reforms. Campbell-Bannerman, a wealthy and cultured Scot who became Liberal Premier in 1906, was not a great speaker but was sincerely devoted to the radical cause and to his party. He gathered around him a brilliant team of ministers which included Asquith as Chancellor of the Exchequer, R. B. Haldane at the War Office, Lord Morley at the India Office, Lloyd George as President of the Board of Trade, and John Burns at the Local Government Board. Among rising young ministers outside the Cabinet were Reginald McKenna, Winston Churchill and Herbert Samuel. These talented men were backed by a majority of eighty-four over all other parties, Liberals having captured 377 seats in the election of January, 1906; but in the House of Lords they faced a strong and obstructionist Conservative majority.

Union of South Africa, 1909

Campbell-Bannerman's great triumph was his settlement of South Africa. Using letters-patent to avoid obstruction from the House of Lords he gave independence to the Transvaal and the Orange Free State. After his death but as a result of his work came the establishment of the Union of South Africa in 1909. Campbell-Bannerman also promptly put an end to the employment of Chinese labour in South Africa.

Haldane's Army Reforms

A vital piece of work carried out during the Liberal spell of office was re-organization of the army. Haldane created a General Staff and reorganized the home military forces on two lines. An expeditionary force of six infantry divisions and one cavalry division was established ready for rapid mobilization; and by the Territorial and Reserve Forces Act of 1907 Haldane combined yeomanry and volunteers into a territorial force. In 1909 Officer Training Corps were established in public and secondary schools, and these O.T.C.s provided an indispensable supply of young officers during the First World War.

In August, 1914, as a result of Haldane's preparations, twenty divisions were mobilized punctually and without a hitch; yet during his tenure of office

Old ladies on an outing. In 1909 old-age pensions were introduced.

Haldane actually managed to reduce military expenditure. He had also seen that the divisions were properly equipped.

Domestic Reforms

During the first year of the Campbell-Bannerman ministry, the Conservative majority in the House of Lords threw out an Education Bill and a bill to abolish plural voting, though they allowed through a Trades Disputes Act which reversed the Taff Vale decision (see pages 383-4). The energies of Lloyd George led to the passing of a Merchant Shipping Act in 1906 to confine pilots' licences to British subjects, and of a Patents Act in 1907 which compelled patentees to work their patents in the United Kingdom within three years. In 1906 Labour pressure led to an act enabling local authorities to provide meals for poor school children, and in 1907 McKenna steered through the House an act to provide for medical inspection of school children. The Liberal government stood firm in the face of a militant demand for votes for women. In 1907, however, they secured the passing of the Qualification of Women Act which for the first time enabled women to sit as councillors, aldermen, mayors and chairmen on county or borough councils. In 1908 a single Port of London Authority was established to replace the chaos of overlapping private dock companies.

Asquith Succeeds Campbell-Bannerman, 1908

In 1908 Campbell-Bannerman resigned because of ill-health, and H. H. Asquith became Premier. Lloyd George succeeded him as Chancellor of the Exchequer, and Winston Churchill became President of the Board of Trade. Asquith, a Yorkshireman, was no crusader and rarely planned ahead, but he was a powerful debater and at fifty-six was at the height of his powers.

Social Legislation, and Naval Construction

Haldane's economies permitted the introduction of an old age pensions scheme in 1908. It was non-contributory and provided only five shillings a week at the age of seventy. It was only available to those earning less than ten shillings a week from other sources, and a seventy-year-old married couple received only 7*s*. 6*d*. Nevertheless it was a beginning.

The Liberals introduced a well-framed Licensing Bill in 1908 to curb excessive drinking of alcohol, which was certainly a social evil; but Conservatives in the House of Lords, espousing the brewers' cause, killed this measure.

When it was learned that the German Admiral Tirpitz was laying down four great battleships to Britain's one in 1908 the public took up the cry "we want eight and we won't wait." As a result R. McKenna, First Lord of the Admiralty, laid down eight Dreadnoughts in 1909, five in 1910, and five in 1911. It was this provision which gave Admiral Jellicoe his margin of superiority in Dreadnoughts in 1914. All this inevitably meant increased expenditure to the tune of £15 million, and paved the way for Lloyd George's famous budget of 1909.

Lloyd George's Budget of 1909

Lloyd George's budget was a masterpiece of political strategy. In order to raise the additional revenue needed, he levied special taxes on petrol and motor licences to provide for road improvement; he increased death duties, the tobacco tax and taxes upon spirits, and raised income tax from 1*s*. to 1*s*. 2*d*. Super-tax was created, and levied on incomes of over £3,000. There were special taxes on profits from land sales and on undeveloped mineral resources, making a complete land valuation necessary. One hundred thousand pounds was set aside to provide labour exchanges. Allowances for children were made for the first time to income tax payers. Conservatives attacked the budget tooth and nail, showing no restraint whatsoever, but this was just what Lloyd George wanted. The budget passed through the Commons by 379 votes to 149, but was rejected in the Lords on the second reading by 350 votes to 75.

The deadlock led to an election in 1910 which resulted in a Unionist defeat, Liberals, Labour and Irish Nationalists mustering 397 seats against the Unionists' 273. The sudden death of King Edward VII suspended the

1911: Railway strikers marching through Willesden.

constitutional crisis for a time; George V, his successor, tried to ease the situation by summoning a conference of leaders of both sides but the conference failed. A second election held in December, 1910, confirmed the government majority, producing almost exactly the same result. The Lords meanwhile had allowed the Lloyd George budget to go through before the election, but the Liberals were now determined to remove the Lords' veto.

Parliament Bill, 1911

In February, 1911, Asquith introduced his Parliament Bill which provided that the Lords could not alter a money bill and could only suspend the operation of a general bill for a limited time. The duration of a Parliament was to be reduced from seven to five years. Die-hards in the House of Lords sought to reject the bill but, threatened by the creation of a host of new Liberal peers (to which George V had agreed), they gave way and the Parliament Bill passed through the Lords by 131 votes to 114. (Asquith had actually prepared a list of 250 new Liberal peers!) The intransigence of Lord Lansdowne and the die-hards had resulted in a serious reduction of the powers of the Upper House.

During the Asquith ministry a first cautious step was taken towards establishing self-government in India. Morley and the Viceroy, the Earl of Minto, made legislative councils partially elective, and admitted Indians to executive councils.

Labour Troubles 1911-12, and Further Liberal Legislation

In 1911 there was a great wave of strikes which affected railway workers, miners, cotton workers, boiler-makers, seamen, engineers and dockers, and caused considerable violence. It was caused partly by the anger stimulated by the Osborne judgment of 1908, which made compulsory political levies by unions illegal and deprived Labour M.P.s of their incomes, and partly by the influence of French syndicalism.

These troubles did not hold up the spate of Liberal legislation, for in 1911 a Shops Act introduced a legal weekly half-holiday, a Coal Mines Act amended laws relating to coal-mining, an Aerial Navigation Act enabled the Home Office to prohibit flights over prescribed areas and a Payment of M.P.s Act gave M.P.s a salary of £400 per annum.

National Insurance Act, 1911

Lloyd George was responsible for the National Insurance Act of 1911, a vast contributory scheme to insure the whole working population against sickness, and certain sections of it against unemployment. Compulsory contributions were to be collected from employers and employees by means of stamped cards. There was much prejudice against the measure in the country, and discontent was fomented vigorously by the Unionists. It must have caused the Liberals to lose much ground electorally, but the value of the act would hardly be disputed now.

Third Home Rule Bill, 1912

In return for recent support from Irish Nationalists, the Liberals were more or less obliged to introduce a measure of home rule for Ireland. The Third Home Rule Bill differed from those of 1886 and 1893 in its federalist conception. The British parliament was to remain the Imperial parliament, and a reduced representation of forty-two Irish members was to be sent to it. Its authority was to remain supreme.

This Home Rule Bill was passed through the Commons in two successive sessions by large majorities, but was twice rejected by the Lords. It should have come into operation in the summer of 1914 under the terms of the Parliament Act, but the international crisis caused its operation to be suspended. Meanwhile Bonar Law, and Carson, with their Unionist and Ulsterite supporters, became more and more violent and irresponsible. There would have been vast bloodshed in Ireland had it not been for the outbreak of the First World War. Asquith revealed a lack of determination and decision in this crisis.

By 1914 the Liberal ministries had many great achievements to their credit, but their reforming activities were largely suspended by the outbreak of the First World War in 1914.

QUESTIONS

1. Describe the reforms carried out by Liberal governments between 1906 and 1914.

2. Assess the importance of the work of H. H. Asquith.

CHAPTER 68

DAVID LLOYD GEORGE

DAVID LLOYD GEORGE was born in Manchester in 1863, the grandson of a well-to-do Pembrokeshire farmer. David's father died in 1864 and the boy was brought up by his uncle in Caernarvonshire, in an atmosphere of Nonconformity and Liberalism. He qualified as a lawyer, was an advocate of temperance and Welsh home rule, and became an alderman for Caernarvon County Council. In 1890 he was elected to represent Caernarvon Boroughs in Parliament and held the seat for fifty-five years. He soon made a name for himself as an orator, and must have had great stamina, for he kept two legal practices going and attended parliament assiduously at the same time. Welsh Disestablishment concerned him greatly at this stage of his career. He was soon referred to as "the finest parliamentarian Wales has yet sent to the House of Commons." His reputation grew as he made speeches throughout Britain. When the Boer War (1899-1902) broke out, Lloyd George opposed it vigorously, feeling strong sympathy for the Boers. He was no pacifist or anti-Imperialist, but he likened the Boer struggle to that of the Welsh. His attitude earned him hatred, because the war was generally popular in the country.

Another issue he bitterly contested was the rate-aid given by the Balfour Education Act of 1902 to schools not fully under state control. In this he shared the hostility of Welsh Nonconformity to Anglican schools.

Cabinet Minister in the Liberal Governments, 1906-14

At the age of forty-two Lloyd George, having established a prominent position among parliamentary Liberals, was made President of the Board of Trade by Campbell-Bannerman in 1906. He soon made his mark by skilfully settling labour disputes in the mining, cotton, engineering and shipbuilding industries. When Campbell-Bannerman resigned in 1908 and Asquith became Prime Minister, Lloyd George took Asquith's place as Chancellor of the Exchequer, though he had no great experience of finance. In 1908 he went to Germany, Austria and Belgium to study social legislation. Many of his Liberal colleagues opposed him over the revolutionary aspects of his 1909 Budget, but Lloyd George said that "all down history nine-tenths of mankind have been grinding corn for the remaining tenth and have been paid with the husks and bidden to thank God they had the husks"; Asquith and Grey loyally supported him. Details of the Budget and the subsequent constitutional struggle which led to a reduction of the powers of the House of Lords have been described in Chapter 67. No one played a greater part than the fiery Chancellor of the Exchequer.

In 1911 Lloyd George fashioned the National Health and Unemployment Bills for which there was an urgent need. Many friendly societies were facing bankruptcy, and the principal trade unions were crippled by a burden of sickness, unemployment and superannuation benefits. Lloyd George proposed that nearly all manual workers between sixteen and seventy earning less than £160 per year should be insured against ill-health by the joint contributions of themselves, their employers and the state. In addition 2,250,000 workers in ship-building, engineering, building and other trades were to participate in a contributory scheme of unemployment insurance with benefit at seven shillings per week. It was a tremendous task to get the scheme under way. Lloyd George's career had already earned him the hatred of the privileged classes.

Cabinet Minister in War, 1914-16

By 1914, Lloyd George had had nine years' experience as a Cabinet minister. He knew little of foreign affairs, though in 1911 a speech of his at the Mansion House warned Germany not to go too far over the Agadir crisis (see pages 435-6). Like many other people, Lloyd George was not convinced of the need to make war on Germany in 1914 until she ruthlessly invaded Belgium. To him fell the task of finding the tremendous sums needed to pay for the war. He did so by increased taxation, by borrowing and by a policy of monetary inflation. He became intensely interested in the military campaigns of the war, and was soon convinced of the ineptitude of the British generals, who angered him by treating him as an amateur. He was also soon convinced that the slaughter on the Western Front was needless, and that it would be better to attack the Central Powers through the Balkans. He favoured Churchill's campaign in the Dardanelles in 1915, but it failed. When munitions were in short supply Lloyd George was angered by the seeming complacency of his colleagues. He helped Asquith to construct a coalition government in 1915.

In May, 1915, Lloyd George became Minister of Munitions, a post which he held for thirteen months. Beginning with a table, a chair and two private secretaries, he finished with a staff of 25,000! He was full of ideas. His natural executive ability came into full play. Red tape was cut. He told parliament, "What we stint in materials we squander in life .. . . What you spare in money you spill in blood."

Who could resist such words? He toured factories and brought businessmen into government service. Ninety-five new factories were built and the quantity of munitions soon leapt, though quality sometimes suffered.

In July, 1916, Lloyd George became Secretary of State for War, and was soon clearing up the military confusion in Mesopotamia and improving railway communications in France.

Prime Minister, 1916-18

In December, 1916, Lloyd George replaced Asquith as Prime Minister. Asquith never forgave him, because he considered that Lloyd George had deliberately plotted to replace him; but Lloyd George was without doubt the greater war-leader. The division proved fatal for the Liberal Party, which never recovered. Lloyd George's great powers of leadership now came into full play. He radiated energy and optimism, and worked from early morning till late at night to win the war. Many formidable problems faced him, among which were the submarine menace, lack of unity of command in France, and lack of an overall strategy. Lloyd George badgered the slow-moving Admiralty into employing a convoy system, stimulated ship-building and introduced food rationing. He was unable to override Robertson, Chief of the Imperial General Staff, and Haig, Commander-in-Chief in France, and relations between him and these two soldiers became very strained. He later described their attitude as "epauletted egoism impenetrable to ideas." He would have liked to sack Haig, but was unable to do so. Only in the desperate days of the German spring offensive of 1918 did Lloyd George succeed in arranging for Marshal Foch to exercise supreme command in France. When the Germans collapsed in autumn, 1918, Colonel House, President Wilson's personal agent in Europe, told Lloyd George, "No one has done more to bring about this splendid victory than you have done."

The Coupon Election, 1918

No one could deny that Lloyd George was a wily politician. Before war was over, he prepared to go to the country to gain a fresh mandate. The election of December, 1918, gave him a huge majority and he continued for four more years to lead a coalition government. He has been severely criticized for holding the election so quickly, when many troops were still abroad; but he could plead that parliament was eight years old. Some Liberals had recently opposed his conduct of the war, and Lloyd George now refused to treat them as political supporters, giving his blessing ("coupon") only to those he deemed faithful. This had the effect of destroying Liberal unity even more.

Lloyd George's election programme may be summarized as:

(*a*) prosecution of the Kaiser;
(*b*) punishment of those guilty of war atrocities;
(*c*) exaction of war indemnities from the Central Powers to the limit of their ability to pay;

Lloyd George addressing a crowd at Elgin in 1925.

(*d*) rehabilitation of those broken by the war;
(*e*) domestic reform in all spheres.

Lloyd George was guilty of misleading the public into thinking that Germany would be able to pay most of the cost of the war. At Bristol he made a speech in which he hinted that Germany would be squeezed to the last farthing, and to secure a temporary advantage he played on the baser passions of the electorate.

Peace of Versailles, 1919

Lloyd George found it as hard to unite the Allies in making peace as in making war. Wilson of the United States, Clemenceau of France and Lloyd George dominated the peace conference. Lloyd George's chief concern was to restore the balance of power in Europe, though he helped Wilson to establish the League of Nations with greater enthusiasm than Clemenceau showed. He soon began to realize that Germany would not be able to find vast sums of money in reparations, and said, "We cannot both cripple her and expect her to pay."

He paved the way for Germany's later entry into the League. If his aims were to destroy German militarism and prevent another war, Lloyd George failed at Versailles. In effect Germany paid no reparations; between 1920 and 1931 she received thirty-seven milliard marks from abroad, and paid only twenty-one milliard marks in reparations. In his defence it may be said that it was not Lloyd George's fault that the treaty was never properly enforced in the years after 1922.

Post-War Problems, 1919-22

For a time Lloyd George was the most prominent statesman in Europe. He had none of the British shyness with foreigners. Unlike French leaders he was ready to scale down reparations and to resume economic co-operation with Germany in order to woo her away from Communist Russia; yet at the same time he did not wish to close the door on Russia.

Ireland gave Lloyd George much concern for civil war raged between Sinn Fein and the Royal Irish Constabulary. By tenacity, good-temper and fairness, Lloyd George succeeded in negotiating a settlement with Sinn Feiners Arthur Griffiths and Michael Collins in 1921 (see page 398).

Relations between Greece and Turkey also gave Lloyd George concern. He became very friendly with the Greek statesman Venizelos, and encouraged the Greeks to establish themselves at Smyrna and in Thrace at the expense of the Turks. With the rise of Kemal Ataturk, the Turks drove back the Greeks, and at one point threatened a British force at Chanak near the Dardanelles. War came close until General Harington came to terms with the Turks.

The Fall of the Lloyd George Coalition, 1922

Since 1918 Lloyd George had relied on the support of the Conservatives in the Commons; but by 1922 the Conservatives were much less ready to support him. Labour difficulties had arisen, and by 1921 there were two million unemployed; taxation was increased to support them. The India Act of 1919 which extended democracy, and the Irish settlement were not popular. It had been difficult to carry out election promises concerning land reform, housing and employment. Pacifists disliked Lloyd George's "forward" policy in Turkey. As a result, the election of 1922 gave the Tories a comfortable majority over all parties, and Bonar Law succeeded Lloyd George as Premier.

Largely due to the eclipse of the Liberal Party, for which he must bear a

By 1915 there was a severe shortage of ammunition. Here bombs are being made by fitting an explosive charge to old tins filled with metal scraps.

large share of the blame, Lloyd George never held office again. In the years that followed he earned a handsome income from journalism and became a wealthy man. Between 1931 and 1934 he wrote his war memoirs. He met Hitler in 1936 and for a time came under his spell. Perhaps his last contribution to history was his speech calling on Neville Chamberlain to resign in 1940. He died in 1945, shortly after being made Earl Lloyd George of Dwyfor.

Conclusion

Lloyd George's two great achievements were his social reforms of 1909-11, which laid the foundations of the Welfare State, and his massive contribution to victory in the First World War. For these, he ranks among the greatest of British statesmen.

QUESTIONS

1. Describe Lloyd George's main achievements between 1906 and 1922.

2. Estimate Lloyd George's services to Great Britain.

CHAPTER 69

THE END OF "SPLENDID ISOLATION"

EVER since the Crimean War, Britain had tended to avoid entanglement in Europe. Able to shelter behind the might of her navy, she felt secure. Yet towards the end of the nineteenth century her isolation began to give her a sense of insecurity for a variety of reasons. The hostility of President Cleveland over the Venezuelan dispute in 1895, the attitude of the Kaiser at the time of the Jameson Raid of 1896, the pro-Boer sentiments of Germany, Holland and France during the Boer War of 1899-1902, and competition from an arrogant Germany in the Far East, on the sea and in commerce all contributed to Britain's growing feeling of isolation.

Lord Salisbury had made approaches to Russia and France in 1898, and twice to Germany through Chamberlain in 1898 and 1899 but no alliance resulted. The German Naval Law of 1898, which provided for a tremendous expansion of the German fleet in the ensuing six years, caused great alarm in Britain. Our security was threatened indeed.

In the Far East, Japan greatly resented Russia's occupation of Port Arthur in 1898 and her seizure of Manchuria in 1900, and Britain too was suspicious of Russian expansion. Mutual interests drew Britain and Japan into an alliance in 1902, according to which Britain was to give military help to Japan if she were attacked by more than one power. In effect it shielded Japan from intervention should she make war upon Russia, as indeed she did from 1904 to 1905, winning a striking victory on land and sea.

Entente with France, 1904

In Europe the Great Powers were ranged against each other in the triple alliance of Germany, Austria-Hungary and Italy, and the dual alliance of France and Russia. Under the guidance of Lord Lansdowne, Foreign Secretary in the last Salisbury ministry and in the Balfour ministry, Britain finally came down from the fence on the French side.

Joseph Chamberlain had set things going by proposing to the French ambassador that Anglo-French colonial disputes should be settled. Edward VII's famous visit to Paris in May, 1903, did much to win over previously hostile French public opinion. President Loubet of France and the French Premier Delcassé came to London and were cordially received. Britain agreed to give France a free hand in Morocco, in return for a free British hand in Egypt. Thus the Dual Entente was born, though Britain's hands were not very firmly bound. When the flamboyant Kaiser William II of Germany visited Tangier in 1905 and asserted the independence of Morocco, it was a direct challenge to the infant Entente, but the Entente stood firm.

Grey and the Entente with Russia

Sir Edward Grey, Liberal Foreign Secretary under Campbell-Bannerman and Asquith, continued the policy of Lord Lansdowne, authorizing military conversations between Britain and France. In 1906 the Algeciras Conference met in Spain to deal with the question of Morocco. Once again the Franco-British Entente held firm and France and Spain obtained mandates to police the Sultanate of Morocco whilst Germany was left empty-handed. Nevertheless, the British government sincerely tried to work for peace by reducing its naval programme, but Germany's suspicions were not appeased.

Since France was linked with Russia by the dual alliance of 1895, it was inconsistent that Britain and Russia should remain hostile towards each other. In 1907, therefore, the two governments signed a convention by which they agreed to de-limit their spheres of influence in Persia and to avoid stealing a march in Tibet and Afghanistan, other disputed spheres of influence. This new Entente was embarrassing to the British Liberal Government because the repressive domestic policy of the Tsar was repellent to British opinion.

Britain's link with France and Russia was not allowed to put an end to attempts to improve relations with Germany, and during the two years after Algeciras Edward VII and the Kaiser exchanged visits.

Pre-war Crises

The international situation darkened in 1908 when the Young Turk party carried out an armed rebellion against Sultan Abdul Hamid. Austria-Hungary and Russia had no wish to see tottering Turkey recover. Austria swiftly annexed Bosnia and Herzegovina, Bulgaria proclaimed complete independence from Turkey, Crete broke away from Turkey and the danger of war loomed up. Serbia gained no compensation and Russia stood by her, but Germany warned her off with an ultimatum. Europe lived dangerously from this time, the two armed camps of Great Powers watching each other suspiciously. Yet the appointment of Bethman-Hollweg as German Chancellor brought friendlier relations between Germany and Britain (1909), and the Kaiser's sympathetic attitude at Edward VII's funeral in 1910 created a good impression; but the Germans were unable to persuade Grey to throw over the Franco-British Entente. Haldane induced Asquith to authorize preparation of a war-book by the Committee of Imperial Defence; it prepared details for immediate action in the event of war, and proved invaluable in 1914.

In 1911 Morocco became the scene of another international crisis when the

Germans despatched their gunboat *Panther* to Agadir. It was a challenge to the French position in Morocco, but Lloyd George's speech at the Mansion House in London, threatening war if necessary, checked German aggressiveness and brought France and Britain even closer together. Nevertheless attempts were still made to improve relations with Germany. Haldane was sent there on a mission, though with little result.

The Balkan Crises

The Balkans, destined to be the scene of the assassination that sparked off war in 1914, were in ferment from 1912 to 1913. In 1912 Bulgaria, Serbia and Greece launched an attack upon a Turkey already weakened by war against Italy in 1911 which had cost her Tripolitania in North Africa. Austria-Hungary and Russia, both having strong interests in the Balkans, watched events closely. At a conference in London (summoned by Grey), Britain threw her weight firmly on the side of Germany and Austria, much to the annoyance of France and Russia. Grey wanted to prove to the Central Powers that there was no attempt to encircle them, but his gesture was lost on Germany.

The Balkan powers were soon quarrelling among themselves, Serbia and Greece ranging themselves against Bulgaria. Bulgaria, weakened by the recent war, was then attacked by Roumania. Serbia was enlarged by both Balkan Wars, and Austria-Hungary found herself faced by a formidable barrier to her intended expansion south-eastwards.

By 1913 Germany had concluded that war between the triple and dual alliances was inevitable, and began to raise the number of her conscripts and to build up her war finances; yet British statesmen took surprisingly little notice. They did, however, notice Germany's growing influence on

On June 28, 1914, the assassination of the Archduke Franz Joseph sparked off the First World War. In the confusion which followed this arrest was made.

Turkey with alarm, and were disturbed by German naval preparations. In March, 1913, Churchill proposed a "naval holiday" by which Germany and Britain would agree to suspend naval construction, but the Germans would not accept his proposal.

Outbreak of the First World War, 1914

By the late spring of 1914, the Germans had widened the Kiel Canal and were rapidly gathering in their capital from abroad. They could hardly disguise their preparations for war. In Britain, Liberal ministers favoured peace, but the assassination of Austrian Archduke Ferdinand, heir-apparent to the throne of Austria and Hungary, on 28 June, sparked off a sequence of events which led Britain into war.

Ferdinand was unpopular in Austria among the ruling classes, and his death was not regretted, but his murder was an excellent excuse for issuing an ultimatum to Serbia, with the intent of attacking her upon her almost inevitable refusal to accept terms. Serbia accepted all but two of them and agreed to submit these to international arbitration, but Austria wanted war. Russia mobilized in support of Serbia, for she could not stand aside and watch Austria score another success at her expense in the Balkans: her pride would not permit it. Germany mobilized in support of Austria, and France prepared to meet her obligations to Russia. What would Britain do?

Grey did all he could to avert war. He sought to persuade France, Italy and Germany to send representatives to a conference to settle the dispute between Russia and Austria-Hungary, but met with no success. Some Liberals in the country were pro-German and anti-French, and the Cabinet was far from united on the issue of peace or war. Meanwhile on 2 August, 1914, Germany declared war on Russia, and on the following day, 3 August, she declared war on France.

When the Germans invaded Belgium because it provided the most convenient route to France, British public opinion changed overnight, and a parliamentary majority supported Grey's entry into the war on the side of France and Russia. Britain had been one of the guarantors of Belgium's neutrality since 1839, and had a legal right and obligation to defend her. In any case, it had always been Britain's traditional policy to prevent a major European power from controlling Belgium, an ideal area from which to launch an attack on Britain, though sooner or later Britain's ties with France would have brought her into the war, had Germany not invaded Belgium.

QUESTIONS

1. Why did Great Britain declare war on Germany in 1914?
2. Contrast relations between Britain and France before and after the *Entente* of 1904.

CHAPTER 70

BRITAIN AND THE FIRST WORLD WAR

BRITAIN has often entered great wars ill-prepared, but in 1914 she was comparatively ready, though she did not possess a large standing army. Few in 1914 thought that the war would last four years or realized how total it would be.

The Land War

Britain rapidly despatched an expeditionary force of ninety thousand men across the Channel to France under Sir John French. The troops were mostly skilled riflemen who took up their position on the left of the French. When the French were driven back, the British army was in a position of peril, but it fought brave rearguard actions at Mons and Le Cateau, and helped to halt the German advance and to stabilize the line which by the end of 1914 ran from the Channel ports to Alsace-Lorraine. At Ypres the British army took the full brunt of a German attack with great fortitude, though the battle left little of the original expeditionary force. Afterwards it could hold only 21 miles of the line, as opposed to the 430 miles held by the French.

In 1915, Lord Kitchener, Minister for War, marshalled fresh armies. Fighting on the Western Front settled down to costly trench warfare. Commanders on both sides were largely uninspired. The British army lost heavily in offensives at Neuve Chapelle (March, 1915) and Festubert (May, 1915) and on the Ypres salient, though its strength had now risen to twenty-one divisions. Resuming the offensive at Loos, it was defeated and suffered heavy casualties. Sir John French was replaced as commander by Sir Douglas Haig.

Encouraged by the presence of the German warships *Goeben* and *Breslau* at Constantinople, Turkey entered the war in 1915. Her entry inspired the allies to attempt a passage of the Dardanelles, which failed. It was decided to land a force on the Gallipoli peninsula to control the straits. Sir Ian Hamilton commanded 120,000 men, including Australians and New Zealanders, who fought brilliantly but were unable to gain control over the peninsula and had to be withdrawn, leaving many dead behind them.

The Turks were attacked in another area when Indian troops landed at Basra on the Persian Gulf to safeguard the oil-base. General Townshend planned to drive the Turks northwards up the Tigris, but having pressed

Ypres in October, 1917, one of the many areas devastated by war.

forward to Kut he was besieged there and, after a brave resistance, he had to surrender with eight thousand men.

By 1916 the French had lost two million men and the British 500,000. The Germans launched a great attack on the French position at Verdun; and in order to relieve pressure on them, the British attacked on the Somme. An elaborate bombardment of German positions failed to achieve the results hoped for, and advertised the coming attack. British soldiers were weighed down by the sixty-six pounds of equipment which each man carried. On the first day alone sixty thousand men were lost, and when October rains brought the attack to a halt the British had suffered 420,000 casualties, having advanced only seven miles on a thirty-mile front. Tanks had been introduced, and had taken the Germans by surprise, but there were too few of them to be decisive.

In 1917 a British victory at Vimy Ridge in front of Arras was followed by a bitter hundred-day offensive in mud and rain at Passchendaele, which cost 300,000 casualties.

When Russian resistance collapsed in 1917 the Austrians were able to exert greater pressure on the Italians, who needed French and British help on their front.

During the same year the British endeavoured to restore their position in Mesopotamia. General Maude moved up the River Tigris to recover Kut, and went on to capture Baghdad. The British also invaded Palestine and, after a long campaign, took Beersheba, Gaza and Jaffa. In December, 1917, General Allenby entered Jerusalem, which had been in Mohammedan hands since 1087.

When the Germans made their last all-out effort to break through on the Western Front in 1918 they attacked General Gough's Fifth Army and drove it across the Somme. During the crisis which followed, Haig accepted the Frenchman, Foch, as Commander-in-Chief. The Germans reached a point within thirty-seven miles of Paris, and were then held. American troops, now reaching France in great numbers, were fresh and enthusiastic, and made a considerable impact. In September, 1918, Haig exerted great pressure on the German army, and it cracked. Its resistance was undermined by the fact that morale at home had declined under the strain of food shortage. The "contemptible" British army had triumphed in the end. Britain had raised larger armies than ever before in her history, and had truly played her part alongside the French on the Western Front.

War at Sea

When war began, the British navy was disposed in three main stations. The battle fleet of Dreadnoughts and Super Dreadnoughts was at Scapa Flow and the Orkneys under Admiral Jellicoe, the cruiser squadron under Admiral Beatty was stationed at Rosyth in the Firth of Forth, and a group of older battle ships with accompanying destroyers kept a watch on the Channel.

Most units of the German navy were recalled to port at the outset of war, but a formidable German fleet was at large in the Pacific under Admiral von Spee who had five fast cruisers. He caught an inferior British force at Coronel, off Chile, and destroyed it, but Admiral Lord Fisher and Winston Churchill at the Admiralty despatched a powerful squadron to intercept him as he tried to cross the South Atlantic, and Spee's force was destroyed in turn at the Falkland Islands in December, 1914. All save one of the German warships at large had been run down by the end of that year. The main German fleet preferred to avoid combat until 1916.

In 1915 Beatty's squadron met a German cruiser squadron at Dogger Bank but a pitched battle failed to develop and the Germans, mauled, returned to their base. Their retirement seemed to stress British supremacy. The British navy stifled Germany's overseas commerce and provoked the Germans into an all-out submarine campaign. It was in 1915 that the *Lusitania* was sunk without warning off the coast of Ireland, with loss of over a thousand lives including those of many women and children.

On 31 May, 1916, the German High Seas Fleet sailed into the North Sea. Beatty lured them towards Jellicoe's fleet, but Admiral Scheer skilfully led his fleet to safety under cover of darkness after inflicting heavier damage on the British than he suffered himself. The British lost six cruisers and eight destroyers, while two Super-Dreadnoughts were badly damaged. The Battle of Jutland cost the British 115,025 tons of shipping and nearly seven thousand sailors, the Germans lost 61,180 tons and three thousand men. Both sides claimed a victory—the British, because the German High Seas Fleet never ventured out again.

The peak of the German submarine campaign came in 1917. Having lost 300,000 tons of shipping in October, 1916, the Allies lost 875,000 in April, 1917. The navy strained every nerve to combat the submarine menace, and by 1918 had triumphed. German submarine activity helped to bring the Americans into the war, an unfortunate consequence for Germany.

In 1918 two daring exploits by the British navy blocked Zeebrugge and Ostend, when ships were sunk in the harbour entrances. Throughout the war the navy blockaded Germany, protected merchant ships and convoyed troop transports all over the world, making a massive contribution to victory.

Commonwealth Contribution

The war served to prove the unity of the British Commonwealth and Empire. Anzac (Australian and New Zealand Army Corps) forces served with distinction at Gallipoli; Indian troops played a great part in the long campaign in Mesopotamia, defended Egypt, helped to conquer Palestine, and assisted the British in a difficult campaign in East Africa where the German colonies were captured; South African troops conquered German South West Africa. In the Far East the Australians and New Zealanders occupied German New Guinea and Samoa; Indian troops helped to capture Kiao-Chau in China. Canadians, Australians and New Zealanders proved themselves capable of standing up to the finest regiments in the German army. In all, the self-governing Dominions supplied 1,500,000 men out of a total population of twenty million, and an equal number came from India.

The Home Front

In 1914 the three most important men in the direction of war were Lord Kitchener (Secretary for War), Winston Churchill (First Lord of the Admiralty), and Asquith (Prime Minister). During the war the political parties observed an electoral truce. Inevitably taxation had to rise, and Lloyd George's special war budget raised income tax from ninepence to 1*s.* 6*d.*

War put an end to unemployment. Women worked in canteens, munition factories, banks and on the railways. Through the formation of the Women's Auxiliary Army Corps (W.A.A.C.) men were released for service at the front. With food shortages, prices inevitably rose. The National Debt increased from £650 million to £7,000 million. The powers of the state were greatly

By 1917 women had taken over many jobs from the men: here is a group in an engineering shop.

extended and brought about a vast expansion of the Civil Service. Mines and transport came under government control. Hotels and private houses were commandeered. When war was over things were never quite the same again.

Conclusion

The First World War cost Britain 750,000 men killed and 1,750,000 wounded. Another 200,000 from the Empire lost their lives. Altogether six million men enlisted and Britain was left almost as exhausted as the defeated enemy.

QUESTIONS

1. Estimate the social effects of the 1914-18 war on Great Britain.

2. Describe the part played by British armies in France in defeating Germany during the 1914-18 War.

CHAPTER 71

FOREIGN AFFAIRS, 1918-39

THE Armistice which ended fighting in the First World War took effect on 11 November, 1918. Peace-making after a war is always difficult, and the Versailles settlement proved no exception. The task fell to President Wilson (United States of America), Clemenceau (France), and Lloyd George (Britain). Lloyd George was not impervious to Wilson's idealism, but was tied to election promises to "hang the Kaiser"; and he was reminded in a telegram sent by 370 M.P.s in 1919 that he had sworn to make Germany pay the entire cost of the war.

Germany was treated severely. She was expected to pay vast annual reparations to finance Allied reconstruction. Most of the industrial Rhineland was to be occupied by Allied troops for fifteen years, and France was to occupy the Saar coalfield for a similar period to compensate France for damage done to her own coalfields. Germany was diminished by 25,000 square miles, and lost seven million inhabitants; she restored Alsace-Lorraine to France, and gave up land to Poland which had hitherto joined East Prussia to the rest of Germany. She surrendered all her overseas territories and was obliged to reduce her army to 100,000 men.

The old Austro-Hungarian Empire came to an end by the Treaty of Saint-Germain of 1919; Austria and Hungary separated, and the new states of Czechoslovakia and Yugoslavia came into being.

Largely due to the idealism of Wilson, the League of Nations was created to provide machinery whereby international disputes could be settled by discussion. Each member was to accept the terms of the League's covenant.

After the Peace of Versailles Germany was prostrate, and France had suffered terribly from the ravages of war. The United States sought once again to withdraw from European entanglements and on the defeat of Wilson in the presidential election of 1920 she resigned from the League. Perhaps the main hope for the League would have been firm Franco-British co-operation, but the war-time allies failed to maintain their unity. France was bitter and anxious, fearing a German revival. Britain's determination to "squeeze Germany till the pips squeak" soon waned, but France remained determined to force full reparations out of Germany. Losing patience at Germany's failure to meet her obligations, Raymond Poincaré, the French Premier, ordered military occupation of the Ruhr industrial area in 1923, though his action increased Germany's inability to pay. Bonar Law, Conservative Prime Minister of Britain, expressed disapproval of the French action, and thus increased the growing coolness between the two countries.

In 1924 a committee of financial experts, led by General Dawes of the United States, eased the burden of reparations upon Germany. Relations between France and Britain improved in that year because of the attitude of co-operation shown by the two prime ministers, Edouard Herriot and Ramsay MacDonald. This better understanding was continued by Baldwin's Foreign Secretary, Austen Chamberlain, with Aristide Briand of France and with Gustav Stresemann of Germany.

Stresemann proposed at the Locarno conference of 1925 that Britain, France, Germany and Italy should recognize and guarantee the existing Franco-German frontier, and then proceeded to negotiate a similar agreement with Poland and Czechoslovakia over Germany's eastern frontiers. Britain accepted the Locarno agreement, which was a praiseworthy attempt to establish collective security; and the three years from 1925 to 1928 were comparatively tranquil. The Allies evacuated the Rhineland and in 1926 Germany entered the League of Nations.

In 1928 Frank Kellogg, American Secretary of State, persuaded sixty-three states to accept the Kellogg Pact, by which they agreed to renounce war as an instrument of national policy, but the pact proved merely a pious aspiration. The trading slump of 1929 darkened the international scene. In spite of the energies of its British chairman, Arthur Henderson, the Disarmament Conference of 1932 achieved little. Equally unproductive was a World Economic Conference which met at the same time. Nations were unwilling to sacrifice one iota of their national sovereignty.

Turn of the Tide

The first great challenge to the League of Nations came in 1931 when Japan (a member) invaded Manchuria, a province of China. China, also a member, appealed to the League. After some hesitation, Britain and the United States stood aside, and the League felt unable to stop Japan, although her aggression was condemned. This was a tragedy, for inevitably it paved the way for further acts of aggression. It revealed the League's weakness, and showed that the covenant could be defied with impunity.

The next blow to peace and to the League came when Mussolini, dictator of Italy, picked a quarrel with Abyssinia and invaded her in 1935. He gambled that the British government would not fight, and he was right; but when the Foreign Secretary, Sir Samuel Hoare, agreed with the French Foreign Minister, Laval, on a plan which would give most of Abyssinia to Italy, a public outcry occurred in Britain which caused Prime Minister Baldwin to replace Hoare by Anthony Eden, a firm supporter of the League. Eden tried to check Italy by persuading the League to impose economic sanctions, thus depriving her of war materials; but the supply of vital oil was not checked, and by 1936 Mussolini had completed his conquest of luckless Abyssinia. For a second time the League had failed to stop aggression.

The appointment of Adolf Hitler as Chancellor of Germany in 1933 was another blow to the prospects of world peace, for he was determined to tear the Treaty of Versailles to shreds. Germany began to re-arm, and the British and French governments did little to stop her. In March, 1936, Hitler took the first step on the path which three years later led to another World War: he sent troops into the Rhineland, which had been de-militarized by the Versailles Treaty. Next he drew closer to two other dissatisfied powers, Italy and Japan. When civil war came to Spain in 1936, Germans and Italians openly gave assistance to the Nationalist side, but the British did not intervene. By 1939 the Nationalists had won, and in General Franco Europe gained another right-wing dictator. To many abroad, Britain and France appeared ineffective and declining powers.

Neville Chamberlain and Appeasement

Neville Chamberlain became Prime Minister in May, 1937. His attempts to deal with the dictators of Europe have received the unflattering description of "appeasement." Chamberlain and his Foreign Secretary, Lord Halifax, recognized the Italian conquest of Abyssinia.

In March, 1938, Hitler and his army marched into Vienna.

Hitler, sensing Britain's weakness, marched troops into Austria in March, 1938; and once again Britain and France failed to take any strong action. His next victim was Czechoslovakia, within whose frontiers lived 3,500,000 Germans. President Benes of Czechoslovakia could not have been more conciliatory, and agreed to the suggestion of Lord Runciman, a British intermediary, that Germans within his country should be given full self-government; but this did not satisfy Hitler, who wished to annex Sudetenland where most of the German minority lived.

A crisis arose in September, 1938, during which the British Prime Minister met Hitler three times, at Berchtesgaden, at Godesberg and finally at Munich, where they were joined by Daladier (the French Premier) and Mussolini. Though they were prepared to fight, and possessed a well-equipped small army, the Czechs, who were not even admitted to the Munich conference, were told that they must cede Sudetenland to Germany; naturally they felt betrayed. Chamberlain spoke of "Peace in our time," but Winston Churchill, who had persistently warned the British government of danger from Germany and who had pressed for re-armament, spoke of "defeat without war." When Hitler occupied the whole of Czechoslovakia in March, 1939, it was quite clear that he meant to dominate Europe. Mussolini proved no worthier of Chamberlain's trust, for he invaded Albania in 1939 in spite of a recently-concluded Anglo-Italian agreement. Appeasement had failed.

Outbreak of War, 1939

Chamberlain was at last convinced that force would have to be met by force, and announced that Britain would take up arms to defend Poland, Greece or Roumania if they were attacked. Russia was cool towards Britain, for she had not been invited to take part in the Munich negotiations of 1938. When negotiations did take place between Britain, France and Russia in the summer of 1939, Britain did not deign to send her Foreign Secretary to Moscow but sent a subordinate official of the foreign office instead. Britain was astounded and dismayed by the non-aggression pact signed by the Russians and Germans in August, 1939. It relieved Hitler of fears that he would have to fight on two fronts at the outset of war. On 1 September, 1939, Hitler launched his attack upon Poland, thus plunging Europe once more into war. Chamberlain told the House of Commons that everything he had worked for was in ruins. He has been criticized for not defending Czechoslovakia, but his advocates say that he gave Britain a vital year to build up her armaments.

QUESTIONS

1. Describe the part played by Great Britain in setting up the League of Nations and in assisting its work.
2. Describe Anglo-French relations from 1918 to 1939.

CHAPTER 72

THE INTER-WAR YEARS: STANLEY BALDWIN

STANLEY BALDWIN was born in 1867 at Bewdley in Worcestershire, and educated at Harrow and Trinity College, Cambridge. His family was wealthy, possessing a large iron and steel concern into which young Stanley moved. Having served without distinction on Worcestershire County Council, he took over his father's seat as member for Bewdley in 1908. Entering parliament at forty-one he had no great expectation of achieving eminence there. In six years he spoke only five times. Little-known but well-liked, he even thought of quitting parliament after seven or eight years. It was Bonar Law's esteem for Baldwin's father that brought Baldwin his appointment in 1917 as Financial Secretary to the Treasury when Bonar Law was Chancellor of the Exchequer. The House came to appreciate Baldwin's lucid expositions of finance. In 1919 he expressed his patriotism when he gave £150,000 anonymously to Britain to help her in her post-war difficulties. By 1921 he had become President of the Board of Trade in the Lloyd George coalition, at a time when there were 1,750,000 unemployed. He revealed patience, good humour and a readiness to answer questions and earned the trust of the House, though he was still almost unknown to the public and had no great standing within the Conservative Party.

Chancellor of the Exchequer and Prime Minister

Britain's debts, lost markets, and difficulties over the French alliance, the Turk, the League of Nations, and the Irish question all combined to bring about the fall of Lloyd George in 1922. At the age of fifty-five, Baldwin was made Chancellor of the Exchequer by Bonar Law in the new Conservative administration. Baldwin was called upon to settle the problem of the debt to America contracted during the 1914-18 war. Largely on his own responsibility he settled for an annual repayment of £33 million which Bonar Law accepted reluctantly. Bonar Law was a dying man, and in 1923 he departed from the political scene. Either Lord Curzon or Baldwin was likely to be called upon to replace him. To the bitter disappointment of Curzon, the King preferring to appoint a Commons man, and having consulted Balfour, made Baldwin the new Premier. Almost by chance the great office had fallen upon Baldwin, and he was to hold it three times. He had now the difficult task of re-uniting the Conservatives. Curzon served as Foreign Secretary and Neville

Chamberlain as Chancellor of the Exchequer in the new ministry. Churchill later called Baldwin "the greatest party manager the Conservatives ever had." He possessed an air of unruffled confidence; he was seen as a solid pipe-smoking Englishman, and was regarded widely with affection. His attendance in the House of Commons was assiduous but he scamped the administrative burdens of his office.

One of the first problems that Baldwin had to face as Premier was that of relations with France, who feared a German revival and marched her troops into the Rhineland in 1923. Britain preferred a long-term policy of reconstruction. Baldwin never really understood foreign affairs or foreigners; he could not speak their language or understand their emotions. He was very insular, and foreign affairs bored him. He was much more concerned with unemployment at home. As a result he exercised no influence to concert Anglo-French policies.

Baldwin was eager to gain a release from Free Trade pledges, and wished to deal with unemployment by means of a tariff. He persuaded a reluctant Cabinet to go to the polls in 1923 on a platform of absolute freedom in all fiscal measures, no further taxes on essential foods, protection for particular industries, assistance to agriculture and "a sound foreign policy based on the principles of the League of Nations." He lost the election and appeared to have made a bad decision, yet he did not lose the leadership of his party.

Baldwin's Second Ministry, 1924-29

Twelve months were enough to show the electorate that the Socialists were no more competent to deal with the malady of unemployment than their opponents. Hence Baldwin's Conservatives won the 1924 election with a majority of 211 over all other parties combined. Winston Churchill became Chancellor of the Exchequer, and Austen Chamberlain Foreign Secretary.

At home, depression in the coal-mines transcended all other problems. Baldwin favoured a subsidy to keep the mines going. In 1926 he did his best to mediate between miners and owners, but was unable to prevent the trouble spreading into a general strike. Convinced that a general strike was always a possibility, Baldwin had revived the Supply and Transport Committee in 1923 and it was this organization that enabled the government to deal so capably with the crisis of 1926. After the strike the king congratulated Baldwin, and his stature was considerably enhanced; but he did little to follow up his success. Under pressure from colleagues he agreed to support the Trades Disputes Bill of 1927, which declared general strikes illegal. From 1927 to 1929 he seemed little more than an observer of events at home and abroad. He never believed in interfering in the work of a minister; foreign policy was Chamberlain's concern, and finance Churchill's. Though protectionist by conviction, Baldwin did not insist on it as a policy. Having

1936: a policeman turns away a demonstrator from Downing Street. The placard reads, "We want Edward VIII, not Baldwin."

given women over twenty-one their "flappers' vote" in 1928, he expected to win the 1929 election, but it was not to be won by a recitation of Conservative achievements: schools, cheap electricity, a million houses, peace at Locarno and 600,000 more men in work. People were tired of the Conservatives.

One aspect of Baldwin's work in this ministry must not be overlooked. He ordered the appointment of the Simon Commission in 1927 to go to India and investigate the possibilities of Dominion status for India. His attitude to the problem was an enlightened one, though he was strongly opposed by Imperialists (such as Churchill) within his own party.

The National Government of 1931

The Labour government of 1929-31 ran into many difficulties. Unemployment figures rose from one million to 2,600,000, and there was a crisis over the cost of insurance benefits. Baldwin agreed to join a new National government in 1931, serving as President of the Council under MacDonald. The 1931 election gave the National government 554 seats and the opposition only fifty-two. Baldwin went off to Ottawa, where his even temper had its usual happy effect. A policy of imperial preference was launched, though it drove free traders like Herbert Samuel out of the National ministry.

In 1933 Hitler began to re-arm Germany. Baldwin recognized the need to look to Britain's defences, but allowed himself to be far too conscious of the unhealthy pacifism which prevailed among many in Britain. He lacked the drive to tackle the question of re-armament efficiently and courageously.

MacDonald also failed to grasp the deep threat to peace created by Hitler's rise to power in Germany.

In spite of his failures in foreign policy, Baldwin deserves credit for giving support to the India Act of 1935 which took responsible government a further step forward in India.

Baldwin's Third Spell as Prime Minister, 1935-37

In 1935 the National government was re-organized, and Baldwin became Prime Minister once more.

He had to declare Britain's attitude towards Mussolini's invasion of Abyssinia. The British fleet in the Mediterranean was reinforced, but Laval of France would not co-operate with Britain in taking firm measures against Italy. In the quiet election of 1935, the Conservatives won 428 seats which gave them a reduced majority. When the Foreign Secretary, Sir Samuel Hoare, met Laval to try to arrange for Italy to be given part of Abyssinia, there was a tremendous outcry in Britain which was a great shock to Baldwin. Always loyal to colleagues, he regretted having to accept Hoare's resignation but again he failed to exert a powerful influence abroad.

The accession of Edward VIII in 1936 brought Baldwin another burden for which he was little prepared. The new king was indiscreet and extravagant, though very popular, and his association with an American lady, Mrs. Simpson, was viewed by Cabinet and Church with great concern; she had been twice married and was now again involved in divorce proceedings. Edward had the choice of marrying her and abdicating, or giving up the idea of such a marriage. Baldwin handled the situation with great courage and tact, though he suffered weeks of anxiety before the king finally abdicated.

By 1937 Baldwin was worn out. His complacency, lack of scientific interest and indifference to administrative work were in part responsible for Britain's military weakness in 1939. He became Sir Stanley Baldwin and then moved up to the Lords as Earl Baldwin. He spent the war years (1939-45) in quiet retirement, knowing that thousands of British men and women regarded him as a man who left his country defenceless in order to gain a few years of office for his party; but he could claim to have saved Britain from civil strife and internal political violence during the inter-war years by his reasonable and calm approach, and to have trained the British Socialist movement to operate through constitutional and parliamentary channels by his friendly attitude. He died in 1947.

QUESTIONS

1. Assess the achievements of Baldwin, as Chancellor of the Exchequer and Prime Minister.
2. Comment on the importance of Baldwin's work up to 1931.

CHAPTER 73

THE INTER-WAR YEARS: RAMSAY MACDONALD

RAMSAY MACDONALD was born in 1866 in humble circumstances at Lossiemouth in Scotland. After journeying to London he worked as clerk and a journalist, his socialist leanings drawing him into the Fabian Society and later into the Independent Labour Party (1894). He became secretary to the Labour Representation Committee from which the Labour Party grew, and entered parliament in 1906 as M.P. for East Leicester. His opposition to the First World War made him very unpopular and cost him his seat in the Coupon Election of 1918, but he re-entered parliament in 1922.

His Aims and Character

MacDonald was something of an intriguer and could be very jealous. Criticism hurt him deeply. Never an extremist, he usually leaned towards compromise: some of his enemies said that he was not really a socialist at all! He wished his party to be respectable so that it could embrace the middle classes within its ranks. The good manners and good taste of the upper classes

Ramsay MacDonald at the great Labour Victory Demonstration.

attracted him strongly. MacDonald cut a very fine figure with his handsome face, brilliant eyes, wavy hair and warm Scottish accent.

Prime Minister, 1924

MacDonald served three times as Prime Minister, first in 1924, then from 1929 to 1931 and finally from 1931 to 1935. The general election of December, 1923, gave the Labour Party 191 seats but since the Conservatives won 258 seats the Socialists had to rely on Liberal support to form a ministry. Their record was disappointing, but they proved that men of working class origin could carry on the government of the country and they were not without some solid achievements. Five cruisers were laid down, council-house building was stimulated by a grant of £9 million per year, free places in secondary schools were increased, state scholarships to universities were revived, and £28 million were found by Philip Snowden, the Chancellor of the Exchequer, for road-building and the increased provision of electricity.

MacDonald acted as his own Foreign Secretary and performed well in that capacity. He brought together Herriot, the French Premier, and Stresemann, the German statesman, in London, and successfully relieved international tension. The League of Nations received his full support, and he tried hard to establish good relations with Russia by recognizing her new government, establishing trade with her, and arranging a loan.

The collapse of the first Labour government occurred rapidly when it was accused of political motives in withdrawing the prosecution of J. R. Campbell, editor of a Communist weekly, on a charge of trying to reduce the allegiance of servicemen. Talk of Red designs on Britain was strengthened by publication in the *Daily Mail* of the famous Red Letter signed by Zinoviev, President of the Praesidium of the Communist International in Moscow, and addressed to the British Communist party: it urged the promotion of a Communist revolution in Britain. The Liberals withdrew their support and at the 1924 election the Conservatives won 415 seats as compared with 152 won by Labour and 42 by the Liberals.

Second Labour Government, 1929-31

From 1923 to 1929 MacDonald led the Opposition in the Commons; when the Labour Party won 287 seats in the General Election of 1929 he returned as Prime Minister, though once again he was dependent upon Liberal support. Few governments have entered upon office with higher hopes and more goodwill than the Labour government of 1929 but it was unfortunate to encounter a desperate economic crisis. MacDonald was incapable of making big decisions, and his remedies were half-hearted. Unemployment figures rose from 1,300,000 in November, 1929, to 2,300,000 by 1930. Snowden, again Chancellor of the Exchequer, would allow no

Philip Snowden, Chancellor of the Exchequer in MacDonald's government.

extravagant expenditure; the House of Lords obstructed Labour measures; and the Liberals were once more inconstant.

The Labour Foreign Secretary, Arthur Henderson, made a very good impression in the Assemblies of the League of Nations at Geneva, working hard to bring about disarmament; and MacDonald successfully negotiated an agreement with America and Japan to curtail naval construction.

Faced with the collapse of international confidence in Britain's financial stability, Snowden proposed to cut unemployment benefits but was bitterly opposed by his colleagues and, as usual, MacDonald lacked the force of character to deal with the situation. By 1931 he had grown away from many of his fellow ministers. When he agreed to form a National ministry with the Conservatives and Liberals in that year because of the economic crisis, most of his colleagues regarded him as a traitor and only J. H. Thomas and Snowden joined him. An election followed the formation of the National government, and it reduced Labour representation in parliament disastrously to only forty-six members. Under the leadership of George Lansbury and Henderson this remnant attacked MacDonald vigorously, causing him considerable embarrassment.

Third MacDonald Government 1931-35

MacDonald, now dependent on Conservative votes, again failed to solve his country's problems. His health began to fail and Neville Chamberlain increasingly dominated the National Cabinet.

By the Import Duties Act of 1932 a substantial return to protection took place, though the Imperial Economic Conference at Ottawa in that year failed to do much to boost the economic strength of the Commonwealth. Gradual economic recovery at home did take place but this was due more to low prices, increasing consumption and rising productivity than to MacDonald's leadership. The introduction of a means test in determining unemployment benefit made him even more unpopular among his erstwhile Labour supporters, and the departure of Herbert Samuel and Snowden from the Government in 1932 made its claim to be national even weaker than before.

Perhaps MacDonald's best achievements in this ministry were the Statute of Westminster of 1931 which legalized and defined dominion status and the India Act of 1935 which extended self-government in India, though the development of the Commonwealth received a set-back in 1932 when de Valera became Prime Minister in Eire and adopted an attitude of hostility towards Britain (see page 398).

MacDonald's government, with Sir John Simon as Foreign Secretary, failed to react vigorously when Japan invaded Manchuria in 1931 and generally pursued a feeble foreign policy in the face of the rise of ruthless dictatorships in Europe.

Ironically enough, one of MacDonald's last acts as Premier was to sanction a modest return to re-armament. He was succeeded as Prime Minister in 1935 by Baldwin and suffered the humiliation in the November election of being defeated at Seaham by Emmanuel Shinwell, a Labour opponent. Another seat was found for him and he served as Lord President of the Council in Baldwin's National government until May, 1937, when Chamberlain became Premier. He died in November, 1937.

Conclusion

MacDonald played a leading part in the formation of the Labour Party during the last years of the nineteenth century and proved to the British middle classes that a Labour government was not the ogre that they feared it would be. If he had allowed the early Labour governments to plunge headlong into wild experiments he might have set the Labour movement back for many years. It was his misfortune to lead governments in 1924 and 1929-31 which had no absolute majorities. After the First World War his sincere efforts to establish lasting peace abroad were highly praiseworthy though they were destined to fail.

QUESTIONS

1. Outline the career of Ramsay MacDonald.
2. Write an account of the achievements and failures of Ramsay MacDonald.

CHAPTER 74

THE INTER-WAR YEARS: NEVILLE CHAMBERLAIN

NEVILLE CHAMBERLAIN, son of Joseph Chamberlain, was educated at Rugby school. In 1886 he studied science and engineering design at Mason College, Birmingham. After this came a successful apprenticeship with a firm of accountants. His father sent him to the Bahamas in 1890 to establish a sisal-growing business there, but after seven years of toil in a difficult climate he had to wind up the venture. Returning to Birmingham he plunged into business and local politics, interesting himself in the University and helping to found the Queen Elizabeth Hospital. In 1911 he became a member of the town council, and by 1915 was Lord Mayor. Lloyd George made him Director of National Service in 1916, though he was not yet in parliament, but Chamberlain gave up the post in 1917, having received little support from Lloyd George.

For much of his life Chamberlain was physically and mentally tireless. He seemed bleak and austere, and made many enemies. Too rarely was he conciliatory, but this may have been due to the strength with which he held his convictions. As a speaker he was dry and matter-of-fact. No one, however, could accuse him of lacking drive. He was almost fifty when he entered parliament, and to attain the Premiership was a remarkable achievement.

Neville Chamberlain entered the House of Commons in 1918 after winning the Birmingham seat of Ladywood. He soon established himself as an effective debater and as a good committee man. His failure as Director of National Service was not held against him, and he found that he liked parliamentary life. In 1922 he became Postmaster-General in the Bonar Law government, and soon afterwards Minister of Health. In this capacity he steered through Housing and Rent Restriction Acts to deal with post-war housing problems. In 1923 Baldwin retained him as Minister of Health, and then made him Chancellor of the Exchequer. Only marked administrative ability could have earned such rapid preferment.

Minister of Health, 1924-29

After returning to the Ministry of Health when the second Baldwin goverment was formed in 1924, Chamberlain was responsible for a prodigious legislative programme.

The Rating and Valuation Act reduced rating authorities from 15,546 to

October, 1938: Chamberlain meets Hitler in Munich at the time of the Czechoslovakian Crisis.

1,767; and a Widows, Orphans and Old Age Pensions Act was based on compulsory contributions. National Health Insurance was linked with Workmen's Compensation and Unemployment Insurance to provide a fairly complete scheme of protection against the major risks which might affect the working classes. Economies were effected in the National Insurance scheme and Poor Law administration. Eight hundred thousand new houses were built. The National Health Insurance Act of 1928 greatly improved health insurance benefits. In four years 440 infant welfare centres were opened and three hundred ante-natal clinics, and as a result there was a noticeable decrease in infant mortality. There was also legislation on clean food, clean air and clean water. Chamberlain and Churchill co-operated over the Local Government Act of 1929, which introduced block grants to local authorities.

If Chamberlain's political career had ended in 1929, he would already have earned the lasting gratitude of his countrymen. Unfortunately he is more readily remembered for his handling of Hitler before the Second World War.

Chancellor of the Exchequer in the National Government, 1931-35

In 1931 Chamberlain played a strong role in forming the National government which was headed by Ramsay MacDonald. He entered it as Minister of Health, but after the 1931 General Election he was moved to the post of Chancellor of the Exchequer. In this office he was able to fulfil his father's policy of tariff reform. An Abnormal Importations Act gave immediate protection against dumping of goods by foreign powers. A Horticultural

Tariffs Act put duties upon certain vegetables, fruit and flowers. In 1932 a general tariff of 10 per cent was established to correct the adverse balance of payments, to raise fresh revenue, to prevent further depreciation of the pound, and to check unemployment.

Interest on government stocks was reduced from 5 per cent to 3½ per cent, saving the Exchequer some £40 million a year. At Lausanne Chamberlain dealt ably with the problem of German reparations in 1932, and played a prominent part in Imperial trade talks at Ottawa. He was, in fact, the dynamic element in Baldwin's government; though ranking behind Baldwin and MacDonald, he was doing most of the work. Much credit for Britain's economic recovery after the 1931 slump was rightly his. In 1931 there had been an unfavourable trade balance of £104 million, but by 1935 there was a surplus of £32 million. In 1931 there had been nearly three million unemployed, but by 1935 the figure was two million.

Prime-Minister Designate, 1935-37

Though Chamberlain is remembered as an appeaser of dictators, he branded Mussolini's Abyssinian aggression of 1935 as barbarous and spoke of Hitler in 1936 as a "mad dictator." As early as 1935 he favoured rearmament and was pilloried by Labour leaders as a warmonger.

Though grumbling that four years of fruitful finance were to be undone, he was principal architect of the Defence White Papers of 1936 and 1937, in which plans were made for constructing five new battleships, twenty cruisers and four aircraft carriers, and for the steady replacement of old destroyers and submarines. The regular and territorial armies were to be expanded, and the R.A.F. was to receive a front-line strength of 1,750 aircraft.

An expenditure of £1,500 million over five years was contemplated. Attlee, the Labour leader, spoke of "a sequence of war budgets." If Britain was inadequately prepared to deal with the dictators, the Opposition of the pre-war years must take a share of the blame. Defence plans forced Chamberlain to raise income tax from 4*s.* 6*d.* to 5*s.* in 1936. In government policy towards the Spanish Civil War, and in Baldwin's handling of the Abdication crisis of 1936, Chamberlain's influence was decisive.

Prime Minister, 1937-40

In June, 1937, Chamberlain, then sixty-seven, succeeded Baldwin as Premier upon the latter's retirement. Few Prime Ministers have worked harder. He continued his interest in social reform and during his ministry a comprehensive Factories Act was passed and a pension scheme established on a voluntary basis for black-coat workers. There was also a New Housing Act dealing with slum clearance, and a Physical Training and Recreation Act.

The excesses of the Nazi régime in Germany appalled Chamberlain.

Necessity was the reason for his policy of appeasement, for he knew that Britain was not ready to fight. In his defence it must be admitted that appeasement expressed the general desire of the British people at that time. The resignation of Anthony Eden from the Foreign Office in 1938 was partly due to Chamberlain's strong interference in foreign affairs, the occasion of it being Chamberlain's readiness to negotiate with Mussolini. When Hitler annexed Austria in March, 1938, Chamberlain was still very conscious of Britain's unreadiness for war.

The next crisis which he had to face was that concerning Czechoslovakia. He has been accused of cold-shouldering Russia over the defence of Czechoslovakia, but there is little evidence that Russia was prepared at that time to defend it. Chamberlain showed great courage in making his first-ever flight to see Hitler at Berchtesgaden in September 1938, and though he was accused of lowering the prestige of the British Prime Minister, he did not allow Hitler to browbeat him. Two other meetings took place over Czechoslovakia, one at Godesberg near the Rhine where Hitler told Chamberlain that he was the only man to whom he had ever made a concession, and the other at Munich. Chamberlain was unable to save Czechoslovakia from partial dismemberment. He considered that Sudeten Germans under Czech rule had definite grievances, and that vital British interests were not at stake. Britain was still under-prepared for war for she had only one-tenth of the anti-aircraft guns needed. When war broke out in 1939, provision of these guns had increased fourfold to 1,653, and a chain of radar stations had been built. Monthly output of aircraft in 1938 was 240: in 1939 it became 660. Chamberlain gained for Britain a vital breathing space in which to prepare herself for war.

Chamberlain should have resigned at the beginning of the war, for he was no war minister. He lived to see Hitler gain domination over much of Europe. Debates over the British failure in Norway led to his downfall in 1940, though he served on under Churchill until his death in November, 1940.

Neville Chamberlain's Achievements

Chamberlain did much for the welfare of his native city, Birmingham. His prudent finance restored confidence after the financial crisis of 1931, and he helped to bring about Britain's economic recovery by 1939. He championed social reform, and encouraged a progressive policy towards the Empire.

He strove hard for peace, and gave his country a year's respite (1938-9) during which she gathered strength for the war which lay ahead.

QUESTIONS

1. Outline Neville Chamberlain's achievements between 1918 and 1939.

2. Describe the career of Neville Chamberlain.

A NOTE ON FREE TRADE AND TARIFF REFORM

In the eighteenth century the Mercantile theory of trade prevailed. It was believed that the only real source of wealth was bullion and that if two countries traded with one another, the one which sold the less must lose.

Mercantilism was attacked by Adam Smith in his book *The Wealth of Nations*, published in 1776. He preached that governments should not interfere with trade, which should be allowed to flow freely; in this way wealth would be increased.

Pitt the Younger was impressed by his views and put them into effect in his Commercial Treaty with France of 1786 (see pages 278-9). The long French wars which began in 1793 suspended further experiment with free trade until William Huskisson took up the cause again between 1823 and 1828 (see pages 315-6).

In his two famous budgets of 1842 and 1845 Peel did much to extend free trade, and the repeal of the Corn Laws in 1846 was another great step towards its completion (see pages 335-6).

Gladstone, a disciple of Peel, carried through the completion of free trade as Chancellor of the Exchequer in the Aberdeen coalition of 1852-55 and in the Palmerston ministry of 1859-65 (see pages 367-8). The Cobden Treaty with France of 1860 was another landmark (see page 344).

Between 1850 and 1870 Britain enjoyed a period of unprecedented prosperity which was naturally credited to free trade. To go back to a policy of protection would have been politically suicidal, as Disraeli clearly saw; but with increasing industrial competition from France, Germany and the U.S.A. some form of protection for British industry became desirable. British agriculture could not stand up to the invasion of cheap grain from the New World.

The man who openly advocated a return to protection was Joseph Chamberlain. His aim was not so much to protect home industries as to impose tariffs on foreign goods entering Britain so that more favourable terms could be offered to dominions and colonies in order to draw closer the bonds of the Empire. The crushing defeat of the Conservatives in the General Election of 1906 proved that the country was not ready to support Chamberlain's policy (see page 422).

The first step towards a policy of protection was taken in 1915 when the

British government imposed the McKenna duties (named after the Chancellor of the Exchequer). A $33\frac{1}{3}$ per cent duty was placed on cycles, motor-cycles, clocks, watches, musical instruments and films, all luxury goods, in order to suspend their importation in wartime. A Safeguarding of Industries Act was passed in 1921 to shut out German optical glasses, electrical instruments and chemicals, but the Liberal and Labour Parties remained firmly attached to free trade.

The National government formed in 1931 went back fully to protection in order to deal with the economic crisis which it faced. Neville Chamberlain Joseph's son, as Chancellor of the Exchequer, imposed a 10 per cent duty on almost all imports except Empire products. After the Imperial Conference at Ottawa in 1932, Britain and her Dominions raised tariff barriers against foreign goods. Britain has never since been able to return to free trade.

REVISION SUMMARY OF CHAPTERS 56-74

BENJAMIN DISRAELI

WILLIAM EWART GLADSTONE

TRADE UNIONISM

OCL/HIST/1—2F*

IRELAND, 1780-1848

IRELAND, 1848-1939

INDUSTRY AND AGRICULTURE AFTER 1870

DEVELOPMENT OF EDUCATION

LORD SALISBURY

Page

CAMPBELL-BANNERMAN AND ASQUITH, 1906-14

DAVID LLOYD GEORGE

Page

FOREIGN AFFAIRS, 1918-39

THE INTER-WAR YEARS: STANLEY BALDWIN

SUGGESTIONS ON EXAMINATION TECHNIQUE

1. Before you reach the examination room find out the time given for the paper and the number of questions required. Allow five or ten minutes for reading through your finished script, and divide the remaining time by the required number of questions, and spend approximately equal time on each question. However much you know about one question, do not exceed your allotted time-per-question by more than five minutes. All questions carry equal marks; the specified number of questions competently answered will earn a better total mark than a small number exhaustively treated, and any question over the specified number will be ignored.
2. In the examination room you may open the paper, and quickly read all the questions on your section of the paper. Those you hoped to find will stand out, and while you work on these, ideas about others will be forming in your mind. Ignore the questions you can not possibly tackle. If you have prepared yourself soundly there will always be at least the required number which you can do.
3. Before writing any answer, make an outline plan similar to those provided for the specimen questions in this book. This will prevent serious omissions, and also the inclusion of irrelevant matter.
4. Irrelevance is the most serious weakness of most history scripts. If asked for an account of the new farming in the eighteenth century, do not give a lot of padding about the evils of the three-field system. Confine yourself to what is wanted, namely the work of Townshend, Coke, etc. "Account *of*" and "describe *how*" demand a narrative; "account *for*" and "explain *why*" call for explanations.
5. There is sometimes a bonus, sometimes a penalty for "presentation," which includes spelling, punctuation, grammatical accuracy and legibility. Be as accurate and neat as time permits. Never use a ball-point pen.
6. Write essays unless the question asks for notes. Even then it is desirable to write in complete sentences. In questions which ask for notes, confine yourself to the essential facts and a brief indication of the importance of the subject concerned.
7. The examiner may sometimes try to help you; if so, do not let this hinder you. A question may read "Give an account of the main attempts to reform parliament between 1830 and 1930. Refer to the measures to 1832, 1867, 1884, 1885, 1911, 1918, 1928." Do not avoid this question because *one* of the dates means nothing to you. If you know the rest well you will still get far more than the pass mark.
8. Remember that no amount of advice on examination technique will remove the necessity for hard work and diligent preparation. Read, make your notes, learn, revise; these are the indispensable foundations of success.

NOTE ON EXAMINATION PAPERS

As has already been stated in the Foreword, there are so many variations in the syllabuses set by the different examining boards, and so many alternative schemes within any given syllabus that any specimen paper can only be a rough guide. Generally, any one examining board offers at least three alternative schemes (such as British Political History, European History, and Social and Economic History). Because this volume is concerned mainly with British Political History the following

OCL/HIST/1—2G

"Specimen Paper" is limited to that alternative. The syllabus is divided into chronological sections. Sometimes the candidate is allowed unrestricted choice of questions throughout the whole range of the paper; sometimes choice is restricted to two periods. The number of questions to be attempted is usually four or five, and the time allowed for the paper two and a quarter, or two and a half hours.

Types of questions also differ. Essay questions form the bulk of those set, and may call for the presentation either of argument or narrative. A modified essay type is that which asks the candidate to "write briefly about" two, three or four topics. A more extreme form of such a question lists perhaps half a dozen topics or more, and asks for three or four specific facts about a given number. At least one board includes for each section of the paper an outline map and asks for certain features to be identified. Unless the candidate has made an approach to the study of his period by means of sketch-map histories, such a question is best left alone. In any case a candidate is not usually allowed to include in his answers more than two such map questions. The same examining board has recently shown a tendency in some of its essay questions to suggest the main points which should be covered in the answer. This type of question should not be avoided merely because the candidate feels there are one or two points on which he is ill-informed.

The Specimen Paper which follows is limited to a particular syllabus and designed to indicate the range of all types of question save that of the outline map. It is always worthwhile studying recent papers set by the examining board for which the student is working.

SPECIMEN EXAMINATION PAPER

Syllabus: "Outlines of British Political History, 1066-1939." *Five questions to be answered chosen from not fewer than two sections of the paper (choice of questions marked with an asterisk might be restricted to not more than two). Time:* $2\frac{1}{2}$ *hours.*

SECTION 1 (1066-1272)

1. What were the dangers of feudalism to the Crown and how did William the Conqueror attempt to safeguard himself against them?

2. Outline the relations of Anselm with William Rufus and Henry I.

3. Account for the anarchy of the reign of Stephen and show how it was finally resolved.

4. How did Henry II reform the government of England and what was the importance of his work in this respect? *In your answer you should refer to as many as possible of the following:* the Exchequer Court, the Assize of Clarendon, the Jury System, scutage, the Inquest of Sheriffs, the Assize of Arms, writs.

5. Describe the part played by England in the Third Crusade.

6. Why did King John quarrel with his barons and what "liberties" did they gain by Magna Carta?

7. What aspects of the government of Henry III during the period 1216-64 gave rise to general discontent?

***8.** Explain each of *five* of the following terms: **a.** fealty; **b.** boon work; **c.** villein; **d.** Curia Regis; **e.** motte and bailey; **f.** cloister; **g.** scriptorium; **h.** chapter house.

9. Write briefly on each of *four* of the following: **a.** Norman Forest Laws; **b.** Robert of Bellême; **c.** the Constitutions of Clarendon 1164; **d.** the rebellions of 1173 and 1188; **e.** Bouvines 1214; **f.** Strongbow in Ireland; **g.** the Parliament of 1265.

SECTION 2 (1272-1485)

10. Outline the steps taken by Edward I to unite Britain and estimate his success.

11. What were the reasons for the deposition of *either* Edward II *or* Richard II?

12. Give an account of the work of the Dominican and Franciscan Friars.

13. Why did England go to war with France in the reign of Edward III and why was the conflict renewed under Henry V?

14. Describe the course and the consequences of the Peasants' Revolt of 1381. *In your answer you should discuss as many of the following aspects of the topic as possible:* events in Essex, Kent, London, Norfolk, revocation of the Charters, effects of serfdom, Richard II.

15. Account for the loss of France in the reign of Henry VI.

16. Why was Edward IV able to establish a royal despotism after 1471?

17. Write briefly about *four* of the following: **a.** the main features of Decorated and Perpendicular Gothic architecture; **b.** the Black Death; **c.** the Craft Gilds; **d.** the Wool Staple; **e.** the Model Parliament of 1295; **f.** the Merciless Parliament of 1388.

***18.** Indicate the circumstances which led to, and the main provisions of, each of *five* of the following: **a.** the First Statute of Westminster 1275; **b.** the Statute of Mortmain 1279; **c.** the Statute of Gloucester (Quo Warranto) 1278; **d.** the Bull Clericis Laicos 1296; **e.** the Statute of Provisors 1351; **f.** the Treaty of Brétigny 1360; **g.** Statute of De Heretico Comburendo 1401; **h.** the Treaty of Troyes 1420.

SECTION 3 (1485-1660)

19. Outline the work of the Reformation Parliament between 1529 and 1536.

20. Why was (**a**) Somerset deposed as Protector in the reign of Edward VI, and (**b**) Northumberland executed on the accession of Mary Tudor?

21. Why was the Spanish match so unpopular, and why did Mary Tudor persist in it?

22. Did Mary Queen of Scots deserve execution?

23. Describe how Crown and Commons quarrelled on religion, finance and parliamentary privilege between 1603 and 1629.

24. Account for the failure of the royalists in the Civil Wars of 1642-49.

25. Give an account of the constitutional experiments of the Interregnum. *In your answer you should refer to as many as possible of the following developments:* Barebone's Parliament 1653; the Instrument of Government 1653; the First and Second Protectorate Parliaments; the Rule of the Major-Generals; the Humble Petition and Advice; Parliamentary Reform.

26. Write briefly on *four* of the following: **a.** Henry VII and Ireland; **b** the First and Second Prayer Books (1549, 1552); **c.** the Marian Persecution; **d.** Elizabeth I and the Netherlands; **e.** the voyages of Sir Francis Drake; **f.** the Hampton Court Conference; **g.** the Levellers.

***27.** Give *two* provisions and indicate very briefly the importance of each of *five* of the following: **a.** the Navigation Act of 1485; **b.** the Acts of Uniformity and Supremacy 1559; **c.** the Poor Law of 1601; **d.** the Petition of Right 1628; **e.** the Grand Remonstrance 1641; **f.** the Solemn League and Covenant 1644; **g.** the Self-Denying Ordinance 1644; **h.** the Declaration of Breda 1660.

SECTION 4 (1660-1783)

28. Describe the part played by Shaftesbury in the reign of Charles II.

29. Why did James II lose his throne?

30. Why was England continually at war between 1695 and 1714?

31. Illustrate Walpole's policy of "letting sleeping dogs lie." *In your answer you should write about as many as possible of the following points:* proposed extension of Bonded Warehouses 1733; Indemnity Act for Nonconformists; Treaty of Hanover 1725; Second Treaty of Vienna 1731; War of the Polish Succession 1733; War against Spain 1739; Wood's Halfpence.

32. "A great War Minister"; justify this verdict on the Elder Pitt.

33. Describe the aims of George III and outline his relations with the ministries of years 1763-70.

34. Explain (**a**) the evils arising from the Industrial Revolution; and (**b**) the advantages arising from the Agricultural Revolution of the eighteenth century.

35. Write briefly about *three* of the following: **a.** the Clarendon Code; **b.** the Trial of the Seven Bishops; **c.** the foundation of the Bank of England 1694; **d.** the South Sea Bubble; **e.** the Gordon Riots 1780.

***36.** Give *three* reasons for each of *six* of the following: **a.** the decision to restore the monarchy in 1660; **b.** the ability of Charles II to dispense with parliament 1680-85; **c.** the failure of Monmouth's Rebellion 1685; **d.** the Union of England and Scotland 1707; **e.** the Accession of the Hanoverian Dynasty 1714; **f.** the failure of the Jacobite Rebellion of 1745; **g.** the importance of John Wilkes; **h.** the success of the preaching of John Wesley; **i.** the concessions to Ireland 1780-82.

SECTION 5 (1783-1939)

37. Either

(**a**) Describe the main policies of the younger Pitt before 1793, or

(**b**) Account for the success of Britain in the Napoleonic Wars 1803-15.

38. Outline the Whig Reforms of the periods 1833-41. *In your answer you should discuss as many as possible of the following issues:* slavery; factory legislation; education; Poor Law; Local Government; births, marriages and deaths; church reform.

39. Give an account of the foreign policy of Palmerston *either* as Foreign Secretary 1830-41 and 1846-51; *or* as Prime Minister 1855-58 and 1859-65.

40. Describe the work of *either* Disraeli with regard to social reform; *or* Gladstone with relation to Ireland.

41. By what means and for what reasons was the policy of "Splendid Isolation" abandoned?

42. Describe the effects of the war of 1914-18 on British agriculture and industry.

43. Describe the ways in which the problem of unemployment was dealt with by Conservative, Labour and National Governments between 1927 and 1939.

44. Write briefly on *four* of the following: **a.** Peel and the Conservative Party; **b.** the extension of the franchise between 1833 and 1928; **c.** Joseph and Neville Chamberlain and the decline of Free Trade; **d.** developments in State Education 1890-1902; **e.** the work of Lloyd George as Chancellor of the Exchequer; **f.** the General Strike 1926; **g.** the foreign and imperial policies of the Labour Government of 1929-31.

***45.** Give the main provisions and briefly indicate the importance of each of *five* of the following: **a.** the Treaty of Paris 1856; **b.** the Trades Union Act of 1871; **c.** the Local Government Act of 1888; **d.** the British North America Act of 1867; **e.** the Morley-Minto reforms in India 1909; **f.** the Taff Vale Case 1901 and the Osborne Judgment 1909; **g.** the Irish Free State Act 1922; **h.** the Hoare-Laval Pact 1935.

OUTLINE ANSWERS TO TEXT QUESTIONS

CHAPTER 1

1. **Trace Anglo-Norman connection:** marriage of Ethelred II and Emma of Normandy (1002), Emma and Cnut (1017), Cnut's sister, Estrith, and Duke Robert of Normandy (1027). Ethelred in exile in Normandy (1013), his sons Alfred, Edward grew up there. **Edward the Confessor and Norman influence:** his twenty-five years in Normandy gave Edward an outlook more Norman than English so appointment of Normans to lay and clerical office was natural, and they were deliberately recruited to counter political and territorial influence of House of Godwin. **Promise of crown to William:** was probably made in 1051 and "oath" of Harold also pointed to William's accession. Everything seemed in William's favour, but his success not inevitable (see answer to next question).

2. **Personal ambition:** he had prepared the way for a take-over in England on Edward's death, he had opposed influence of House of Godwin and had succession promised by Edward, and support promised by Harold. Harold's "election" as king called for immediate response, delay would strengthen Harold's position. **Reasons for success:** Harold engaged on two fronts, William's landing unopposed, Normans established before Hastings. **Harold's errors of judgement:** in giving battle immediately when his force was weakened by march from Stamford Bridge, his failure to wait for reinforcements, half-hearted support from his brothers-in-law, Earls of Mercia and Northumbria, superior Norman battle tactics, armoured, disciplined mounted knights, death of Harold, "scorched earth" policy of William after Hastings and calculated isolation of London.

CHAPTER 2

1. **Rapid and ubiquitous castle-building** ("motte-and-bailey"), in particular to guard South-East coast against Continental attack, northern border against Scotland and Welsh frontier; defeat of Mercian and Northern risings prompted further building. **Checked rebellions** against him in Kent, Exeter, York, East Anglia—and by his "Devastation of the North" demonstrated his authority. **Confiscated estates** of Englishmen killed at Hastings and in rebellion. Norman plantation of North; after 1069 Englishmen replaced by Normans as holders of land. **Adaptation of feudal system** to provide army of knights bound by oath of fealty, thus curtailing risk of baronial revolt. **Emphasized continuity** between his and Confessor's reign, preserved Saxon partnership of Crown and Church. *Domesday Survey* gave details of land and people.

2. **Feudal System not Norman invention** but given distinctive pattern by William I; a military society based on land. Keeping a quarter of all land himself, distributed remainder as fiefs among lay and ecclesiastical tenants-in-chief; each required to provide king with fully-armed knights in proportion to amount of land each held. Homage and oath of fealty required directly from all tenants-in-chief, lesser tenants, knights (see page 28); additional feudal obligations: regular aids, relief, wardship. **Limitations of system:** military needs not satisfied, unrealistic assessment for knights, recourse to mercenaries, scutage. Effectiveness of system depended on personality of king (see pages 26-31).

CHAPTER 3

1. **Two main issues:** lay investiture, church courts and "criminous clerks." Relations between Crown and Church affected by character and policy of king, and character and principles of Archbishop (e.g. harmony of William I and Lanfranc, deadlock between William II and Anselm). Reconciliation with Church by Henry I on his accession shattered by lay investiture issue. Compromise reached by Henry and Anselm reduced royal power over Church. Under Theobald Church exploited weakness of Stephen to secure charter (1136) acknowledging Church jurisdiction over ecclesiastical persons and property. Point at issue in struggle between Henry II and Becket: church courts and lay control. Neither prepared to give way. Murder of Becket symbol of triumph of Church.

2. (See also above.) As Archbishop, Becket was champion of Church independence of lay control. Position threatened by aims of Henry II; king protagonist of royal supremacy and administrative order (abuses in clerical jurisdiction). Character of two men key to struggle. In early deadlock (1162-70) Henry had slight advantage, but this wiped out by Becket inciting Henry to murder. **Becket's achievement:** victory for Church independence, unchallenged until Reformation of 16th century.

CHAPTER 4

1. **Sketch situation on Stephen's death:** aftermath of civil war, diminished authority of Crown, alienation of Crown estates, disproportionate power of nobles, abandonment of law and order. Henry's aim to continue work of Henry I. **Immediate actions:** demolished adulterine castles, dismissed mercenaries, reclaimed Crown lands, stabilized frontiers. **Long-term measures:** reform of law; itinerant justices, Courts of King's Bench and Common Pleas, writs for settlement of land disputes. Remarkable for his energy, dynamic purpose, administrative skill, and extent of his empire.

2. **Basic trouble:** disputed succession on death of Henry I (1135). Rival candidates Mathilda, Stephen, were each supported by noble factions greedy for power at expense of Crown. **Stephen made concessions:** privileges to London, cession of land to Scotland, estates to barons, which won him title, but not authority of king. **Civil War (1139-48):** barons rejected their feudal obligations ("diffidatio"), played one side off against other, pursued private feuds; unlicensed castles mushroomed, Normandy lost. Mathilda withdrew (1148), agreed with Stephen (1153) succession in favour of her son, Henry II.

CHAPTER 5

1. See pages 32-5 and 37 for answer to this question.

2. **Many shortcomings, little success.** Obsessed by war (killed besieging an obscure castle); no interest in government, or in England except as a source of campaign funds (only five months of a 9½-year reign spent in England). Treacherous and untrustworthy: rebellion against his father; repudiation of Alice, sister of Philip of France. Brave and skilful as a soldier, but even his military success limited: captured Messina and Cyprus, mainly responsible for fall of Acre, but failed to recover Jerusalem and glad to conclude truce with Saladin. **Only successes:** quality of administrative measures of Henry II and work of four justiciars (Hubert Walter the most important), which held England together in spite of Richard.

CHAPTER 6

1. **John traditionally a "bad king,"** a view largely derived from hostile but often false stories of Roger of Wendover. Had many faults; spoilt, cruel (treatment of hostages, of Matilda de Briouze), vile-tempered, suspicious, treacherous (towards his father, his barons, murder of Arthur), untrustworthy (Magna Carta). **But did not hanker after extension of royal power:** took his job very seriously; constant progresses, keeping watch on administration, dispensing justice, fostering efficient bureaucracy. Intelligent, excellent military tactician (baronial absenteeism partly responsible for French defeats), saw importance of fleet; effectively administered Ireland (after earlier ineptitude), contained Scotland and Wales.

2. **Alienated clergy:** Canterbury election (1205), his attitude to Langton, appropriation of Canterbury revenues (1208-13) and of opposition bishops (1209-13), Interdict. **Alienated barons:** demand for hostages, crushing financial demands (excessive scutages, reliefs, abuse of wardship), murder of Arthur. **Alienated remainder of his subjects:** Interdict (1208), murder of Arthur, loss of French lands. Magna Carta a feudal document, not legendary source of our modern liberties, but was the first limitation of royal authority, and with many later confirmations (including one in 1660) symbolized triumph of "lex" over "rex."

CHAPTER 7

1. **Career:** de Montfort (1208-65) a Gascon; came to England to secure claim through his father for Earldom of Leicester (1229); married Henry III's sister, Eleanor (1238); Earl of Leicester (1239); on crusade (1240-41), having fallen out with king (1239); Lieutenant of Gascony (1248), returned to England (1254). In opposition to king was one of authors of Provisions of Oxford (1258) and member of Great Council set up to reform administration; defeated king at Lewes (1264) and himself governed England in accordance with Provisions of Oxford. Position undermined, defeated and killed at Evesham (1265). **Importance:** contributed to development of Parliament (see page 60), unselfish leadership of baronial reformers and devotion to good government.

2. **Character** (page 46). **Difficulties:** alien influences, appointment of Poitevin Peter des Roches, relations of Queen Eleanor of Provence, offspring of Henry's mother's second marriage. **Financial complications:** personal extravagance, building schemes, Papal demands for "provisions" and subsidies. **Sicilian project:** forfeiture of baronial trust. **His own character:** a monarchical misfit.

CHAPTER 8

1. **Possessed all kingly attributes:** believer in strong royal authority and good laws. He must be judged on his work from coronation, 1274-94 (point of uncertainty, disappointment and rising opposition). **Outstanding as administrator and lawgiver:** inquiry into extent of Crown lands and baronial jurisdictions, Statutes of Westminster (1275, 1285, 1290), Gloucester (1278, "Quo Warranto" inquiry), Mortmain (1279), Winchester (1285); Exchequer, Chancery and Wardrobe flourishing departments of administration; development of Courts of Exchequer, King's Brench and Common Pleas, extension of work of itinerant justices; contribution to development of Parliament (see page 60). All this and conquest and settlement of Wales achieved in twenty years.

2. See page 60 for answer to this question.

CHAPTER 9

1. (a) See page 61.
(b) Marks peak of English fortunes in Edward III's reign (see page 63).
(c) See page 66 for terms. Marks nadir of French fortunes; had Henry V not died in 1422, or had he had a grown son to succeed, treaty would have meant end of French independence and Valois line of kings.

2. Henry anxious for military glory, deliberately exploited war fever in England; a national war, if successful, would remove stigma of Lancastrian usurpation of throne in 1399; as descendant of Edward III Henry maintained his valid claim to French throne. **His success:** took Harfleur, decimated French cavalry at Agincourt (1415); completed conquest of Normandy (1417-19); established high military reputation. By Treaty of Troyes had French crown within his grasp.

CHAPTER 11

1. **Fundamental causes:** social upheaval arising from break-up of the manor, process hastened by Black Death, labour scarce, peasants mobile, demanding higher wages, Statute of Labourers, 1351 (reissued 1357, 1361), government attempt to peg wages and rents and check mobility of labour. This aroused resentment, as did enclosure, continuation of feudal services, war taxes, corrupt court, privileges in trade and Church granted to foreigners. **Immediate causes:** poll taxes of 1377, 1379, 1380; violent resistance to tax collectors in Essex sparks off revolt. **Results:** manorial system in decline, poll taxes not reimposed, landed classes in control but change inevitable.

2. See pages 80-1 for answer to this question.

CHAPTER 12

1. Established primarily for trade. **Sites:** fords (Oxford), crossroads (Winchester), unloading points for ships on navigable rivers (London), castles (Devizes), places of pilgrimage and monastic sites (Peterborough), river loops (Shrewsbury), hills above a river (Malmesbury). Also developed for strategic purposes (Newcastle), "gap" sites (Stirling), and for some special feature (Bath). Sites chosen by Romans, Saxons, Vikings, and many new towns formed in twelfth and thirteenth centuries. Establishment of towns gives rise to new townsman class; extension of trade as result of Crusades increased wealth and potential influence of merchants (seen in acquisition of charters). External trade regulated by Merchant Gild, internal by Craft Gilds, both controlled ultimately by Mayor and municipal authority through the control of weekly markets and annual fairs.

2. See page 85 for answer to this question.

CHAPTER 13

1. See pages 91-2 for answer to this question.

2. See pages 96-7.

CHAPTER 14

1. **Rival claims to throne** (see page 99): House of Lancaster usurped throne, 1399 (claim through third son of Edward III), House of York claimed superior title

(through second and fourth sons of Edward III). Henry VI weak and ineffectual, dominated by Queen Margaret of Anjou; reform of government demanded by York. **Over-mighty subjects:** weakness of king meant strength of nobles; feuds among them, many related to Lancaster or York (through numerous children of Edward III); "livery and maintenance" meant they had private armies. Failure in Hundred Years War (Castillon, 1453) blamed on peace policy of Queen, York wanted maximum war effort. Henry VI's madness (1453); Duke of York was heir to throne, Protector; reformed government. Recovery of Henry, birth of an heir—York out of the running now—Queen out for revenge on York who rallied support in his own defence.

2. See page 104 for answer to this question

CHAPTER 15

1. **By Treaty of Medina del Campo (1489):** Ferdinand of Spain alarmed by growing power of Charles VIII of France; Henry VII approached Spain; treaty guaranteed mutual protection. Thus Spain recognized Tudor dynasty. Henry's security was enhanced; marked him as a powerful ruler whose alliance was worth having. **Marriage of Arthur to Catherine of Aragon:** strengthened Tudor dynasty; gained for Henry further recognition abroad; increased England's status abroad to the same level as the two greatest powers of the time. **By Treaty of Etaples (1492):** Charles VIII bought off Henry's military support for Spain; implying that England was a powerful state; treaty honoured Henry as arbitrator between two greatest powers. Anglo-Flemish trade threatened by Flemish support of Yorkist pretenders, therefore Henry moved English wool market from Antwerp to Calais. **Result:** *Intercursus Magnus* granted English traders a free market without pass or licence in Flanders. Successful protection and extension of English trade; increased respect for Henry and English power. English position of great international power restored; increase of international prestige; English trade protected, extended and privileged; recognition of Tudor dynasty secured.

2. *N.B.:* **Threefold aspect of this question. Aim:** to establish Tudor dynasty. **Methods:** ending York-Lancaster rivalry by marriage; securing recognition by France, Spain, Papacy. **Aim:** restoration of peace and ordered government based on strong central monarchical power. **Methods:** suppression of Baronage; building up financial strength of central government (give details in each case). **Aim:** to protect national interests. **Methods:** Intercursus Magnus; refusal to enter Italian Wars; commercial treaties with Italian states to promote English Mediterranean trade; Navigation Act (1485) to increase size of the navy. **Comments on methods:** Little that was new, but in seeking to build up the Crown independent of faction he was reverting to policy of great medieval rulers. He merely gave new form to this policy by his prerogative courts.

CHAPTER 16

1. *N.B.:* **Wording of the question; not services to England, but to Henry VIII. Remember second part of question.** In early years of the reign Wolsey relieved Henry of routine administration, leaving the king free to be Prince of the Renaissance, following his interests in literature, art, music, theology, sport and pleasure. Wolsey used his position loyally to strengthen power of the King (explain his measures to assert power of central government against the Baronage, the Church, lawyers and parliament). Sought to satisfy the king in annulment of

marriage to Catherine; failure due as much to Papal non-co-operation as to Wolsey's desire to further his own ambitions. **Conclusion:** He taught Henry the extent to which a king might push his power; sent Henry on way towards freedom from control of an alien religious authority; laid foundations of Henry's later Tudor Despotism. **Reasons for fall:** Failure to accomplish King's Great Matter; made too many enemies (nobility, clergy, lawyers, merchants); excessive ambition and over-estimation of his indispensibility to King.

2. See pages 121-2 (Wolsey and the administration of justice).

CHAPTER 17

1. **Problems:** a second marriage in interests of succession, dynasty and nation; to break with Rome and assert royal will; to avoid in doing so the dangerous opposition from the clergy and the nation (which was anti-clerical rather than anti-Catholic and pro-Protestant). **Solution:** attack on clergy (invocation of Statute of Praemunire, appointment of Protestant Cranmer. These measures forestalled clerical revolt and pleased the nation which was anti-clerical); enlistment of Parliament on his side (the work of the Reformation Parliament was legislation effected by Parliament but which represented royal will and policy). With the clergy intimidated and the King declared Supreme Head of the Church, Convocation was used to give appearance of legality to Henry's second marriage. The clergy were now identified with the breach with Rome and the State Church. Henry's defence of Catholic doctrine and the Six Articles appeased people's attachment to teachings and practices of old church.

2. *N.B.:* **Threefold nature of the question. Why:** fear for dynasty and of civil war in absence of male heir; unlikelihood of a son by Catherine; infatuation for Anne Boleyn; scruples (sincere or otherwise) about validity of marriage to Catherine. Personal and national desire to be free from alien ecclesiastical authority (papacy). Failure of Wolsey in the King's Great Matter. **How:** Prohibition of payments and appeals to Rome; intimation of clergy (give details); enlistment of parliamentary and Convocation support; enlistment of Cromwell and Cranmer in King's service; suppression of papal outposts in England (i.e. monasteries); Henry's new title, Supreme Head of Church. **A Protestant:** Yes, in so far as he protested successfully against, and rejected, authority of papacy in English church. No, so far as doctrine was concerned; Fidei Defensor, Six Articles in spite of Cromwell and Cranmer.

CHAPTER 18

1. *N.B.:* **The limits of the question, 1540-53.** Answer here falls into two parts. **Under Somerset:** the Catholic Wriothesley dismissed from the Council; the Catholic Gardiner imprisoned for refusing to obey orders to place New Testament in English in every church; repeal of the Six Articles; attack on veneration of saints; use of candles prohibited; clerical marriage allowed; 1549 First Prayer Book and Act of Uniformity; Roman doctrine and practice now illegal for clergy; attack on doctrine of Purgatory; chantries dissolved. **Under Northumberland:** pro-Catholic bishops replaced by reformers (give names); the Ordinal (1533) reduced clerical orders to Bishop, Priest and Deacon in place of longer Catholic list; further attack on veneration of saints, also removal of images and stained glass; attack on ritual; simpler vestments; no private confessions; Second Prayer Book and Act of Uniformity 1552; Holy Communion rather than Mass;

communion commemorative not sacrificial; tables instead of altars; Transubstantiation condemned; uniformity to apply to laymen as well as clergy; the Forty-two Articles asserting Protestantism and condemning Catholicism teaching.

2. **Early popularity due to:** sympathy for her sufferings under Henry VIII and for her loyalty to her mother; public opinion anti-clerical rather than pro-Protestant, hence rapid religious changes of Edward VI had not been popular; the hope that under Mary a State Church would revert to old teaching and practice; Northumberland unpopular because of his opposition to needed social and economic reform; relief at deliverance from the prospect of civil war raised by Northumberland's exploitation of Lady Jane Grey; loyalty to a daughter of Henry VIII. **Later unpopularity:** attempt to restore Church lands (angered the landowners and nobility who held these lands); willingness to re-submit the country to authority of Pope; Mary willing to abandon the ecclesiastical independence of nation as well as anxious to restore old teaching and practice; the Spanish marriage offended merchants prohibited from trading with Spanish colonies, and the nation who feared the subordination of national interests to those of Spain; the Marian Persecution made England Protestant in sympathy for the first time; disgrace of the loss of Calais and that in the course of a war fought in Spanish (not English) interests.

CHAPTER 19

1. **Causes:** rise of new land-owning class (state why) with a new attitude to land-ownership (define it); the new farming, the consequence of these factors necessitated enclosures if it was to succeed; the old medieval system of farming had already begun to break up. Tudor enclosures were a natural continuation of an historical trend. **Effects:** some distress (not universal), due more to rising prices and rents; reduction of yeoman class by reduction of proportion of population engaged in farming; new inequalities of wealth, new rich, new poor; divergence of interest between landlord and tenant; beginnings of state regulation of economic life by government measures to control enclosures.

2. Rise of new social group to power through land ownership, and parliament (i.e. middle class merchants); changes in land ownership caused by passage of monastic and diocesan lands into lay ownership, new owners in search of profits, rise of rents; state replaces Church as agent for relief of poverty; growth of social unrest; nation divided on religion; individualist, materialist approach to life.

CHAPTER 20

1. **Policy:** see pages 148, 151. **Degree of success:** in neither case wholly successful. Although Catholicism was worse affected it was not completely destroyed; it was merely driven underground; Puritanism was less adversely affected because it had its champions in Parliament.

2. See text on Elizabethan conspiracies, pages 148, 151.

CHAPTER 21

1. **Explain:** Franco-Scottish links (the Guise connection and marriage); the attitude of Elizabeth to Regent Mary of Guise, Murray and the Protestant cause, and John Knox. Review Elizabeth's dealings with Mary Queen of Scots (Mary's desire to be recognized as Elizabeth's heir; if not herself then her son; Elizabeth's refusal to commit herself). **Mary in England:** as refugee guest, as prisoner.

Give reasons for: Elizabeth's efforts to avoid Mary's execution; Mary's ultimate execution. **Weakening of the Franco-Scottish links:** death of Francis; progress of Protestantism in Scotland, Alliance 1570-72.

2. **Justification of Elizabeth:** Mary's early actions were provocative in demanding recognition to the succession, in seeking refuge in England, in associating herself with conspiracy. **Mary was a danger to Elizabeth:** because she was a Catholic and therefore an inevitable focus for Catholic plots whether she encouraged it or not; because Elizabeth was childless and the succession uncertain. **Elizabeth exercised great patience:** in refusing to deliver Mary to her Scottish enemies; in delaying extreme action, thereby prolonging danger to herself, the country and Protestant cause in England. Ultimately she was right in sacrificing Mary. Catholic succession in England contrary to national interest. **Criticism:** might have mitigated the danger by recognizing James VI as heir; Mary's complicity in conspiracy is doubtful; kinship and kingship ignored; Mary had thrown herself on Elizabeth's protection; Elizabeth's attitude to execution was dishonest; execution led to papal pressure for action against England by Spain.

CHAPTER 22

1. **Elizabeth:** lack of money for war; expense of French wars in Mary's reign; rising prices diminished value of Crown's fixed income; desire to further English trade with Flanders (since this territory controlled by Spain, war with Spain would interrupt trade and so diminish Crown's revenue and displease merchants). Traditional policy to be on friendly terms with whatever power controlled the Low Countries. Fear that war with Spain (or France) might lead to Catholic uprising in England. **Philip:** while Francis lived he had no desire to see Queen of France and Scotland become Queen of England; this would tilt the balance of power in Europe against Spain; pre-occupation with the Netherlands; hope of peaceful restoration of Catholicism in England by diplomatic negotiation; possibility after 1572 of Franco-English alliance.

2. *N.B.:* **A narrative of the foreign policy of Henry VIII followed by a narrative of the foreign policy of Elizabeth will not do. Similarities and differences must be looked for and discussed side by side throughout the answer.** Intervention on the side of Spain or France to preserve the balance of power (Henry VIII). Diplomatic support of France or Spain as circumstances demanded but in order to avoid attack and to preserve peace and national independence (Elizabeth). Henry VIII's foreign policy governed mainly by desire to secure national religious independence. Elizabeth's foreign policy determined by desire to secure national political independence and preserve national sovereignty; religion a secondary consideration. Henry's foreign policy anti-papal but not anti-Catholic and pro-Protestant. In both cases complicated by succession question (Henry's desire for male heir, Elizabeth lacked direct heir).

CHAPTER 23

1. See text. Select any three voyages.

2. Suppression of a rebellion by Shane O'Neill in Ulster, 1567. **Give a detailed narrative of:** rebellion and its consequences by Earl of Desmond in Munster (1579-83); rebellion of Hugh O'Neill, Earl of Tyrone and the policy of Essex and Mountjoy in Ireland (1598-1603).

CHAPTER 24

1. **The Tudor monarchy had afforded the country protection against feudal anarchy; such protection was no longer necessary under the Stuarts because:** feudalism had been broken and was in rapid decline; Parliament and Convocation had been taught by the Tudors how to play a part in government, even though that part had been dictated by the Tudor sovereigns. These bodies had learned the lesson and were now ready and desirous of playing an independent part; foreign danger had been diminished by the exhaustion of France and the beginning of the decline of Spain after the Armada, there had been no foreign threat to the accession of the Stuarts and there was no succession problem. The challenge had already been made at the end of the Tudor period (in the last ten years of Elizabeth's reign by the assertion of parliamentary privileges and the right of freedom of speech in parliament); the Tudors were content with the reality of power and knew when to make timely concessions, the Stuarts forced the issue by the assertion of principle and lacked the art of compromise; this assertion of principle might have mattered less if the Stuarts and their parliaments had seen eye to eye on policy, but they did not (give general examples but avoid detailed narrative of quarrels between Stuarts and parliaments); Crown under the Stuarts more heavily dependent on Parliament for finance than were the Tudors owing to the rise in prices and fall in value of Crown's fixed revenue, this put Parliament in a stronger position to challenge power of Crown than had been the case in Tudor times.

2. Description of theory, pages 171-2, effect on relations page 172.

CHAPTER 25

1. Write a paragraph on the offence James I gave to Puritans, and one on offence given by his sympathy towards Catholicism (*N.B.:* do not make the mistake of saying that he was a Catholic). Offence given by peace with Spain and marriage alliance of his son with France. James I's unpopular financial measures. His tactless insistence on Divine Right of Kings. Made himself unpopular by his failure to give strong support to his daughter and her husband and the Protestant cause in the Thirty Years' War. His unfortunate choice of advisers after the death of Cecil, his attempts to subordinate the law to the royal will.

2. See pages 179-180.

CHAPTER 26

1. **Strafford. Action taken:** impeachment, charges, evidence: change to Bill of Attainder. Why? Riots in support of action and to intimidate the king. Execution with the king's unwilling consent. **Reason:** Strafford seen as the strongest supporter of the king and as his most efficient adviser in politics. The threat of Strafford's Irish army; he personified the king's personal rule, without him the eleven years of personal rule would not have lasted so long, and it was not likely to end until he had been removed. **Laud. Action taken:** impeachment, charges, Bill of Attainder. Why? Coercion of Lords by Commons at trial. Sentence, imprisonment, execution. **Reason:** his belief in the royal supremacy in church matters, his opposition to Puritanism, intolerance of the Presbyterians, pressure of the Scots who regarded Laud as originator of attack on Presbyterianism.

2. See pages 181-2.

CHAPTER 27

1. Better financial resources (explain why); control of the navy prevented foreign intervention on the King's side; possession of London, the ports, and their revenue; the New Model Army; skill, leadership, and determination of Cromwell was superior to Royalist leadership. Refusal of the anti-Royalist factions to allow themselves to be divided by King's attempt at separate negotiations; Scottish support (Solemn League and Covenant); strong sense of conviction both political and religious.

2. **Show how the Bishops' War led to the summoning of the Long Parliament and brought to an end the eleven years of personal royal rule;** Solemn League and Covenant with Parliament (1644); contribution of Scots to Parliamentary victory at Marston Moor; serious weakening of Royalist cause by failure of Montrose at Philiphaugh in 1645. Parliament's efforts could now be concentrated in England; it was the Scots who surrendered Charles to Parliament; it was the Scottish demand that Parliament should enforce Presbyterianism, and Parliament's unwillingness to do so that led to the breach between Parliament and the army; alliance of Scots with the King after the defeat of Parliament by the more tolerant army on the issue of enforcing Presbyterianism led to the second civil war and Scottish invasion of England in support of the King; defeat of Scots at Preston and Warrington by Cromwell led to final collapse of Royalism; the King's alliance with the Scots and their defeat made the King's execution inevitable.

CHAPTER 28

1. **Cromwell and Scotland:** alliance of Prince Charles and the Covenanters after the defeat and execution of Montrose by the Covenanters (1650); Cromwell's march on Edinburgh and his defeat of David Leslie at Dunbar (1650); Covenanters crown Prince Charles at Scone (1651); Cromwell captures Perth; Charles invades England; Cromwell follows south, overtakes and defeats Scots and Charles at Worcester (1651); Parliamentary union of England and Scotland (1652), freedom of trade, Presbyterianism the official religion but toleration of other denominations. **Cromwell and Ireland:** Cromwell aimed at destruction of the Royalist cause in Ireland, the establishment of English supremacy and the Protestant faith. Conquest of the North-East, massacre at Drogheda, capture of Dunkirk in France, conquest of the South of Ireland, Wexford captured, surrender of Cork, defeat of Royalist fleet at Kinsale, completion of conquest by Ireton after Cromwell's return to England, Wexford 1650, Limerick 1651. **Settlement:** Articles of Kilkenny (1652); Abolition of Irish Parliament, thirty Irish representatives to sit at Westminster, confiscation of Roman Catholic estates, plantation on these estates of Cromwell's soldiers.

2. See pages 194-7. Describe Barebone's Parliament, Instrument of Government, Protectorate Parliaments, Rule of the Major Generals. Failure: see pages 197-8.

CHAPTER 29

1. See pages 203-4.
2. See pages 203 and 204.

CHAPTER 30

1. **Define the undertakings given in the Declaration of Breda:** religious toleration for all except "disturbers of the peace," confirmation of sales of land during

the Commonwealth subject to Parliamentary approval, amnesty for all political offenders except such as should be excluded from the amnesty by Parliament, arrears of pay for the army. Note the ambiguity of these terms and the reason for it, namely Charles's desire to recover the throne at all costs and his desire to leave Parliament to implement the terms of Breda. How far honoured? Religious toleration. **Proposals for the Convention Parliament were:** restoration of Episcopalians expelled under the Commonwealth, but Presbyterians legally presented to livings which had fallen vacant in normal course of events to retain their places, amalgamation of Episcopacy and Presbyterianism by appointment of assistant bishops to preside over the local synods, some Puritans to be offered Bishoprics, a conference to revise the Liturgy to appease Presbyterians, these proposals rejected by the Cavalier Parliament who proceeded to pass the Clarendon Code (give details of Code, see page 207), failure of Savoy Conference. **Land question:** see text page 206. **Amnesty:** Act of Indemnity and Oblivion but excluding the Regicides from the benefits of the Act, desecration of the bodies of Cromwell and Ireton but no persecution of their families. **Army:** arrears paid but army disbanded except for Coldstream and King's Horse Guards.

2. See text pages 207-8 but emphasize the difference of motives between Charles II and Cromwell in foreign policy.

CHAPTER 31

1. *N.B.:* **Since the question is "how" the answer needed is a narrative, reviewing main issues on which Charles and Shaftesbury were opposed.** Up until 1672 Shaftesbury supported the King and the royal policy (e.g. 1668 supported the Triple Alliance, 1672 defended the Dutch War). Went into opposition on learning that in the Treaty of Dover (1670) Charles had promised to attempt to restore Catholicism. **Strong opposition to the King's sympathy with Catholicism:** supported the Test Act; opposed marriage of James, Duke of York and heir to the throne, to the Catholic Mary of Modena (1673), hence Shaftesbury dismissed from the Privy Council, supported Oates and the Popish Plot though he may well not have believed it. **Opposition to royal power:** organized the Country Party and by speaking tour secured an anti-court majority in the 1679 Parliament, urged the passing of the Exclusion Bill, supported Monmouth in preference to the Duke of York as successor to the throne, organized petitions for the recall of Parliament after its prorogation in 1679. **Results:** beginning of organized political groups, Petitioners and Abhorrers, leading later to Whigs and Tories. To this extent contributed to development and progress of party government, made a notable contribution to the safeguarding of the subject's liberty by his support of Habeas Corpus, provoked a reaction in the King's favour by supporting Monmouth and thus exposing the country to the possible risk of civil war (by thus over-playing his hand was the author of his own defeat), helped to make public opinion of the masses especially of London a factor in political life.

2. By leaving Parliament to work out the Restoration settlement and accepting their decisions even when these did not conform to his own wishes, Charles ensured that in so far as the settlement was unpopular, the unpopularity fell on Parliament and ministers not on the King; by secret diplomacy (e.g. the terms of the Treaty of Dover were only partially revealed at the time to those of his ministers who were likely to find the terms unacceptable) and by the employment of unofficial agents whom he could trust implicitly, i.e. his sister Henrietta Maria

(Minette), by a financial bargain with France, by circumstances he could not have engineered (e.g. the increased revenue from increase in trade, which helped to make him independent of Parliament, and in a large measure accounts for the fact that he was able to dispense with Parliament for the last few years of his reign); by knowing when it would be unwise to prolong his direct resistance to the wishes of parliament (e.g. failure to persist with the Declaration of Indulgence and his acceptance of the Test Act); by his skill in ridding himself of unwanted ministers (e.g. Clarendon and Danby); by allowing his opponents to overplay their hand (e.g. he let the Popish Plot burn itself out, he let Shaftesbury over-reach himself). Popular reaction in the King's favour due to his illness, revulsion against the extremism of Shaftesbury and the Country Party, fear of civil war.

CHAPTER 32

1. **Charles II's support:** Declaration of Indulgence (attempt to win Nonconformist support), appointment of Catholics as ministers of state, promise to Louis XIV, defence of James, Duke of York after latter's conversion to Catholicism and approval of his marriage to Catholic Mary of Modena. **Opposition:** non-co-operation of Nonconformists, Parliament insisted on withdrawal of Declaration of Indulgence, opposition of Shaftesbury and Country Party, Parliament's anti-French policy, the Exclusion Bill and the candidature of Monmouth for the succession. **James II's support:** Declaration of Indulgence, claim to Suspending and Dispensing Powers enabling him to override Parliament to advantage of Catholics, intrusion of Catholics into army and political office (give examples), intrusion of Catholics into the universities (give details), attempt to pack Parliament. **Opposition:** from magistrates, bishops and clergy, army; finally parliamentary invitation to William and Mary.

2. **Terms of Revolution Settlement:** see pages 221-3. **Reasons for joint accession:** Mary refused out of regard for her husband to rule alone, William refused to accept anything less than Crown in hope of ruling as well as reigning; wanted to align English foreign policy with that of Holland, desire of Parliament to ensure Protestant succession through either partner.

CHAPTER 33

1. **Causes:** pages 225 and 226. **Terms of Peace of Utrecht:** pages 228-9.

2. A factor in William's acceptance of the English throne; by alliances (e.g. Grand Alliance, French War of Spanish Succession); by diplomacy (the Partition Treaties); by war (Marlborough's campaigns).

CHAPTER 34

1. See text pages 230-2.

2. **Unrest:** pages 232-3. **Scotland's gains and losses:** pages 233-4.

CHAPTER 35

1. Movement originated in 1688 but its two major efforts in 1715 and 1745. **Failure of 1715 rebellion due to:** poor leadership, Old Pretender out of touch, Whigs energetic, Stair informative, death of Louis XIV a blow, no help from abroad, English Jacobites feeble, no great sense of injustice in England, Campbells pro-

Hanoverian, Jacobite clans quarrelled, highlanders not good as regular troops, Old Pretender Roman Catholic, Whig resources far greater than Jacobite, Dutch help for Whigs. **Failure of 1745 rebellion due to:** lack of response in England, people enjoying peace and prosperity under Hanoverians, Jacobite resources again scanty, Hanoverian army much stronger than Jacobite army, highlanders again quarrelled, highland army dispirited in England, Pretender Roman Catholic, George II had Dutch and Hessian mercenaries, no help from abroad for Jacobites. The two rebellions failed for very similar reasons.

2. Prospects for success much greater in 1715 than in 1745, yet the 1745 Rebellion came much nearer to success. **Reasons:** George's best troops abroad in Netherlands and just defeated at Fontenoy, Hanoverians at war in 1745 but at peace in 1715, more harassed in 1745, Charles Stuart much more dashing leader than any in 1715, Hanoverian forces weak in Scotland where rebellion began, Cope was mediocre, rebels reached Derby but only Preston in 1715, Hanoverian government in greater state of panic, if rebels had gone on to London there might have been foreign intervention, Walpole had neglected army and navy. 1745 Rebellion came remarkably close to success but was to be last serious Jacobite effort.

CHAPTER 36

1. **Walpole pursued policy of "letting sleeping dogs lie":** to promote contentment and therefore to prolong his own rule. **Give details:** Wood's Halfpence (1725), Excise Scheme dropped (1733), Porteous Riots (1736), use of Sinking Fund to avoid increasing taxation, did not effectively apply Molasses Act of 1733, no positive part in War of Polish Succession to avoid expense of war. Walpole tended to preserve peace at any price but could be firm on occasions (he muzzled Pitt and dismissed Chesterfield at time of Excise Scheme).

2. Walpole became leading minister in 1721 and remained in that position for twenty-one years. **Finance:** Sinking Fund, new book of rates, excise, reduction of duties, low taxation. **Religious Policy:** no persecution, help to dissenters. **Opposition:** sometimes vigorous in dealing with it, undermined it by creating contentment. **Constitution:** established status of Prime Minister, party government, Cabinet solidarity. **Jacobites:** played upon threat to maintain himself in office. Neglected army and navy. "Let sleeping dogs lie" attitude in general. Outbreak of Spanish Succession War brought down Walpole. His fall was not due to his domestic unpopularity.

CHAPTER 37

1. Pitt rose to high office by national demand, not by usual eighteenth-century methods. **Early career:** M.P. for Old Sarum and Cornet 1735, attacked Walpole, lost commission but helped bring Walpole down in 1742, Paymaster under Pelham 1745, resigned 1755, disgusted by Newcastle's ineptitude, returned 1756 to direct Seven Years' War, briefly out of office 1757, then in coalition with Newcastle. War Minister, turned defeat into victory almost everywhere between 1757 and 1761, resigned because colleagues refused to make war on Spain, greatest part of career over. **Subsequent career:** upheld Wilkes 1763, formed unsuccessful ministry 1766-68, upheld cause of American colonists and tried to avert loss of colonies, Chatham 1766, attacked abuses in East India Company, died 1778. Incorrupt in a corrupt age, won Seven Years' War, established First British Empire, championed liberal causes fearlessly.

2. As Paymaster (1745-55) Pitt studied military strategy, foreseeing world-wide struggle with France. Policy upon Newcastle's fall in 1756 directed country's war effort, raised highland regiments, established Army of Observation, raised additional soldiers and sailors, sent reinforcements to North America, out of office briefly in 1757, grasped war as whole, subsidized Frederick II regularly, blockaded French fleets in ports, gained supremacy of seas by Lagos and Quiberon Bay (1759), chose able leaders such as Boscawen, Wolfe, Howe, backed Clive in India, made landings on French coast, attacked French colonies, planned conquest of Canada, western Louisiana, Senegal, Tobago, Grenada (from France), Florida and Minorca (regained from Spain). Britain became supreme in North America and India. **Gains:** see page 261.

CHAPTER 38

1. George III only twenty-two when he became king. He wanted to make impact, no definite political programme, did not aim at absolutism. **Methods:** resumed control over Crown patronage, gave him vast influence, did little to bolster up early ministries, their brevity increased royal influence, found pliant premier in North (1770-82) and was able to assert his will strongly. **Decline:** influence waned with loss of American colonies (he was blamed), resignation of North in 1782 caused decline of royal influence, emergence of Pitt, a strong character, and George's ageing added to decline, Crewe's and Clerk's Acts reduced king's influence through Treasury. Until he became insane in 1811 George could exercise powerful influence (e.g. stopped Catholic Emancipation 1801, kept out Fox 1804).

2. As in Question 1. George III wished to purify politics and to break down party politics, yet no great break in constitutional development. In part responsible for succession of short ministries 1760-70, played prominent part in dispute with American colonists and in conduct of war (1775-83), impact upon politics, responsible for growth of economical reform movement and parliamentary reform movement, strong enough to defeat Whig clans for second time 1782-83 and to steer Pitt into power. George failed to destroy party politics.

CHAPTER 39

1. Clive paid three visits to India (1743-53, 1756-60 and 1765-67), began as humble clerk, became Governor of Bengal. **Achievements:** Arcot, 1751, restored British prestige in southern India, placed pro-British Mohammed Ali on throne of Carnatic, saved Madras, Dupleix's plans foiled, he was recalled to France, turning point in history of Britain's power in India. Plassey, 1757, Clive's victory over Sirajud-dowlah gave East India Company control over Bengal, the richest province of India. Britain became supreme power. **Reform:** on last visit Clive tried unsuccessfully to place administration of Bengal on even keel, established dual system, treaty with Oudh, abolition of corrupt trading, failed, needed more time. Clive greater as soldier than as administrator.

2. Hastings became Governor of Bengal in 1772. Inherited problems left by Clive. **Reforms in Bengal:** swept aside Clive's dual system, made Calcutta centre of administration, established new system of justice, made taxation more equitable, reduced corrupt trading, all with opposition of council. **War of American Independence:** Hastings saved British India almost single-handed against French, Mahrattas, Hyderabad and Mysore, seized French bases, raised armies, broke

up hostile confederacy by diplomacy. **Impeachment because of:** jealousy over large fortunes made in India, political spite of Whigs, genuine desire to check ill-treatment of subject peoples. **Four main charges:** cruel treatment of Rohilla tribe (1774), judicial murder of Nuncomar (1776), deposing of Rajah of Benares (1780) and harsh treatment of Begums of Oudh (1782). Trial lasted 1788-95. Hastings did not deserve treatment given him, cleared on all main charges.

CHAPTER 40

1. England ripe for religious revival during eighteenth century. **Rise of Methodism:** term originated from activities of a small group of men at Oxford (1729) with whom John and Charles Wesley associated. Wesleys went to America 1735, year of Charles's ordination, returned and in 1738 John experienced sudden personal "conversion" at Aldersgate Street in London, began open-air preaching, Whitefield assisted, local societies of Methodists set up, lay preachers trained, 1744 Methodist Annual Conference established, by 1797 Methodist movement quite separate from Anglican Church, 100,000 members, spread to Ceylon, U.S.A., West Indies. **Effects:** improved general morality, civilizing effect on new industrial masses, stimulated primary education, diverted minds of poor from revolutionary political activity and brought about a religious revival.

2. Methodism made great impact on eighteenth-century society. **Reasons for dissatisfaction:** Anglican Church complacent, no enthusiasm, too political, little attempt to provide for spiritual needs of new working classes, too few new churches built in industrial areas, pluralism abounded, Bishops concerned mainly with scholarship, moral standards low. Social changes were unable to stir Anglican Church, Wesleys acted outside Church, took religion to people in fields, preached with great fervour, wrote hymns, emotional impact, ordained own priests for spread of movement, established local Methodist societies, controlled movement through annual conferences, travelled thousands of miles in Scotland, Ireland, Wales, sent preachers abroad. John Wesley died in 1791, 100,000 Methodists by 1797.

CHAPTER 41

1. **Many fundamental causes of friction during eighteenth century but unfortunate sequence of events following Seven Years' War ensured that independence came by violence:** Stamp Act 1765, its repeal 1766, Declaratory Act 1766, Townshend's duties 1767, Boston Massacre 1770, Gaspee incident 1772, Boston Tea Party 1773, Continental Congress 1774, punishment of Massachusetts 1774. Declaration of Independence (4 July, 1776) marks real outbreak of War of Independence.

2. **Fighting began with skirmishes of Lexington and Bunker's Hill 1775, war lasted eight years:** colonists struggling at first, Saratoga turning point, Howe's defeat of Washington in same year at Brandywine insignificant. France (1778), Spain (1779) and Holland (1780) joined Americans, Great Britain isolated and harassed by Armed League of Neutrality, Clinton captured Charleston for British in 1780 and Cornwallis surrendered at Yorktown 1781, ensured American victory, Rodney's victory over de Grasse at Les Saintes (1782) retrieved Britain's reputation, war ended by Treaty of Versailles 1783. **Reasons for Britain's defeat:** British army far from base, terrain unmapped and difficult, no single centre of resistance, Americans dedicated, George III's mercenaries not, Howe and Clinton

mediocre, Washington great leader, British directors of war (Sandwich and Germaine) uninspired, Britain lost command of seas and had no allies. War was most disastrous in modern times for Britain.

CHAPTER 42

1. During early part of his career Pitt had liberal tendencies, attempted parliamentary reform (1785), but French Revolution, at first welcomed by him, made him into "thorough-going Tory." **Repressive policy:** Act to submit immigrants to police supervision (1793), suppression of Corresponding Societies, suspension of Habeas Corpus Act (1794), new Treasons and Seditious Meetings Act (1795), and Combinations Laws (1799 and 1800). War of 1793 killed Pitt's policy of freer trade with France and impaired his work for financial recovery. French Revolution turning point of Pitt's career.

2. Pitt entered Parliament in 1780 as Whig, later established new Tory Party (1782), Chancellor of Exchequer under Shelburne and by 1783 youngest-ever Prime Minister, tried in vain to secure parliamentary reform, freer trade for Ireland and restriction of slave-trade. **Finance:** sinking fund, economy, purchase of government stock open to competition, reduction of duties, taxes on luxuries. **Commerce:** treaty with France (1786). **Empire:** India Act (1784), settlement of Australia (1788), Canada Act (1791). **Foreign policy:** Triple Alliance (1788), Nootka Sound (1790), Oczakoff (1791). **Conclusion:** Pitt strengthened Britain's economy, rebuilt her Empire, restored her prestige abroad and gained allies.

CHAPTER 43

1. In 1700 age-old open-field system still widespread. Expansion of population made it inadequate, could no longer supply enough food. Widespread enclosure movement (to permit experimental scientific, capitalist farming) took place. **Agricultural experimenters able to try new methods:** Tull economized on seeds and introduced mechanical hoeing. Townshend introduced Norfolk rotation, Bakewell and Colling improved livestock, Coke, George III and Arthur Young popularized new ideas. **Results:** heavier crops, better cattle and sheep, more food, higher profits, autumn slaughtering reduced, more winter fodder, compact farms replaced open fields. Subsistence farming gave way to capitalist farming.

2. Enclosure necessary so that landowners could consolidate land to experiment, open-field system discouraged experiment. **Defects of open-field system:** fallow-field was wasted land, time wasted travelling to and from strips, breeding not carefully controlled, disease spread easily among cattle, shortage of winter fodder, little room for initiative, disputes over boundaries, overcrowding of common land. **Results of enclosure:** squatters lost common rights, poor men tended to lose, but labour needed to carry out enclosures and work on enclosed land, no mass unemployment, no mass eviction, high wages in towns tempted away labourers, cottagers able to buy small parcels of land from wealthier landowners needing money, Tull, Townshend and others able to experiment. Enclosure inevitable, evils exaggerated, led to better farming and increased production.

CHAPTER 44

1. Woollen industry mainstay of Britain for centuries but during eighteenth century was outstripped by cotton industry. **Domestic System:** before industrial revolu-

tion spinning and weaving done in homes, now processes to be transferred to factories, chronic shortage of yarn at beginning of century. **Inventions:** Kay's Flying Shuttle (weaving) 1733, Hargreaves' Spinning Jenny 1767, Crompton's Mule (spinning) 1779, Cartwright's Power-loom (weaving) 1785, revolutionized cotton industry, woollen industry followed. Factory system established, cotton industry concentrated in Lancashire, woollen in West Riding of Yorkshire.

2. Improvement in road- and water-transport necessary for industrialization. In 1700 roads few and poor in summer and winter, few canals. Turnpike trusts began process of road improvement, employed engineers like Metcalf, Telford and MacAdam who set new standards. Many canals dug after success of Brindley's Worsley to Manchester canal (1761). Grand Trunk Canal (1777), Grand Junction Canal, Caledonian Canal, etc., cheap transport for bulky goods. Travel speeded up, industrialization stimulated, railways 1820 onwards (a blow to roads and canals).

CHAPTER 45

1. Prestige of British Navy low at end of War of American Independence but it was to establish complete supremacy during French Wars (1793-1815). **General activity:** sealed French fleets up in their ports, ferried army all over world, attacked French commerce, blockaded French-controlled Europe, convoyed British merchant ships. **Battles (a series):** Glorious First of June, 1794, Cape St. Vincent 1797, Camperdown 1797, Aboukir Bay 1798, First Battle of Copenhagen 1801, Trafalgar 1805, Second Battle of Copenhagen 1807, enemy ships destroyed, invasion averted, attacks on British Empire foiled, Armed Neutrality broken up. Navy also played major part in securing victory in Spain and in defeating Napoleon's Continental System. It also seized French, Spanish and Dutch possessions overseas. Navy played major part in overthrowing Napoleon.

2. Nelson thwarted French plans and was Britain's greatest sailor. **Fought in four major battles:** Capt St. Vincent (1797), Aboukir Bay (1798), First Battle of Copenhagen (1801), and Trafalgar (1805). At Cape St. Vincent sailed out of line to prevent Spaniards from joining French to invade Britain. At Aboukir Bay surprised French by sending some ships between them and shore, suspended Napoleon's plans for conquest of East. At Copenhagen continued attacking in spite of order to withdraw, Armed League of Neutrality broken up. At Trafalgar, after chasing Franco-Spanish fleet to West Indies and then averting invasion, destroyed enemy fleet, gave Britain supremacy on seas and drove Napoleon into fatal Continental System. Nelson's death a tragedy but his work completed.

CHAPTER 46

1. Britain's success in the Peninsular War restored her military prestige and proved to be an important cause of Napoleon's downfall. **Course of War:** Britain responded to Portugal's appeal, sent Wellesley with 10,000 men, he defeated Junot at Vimeiro (1808), was superseded, Convention of Cintra, Wellington returned 1809, meanwhile Moore's retreat to Corunna had occurred. Wellesley drove Soult from Portugal and defeated Joseph Bonaparte at Talavera (1809), retired on Lisbon, built lines of Torres Vedras, defeated Masséna at Busaço 1810, took Almeida 1811, and Ciudad Rodrigo and Badajoz 1812, cleared frontier of French, Marmont then defeated at Salamanca 1812, Joseph Bonaparte driven from Madrid, Wellington again retired on Portugal, 1813 left Portugal for good, defeated Joseph Bonaparte at Vittorai, war won. **Importance of War:**

proved Napoleon was not invincible, set example of resistance, bottled up French troops badly needed elsewhere.

2. **Wellington's military reputation made in India:** Seringapatam (1799), Assaye and Argaum (1803), thwarted French plans for overthrow of British power in India. **Peninsular War:** helped to capture Copenhagen in 1807, defeated French in Spain by long-drawn-out war; made them fight on his terms, co-operated with navy, excellent staff work, made Peninsular army into a brilliant fighting unit. Waterloo (1815) with mixed army and new staff brought about final defeat of Napoleon with Prussian aid. Great soldier, restored military prestige.

CHAPTER 47

1. Any long war inevitably followed by difficult years, those after 1815 especially hard because of effects of Industrial and Agricultural Revolutions, disruptive results of Napoleon's trade wars, overswift demobilization of servicemen, distress among hand-loom weavers, low wages generally, high prices, increased indirect taxation, dear bread due to Corn Law of 1815, domination of Parliament by landed class, slow recovery of foreign trade, illegality of trade unions, inadequate poor relief, fierce game laws. **Government policy:** repression only; spies, informers, agents provocateurs, suspension of Habeas Corpus Act, Six Acts. Only a change of attitude after 1822 averted political upheaval.

2. Answer as above.

CHAPTER 48

1. Castlereagh Foreign Secretary 1812-22. Much maligned in his time, was one of Britain's ablest holders of the post. **Policy:** construction of Fourth Coalition 1813, Treaty of Chaumont 1814, kept allies together, ended Anglo-American War 1814, played major part in peace settlement of Vienna 1815, wise treatment of France, made additions to British Empire, established Congress System, rejected Holy Alliance 1815, approved of rehabilitation of France at Aix-la-Chapelle 1818, opposed general intervention against revolts at Troppau and Laibach, 1820 and 1821, opposed unilateral intervention by Russia over Greek Revolt against Turks. Settled North American frontier 1818. **Conclusion:** successful and constructive foreign policy, helped to restore peace to Europe.

2. **Foreign Secretary 1807-09:** ordered seizure of Danish fleet 1807, launched Peninsular campaign, fought duel with Castlereagh over Walcheren expedition 1809, resigned, returned as President of Board of Control for India 1816-20, succeeded Castlereagh as Foreign Secretary, 1822. **Policy:** opposed French intervention in Spain at Verona, lukewarm towards Congress System, threatened to use navy to stop French intervention in South America 1823, sent troops to Portugal (1826) to assist constitutionalists, refused to see Russia act alone over Greek independence, sent Anglo-French fleet, Premier briefly in 1827. **Domestic policy not so often liberal as sometimes thought:** supported Six Acts and opposed parliamentary reform, but favoured Catholic Emancipation. Played major part in break-up of Congress System and broke up unity of Quadruple Alliance.

CHAPTER 49

1. **With suicide of Castlereagh in 1822 Tories adopted more liberal attitude and tried to remove some of causes of social and political discontent:** Huskisson and

Robinson relaxed navigation laws, reduced duties, made reciprocity treaties, and established colonial preference. Peel reformed prisons, made penal code more humane and established Metropolitan Police. Combination laws repealed but Amending Act followed. Sliding Scale introduced by Wellington to replace Corn Law of 1815. Test and Corporation Acts repealed and Catholic Emancipation passed (1828 and 1829). Tory reforms valuable but not enough to keep them in office.

2. In years between 1815 and 1822 Liverpool ministry pursued policy of repression but Castlereagh's suicide in 1822 marked a change of attitude. Canning replaced Sidmouth at Home Office, series of useful reforms followed, for detail see answer above. **Conclusion:** these reforms probably averted revolution but Tories could not agree over parliamentary reform and were replaced by Whigs in 1830.

CHAPTER 50

1. By 1830 parliamentary reform was long overdue for many reasons, though Reform Act of 1832 did not prove to be drastic. **Need for reform because:** Parliament dominated by landowning class, no heed paid to considerable population changes caused by Industrial Revolution, large cities unrepresented, no uniformity in boroughs, many rotten and pocket boroughs. Matters came to a head in 1830 because Whigs came into office, reform societies active, new and less reactionary king (William IV), example was set by Paris Revolution. Struggle to pass Bill took over a year, involved election in 1831, resignation by Grey, and threat to create fifty new peers. Terms and results of Act see pages 320-2.

2. Between 1832 and 1872 the parliamentary franchise was considerably extended but the largest class of all, that of the agricultural labourer, was left without vote and women were not given vote. **In 1832 floodgate of reform opened (see pages 320-3 for detail):** Corrupt Practices Act 1854, Jews admitted to Parliament 1858, property qualification for M.P.s abolished 1858, Second Reform Act of 1867 extended franchise further and re-distributed seats (see pages 322-3). In 1872 Gladstone introduced secret ballot. By 1872 Parliament much more popularly based, but process not complete until 1928.

CHAPTER 51

1. Two of the most important of Whig reforms were Poor Law Amendment Act, 1834, and Municipal Reform Act, 1835. Speenhamland system had failed; agrarian disorder made it necessary to make new provisions. Whig Poor Law based on report of commission, workhouses (indoor relief) introduced, conditions harsh, soon hated. Before 1835 no adequate provision for government of new large cities, parish meetings could not cope, boundaries overlapped, no democratic control in majority of existing municipalities, another commission appointed. Municipal Reform Act introduced uniform voting: councillors, aldermen and mayors, proper accounts. **Conclusion:** new cities more adequately provided for but improvements slow. New Poor Law better than ignoring problem.

2. **After Great Reform Act of 1832 Whigs embarked upon a whole series of reforms often because of outside pressure:** in 1833 they abolished slavery within the British Empire, passed first effective Factory Act, and made first state grant towards primary education; in 1834 came Poor Law Amendment Act and in 1835 the Municipal Reform Act. Later there were other minor reforms, ecclesi-

astical reforms, registration of births, marriages and deaths (1836), penny postage 1840. In spite of reforms Whigs unpopular by 1841 and lost office.

CHAPTER 52

1. **Chartism a working-class political movement, three main phases:** 1839, 1842 and 1848. **Aims:** to win for workers greater share in nation's political life, to raise their social and economic status, six-point programme drawn up in Charter of 1838. **Methods:** to obtain millions of signatures for great petitions to be presented to Parliament, general strike attempted in 1839, failed, bloodshed at Newport. **Reasons for failure:** too many mad conflicting schemes, poor and divided leadership, firm government action, middle classes preferred better-run Anti-Corn-Law League, improvement in economic conditions after 1846. Chartism an apparent failure, but produced enquiry into working-class conditions, and most of its programme ultimately achieved.

2. **Chartism a working-class movement, coincided with hungry forties. Arose for a number of reasons:** workers disappointed with Great Reform Act of 1832, no vote for them, yet they worked hard for reform, collapse of G.N.C.T.U. turned them away from trade unionism, labourers greatly resented new Poor Law, economic depression from 1836 caused distress and discontent, workers not attracted by Disraeli's Young England Movement, wanted to place own M.P.s in Parliament, resentment against Whigs. Reasons for failure as in answer above.

CHAPTER 53

1. Though a Tory all his life, Peel had innate liberal tendencies. **Finance:** return to gold standard, budgets of 1842 and 1845, Bank Charter Act (1844). **Commerce:** repeal of Corn Laws 1846, movement towards full free trade. **Social Reforms:** reform of prisons and penal code as Home Secretary, 1822-27, establishment of Metropolitan Police 1829, Mines Act 1842, Factory Act 1844. As a result of Peel's work social evils removed, trade stimulated, cost of living reduced and country's finances put on sound footing.

2. Peel, son of wealthy manufacturer, entered Parliament 1809, soon Under-Secretary for War and Colonies (1810), then Chief Secretary for Ireland (1812-18 and 1828-30), valuable reforms, accused of betraying party by supporting Catholic Emancipation 1829, lost seat, represented Tamworth, opposed Great Reform Bill of 1832, first Ministry 1834-35, Tamworth Manifesto, second Ministry 1839, Bedchamber incident, third Ministry 1841-46. **Importance of last ministry:** good finance, movement towards free trade, valuable social reforms, sound foreign policy (improved relations with France and America, Opium War ended). Peel was one of outstanding nineteenth-century statesmen.

CHAPTER 54

1. Palmerston called upon to replace Aberdeen as Prime Minister in 1855, served in two spells 1855-58 and 1859-65. **Foreign affairs:** brought Crimean War to successful conclusion, checked Indian Mutiny, forced China to admit British commerce (Arrow incident), defeated over Conspiracy to Murder Bill 1858, promoted Italian unity, dealt with difficulties arising from American Civil War (Trent and Alabama incidents), suffered reverses over Poland (1863) and Schleswig-Holstein (1864-65). **Home affairs:** during last ministry full free trade established, factory conditions improved, but he opposed parliamentary reform.

Generally made Britain respected abroad but influence declined in his last years. At home was less opposed to reform than is sometimes thought.

2. Palmerston began career as Tory, became Whig and served as Foreign Secretary twice (1830-41 and 1846-51). **Work:** successful intervention over Belgian independence (1830-39), support given to constitutionalism in Portugal and Spain, Straits Convention removed undue Russian influence over Turkey 1841, bullied China 1839, reverse over Spanish Marriages 1846, liberal sympathies during 1848 revolutions but no active intervention, wished to preserve Hapsburg Empire, Don Pacifico and Haynau incidents (1850), revealed hostility to foreigners, message of congratulation Louis Napoleon (1851) brought dismissal. A very active and hard-working minister but poor diplomatist, upheld British interests, annoyed Queen, popular with people.

CHAPTER 55

1. Crimean War only major war in Europe in which British participated between 1815 and 1914. **Causes:** general hostility towards Russia, jingoism in Britain, fear of Russian expansion towards Mediterranean, into Persia and into Afghanistan, Tsar's talk of partition of Turkey, Nicholas I hated as persecutor of Poles and Hungarians and upholder of serfdom. Stratford de Redcliffe's presence in Constantinople bolstered up Turkish resistance to Russia, Napoleon III wanted war to strengthen his position in France and had personal grudge against Tsar, invasion of Moldavia and Wallachia by Russia, sinking of Turkish fleet at Sinope. **Events of War:** allies landed at Varna, Russians withdrew from Wallachia, landed at Eupatoria, Alma, Balaclava (charge of Light Brigade), Inkerman, Russian winter, 1854-55, Florence Nightingale's arrival at Scutari, fall of Sebastopol 1855. For results of war and Treaty of Paris see next answer.

2. Introduction and reasons for Britain's intervention as in answer above. **Terms of Treaty of Paris:** Russians surrendered Southern Bessarabia, Dardanelles closed to foreign warships in peace-time, Black Sea de-militarised, Turkey recognized as major power, Moldavia and Wallachia independent. **Comments:** Russia temporarily checked, no permanent settlement of Eastern question, Napoleon III had his military success, Sultan's promise to treat his Christian subjects better not kept, Russia ignored demilitarisation clause in 1870.

CHAPTER 56

1. Disraeli's main work concentrated into his ministry of 1874-80. **Empire:** strongly imperialist, purchase of Suez Canal shares 1875, Royal Titles Act 1876, annexation of Transvaal 1877, Zulu War 1879, Afghanistan. **Foreign policy:** mainly concerned with Eastern Question, Bulgarian atrocities, Russo-Turkish War 1877, San Stefano 1878, Disraeli's pressure upon Russia, Congress of Berlin a triumph, (became Beaconsfield), war averted, Russian gains by Stefano reduced, Cyprus gained, settlement unsatisfactory in many aspects. **Conclusion:** Disraeli strengthened British Empire and made Britain's influence felt in Europe.

2. Disraeli a radical in his early career, sincere when he preached Tory Democracy. Social reforms concentrated in ministry of 1874-80, Richard Cross performed spade-work; Factory Act 1874, Artisans' Dwelling Act 1875, Public Health Act 1875, Conspiracy and Protection of Property Act and Employers and Workmen Act to assist trade unionists 1875, Education Act 1876, Act restricting enclosures 1876, Agricultural Holdings and Rivers Pollution Acts, Sale of Food and Drugs Act, reform of Oxford and Cambridge. Disraeli one of important reformers of nineteenth century.

CHAPTER 57

1. Between 1868 and 1894 Gladstone served four times as Prime Minister and on every occasion grappled with the problem of Ireland. **First Ministry (1868-74):** Fenian outrages, Disestablishment of Irish Church 1869, first Land Act 1870. **Second Ministry (1880-85):** second Land Act (three "F.s"), fine attempt to solve agrarian problem, Parnell imprisoned, Kilmainham Treaty 1882, work shattered by Phoenix Park Murders 1882. **Third Ministry (1886):** Gladstone converted to Home Rule, first Home Rule Bill defeated in Commons, Liberals split, Ulster problem difficult. **Fourth Ministry (1892-94):** second Home Rule Bill defeated in Lords. Gladstone's praiseworthy efforts defeated by English prejudice against Irish, Tory domination of Lords, Ulster problem, Parnell's disgrace, violence in Ireland, division within own party.

2. Gladstone over seventy in 1880, ministry beset by divisions and harassed by Parnell's Irish Nationalists and Randolph Churchill's Fourth Party. **Ireland:** second Land Act, Kilmainham, Phoenix Park Murders, Arrears Act. **Domestic Reforms:** legislation of J. Chamberlain, Corrupt Practices Act 1883, third Parliamentary Reform Act 1884, and Re-distribution Act 1885. **Empire:** Majuba Hill, Pretoria Convention, Afghanistan, occupation of Egypt 1882, death of Gordon 1885. **Reasons for downfall:** government divided by Chamberlain plan for Irish local government, Parnell withdrew support, Gladstone's weakness with Boers criticized, blamed for Gordon's death.

CHAPTER 58

1. **Conditions in factories and mines very harsh in 1830:** Improvement came as result of work of humanitarians such as Robert Owen, Fielden, Oastler, Sadler and Shaftesbury. **Improvement:** 1833 Act (page 325), 1842 Act (page 335), Ten Hours Act 1847, 1853 normal day for children, Print Works Act, Acts concerning bleaching, dyeing, calendering and finishing. Lace Works Act 1861, Factory Extension Acts 1864 and 1867, Disraeli's Act 1874, Factory and Workshop Act. By 1878 conditions and hours of employment in factories and workshops considerably improved but still much reform necessary.

2. Introduction as in answer above. Mines Act 1842 (page 335), then as above. **After 1878:** Factory Acts of 1901 and 1937, safety measures, Employers Liability Act 1880, Act concerning fire-escapes 1891, Workmen's Compensation Act 1906, regulations concerning dangerous trades. **Arbitration:** trade boards 1850 onwards, Industrial Courts Act 1919, Coal Mines Regulating Act 1908. Vast improvement between 1832 and 1937.

CHAPTER 59

1. **Turning point in history of trade union movement had been formation of Amalgamated Society of Engineers in 1851.** Royal Commission on trade unions 1867, T.U.C. founded in 1868, Trade Unions (Protection of Funds) Act 1869, Gladstone's Act 1871, Criminal Law Amendment Act 1871, Conspiracy and Protection of Property Act 1875, Employers and Workmen Act 1875, beginning of unions of unskilled workers, agricultural workers, gas workers, match-girls, dockers, strikes in mines 1893 and 1898, Taff Vale Case 1901, Trades Disputes

Act 1906, Osborne Judgment 1909, Trade Union Act 1913, strikes 1910-12, miners' strike 1921, General Strike 1926, Trades Disputes Act 1927, period of decline 1927-39. Trade Unions are now very strong.

2. **London Dockers' Strike 1889, Taff Vale Judgment 1901, and Osborne Judgment 1909, General Strike 1926.** In 1880s unskilled workers began to form unions 1889, dock workers of Port of London struck for minimum wage of sixpence an hour, public sympathy, strike successful, strengthened faith of unskilled workers in trade unionism, stimulated growth of other unions of unskilled. Taff Vale Railway Company; company won damages from Amalgamated Society of Railway Servants, union lost £23,000. If similar actions occurred unions would lose funds after each strike. Trades Disputes Act, 1906, righted matters for unions. Osborne Judgment another setback, Osborne contested use of subscriptions to support Labour Party, Lords upheld him, blow to Labour movement, payment of M.P.s in 1911 relieved situation somewhat but Trade Union Act, 1913, helped more. For importance of the General Strike see page 385.

CHAPTER 60

1. **Ireland seething with discontent in late eighteenth century:** grievances political, agrarian, commercial and religious. In 1780 commercial concessions made, 1782 Irish Parliament made independent. French Revolution stirred spirit of rebellion, 1791 Society of United Irishmen formed, 1793 Catholics received vote, not grateful, Fitzwilliam episode caused Irish to look for violent means of redressing grievances, French landings 1796, martial law, terrible rebellion in 1798, another French landing, caused Pitt to decide upon parliamentary union, bribery used, Catholic Emancipation promised, for Terms of Act see pages 388-9. Irish felt cheated, soon sought repeal, no Catholic Emancipation.

2. O'Connell, a great orator and lawyer, wanted independent Irish Parliament, emancipation of Catholics, disendowment of Anglican Church, fixity of tenure for peasants, compulsory lease of land and taxation of absentee landlords. Known as "Liberator," did not want violence. Formed Catholic Association 1823, £1,000 per week, won Clare election 1828, caused British Government to give Catholic Emancipation 1829. Sought concessions from Whigs. Poorest Irishmen relieved from payment of tithes 1832, ten Anglican sees abolished 1833, remaining bishoprics taxed, poor law introduced to Ireland after Lichfield House Compact, 1838 tithes replaced by rent-charges. In 1840s O'Connell began to use mass meetings, sought repeal of Union, Clontarf 1843, gave way to Peel in calling off a meeting, lost influence. O'Connell died in Genoa 1847. Achieved much for Irish but failed in chief aim, to secure repeal of Union.

CHAPTER 61

1. Parnell a Protestant Irish landowner with a passionate hatred of England. Entered Parliament 1875, by 1878 was leader of Irish Nationalists, used obstruction in Parliament to further Irish cause. **Home Rule was Parnell's aim, he refused to co-operate with Gladstone** over the second Land Act (1881) because he wanted nothing short of Home Rule, did not care from which party it came, gave parliamentary support to Gladstone in 1886 when Gladstone became converted to Home Rule but Home Rule Bill defeated. Disapproved of plan of campaign of Dillon and O'Brien, *Times* letter concerning Phoenix Park murders a setback, discovery that they were forged brought wave of sympathy, lost

when Parnell involved in divorce case 1890, schism which resulted in Irish Nationalist party a set-back to Home Rule movement. Parnell brought Irish affairs to the forefront of British political scene but his erratic career as much a drawback to cause of Home Rule as advantage.

2. **Agrarian discontent as much a cause of violence in Ireland during eighteenth and nineteenth centuries as any other factor:** absentee landlords, shortage of land, poor standard of farming, lack of secure tenure, no compensation for improvement. Gladstone's first Land Act of 1870 did not go far enough, agricultural depression hit Ireland in 1875, Davitt's Land League 1879, voiced discontent, outrages, Gladstone's second Land Act 1881, brave measure, three "F.s," Parnell unco-operative, Arrears Act, Ashbourne's Act 1885, beginning of state-aided land purchase, campaigning of Dillon and O'Brien against landlords, evictions, Balfour, 1891 another Land Purchase Act, 1903 Wyndham's Land Purchase Act, excellent measure, loans from government, repaid faithfully by peasants until 1932. Agrarian problem solved by land purchase.

CHAPTER 62

1. Great Exhibition of 1851 displayed Britain's industrial strength, until 1870 she maintained her lead but thereafter experienced a decline. **Reasons for failure to maintain lead:** full industrialization of France, Germany and America, discovery of Gilchrist-Thomas method of making steel, enabled Germany to exploit phosphoric ores of Lorraine, better German and American techniques, American industrialists more enterprising, more capital in America, energy of state in Germany, British industrialists too complacant, trade union activity impeded Britain, foreign states set up tariff barriers against British goods, machines exported from Britain enabled foreign states to compete with Britain. Britain has fought back but has never regained her mid-nineteenth-century lead.

2. Protectionists forecast the decline of British agriculture after repeal of Corn Laws 1846, but decline did not set in until after 1870. **Reasons:** influx of cheap North American wheat from prairies, failure of Britain to impose protective tariffs, and 1875-79 succession of wet summers and bad harvests, decline in agricultural prices caused by world monetary depression, attacks by various diseases upon cattle and sheep in 1870s. Only during and after First World War did state intervene to support British agriculture, which has since recovered.

CHAPTER 63

1. **No state education in 1800.** Need for primary education grew as Britain became fully industrialized. Voluntary provision, dame schools, charity schools and Sunday schools, schools established by Anglican National Society (1811), and Nonconformist British and Foreign Society (1814). Monitorial system used. **State activity:** grant of £20,000 in 1833 to these two societies, £30,000 in 1839, £125,000 by 1848, provision of primary education still very inadequate, Committee of Privy Council established, 1858 Newcastle Commission, payment by results introduced, bad effects, Forster Act 1870, board schools, 1886 education available to all, compulsory through Sandon's Act 1876 and Mundella Act 1880, Cockerton Judgment 1900 a setback, Balfour Act 1902, education committees established, leaving age raised to fourteen in 1918, after Hadow Report eleven-plus tests introduced. Continual progress made after 1870.

2. After lagging behind Germany and America, Britain made rapid progress after 1870. Primary education see answer above. **Secondary education:** ancient grammar schools existed at beginning of century, out-of-date curricula, some grew into public schools such as St. Paul's and Shrewsbury, efforts of Arnold of Rugby, Thring of Uppingham and Butler of Shrewsbury slowly revolutionized standards in public schools; state secondary education grew from Balfour Act 1902. **Universities:** 1871 University Tests Act, new universities founded at end of nineteenth and early twentieth centuries, e.g. Aberystwyth, Cardiff and Bangor 1893, Birmingham 1900, Manchester and Liverpool 1903. Adult education grew, lectures from Oxford and Cambridge, trade union and Co-operative movement activity, W.E.A., 1903. Education available to all by 1939.

CHAPTER 64

1. **Salisbury's main interest was in foreign affairs:** sent to Constantinople in 1876 over Balkan question, 1878 became Beaconsfield's Foreign Secretary, helped to bring about Congress of Berlin which he attended, expert on Eastern Question, as Premier in 1885 sanctioned union of Eastern Rumelia and Bulgaria, change of attitude, watched over "scramble for Africa" and averted war, tended to be passive, suspicious of France and Russia during second ministry (1886-92), dealt with Venezuelan dispute during third ministry 1895-1902, avoided war over Fashoda 1898, sanctioned approaches to Germany 1898 and 1899 to end Britain's isolation, Britain unpopular and isolated during Boer War. His calm wisdom valuable to Britain and Europe at end of nineteenth century.

2. During Salisbury's three ministries European powers increasingly imperialistic, some jealousy of Britain's strong imperial position. **As Secretary for India in 1874:** Salisbury supported Lytton's "forward" policy in Afghanistan, in short ministry of 1885 authorized annexation of Lower Burma, watched over "scramble for Africa," agreements with Germany, France and Portugal, 1890 control over Zanzibar, powerful Chamberlain at Colonial Office during last ministry, interests of British Guiana upheld, struggle with Boers in South Africa, Jameson Raid 1896, reconquest of Sudan 1898, Fashoda 1898, Boer War 1899-1902, Vereeniging. Great colonial issues arose during Salisbury's time; dealt with firmly and wisely. Britain still a great imperial power when Salisbury died.

CHAPTER 65

1. **Much accomplished during Balfour's short ministry of three years:** Education Act 1902, beginning of modern primary and secondary education, Wyndham's Land Purchase Act, best of such measures for Ireland. Licensing Act 1904, courageous measure of social reform. Creation of Committee of Imperial Defence, much value during First World War. Naval reconstruction (1905) strengthened Britain's naval position at vital time. Anglo-French *entente* ended Britain's isolation in Europe. Unemployed Workmen Act another useful measure. Although Balfour allowed his party to become split over tariff reform and mishandled question of Chinese labour in South Africa, much of value achieved.

2. Balfour a Scottish aristocrat, nephew of Salisbury, one of brilliant Fourth Party, President of the Local Government Board in Salisbury's first ministry of 1885, Chief Secretary for Ireland (1887) in Salisbury's second ministry, unexpectedly firm, Crimes Act and land purchase. In 1891 Leader of the House and First

Lord of Treasury. Prime Minister 1902-05 (for his work see answer above). Suffered disastrous electoral defeat 1906, party eclipsed, impeded Liberal measures 1906-14, First Lord of the Admiralty 1915-16, Foreign Secretary, 1916-18, helped negotiate Versailles settlement, helped to settle Jews in Palestine, died 1930. Important part of career before First World War, very able, not always wise in judgment.

CHAPTER 66

1. **Chamberlain reared in local politics in Birmingham:** Lord Mayor, slum clearance, entered Parliament in 1876 for Birmingham constituency, soon leader of radical section of Liberal Party, President of Board of Trade under Gladstone, proved administrative skill with Bankruptcy and Patents Bills, put forward own "unauthorized programme." Joined Gladstone's third ministry in 1886 as President of Local Government Board, opposed first Home Rule Bill, brought about Gladstone's defeat. Also attacked Gladstone's second Home Rule Bill in 1893. Deserted Liberals in 1895 and became Colonial Secretary under Salisbury, actively and energetically imperialist, annexed Ashanti territory, defended Uitlanders of Johannesburg, sent Molner to South Africa, firmness partly cause of Boer War though he did not want it. Used Diamond Jubilee to boost Empire, helped to establish Dominion of Australia 1901, Colonial Conference 1902. **Foreign affairs:** tried to establish alliance with Germany, failed, helped to settle Venezuelan dispute 1899. **Tariff reform:** put forward policy under Balfour 1902-03, resigned, split Conservatives, had stroke 1906, died 1914. Great administrator, empire builder, genuinely radical, stormy career, not docile party man.

2. Chamberlain had vision of great and expanding Empire and deliberately chose post of Colonial Secretary in Salisbury ministry 1895, raised stature of office, for work see answer above. Successfully defended, strengthened and extended Empire, made Englishmen conscious of it.

CHAPTER 67

1. **Having won great electoral victory in 1906 Liberals under Campbell-Bannerman and Asquith embarked upon tremendous series of reforms:** Haldane's Army Reforms, Trades Disputes Act 1906, Merchant Shipping Act 1906, Provision of School Meals 1906, Patents Act 1907, medical inspection in schools 1907, Qualification of Women Act 1907, Port of London Authority 1908, Old Age Pensions 1909, naval expansion (dreadnoughts), Lloyd George's budget 1909, Parliament Act 1911, payment of M.P.s 1911, Shops Act 1911, Coal Mines Act 1911, Aerial Navigation Act 1911, National Insurance 1911, third Home Rule Bill 1912. Liberal reforms paved the way for establishment of Welfare State.

2. Asquith, a Yorkshireman, succeeded Campbell-Bannerman as Premier in 1908. Naval reforms prepared Britain for struggle 1914-18, so did Haldane's army reforms, social reforms laid foundations of Welfare State, constitution re-shaped by Parliament Act 1911, Morley-Minto reforms paved way for eventual self-government in India, third Home Rule Bill might have averted disaster in Ireland, Grey's sage foreign policy received his support. Conducted war 1914-16, resentment at replacement by Lloyd George in 1916 caused division within Liberal Party from which it has never recovered. Last Liberal premier, should be remembered for part in great era of reform before First World War.

CHAPTER 68

1. Lloyd George entered Parliament in 1890, Welsh Nonconformist background. President of the Board of Trade in 1906 in Liberal ministry of Campbell-Bannerman, secured passing of Merchant Shipping and Patents Acts and established single Port of London Authority. Chancellor of Exchequer 1908, forced through People's Budget of 1909, secured reduction of powers of House of Lords, responsible for National Insurance and Unemployment Acts, played part in foreign affairs, warned off Germany at time of Agadir Crisis 1911, achieved wonders as Minister of Munitions 1915-16, putting end to shortage of shells, 1916 Secretary of War and then Prime Minister, did much to bring war to successful conclusion, won Coupon Election 1918, leading figure at Versailles Peace Conference, helped to establish League of Nations, leading statesman of Europe 1918-22, negotiated Irish Treaty 1921, split Liberal Party. Wily politician, achieved greatness as social reformer and war leader.

2. See answer above.

CHAPTER 69

1. Between 1900 and 1914 Anglo-German relations steadily deteriorated. When Britain was attempting to put an end to her isolation at end of nineteenth century was snubbed by Germany (1898 and 1899). **Reasons for increasing hostility:** expansion of Germany navy made Britain feel less secure, German intervention in North Africa, Tangier and Algeciras crises, Britain jealous of Germany's increasing influence over Turkey, Kaiser unpopular in England, Britain inevitably drew away from Germany as she drew nearer to France and Russia, industrial and colonial rivalry with Germany, resentment of German support for Boers. Britain was still hesitant in 1914 but German invasion of Belgium brought her rapidly into war.

2. For much of last decade of nineteenth century relations between Britain and France hostile, France openly sympathized with Boers, clashed with Britain in Sudan (Fashoda). After 1900 improvement, Edward VII's visit to Paris 1903. Delcassé's visit to London. After *entente* of 1904 Britain gained free hand in Egypt, and France in Morocco, eased tension, both feared Germany and wished to keep her out of North Africa, mutual support in Tangier and Algeciras crises, and again in Agadir crisis 1911, naval agreement further improved relations, 1907 Britain came to terms with Russia, ally of France. When Britain joined France in 1914 in war against Germany, diplomatic revolution complete.

CHAPTER 70

1. Through Cawdor-Fisher naval reforms 1906 (page 416) and Liberal naval construction, 1909-11 (page 425), British navy was well prepared for war in 1914. **Had three main stations:** Scapa Flow and Orkneys, Rosyth, and the Channel. British defeated at Coronel but victorious at Falkland Islands 1914, German naval units cleared from seas, 1915 Dogger Bank, navy imposed full blockade upon Germany, Battle of Jutland 1916, British suffered more heavily than Germans but German High Seas fleet never ventured out again, 1917 navy fought against German all-out submarine campaign, triumphed by 1918, blocked Zeebrugge and Ostend 1918. All through war it protected merchant ships and convoyed troops all over world, navy made massive contribution to victory.

2. British army, though small, well prepared for war by Haldane's reforms (page 423). **Western Front:** expeditionary force soon smoothly across Channel, at Mons, Le Cateau skilled riflemen held up German advance, took full brunt of attack at Ypres. In 1915 Kitchener marshalled fresh armies, prolonged trench warfare, British suffered heavily at Neuve Chapelle and Festubert 1915, again at Loos, 500,000 men lost by 1916. Attack on Somme to take pressure off French 1916, tanks used, terrible casualties, few miles gained, success at Vimy Ridge 1917, and reverse at Passchendaele. Final German attack drove back Gough's Fifth Army 1918, but Haig exerted counter-pressure, Germans collapsed. **Gallipoli:** British and Dominion forces tried to effect passage of Dardanelles in vain (1915). **Mesopotamia:** reverse at Kut 1915, recovery under Maude 1917, Baghdad taken. **Italy:** 1917 British troops bolstered up Italian resistance to Austria. **Palestine:** 1917 Allenby took Jerusalem from Turks. British raised larger armies than ever before and played role of major military power.

CHAPTER 71

1. Lloyd George played prominent part in establishing League of Nations at Versailles, had not Wilson's idealism, but gave steady support to League, Britain a full member, withdrawal of America (1920) and failure of France and Britain to co-operate in years immediately after war undermined League's prospects of success. Britain supported Germany's entry 1925, Henderson, Labour minister, worked hard at Disarmament Conference, Geneva 1932, and World Economic Conference, Britain stood aside when Japan invaded Manchuria in 1931, giving League its severest test to date. At time of Mussolini's invasion of Abyssinia (1935) again Britain did not take strong action, League undermined but Eden replaced Hoare; Eden strong supporter of League, Britain's weakness in face of Hitler's aggression no help to League. Britain's lack of strength considerably undermined League and played part in its decline.

2. **Britain and France strove in unity during Great War but were soon at variance afterwards:** France had suffered more severely, wanted harsh treatment of Germany, Britain willing to be more generous, desired rehabilitation, France feared German revival, occupied Ruhr 1923, Britain cool, Herriot and MacDonald and later Chamberlain and Briand improved relations, both states signed Locarno Treaty 1925, Rhineland evacuated, Hoare-Laval pact over Abyssinia 1935, short-lived, France and Britain both pacifist and weak in face of Fascist aggressions, Hitler allowed to remilitarize Rhineland, no intervention in Spanish Civil War. Although ill-prepared, Britain and France declared war against Germany in 1939. France and Britain often hostile towards each other during inter-war period and had failed to meet threat from European dictators.

CHAPTER 72

1. Baldwin entered Parliament in 1908 as a Conservative, 1917 Financial Secretary to Treasury, built reputation for financial wisdom. **Achievements:** became Chancellor of Exchequer in 1922 under Bonar Law, went to America to settle problem of debt, arranged to pay £33 million annually, 1923 Prime Minister for first time, failed to secure Anglo-French co-operation and lost election over tariff issue. **Premier again 1924-29:** coped well with General Strike 1926, new schools, cheap electricity, new houses, re-rating, franchise extended, B.B.C., Simon Commission on India. **Served under MacDonald 1931-35:** launched imperial

preference, supported India Act of 1935. **Prime Minister, National Government 1935-37:** won election of 1935, handled 1936 abdication crisis well, weak foreign policy in face of fascist aggression, resigned in 1937. Calmness averted civil strife during inter-war years but did not provide strong leadership.

2. See answer above to 1931.

CHAPTER 73

1. Ramsay MacDonald was born in 1866 in humble circumstances in Scotland, joined Fabian Society and Independent Labour Party, became Secretary to Labour Representation Committee, entered Parliament 1906, lost seat 1918, returned 1922. **First Labour Prime Minister 1924:** progress in education and housing, League backed and international tension eased. **Prime Minister again 1929-31:** failed to solve country's economic difficulties, unemployment figures grew, MacDonald and Henderson worked hard through League for disarmament. **Formed National Government 1931:** won election that year, split Labour Party, 1932 return to protection, imperial preference, unpopular because of means test, Statute of Westminster 1931, India Act 1935, failed to stop Japanese aggression in Manchuria 1931, replaced by Baldwin 1935, served on as Lord President, died 1937. Prominent founder of Labour Party and proved it able to govern.

2. **MacDonald served three times as Prime Minister 1924, 1929-31 and 1931-35. Achievements:** helped to form Labour Party, proved party's capabilities, useful reforms 1924, houses, naval construction, educational progress, electricity, made good contribution towards international peace and working of League. **As Premier 1929-31:** worked hard for peace and League again. **As Premier 1931-35:** guided development of Empire and Commonwealth, Statute of Westminster 1931, Ottawa Conference 1932, India Act 1935, some national economic recovery achieved. **Failures:** no cure for unemployment and no removal of economic weaknesses 1929-31, weak in face of Japan's aggression (1931), split Labour Party in 1931, failed to provide strong national leadership. It was his misfortune to be without strong Labour majority.

CHAPTER 74

1. Chamberlain entered Parliament in 1918, Conservative, son of Joseph Chamberlain. In 1922 Postmaster-General and then Minister of Health in Bonar Law ministry, Housing and Rent Restriction Acts. **Minister of Health in second Baldwin ministry 1924-29, much valuable legislation:** Rating and Revaluation Act, Widows, Orphans and Old Age Pensions Act, extension of Health Insurance Scheme, changes in poor law, infant welfare, Local Government Act 1929. **Strong part in formation of National Government in 1931:** served as Chancellor of Exchequer, carried through tariff reform, helped settle reparations problem, led way at Ottawa Conference 1932, guided economic recovery. **Under Baldwin 1935-37:** produced Defence White Papers 1936 and 1937. **As Premier after 1937:** responsible for extension of pensions and housing, failed to deal adequately with threat from Hitler, but gained breathing space 1938-39. He is remembered too much for appeasement and too little for valuable social and financial work.

2. **Introduction:** business experience when young, seven years in Bahamas, local politics in Birmingham, Lord Mayor 1915, Director of National Service 1916, entered Parliament in 1918. Then as answer above.

OUTLINE ANSWERS TO EXAMINATION QUESTIONS

SECTION 1 (1066-1272)

For the first question a fully expanded specimen answer is given, for the rest of the questions outline answers are provided.

1. The greatest danger to the Crown under the feudal system lay in the king's complete dependence on the loyalty of his tenants-in-chief for military support. It was their duty to bring into William's service the knights who formed the core of the Crown's military strength. Any tenant-in-chief who chose to disregard his oath of loyalty to the king could either withhold his support, or more dangerous still, employ it in rebellion. Should two such disloyal tenants unite in rebellion their combined strength might prove more than a match for the king's personal forces. In Normandy William himself had established his independence of the French king by precisely this method, and if English tenants-in-chief chose to follow his example, the country might easily be split into a number of small separate kingdoms, and William become merely one of many rulers of such kingdoms.

William attempted to safeguard himself against such a threat when in 1086 he summoned all landowners to do homage directly to himself on Salisbury Plain. Formerly sub-tenants had been bound only to their immediate overlord, but they were now bound directly to the king himself. If a rebellious tenant-in-chief now called upon his sub-tenants to rise against the Crown, they could always plead that their oath to the king took precedence over their oath to their immediate overlord. After 1086 they were under a dual loyalty to Crown and overlord, and should the two obligations conflict, they were expected by William to give precedence to their loyalty to the Crown.

A second threat to the Crown under feudalism lay in the danger of civil war. Tenants-in-chief had the means of waging war upon each other should they fall out amongst themselves, and this could disturb the king's peace and undermine the strength of the kingdom.

William countered this possibility by scattering the holdings of the tenants-in-chief throughout the kingdom rather than concentrating them in one geographical area. The only exceptions were in such regions as the Welsh marshes, the Scottish borders, and the South-east coast where there was danger of invasion, and consolidated holdings were in the nation's interest.

The danger of concentrated holdings was shown up when William's half-brother, Odo of Bayeux, led a rebellion, but William was prepared to make an example even of a member of his own family. By doing so he further discouraged any like-minded "over-mighty subjects" from similar ventures, and further safeguarded his own position.

A third danger was the possibility that some tenants-in-chief might deprive the Crown of services legally due by misrepresenting the extent and resources of their holdings. At the Council of Gloucester in 1085 William sought to forestall this type of disloyalty by conducting a survey of the whole kingdom. The resulting Domesday Survey of 1086-87 was a record of all land, who owned it, what its resources were, and thus what the obligations of the owner were to the Crown.

Finally, William reinforced all these precautions by his ruthless suppression of all rebellion, not only by his treatment of Odo, but by the more savage and general Devastation of the North in 1069-70. Having perceived and successfully exploited the dangers of feudalism to the Crown against his own overlord in France, William took care to see that similar opportunities were denied to his subjects in his new kingdom of England.

2. See narrative, pages 21-2.

3. **Reasons for anarchy of Stephen's reign:** (*1*) Disputed succession (infant heir and female guardian).
(*2*) Weakness of Stephen (chosen by barons as likely to be less effective in asserting Crown's authority than Henry I had been).
(*3*) Stephen's unwise concessions to ensure his retention of the Crown (*e.g.* to London, Scotland and the Church).
(*4*) Barons' readiness to play off interested parties against each other to ensure the growth of their own independence.
(*5*) Baronial resentment of the strong administration of Henry I and desire to prevent its continuance under any successor.
Resolution of anarchy: (*1*) Collapse of Matilda's cause (in spite of capture of Stephen at Lincoln, 1141, and acceptance of Matilda as Queen) *was due to*:
   (*a*) Alienation of London by her refusal to confirm laws of Edward the Confessor.
   (*b*) Flight of Matilda to Oxford. Henry rejoined Stephen. Robert of Gloucester captured at Winchester; Stephen freed in exchange for Robert.
   (*c*) Matilda besieged in Oxford, Oxford taken, escape of Matilda to Wallingford.
   (*d*) Exhausting civil war, 1142-47.
   (*e*) Death of Robert of Gloucester, 1147, flight of Matilda to Normandy, 1148.
(*2*) Henry Plantagenet consolidated his power in Normandy 1147-53, and was strong enough to invade England in 1153.
(*3*) Death of Stephen's son Eustace, 1153, reduced Stephen's will to continue struggle when he had no heir. Way open for peace.
(*4*) *Treaty of Wallingford 1153:* Stephen to retain English crown for his life, Henry Plantagenet recognized as Stephen's heir.
(*5*) Stephen died in 1154.

4. For **Henry's reforms** see pages 29-30.
Their importance: (*1*) The beginnings of a national legal system.
(*2*) Disputes settled by rational process rather than by superstitious appeal to divine justice and intervention.
(*3*) Beginning of idea of, and respect for, "King's Justice."
(*4*) Strengthened Crown power by replacing manorial justice with Crown justice.
(*5*) Judicial decisions recorded; beginning of Common Law.

5. See pages 35-7.

6. **Points at issue between John and Baronage:** (*1*) His strict watch (by Progresses) on the administration of the whole country.
(*2*) Distrust and dislike aroused by John's personality and methods (see page 38).
(*3*) Unpopularity of John's heavy financial demands (but note that these were

created partly by price-rise without corresponding increase in Crown revenue).
(*4*) Abuse of feudal processes (see page 40).
(*5*) Failure of adequate baronial support in Normandy campaign, but baronial resentment at loss of Normandy.
(*6*) Exclusion of baronage from positions of prestige and influence.
(*7*) Failure of French campaign of 1214.
Liberties granted (note that "liberties" are baronial privileges): (*1*) No scutage or aid without consent of Common Council.
(*2*) Heirs to succeed without exaction of swollen fines, similar protection of widows' dowries.
(*3*) Restoration of castles, etc., illegally seized by Crown.
(*4*) Barons to be tried by their equals in rank, not by king's paid officials of humbler birth.
(*5*) Participation of Baronage in administration through Committee of Twenty-five.

7. **Aspects of government arousing discontent:** (*1*) Unpopular administration of Hubert de Burgh.
(*2*) Henry's financial extravagance (*e.g.* re-building of Westminster Abbey, excessive payments to pope for support given, expense entailed by acceptance of papal Sicilian and German projects).
(*3*) Henry's reliance on foreigners (*e.g.* Peter des Roches and Peter des Rivaux).
(*4*) Baronial demand for voice in appointment of chief Crown officers (see page 47 for demands of Parliament of 1244).
(*5*) Henry's exploitation of baronial divisions to evade the Provisions of Oxford.
(*6*) Refusal of baronage to accept the Mise of Amiens.

8a. **Fealty:** Loyalty of tenant-in-chief to king, or of sub-tenant or vassal to immediate overlord. Formal oath taken on receiving land and doing homage. It bound tenant to faithful obedience, implied he would faithfully perform his feudal duties in return for land granted.

b. **Boon work:** Most villagers (villeins) held land in return for services which took form of work. Normal requirement was week work, but at such times as harvest additional work required which was boon work. In return the villager received daily food and drink while thus engaged.

c. **Villein:** See pages 71-2.

d. **Curia Regis:** Was originally the king's court (a post-Conquest development) which travelled with the king, and was joined by the Great Council three times a year. Under Henry I was smaller body in permanent attendance on the king, consisting mainly of great officers of royal household (Chancellor, Justiciar, Treasurer, Chamberlain). A branch of the Curia Regis specially devoted to finance became Court of the Exchequer. Under Henry II judicial officers first increased to eighteen and then dwindled to five; this limited body ceased to be a court of final appeal, cases in which Curia might fail to do justice being reserved for the king's personal hearing in council. The limited body became the Court of Common Pleas and ultimately sat always at Westminster (after 1215), instead of travelling with the king. By the end of the reign of Henry II Curia Regis had divided into three bodies: Exchequer, Common Pleas, Court of King's Bench.

e. **Motte and bailey:** Simplest and earliest form of Norman castle. Motte was a huge mound of raised earth surrounded by dry ditch, approached by bridge. It was surmounted by a wooden fortification or house, the origin of the later Norman keep. The fortification was protected by a palisade. The bailey was an open space between palisade and keep (inner ward of bailey). If mound surrounded by palisade, the enclosed space this provided was the outer bailey. These primitive castles were erected immediately after Conquest on Welsh and Scottish borders and elsewhere at strategically important points along south coast, in Thames valley, Midlands and along Pennines.

f. **Cloister; g. Scriptorium; h. Chapter house:** Parts of monastic buildings. *Cloister* was central leisure area, grass square surrounded by paved covered walks. Access from all principal quarters (*e.g.* church, refectory, chapter house, lay quarters). *Scriptorium:* monasteries were the home of learning and book production by copying; letter-work carried out in scriptorium which was a room set apart for writing and copying of books either for monastery library or as gifts to other abbeys or churches. *Chapter house:* was the business office, meeting place of Abbot and monks after High Mass to discuss the economy of the monastery or other matters affecting daily routine. Rectangular or circular stone benches there were called "stalls."

9a. See pages 14-5 for **Norman Forest Laws.**

b. **Robert of Bellême:** On death of William II (Rufus) his brother Henry made good his possession of English throne in the absence of brother Robert in Normandy. In 1101-02 baronial revolt against Henry in Robert of Normandy's favour was led in England by Robert of Bellême. Invasion by Robert of Normandy supported by Bellême. Henry and Normandy came to terms and Normandy withdrew. Henry besieged Bellême's castles of Bridgnorth and Shrewsbury. Bellême was forced to surrender, his estates were confiscated and he was banished, and took refuge in Normandy. His presence there was a reason for Henry's conquest of Normandy, 1106, to forestall a possible second invasion of England by Robert of Normandy.

c. **Constitutions of Clarendon:** (*a*) Circumstances leading to the Constitutions see text pages 24-5.

(*b*) *Terms:* clerics accused of crime to be tried in king's court. If convicted to be degraded by church courts and returned to royal court for sentences according to king's law; Curia Regis to decide whether disputes between laymen and clerics should be heard in church or royal courts; no bishops to leave the country without royal consent; no appeals to be made to Rome without royal consent; bishops to be elected by royal summons and consent; clergy to hold land as feudal barons.

d. **Rebellions of 1173 and 1188:** against Henry II, organized by his sons.

1173: Henry II's fondness for his youngest son John aroused the jealousy of older sons, especially when Henry attempted to create a domain in France for John. Elder son, Henry, rebelled and was supported by Anglo-Norman baronage in both France and England (lesser barons supported king). Revolt in Midlands led by Earl of Leicester, and supported from Scotland by William the Lion, who invaded north of England. North resented Scottish invasion and rallied to king's side. William captured at Alnwick and compelled to do homage to Henry II. In France main leaders were Henry's sons, Geoffrey and Richard, and great nobility in Brittany, Normandy and Acquitaine. Rebellion defeated in both countries by 1174.

1188: By Henry's son, Richard, with the help of Philip Augustus of France.

John, the favourite son, joined the rebel cause and Henry II was defeated, forced to make peace.

e. **Battle of Bouvines, 1214,** see page 43.

f. **Strongbow in Ireland** (in reign of Henry II): Strongbow was Richard, second Earl of Pembroke who had extensive territory in Wales. Ireland in twelfth century was divided into several kingdoms, tribal in character. Only a nominal king of Ireland. Constant tribal warfare. An Irish tribal chief, Dermot MacMurragy was exiled after tribal defeat, took refuge in Wales. Allowed to recruit an army among Pembroke's tenantry. Dermot returned to Ireland to recover his territory. Joined by Strongbow with group of volunteers, 1170. Strongbow captured Waterford and married Dermot's daughter, an only child. Went on to capture Dublin and Meath. Dermot proclaimed himself King of Ireland, and promised succession of Leinster to Strongbow. On Dermot's death Strongbow claimed Dermot's territory and successfully defended Dublin against Danish invasion and against Roderick, another claimant to kingdom of Ireland. Activities viewed with misgiving by Henry II who was anxious to add Ireland to his empire and convert Irish from Celtic to Roman faith. Henry crossed to Ireland 1171, and Strongbow paid homage. Given Leinster in fee by Henry, and appointed "Custos" of Ireland. General submission of Irish chiefs in southern and eastern Ireland.

g. **Parliament of 1265:** (*1*) For background see pages 52-3.

(*2*) **Composition:** Lay and ecclesiastical barons as was usual in the Great Council, with the addition of knights of the shires.

(*3*) In 1255 Simon de Montfort was beginning to sense that he was losing the support of some of the baronage. To strengthen his support in the Great Council he summoned representatives of the boroughs to the meeting of 1265.

(*4*) Only those boroughs which were thought likely to return supporters of Simon were invited to send representatives. Hence Simon was not attempting constitutional reform, he was seeking partisan support.

(*5*) The novel feature he introduced was not always followed in the years between 1265-95. Nevertheless he introduced an idea which when followed after 1295, and when the knights sat with the borough representatives, was a step towards the transformation of the Great Council into Parliament, and the formation of the House of Commons as distinct from the House of Lords.

(*6*) See also page 60.

SECTION 2 (1272-1485)

10. See pages 57-9.

11. **Reasons for the unpopularity of Edward II:** (*1*) His character and temperament, lack of interest in military achievement or in politics, his interests were acting, games, hedging, ditching, forging as a blacksmith, which were undignified for a king. He showed no interest in tournaments (the aristocratic sport).

(*2*) His preference for foreigners such as Piers Gaveston (1307-10).

(*a*) Gavestone was a Gascon by birth, irresponsible and with a malicious wit. He had been banished by Edward I because of his unwholesome influence on Edward as heir to the throne, was recalled by Edward II and made Earl of Cornwall. In 1310 was banished on baronial demand, but by 1311 was back in favour. He was attacked by barons and surrendered at the Siege of Scarborough Castle. Earl of Warwick seized him from his captors, illegally tried and executed him outside Warwick. Result: baronage offended by Edward's persistent favour to Gaveston, and Edward by Gaveston's illegal execution.

(*b*) The Despencers, 1322-26: from 1312-22 government was by a baronial committee, the Lords Ordainers led by Thomas Earl of Lancaster, Edward found new foreign favourites, the Despencers who encouraged him to resist the Lord Ordainers and to defeat the Lancastrian party when they resorted to arms. The Despencers also encouraged and enabled Edward to break his undertaking in 1322 to rule by the assent of the prelates, earls, barons and commonality.

(*3*) His loss of prestige by military failure (Scotland, Bannockburn. See pages 58-9).

(*4*) Defection of his wife, Queen Isabella: sent to arrange a treaty with the French, Isabella failed to return and joined with Lord Mortimer in Flanders to intrigue against Edward. She and Mortimer invaded England, winning support of substantial part of baronage. The Despencers were caught and executed, Edward imprisoned in Kenilworth Castle and induced to resign the crown in favour of his son aged thirteen.

Reasons for deposition of Richard II, see pages 80-1.

12. See pages 96-7. **13.** See pages 61-5. **14.** See pages 77-80.

15. **Reasons for loss of France under Henry VI:** (*1*) Sound administration of Bedford undermined by loss of Burgundian support.

(*2*) Inspiration and leadership of Joan of Arc.

(*3*) Rise of peace party in England under Henry Beaufort, Suffolk, Queen Margaret and Henry VI.

(*4*) Alliance of Burgundy with Charles VI.

(*5*) Growth of anti-English sentiment in France.

(*6*) Disunity in England leading to outbreak of civil war.

16. **Reasons for ability of Edward IV to establish Royal Despotism after 1471:**

(*1*) Temporary but lengthy Lancastrian exhaustion after Tewkesbury.

(*2*) Strength of Edward's grasp on the crown, descendants of Henry IV eliminated, Edward's double claim through male and female line.

(*3*) Support of traders and merchants for king; peace with France meant the re-opening of the French markets, growth of prosperity and so contentment with the regime.

(*4*) Crown financially independent of parliament; trade expansion increased Crown port revenues, personal wealth of Crown by confiscation of Lancastrian estates, revival of Crown justice led to increased revenue from legal monetary penalties, parliamentary grant for war with France (1475) not used, but also pension from France for not using it.

(*5*) Nation ready for peace at almost any price.

17a. **Decorated Gothic architecture:** at first geometric, designs based on natural phenomena such as leaves, flowers, but stylized into geometric patterns. Later became curvilinear. More faithfully reproduced natural shapes in curves and hollows. Became excessive after 1350. Other features were bar-tracery in windows, lighter masonry, larger windows with wrought iron support.

Perpendicular Gothic architecture: continued development of windows, extending upwards without deflection, and meeting or cutting at right angles the horizontal lines of the building in their path. Unity of whole building, space division either longitudinal or transverse. New attention to proportion, fewer pillars.

b. **Black Death:** see page 76.

c. **Craft Gilds:** see pages 85-6.

d. **Wool Staple:** see pages 89-90.
e. **Model Parliament:** see page 60.
f. **Merciless Parliament:** see pages 80-1.

18a. **First Statute of Westminster:** see pages 55-6.
b. **Statute of Mortmain:** see pages 55-6.
c. **Statute of Gloucester:** see page 55.
d. **Bull Clericis Laicos 1296:**
(*1*) Occasioned by Edward I's action in preparation for war against France in an attempt to hold Gascony. Needing money, he taxed clergy as well as laity. This raised the old question of relations between Church and State, and the extent of the power of the former over the latter.
(*2*) Papal reply: the Bull Clericis Laicos which was issued by Boniface VIII forbidding the clergy to pay taxes levied by any lay authority. This in turn re-opened the issue of the Crown's power over the Church in England.
(*3*) Consequences: Archbishop Winchelsey refused to support Edward's war plans. Edward replied by outlawing the clergy. Archbishop declared the king excommunicate. Barons and merchants supported clerical opposition to the king not because of sympathy with the church so much as to welcome an excuse to resist the king's demands for money.
(*4*) Resolution of conflict: Archbishop allowed clergy to make voluntary contributions, king restored archbishop's confiscated property, compromise made possible by modification of bull by the pope.
e. **Statute of Provisors, 1351:** (*1*) Reasons for the statute were: the conflict of interests between king and papacy over the degree of self-government the church should enjoy in England and the extent of the king's right to control church affairs, papal power of appointment in the English church led to absenteeism of higher clergy, exodus of finance.
(*2*) The terms prohibited papal patronage in the English church.
(*3*) The object was to prevent papacy providing for its supporters and friends at England's expense by appointment to English livings.
f. **Treaty of Brétigny:** see page 63.
g. **De Heretico Comburendo, 1401:** (*1*) Occasion: From 1360-84 John Wycliffe, Divinity Professor at Oxford sought church reform. He attacked the wealth of the church and the immorality of some clergy, and denied the doctrine of Transubstantiation. In furtherance of his opinions he translated the Bible into English. He was supported by John of Gaunt and strongly opposed by Countenay, Bishop of London. Those who accepted his views became known as Lollards. Gaunt frustrated Wycliffe's trial by the Bishops in 1377, but after the Peasants' Revolt in 1381, for which Lollardry was held partly responsible Wycliffe's teachings were condemned as heretical. The movement survived both his death in 1384, and its persecution in the reigns of Henry IV and V.
(*2*) Terms: burning had been the traditional punishment for heresy and this punishment was now formally legalized by parliamentary legislation.
(*3*) Later developments: the Statute was repealed under Somerset in the reign of Edward VI, but re-enacted under Mary Tudor.
h. **Treaty of Troyes:** see page 66.

SECTION 3 (1485-1660)

19. See pages 129-30.
20a. Reasons for the fall of Somerset: (*1*) Protestant sympathies alienated not

merely Roman Catholics, but also those who willingly accepted a national church but did not wish to see changes in doctrine and ritual.
(*2*) His Protestant sympathies not strong enough to please those who wanted doctrinal and ritualistic changes.
(*3*) His Enclosure policy alienated the landowners.
(*4*) His sympathy with the need for social reform alienated the Council.
(*5*) Northumberland ambitious for power.

b. Reasons for the execution of Northumberland: (*1*) Religious policy split the nation into two opposed camps.
(*2*) He was too committed to Protestantism to survive a Roman Catholic succession. He knew this, and felt compelled to try to prevent it happening.
(*3*) Too fond of power to be trusted to accept defeat; Mary could not be secure while Northumberland lived.
(*4*) His antipathy to social reform lost him any popular support.
(*5*) His rebellion opened up the prospect of civil war; the country was not prepared to see a revival of the disasters of the fifteenth century.

21. **Reasons for the unpopularity of the Spanish Match:** (*1*) Too many people of influence and power had a vested interest in the Reformation; they could not countenance a step which would lead to the re-establishment of Catholicism.
(*2*) Fear of subordination of English to Spanish interests. Spain likely to be the dominant partner of the alliance; Mary too much in love with Philip to be likely to resist his policies which were sure to be Spanish and Catholic.
(*3*) Fear of entanglement in Franco-Spanish rivalry.
(*4*) Resentment at Spain's exclusion of English merchants from Spanish overseas possessions. Such exclusions not likely to be reduced by the marriage.
(*5*) Fear of introduction into England of Spanish Inquisition.
Reasons for Mary's persistence in the Spanish Match: (*1*) Her genuine affection for Philip.
(*2*) Her admiration for Spain arising from sympathy with her mother.
(*3*) Her desire to ensure a Catholic succession.
(*4*) Her desire to restore England to Papal obedience, and the realization that she would need support to counter English opposition.
(*5*) She hoped that marriage with the dominant Catholic power would ensure foreign support for her plans.
(*6*) She had her share of Tudor self-will; was fanatically Catholic; felt a religious obligation to restore what she was convinced was the only true faith.

22. See pages 155-6 and also answers to text questions on Chapter 21, Question 2 on page 484.

23. See pages 173-80. **24.** See pages 191-2. **25.** See pages 193-8.

26a. See page 120.

b. First Prayer Book: *Under Somerset:* Little change of doctrine; Cranmer was the author. Was largely translation of older Latin prayers and service forms, simplified ritual, its use made compulsory in First Act of Uniformity 1549. Aroused strong protests in Cornwall and Devon. **Second Prayer Book:** *Under Northumberland:* Communion service instead of Mass; therefore doctrinal changes; denial of Transubstantiation, table instead of altar, minister instead of priest. Enforced by Second Act of Uniformity.

c. See pages 137-8. **d.** See pages 159-60.

e. Voyages of Sir Francis Drake: First voyage in 1572. Two ships sailed from Plymouth, made land at Nombre de Dios in Gulf of Panama. Crossed isthmus from Pacific to Atlantic, interception of Spanish silver train from Peru, aroused Spanish protests. Second voyage 1577-80: round the world, England to South America, disasters on passage through Magellan Straits (Golden Hind sole survivor). Raids on Spanish ports of Lima and Valparaiso, then went north with treasure to California, then to East Indies, Indian Ocean, Cape, Plymouth. An enterprise in which the Queen had shares. Spain protested, Drake knighted. Provocation to Spain. Other exploits: 1585 raids on Cape Verde Islands and Spanish main, 1587 raid on Cadiz to weaken Armada.

f. See page 173.

g. **The Levellers:** Political radicals in the parliamentary army ranks. Led by Rainborough and Lilbourne. Programme drafted by latter, a London journalist. Advocated manhood suffrage, complete religious toleration, abolition of monarchy and establishment of a republic. Opposed to all forms of social distinction. They argued with Cromwell and officers against the Heads of Proposals. Their argument overruled, but it influenced Cromwell in the interests of army unity to bring Charles I to trial and execution. Subsequently they criticised government by Major-Generals and plotted against Cromwell's life. Formed part of the opposition to Richard Cromwell.

27a. **Provisions of Navigation Act 1485:** imported Bordeaux wines to be brought only in English ships manned by Welsh, English or Irish sailors only. Importance: one of Henry VII's measures to build English trade which had been disrupted by the civil wars of the fifteenth century. An attempt to rebuild a Merchant Navy and since no clear distinction was drawn between merchant shipping and warships, to add to the country's naval security. It was one of a series of Navigation Acts between 1381-1854, most of the later Acts being designed to promote English trade against that of her continental competitors.

b. See pages 144-6.
c. See page 143.
d. See pages 179-80.
e. See page 185.
f. See page 189.
g. See pages 189-90.
h. See pages 197-8.

SECTION 4 (1660-1783)

28. **Shaftesbury in the reign of Charles II:** (*1*) 1660-72 was strong supporter of Charles, was created Baron Ashley, appointed Chancellor of the Exchequer. Helped to destroy Clarendon's administration, member of Cabal, Lord Chancellor and Earl.

(*2*) 1672-78. Broke with Charles on discovering real terms of Secret Treaty of Dover. Led resistance to pro-Catholic policy of Charles II, opposed marriage of Duke of York (heir to throne) to Catholic Mary of Modena. Dismissed York from Privy Council.

(*3*) 1678-81. Supported Oates and exploited Popish Plot. Intrigued with France to secure fall of Danby, led the demand for the exclusion of James, Duke of York from succession. Organized Country Party, responsible for Habeas Corpus, organized Petitioners for recall of Parliament 1680. Origin of Whigs and party politics; supported Rye House Plot 1683, but took refuge in Holland. Died in Holland 1683.

29. **Reasons for James II's loss of throne:** (*1*) Different character from that of his brother. Conscientious views on Crown power and religion, and not prepared to compromise. A man of sincere conviction but intolerant. Lacked Charles II's regard for expediency.

(*2*) Provocative measures by which he sought to promote Roman Catholicism (attacks on army, universities, Episcopacy). These were some of his most likely supporters had he been more diplomatic.
(*3*) His policy threatened to re-open issues (Standing Army, royal prerogative) believed settled by the Great Rebellion and the Restoration.
(*4*) Alienation of all sections of nation, even Nonconformists.
(*5*) Birth of an heir, prospect of Catholic succession and continuation of Crown/Parliament conflict.
(*6*) Tactical errors: ignored warnings of Louis XIV, and then his flight.
(*7*) Unity of the opposition (Whigs, Tories, Army, Church); all these groups had members who supported the invitation to William of Orange.
(*8*) Existence of an alternative legitimate succession which would guarantee Protestantism.

30. **Reasons why England was continually at war (1695-1714):** (*1*) Accession of William III involved England in the Franco-Dutch struggle.
(*2*) Desire to preserve Protestant succession against foreign support for Catholic Stuart cause.
(*3*) French domination of Europe a threat to English security and trade. Also possible close association of France with Spain re Spanish succession.
(*4*) France rather than Holland now England's commercial and overseas rival.
(*5*) Revolution Settlement of England's internal difficulties allowed her to resume her interest and position in international European affairs.

31. Follow up points mentioned in question by reference to Chapter 36, page 235.

32. Arrange material on pages 259-61 to illustrate the following points: (*1*) Faculty for choosing able leaders.
(*2*) Willingness to outline broad strategy but leave tactical execution to those in command.
(*3*) Skilful use of navy.
(*4*) Sound general policy: subsidies to Continental allies, main military effort for overseas possessions.
(*5*) Successful extension of Empire.

33. **Aims:** (*1*) To resume legitimate political role of the Crown which George I and II (by their lack of English and pre-occupation with Hanover) had ceased to play: Crown patronage, free choice of ministers, unconditional ministerial acceptance of office, personal participation in executive government.
(*2*) To avoid dependence on "party" management.
(*3*) To purify administration of corruption.
(*4*) See also page 262, first paragraph.
Relations with ministries 1763-70: See pages 262-4.

34a. **Evils of Industrial Revolution:** Expand points made in the last paragraph of Chapter 44, page 293, and from material in earlier sections of the chapter, but confine yourself to evils.

b. **Advantages of the Agricultural Revolution:** Expand points made in last paragraph of Chapter 43, page 288, and from material in earlier sections of the chapter, but confine yourself to advantages.

35a. See page 207.

b. **Trial of Seven Bishops** (Sancroft, Archbishop of Canterbury; Turner of Ely; Lloyd of St. Asaph; Ken of Bath and Wells; Trelawny of Bristol; White of Peterborough; Lake of Chichester): (*1*) Petitioned James II to revoke his order to read the second Declaration of Indulgence by all clergy in churches on

grounds that Parliament had on three occasions declared illegal the use of the Dispensing Power on which the Declaration rested.
(*2*) Bishops arrested, charged with seditious libel and lodged in Tower, tried and acquitted, 30 June, 1688. Popular acclamation.
(*3*) Failure of James to reduce the Anglican Church to unquestioning obedience. Alienation of one of his most likely sources of support.

c. See page 230. **d.** See page 253.

e. **The Gordon Riots 1780:** 1778 Savill's Catholic Relief Bill protected priests from imprisonment for the practice of the faith and allowed Roman Catholics some limited rights of land ownership. 1779 Violent Protestant riots against the Bill in Glasgow and Edinburgh. Formation of Protestant Association for the repeal of the Bill by Lord Gordon. 1780 Gordon led London mob in attack on House of Commons. Damage also inflicted on R.C. churches in London. Attacks also on Bank of England, Newgate prison and houses of known supporters of the Bill. Troops sent in by George III. Gordon tried but acquitted of treason, but imprisoned for libel. Execution of some who had taken part in the riots.

36a. *Develop any three of the following points:* (*1*) Commonwealth too dependent upon Oliver Cromwell, hence unable to survive his death since there was no one of his calibre and acceptability to succeed him.
(*2*) Unpopularity of the Puritan aspects of Commonwealth.
(*3*) Failure of Commonwealth to find a satisfactory solution to constitutional issue, in particular unpopularity of administration by Major-Generals.
(*4*) Differences between Army and Parliament after death of Cromwell.
(*5*) Charles II's concessions in Declaration of Breda.

b. *Develop any three of the following points:* (*1*) Financial independence of Crown due to trade expansion, led to increased revenue from port duties.
(*2*) Accommodation with France.
(*3*) Shaftesbury and his party had been too extreme.
(*4*) Fear of civil war (Monmouth) intensified by illness of Charles II.

c. *Develop any three of the following points:* (*1*) Lower class movement lacking any influential support. Hence militarily badly equipped.
(*2*) Local, not national movement.
(*3*) Nation shrank from the prospect of civil war.
(*4*) Did not command united Whig support.

d. See pages 233-4.

e. (*1*) Act of Settlement, 1701.
(*2*) Desire for Protestant succession.
(*3*) Tory disunity.
(*4*) Suddenness of Queen Anne's death during ministerial crisis.
(*5*) Queen's appointment of Whig as Lord Treasurer.

f. Elaborate points made on page 252.

g. See page 264.

h. **Wesley's preaching:** (*1*) (*a*) Appealed to tough industrial workers.
(*b*) Extended his influence through open air services.
(*c*) His fearlessness, courage and sincerity bred conviction.
(*2*) Wesley's organizing ability (class meetings, circuit system, circuits organized into districts, Annual Conference, lay-preachers, itinerant system).
(*3*) Wesley's hymns and music were evangelical and emotional, his brother Charles wrote thousands of hymns.

(*4*) Alienation of Anglicanism from life of lower classes:
(*a*) Was the formal religion of upper classes, no social content.
(*b*) Was closely identified with the squirearchy, had not adapted itself to the new industrial society.
(*c*) Was rationalist and intellectual in its theology.
(*5*) Methodism's educational and social aspects (establishment of schools, *e.g.* Kingswood; stimulus to radical and social reform, *e.g.* prison reform, Sunday School movement; stimulating effect on Anglicanism, *e.g.* rise of evangical movement within the Church of England).

i. (*1*) English government fully occupied with American Revolt.
(*2*) Fear that Grattan's Volunteers might be used for an attack on English establishment in Ireland.
(*3*) Fear of French invasion of Ireland.
(*4*) English fear of the influence of American example in Ireland.

SECTION 5 (1783-1939)

37a. See page 278.

b. (*1*) *English Naval Supremacy: Preservation of country from invasion;* weakening of French resources by capture of French colonies; frustration of Napoleon's hopes of blockading Britain; successful counter blockade of French and allied ports; contribution to Wellington's military success by maintenance of his lines of sea communication.
(*2*) *Failure of Napoleon's economic warfare:* Orders in Council more effective than Berlin Decrees; British goods essential to Continent (Napoleon had to make exceptions to his exclusion of British goods from Continent or ignore breaches; damage to trade and welfare of countries subject to Napoleon provoked the national uprisings against him. Efforts on his part to check these movements led him into the Moscow and Peninsular campaigns and his ultimate undoing.
(*3*) *Effect of British Agricultural and Industrial Revolutions:* increase in home-produced agricultural produce offset loss of overseas supplies; development of iron and steel industries provided adequate armaments; growth of textile industry and command of seas enabled diminution of continental markets to be counter-balanced by development of American market; wealth from continued trade provided adequate finance for repeated coalitions.
(*4*) *Military success of Wellington:* destroyed the legend that Napoleon could not be beaten on land, hence national movements against him in subject countries encouraged. Liberation of Spain opened the way into France.

38. See pages 324-8.

39. See *either* pages 338-40, *or* pages 342-3.

40a. Artisans' Dwelling Act, Public Health Act, Company and Protection of Property Act, Employers' and Workmen's Act, Education Act of 1876, Agricultural Holdings Act, River Pollution Act, Food and Drugs Act, Merchant Shipping Act.

b. See pages 391-5 and pp. 368, 371, 372-3. Arrange material either under the headings of Land Problem and Home Rule or use chronological arrangement.

41. See pages 434-7.

42. During the War:
Agriculture: (*1*) Improved prices for home-grown agricultural produce owing to diminution of overseas supplies.

(*2*) Reduction of pastoral farming, extension of arable farming (state direction of proportion of the two).
(*3*) Expansion of area under cultivation (hitherto marginal land could now be used owing to good prices).
(*4*) Corn Production Act, 1917, guaranteed minimum price to farmer and minimum wage to farm labourer.
Industry: (*1*) Full employment.
(*2*) Rise in wages and profits.
(*3*) Flourishing iron, coal and engineering industries.
(*4*) Dilution of labour; unskilled employed on hitherto skilled work, employment of women.
Post-War Effects:
Agricultural decline: (*1*) Revival of foreign competition.
(*2*) Fall in prices for home produce.
(*3*) Minimum price discontinued.
(*4*) Minimum wage discontinued 1921, and restored 1924.
(*5*) Return to pastoral farming, reduction of areas under cultivation.
(*6*) Unemployment among farm workers.
Industrial slump: (*1*) Momentum given to industry during war ceased by 1921.
(*2*) Decline of basic heavy industries, *e.g.* coal, iron, shipbuilding, textiles.
(*3*) Steady increase of unemployment in areas dependent upon heavy industries.
(*4*) Concentration of industry in midlands and south where new "light" industries developed, *e.g.* motor industry, electrical engineering.
(*5*) Failure to re-capture markets neglected during the war, which had therefore developed their own industries, *e.g.* Canada, Latin American, Japan.
(*6*) Fall in wages, growth of unemployment.
(*7*) Conflict of interests; management v. trade unions, the former defended private enterprise, the latter advocated socialism. *Result:* strikes and lock-outs.
(*8*) See also pages 441-2.

43. **The Conservatives and Baldwin, 1924-29:** (*1*) *Tariff policy:* on imported foodstuffs, to stimulate British agriculture and reduce rural unemployment. Safeguarding Duties to protect industries from foreign competition.
(*2*) *Unemployment Insurance Act*, 1927*:* lower benefits and contributions but standard benefits for an indefinite period after thirty weeks' contributions paid.
MacDonald and Second Labour Government 1929-31: (*1*) J. H. Thomas became Minister for unemployment; not very successful.
(*2*) Programme of public works; defeated by Snowdon's policy of economy.
(*3*) Unemployment Insurance Act 1929 provided for young unemployed (training, slightly increased benefits; no necessity to prove search for work).
(*4*) Financial crisis of 1931 led to reduction of unemployment benefits; fall of government.
National Government 1931-39: (*1*) 1931 benefits cut, contributions raised.
(*2*) In 1934 Unemployment Assistance Board independent of Ministry of Labour.
(*3*) General improvement 1931-35, gradual world recovery: government measures to help agriculture, engineering, coal, steel. A public works programme. Encouragement of new light industries.

44a. Narrate the three "betrayals." See pages 333-7. *Comment:* He put national interest above personal position or party advantages. This the justification for "betrayals." Performed considerable service to the Conservative Party by changing its attitude of resistance to all change. Turned Tory Party into Conservative Party. A necessary stage in its development from Wellington to Disraeli.

b. See Chapter 50, pages 319-23, and confine yourself strictly to extension of franchise (i.e. the right to vote).

c. See pages 422, 456, 459-60. **d.** See pages 403-8.

e. See pages 425-9.

f. **Causes:** *Unrest in the coal industry:* (*1*) Fall in demand resulting in re-opening of the Ruhr coalfield and the availability of German coal to Europe in lieu of cash reparations.

(*2*) Easiest seams in British pits being worked out because other seams more expensive to mine.

(*3*) Consequent reduction of manpower and wages.

(*4*) Miners attributed difficulties not to these factors but to private ownership and the royal system. Under the influence of socialist economics they advocated nationalization of the industry.

(*5*) Owners anxious to break the power of the union.

General industrial slump: see answer to question 42, pages 517-8.

Failure of the Simon Commission to reach a generally acceptable solution of the mines problem: (*1*) Miners under A. J. Cooke demanded nationalization and pending that, "Not an hour on the day not a penny off the pay."

(*2*) Owners demanded longer hours and lower rates of pay.

(*3*) Commission rejected nationalization and recommended pay reduction though less than owners wanted.

Development: (*1*) Miners locked out.

(*2*) T.U.C. support for the miners, so engineers, electricians, gas workers, iron and steel and transport workers, took strike action in support of miners, also printing trade, newspapers.

(*3*) Government called for volunteers to man essential services, response from students etc., causing great social bitterness.

(*4*) Volunteers assisted or guarded by troops; government produced news-sheet.

(*5*) Law officers of Crown declared such a general strike illegal; alarm of T.U.C.; unions might be actionable at law.

(*6*) General strike called off under mediation of Sir Herbert Samuel. Miners continued alone but met with defeat.

Consequences: Trade Disputes, Trades Unions Act of 1937. See page 448.

g. **Foreign policy of world peace:** based on principle of Collective Security and strong support for the League of Nations. Strenuous, but unavailing efforts to achieve results from Disarmament Conference of 1930 presided over by Arthur Henderson, the British Foreign Secretary. Support for modification of Reparation payments by Germany at the Hague Conference of 1929. Resumption of diplomatic relations with Soviet Russia 1930. Naval agreement with America and Japan to reduce armaments race.

Imperial policy towards India: (*1*) Continued demonstrations against British Rule in India and demand for independence.

(*2*) Simon Commission which had been appointed in 1927 reported to the Labour Government in 1930. It recommended a greater measure of responsible government for the Indian provinces and a conference in London to reform the central government of India. Commission's report accepted by British government but not to the liking of Indian Nationalists.

(*3*) Civil disobedience campaign in India (leaders Ghandi and Nehru arrested).
(*4*) Round Table Conference in London boycotted by Indian nationalists but recommended examination of a possible federal constitution for all India, British and native alike.
(*5*) Imperial Conference 1930: re-asserted the equality of all Dominions with the mother country. Failed to make progress with development of Imperial Preference because Great Britain unwilling to abandon belief in and practice of Free Trade. Governments of each Dominion in future to nominate a Governor-General for appointment by the Crown.

45a. See page 348.
b. See pages 381-2.
c. **Terms of the Local Government Act 1888:** (*1*) Creation of sixty County Councils.
(*2*) Councillors elected by household suffrage for three years.
(*3*) Aldermen to be elected by councillors.
(*4*) County Councils to take over from J.P.s responsibility for roads, bridges, drains.
(*5*) Councils of boroughs of more than 50,000 population to be independent of the Council of the county in which they fell.
(*6*) Special provisions for London: the City to retain its own government by its own mayor and corporation; London police to be administered by the Home Office.
Importance: the extension of democracy into local government and diminution of role and importance of the Magistracy.
d. **Terms of the British North America Act, 1867:** (*1*) Province of New Brunswick, Nova Scotia, Quebec and Ontario to form the Dominion of Canada.
(*2*) Dominion Parliament to consist of two chambers: a Senate with members appointed for life, and a House of Commons proportionately representative of each province.
(*3*) Central Federal Government to be headed by a Governor-General appointed by the Crown.
(*4*) Each province to have its own provincial parliament and to be headed by a Lieutenant-Governor appointed by Governor-General but acting on ministerial advice.
Importance: Canadian unity thus achieved disposed of any possibility of Canadian provinces being absorbed by the U.S.A. This was the beginning of Canadian independence.
e. **Terms of the Morley-Minto reforms in India 1909:** (*1*) Indian Legislative Council (established 1833 and enlarged in 1853, 1861 and 1892) now further enlarged and its powers increased. Its members were still nominated, not elected.
(*2*) Provisions for elected members on the provincial legislative councils. Powers of these bodies also extended.
(*3*) An Indian member to sit on the Executive Council and two Indian members to be appointed to the Council of India in London.
Importance: (*1*) Reforms *not* intended by their authors to be a step towards Indian Independence, but encouraged Indian nationalists to continue to agitate to this end.
(*2*) Inadvertently contributed to advance of India towards independence by extension of Indian participation in responsible government.
f. See pages 383-4. **g.** See page 398. **h.** See pages 444-5.

INDEX

ACKNOWLEDGEMENTS

Illustrations appearing on pages 206, 259 and 263 are reproduced by gracious permission of Her Majesty the Queen.

The publishers also wish to thank the following for the use of photographs and illustrations on the pages indicated: The Royal Collection, Windsor (copyright reserved) 365. Aerofilms and Aero Pictorial Ltd., 57 (R), 93 (T). The Trustees of the British Museum, 43, 45, 79, 135, 153, 156, 161, 188, 195. British Travel Association, 84, 142. The Archbishop of Canterbury and the Trustees of the Lambeth Palace Library, 147. J. Allan Cash, 231, 380. *Country Life*, 73, 126, 213. The Librarian, the Guildhall Library, 234. The Trustees of the Imperial War Museum, 433, 439. A. F. Kersting, 119, 123. The Trustees of the London Museum, 35. The Mansell Collection, 154, 165, 174, 178, 217, 254, 257, 288. Eric de Maré (by arrangement with the Gordon Fraser Gallery), 295. Ministry of Public Building and Works (Crown Copyright), 27. National Portrait Gallery, London, 145, 171, 190, 223, 267, 271 (L), 284, 312, 316, 409. Paramount Film Service Ltd., Hal Wallis's production *Becket*, 23. Pendennis Picture Corporation Ltd., *Fire Over London*, 159. Phaidon Press, London, *The Bayeux Tapestry* edited by Sir Frank Stenton, 12. Paul Popper Ltd., 199, 227. Press Association Photos Ltd., 8. The Controller of Her Majesty's Stationery Office, facsimile of records in the Public Record Office (Crown Copyright), 17. Radio Times Hulton Picture Library, 39, 271 (R), 274, 291, 302, 304, 323, 337, 341, 345, 363, 369, 375, 383, 387, 391, 401, 405, 417, 421, 424, 426, 431, 436, 442, 446, 449, 451, 453, 456. Royal Doulton Potteries, 321. John Rylands Library, Manchester, 309. Dr. J. K. St. Joseph, 287. Two Cities Films, *Henry V*, 64. Victoria and Albert Museum (Crown Copyright), 131, 209. The Earl of Warwick, from the collection at Warwick Castle, 183.